REAL-TIME
PROGRAMMING

REAL-TIME PROGRAMMING

A Guide to 32-bit
Embedded Development

RICK GREHAN

ROBERT MOOTE

INGO CYLIAX

ADDISON–WESLEY

An imprint of Addison Wesley Longman, Inc.

Reading, Massachusetts   Harlow, England
Menlo Park, California   Berkeley, California
Don Mills, Ontario   Sydney   Bonn
Amsterdam   Tokyo   Mexico City

EXECUTIVE EDITOR   J. Carter Shanklin
PROJECT EDITOR   Krysia Bebick
COPY EDITOR   Susan Pink
PACKAGER   Neuhaus Publishing
MARKETING MANAGER   Chris Guzikowski
COVER DESIGNER   Tracy LeBlanc
COMPOSITOR   Alan Convis
MANUFACTURING SUPERVISOR   Chuck Dutton

Many of the designations used by manufacturers and sellers to distinguish their products are claimed as trademarks. Where those designations appear in this book, and Addison Wesley Longman, Inc., was aware of a trademark claim, the designations have been printed with an initial capital letter or all capitals.

The authors and publisher have taken care in the preparation of this book, but make no express or implied warranty of any kind and assume no responsibility for errors or omissions. No liability is assumed for incidental or consequential damages in connection with or arising out of the use of the information or programs contained herein.

The publisher offers discounts on this book when ordered in quantity for special sales. For more information, please contact:

AWL Direct Sales
Addison Wesley Longman, Inc.
One Jacob Way
Reading, Massachusetts 01867
(781) 944-3700

Visit AWL on the Web: http://www.awl.com/cseng/

Library of Congress Cataloging-in-Publication Data
Grehan, Rick.
    Real-time programming: a guide to 32-bit embedded development /
  Rick Grehan, Robert Moote, Ingo Cyliax.
        p.   cm.
    Includes bibliographical references and index.
    ISBN 0-201-48540-0
    1. Real-time programming.   2. Embedded computer systems —
  Programming.   I. Moote, Robert   II. Cyliax, Ingo.   III. Title.
  QA76.54.G74   1998
  005.2'73 — dc21   98-37204
                                                             CIP

Text printed on recycled and acid-free paper.

ISBN 0201485400

2 3 4 5 6 7   CRS   03 02 01 00

2nd Printing   February 2000

Contents

CHAPTER 18   Floating-Point Programming 537

CHAPTER 19   Dynamic Link Libraries 561

CHAPTER 20   C++ Exceptions and Structured Exceptions . . 583

CHAPTER 21   ROMing an Application 607

Acknowledgments

Many people contributed to this book. At the top of the list is my wife, Judy, and my three sons, Aaron, Ben, and Connor. Although they provided not a scrap of technical help, their patience at Dad's repeated vanishings into the basement contributed more to the well-being of my portion of the book than anything else. Pulling a close second are Trudy Neuhaus — editor, writer, driving force behind the book — and Bob Moote — coauthor, techno-wizard, and one of the founders of Phar Lap. They were forever calm, forever helpful, forever wise. Trudy's edits and Bob's technical insights were always on the money. Most of what this book *is* is because of them.

I would also like to thank coauthor Ingo Cyliax and contributor Peter Varhol. None could have performed better. Finally, thanks to Richard Smith, Phar Lap's President and cofounder, and the various engineers who provided feedback throughout the writing. Last but not least, thanks to God for making it all possible.

—Rick Grehan

Thanks first and foremost to my wife, Faith Justice, and son, Jaryd, for their love, support, patience, and understanding. Trudy Neuhaus did a tremendous job editing the book and managing the project; this book could not have happened without her. Alan Convis's work on layout and production and Susan Pink's copy editing improved the book immeasurably. Thanks to my coauthors, Rick and Ingo, for their hard work and insightful writing. Rick also created most of the excellent illustrations in the book. Nancy Nicolaisen, Ed Nisley, Pat Timpanaro, and Peter Varhol all contributed to the book's contents. Finally, the entire development and technical support staff at Phar Lap provided assistance and information on countless occasions; in particular, thanks to Rob Adams, Marty Bakal, John Benfatto, Paul Desjarlais, Mike Feldhusen, Clark Jarvis, Karl Kinsella, Adrian Michaud, Jim Phillips, Andre Sant'Anna, Richard Smith, Maria Vetrano, and Bill Westland.

—Robert Moote

My thanks to Lisa, my wife, for her patience while I worked on this project. Thanks also to my daughters, Keisha and Lucie, and my son, Albert, whose question, "When will the book be done?", is now answered. Many thanks to my friends and coworkers for putting up with me while I worked on this, and to Bob Moote, Rick Grehan, and Trudy Neuhaus for making this book possible. And finally, thanks to Janice Hughes for her words of encouragement.

—Ingo Cyliax

Introduction

This is a practical, hands-on guide to building real-time embedded software. You read right. Plenty of books take a high-level, theoretical approach to real-time embedded systems development; other texts take a hardware-specific approach, emphasizing building applications for atypical hardware. Few books, however, focus on developing real-time embedded software.

We understand why authors have gravitated to one of these two extremes. The absence of standard hardware, standard development tools, and a standard operating system virtually demanded that authors pursue either a theoretical or hardware-specific approach.

The world is changing, however. As time to market becomes ever more important, developers of embedded systems are starting to turn more to off-the-shelf boards and components. In particular, the PC architecture, with its high-volume cost advantages, standardized interfaces, and plethora of suppliers, is an attractive choice for systems produced in low to medium quantities.

This shift — that is, the emergence of a standard platform that is also already widely used and understood by developers — enabled us to carve out a middle ground: a book that focuses on software issues surrounding real-time embedded application development. From the beginning, we cover everyday programming topics such as designing, developing, and debugging real-time embedded applications. We show you how to implement interrupts, timers, threads, and more in real-time embedded programs. And we illustrate all topics with code examples. Because you're probably already familiar with the PC architecture, and because it's been exhaustively explored and documented, we don't spend time on hardware details — and neither do you. Both the host and target development platforms are PC-based, so you should have all the hardware you need to get started; you don't have to spend time or money building custom hardware.

At least half the value of using standard hardware is using standard software. This is where Phar Lap Software's ToolSuite Lite comes in. Included on the CD-ROM, ToolSuite Lite is a limited version of Phar Lap's TNT Embedded ToolSuite, Realtime Edition. TNT Embedded ToolSuite supports off-the-shelf compilers and tools, and enables you to build and deploy real-time embedded applications that use the PC architecture.

ToolSuite Lite includes a real-time embedded operating system (ETS Kernel) that supports a subset of Microsoft's Win32 API — the same API used for Windows 95, 98, and NT. (ETS Kernel is not Microsoft Windows. The kernel looks and acts like Windows, but that's as far as the similarity goes. Phar Lap's ETS Kernel is compact, scalable, and optimized for real-time embedded systems.) ToolSuite Lite also includes support for the Microsoft Visual C++ compiler and run-time libraries, Microsoft Developer Studio Integrated Developer Environment (IDE), and the use of the Developer Studio debugger as a cross-debugger for real-time embedded programs.

> **Note:** According to *Microsoft Visual C++ 6.0 Programmer's Guide* (Microsoft Press, 1998), with the release of Visual C++ 6.0, Microsoft no longer distinguishes between Visual C++ the product and Developer Studio the IDE, and uses Visual C++ to refer to both. For the purposes of our discussion, however, we continue to refer to the IDE in Visual C++ 6.0 as Developer Studio.

We included ToolSuite Lite because the best way to learn how to write programs is to, well, write them. With the software on the CD-ROM, a copy of Microsoft Visual C++, two PC-compatible computers, and a LapLink-compatible cable, you can build, run, and debug all the programming projects in this book.

IS THIS BOOK FOR YOU?

Does this book target only PC and Win32 developers? Not at all. We had to choose specific hardware and software platforms so that you could actually build and run the real-time embedded programs in this book. But you can apply the principles of embedded systems development described here to the design and development of any embedded product, regardless of which specific processor, real-time operating system, and software tools you use.

You'll find this book worthwhile if you are one of the following:

- A programmer who is new to or had limited exposure to embedded systems and wants to acquire a good, overall understanding of embedded systems programming.

- A programmer who is familiar with at least one of the Windows operating systems, has never explored real-time embedded systems programming, and wants to experience it firsthand.

- A programmer who has worked on non-Intel hardware and wants some hands-on experience with the kind of embeddable PC systems supported by ToolSuite.

- A programmer with a hardware/software project you've been toying with. You suspect the implementation solution to this project is some sort of embedded system, but you don't know how to go about turning your idea into a reality.

- A student or a teacher in the engineering or scientific disciplines who anticipates building projects that will require computer control.
- Someone who is already familiar with ToolSuite and wants an adjunct to the examples given in the ToolSuite documentation.
- An inquisitive person who wants to explore embedded systems just because you find them interesting.

We have only one prerequisite. You should be conversant in the C programming language so that you can read the source code (most examples are in C) and understand what's going on. A few projects are written partially in C++, and one of the programming projects includes a Java applet. Nevertheless, C is the only requirement. Knowledge of C++, the Win32 API, and Java, however, would provide a headstart.

EMBEDDED SYSTEMS: WAVE? YOU MEAN TSUNAMI

The number and types of embedded systems available make it almost impossible to miss the trend toward embedded systems. Your programmable microwave is an embedded system. Your VCR is an embedded system. Your TV remote is an embedded system. And if your TV is programmable, it's embedded, too.

You can expect the embedded systems trend to continue. In the September 1996 issue of *Computer Design* magazine, Ray Weiss wrote an article titled, "Embedded Advances in Auto, Communications, Office, Industry, and Consumer Markets." Based on information released by Motorola, Weiss wrote that the average 1990 car contained about 14 microprocessors; by the year 2000, that number is expected to reach 35.

Now combine this with another trend that's even more difficult to miss: that wildfire called the Internet. The same *Computer Design* article mentioned earlier continues:

> Home set-top-box and Internet connections via ISDN or higher home-connection technologies like 8-Mbit ADSL (Asymmetric Digital Subscriber Line) have the potential to feed huge communications growth as homes tie into advanced digital services for set-top or cable boxes. And expect these boxes to become integrated into TV sets soon...VMEbus and PC-based systems are expected to play a major role as system bases for these applications.

Set-top boxes, routers, modems — in short, the infrastructure of the Internet — are embedded systems, a fact that further supports the expectation that embedded systems will become increasingly prevalent.

Although the growth of the embedded market is largely due to new uses and applications for embedded systems, it's also been fueled by advancements in microprocessors. Increases in processor speed, bus width, and the number of peripherals that manufacturers can squeeze on a chip have increased the variety of chips available for embedded systems and their suitability to a wider variety of tasks. RISC chips are now common in high-end embedded applications and even in not so high-end applications, if you look at consumer electronics products such as video games. The Sega Saturn, for example, has three 32-bit Hitachi SH RISC processors. Small, embeddable, complete PC-based boards are common in mid-range systems. And super-small microprocessors dominate low-end systems. For example, Parallax's BASIC Stamp is a complete development system based on Microchip's PIC line of super-small microprocessors, including a BASIC interpreter, that's programmed from your desktop PC and comprised of two chips and a thimbleful of passive components.

Embedded systems are everywhere. If you're like us, you want to figure out how to use this stuff before you find yourself tripping over a technology you don't understand.

REAL-TIME EMBEDDED SYSTEMS

All this talk of embedded systems has left out an important aspect of the applications we'll be talking about: real-time. Some definitions of real-time systems that we've seen would make every embedded system a real-time system. Those definitions classify a real-time system as one that interacts with real-world activities (buttons being pushed, temperatures being monitored, robot arms being moved, and so on). Such a definition is correct but incomplete.

The complete definition can wait until later. For now, note that we cover not simply embedded systems development, but *real-time* embedded systems development. In fact, when we say *embedded* in this book, we mean *real-time embedded*. Real-time systems, which usually perform critical and timer-sensitive functions, account for a significant segment of the total population of embedded systems. Many embedded applications *demand* real-time performance. The anti-lock braking system (ABS) in your car is a good example. When you put your foot on the brake, you want the brakes to respond immediately. If the ABS decides to defragment some memory instead of responding, a few moments later a lot more than its memory could be fragmented. This book covers how to determine whether your project requires real-time functionality and, if so, how to implement it.

WHAT'S IN THIS BOOK

This book is not a high-level, abstract discussion of software development. Instead, you look at the nitty-gritty of building real-time embeddable software. This will necessarily lead you into some low-level details. For example, we go over the ins and outs of multithreading: when multithreading is and isn't a good idea, how to manage thread priorities, and how to synchronize threads. We also explore building interrupt handlers, how to control the serial I/O port, how to use timers in your applications, and more.

We illustrate all the concepts in this book using tutorial examples, or projects. We chose projects that encompass everyday programming tasks and illuminate challenges you're likely to encounter. As we point out in Chapter 1, however, embedded software is closely tied to embedded hardware — so close, in fact, that it's hard to develop one without the other. More often than not, you should start developing the software first or in parallel with the hardware. To get software development underway, then, programmers of embedded systems often create hardware simulations so that they can run and debug their software while the final hardware is unavailable.

Building hardware simulations is what you do in the programming projects in this book. We had a practical reason for this approach: Our projects are actual (if somewhat simplified) embedded systems you'd encounter in the real world, and as such, they require specialized hardware that isn't present on a PC. Therefore, we simulate the hardware that isn't present to run the rest of the program. We had an instructive purpose as well: Simulation is critical to developing embedded systems. Creating hardware simulations for our projects lets us demonstrate this technique.

After your application is running on the hardware simulation, however, you must migrate it to the target hardware. We show you what would need to change in each project in a "Beyond Simulation" sidebar in each project chapter.

Before you can begin building the projects, you need to set up ToolSuite Lite. We show you how to do this in Chapter 3, "Software Installation and Setup." We also present a simple, embedded version of the Hello World program to expose you to the fundamental ins and outs of compiling a program, downloading it to the target, and running it. Chapter 4, "Debugging," covers the debugging solutions used for embedded development, and then shows you how to use the Microsoft Developer Studio debugger to debug the example projects.

Hello World is followed by a point-of-sale (POS) terminal application (that is, a smart cash register like the ones you see in department stores) in Chapter 5. We simulate the POS terminal application so that you can enter SKU numbers, enter quantities, and retrieve information from a fictitious inventory.

From the POS terminal, you proceed to a more ambitious project, a UPS simulation in Chapter 8. Actually, you simulate the brain of a UPS, but the mimicry is true enough so that you can simulate a power outage and witness how the UPS responds. In Chapters 11 and 14, you add functionality to the UPS (read: make it smarter), to the point of inculcating it with the capability to generate HTML pages and communicate over a network to a web browser.

The chapters in the final third of the book include a series of smaller programming projects that illustrate other concepts. We hope the projects don't end here, however, and that you'll use the examples as springboards for more elaborate projects of your own.

After each project chapter, we present chapters that discuss the specific programming topics and techniques illustrated in that project. For example, the POS terminal project in Chapter 5 illustrates implementing keyboard I/O, screen I/O, and file systems in an embedded system; Chapters 6 and 7 explore these topics in-depth. The first half of each topic chapter presents an in-depth discussion of the subject so that you'll be able to use the information on whatever platform you choose. In the second half of each chapter, we examine the code from the programming project, so that you can see working code running on the PC and ETS Kernel platform.

Here are some of the subjects we go over:

- **Interrupts.** You see how to write interrupt service routines, properly fielding interrupts in your application to ensure real-time responsiveness.

- **Timers.** You see how to set and respond to software timers to perform synchronous operations.

- **I/O ports.** Because serial communication is so prevalent, we illustrate I/O to hardware peripherals by programming the serial I/O port to communicate with another system.

- **Multitasking.** Multiple, concurrent tasks form the heart of many real-time systems. We show you the advantages — and challenges — of writing a multitasking application.

- **Networking.** Networking is an increasingly important requirement for many embedded systems. We cover networking in general and take a detailed look at the TCP/IP protocol suite. Then we implement a network between an embedded PC running ETS Kernel and a Windows machine, using a serial PPP link for the network connection.

- **HTTP servers.** Including an HTTP server in your embedded product is a great way to remotely monitor and configure your embedded system using a standard program available to almost anyone with a network connection: namely, a web browser. We describe how the HTTP protocol works and show you how to easily build an HTTP server into an ETS Kernel application.

We also introduce other techniques and technologies, such as burning your application into ROM, that are pertinent to real-time embedded development.

HARDWARE AND SOFTWARE REQUIREMENTS

The CD-ROM contains ToolSuite Lite plus full source code to all the sample programs in the book. To run ToolSuite Lite, your host computer (where you do your development work) must be a 486 or later PC running Windows 95, 98, or NT. To compile the programs in this book or to write new ones, you need a copy of Microsoft Visual C++, version 5.0 or later. (For a list of the components included in ToolSuite Lite, see Chapter 3.)

For the target computer (where your embedded programs run), you need a 386 or later PC with a BIOS, a floppy disk drive, a monitor, a keyboard, and serial and parallel ports. A floating-point coprocessor is desirable but not required.

You also need a LapLink-compatible parallel cable for downloading and debugging applications. (If necessary, you can use a serial cable, but downloading and debugging over a parallel cable is faster.) For the sample programs that use TCP/IP networking, you need a LapLink-compatible serial cable for the network connection.

After you have your system set up, you can run the programs in this book, extend and rebuild them, or write your own embedded programs from scratch. So roll up your sleeves, dive in, and have fun.

1

An Introduction to Embedded Systems

I n the Introduction, we wrote of the ubiquity of embedded systems. We probably gave you the idea that if you weren't careful, you might accidentally step on one. (Perhaps you already are — purposefully, of course — if you're weighing yourself.)

The infiltration of embedded systems into the nooks and crannies of our lives — into appliances, toys, automobiles, TVs, VCRs, medical instruments, aircraft, and on and on — makes the term *embedded system* difficult to define. The range of embedded systems magnifies this difficulty.

Here's a comparative example. Should we consider your TV's handheld remote control an embedded system? Probably so. Should we consider the computer system controlling a hospital's portable ultrasound unit an embedded system? Probably so. Yet if you compare the capabilities of the microcontroller in the TV remote control to the system in the ultrasound machine, you come away with the sense that these two processors so differ from one another in function and capability that their only common attribute is that they are both called microprocessors.

These two systems, however, share two more admittedly abstract aspects. First, they both involve the immediate control of hardware. The TV control must respond to key presses and transmit appropriate infrared signals to your TV set. The computer system in the ultrasound machine must generate and receive the sonic signals that it ultimately interprets for display on the viewscreen. In both cases, the microprocessors have a close connection with hardware that is, in turn, in close communication with the outside world. Contrast this with the operations that take place as a desktop computer queries a database. Although hardware is being controlled — for example, the read/write head of the disk drive is moved so that data can be transferred — the hardware is internal to the operation of the computer system, rather than external, such as an infrared transmitter, a sonic probe, a valve, or a robot arm.

RAM and ROM and In-Between

In the past, you could define an embedded system as a computer system that has all its software in ROM, or read-only memory — with the understanding that some RAM, or random-access memory, was involved to provide read/write memory for data and the stack. Today, embedded systems developers must be conscious of the differences between RAM and ROM and how they are utilized by running programs. Here is a quick review of the differences between these two types of memory. (In Chapter 21, "ROMing an Application," we discuss using ROM in embedded systems in more detail.)

ROM is a type of permanent memory storage. Information stored in ROM can be read but not modified. Instructions are stored in ROM through a programming process called burning. This process is not complex but does require special hardware. After you burn a program in ROM, it's always there (like writing in indelible ink), ready to be executed. ROM is suitable for holding programs that you want the microprocessor to remember after you've turned off the power. That way, when you turn the hardware back on, the microprocessor begins executing the program in ROM.

RAM, on the other hand, is volatile memory. Information stored in RAM can be read and modified. Information in RAM is lost when the power is cut. When you turn the power back on, whatever needs to be in RAM must be rewritten to it. Because it can be written to, RAM can run any program at any time . . . unlike ROM.

In between RAM and ROM is a special type of ROM called EEPROM, or electrically erasable programmable read-only memory. EEPROM works like ROM in that it remembers information you write to it, even after you turn off the power. However, like RAM, EEPROM can be written to. Admittedly, you have to send special signals to EEPROM to tell it that it's about to be reprogrammed, but most microprocessors can easily generate those special signals with a little additional hardware. Most EEPROM devices can be rewritten only hundreds of times. This makes them unsuitable for holding data that changes frequently but ideal for uses such as software upgrades to the BIOS or other firmware.

Finally, flash memory — sometimes called flash EEPROM — is a variation of EEPROM. As with EEPROM, flash memory retains its contents after power is removed. However, whereas standard EEPROM's contents are read and written on a per-byte basis, flash memory's contents must be modified in blocks. Flash memory is more expensive than EEPROM but can be rewritten thousands of times rather than hundreds of times. One common use of flash memory is for file systems. Because there is a limit to how many times flash memory can be rewritten, file system drivers for flash memory perform wear-averaging to try to average out disk writes over the entire device and bad block management to detect and stop using bad blocks.

Second, both the TV remote control and the ultrasound unit are limited in function. Actually, it's probably more accurate and gentler to say that both systems have a specific function. This notion holds up even though a TV remote performs fewer and less complex operations than an ultrasound machine does. Neither a remote control nor — for all of its power — an ultrasound machine can be used for another function. Again, contrast this to a PC, which can perform complex mathematical calculations one minute and difficult sorting feats the next.

To summarize, we'll settle on the following definition:

> An embedded system includes a microprocessor, involves the immediate control of hardware, and is limited to performing a specific function.

Before we move on, we would like to leave you with one thought that is not so much a definition as a guideline. Don Lancaster, a long-time luminary in the microcomputer industry, once wrote in *Kilobaud Microcomputing* — a magazine long dead — that the optimum solution to any application involving computers is not all software and not all hardware; it is a proper combination of the two. That's the key to a successful embedded design: the proper marriage of hardware and software.

The Microcontroller

Everyone knows what a microprocessor is, but do you know what a microcontroller is? A *microcontroller* is a specific kind of microprocessor whose primary job is to *control* the hardware it's attached to, such as a light, a switch, or a motor. A microcontroller chip typically has more pins dedicated to carrying input/output signals than a run-of-the-mill microprocessor. The additional pins allow designers to connect the microcontroller directly to the external I/O hardware. (Most microprocessors, on the other hand, access I/O hardware as if it were memory — this is referred to as *memory-mapped I/O* and requires additional external logic circuitry.) Also, a microcontroller usually has internal timer hardware, which is useful for creating interrupts at regular intervals. Some microcontrollers are even available with built-in analog-to-digital converters. In small embedded systems, a microcontroller often is the CPU; larger systems often use microcontrollers to manage specific pieces of hardware in the system, such as a disk drive or a joint in a robot arm, with a more powerful microprocessor as the system CPU.

REAL-TIME SYSTEMS

Although we had to fish around for a definition for embedded systems, we needed to do far less groping for a definition of real-time systems. *The Oxford Dictionary of Computing* provides one:

> Any system in which the time at which output is produced is significant. This is usually because the input corresponds to some movement in the physical world, and the output has to relate to that same movement. The lag from input time to output time must be sufficiently small for acceptable timeliness.

This quote is from *Real-Time Systems and Their Programming Languages*, by A. Burns and A. Wellings, which in turn quotes the *Oxford Dictionary of Computing*. The authors go on to point out that the notion of "acceptable timeliness" is relative and should be considered in the context of the application. Timeliness in a guided missile system might be on the order of microseconds; timeliness in an assembly line might be on the order of seconds. Both are real-time systems, nonetheless, because the timeliness of the response is at the top of the requirements list.

Real-time systems are distinguished from desktop systems by the former's timeliness requirements. The timeliness of a response in a real-time system is a predetermined, inflexible, and necessary ingredient for correct operation. In other words, if a real-time system fails to respond to some event within a set amount of time (with the event, the response, and the speed of the response all specified), the system is wrong, just as much as a spreadsheet application is wrong if it adds two and two and gets five. However, the timeliness of a response in a desktop system varies and isn't necessary for correct operation. If it takes a PC a few seconds longer to load a program under certain conditions, the delay is acceptable. Timeliness in a desktop system is important; timeliness in a real-time system is critical.

In addition to providing timely responses to external events, real-time systems often must provide multiple simultaneous responses. Real-time systems are closely tied to hardware that, in turn, is closely tied to the real world where multiple events and multiple requests for service rarely occur independently and in sequence. Real-time systems accomplish the appearance of responding to and handling multiple events thanks to the raw speed of the computer hardware coupled with the careful engineering of the system's software and the operating system. When a heavy traffic of multiple events must be serviced, multiprocessor real-time systems can be employed, but their complexity is beyond the scope of this book.

Real-time systems are divided into two categories: hard real-time and soft real-time. Membership in one of these two categories usually depends on the importance of the system's timeliness in response to external events.

Hard Real-Time

A system is a hard real-time system if failure to respond to an event within a specified time is considered complete system failure. Our use of the word *complete* is not superfluous. When we say *complete failure,* we mean a failure that the system designers consider unacceptable. In other words, a designer wouldn't witness such a failure and say: "Okay, so the system failed that one time. Not a big deal." Just the opposite. If a hard real-time system misses a deadline, the designer would say: "Holy smokes! How did that happen? If it's my fault, I'm dusting off my resume." (Hard real-time systems are in, for example, shuttle-craft flight controls, where the computer system must perform precisely as and when needed — or people die.)

And when we say *misses a deadline,* we mean misses any deadline. One missed deadline out of a hundred is unacceptable. One missed deadline out of a thousand is unacceptable. (Remember, a real-time system may experience hundreds or thousands of deadlines — that is, requests for service — every second.) A hard real-time system must make all its deadlines all the time. This requirement is a result of the fact that the correctness of the system is tied to the timeliness of its response.

In Chapter 12, which is about multitasking, we visit longer with the notion of meeting deadlines. As you'll discover, this is an area of much effort and research in the realm of real-time systems. Real-time developers at work on hard real-time systems spend much of their up-front design work detailing how a system will meet all its deadlines all the time.

SOFT REAL-TIME

In a soft real-time system, timeliness of response is important but not a matter of life and death. Designers of a soft real-time system, having witnessed a missed deadline, might say: "Okay, so the system failed that one time. Not a big deal."

The acceptable frequency of missed deadlines is dictated by the design. One soft real-time system may function within tolerances if one deadline out of every five is missed. Another may function within tolerances if no more than one deadline in fifty is missed.

Designers of soft real-time systems must also consider by how much the system misses a deadline and what size delay is acceptable. For example, designers of a remote-controlled TV system (a classic soft real-time system) might consider it acceptable if the TV responded to a change channel request within $\frac{1}{20}$ of a second usually and $\frac{1}{10}$ of a second occasionally.

The vast majority of real-time systems are soft real-time systems. For example, most real-time systems controlling appliances and consumer devices (such as a remote control) are soft real-time systems. The fewer hard real-time systems tend to be far more complex.

A Different Classification of Real-Time Systems

Another way to categorize real-time systems appeared in *Embedded Systems Programming* magazine, in an article titled, "Eliminating the Hard/Soft Real-Time Dichotomy," written by E. D. Jensen. He refers to this new model as the *benefit accrual model*.

The benefit accrual model measures a system's timeliness as a continuous variable, rather than a Boolean (the task is on schedule or not). The timeliness of a task is measured based on its benefit to the system. Programmers working in a real-time system that implements the benefit accrual model would program timeliness functions, which serve the same purpose as priorities in conventional real-time systems. These timeliness functions guide the *scheduler* — that part of the real-time system that decides which task can run.

Additionally, the scheduler in such a system — rather than select the highest priority task as the next to run, as in classical scheduling — considers the timeliness of all tasks in the system as a whole. The scheduler tries to optimize task scheduling based on what it knows about the importance of tasks in the system. One way to do this is for the scheduler to build potential scheduling scenarios and attempt to schedule tasks based on the most acceptable scenario first; barring that, schedule according to the second most acceptable scenario, and so on down the line of scenarios.

Using this scheme, a system is not categorized as being hard real-time or soft real-time. Rather, the real-time world is seen as a spectrum of rigidity, ranging from super-soft at one end (where the scheduler has lots of scenarios to choose from) to hard at the other (where, at any given time, only one scheduling scenario is available).

REAL-TIME EMBEDDED SYSTEMS

The terms *real-time* and *embedded* are close cousins. So close, in fact, that in their book, *Real-Time Systems and Their Programming Languages*, Burns and Wellings use the two words interchangeably. Although we're not convinced yet that real-time systems and embedded systems are synonymous, we admit that an embedded system is at least a soft real-time system. This leads us to a relationship similar to the relationship between rectangles and squares: all squares are rectangles, but not all rectangles are squares. All embedded systems are real-time systems, but not all real-time systems are embedded systems.

Philosophical rambling aside, the focus of this book is real-time embedded systems: systems designed to carry out specific functions that adhere to at least soft real-time performance. Because the term *real-time embedded systems* is a bit long and awkward, we shorten it to just *embedded* throughout this book. Whenever you see the term *embedded*, remember that we mean *real-time* too.

The projects we chose for the book satisfy the criteria for real-time embedded systems — hard and soft. The first project you'll see — the point-of-sales terminal in Chapter 5 — is illustrative of a typical soft real-time application. Then, in Chapters 8, 11, and 14, we develop a simulated uninterruptible power supply to explore the details of hard real-time systems.

In addition, we're interested in the aspects of embedded systems that aren't directly related to deadlines or real-time behavior. Thus, the projects also expose the challenges of topics such as direct manipulation of hardware, interrupts, and timers.

EMBEDDED PROCESSORS

The world of embedded hardware — particularly processors — stretches along a broad horizon. An entire book could be written about nothing more than a guided tour of all the processors used in embedded designs. At one end of the horizon are 4-bit (yes, that's right, 4-bit) processors still at work in some super-small applications such as the control of household appliances.

Not far past 4-bit processors are 8-bit machines. For those of us who have lived most of our adult lives using desktop machines, 8-bit processors are no more than ghostly reminders of dimly remembered things such as CP/M, S-100 buses, and Apple II computers. Among developers of embedded systems, however, the 8-bit processor is alive and doing well. Intel's 8051 microcontroller continues to be the mainstay of 8-bit embedded development, though plenty of systems are built around the Zilog Z180 (a descendent of the Z80) and the Motorola 68xx series of microcontrollers.

The 16-bit machines are represented by such processors as the Intel 80188/80186, the Intel 8096 processor, and Motorola's 68HC11 — a favorite among robotics enthusiasts. (We put the HC11 in the 16-bit group, which some may consider incorrect. Although the A and B accumulators of the HC11 are 8 bit, they can be combined to form a 16-bit D register, with which 16-bit mathematics can be carried out. We apologize if you don't agree.)

At the high end of the embedded processor market, you find the 32-bit machines. This segment of the embedded market is growing rapidly — not only in quantity of chips shipped but also in the variety of processors available. Intel's embedded x86 and I960 chips, AMD's Am29K, Hitachi's SH RISC, IBM's and Motorola's PowerPC, Advanced RISC Machines' ARM, and Silicon Graphics' MIPS chip are just a few of the 32-bit embedded CPU offerings. (Even 64-bit embedded processors are seeing action. Certain members of the MIPS embedded processor family are 64-bit CPUs.) The growth in the 32-bit arena is driven mainly by two factors: the reduction of hardware costs and the increase in complex and feature-rich embedded applications that require more horsepower.

The software in this book targets the Intel x86 32-bit embedded processors and compatibles. Processors in this group include Intel's 386EX, 486, Pentium and Pentium Pro, National Semiconductor's NS486SXF, and AMD's Am386EM. The principles we discuss, however, apply across the spectrum of embedded processors.

THE ADVENT OF PC EMBEDDED SYSTEMS

As its name implies, an embeddable PC consists of hardware based on the PC architecture. Another implication of its name is that the hardware doesn't look quite like the motherboard you find in a current desktop machine (or even in an old PC machine, if you could find one). PC embedded systems are single-board computers (SBCs), whose form-factors are surprisingly small (3.55" x 3.75" in some cases) and getting smaller. Their small size makes them viable as embeddable engines. As we stated, however, they are PC-compatible machines, so software running on such a device acts like it's running on a PC-compatible machine.

(You might get the idea that, because the original AT was an 80286, a PC-based single-board computer's processor is an 80286. Not so. Although you can get single-board 80286 machines — you can even get single-board 8088 machines — the trend is to use 32-bit embedded processors of the 80386 family line. The trend is so powerful that soon it might be difficult to find an embeddable PC system with anything less than an 80386-class processor.)

In addition to its small size, the single-board PC is a viable platform for embedded applications due to the influence of the following market forces:

- **The ongoing price-wars on the PC desktop.** As system designers try to undercut one another in pricing and features, they provide the marketplace with plenty of basic PC hardware components: microprocessors, bus logic, I/O port logic, and so on. As a result, the fundamental pieces of PC hardware are abundant, inexpensive, and well-defined. And perhaps that last attribute — well-defined — is the most important. Even as manufacturers compete with one another, they are all carried along by an irresistible current of compatibility. They want their hardware working with as much hardware from other manufacturers as possible. You do, too.

- **The growing demand for smaller and more powerful laptops.** Curiously, research conducted by manufacturers of laptops pours benefits into the embedded bowl. This is simply because the push for laptops that are lighter, housing more resources, and faster forces the development of higher tolerances and tighter integration in PC electronics. More power in smaller spaces called for by laptop users produces hardware that the embedded system builders can use.

- **The growing activity in small form-factor interfaces**. Several existing and evolving standard interfaces are intended for the kind of compact hardware designs often required in embedded systems. These interfaces include the PC/104 interface, a stackable bus architecture standard that calls for small form-factor boards (3.55" x 3.75") and pin-and-socket bus connectors (more rugged than PC edge connectors); the Compact PCI, a variant of the desktop version of PCI that uses Eurocard connectors (another pin-and-socket style of connector); the PC/104 Plus (evangelized by the single-board computer manufacturer Ampro); the Small-PCI; and the Cardbus. The Small-PCI and Cardbus designs resulted from credit-card form-factor peripherals, much like PC Card. This healthy activity will only further improve the PC's position in the embedded systems marketplace.

- **The growing number of embedded 32-bit PC-compatible processors**. Embedded PC-compatible processors incorporate standard I/O devices and bus control logic from a PC motherboard — such as interrupt control, serial ports, parallel ports, timers, DMA, and RAM refresh — on a single chip. This integration reduces the chip count required in an embedded design. Currently shipping PC-compatible embedded processors include the Intel 386EX, the National NS486SXF, and the AMD Elan family of microcontrollers.

PC HARDWARE COMPONENTS

Because the PC is a standard platform, many of its hardware components are standardized as well. Some of the important hardware components found in embedded PC systems are listed in the following:

- **Processor.** All manufacturers of PC SBCs use 80286-compatible or later processors, although by most accounts an 80386-compatible processor is considered the baseline (and by the time this book is printed, may even be a step beneath baseline). Intel, AMD, and National Semiconductor all manufacture SBCs with 386-, 486-, and Pentium-compatible chips. Consequently, for the remainder of this book, we presume that any embeddable PC we write about is at least an 80386-compatible.

- **Memory map.** All PC systems map their hardware peripherals to the PC memory system at standard memory and I/O locations. For example, graphics peripherals map their graphics, or screen, memory to a known location; I/O devices such as serial ports map their I/O to standard I/O addresses. Using a standard memory map makes it easier to write programs that need to find and access hardware. Whenever a PC system boots up, it looks for hardware peripherals at one of several known locations in memory. Each peripheral's initialization code is stored in its ROM. As the system is coming up, it checks for the presence of peripherals and — if found — executes each peripheral's initialization code. This allows attached hardware to initialize itself and wire its controlling code into the system.

- **Serial and parallel ports.** The manufacturers of SBCs use standard hardware to control serial and parallel ports. Therefore, the interrupt system that manages the ports is also standard.

- **Keyboard and screen controllers.** If your embedded applications require a keyboard and a screen, note that SBC manufacturers make standard onboard controllers.

- **Motherboard.** For a PC motherboard to be called standard, the board must contain timers, an interrupt controller, and a DMA controller.

THE ADVANTAGES OF THE PC ARCHITECTURE

Building real-time embedded systems using PC hardware has many advantages. The key benefit that begets all others, though, is the long-time standardization of the PC design.

The widespread and long-time acceptance of the PC architecture has resulted in a proliferation of reference material such as books, magazine articles, and manuals; numerous software tools that can be used or easily adapted for embedded development; and hardware devices and software interfaces that are compatible, readily available, reliable, and inexpensive.

Additionally, many embeddable PCs are available with varying kinds and quantities of peripheral hardware. If your embedded application needs a video display, you can find systems with onboard display hardware ranging from monochrome LCD controllers all the way up to color SVGA (super VGA) hardware. If your design doesn't require a PC-style keyboard, you can get a system without the keyboard controller hardware. Or, if you want to keep your options open, you can get an embedded PC that accepts a standard card interface, such as PC/104, PCI, or PC Card. The availability of different types of peripherals makes it easy to upgrade, adding hardware such as network adapters and hard-disk controllers at a later time.

Time to market is another major advantage. If you use standardized components, you don't have to spend time designing, building, and testing custom ones. Similarly, you can easily prototype your software on a plain-vanilla PC, secure in the knowledge that your final hardware will closely resemble that PC in many respects. In today's world of accelerated product release cycles, gaining even a few months can mean the difference between success and failure in the marketplace.

In short, you can reduce turnaround times, lower software and hardware development costs, and easily upgrade systems if you use standard PC hardware. John Gabay, writing in *Embedded Systems Programming* magazine, summed it up nicely when he wrote:

> ...almost every problem has already been solved. Inexpensive standard interfaces to storage devices, video, printing, sound, and networking are widely available. Designers do not have to tediously design their own floppy interface (for example) if they are using an embedded PC in their design. Odds are, designers can buy the floppy controller cheaper than it would cost to manufacture, and without any design time and R&D dollars.

On the first reading, you may accept this as simple common sense and be tempted to quickly move on. But before you do, stop and think about what we just said: In your heart of hearts, do you really agree? Or are you more likely to think, "Why should I use off-the-shelf hardware and software that solves *almost* every problem when I can build something that solves *every* problem?"

The intent and objective are admirable but rarely practical. Constraints such as time and money increasingly dictate that we not reinvent the wheel and that we spend reasonably and proportionately when solving problems. There's perhaps no better example of this than the Mars Pathfinder.

In 1976, the Viking probe was built from scratch to the tune of, in today's dollars, $3 billion. Challenged to build a faster, cheaper, and better probe, the Mars Pathfinder crew sought off-the-shelf components and adapted them for use on Mars. The result: They designed and built the Pathfinder and Sojourner for $171 million — the cost of a movie, albeit an expensive one. The reduced costs and time enabled NASA's Mars program to launch the Pathfinder mission seven years earlier than if they had followed traditional design procedures. Going forward, it enables the program to launch a probe every 26 months rather than once a decade.

The Pathfinder and Sojourner were built faster and more cheaply, but were they better? It depends on what you mean by *better*. For many of us engineers, that's the rub. We're skeptical that anything built faster and more cheaply can be better — often because we have a narrow definition of *better* in mind. We equate better with more features, more power, more precision, and the like, when a correct interpretation could be that better simply means better-suited — whether to a task, a customer, or an organization's objectives. In this regard, the Pathfinder was better.

So the next time you're tempted to build something from scratch rather than buy off-the-shelf components, think hard: How much are you really gaining? Does it advance the goals of the project? Could your time be better spent elsewhere? And remember the success of the Mars Pathfinder mission.

DOES AN EMBEDDABLE PC SUIT YOUR APPLICATION?

For all the advantages of the PC architecture, you would think it would have some disadvantages. But we can't cite even one. Rather, whether or not you build custom hardware or use PC hardware will likely hinge not on a fault or failing of the embeddable PC concept (or any particular manufacturer's design) but on its appropriateness to your application. You should examine three criteria to determine whether an embeddable PC is suitable: power, cost-effectiveness, and uniqueness.

Power

How much horsepower do you need? If your application would be satisfied with a 4- or 8-bit processor and minimal RAM, a 16- or 32-bit embeddable PC is overkill. Too much processing power in and of itself isn't a bad thing. Rather, making sure you have enough but not too much power is important so you don't incur unnecessary overhead and costs.

For example, suppose you're designing an application that will read a temperature sensor and open and close a switch that activates a heater. The switch position is based on current and past temperature readings (because the computer needs to know whether the system is heating up or cooling down and at what rate). That's all: The application inputs temperature, does some calculations, and decides whether to alter the position of a switch.

Given the extent of this application, using an embedded PC as the hardware platform is like killing a small insect with a large gun. However, while the processing power is much greater than the task requires, more important is what this unneeded power costs you. Perhaps with a less powerful chip, the system could run on a smaller battery and be smaller in size, costing less to produce.

Cost-Effectiveness

Is using embedded PCs cost-effective? This is a buy-versus-make decision. Based on the number of units to be produced, estimate and compare the cost of building systems with embedded PCs to the cost of building systems containing your own hardware. For certain quantities, purchasing embedded PCs will be less expensive; for others, creating custom hardware will prove to be your best bet.

Uniqueness

What type of application are you creating? This is critical in determining whether using an embedded PC is appropriate. For some projects, such as a graphics-intensive application, a RISC chip rather than an embedded PC may be more appropriate. For others, such as a distributed data gathering system, an embedded PC in combination with custom hardware may be best. In this case, an embedded PC would do well as a robust, central controller, while smaller microcontrollers could be attached on the periphery and dedicated to gathering data.

SUMMARY

In this chapter, we defined real-time embedded systems and examined the advantages and disadvantages of using embedded PC hardware as a platform for embedded projects. In the next chapter, we provide some practical guidelines for designing and developing real-time embedded systems and for choosing a processor, an operating system, a language, and development tools.

2

Designing and Developing Your Real-Time System

Before you embark on any programming project beyond writing a simple routine or two, your first task should be to create a plan. Without a plan, you risk programming for days (perhaps even weeks or months) only to discover something you hadn't anticipated — something that causes you to redo a lot of work. We've experienced this self-inflicted misfortune more than once. We call it programming ourselves into a corner.

In this chapter, we show you how to plan a real-time embedded project. For small undertakings, a back-of-an-envelope sketch may be sufficient. For any moderate-sized computer project, however, you need to methodically map all aspects of the project and then troubleshoot your plan. That way, you are less likely to overlook important details and make costly mistakes. Later in the chapter, we give you pointers on choosing the right hardware and software for your projects.

A PRACTICAL APPROACH

Our approach to planning a real-time embedded project consists of three phases:

- Analysis
- Design
- Implementation

Each phase is a sequence of related activities. During analysis, you learn and document the goals of the system, as well as its constraints. During the design phase, you decide how to fulfill those goals given the constraints. Think of the design phase as the point in the building process at which you draw the blueprints. In the implementation phase, you carry out the design, building, and testing the system. (Many people jump into the implementation phase directly, which is usually a bad idea. Up-front analysis and design are a necessary part of development on anything but the smallest of projects.)

So, during analysis, you determine *what* the system should do. During design, you determine *how* the system will do it. In the implementation phase, you make the system do it.

It's common for real-time embedded projects to include two additional phases: testing and maintenance. Because this book focuses on the *building* of real-time embedded applications, however, we do not discuss a maintenance phase, which focuses on the upkeep and extension of a deployed application. We do discuss testing in the implementation process, and phase testing, or verification, in the analysis and design sections.

> **Note:** Many books have been written on various development methodologies — formalized step-by-step guidelines that lead you through the analysis, design, and implementation processes or comparable processes. Although most methodologies provide guidelines for developing software in general, some are tailored to developing embedded and real-time systems. Much of what we describe in this chapter is a distillation of methodologies we've used or studied over the years. You can, however, choose from plenty of methodologies. In Appendix D, "Development Methodologies for Real-Time and Embedded Systems," you'll find a survey of several methodologies for building embedded and real-time systems.

THE ITERATIVE APPROACH

We're not advising that you proceed linearly through the analysis, design, and implementation phases. Rather, we think that using an iterative approach is best.

The idea is this: When you begin work on a project, your information regarding that project's solution — the system you're going to build — is incomplete. You haven't yet figured out the whole problem (much less the solution), so you begin gathering information regarding the problem and its solution. You put that information into a framework that lets you make sense of all the facts. As you progress, your knowledge of both the problem and the solution becomes more detailed. Ultimately, it becomes detailed enough so that you can begin writing code and building hardware.

Sometimes, however, as you uncover details about the problem and its solution, you discover that something you *thought* would work, won't. For example, suppose that you're working on a project that requires a sorting routine. You choose an algorithm that you believe will perform as required using the hardware available. When implementation time comes, you discover that the sort routine doesn't execute as rapidly as you'd hoped. Maybe you goofed in its projected performance during your design phase. You do some quick testing and settle on an algorithm that's fast enough, but whose memory requirements are such that you need to add a little extra RAM to the final product. The result is that you find yourself revisiting a higher-level phase (the design phase, in this case) to make alterations because of something discovered in a lower-level phase (the implementation phase).

This iterated fashion of building projects is not something that we make explicit in the upcoming descriptions of the individual phases. But we suggest that you keep it in mind while reading this chapter and, later, as you work through designing and constructing any computer-based system (software, hardware, or both). Be flexible enough — willing enough — to stop, back up, and refine a component that you recognize was incorrectly or poorly designed. Don't try to pave over analysis and design errors with the expectation of revisiting and patching the error later.

THE ANALYSIS PHASE

In the analysis phase, you define the problem to be solved or the goals to be accomplished. The analysis phase is often referred to as the *requirements phase*, or the *system requirements phase*. Five steps make up the analysis phase:

- State the problem.
- Specify the project constraints.
- List the customer requirements.
- Specify hardware and software.
- Verify your analysis.

We mentioned that the best approach to the analysis, design, and implementation phases is iterative. An iterative approach is also best when working within any of these phases. If, for example, you realize that you should refine your statement of the problem after reviewing the customer's requirements, don't hesitate to do so.

STATING THE PROBLEM

The first step in the analysis phase is to write a problem statement that clearly defines the problem or objective. Depending on the complexity of a project, a problem statement could be anything from a single sentence to several pages. What's most important is that it clearly and thoroughly defines the problem or goal; this document shouldn't offer any solutions. To make sure that the problem is clear and everyone agrees on the objectives of the project, have your customer(s) review the statement. (For our purposes, a *customer* is anyone — a person, a department, or a company — to whom you provide a service. A customer isn't necessarily only the organization that pays for your services or the person who uses your product.)

SPECIFYING PROJECT CONSTRAINTS

Next, make a list of all the constraints imposed on your project. Think broadly: Constraints come in all shapes and sizes and from internal and external sources. Despite their differences and origins, though, constraints have one thing in common: They can wreak havoc with your project if you don't anticipate and plan for them. For example, you may find your development options limited by your company's management policies or your staff's experience; or you may find constraints imposed by external forces such as the market. So no matter what the constraints, or who or what imposes them, you should enumerate them now and keep them in mind as the project develops. Here are some questions to help you begin thinking of possible constraints:

- Do you have interim or final project deadlines that must be met?
- Do you have a fixed budget for the project or parts of the project?
- What's the maximum number of people who will be assigned to the project?
- What's the maximum number of hours per week that each person can work on the project?
- Is the staff's technical knowledge and experience sufficient?
- Is the staff familiar with the problem you're trying to solve?
- Where are the staff and other critical resources located?
- Do you have to use certain hardware components?
- Do you have to use certain software tools?
- What are the approval milestones and process?
- Can you depend on your regular suppliers for this project?

Sometimes the constraints aren't what you'd expect, nor do they originate from where you'd expect. Marketing, for example, may view an interim date for delivering a working demo as more critical to the success of the product than making the final delivery date. You may view having staff in more than one location a hindrance. Purchasing may have only one microprocessor supplier on its approved vendor list. Or management may have very few approval milestones but take weeks at each point to provide feedback.

It's important to keep an eye on project constraints for four reasons:

- **Constraints can surface at any time.** It would be nice if all constraints were obvious at the beginning of a project, but that's rarely the case. More often than not, more constraints become apparent as a project evolves.
- **Constraints affect the solutions you choose.** The choices you make in the design phase will be less effective and may not work at all if they aren't developed with a project's constraints in mind.
- **Constraints breed constraints.** A limitation in one area often affects other aspects of a project. For example, supplier constraints may dictate hardware restrictions that, in turn, may result in limited software options. You may have more constraints than it appears.
- **Too many constraints can make executing a project impossible.** When limitations pile up and begin to threaten a project, it's time to revisit or rework a project's priorities and goals.

LISTING CUSTOMER REQUIREMENTS

After you've written a problem statement and started your list of constraints, your next task is to start a list of customer requirements. A good way to define customer requirements is in terms of what they're not: They're not engineering-driven specifications. Rather, customer requirements are features requested by nonengineering folks such as your customer and the marketing department. When you make a list of customer requirements, you gain a better understanding of the project's problems and objectives. Hence, you could think of specifying customer requirements as elaborating on the problem statement you wrote earlier.

Getting the information you need to formulate a complete picture isn't always easy. You and your customer will make assumptions; your customer may not realize information that he has would be helpful to you; or your customer may forget to specify certain requirements because he uses them so often or so rarely. These are just a few of the things that can prevent you from gathering necessary data.

To build a product that meets your customer's expectations, then, you have to start thinking about a project from various angles, act like a troubleshooter, and ask a lot of questions. Following are some questions to jog your thinking. Not every question on this list will apply to your project, and some are undoubtedly missing. Our purpose here is simply to help you begin looking at projects critically.

- What tasks will the system be used for?
- What input will the system receive from users and other sources?
- What output should the system provide users and other sources?
- How do users want to physically interface with the system?
- What should the system's size and weight be?
- What peripherals should the system connect to?
- Does the system need to run any existing software?
- What type of data will the system process?
- Does the system need to communicate with other systems?
- Is the system a standalone or networked system?
- What is the expected response time of the system?
- What security safeguards are required?
- Under what environmental conditions will the system be operated?
- What are the physical storage and memory capacity requirements?
- What are the scalability, reliability, and robustness expectations for the system?
- How should the system be powered?
- How should the system notify users of malfunctions?
- Are any manual or mechanical overrides necessary?
- Will the system have a capability to remotely diagnose and correct problems?

You may notice that some questions could have more than one answer, and two different questions could have the same answer. This is intentional. Very often, people interpret words and questions more narrowly than we expect. For example, ask a customer about their communications needs and they may think in terms of modem connections. Unless you specifically ask whether a system should connect to a network, that crucial bit of information may not surface until later. Asking questions that may have more than one answer, or multiple questions that may have the same answer, is a good way to uncover information.

As with constraints, itemizing customer requirements is important because requirements often breed other requirements that will, in turn, affect the solutions you choose. For example, your I/O and network specifications for a device connected to a network periodically would be different than specifications for a device that must be able to exchange information on a network at any time. Taking time to ferret out requirements is time well spent.

It's also important to be thorough when listing customer requirements. For example, suppose the problem is to build a home thermostat control. Your list of the system inputs and outputs should enumerate the I/O between the system and the user and the I/O with all external sources, such as a temperature sensor. In addition, you should document each I/O channel and its characteristics in as much detail as possible. Note if the input will be analog or digital; note the input source, such as a pushbutton; and note the frequency — that is, will a user be allowed to push a button once a second or once every half-second; and so on.

You may find it difficult to decide whether something is a customer requirement or a project constraint; it may be both. Admittedly, this is a gray area with no hard and fast rules to go by. The best way to handle a specification that's a customer requirement and has the slightest chance of being a project constraint is to include it on both lists. It's far better to list it twice than to overlook it.

SPECIFYING HARDWARE AND SOFTWARE

The next step is to take a first cut at a list of hardware and software you'll use to build the system. Although many choices won't be clear this early in the development process, it's worthwhile to narrow your options and reduce the number of variables you have to consider in the design stage. Some items to consider at this time include the following:

- Processor speed
- Bus size
- Operating system
- Programming language
- Third-party software components or libraries
- Third-party hardware components

The earlier you can pinpoint the microprocessor that will be at the heart of your system, the better. Specifying the processor speed and bus size are a first step in this direction.

The operating system you'll use is another critical decision. Although it's probably too early to make that decision, you may be able to decide the type of operating system your design will require. For example, do you need a hard real-time operating system, or a small single-tasking kernel with limited services, or no operating system — just a collection of drivers for your hardware?

If you can anticipate your language or third-party requirements, add them to the list. For example, if you know that you need to use a language with low overhead, you might specify C and assembly as your options.

We discuss at greater length making these and other choices later on, in the design phase.

VERIFYING YOUR ANALYSIS

Verification, also known as *phase testing,* is checking the documentation produced in a particular phase for clarity and completeness. Verification of the materials that you generate in the analysis phase is important, because believe it or not, most of the errors that you'll encounter in your project stem from the analysis phase. According to *Design for Debug and Test, An Applied Microsystems Whitepaper* (available at http://www.amc.com), 56 percent of a project's errors are generated when you are working to "...lay down the requirements and specifications of the system." These errors can be the result of ambiguity in the documentation, omitted information, or other problems that we enumerate shortly.

Briefly, the goal of verification at the analysis phase is to confirm that the documents from this phase clearly and completely describe what the system does. Now, *clearly* and *completely* are admittedly subjective terms; no process exists through which you can pass documentation such that the result will be completely clear and clearly complete. Some guidelines, however, can aid you in this endeavor. In *Software Engineering, Methods and Management,* published by Academic Press, Anneliese von Mayrhauser suggests auditing your documentation using the following criteria:

- **Noise.** Irrelevant information.
- **Silence.** Omitted information.
- **Overspecification.** Information that should be withheld until the design phase.
- **Contradiction.** Incompatible specifications or constraints.
- **Ambiguity.** A specification or constraint that permits more than one interpretation.
- **Forward reference.** A feature referenced in the documentation before that feature has been clearly defined.
- **Wishful thinking.** The definition of a requirement such that there is no way to verify that the requirement has been fulfilled.

Three of these criteria, overspecification, forward references, and wishful thinking, need further explanation.

Implementation details have a way of creeping into analysis documents. When von Mayrhauser warns against overspecification, she's advising us to keep an eye out for just this.

Documents generated in the analysis phase are supposed to describe what the system should do. Documents generated in the design phase are supposed to describe how the system will do it. If you find that your analysis documents include implementation details, move that information to the design documents.

Forward references make documents hard to read. Using the iterative approach to analysis, design, and implementation, it's easy for references to creep in to a document ahead of explanations. One simple example is using an acronym before you explain it and define the term in its entirety. To solve the problem, you should delete the premature reference or move the explanation of the reference forward in the document.

Wishful thinking refers to requirements that cannot be verified or tested. If you can't create a situation to test the requirement, the requirement is unnecessary or too strict. For example, it's ridiculous to specify that a pushbutton input operated by a person must be able to respond to 1,000 presses per second.

The most effective way to critique your analysis is to have it reviewed by people who have different perspectives on the project. Ask users, customers, technical staff, and others to use these criteria to examine the documents you've generated in the analysis phase. Not only will people with different perspectives catch different errors, but multiple reviews of any document lessens the likelihood of an error sneaking through. Depending on the verdict, you then proceed to the design phase or redo part of your analysis.

An Example

To illustrate the steps we've just described, suppose we've taken on a project for a TV manufacturer to build a simple infrared (IR) TV remote control. Here, we give examples of some of the information to gather in the analysis phase and how to document it.

Problem Statement

The problem statement should be a clear and thorough statement of the problem or goals of the project. Our statement for this remote-control device is as follows:

> To develop a simple handheld remote that has a three-button controller that can remotely operate this manufacturer's television sets. The remote will be lightweight and battery powered. It will control a television through a built-in infrared transmitter. (The customer's televisions have an infrared receiver.)

> One button on the remote will control the TV's power and be labeled "power." The other two buttons will be used to cycle through the available channels. A button with an up arrow will change channels in increments; a button with a down arrow will change channels in decrements.

Constraint Specification

Now we list the project constraints. This project has just two, and both are combined hardware/software constraints:

- The remote must use a customer-supplied ROM. The manufacturer's TVs respond only to signals that adhere to a unique protocol. This protocol is comprised of the manufacturer's signature code, commands, and timing specification. The signature code is a unique code stored in a ROM available only from the manufacturer. Consequently, the handheld remote must use this ROM.

- The remote must adhere to the customer's timing specifications. The timing of the transmission of each bit of the signature code is important. When the remote sends a signal to the TV, the signal is in two pieces: the signature code and the command. The TV may not recognize a command if the timing does not meet specifications. The software in the remote must transmit the signature code and commands according to these specifications.

Of course, the final documentation will need more detail than we show here. We would include a diagram of the masked ROM for the benefit of the hardware design engineers who must ultimately incorporate it in the remote. We would also include the detailed description of the signature signal's timing for the benefit of the programmers.

Customer Requirements

The customer requirements detail the product specifications. They should elaborate all specifications mentioned in the problem statement, and list and explain any additional product features or attributes that aren't specified in the problem statement. For this example, our customer requirements are

- The remote will be battery powered. It will require no more than 2 AAA batteries. The current draw of the entire system should be such that the average time between battery replacements will be no less than 10,000 button presses.

- The remote must weigh less than 100 grams and measure less than 10 cm. x 5 cm. x 1.5 cm.

- The remote must be manufactured from high-density black plastic.

- The power button must be red and circular. The channel up/down buttons must be black and rectangular.

- The remote must be able to withstand a fall of 1.5 meters to a wooden floor with no cracking of the case or damage to the electronics.

- The infrared signals transmitted by the remote must conform to the timing specification provided by the customer.

- The remote must work within a range of up to 10 meters from the TV set. The remote must operate correctly when positioned within 45 degrees of the front of the TV set and when pointed within 20 degrees of the infrared detector on the TV.

- The correct infrared signal must be transmitted within 20 milliseconds after a button is pressed.

Notice that the description is very general. We don't mention anything yet about the details of the transmission timing, where the software goes in the ROM to find the identification code, and so forth. We're still describing what the system does, not how it does it.

Hardware and Software Specifications

Now we can make a first pass at specifying the hardware and software we'll use:

- **Processor.** The design will not require anything beyond an 8-bit microcontroller. We might even use a 4-bit microcontroller. At this point, we would begin researching candidate processors — perhaps by searching through the trade journals or spelunking on the Internet.
- **Operating system.** The software requirements for this system are uncomplicated enough that even a simple operating system kernel is not needed. We'll write directly to the hardware.
- **Programming language.** Because we'll code directly to the hardware, we need to use a low-level language. Our first choice is C, assuming a reasonable C compiler/debugger combination is available for the processor we choose. If not, we'll use assembly language.
- **Third-party software components.** The project's software requirements are so minimal that we're unlikely to need any third-party software.
- **Third-party hardware components.** There obviously isn't any need for board-level or above hardware components in this project. We'll start identifying components such as the pushbuttons and infrared LED at this stage.

For now, set this example aside and go on to the theory of the design phase. We come back to the example when we illustrate the steps of the design phase.

THE DESIGN PHASE

In the analysis phase, you learned what the system is supposed to do. In the design phase, you determine how the system will fulfill the customer's requirements given the constraints on the project. The steps in the design phase are

- Review the analysis.
- Specify hardware components.
- Define hardware interfaces.
- Specify software subsystems.
- Define software interfaces.
- Specify the start-up and shutdown processes.
- Specify error handling.
- Verify your design.

Although you're supposed to focus on the *what* in the analysis phase and save the *how* for the design phase, we've found that we occasionally jump ahead to the design phase when we know how a particular piece of the system is going to work. Consequently, by the time we complete our analysis, substantial chunks of the design are already worked out. There's no harm in doing this; as we've said, the process is iterative.

REVIEWING THE ANALYSIS

The following may sound ridiculously obvious, but you'd be surprised how often it's forgotten: Before you begin designing your system, review the problem statement and the customer requirements. It's always a good idea to have the end in sight before you embark on a project. So, refresh your memory by reviewing the documents that define the problems to solve and the goals to achieve.

At the same time, review the constraints. These limitations will determine what options are available to you and how you build your system. For example, suppose the project requires floating-point calculations, but the budget doesn't allow for a processor that includes a floating-point coprocessor. This means the design must specify that the floating-point calculations will be performed by software. It also means that you will have to write a floating-point library yourself or obtain one from a third party.

Review the analysis documents not only at the outset but also throughout the design phase. This helps keep the goals and constraints in mind and the project focused. A project can get derailed at many points — even by good intentions and suggestions. By frequently consulting the analysis documents you can keep a project on track.

SPECIFYING HARDWARE COMPONENTS

Now it's time to turn your attention to the hardware in the system. Break the hardware down into components, and construct a block diagram or diagrams of the hardware components. Create one block diagram showing individual circuit boards, peripherals, and so on. Unless the hardware design is fairly simple or uses all off-the-shelf boards, you probably need block diagrams also for one or more of the circuit boards; partition the board logic into components that correspond roughly to functionality provided by an off-the-shelf chip, a PAL (Programmable Array Logic) chip you will create, and so on.

By identifying hardware components, you break up the project into more manageable pieces that can be thought about and possibly worked on independently. Also, it will help you identify which components can be off-the-shelf or adapted from a previous project rather than designed from scratch.

The hardware block diagrams produced in this step are extremely useful not only to the hardware designers but also to the software engineers and project managers. The diagrams provide a quick visual reference showing how to communicate with the hardware and how the hardware components interconnect. In addition, the diagrams help you create a high-level mental picture of the system.

Perhaps some functions of the system could be implemented in either hardware or software. No clear-cut method can swiftly and flawlessly guide you through determining which functions should be assigned to hardware and which should be assigned to software. Often, your list of constraints dictates this decision. Determining whether to implement a function in hardware versus software is usually a tradeoff between cost and system performance or between development costs (additional time) and manufacturing costs (additional hardware). For example, suppose your system requires a time-of-day clock. Should you implement that timer as a hardware real-time clock, which will add the cost of an additional hardware component to each system manufactured? Or should you implement the timer as a routine that is repeatedly triggered by a hardware interrupt and keeps track of time in software, and therefore could potentially be affected by an overcommitted CPU?

For functions that do not have a clear preferred implementation, put off the decision as long as possible. As the specification for the rest of the system evolves, it may become obvious whether hardware or software is the best choice.

Hardware or Software: Which Comes First?

The design approach we presented attacks the design of the hardware components and interfaces first and then moves to software design. In general, this is a good, practical approach for many projects. It's helpful to have block diagrams of the hardware design available as a reference during the software design. It's often possible to specify the high-level hardware design faster than the software design, either because the project constraints dictate the hardware design or because a lot of off-the-shelf hardware is used.

If the system is large or complex, you'll probably want to design the hardware and software in parallel. You can speed up the overall design time (assuming you have sufficient staffing) with parallel design efforts. The hardware and software designers need to communicate well and periodically revisit earlier design decisions to ensure that the hardware and software designs are kept consistent.

In some cases, you may need to design the software first. Although it's difficult to design software without a clear idea of what hardware it will run on, external circumstances such as a staffing problem or a holdup in an executive-level decision on what processors are approved for use may delay the hardware design effort. Work on hardware-independent portions of the software design (in many systems, most of the software is hardware independent), and leave the design of subsystems that interact directly with hardware until later in the design process, when the hardware design has jelled.

DEFINING HARDWARE INTERFACES

The next step is the design of the interfaces that allow the software to communicate with the hardware. Specifying the interfaces helps drive the rest of the hardware and software design by providing some concrete details that keep the designers focused. At a minimum, the hardware interface specification should specify the following:

- **I/O ports.** You need a list of all I/O ports used by the hardware, the port addresses, and all the commands and command sequences that can be written to each port.

- **Hardware registers.** For each register, you need its bit assignments, a description of how the register is read or written to (for example, by reading or writing to an I/O port or through a command sequence), and any timing requirements or other restrictions on the use of the register.

- **Memory addresses for shared memory or memory-mapped I/O.** For memory-mapped I/O, you must also specify the sequences of reads and writes required to perform each possible I/O operation.

- **Hardware interrupts.** If the system uses hardware interrupts, list the interrupt numbers used and the hardware events to which they are assigned.

SPECIFYING SOFTWARE SUBSYSTEMS

After defining the hardware interfaces, you partition the system's software into reasonably well-defined subsystems. The intent is to identify self-contained pieces or subsystems that you can think and talk about more easily as pieces than as a whole and that can be parceled out and worked on semi-independently and in parallel. This will also help you to identify subsystems that don't have to be written from scratch. Perhaps you can license third-party software or reuse code from a previous software project.

We advocate a top-down approach. Start by identifying the major subsystems: user interfaces, data collection from hardware devices, data processing, and so on. Then drill down, dividing the major subsystems into smaller subsystems, the smaller subsystems into smaller ones, and so on, until you feel you have reduced each to a manageable-sized subsystem. For anything beyond a small- to medium-sized project, this is usually a multistep endeavor.

> **Note:** In the opening paragraph of this section, we used the admittedly vague term *reasonably well-defined* to characterize subsystems. It's not easy to explain the differences between a well-defined subsystem versus an ill-defined one. Generally, a subsystem is a collection of related software routines and data that work together to perform a specific function. Other parts of the system have no direct access to the subsystem data, and make calls into the subsystem only through a small number of interface routines. To use the subsystem, you shouldn't need to know anything about how it works internally — you only need to know what it does and how to use the subsystem interface.

Then detail the functionality of each subsystem. You already started this process by identifying the subsystems, because that task required an understanding of each subsystem's responsibility. Flesh out your understanding of what each subsystem does, the services it provides to other subsystems, and the services it needs from other subsystems.

DEFINING SOFTWARE INTERFACES

Next, you should specify the software interfaces that each subsystem furnishes. Detail the APIs (application programming interfaces) by specifying function calls, data structures, and global data used in each subsystem's interface. Create header files with function prototypes, data structure declarations, class declarations, and so on.

Like the hardware interfaces, specifying the software interfaces helps drive the design by providing a common reference point. You'll also find that defining a subsystem interface often helps you refine and clarify your understanding of the functionality provided by the subsystem.

SPECIFYING THE START-UP AND SHUTDOWN PROCESSES

Describe the sequence of events that occur during system start-up and shutdown. For start-up, specify the details of hardware component and software subsystem initialization, and in what order the subsystems should be initialized. Often this is obvious, but sometimes intricate interdependencies or an external requirement for start-up exists, such as a communications link that must be established. Likewise, for shutdown, describe any actions that each subsystem must perform, such as flushing files to disk or closing network connections.

SPECIFYING ERROR HANDLING

Error handling can be critical in an embedded system, which is often required to run unattended for days or weeks at a time. It's important to create an error-handling strategy during the design phase and create error-handling routines early in implementation, even if they're only placeholder routines at first. Defining error routines early helps ensure that programmers include error-handling code from the beginning, rather than ignore error conditions during the early stages of implementation because no error-handling capability is in place yet.

Many potential error conditions that crop up during implementation can be ignored or easily worked around. But what should the software do when an error occurs that can't be ignored or when something nonsensical occurs that means the software has a bug or the system has been corrupted? Your error-handling strategy should include dealing with fatal errors.

We can't give you specific guidelines, because the correct approach depends on your system's user interface, communication capabilities, and mission-critical nature, as well as other system-specific characteristics. Here are some points to consider, though:

- What is your user interface? Can you report errors to a system operator? Or should you log errors to a file for post-mortem analysis?

- Does your system have the capability to communicate with other devices? Can you use that capability to report errors to a remote station?

- What are the consequences of system shutdown or a crash? If a shutdown is unacceptable, fatal error conditions may have to trigger a restart of the system. And you may need a watchdog timer capability in the system that can detect a system crash and restart the system automatically.

Watchdogs

Some embedded systems are deployed in severe operating conditions where anything (literally) might happen. Designers must plan for cases in which the system fails so severely that it crashes, and yet must somehow rise phoenix-like from that crash. This system resurrection is accomplished with the help of a watchdog timer.

A *watchdog timer* is a little alarm clock that designers have built into some CPUs. After the CPU has been powered up, software turns on its watchdog timer, and from that moment, the executing software has a contract with the watchdog. That contract goes something like this: "I'm ticking down toward zero," says the watchdog. "You have so many ticks (a certain amount of time) to go before I reach zero. Now, if you reset me before I reach zero, I'll start over and start ticking down again. But if you *don't* reset me before I reach zero, I'm going to reset *you.*"

So, during normal operation, the software periodically resets the watchdog timer. The watchdog never counts down to zero and nothing remarkable happens. (Not unlike security guards who make regular rounds, checking in at stations within a fixed amount of time during those rounds.)

If something should happen such that the software is unable to reset the watchdog in time, however, the watchdog reboots the whole system. To be prosaic: If the system goes into a crash-induced coma, the watchdog wallops it back to its senses. Some watchdog-enabled CPUs even provide a means by which software that's going through reset initialization can determine whether the system is just powering up or is recovering from a watchdog-induced reset. If the latter, the software can examine the environment and attempt to determine what caused the crash.

VERIFYING YOUR DESIGN

Just as you verify the quality and completeness of documentation you generate at the conclusion of the analysis phase, you should check the caliber of your design documents. For small projects, involving one- or two-person teams, review the design documents for the seven criteria: noise, silence, overspecification, contradiction, ambiguity, forward references, and wishful thinking. For medium-sized projects, review your design in an informal design walkthrough. This task can be as simple as turning to a colleague or cohort and explaining the design to them. Ask your colleague to keep the seven criteria in mind as you go over the design.

For the largest projects, you should do a more formal presentation. Because this is a design review, assemble a group consisting primarily of engineers, but try to include a few members who have different perspectives on the project, such as marketing people and end users. Explain the seven criteria by which they should judge the design, then "teach" them the design. Although you may find it difficult to explain some of the technical material to those not technically savvy, you'll find that people who have not been too close to the details of a project often spot errors that the designers miss.

AN EXAMPLE

We continue here with the design phase for the infrared TV remote control example. The first step of the design phase is revisiting the customer specifications and constraints. Take a moment at this point to look back at the example in the analysis phase and review it.

Specify Hardware Components

We suggested that a diagram would be useful when specifying hardware components. The diagram should not be a detailed circuit diagram but rather a high-level diagram that helps you identify the major pieces in the final system. Figure 2-1 shows what we mean.

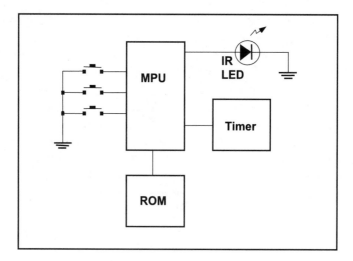

Figure 2-1: This is a block diagram of the system. It helps you identify the system's major components. Details, such as actual part numbers, pin assignments, and power supply connections are not shown. They are added later, as you sharpen your view of the system.

This diagram is already helping us recognize which functions could be implemented in either hardware or software. Notice that we've identified that a timer is necessary. (Remember, the timing of the delivery of the bit-stream messages to the TV is important.) We have a choice of implementing that timer in software — counting instruction cycles for the part of the program that sends the data — or using a hardware timer. The latter would certainly be less of a programming headache, so we'll probably choose the hardware route.

Our choice of a timer is also a factor in the process of hardware product selection. Some microprocessing units (MPUs) carry on-chip timers. We'll note that fact in our list of candidate processors, because using an on-chip timer would mean one less piece of silicon taking up space on the circuit board. (Remember, this is a small handheld unit, so space is an issue.) If we can use an on-chip timer, we'll redraw the diagram to show the timer as part of the processor.

Notice also that at least one component on this diagram is specified by the customer constraints: the ROM. Back in the analysis phase, we learned that the customer would supply a ROM chip that carries the special identification codes; the device *must* use this ROM. Some microcontrollers provide onboard ROM. Because constraints force this ROM to be external, we'll keep it that way on the diagram.

Define Hardware Interfaces

Referring to the system block diagram in Figure 2-1, we see that hardware interfaces are needed to the pushbuttons, the LED, the timer, and the ROM. We'll assign I/O pins or I/O addresses (depending on the I/O architecture used by the processor we settle on) to read the state of the three buttons and to control the LED. We'll also assign I/O addresses to program the timer chip and choose an interrupt to use for the timer interrupt. The final assignment are the memory addresses for the customer's ROM.

Specify Software Subsystems

The hand-held remote is simple enough that partitioning the software into subsystems is elementary. We identify three subsystems:

- **Button monitoring.** This subsystem waits for a button to be pressed and then returns a code identifying which button was pressed.
- **Command lookup.** This subsystem looks up the command corresponding to the button that was pressed. Commands are kept in a table of global data in ROM.
- **Command transmission.** This subsystem transmits the command. It is responsible for turning the LED on and off, and using the timer to ensure that the command's timing requirements are met.

We use a high-level flowchart, shown in Figure 2-2, to show the control flow relationship between these subsystems. In a more complex system, a data flow diagram rather than a control flow diagram might be more helpful.

Define Software Interfaces

Because we're using the C programming language to write the code for this project, we define the software interfaces in terms of C data structures and function prototypes.

The button monitoring subsystem needs only one interface function, which waits until a button is pressed and then returns a value identifying the button. A more versatile interface is unnecessary in this project, because the system doesn't need to do any work while it's waiting for button presses.

```
#define BUTTON_UP 0
#define BUTTON_DOWN 1
#define BUTTON_POWER 2
int GetButtonPress(void);
```

The command lookup subsystem also has one interface function, which takes a button code as input and returns a command to transmit to the TV. We need to define a data structure for a TV command. For this simple example, we need only a variable-sized array of data structures identifying LED on or off, and a duration in microseconds.

```
typedef struct
{
    int     fLEDOn;         // T if LED on, F if LED off
    int     nmicrosec;      // number of microseconds
}
LED_COMMAND;
typedef struct {
    int     nLEDCommands;   // number of LED_COMMAND structs
    LED_COMMAND LEDCmd[1];  // variable-sized array of commands
}
TV_COMMAND;

TV_COMMAND *LookupCommand(int Button);
```

The command transmission subsystem also consists of one function, which accepts a TV_COMMAND structure as input, and returns after transmission is complete.

```
void TransmitCommand(TV_COMMAND *pCommand);
```

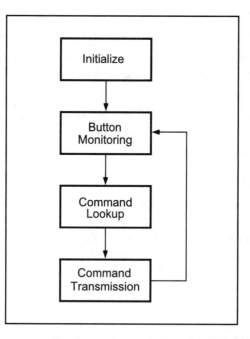

Figure 2-2: From the software perspective, the remote control will consist of three subsystems. First, the device executes any initialization code when a battery is inserted. Then, it enters an eternal loop, watching for button presses. When the user presses a button, the system retrieves the corresponding command to be sent to the TV, transmits the command, and returns to watching for button presses.

Specify the Start-up and Shutdown Processes

At start-up time, two subsystems perform initialization functions:

- The button monitoring subsystem performs any hardware reset necessary for the button hardware.
- The command transmission subsystem initializes the hardware timer and installs an interrupt handler to process timer interrupts.

No shutdown is required for this system.

Specify Error Handling

The next step in the design phase is to specify error handling. This system has no user interface and no communications path over which it can report errors. Therefore, any error conditions must be dealt with internally, and the device must continue to operate correctly. Most errors should just be ignored. (For example, if a nonsensical button press is received, the button monitoring subsystem should ignore it and continue waiting for another button press.) If any part of the system detects an error that indicates some part of the system may have been corrupted, it should reboot the system to reinitialize and continue operation.

SOME DECISIONS

During the design phase, you finalize the choices of the hardware and software you'll employ to carry out the project. You began the process of hardware and software selection toward the end of the analysis phase, but that was only a first cut. Now it's time to confirm the decisions you've made and make others.

We've separated the hardware and software you have to select into the following categories. You won't need components from all these categories in every embedded project, but some choices (such as the processor and the programming language) must be made for any project:

- Processor
- Hardware components
- Operating system
- Programming language
- Software development tools
- Hardware debugging tools
- Software components

This list doesn't have a sequential path. We find that the relative importance of categories varies from project to project; usually the processor is the most important selection, but sometimes the operating system or the programming language choice is the most critical. You will find no universal or pat answers when making these choices.

In the following sections, we outline the criteria that we think are most important for you to consider as you make your decisions for each item. We have cast the criteria as questions. None of the collections of criteria are exhaustive; that would be impossible. Nor are they arranged in a particular order. We've found that the questions you must ask as you work through the selection process have cross-dependencies. Which processor you choose can limit your operating system choices; which language you choose limits your development tools choices; which operating system you choose can limit your development tool choices as well; and so on.

Choosing a Processor

Criteria to consider when choosing a processor include the following:

- **What sort of processing horsepower does the design require?** This is not an easy question to answer. A little investigating will uncover a vast body of literature and popular press discussing how to judge processor performance — with no consensus. A processor's performance is dependent on many things: clock speed, the size of the processor's internal registers, whether registers are treated orthogonally (instructions treat all registers equally), special on-chip hardware to facilitate time-consuming operations (for example, a hardware multiplication unit), and so on.

  You should match the processor's capabilities to the project specifications. (You started this back in the analysis phase, where we suggested that you take a first whack at processor characteristics.) For example, will the predominant data types operated on fit into 8 bits? (In other words, will the bulk of the data being processed by the embedded application be in the form of bytes?) If so, perhaps an 8-bit CPU would be sufficient for the task. If the design calls for the manipulation of 16-bit integers, you may need to investigate 16-bit processors (such as the 80188). Lots of big integers? A 32-bit embedded x86 CPU might be called for. Familiarize yourself with the offerings of the marketplace and recognize that selecting a processor with capabilities that exceed what the job requires can often be as detrimental as selecting one with capabilities that fall short. (In the former case, you spend money unnecessarily; in the latter, the system won't perform to spec.)

- **What is your staff's processor expertise?** This might seem like an odd question, but it's not. Suppose you're working through the design of your system, and during your research you stumble across a processor that appears to meet your exact requirements. Unfortunately, no one on your staff (and your staff might be just you) is familiar with that processor. You have to gauge the repercussions of using that processor: The programmers and hardware designers will have to not only expend energy solving the application itself, but also spend some of that energy figuring out how to work with that processor. Will your schedule allow that?

- **What are the design's I/O specifications?** Today, many embedded processors provide on-chip peripherals, reducing chip-count and, therefore, overall system cost. Find out, up front, if the hardware your application requires can be connected to the processor without undue amounts of glue logic and bulky hardware driver software. In addition, consider the availability of support chips for the processor (DMA controllers, memory management chips, interrupt controllers, and so on). Explore the available processor offerings — you might find a match to your application that reduces hardware costs considerably.

- **What software support tools are available for the processor?** A processor sitting on a circuit board isn't much help without a good set of development tools to put software into it. Also, what other software — real-time operating system (RTOS), for example — is available for the processor?

- **Does the processor provide on-chip debugging support?** Some new processors actually provide *debug pins* that facilitate the connection of external debugging hardware. The debugging hardware is not only less expensive than equivalent hardware for processors not so outfitted, but the entire laborious process of tracking down hardware problems is considerably simplified.

- **How trustworthy is the processor's vendor support?** Before you settle on a processor, you should confirm that it is readily available in good quantity, and that the manufacturer will continue to support that processor as long as your project will require it. (This is no joke. While we were writing this book, we came across a posting on the Internet from a fellow whose company had committed to supporting its real-time systems for the next 20 years. Unfortunately, the manufacturer of the processor that the systems used was dropping support for that processor. The note we read was a plea for sources of compilers and assemblers for the processor. We never found out if the plea was answered.) Some processor vendors offer guarantees of long-term support for embedded CPUs. If the estimated life span of your target system is three or more years, investigate such guarantees for your chosen processor.

CHOOSING HARDWARE COMPONENTS

Hardware components cover a lot of territory — everything from individual IC (integrated circuit) chips and components to complete circuit boards to disk drives to entire self-contained systems. We can't give general guidelines that apply to all the possibilities. We can, however, give you criteria to help you decide what you should build and what you should buy:

- **How many units of your system do you expect to build?** The higher the volume, the more worthwhile it is to design and build all the hardware yourself to keep unit costs low. On the other hand, if unit quantities are low, design costs can swamp any savings in manufacturing, and you may be better off purchasing motherboards and I/O boards from a third party.

- **What is the window of opportunity for your target market?** If you need to get your product released as soon as possible to stay competitive, buy as much predesigned hardware as you can and build as little as possible. If you have the luxury of a longer design cycle, you may want to design custom hardware in order to lower costs.

- **Is software development critically dependent on having hardware available, or can most software development be performed on a prototyping system, such as a PC?** The sooner the software team needs final hardware, the more attractive it is to buy off-the-shelf hardware to avoid delays that snowball and cause the overall product delivery date to slip significantly.

CHOOSING AN OPERATING SYSTEM

Criteria to consider when selecting an operating system, or OS, include the following:

- **How much functionality do you need from an OS?** Do you need all the capabilities of a general-purpose OS such as UNIX or Windows NT? Do you need a real-time OS with deterministic multitasking support and better scalability than a general-purpose OS? Do you just need a modest set of system services with no multitasking capability? Or are your requirements so minimal that you'd be better off rolling your own — writing your own start-up code and low-level services?

- **What development tools are available for the OS?** Some real-time operating systems have only vendor tool support. That is, you must acquire compilers, debuggers, and so on from the OS vendor. On the other hand, if the OS is in widespread use and third-party tools are available, you'll have alternatives to choose from.

- **How difficult will it be to port the OS to your hardware?** If you're using an off-the-shelf motherboard, does the OS vendor already have a port for that board? For a custom design, how close is your design to existing hardware the OS already runs on? After the OS is up and running on your hardware, the debugging process is usually straightforward. But the initial porting of the OS to the hardware can be frustrating and time-consuming, causing schedule slippage.

- **Does the OS include special debugging support?** Some operating systems allow you to activate a special debugging layer and get inside the OS to access functions that facilitate the task of tracking down application bugs.

- **What are the operating system's memory requirements?** If the OS requires a lot of memory, you may wind up paying for RAM or EEPROM simply to keep a bloated operating system happy.

- **Are your programmers familiar with the OS or with the API the OS uses to provide system services?** If not, remember that your schedule will have to include extra time to enable your programmers to familiarize themselves with the OS.

- **Does the OS include all the system-level components you need?** If not, you have to write them or purchase them elsewhere and integrate them. Commonly required components include networking support, the file system, the flash file system, PC Card support, CD-ROM support, floating-point emulation, and serial I/O support.

- **Does the OS have I/O drivers for your target hardware?** Again, you have to write anything that's not provided. You may want to reconsider your choice of an I/O card — such as an Ethernet card — based on what hardware the OS includes drivers for.

- **Is the OS scalable?** You want to be able to remove all unnecessary system features. If you can't, you wind up with additional memory costs for code that isn't being executed.

CHOOSING A PROGRAMMING LANGUAGE

Criteria to consider when choosing a programming language include the following:

- **What language is your staff proficient in?** You should not only concern yourself with the learning curve that your staff will have to pass through if you choose a language that's new to them, but also watch for increased bugginess, which happens when a programmer works in unfamiliar territory.

- **Is the language in widespread use?** If not, you might have difficulty obtaining good educational materials or finding programmers should you need to hire additional staff temporarily or permanently. (Here's an example: Forth has often turned up as a potential language for embedded projects. But take a trip to your local bookstore and count the number of Forth books as compared to the number of C/C++ books. Even if you want to make an argument that quality, not quantity, counts, odds are you'll find more good C/C++ books than good Forth books. We say this with a twinge of sadness, because we happen to like Forth a great deal.)

- **Will the language provide the performance required by your application?** In general, the higher the level of the language, the more overhead is imposed by the compiler and run-time library and the bigger and slower your application will be. For example, it's widely accepted that you can write the smallest and fastest applications in assembly language, the next smallest in C or Forth, then bigger in C++ or Basic, and so on.

  The tradeoff is development time versus run-time performance. If you write everything in assembly language, you can (if you spend enough time) produce code that is optimal for the processor — but you might miss your project deadlines. On the other hand, if you write your application in a high-level language, the resulting executable may be slower than the assembly language version and require more memory than your specifications can tolerate. You have to weigh all the pros and cons according to the requirements of your application.

CHOOSING SOFTWARE DEVELOPMENT TOOLS

Criteria to consider when choosing software tools include the following:

- **What are the capabilities of the system's debugger?** Remote debugging, in particular, is an important feature. *Remote debugging* means that you connect a host development system to the target by means of some cable, and run the application on the target under the control of a debugger on the host. The debugger should support source-level debugging for the language you've chosen, and should have full support for debugging code in ROM, including setting breakpoints in ROM. Two other important features of a debugger are its capabilities to debug multiple threads (tasks) and to allow you to examine and modify system data structures.

- **If you've chosen a compiler, does it include an assembler?** Some compilers allow in-line assembly as an alternative to a separate assembler. Although some applications are small enough to assault with assembly language, many aren't. Even for the larger jobs, however, it's nice to have an assembler around in case you have to hand-tune a section of code that compiler optimizations just can't improve. Also, if your application needs access to system-level instructions, an assembler is a must.

- **What sort of supporting libraries are available?** Many development systems now come with piles of useful libraries and sample code. Not only does the sample code provide additional educational material that you can draw from, but this is another case of avoiding wheel-reinvention: If someone else has already written code to implement a feature you need (and you're getting that code for free), use it. For example, most C++ compilers today are available with the standard template library, which provides a set of templates for defining all sorts of useful container, storage, searching, and sorting objects.

- **Has the compiler vendor kept the compiler up-to-date?** This is usually not a problem if the compiler vendor targets a range of embedded and full-blown operating systems rather than only one embedded kernel. Nevertheless, check to see whether the vendor has made timely releases with standardized changes to the language, better code optimizations, new instructions from later generations of processors, and so on. (This question could be applied to an interpreter as well as a compiler.)

- **Does the linker support all the file and symbol formats used by your other tools?** On the input side, it needs to read object modules produced by the compiler and assembler and libraries produced by a librarian. On the output side, it must generate an executable format the OS will load, a symbol format the debugger can read, and — if you're using an ICE or other hardware debug tool — the executable and symbol formats required by the hardware debugger. In particular, make sure no symbolic information is lost in the translation from input to output, so that you have full source-level debug capability.

- **Is there some sort of easy-to-use system builder tool for customizing the operating system?** Most real-time operating systems are scalable, allowing you to remove functionality you don't need to save memory. You want this capability to be easy to learn and use.

- **What vendor produces the development system?** Given that you're about to make an investment in the development system itself and that your staff will expend time coming up to speed with new software, it is worthwhile to become familiar with the company whose products you're going to buy. Find out how responsive the company is to its customers, how long it's been in business, whether it's growing or scaling back its operations, and so on. Most companies will provide you with a list of customers whom you can contact. User groups on on-line services or the Internet can also be a source of information.

CHOOSING HARDWARE DEBUGGING TOOLS

A good software debugger is all you need to find most bugs efficiently. Sometimes, however, hardware-assisted debugging can save you days or weeks of sleuthing. For example, to port an OS to new hardware, you have to get some amount of software working on your target hardware before your software cross-debugger can work. How would you debug that initial code if it doesn't come right up? You could write code that lights LEDs or writes to a serial port to let you know whether you've reached a certain point in the code, but using a hardware debugger is a lot faster and easier.

Hardware debugging tools include the following product categories:

- **In-circuit emulators (ICEs)** connect to the target system by means of a short cable that ends in a pod that plugs into the processor socket. The actual processor then plugs into the top of the pod. Because no debug software is needed on the target hardware, you can start debugging before any software (or hardware) is working correctly. ICEs support the usual debugging operations: single stepping, breakpoints, disassembly, examining memory, source-level debugging, and so on. They also let you see (and trigger on) hardware events such as interrupts and memory accesses. Most ICEs also have a memory overlay feature that enables you to load a program into memory located in the ICE and make it appear (overlay the target memory) at any location in the target's address space.

- **Logic analyzers** are most often used to debug hardware, but they can be used for software debugging as well. A logic analyzer is a passive device that watches everything that happens on the system bus. Because it's passive, you can't set breakpoints or examine memory, but you can trigger on events on the bus (such as interrupts or memory fetches from a specific location) and capture and disassemble a sequence of instructions and data reads and writes. Although a logic analyzer is a bit tedious to use for software debugging, it can be the next best choice for tracking down difficult bugs if you don't have an ICE.

- **Hardware-enabled software debuggers** use the debug port built into many processors to add hardware-level debugging capabilities. They usually require some code to be running on the target hardware before the debugger can work, but typically the amount of target-side code required is much less than that required for other software debuggers. Less code translates into less work to get to the point where your software debugger can help you.

- **ROM emulators** are devices that plug into a ROM socket on the target to emulate a ROM chip. You download your program to the ROM emulator and then debug the program on the target as if it were burned into PROM. This makes for a much quicker edit-compile-download-debug cycle than would be possible if you had to actually burn a PROM each time you modified the program.

CHOOSING SOFTWARE COMPONENTS

You can often identify software subsystems that could potentially be licensed rather than written. Some examples are math packages for scientific applications, graphics libraries, file systems, and networking stacks. Some or all of the components you need may be provided by the RTOS vendor, but software that isn't provided can often be licensed from a third party. The primary advantage of licensing software is less work for your programming staff, resulting in quicker time to market or more flexibility to work on other features. Existing software packages have also (usually) been fairly well tested and are reasonably solid, saving you time during the testing of the system. You have to weigh these advantages against the cost of licensing the software to decide which approach is best for your project.

THE IMPLEMENTATION PHASE

Many different, equally valid approaches to implementing a software system exist. We present a simple, direct approach that we've found works well in practice. We emphasize two aspects of implementation: planning and testing. Regardless of how you structure the implementation of your product, make sure a clear schedule is in place early and that the schedule includes adequate time set aside for testing and debugging. If you don't get your plan in place from the start, you'll be amazed at how fast the implementation process can get out of control.

PLANNING THE IMPLEMENTATION

Planning is a prerequisite to the hands-on work of implementation. We've identified four areas of planning and preparation that we think are the most important. They are

- Prototype planning
- Test planning
- Source-control setup
- Scheduling

We address each in the sections that follow. You should understand that, depending on the nature of a project, you may have other planning requirements that aren't shown here. Some examples might include equipment rental requisitioning and scheduling, personnel requisitioning, and training (the project may employ some hardware or software that you and your staff are unfamiliar with).

Prototype Planning

Prototyping is such a worthwhile accompaniment to the development process that it pays to do some up-front planning for the prototyping process. First, what is prototyping?

Prototyping amounts to building experimental models of pieces of the final system so that developers can begin work before the target system is available. Let's face it, implementation never proceeds smoothly. Often in the life of a project, different elements necessary for development are available at different times. Hardware components, for example, are frequently unavailable for the software designers to begin their work. This is a polite way of saying that sometimes the stuff is late. Politeness aside, you don't want to sit around twiddling your thumbs. Prototyping is a way around this problem.

For example, suppose you discover that the particular microcontroller you've selected for the handheld remote-control system is available also on a development board. This board includes the processor, RAM, a small amount of ROM, and the capability to connect the board to a host PC system (on which you do the programming). It also comes with development software and a debugger. (Writing and compiling code on a host and then downloading the result to a development board is referred to a *cross-development*.) This setup would let you test and debug most of your code on the processor that will be the heart of the final system. (Some such boards actually provide a hardware prototyping area — a region on the board where you can construct custom hardware and wire it into the processor.)

Prototyping can serve software as well as hardware development efforts and also contain an element of simulation. The development board doesn't have buttons or an infrared transmitter, but you could simulate those in software. On a desktop PC, you could write all the routines for watching buttons, fetching codes, and transmitting signals, simulating the as-yet-unavailable hardware. The upshot of all of this is that developers can complete substantial pieces of the system using an environment that is an approximation of that system.

Prototype planning is a four-step process. First, you determine what pieces of the final system are amenable to being prototyped. Perhaps you can prototype the whole thing: software packages are appearing that come close to allowing designers to build remarkably complete software mockups of hardware. Or perhaps the system is so complex that you have to wait for final hardware, and you can prototype only portions of the system.

Second, determine how you will prototype. Will you be prototyping entirely in software? Or are usable hardware tools available? Perhaps your system is so simple that you could buy a single-board development system and custom-make a test version of the additional hardware yourself.

Third, map out precisely how the system will evolve from the prototype to the final platform. Prototyping will take you only so far; determine the point at which the prototype will break down and you'll need final hardware. This information will be important as you work out the scheduling for the implementation phase (something we talk about shortly).

Finally, find and allocate the resources you need for prototyping.

Test Planning

Few systems, if any, are built error free from start to finish. Testing is a fact of system development life, so plan for it. Furthermore, testing is not something you want to leave until the final stages of the implementation cycle. Devise a continuous testing strategy that starts early.

Testing *ad hoc* — as the need arises — not only upsets your scheduling, but is likely to be fraught with holes. Too many errors will slip through.

Your first step in test planning is to make sure that your implementation schedule includes time for the testing process. The amount of time you allot depends entirely on the complexity of the project.

Plan on testing at two recurring points in the implementation phase:

- When a subsystem is complete; this is called *unit testing*
- When that subsystem has been integrated into the larger system; this is called *integration testing*

You apply three types of tests during unit and integration testing in the implementation phase:

- Code-based testing
- Functional testing
- Regression testing

For the most part, unit testing employs code-based testing and integration testing employs functional and regression testing. We'll first describe the three types of testing. Then we'll go into more detail on good strategies to use for unit testing and integration testing.

Code-based testing
The goal of code-based testing is to verify that software performs as designed. Consequently, code-based testing of a particular piece of software is best performed by the programmer who wrote that software. Knowing the nature of a given routine's input data, how the routine processes that data, and the after-effects of the routine's execution, the programmer can generate test patterns to throw at the routine to verify correct execution. For example, suppose you've written a routine designed to sort in ascending order text strings consisting of people's names. It would make sense to generate an array of random text strings that look like peoples' names, hand that array to your sort routine, and ascertain that the result is indeed sorted.

Verifying the correct execution of a program is only part of code-based testing. The other half of the job is making sure that testing has exercised each and every statement of source code. This is referred to as *code coverage* testing. Again, the programmer uses his knowledge of the internals of the software (all the `if` statements and `switch()` statements and other control structures) and builds dummy data that will explore every possible path of execution through the code.

Code-based testing should also thoroughly exercise the APIs that make up the interface to each software subsystem. All reasonable (and some unreasonable) inputs should be passed to each API to ensure that it performs as specified.

Finally, keep the data sets and test programs you wrote to perform your code-based testing. You'll use the code-based tests you construct for each subsystem as the basic building blocks for your regression tests.

Faking Devices

Sometimes the hardware isn't there when you need it. You want to get started on your project, but that custom I/O card hasn't arrived in the mail. What do you do?

In the article "Device Drivers for Nonexistent Devices," which appeared in the August 1996 issue of *Embedded Systems Programming*, author Larry Mittag shares his technique for dealing with nonexistent devices. Mittag's idea is a device-driver stub. He uses a top-down approach that identifies the ways in which application software will talk to the hardware, so that the developer can create those interfaces and begin writing to them. Initially, the interfaces might be empty; that is, a call to one of the functions either returns nothing or returns a dummy value. As time goes on and details of the hardware become clear (and the hardware actually arrives), the stubs are inflated into their final form.

This arrangement allows software developers to be developing before final hardware arrives. It affords the means to at least shake bugs out of a portion of the application. Bugs in the hardware and hardware drivers (and interactions between drivers and the application) can be attacked when hardware and drivers are finally in place.

A key to making this work is identifying a set of universal entry points that all device drivers support. Mittag specifies six:

- **Create.** The entry point called by the application to initialize the hardware.

- **Open.** Called to set up communications between the hardware and a specific task. (That is, one piece of hardware may be simultaneously accessed by several tasks. The Open call lets a task set up with the hardware a session that is unique to that task.)

- **Close.** Shuts down communications between the task and the hardware.

- **Read.** Self-explanatory. Provides input from the hardware.

- **Write.** Self-explanatory. Provides output to the hardware.

- **Control.** A catchall routine that the application calls to manipulate the hardware beyond reading and writing data. For example, in a serial port driver, the Control entry point might be used to alter the serial port's baud rate.

Functional testing

Functional testing verifies that the system performs as specified. Although this definition sounds identical to the one for code-based testing, it's not. Code-based testing verifies the operation of individual pieces of code; functional testing verifies the operation of the system as a whole. To illustrate, we'll use the sort routine example from several paragraphs back: Whereas code-based testing of the sort routine checks that the data was sorted correctly, functional testing checks that the system uses the sort routine appropriately. If the system requirements specified that a database is sorted by last name but the system asks the sort routine to sort by first name, the sort routine is working properly but the system is not working as specified.

Functional testing, therefore, is best carried out by someone approaching the system from the customer's point of view. You can use the documentation from the analysis phase to create test suites; each test in such a suite would consist of user input and expected output (or system behavior). For example, one test suite in the remote project would include all the possible button presses and the associated output data-streams to the IR LED.

Regression testing

Finally, regression testing checks that the system can still correctly process data sets whose results have been previously verified. As the implementation phase progresses, your system moves from one build to another. You get one subsystem working, you get another subsystem working, and you put those two together; you get a third working and add that; and so on. As you tack on new subsystems and the final system begins to take shape, you use regression testing both to exercise as much of the code as possible in the system and to confirm that old bugs have not reappeared.

You can use the code-based test suites from the unit testing as a basis for regression tests (to confirm that code that worked on its own also works when it's integrated). Then keep adding to your suite of regression tests. As bugs are discovered and corrected, add a test for the condition that caused the bug. As new subsystems are integrated, integrate their code-based test suites into your regression test suite.

When your product is released, don't throw that regression test suite away! You'll need to use it — and keep adding to it — with each future release of your product.

Unit and integration testing

Unit testing verifies the proper functioning of subsystems independent of the larger system into which they will be incorporated. On a development team, each programmer will have been assigned a subset of the overall application. As each programmer completes subsystems, he should pass that subsystem through unit tests. This confirms that the subsystem is functioning properly before being integrated with other subsystems.

In unit testing, programmers should employ code-based testing as each subsystem is completed. As just described, in code-based testing, each programmer constructs test patterns for verifying a subsystem's correct execution, as well as code-coverage test data for exploring all execution paths.

As each subsystem is completed and integrated into the final system, it's time for integration testing. It's important that you do integration testing in small steps. If at all possible, refrain from integrating a large number of modules at once and attempting to test the resulting system. You could end up with what is called the big bang effect: lots of interrelated errors that are difficult to track down. (Admittedly, when you're just getting a system on its feet, this is often unavoidable.)

Integration tests will be comprised largely of functional and regression tests. Your test suites should grow as bits and pieces of the system come together. At the end, you'll have a single, comprehensive functional and regression test suite through which you can pass the end product as a final verification.

Source-Control Setup

Before any programmers on your staff begin writing, you should have in place a system for keeping track of the generated code. This involves not only a *repository* (a central database) so that you know where the source code is, but also a mechanism for tracking the status of the bits and pieces of the project. Such a mechanism will enable you to determine whether a specific routine is still under construction, is being debugged, or has been flagged as completed.

Numerous software control systems are on the market for managing team programming projects. They maintain a repository where all the source-code components of the growing application are kept. Anyone wanting to work on a particular piece of the application must check it out of the repository. A control system tracks who has checked out the code and for what purpose. Such systems also have the means of storing multiple versions of the same piece of software. (This is handy in case version 2 of a particular routine, for example, introduced a bug that was not in version 1. You can compare the two pieces of source code, locate the difference, and be that much closer to tracking down the bug.)

We strongly recommend that you select one of these source-control systems and put it in place before any implementation work. This will not only guard against pieces of source code being misplaced or misused, but will also aid in keeping track of deadlines. Source-control packages attach time and date stamps to software that a programmer checks into the repository, so you can see when a particular piece of code was completed.

Scheduling

Finally, before any fingers hit the keyboards or solder hits the boards, put in place a schedule to govern the implementation process. This schedule should take into account the different types of work that will occur during implementation: programming, hardware construction, testing, and debugging. It should account for deadlines in each of these areas, as well as interrelated tasks. For example, you'll want to monitor each subsystem's completion date so that integration tests are ready when those subsystems are plugged into the final application.

Revisit this schedule regularly and be willing to modify it. You cannot accurately estimate the time to complete large software components; you will always underestimate the required work. Instead, you have to break large software tasks down into a collection of smaller tasks and estimate the work for each of the smaller tasks. A good rule of thumb is that any task whose estimated duration is more than 2 or 3 days is still too big; you need to break it down into smaller pieces to make a more accurate time estimate. Of course, you won't be able to break down all the components of the system up front, and along the way you'll have to revise and change earlier choices, which is another reason (besides slippage) that your schedule needs constant updating. To have a more realistic schedule, strive to have as detailed a picture as possible, as early as possible.

IMPLEMENTING THE DESIGN

After you finish planning, you can start to implement your design. Following are the first set of tasks you need to tackle (in the order listed):

- Create a program framework.
- Assign subsystem development.
- Write function interfaces.

Once you've performed these tasks and got implementation rolling, you'll need to continually monitor the progress of the implementation to make sure it stays on track; we'll say more about that below.

Create a Program Framework

As mentioned, we recommend a top-down approach to design. We attack programming in the same fashion. Consequently, the first source code built should be a kind of software exoskeleton. Write the main routines first, so that you can determine overall program flow. You will then be able to not only get a framework for the final software running quickly, but also see which lower-level functions are called from where. This top-down approach will also help you work out the details of the global data that all routines will share.

Low-level functions can be *stubbed out*; in other words, they can appear in this framework code as empty routines — just a return statement.

Use the information in the design phase to drive the creation of the program framework. Revisit the design phase documents frequently so that what you implement properly tracks what you designed. Identify and resolve any deviations. (A deviation could be an error in the implementation or the design.)

Assign Subsystem Development

In the design phase, you identified software subsystems that can be worked on independently. As project staffing permits, assign people to subsystems so that as much parallel work as possible can take place. Obviously, the more parallelism you can harness, the quicker the implementation.

Write Function Interfaces

For each subsystem, insist that the programmer begin by producing an implementation of the subsystem interface. The structure of the subsystem's interface will have been worked out in the design phase. Finalize those interfaces at this point (answer any outstanding questions with regards to the details of each interface), and have each programmer produce source code for the interface. If you're using the C language, a well-documented header file of function prototypes will serve the purpose here.

Requiring a hard copy of each subsystem interface gives other project members an exact view of the services that the subsystem will provide and keeps programmers from going off in the weeds by making sure they start with clear design goals and a reasonable approach toward solving problems.

It might be worthwhile to have programmers take the same top-down approach with subsystems as you did with the overall program. In other words, a subsystem will consist of an API that it presents to the other subsystems, as well as internal routines that will be called only from within the subsystem. Have programmers put together a skeletal version of a subsystem, identifying not only its external APIs but also the prototypes for the internal routines (function names, arguments, and so on) and important internal data structures.

Monitor Progress

At this point, the programming and hardware construction will be underway. Implementation, however, doesn't consist solely of programming and soldering. Properly seeing a project to its completion is a combination of applied management plus software and hardware engineering. After programming and hardware development have begun, you must continuously monitor the project's progress. You must also perform certain tasks (such as testing) on a recurring basis as the system evolves.

Don't forget to revisit the schedule regularly. This will help you identify and correct problems early. It will also keep you aware of approaching deadlines — rather than being startled by them the day before they arrive. Schedule regular progress meetings to keep everyone synchronized.

Keep using the software control system. Without it, version control will become more and more nightmarish as the project proceeds and the number of subsystem versions pile up. Also, the repository fosters reuse of frequently used routines, and may serve as a source for code in some future project.

Encourage prototyping throughout the process; prototyping fits in nicely with the top-down approach we've presented. Even if a system is so complex that a hardware prototype would be infeasible, designers can apply prototyping principles to subsystems.

Finally, remember that testing takes place throughout the development process as programmers complete subsystems, and intermediate versions of the final product become available. Put someone (perhaps yourself) in charge of maintaining your growing library of test suites.

SUMMARY

This chapter provided guidelines, in the sense that we've given an outline of a project development process suitable for real-time embedded systems. We emphasized the use of practical, straightforward, time-tested techniques for ensuring that your product does what it's supposed to, you reasonably and accurately predict when the project will be completed, product costs are kept under control, and unpleasant surprises don't crop up. Although this is not a formal design methodology, this development process can work well with the design methodology of your choice. Throughout the development cycle, if you can ensure that goals and specifications are stated clearly, that people are communicating well, and that you have some basic control mechanisms such as source control and formalized regression testing in place, you'll maximize your chances of success.

But now, put theory aside. It's time to take a look at what's on the CD-ROM in the back of the book and put it to use. We've talked enough about real-time embedded systems; let's do some hands-on work.

3

Software Installation and Setup

I t's brass tacks time.

Much of what we've discussed so far has been theory; now it's time to focus on the practical. In this chapter, we present the target and host hardware platforms and the software tools we use in this book. Then we lead you through setting up the hardware and installing the software on the CD-ROM. Next, you download and run a program to make sure all hardware and software components are working properly. Finally, we demonstrate how to build, compile, and link an application with the software on the CD-ROM. When we're finished, you'll have a development system that's ready to build and run the projects in this book or programs of your own.

CHOOSING A PLATFORM AND TOOLS

In the Introduction, we alluded to our choices for a target platform and toolset. Here's the itemized list:

- **Target hardware platform:** The PC platform
- **Programming language:** C (with some C++)
- **Development tools:** Microsoft Visual C++ and Phar Lap TNT Embedded ToolSuite
- **Target real-time operating system:** Phar Lap Real-Time ETS Kernel
- **Target processor:** A 32-bit x86 or compatible processor

As we noted in Chapter 2, "Designing and Developing Your Real-Time System," no set order exists for selecting the target platform and tools. Sometimes choosing the operating system first makes sense; other times you might choose the language first. We started with the target hardware platform and chose the PC, a readily available, off-the-shelf desktop and embedded platform that most programmers either own already, have access to, or can buy cheaply. For real-world, real-time embedded development, PC desktop machines are handy for prototyping embedded applications, and PC SBCs are inexpensive, compatible with a large selection of hardware and software, and use a widely understood and well-documented architecture.

Although a few projects have some C++ code, we chose to write mostly in C because it is one of the most widely used languages for embedded programming. The combination of low overhead, fairly easy hardware access for a high-level language, good standardization of the language across platforms, and the language's popularity resulting in the availability of lots of off-the-shelf code make C a good choice for embedded projects.

An obvious choice for a compiler is Microsoft Visual C++, because it is by far the leading C/C++ compiler in the PC world.

We use Phar Lap's TNT Embedded ToolSuite for the real-time operating system and the rest of the development tools. ToolSuite's ETS Kernel runs on the PC platform, uses a subset of Windows Win32 API as its API, and is designed to work with Visual C++. Hence, ToolSuite ties together what were once two separate worlds: a Win32 development environment and the writing of real-time embedded applications. Using Win32 has many of the same advantages as using the PC platform. Win32 is a good teaching platform because it's so widely used; it's also a good real-world platform because the tools are relatively inexpensive, widely understood, well-documented, and compatible with much third-party hardware and software.

Finally, our target has a 386 or later Intel-compatible CPU. Visual C++, ETS Kernel, and the Win32 API all require a 32-bit processor. For developers who want to design their own hardware, Intel, AMD, and National Semiconductor all offer embedded versions of 32-bit x86 chips that include PC-compatible I/O devices on the chip, thereby further conserving board real estate and reducing costs.

TOOLSUITE LITE COMPONENTS

The book's CD-ROM includes ToolSuite Lite, a limited version of Phar Lap's TNT Embedded ToolSuite, Realtime Edition. It's worthwhile to take a few minutes at this point to briefly introduce the components of ToolSuite Lite.

EMBEDDED STUDIOEXPRESS

Embedded StudioExpress is an add-in for Microsoft Developer Studio, the Visual C++ IDE. Embedded StudioExpress provides support for downloading and debugging ToolSuite applications with the Microsoft IDE debugger. StudioExpress also includes ETS Project Wizard, which guides you through the process of creating a Developer Studio workspace for a program that targets ETS Kernel.

LinkLoc

LinkLoc is a linker/locator for building embedded programs. You'll use this linker to build all the projects in this book.

Real-Time ETS Kernel

Real-Time ETS Kernel is a real-time operating system for running real-time embedded programs. It provides several APIs, including Win32, WinSock, and ETS; initializes 32-bit protected-mode operation; and has a number of pluggable components you can use to customize ETS Kernel. The components include a real-time scheduler, a TCP/IP stack, the MicroWeb server, an MS-DOS-compatible file system, a floating-point emulation library, and a DLL loader. The advantage to pluggable components is that you can use only those your application requires, keeping the kernel's size to a minimum. ETS Kernel also supports structured exception handling and event logging.

ETS Kernel is physically divided into ETS Monitor and a set of libraries that are linked with your application. ETS Monitor is placed on the ETS Kernel boot diskette. When you boot the target system, ETS Monitor is loaded into memory, initializes the target's hardware, and then waits for an application program to be downloaded from the host system. The linkable libraries embody the bulk of ETS Kernel and include all the kernel APIs plus the pluggable components. When you download the application, you're actually downloading the application plus the linked-in ETS Kernel components.

Win32 API

ETS Kernel provides a subset of the Win32 API that's present in the Microsoft Windows 95, 98, and NT operating systems. (Remember: ETS Kernel is *not* Windows; it merely provides an API that makes the kernel *look* like it's a stripped-down version of Windows.) By building on the Win32 API, ToolSuite

- **Minimizes the embedded programming learning curve.** If you're a Windows programmer, you are already familiar with the ins-and-outs of the Win32 API (particularly those portions provided by ETS Kernel) and will find the transition to ETS Kernel easy. If you're not a Windows programmer, you'll find that the Win32 API is well-documented in a number of sources.

- **Supports the C/C++ run-time libraries.** The routines in the C/C++ run-time libraries call the Win32 API. Because the kernel implements a subset of Win32, it supports the run-time libraries. The obvious benefit is that you can use in your embedded programs the same routines you use in your desktop applications — you won't have to write replacement code. In addition, just as you do on the desktop, you can use the run-time libraries' I/O calls to prototype and debug an embedded application and get it up and running quickly.

In addition to the Win32 APIs, ETS Kernel supplies a number of APIs (all prefixed by Ets) to perform actions not supported in Win32. These actions include such operations as installing and removing interrupt service routines and configuring and programming the ETS Kernel components. Appendix B, "APIs," contains a brief description of all supported APIs. More detailed descriptions of the APIs can be found in the Microsoft Word file APIS.DOC, in the directory \TSLITE\DOCS.

Real-Time Scheduler

The scheduler is the kernel component that supports real-time multithreaded applications. A quick reminder: multithreading means multitasking. By this we mean that threads are one way to implement multitasking. Threads give applications the capability to multitask in a single address space, usually the preferred configuration for real-time systems.

Although ETS Kernel provides multitasking based on the Win32 multithreading support in Windows 95, 98, and NT, the internal operation of threads differs in ToolSuite and Windows. The system calls that you use to create and manage threads in ETS Kernel are identical to the calls you would use in Windows. ETS Kernel, however, implements a different scheduler.

The *scheduler* is the part of the operating system whose job it is to figure out which thread runs when. The scheduler in ETS Kernel implements *deterministic* scheduling; the one in Windows does not. (This is the one of the reasons why Windows 95, 98, and NT aren't suitable as hard real-time operating systems.) We describe what deterministic scheduling means in detail in Chapter 12; what it means in general is that you, the developer, at a given time and with a given set of circumstances, can know what thread will run next. In other words, the behavior of the system in regards to thread scheduling is predictable.

Suppose you're designing a real-time system and someone asks: "If your system is running thread A and the time-slice concludes, which of four threads will the scheduler run next?"

With a nondeterministic system, your answer would be: "Probably this one" or "Maybe that one." These answers, however, are unacceptable in a real-time system; the designer must know whether a critical event will be serviced on time or not. With a deterministic system, you would always be able to point to a thread and say, with confidence, "That one." Which thread you would point to is determined by several factors, such as the priority you assign to each task and the state of the thread. We get into all these things in Chapter 12, "Multitasking."

Predictability is a necessary characteristic of a real-time system. It enables the developer to design a program and examine its behavior before code is written or hardware is built. In so doing, the developer can verify that the system will work according to specification.

TCP/IP Networking and MicroWeb Server

Network programming on ETS Kernel is supported with a TCP/IP stack, which is programmed with the WinSock APIs used for network programming under Windows. TCP/IP stands for Transmission Control Protocol/Internet Protocol. TCP/IP is the protocol stack used for communications on the Internet, and for that reason is the most common set of networking protocols used worldwide.

ETS Kernel also includes a component called MicroWeb Server, which simplifies the task of connecting your embedded system to the Internet or a corporate intranet. MicroWeb

Tasks, Processes, and Threads

When you delve into the mechanics of multitasking, you will often encounter three words: *task, process,* and *thread.* Let's take a few minutes to review each.

Of the three words, *task* is the most abstract. A task could be either a process or a thread. It simply refers to a sequence of related computations that all work together to achieve some end. For example, you might build a system that includes a task whose job it is to read data from a serial port and place it in memory. That task could be implemented as a thread or as a process (or as an interrupt service routine).

A multitasking system can run multiple tasks simultaneously, or more precisely, *appears* to run multiple tasks simultaneously. (How that appearance is achieved is covered later in Chapter 12, "Multitasking.") Those tasks might be processes, threads, or both.

You can think of a *process* as an independent program, complete with its own data space and code space in memory. The data and variables that a process owns, it owns by itself. This is true of all processes running in the system. One process cannot see the variables in another process unless that other process agrees to let it do so (and even then, both processes need the help of the operating system to find one another's variables).

To put this in the real world, imagine that you are running Windows 95 and opened up both a word processor and a spreadsheet. The program controlling the word processor is a separate process from the program controlling the spreadsheet. Each is unaware of the other, unless some outside intervention (such as cutting and pasting through the clipboard) provides a communications path between them.

A *thread* is a separate execution path within a process; that is, threads exist in processes. Each thread shares the same code and global data, but has its own stack. Because the stack is per-thread, local variables are private to each thread. To create a new thread, your program executes a call to the operating system that says: "Make a new thread of execution for me, and start it executing at function X." Your program can make multiple such calls, and so create multiple threads, each executing independently (multitasking).

The most blatant difference between a process and a thread is that a process has its own global data. Threads exist within processes, so the global variables of a process are shared by all the threads. This, as you will see, has important ramifications when it comes to allowing threads to access those global variables.

Server includes an HTTP (Hypertext Transfer Protocol) server and a collection of tools for building web pages on demand. Using HTTP permits standard web browsers to connect to your application, collect data from your system, and remotely configure your system.

DOS-Compatible File System

ToolSuite includes support for an MS-DOS-compatible FAT16 and FAT32 file system. File I/O is supported at both the Win32 (`ReadFile()`, `WriteFile()`, and so on) and the C library (`fread()`, `fwrite()`, and so on) levels.

In addition to file I/O on the target system, ToolSuite allows applications to perform file I/O to files on the host system, using the same standard Win32 and C library functions. File I/O to host files is redirected over the communications cable used for downloading programs to an agent in the download software running on the host system. Host file I/O is useful both for debugging while bringing up your software and for running regression tests that read input from and write results to host files.

Floating-Point Emulation Library

Floating-point emulation amounts to a floating-point or math coprocessor in software. Although processors without on-chip math coprocessors are becoming rare on the desktop, that's not so in the embedded world. A number of Intel-based chips targeted for embedded applications do not include a coprocessor for price and chip-size reasons.

It's all a matter of tradeoffs. Some real-time embedded applications simply don't need floating-point support. In this case, find a processor without a floating-point coprocessor and forget the emulator. Other real-time applications use *a lot* of floating-point numbers (signal-processing applications, for instance). In this case, get a processor with onboard coprocessors and, again, forget the emulator.

Some applications, however, require floating-point numbers, but only a little. In other words, no critical time requirements are placed on the floating-point calculations. In such cases, a floating-point emulation library such as the one in ToolSuite offers a good solution. Granted, performing calculations using an emulation library is slower than if you used a coprocessor, but saving money may be more important than saving time when implementing a noncritical feature.

DLL Loader

ToolSuite allows applications to use dynamic link libraries (DLLs). DLLs are libraries of code and data that are not statically linked into the executable file; instead, the program loads (and links to) and unloads them dynamically while it is executing.

As for executable files, ToolSuite uses the Windows Portable Executable (PE) file format for DLLs. This means Windows tools that manipulate DLLs also can be used on ToolSuite DLLs.

DLLs are useful for such things as adding functionality by loading modules written by third parties, reducing memory requirements by loading only the parts of a program needed to perform a specific task, and modularizing programs by separating well-defined sets of routines into DLL files.

Structured Exception Handling

Windows 95, 98, and NT use structured exception handling to deal with processor exceptions and other errors in a controlled fashion. Using structured exception handling, an error condition in your program can unwind through an arbitrarily deep nesting of function calls to the outermost level where the error is caught. Structured exception handling is exposed to C programs with a Microsoft-defined language construct that allows you to define program blocks with an associated exception routine that runs if an exception occurs anywhere in the program block. The C++ `catch` and `throw` exception handling in Visual C++ is also implemented on top of the operating system's structured-exception-handling support. ToolSuite provides complete support for structured exception handling in both C and C++ code.

Event Logging

The event logging system in ToolSuite allows programs to request the kernel to automatically log system events of interest in a circular buffer in memory. The program can log events of interest also within the program itself. A set of APIs are provided for turning logging on and off, and for accessing the buffer of logged events. Event logging is normally used for debugging hard-to-replicate bugs that tend to disappear when you change the timing by using a debugger or inserting `printf()` statements in your program. Typically, a program turns on event logging while a specific part of the program runs, and then turns it off and uses the event logging APIs to either display the captured events on the screen or write them to a file for later analysis.

WHAT'S LITE ABOUT TOOLSUITE LITE?

ToolSuite Lite has a number of restrictions not present in the full TNT Embedded ToolSuite, Realtime Edition, product. None of these limitations affect the programming projects in this book. If you are writing applications that require functionality not included in ToolSuite Lite, you'll need to purchase the full product from Phar Lap Software.

The following ToolSuite components and features are not included with ToolSuite Lite:

- Visual System Builder (VSB), a point-and-click Windows utility for easily configuring ETS Kernel for custom hardware, is not included.
- Support for Inprise's (formerly Borland) compiler and Turbo Debugger is removed.
- The CodeView debugger and support for versions of Visual C++ before 5.0 are not included.
- The utility programs 386|ASM, 386|LIB, MAPEXE, MAKEHD, REBIND, and PLSTRIP are not included.
- Support for ROMing ETS Kernel and applications is removed.
- Target support for various single-board computers, evaluation boards from processor manufacturers, and in-circuit emulators is removed. (The only supported target is a PC with a floppy disk boot.)

The limitations of ETS Kernel included with ToolSuite Lite are as follows:

- The application must be downloaded from a host computer. Support for loading the application off disk, running from ROM, and for running standalone (with no host connection) is removed.
- The maximum amount of RAM available to the application is 1MB.
- PC Card support is not included.

- The file system supports only floppy disk drives. Support for hard disks, flash file systems, and RAM and ROM disks is removed.

- The TCP/IP system includes serial drivers only for SLIP and PPP. All Ethernet drivers are removed. The FTP server and SMTP mail client components of MicroWeb Server are not included.

- ETS Kernel cannot be customized for special hardware. None of the source code to the kernel is provided. (The full product includes the source to all drivers and all hardware-specific code in the kernel.)

The limitations of the LinkLoc linker included with ToolSuite Lite are as follows:

- The maximum program size is 1MB.

- The program load address is fixed at 64K.

- Standalone symbol files cannot be produced.

ETS KERNEL APPLICATION ENVIRONMENT

ETS Kernel always sets up a protected-mode environment for your embedded application. When your program gets control at the beginning of its `main()` function, the kernel has already performed the low-level details of setting up the environment:

- The processor is in 32-bit protected mode. Intel-compatible processors boot in 16-bit real mode, for backward compatibility with the 8086 processor. The kernel takes care of setting up a protected-mode environment and switching the processor to protected mode.

- The code and data segment registers are loaded with segment selectors for a 32-bit flat address space starting at address 0 and extending to 4GB. Thus, all addresses are physical addresses, and embedded applications can directly access all physical memory in the system.

- Interrupts are enabled.

- The paging hardware on the processor is disabled. ETS Kernel operates on physical memory only; it does not have support for demand-paged virtual memory.

- The C run-time library is initialized.

SEGMENT SELECTORS

ETS Kernel creates a Global Descriptor Table (GDT) in which the segment descriptors for all defined segments are located. The GDT is created with 50 entries, 10 of which are initially used by the kernel. The kernel does not create a Local Descriptor Table (LDT).

The GDT segments of interest to the embedded application have the following segment selector values:

```
#define CODE32_SELECTOR   0x18   // 32-bit flat code segment for App
#define DATA32_SELECTOR   0x20   // 32-bit flat data segment for App
#define TEB_SELECTOR      0x28   // 32-bit data seg mapping thread
                                 // environment block for Win32 code
```

When ETS Kernel finishes initialization and transfers control to the application's entry point, the general registers are all zeroed. The CS (code segment) register is loaded with selector 0x18, the DS (data segment) and SS (stack segment) registers are loaded with selector 0x20, and the FS data segment register (which is used by the C run-time library to access thread-specific information) is loaded with selector 0x28. The other two data segment registers, ES and GS, are both loaded with selector 0x20.

NULL POINTER DETECTION

Segment 0x20, the data segment, is initialized as an expand-down data segment with a limit of 4K. Expand-down data segments permit accesses to any address from their limit up to 4GB. So although the data segment is 0-based, it does not allow access to addresses from 0 to 0xFFF. Any attempt to access data or the stack in the first 4K of memory results in a segment access violation, which causes the processor to generate a general protection exception. This feature is present to help you detect a particularly common programming error: an attempt to access memory through an uninitialized pointer variable. Because uninitialized variables are often zero, trapping accesses to low memory locations helps you catch these bugs.

THE STACK AND THE HEAP

The size of the stack in your application is determined by the linker -STACK switch, which by default is set to 8K. All the projects in this book use the default stack size. The stack is located immediately following the program's data. In ToolSuite Lite, the features that allow you to reposition the program's code, data, and stack independently are disabled.

All memory not used for ETS Monitor (which, as you recall, is the portion of ETS Kernel that loads before the application) and the application's code, data, and stack is automatically used for the C memory heap. ETS Kernel in ToolSuite Lite restricts total memory usage to 1MB, regardless of how much physical memory is in your embedded target system.

THE COMMAND LINE AND THE ENVIRONMENT

Embedded programs downloaded to the target computer inherit the environment variables from the host computer, and get the command line entered by the host user when the program is downloaded. The embedded application can access the environment and the command line with the standard C programming techniques. Specifically, command-line arguments are available from the standard argc and argv parameters passed to the main()

function by the C run-time library. Environment variables are accessed by calling the C library `getenv()` and `_putenv()` functions or by using the `envp` parameter passed to `main()`.

The full version of ToolSuite has techniques for creating command-line arguments and an initial environment when booting an application from ROM or disk on the embedded target. Because ToolSuite Lite supports only downloading applications, these techniques are not available.

INTERRUPTS

ETS Kernel creates entries in the Interrupt Descriptor Table (IDT) for all 256 interrupts possible on Intel processors. The entries for all interrupts not used by ETS Kernel initially point to an interrupt service routine that executes an `IRETD` instruction to return from the interrupt.

ETS Kernel uses the following interrupts:

- Processor exceptions are used for debugging and to implement structured exception-handling support. Processor exceptions occur on interrupts 0, 1, 3, 4, 5, 6, 7, 8, 0xA, 0xB, 0xC, 0xD, and 0xE.

- The coprocessor error hardware interrupt, IRQ13 (interrupt vector 0x75), is used for structured exception-handling support.

- The host communications support uses one hardware interrupt. For parallel communications on LPT1, IRQ7 (interrupt vector 0xF) is used, for LPT2, IRQ5 (interupt vector 0xD). For serial communications on COM1, IRQ4 (interrupt vector 0xC) is used; for COM2, IRQ3 (interrupt vector 0xB) is used.

- The timer driver (which is optional, but which is always linked in by default), uses hardware interrupt IRQ0, which is interrupt vector 8.

- The optional keyboard driver uses hardware interrupt IRQ1, which is interrupt vector 9.

- The optional file system uses hardware interrupt IRQ6 (interrupt 0xE) for the floppy disk and IRQ14 (interrupt 0x76) for the hard disk.

- The serial driver for the optional TCP/IP networking support uses IRQ4 (interrupt 0xC) for PPP/SLIP connections over COM1, and IRQ3 (interrupt 0xB) for connections over COM2.

- Software interrupts 0xFE and 0xFF are used internally by ETS Kernel.

Table 3-1 summarizes this information. You'll notice that, because of the original interrupt vector assignments for hardware interrupts on the IBM PC, some overlap exists between processor exceptions and hardware interrupts. ETS Kernel can differentiate between processor exceptions and hardware interrupts, so applications can separately install exception handlers and hardware interrupt handlers on these overloaded interrupt vectors (interrupts 8 – 0xE).

Table 3-1: ETS Kernel Interrupts

Interrupt Number	Used	Optionally Used	Not Used	Description
0 – 1	x			Processor exceptions.
2			x	Non-maskable interrupt (NMI).
3 – 7	x			Processor exceptions.
8 (exception)	x			Double-fault processor exception.
8 (IRQ0)		x		Timer tick interrupt, used by optional timer driver.
9 (IRQ1)		x		Keyboard interrupt, used by optional keyboard driver.
0xA (exception)	x			Invalid TSS processor exception.
0xA (IRQ2)			x	Used on PC to connect slave 8259A PIC to master 8259A.
0xB (exception)	x			Segment not present processor exception.
0xB (IRQ3)		x		COM2 serial port interrupt. Used for download/debug, or used by optional PPP/SLIP networking driver.
0xC (exception)	x			Stack fault processor exception.
0xC (IRQ4)		x		COM1 serial port interrupt. Used for download/debug, or used by optional PPP/SLIP networking driver.
0xD (exception)	x			General protection fault processor exception.
0xD (IRQ5)		x		LPT2 parallel port interrupt. Used for download/debug.
0xE (exception)	x			Page fault processor exception.
0xE (IRQ6)		x		Floppy disk interrupt, used by optional file system.
0xF (IRQ7)		x		LPT1 parallel port interrupt. Used for download/debug.
0x10 – 0x6F			x	Software interrupts.
0x70 (IRQ8)			x	Real-time clock interrupt.
0x71 (IRQ9)			x	Unassigned hardware interrupt.
0x72 (IRQ10)			x	Unassigned hardware interrupt.
0x73 (IRQ11)			x	Unassigned hardware interrupt.
0x74 (IRQ12)			x	Unassigned hardware interrupt.
0x75 (IRQ13)		x		Coprocessor interrupt, used by optional structured exception handling subsystem.
0x76 (IRQ14)		x		Hard disk interrupt, used by optional file system.
0x77 (IRQ15)			x	Unassigned hardware interrupt.
0x78 – 0xFD			x	Software interrupts.
0xFE – 0xFF	x			Used internally by ETS Kernel.

HARDWARE SETUP

To get started with ToolSuite Lite, you need two computers: one is the development host, and the other is the embedded target. You'll build the projects discussed in this book on the development host and then download and run them on the embedded target.

Our development host can be any 32-bit PC-compatible computer running Windows 95, 98, or NT with the following (minimum) capabilities:

- Intel 486-compatible or later CPU
- 16MB RAM
- 40MB free disk space
- Parallel port
- Serial port
- CD-ROM drive
- 3½" floppy disk drive

The host machine is the home of your development tools: the compiler, linker, debugger, libraries, and so on. So if you want to build the programs, you also need sufficient disk space to install Microsoft Visual C++.

The simulated embedded target must also be a 32-bit PC-compatible computer, with the following capabilities:

- Intel 386-compatible or later CPU
- 1MB RAM
- Parallel port
- Serial port
- 3½" floppy disk drive

In addition, the target must be capable of booting from the floppy disk.

The memory requirements of the projects in this book are modest. You actually need less than 1MB of RAM to run them, but we can't imagine that you would have a PC-compatible computer with less memory!

To use ToolSuite Lite and the projects in this book, you need to establish two connections between the host and target machines. The first connection allows you to download the projects to the target; the second is used by some of the example programs for serial communications with the host machine.

To set up the download connection to use the default parallel option, connect LPT1 on the development host to LPT1 on the embedded target, using a standard LapLink (or compatible) parallel cable. If you choose to connect different parallel ports, make note of the number, because you use it later to configure ETS Kernel.

If one of your computers doesn't have a parallel port or the port is in use, you can use the serial ports for downloading. Use a standard LapLink (or compatible) serial cable to connect a serial port on the host (such as COM1) to a serial port on the target (such as COM1). Again, make note of the serial port you use for the connection so you can configure ETS Kernel with this information.

You must have a separate serial connection to run several of the programming projects, which communicate over a serial link with the Windows host computer. All the projects support either COM1 or COM2 for serial communications. If you're using parallel ports for downloading, you can connect COM1 on the host to COM1 on the target. If you've already used COM1, however, select COM2 on each machine. Use a standard LapLink-compatible serial cable for the connection.

SOFTWARE INSTALLATION AND SETUP

Before you can actually build and run a project, you have to install the development tools on the host and the operating system on the target.

INSTALLING TOOLSUITE LITE

To install ToolSuite Lite, insert the CD-ROM that came with this book in your computer. If Auto Run is enabled, the SETUP program starts automatically. If Auto Run is not enabled, select Run from the Start menu in Windows 95, 98, or Windows NT, and run the SETUP program on the CD-ROM.

After copying files to your hard disk, the SETUP program gives you the option of registering at the book's web site, `http://www.pharlap.com/book/`. Registered users can obtain technical support on installing and using the book software through the web site, and can download updates to the software made available for compatibility with future releases of Visual C++.

By default, ToolSuite Lite is installed in the `\TSLITE` directory on your hard disk with the following subdirectories:

- **`\TSLITE\BIN`**. The `.EXE`, `.DLL`, and `.HLP` files for ToolSuite Lite.
- **`\TSLITE\INCLUDE`**. The C header files defining constants and data structures for ETS Kernel system calls.
- **`\TSLITE\LIB`**. Libraries of C-callable functions, documented in Appendix B, "APIs."
- **`\TSLITE\LINKCMD`**. Linker command files containing default switch settings for building ETS Kernel programs.
- **`\TSLITE\MONITOR`**. ETS Monitor and batch files for building boot disks.
- **`\TSLITE\PROJECTS`**. Code for the sample projects discussed in this book. Each project has a separate subdirectory containing the C source code, an executable version of the program, a Developer Studio workspace, and a make file.
- **`\TSLITE\DOCS`**. Documentation on ETS Kernel APIs.

If your development host system is running Windows NT, the SETUP program optionally installs the ETSIO.SYS parallel device driver. Note that, under Windows NT only, the ETSIO.SYS parallel device driver must be installed if you want to download and debug programs over a parallel connection.

If an error occurs during this installation, you'll receive one of two messages:

> You currently do not have Administrator access. You will have to install the parallel driver manually. See the ToolSuite Lite Installation Instructions for more information.

> Error accessing service control manager. You will have to install the parallel driver manually. See the ToolSuite Lite Installation Instructions for more information.

If you receive one of these messages, click OK and complete the installation of the parallel driver after the SETUP program exits by running the program ETSIOINS.EXE in the \TSLITE\BIN directory. (ETSIOINS.EXE uses other files in the \TSLITE\BIN directory, which is why you must run the program from that directory.)

```
C:\>cd \tslite\bin
C:\tslite\bin\>etsioins install
```

You must specify the parameter INSTALL on the command line.

If at any time you want to remove this device driver from your Windows NT system, run the same program and specify REMOVE on the command line:

```
C:\>cd \tslite\bin
C:\tslite\bin\>etsioins remove
```

CONFIGURING VISUAL C++ AND DEVELOPER STUDIO

ToolSuite Lite has been designed for use with Microsoft Visual C++, Version 5.x and 6.0. You can use the Developer Studio IDE and debugger to modify and compile the projects in this book, and to build and debug new real-time embedded programs. (In 6.0, Microsoft refers to VC++ and Developer Studio as VC++. We refer to each separately.) For this and other discussions in this book, we assume that you have installed these tools in the default \Program Files\Microsoft Visual Studio directory (for Visual C++ 5.x, in the \Program Files\DevStudio directory).

If you're using Visual C++, Version 4.x, you can still compile, link, and run your embedded programs from the command line. You just won't be able to use the IDE or debugger.

Even if you don't have Visual C++, you can still run the sample projects in this book. The \TSLITE\PROJECTS subdirectories contain prebuilt .EXE files for each of the projects. These files are ready to be downloaded to your embedded target, and run.

Note: The prebuilt executables are built with Visual C++ 6.0. If you want to debug a program with Visual C++ 5.x, you must rebuild it first, because the symbol table information from VC++ 6.0 can't be used with VC++ 5.x.

You must do two things to configure Visual C++ to work with ToolSuite Lite. You must set up the directory lists and install Embedded StudioExpress. To begin, start Developer

Studio using whichever one of the following three methods you normally use to start a Windows 95/98/NT program:

- If you use the Start menu, select the icon labeled "Microsoft Visual C++ 6.0" from the Microsoft Visual Studio 6.0 folder (or the icon labeled "Microsoft Visual C++ 5.0" from the Microsoft Visual C++ 5.0 folder) in the Programs folder.

- If you select icons from My Computer, choose the one labeled "MSDEV" in the Common\MSDev98\Bin folder (for VC++ 5.*x*, the SharedIDE\bin folder).

- If you prefer to start your programs from the command line, type `msdev` in a Windows DOS box. If you have trouble starting MSDEV from the command line, make sure the `Common\MSDev98\Bin` directory (for VC++ 5.*x*, the `SharedIDE\bin` directory) appears on your PATH.

If this is the first time you're running Developer Studio, you may see some Microsoft Hints/Tips and possibly other informational dialog boxes.

Our first task is to set up the directory lists used for building programs, as shown in Figure 3-1. During installation, Visual C++ sets up initial values for these lists based on the current contents of the PATH, INCLUDE, and LIB environment variables. To build ToolSuite Lite programs, these lists must also contain the corresponding \TSLITE subdirectories. Choose Options from the Developer Studio Tools menu and then choose the Directories tab.

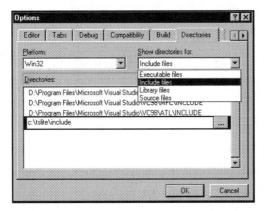

Figure 3-1: To build the programs in this book, add ToolSuite Lite's subdirectories to Visual C++'s directories list.

Select the directory list from the drop-down box and add the following ToolSuite Lite directories:

Directory List	**ToolSuite Lite Directories**
Executable files	\TSLITE\BIN
Library files	\TSLITE\LIB
Include files	\TSLITE\INCLUDE

The directory lists are used for all Developer Studio projects. After you have them set up, you'll be able to build all the projects in this book.

Our second one-time-only task is to install the Embedded StudioExpress add-in so you can use Developer Studio projects for your embedded programs, and debug programs on the target with the Developer Studio debugger. To install it, follow these steps:

1. Choose Tools from the menu bar, and then choose the Customize menu item.

2. Choose the Add-ins and Macro Files tab, and then click the Browse button to open the Browse for Macro File or Add-in dialog box.

3. From the drop-down list associated with Files of type, select Add-ins (.dll). In the File name box, specify the file ETSVC5.DLL from the \TSLITE\BIN directory, as shown in Figure 3-2. You can either type the full path or browse to find and select the directory and the file.

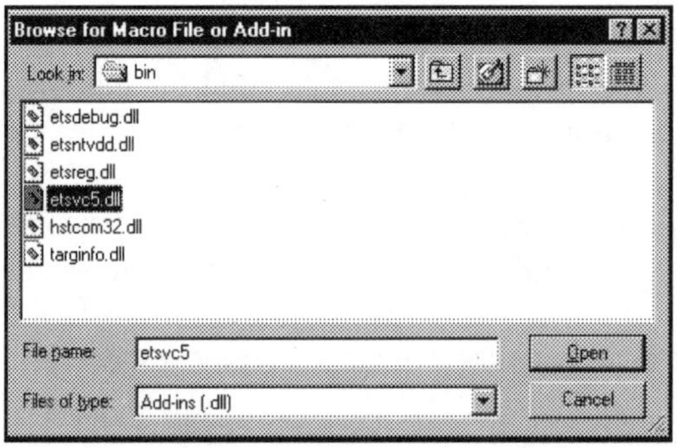

Figure 3-2: Select ETSVC5.DLL to install Embedded StudioExpress in Visual C++, Version 5.*x* or 6.0.

4. Click Open to install Embedded StudioExpress. Wait a few seconds while the file is being installed. Phar Lap Embedded StudioExpress is now included in the list of add-ins and macro files, as shown in Figure 3-3. The check mark in the box indicates that this add-in has been enabled.

5. Click the Close button to complete the installation of Embedded StudioExpress.

The Embedded StudioExpress toolbar is now available. You can move this to the top of the screen with the other toolbars or wherever you find it most convenient. From left to right, the icons on the toolbar are as follows:

- **About Embedded StudioExpress.** This icon displays the standard About window.

- **Target Configuration Settings.** Click this tool to specify communications and download options; this will be described in the "Testing the Host-Target Connection" section in this chapter.

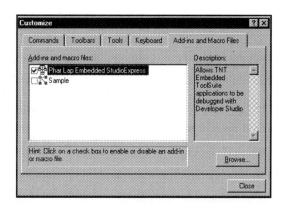

Figure 3-3: Embedded StudioExpress lets you use Developer Studio to debug applications after you've downloaded them to the target.

- **Target Port Input/Output.** This option allows you to perform direct port I/O on your embedded target. When you select this icon, the Target Port Input/Output dialog box in Figure 3-4 opens. Specify a port number and desired operation. That is, select Input to read the specified port on your embedded target and have the result displayed in the Value box; select Output to specify a number in the Value box and have that value written to the specified port on your target. The Access Size options choose the amount of data transferred by the operation.

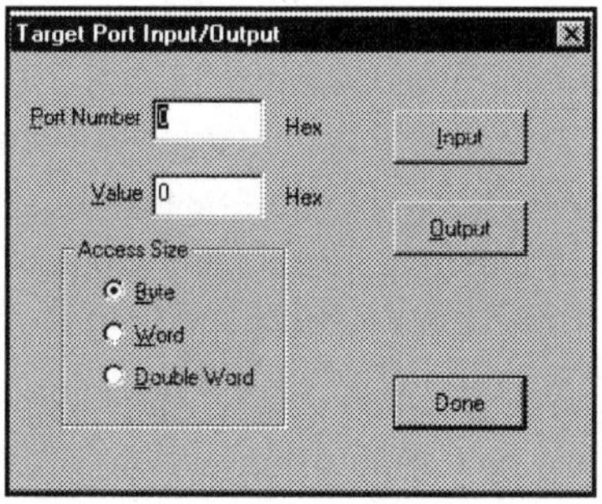

Figure 3-4: Target Port Input/Output lets you perform direct port I/O on your target.

- **Target System Information.** This icon displays a comprehensive view of the current state of the embedded target. In Chapter 4, "Debugging," you see how this information can be used to speed up your debugging.

- **ETS Project Wizard.** This tool creates a new project workspace targeting ETS Kernel. The Project Wizard is described in the section "Creating New Programming Projects."

- **Visual System Builder.** This option is not supported in ToolSuite Lite. If you click this icon, you get the error message, "Error executing VSB.EXE - Error Code 2." Simply click OK.

To complete the configuration of Embedded StudioExpress, you need to enter the communications settings. To do this, click Target Configuration Settings on the toolbar. The dialog box in Figure 3-5 is displayed. In the Communications area, select the appropriate host port from the drop-down list. This is the port on your development host computer that you've chosen to use for downloading programs to your embedded target. If you followed our recommended configuration, you're using LPT1. If you chose another parallel port or a serial connection, select accordingly. In addition, for a serial port you must specify the baud rate. It is usually best to accept the default baud rate of AUTO and let the software determine the fastest reliable rate of communications.

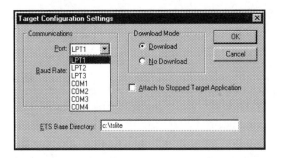

Figure 3-5: Before you can download programs to your target, configure the communications link using the Target Configuration Settings tool.

Next, select a Download Mode:

- **Download** causes a new download of the application each time you debug or run the application. This is the default and is the option you should normally use.

- **No Download** restarts the program without reloading it. This option is safe only if the application code has not corrupted itself, and should be used only if you're sure the code is good.

Finally, click OK and you've finished configuring Embedded StudioExpress! (We've skipped the Attach to Stopped Target Application option because ToolSuite Lite doesn't support it.) Before we continue, you should know a few things for future use:

- Always use the Embedded StudioExpress Target Configuration Settings tool to specify the host/target communications options. You *cannot* use the Debugger Remote Connection item from the Build menu in Developer Studio. In addition, the Debugger Remote Connection defaults to Local. If you have changed it, you must set it back to Local before debugging an ETS Kernel program.

- The Communications options that you specify using the Target Configuration Setting dialog box are set in the Registry and will apply every time you run an ETS Kernel program, even if you run the program from somewhere other than Developer Studio. Your choice for Download Mode, however, applies only to the next time you download a program to the embedded target. The option always reverts to the default, Download.

Embedded StudioExpress is used when you're running or debugging only an ETS Kernel program. If you're building other kinds of programs, it doesn't interfere. Specifically, when you run or debug a program, Embedded StudioExpress looks in the file for an ETS Kernel signature. If it finds the signature, Embedded StudioExpress knows the program is an ETS Kernel application and it sets up communications with the embedded target, downloads your program, and does other behind-the-scenes processing so you can use Developer Studio to debug your program. If it doesn't find the signature, StudioExpress does nothing and Developer Studio works normally.

SETTING UP THE HOST ENVIRONMENT

Now that you've configured ToolSuite Lite, Visual C++, and Embedded StudioExpress, you're ready to set the environment variables that tell these tools where to find the system files. Setting these environment variables allows you to use the command-line compiler, linker, and download tools, in addition to the Developer Studio IDE, to build and run programs:

- **PATH.** The `\TSLITE\BIN`, `\Program Files\Microsoft Visual Studio\VC98\Bin` and `...\Common\MSDev98\Bin` (for VC++ 5.*x*, `\Program Files\DevStudio\VC\bin` and `...\DevStudio\SharedIDE\bin`) directories must appear in the `PATH`.

- **INCLUDE.** The `INCLUDE` environment variable tells the Visual C++ compiler, CL, where to look for include files. This variable should point to the `\TSLITE\INCLUDE` and `\Program Files\Microsoft Visual Studio\VC98\Include` (for VC++ 5.*x*, `\Program Files\DevStudio\VC\include`) directories.

- **LIB.** The `LIB` environment variable tells LinkLoc in which subdirectory to find the C run-time library and libraries for making TNT Embedded ToolSuite system calls. This variable should point to the `\TSLITE\LIB` and `\Program Files\Microsoft Visual Studio\VC98\Lib` (for VC++ 5.*x*, `\Program Files\DevStudio\VC\lib`) directories.

- **PHARCOMM.** The `PHARCOMM` environment variable tells the RUNEMB download program which communications port to use. If you're using parallel download, set this variable to `-LPT 1` (or `-LPT 2` or `-LPT 3`, as appropriate). If you're using a serial connection, set this variable to `-COM 1` (or `-COM 2`, as appropriate).

It is most convenient to set these environment variables in your AUTOEXEC.BAT file so they are automatically set for you when you turn on your computer. Under Windows NT, run the System program from the Control Panel, choose the Environment tab, and set the environment variables in the User window.

BUILDING A BOOT DISK

The DISKKERN.BIN file in the `\TSLITE\MONITOR` directory contains the ETS Monitor portion of the real-time operating system. To load this file on your embedded target, you have to build a boot disk. For ToolSuite Lite, the boot disk is a floppy disk with a boot sector loader in the boot record and ETS Monitor, DISKKERN.BIN, as the first file on the disk. When you boot your embedded target, the boot sector loader loads DISKKERN.BIN into memory and begins to execute it.

The `\TSLITE\MONITOR` directory also contains two batch files for building boot disks:

- `DISK1200.BAT` for use with 1.2MB 5¼" floppy disks
- `DISK1440.BAT` for use with 1.44MB 3½" floppy disks

These batch files run on your host computer and take one parameter, the letter of the drive being used to build the boot disk. The only constraint on using these files is that `\TSLITE\MONITOR` must be the current directory.

Next, we go through the process of creating a boot disk. We assume that the host and the target each have a 1.44MB 3½" floppy disk drive. We assume also that the host's floppy drive is A:. In a Windows DOS box, change to the proper directory by issuing the command

```
cd \tslite\monitor
```

Then execute the following to build a boot disk:

```
disk1440 a
```

Before you can use this disk to boot the target system, you have to configure the correct downloading and debug communications option in the ETS Monitor. By default, ETS Monitor is configured to use LPT1 on the target for host communications. If you're using a serial port or a parallel port other than LPT1, you have to change the default configuration settings in ETS Monitor using CFIGKERN, a utility program. The syntax for CFIGKERN is

```
cfigkern monitorfilename [switches]
```

If you omit `monitorfilename` and `switches`, CFIGKERN prints the list of the accepted switches, as shown in Figure 3-6. The switches are grouped according to functionality.

Figure 3-6: CFIGKERN lets you change the configuration settings of ETS Monitor.

If you specify a `monitorfilename` and no `switches`, CFIGKERN displays a summary of the options configured in ETS Monitor.

The `-lpt` switch is used to select a parallel port, and the `-com` switch is used to select a serial port:

```
cfigkern -lpt n a:diskkern.bin
cfigkern -com n a:diskkern.bin
```

where *n* can be 1, 2, or 3 for the parallel port and 1 or 2 for the serial port.

You're now ready to boot ETS Monitor on your embedded target. Insert the disk you just created in the drive on your embedded target and reboot the machine. When the machine has booted, the following banner appears on the screen:

```
ETS Monitor 9.1 — Copyright (C) 1994-98 Phar Lap Software, Inc.
Code: 7E00h to FAAFh, Data: 1000h to 6D6Bh
Boot Method: Disk (A:)
Parallel Support: LPT1
Application Loader: NONE
Null Pointer Protection: On, Range 0 to FFFh
Ready for debugger commands.
```

TESTING THE HOST-TARGET CONNECTION

At this point, all the pieces should be in place and ready for you to download a program to your embedded target and run it from the host. To make sure, we'll use HELLO.EXE, a prebuilt executable shipped with ToolSuite Lite.

We'll use RUNEMB to download the program from the DOS command prompt. RUNEMB is a host program that launches an embedded program; that is, it downloads a program to the target and executes it. To start an embedded program from the command line, change to the proper directory and specify RUNEMB followed by the name of the program. For example:

```
cd \tslite\projects\hello
runemb release\hello
```

You'll see the Download ETS Application dialog box shown in Figure 3-7. The thermometer displays the progress as the program is downloaded to the target.

If you have a configuration problem, a Communications Error dialog box pops up with the message "A communications error has occurred on port LPT1. The target system is not responding." Click Cancel to return to the DOS prompt. We tell you how to debug that problem in a moment. For now, let's finish running HELLO.EXE.

After the download is complete, HELLO.EXE starts running immediately. Because it's such a simple program, it also exits almost immediately, after printing "Hello World!" in the DOS box, as shown in Figure 3-8. For now, ignore the fact that a simple `printf()` made output appear on the host computer; we explain how that works in Chapter 6, "Keyboard and Screen I/O."

Now, what should you do if the download didn't work? First, check your cable connection. See if another program, such as LapLink, will work over the cable connection you've made. If not, try another cable. Second, make sure ETS Monitor is configured to use the correct port on the embedded target computer. When ETS Monitor boots, the start-up message

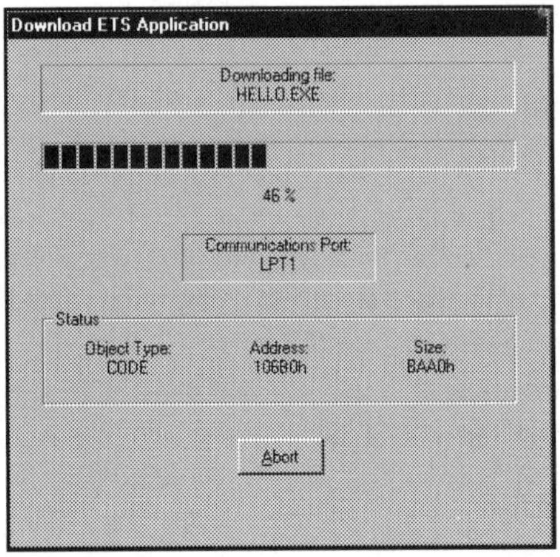

Figure 3-7: After connecting and configuring the download connection between the host and the target, boot the target and test the connection.

on the display includes a line identifying the communications port. Verify that this is correct; if not, use the CFIGKERN utility to set the correct port and then reboot the target computer. Finally, check that RUNEMB is using the correct port on the Windows host computer for the download. The dialog box displayed for the download identifies the communications port. If it's incorrect, set the PHARCOMM environment variable to include the correct communications switch setting, as described in the "Setting Up the Host Environment" section shown previously.

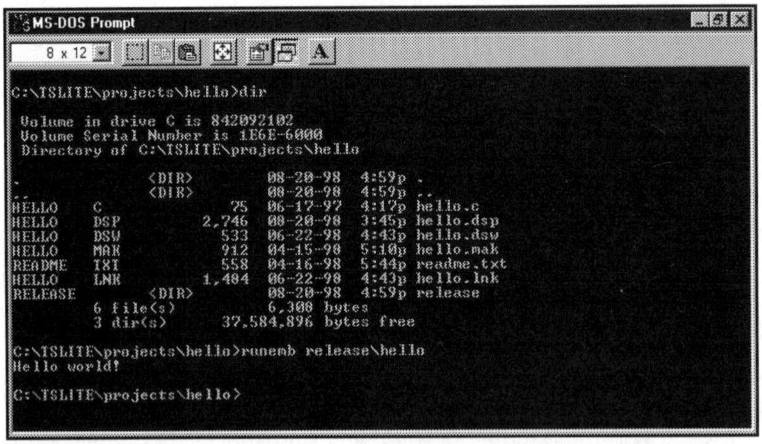

Figure 3-8: The HELLO.EXE program prints a string on the host computer and then exits.

PROGRAMMING PROJECTS

Throughout this book, we make extensive use of sample projects for embedded systems. Each project is in a separate subdirectory of \TSLITE\PROJECTS and has associated with it the following files:

- **README.TXT.** The text file describing the project and how to run and build the project.

- ***.C, *.CPP, *.H.** Source file(s) needed to build the project.

- ***.EXE.** A prebuilt executable version of the product, compiled with Visual C++ 6.0 and ready to run under ToolSuite Lite. For most projects, the .EXE file is in the RELEASE subdirectory; for the projects used in Chapter 4, "Debugging," the .EXE file is in the DEBUG subdirectory.

Note: If you want to debug a program with Visual C++ 5.*x*, you must rebuild it first, because the symbol table information from VC++ 6.0 can't be used with VC++ 5.*x*.

- ***.DSW, *.DSP.** Developer Studio project workspace files.

- ***.LNK.** A linker command file used by LinkLoc to link the project. This file is created automatically by ETS Project Wizard when the project is created. The .LNK file is used by both the Developer Studio project files and the .MAK file which is described next.

- ***.MAK.** A make file for building the project; this file can be used with NMAKE from any version of Visual C++. This file is not used by the Developer Studio project; it is present only for developers who prefer to do builds from a DOS command prompt rather than from Developer Studio.

Remember that the Developer Studio files are for the version of Developer Studio that comes with Visual C++ Versions 5.*x* and 6.0.

OPENING A WORKSPACE

Using, altering, and enhancing the projects in this book is straightforward. We'll step through it using the HELLO program as an example.

Begin by seeing what files are available. Start Developer Studio and then choose Open Workspace from the File menu. The dialog box in Figure 3-9 is displayed. Specify the project you want to change by entering the path and project name in the File name text box. For the HELLO program, we enter C:\TSLITE\PROJECTS\HELLO and then click the Open button.

Open the HELLO.DSW workspace file. After the project is opened, you can use all the Developer Studio tools to manipulate the project files. If you choose the File|View option, for instance, you see that the project has just one source file, HELLO.C. If you double-click HELLO.C, it opens for editing in the main edit window, as shown in Figure 3-10.

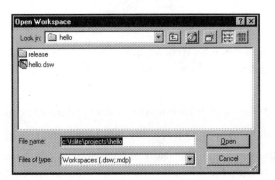

Figure 3-9: Open a workspace by selecting the .DSW file in the project directory.

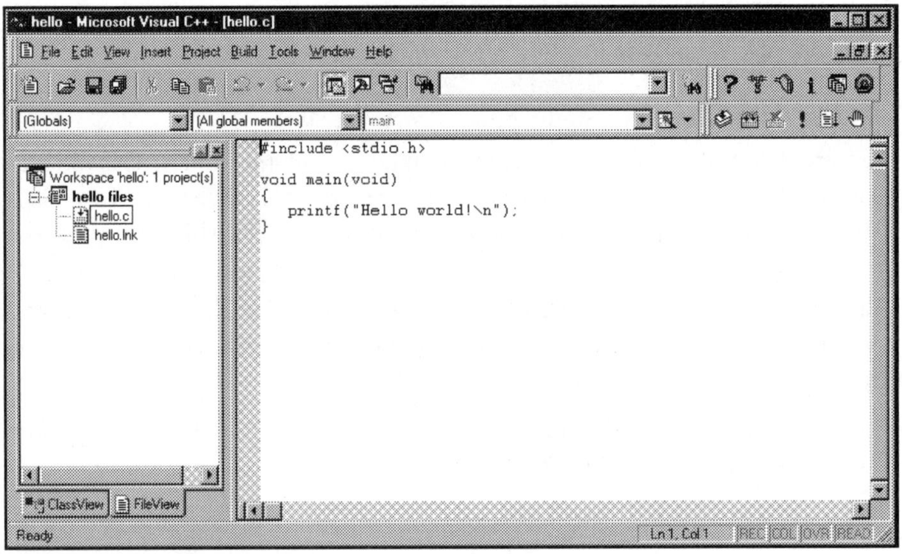

Figure 3-10: Use Developer Studio to modify the source code files in this book.

RUNNING A PROGRAM

You've already seen how to download and run HELLO.EXE from a DOS command prompt. Usually, however, it's more convenient to run programs directly from Developer Studio.

From the Build menu, choose Execute hello.exe. If you carefully watch the screen, you may see a Windows DOS box open. Next the Download ETS Application dialog box you saw in Figure 3-7 pops up. As before, the thermometer displays the download progress. Because you already tested your cable connection with the RUNEMB program, the only reason you should have a problem now is if Developer Studio is misconfigured. Click the Target Configurations Settings icon on the toolbar, and make sure you've selected the correct port for downloading and debugging.

The dialog box disappears when the program has finished loading, leaving the newly created DOS box in Figure 3-11 as the foreground window. As before, the output is generated almost immediately.

Figure 3-11: HELLO.EXE sends output to the DOS box created by Developer Studio to download and run the program.

Press any key on the host keyboard to stop the program. The DOS box disappears, and you're back in Developer Studio.

BUILDING A PROGRAM

The easiest way to build HELLO.EXE is from within Developer Studio. You use the same Developer Studio features you would use to build a native Windows application. Simply choose Build hello.exe from the Build menu, as shown in Figure 3-12.

The HELLO project — as is the case with all the ToolSuite Lite projects except the two used in Chapter 4, "Debugging" — is configured to build a release version of the program. If you want to build a debug version, choose Set Active Configuration from the Build menu to select the Debug configuration. When building a release version, the .OBJ and .EXE files are placed in the RELEASE subdirectory. For the debug version, these files are put in the DEBUG subdirectory.

As shipped with the ToolSuite Lite product, the project is prebuilt; when you select Build hello.exe, Developer Studio just notifies you the project is up-to-date and doesn't build anything. But if you delete the .OBJ file, choose Rebuild All on the Build menu, or edit the .C file, HELLO.EXE is rebuilt. Rebuilding HELLO generates the following output:

```
————————Configuration: hello - Win32 Release————————
Compiling...
hello.c
Linking...
LinkLoc: 9.1 — Copyright (C) 1986-98 Phar Lap Software, Inc.

hello.exe - 0 error(s), 0 warning(s)
```

Output from the build process is displayed at the bottom of the screen in the Build window.

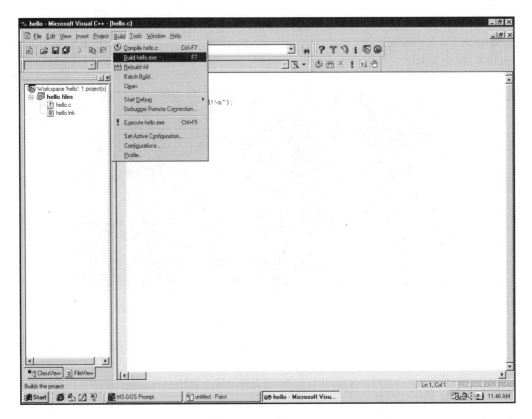

Figure 3-12: Build an embedded program the same way you normally build a Windows application using Developer Studio.

Just as with Windows programming projects, if you edit a source file and then try to run the program, Developer Studio automatically notices that the project is out-of-date and asks whether you want to rebuild the program before running it. In fact, all the Developer Studio features you use with Windows projects continue to work as usual with ToolSuite Lite programming projects.

If you have problems rebuilding files, the most likely culprit is the directory lists in Developer Studio. Select Options|Directories and make sure the Executable files, Include files, and Library files lists contain the appropriate directories for both ToolSuite Lite and Visual C++.

If you prefer, you can use the command-line versions of the compiler and linker to build your programs. This process will also work with versions of Visual C++ earlier than 5.0, where you can't use the IDE. Each project includes a .MAK file you can use to build the project with the NMAKE utility program in Visual C++. For the HELLO project, type the following:

```
cd \tslite\projects\hello
nmake -f hello.mak
```

If the project is up-to-date, NMAKE just exits silently without doing anything. But if you've deleted the .OBJ file or edited the .C file, you'll see the build shown in Figure 3-13.

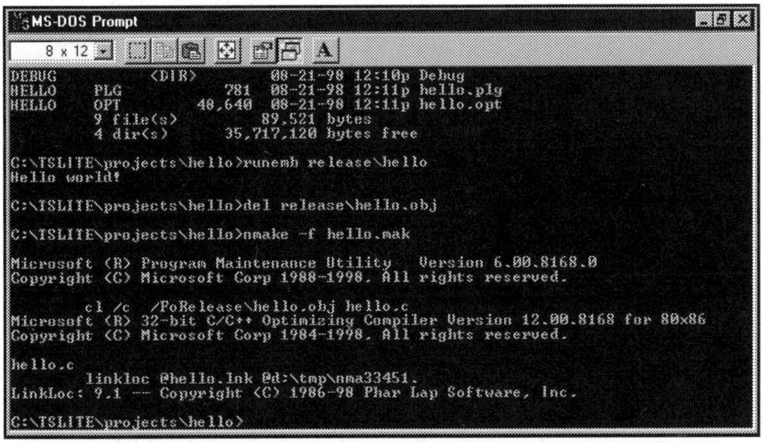

Figure 3-13: Use the included .MAK file to build HELLO.EXE with the command-line tools.

You don't even have to use the NMAKE utility if you don't want to. You can simply enter the cl and linkloc commands directly at a DOS command prompt.

To build the debug version of HELLO.EXE with NMAKE, enter the following commands. We need to create the DEBUG subdirectory first because (unlike Developer Studio) NMAKE won't automatically create it if it's missing.

```
cd \tslite\projects\hello
mkdir debug
nmake -f hello.mak debug=1
```

If you're having problems building programs with the command-line tools, you probably haven't set up your environment variables correctly. Make sure the PATH, LIB, and INCLUDE environment variables contain the appropriate directories for both ToolSuite Lite and Visual C++.

CREATING NEW PROGRAMMING PROJECTS

All the programming projects included on the CD-ROM are prebuilt as Developer Studio projects. To build your own programs using ToolSuite Lite and Developer Studio, use ETS Project Wizard to create a new workspace with a project targeting ETS Kernel. By creating a workspace in this way, you can use the full capabilities of the Developer Studio IDE, including automatic compilation of modified source files, C/C++ compilation options, and linker options set from the IDE.

An ETS Kernel project is basically a Win32 console application project that has the switch /ETS:FILENAME in its link command line. When Developer Studio links the program,

Embedded StudioExpress intercepts the operation and redirects it to the LinkLoc linker, using the filename specified in the /ETS switch as a linker command file. This linker command file is automatically constructed by ETS Project Wizard when you create the project.

To create a new Developer Studio workspace, click New ETS Project in the Embedded StudioExpress toolbar. As shown in Figure 3-14, you need to fill out a dialog box with the new workspace name and the complete path to the workspace base directory. We give each the same name.

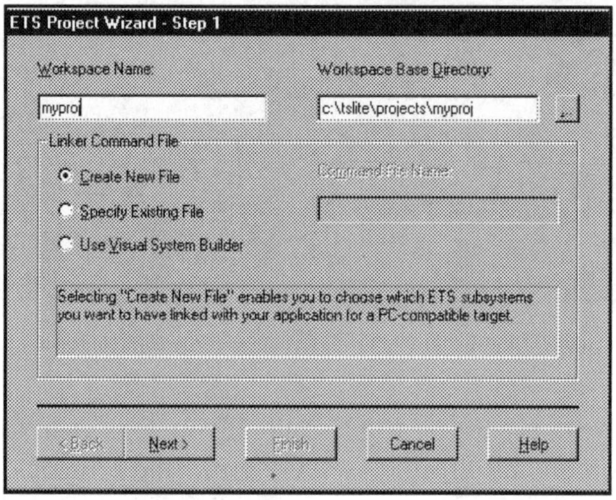

Figure 3-14: When creating a new workspace, it's simplest to make the workspace name and the base directory name identical.

The dialog box has three options for creating the linker command file. The Use Visual System Builder option is not available under ToolSuite Lite. If you select Specify Existing File, you have to create your own linker command file. We recommend you select Create New File.

If you select Create New File and click Next, the Subsystem Selection dialog box in Figure 3-15 pops up to allow you to select ETS Kernel subsystems to be linked with your application.

Select the ETS Kernel components you want to include with your application. As we noted earlier, the M-Systems Flash Disk Support, FTP Server, and PC Card (PCMCIA) Support options are not available with ToolSuite Lite. The more optional components you select, the larger the size of your final executable file. For this example, we've chosen to link in the screen and keyboard drivers so we can perform console I/O on the target system, and we've selected multithread support because we're planning to build a multithreaded application. Click Next to continue, and you'll see the dialog box in Figure 3-16.

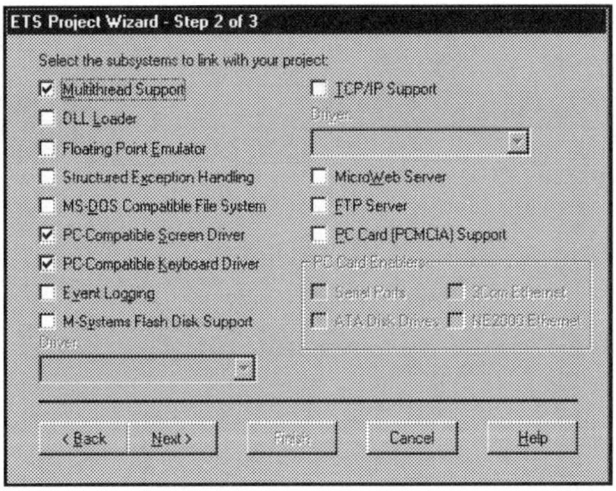

Figure 3-15: ToolSuite lets you select only the subsystems that you need. This lets you customize ETS Kernel yet keep its size to a minimum.

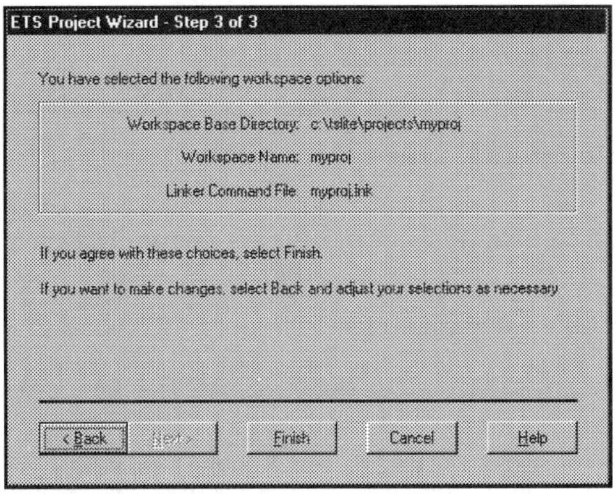

Figure 3-16: This final screen confirms your workspace choices.

The next dialog box shows you the name of the workspace, its base directory, and the linker command file that will be created. Click Finish to complete the creation of the new workspace. Developer Studio will then open the newly created workspace, as shown in Figure 3-17.

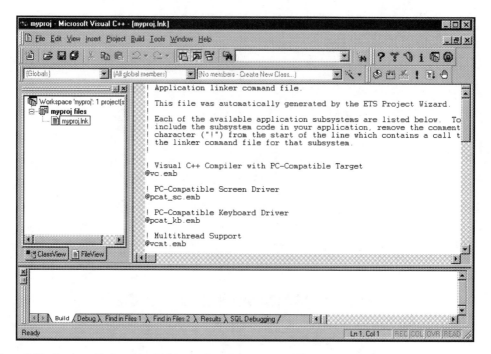

Figure 3-17: Developer Studio automatically generates a linker command file.

Initially, the project contains just one file, the automatically created MYPROJ.LNK file. Take a look at this file:

```
! Application linker command file.
!
! This file was automatically generated by the ETS Project Wizard.
!
! Each of the available application subsystems are listed below.  To
! include the subsystem code in your application, remove the comment
! character ("!") from the start of the line which contains a call to
! the linker command file for that subsystem.
!

! Visual C++ Compiler with PC-Compatible Target
@vc.emb

! PC-Compatible Screen Driver
@pcat_sc.emb

! PC-Compatible Keyboard Driver
@pcat_kb.emb

! Multithread Support
@vcmt.emb
```

```
! Structured Exception Handling
!@strucexc.emb

! Floating Point Emulator
!@fpem.emb

! MS-DOS Compatible File System
!@lfs.emb

! DLL Loader
!@ldr.emb

! TCP/IP Support
!@winsock.emb

! TCP/IP Driver
!@eth-smc.emb          ! SMC 8003/8216/8416
!@eth-smc9.emb         ! SMC 91C92/91C94
!@eth-3com.emb         ! 3Com 3C509
!@eth-ne2k.emb         ! NE2000
!@eth-dec.emb          ! Digital 2114x
!@ppp16550.emb         ! PPP 8250/16450/16550
!@slp16550.emb         ! SLIP/CSLIP  8250/16450/16550

! MicroWeb Server
!@microweb.emb

! FTP Server
!@ftpserve.emb

! Event Logging
!@log.emb

! PC Card Support
!@pccard.emb

! PC Card Enablers
!@cs-ser.emb       ! Serial Ports
!@cs-ide.emb       ! ATA Disk Drives
!@cs-3com.emb      ! 3Com Ethernet
!@cs-ne2k.emb      ! NE2000 Ethernet

! M-Systems Flash Support
!@pcfd.emb         ! PC-FD
!@dochip2.emb      ! DiskOnChip 2000

! Add any additional linker commands here.
```

This file just references other linker command files, which can be found in the \TSLITE\LINKCMD directory. Each linker command file enables a different subsystem or driver.

As you can see, the screen, keyboard, and multithread support command files are activated. All other command files are present but are commented out with an exclamation point (!). If you want to add or remove components, you can edit this file to uncomment or comment the appropriate command file. You can also add any additional linker switches you may need at the end of the file.

Finally, add source code files to the project as you normally do for any Developer Studio project, using the Project|Add To Project command, as shown in Figure 3-18.

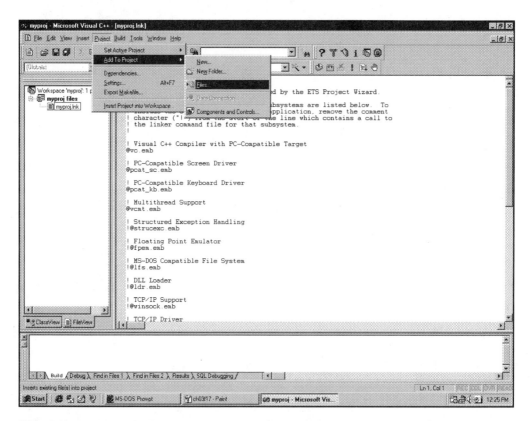

Figure 3-18: Add files to a ToolSuite Lite project just as you would for a Windows programming project.

SUMMARY

This was a burn-in chapter. Our goal was to outline our hardware and software selections, acquaint you with tools, and make sure all the paraphernalia you need to work through the projects — host and target hardware, ToolSuite Lite software, Visual C++ software, target boot diskettes, and LapLink cable — is in working order.

In addition, you've seen how to build, compile, link, and run a real-time embedded application. What we didn't show you was how to debug one. As any programmer knows, writing error-free applications on a regular basis is something that you either dream of or read about in books (although not in this one). In the real world, programs fail and you have to figure out why.

On to debugging.

4

Debugging

If you've developed even a moderate amount of software, you know the importance of a good debugger. As much as we would like to think that the advances in software and hardware technology have made our programming lives simpler and less prone to inadvertent errors, the reality is that all those advances have resulted in an increase in overall software complexity. Consequently, the need for a robust debugger as part of any software development system has grown over time.

Well-known C/C++ development software vendors — Microsoft, Inprise (formerly Borland), and Watcom, for example — recognized many years ago this need for powerful debugging. In addition to implementing powerful source-level debugging features, all have integrated a debugger directly into their software development suites; these suites are known as integrated development environments (IDEs) because the vendors combine compiler, editor, and debugger into what appears to the user to be a single program. Because the debugger is integrated with the rest of the tools, vendors can include powerful features such as the capability to edit source files while debugging and automatic rebuilding for out-of-date executables.

As a developer of embedded systems, you want the same ease of use and power that's available in an IDE. But embedded systems have other debugging requirements that aren't often encountered when debugging desktop applications.

First, embedded applications usually interact closely with hardware. The more capabilities your debugger has to examine hardware, the better. At a minimum, it must be capable of reading and writing to I/O ports so you can examine and modify the state of hardware attached to the system. It's even better if the debugger can present a high-level view of some hardware on the system, so you don't have to go poking around in hardware registers and looking up bits to figure out what's going on. For example, it's helpful if the debugger can read the interrupt controller and tell you what hardware interrupts are active, pending, or masked, or if the debugger can read the real-time clock and tell you the exact time, down to the microsecond. Some debuggers allow you to easily write add-on modules so you can customize the debugger to look at hardware specific to your application.

Hardware-related problems are often also timing-related. Using traditional debugging techniques of setting breakpoints and stepping through code changes the timing and affects the system behavior. For tracking down timing problems, your best bet is a hardware-assisted debugging tool, such as an in-circuit emulator (ICE) that can trace thousands of instructions and hardware signals in real time and allow you to perform a post-mortem examination of a crash.

Second, developers of embedded systems often need to examine what's happening inside the operating system, as well as inside the application. For example, when debugging real-time systems, you may want to see which threads are blocked on which synchronization objects, what the thread priorities are, where each thread is currently executing, and so on. Or you may want to peek inside the network stack and see what TCP connections are currently active. The ability to examine OS data structures can give you a lot of useful additional information when debugging an embedded system. This requirement argues for using a debugger that's closely integrated with your operating system or using an extensible debugger that you can customize to display information about the RTOS.

Third, embedded software often needs to run in ROM. Usually, you'll do most of your debugging with the application running in RAM, and switch over to ROM only after the program is up and running. But even so, you have to be able to debug problems that occur only when the program runs in ROM. At a minimum, your debugger must be able to set breakpoints in code running in ROM. A software debugger may be capable of this using features built into the processor, or you might need a hardware tool such as an ICE. It's also tedious to burn new PROMs each time you fix a bug; a ROM emulator can help you here by allowing you to quickly download new software builds instead of fiddling with physical chips and sockets.

Finally, your debugging solution has to work on a typically nonstandard hardware platform. That means you often have to do some work to get the debugger up and talking to your target system. Make sure you have good documentation for how to accomplish this, as well as access to well-informed technical support staff at the debugger vendor. This is another situation where an ICE can make your life simpler; because an ICE doesn't have a software presence on the target system, it can be operational from day one, before the target hardware is working and before any software is running on the target.

In this chapter, you look at the range of software and hardware debugging tools that developers use to debug their embedded systems. Although a software debugger will probably be your primary debugging tool, we show you a number of other hardware tools that can save you a lot of time in certain situations. In the best of all possible worlds, you'd have an arsenal of debugging tools from which you could select the best tool for whatever particular problem you were having.

After our survey of debugging tools for the embedded market, we tell you how to use the Microsoft Developer Studio debugger to cross-debug ETS Kernel applications. We step you through a sample debug session, and show you some of the specialized embedded capabilities added to Developer Studio by the StudioExpress component of ToolSuite Lite.

SOFTWARE DEBUGGERS

Your primary debugging tool for embedded systems will almost certainly be a software debugger, similar to the debuggers found on the desktop. But you'll also need a good embedded debugger that picks up where a regular debugger leaves off. An embedded debugger should allow you to examine system registers and system data structures, in addition to the general registers any debugger can display. You should be able to directly debug an interrupt service routine, a feature many desktop debuggers lack. The debugger should provide a good view into a system's multitasking operations, showing you which threads or processes are runnable and which are blocked, which synchronization objects are owned by which threads or processes, and so on. Debugger commands should be available to allow you to easily switch between threads and freeze selected threads, so you can control which thread will run in a specific debugging situation.

In addition to these features, your embedded debugger should be capable of cross-debugging; that is, executing on one hardware platform while debugging an application on another. If you've developed mostly desktop applications, a cross-debugger may be new to you. For applications that will ultimately run on the same hardware platform on which they were built, a cross-debugger isn't necessary. However, you need a cross-debugger for embedded applications intended for another platform; you'll be able to debug your applications on the host only up to a point. After that, to thoroughly debug your software, you should download your programs to the target, and finish debugging while they're running on the actual target hardware.

Cross-debuggers usually have two components: the software that runs on the host and a debug agent that runs on the target. The host portion uses a communications link to either download an application to the target's RAM or connect to an application in the target's ROM. Usually, the communications link is a serial cable, a parallel cable, or a network connection. A cross-debugger usually works by sending commands to a debug agent, often called a *debug monitor*, on the target. The debug monitor executes a command on behalf of the debugger running on the host and sends the results of the command back over the communications link.

Getting a debug monitor up and running on a target isn't always easy. First, the monitor and target OS must be integrated. If you purchase your operating system and debugger from a single vendor, the debug monitor is already integrated with the OS. If, on the other hand, you write your own operating system or get your OS and debugging tools from different vendors, you are responsible for integrating them. That may be straightforward if the OS just sits on top of the debug monitor and doesn't really know it's there. But if the debug monitor and the OS need to interact — for instance, to provide the debugger with information about OS data structures or to interface downloading with program loading in the OS — you could spend a lot of time searching through OS source code (or worse, disassembling code for which you don't have source) to find the right place to attach the debug monitor hooks.

Second, you have to bring up the OS and debug monitor on your target hardware. That can be difficult: Until the debugger is working, you often don't have any tools to show you what's happening on the target system, so you're working in the dark. An ICE can be an invaluable tool during this process; without a hardware debug aid, you have to fall back on primitive techniques such as flashing LEDs on the system board to see how far the software gets before it crashes. If your target hardware is similar to a standard system, or you're using a commercially available single-board computer that the OS supports directly, this job is much simpler, because you can start with a working board support package provided by the OS vendor for that standard system.

If integrating the monitor and OS, as well as bringing them up on a target, is up to you, make sure your debugger vendor and your OS vendor have good documentation for performing these tasks and are available to give you technical support.

If you've chosen your language tools before choosing your debugger, verify that the tools and the debugger work well together before buying the debugger. If you purchased the language tools and debugger from the same vendor, they are usually well integrated. If you buy them from different vendors, however, make sure they support the same executable formats and symbol formats. Check that they are compatible for full source-level debugging; small incompatibilities may mean that the debugger is incapable of viewing local symbols or decoding data structures symbolically, for example. Larger incompatibilities might mean that the debugger doesn't understand the name-mangling conventions (which are not standardized) of your C++ compiler, or that the tools to build an image for burning an application into ROM produce a symbol table file that your debugger can't use to debug the code in ROM. If you can, try to purchase tools integrated into an IDE like the ones commonly used for desktop programming. The ease of use and power of an IDE will pay back its cost many times over in time saved during debug sessions.

Debugging embedded systems is often more challenging than debugging a desktop application. Because of the real-time nature of embedded systems, they tend to have more timing-related problems than do desktop applications. Interrupt handlers, because of their asynchronous nature and the fact that they may run very frequently, are difficult to debug; we give some debugging tips in the "ISR Fundamentals" section in Chapter 9, "Interrupts." And debugging multitasking programs presents special problems; see the "Debugging" section in Chapter 12, "Multitasking." Listed below are a few general debugging and programming techniques you may find useful:

- **Program defensively.** Check for error returns from functions (especially the `malloc()` function). Always put a `default` clause inside a `switch()` statement to catch unexpected cases. Use the `assert()` macro to verify that expected preconditions and postconditions are satisfied. (The `assert()` macro prints an error message and terminates the program if the assertion fails. You can turn off all code generated by `assert()` statements by defining a symbol when you build a release version of your program.)

- **Log events of interest as they occur for post-mortem analysis.** You can log information directly to a file, or store it in memory. If you store information in memory, when the program completes or you finish executing your test case, you can print the information or save it to a file. Logging directly to a file doesn't require allocating memory for debug information, which is good if your application uses most of the available memory. On the other hand, writing information to disk changes the program timing much more than logging information in memory, so it doesn't work well for tracking timing-related problems. Many real-time operating systems include some kind of event logging feature that can log both operating system and application events. For example, the ETS Kernel event logging system keeps an in-memory circular buffer of events of interest.

- **Find uninitialized variables.** Uninitialized variables are the cause of some non-reproducible errors (problems that tend to go away when you debug the program, change the inputs to a program, or rebuild the program). Because local variables are kept on the stack, the value in an uninitialized variable changes depending on what code ran (and used that stack region) prior to the code with the bug. Any slight change, including adding or removing code, using a debugger, or performing actions in a different sequence can make the problem appear or disappear.

  Don't ignore problems that go away when you try to track them down! They'll almost always come back to bite you. Be methodical when pursuing this kind of bug; always perform the same steps in the same sequence, and make changes (such as adding debug code) one at a time. When the problem disappears, back up and take a different tack. Remember that the symptom may be far removed from the actual bug. For example, if an uninitialized pointer variable is used to overwrite memory, nothing bad may happen until much later when the corrupted memory location is used.

- **Track down timing problems.** Timing problems are the other common cause of non-reproducible errors. Since debugging a program changes its timing characteristics, debugging can make timing problems disappear. Likewise, adding debug code (especially if it writes to a slow device such as a disk or a serial connection) changes a program's timing. Timing problems can appear and disappear even with repeated runs of the identical executable, loaded at the identical location in memory, with identical inputs. That's because other events over which you have no direct control — namely, hardware interrupts such as timers, network cards, serial ports, and so on — tend to occur in slightly different sequences with each run.

  An ICE or other hardware debugging tool is the preferred method for finding timing problems. If you don't have a hardware debugger, try instrumenting your program, either with an event logging capability or with debug code that checks for suspected erroneous conditions. Then run the program repeatedly in an attempt to make it fail so you can gather additional information. Be a good observer; keep track of all the different ways the program fails. While different nonreproducible crashes may be due to separate program bugs, it's likely they're different manifestations of the same bug.

Finally, formulate theories that can account for all the different failures you've seen, and then prove or disprove each theory. For example, if you suspect a particular interrupt may be the culprit, remove the ISR for that interrupt from your program. If that makes the problem disappear, you can focus on the ISR and the code that interacts with it. If the problem doesn't disappear, try to formulate a different theory.

HARDWARE DEBUGGERS

Developers use a variety of hardware tools to debug both software and hardware on embedded systems. What follows here is a brief introduction to a few of the more important hardware debugging aids. If you will be involved in serious embedded system development, you should familiarize yourself with them. Magazines such as *Embedded Systems Programming* occasionally have product roundups, which are articles that provide extensive coverage of products in a particular category. Such articles give you a good feel for the capabilities of these tools, and they also list prices and suppliers.

IN-CIRCUIT EMULATORS

An in-circuit emulator (ICE) is a standalone microcomputer that uses software and hardware to emulate the inner workings of a particular CPU. A typical ICE consists of two main components: the host controller, which is a specialized computer workstation, and a *pod,* which is a pin-for-pin replacement of the microprocessor used in the system being tested. The pod is tethered to the host controller by a cable — usually a very wide, flat ribbon cable. Using an ICE requires that you pop the processor out of the test system and plug the pod into the CPU socket or circuit (hence the name in-circuit emulator). Through the pod, the workstation takes the place of the processor, emulating it to such a degree that the target system is unaware that its brain has been replaced with a replica. This replica lets you, the operator of the ICE workstation, watch every signal exchanged between the target processor and its environment.

An ICE provides all the usual capabilities of a desktop debugger, such as breakpoints, watchpoints, and reading and writing memory, but also offers a number of additional features. The most important example is an execution trace. To perform an execution trace, you set up a trigger event that will cause the ICE to capture bus cycles around the circumstance you want to debug. An ICE can save information from thousands of bus cycles in a buffer. With most ICEs, the trigger can begin, end, or be in the center of the trace. After the trace is captured, you can examine it with the ICE software. You can see individual memory reads and writes, hardware signals such as I/O and interrupts, and so on.

The ICE software attempts to identify code fetches and disassemble the executed code, though it sometimes can be fooled by processor prefetch, which we describe in a moment. Using an execution trace, you can see which instructions were executed and in what order, what code was interrupted, what happened after an ISR completed execution, and so on. This trace feature is sometimes the only way to gather data on bugs that occur as a result of critical timing conditions; if you try to step through the code with a software debugger or with the ICE, the interactions with the debugger change the timing and the bug doesn't occur.

Another example of a feature found in ICEs but not desktop debuggers is memory overlays. An ICE can overlay memory in the target system with RAM in the ICE system. This is useful for replacing code in ROM on the target with new software you've just built and want to test.

Also, because the ICE doesn't have any software that runs on the target processor, it can debug any code that runs on the target. It can step through the boot process one instruction at a time, if necessary. It can debug any hardware interrupt handler on the system, including interrupts that may be integral to the operation of the OS, such as the system timer or a hard disk interrupt. No matter how critical to system operation a particular section of code is, an ICE can debug it.

In addition to a more extensive set of debugging capabilities, an ICE provides hardware triggers — something even an embedded software debugger doesn't have. You can configure an ICE so that interrupts and port I/O trigger a trace or a breakpoint.

In short, an ICE is the perfect tool for situations in which a system is misbehaving and you're not sure whether the problem lies in the software, the hardware, or the interaction between the software and hardware.

On the downside, using an ICE can be somewhat more awkward than using a software debugger. First, the debugger that comes with an ICE is often primitive by IDE debugger standards. Second, the debugger poses the same potential compatibility problems for language tools that we mentioned in the section on software debuggers. (As we advised there, before you make a purchase, be sure that the executable file and symbol table formats are compatible, and that features such as source-level debugging work with the ICE/compiler/linker combination you choose.) Third, it's not uncommon to end up debugging in assembly language on an ICE, either using a map file to look up global symbols or having only global symbols available in the ICE debugger. One nice solution, if you can find it, is a software debugger that can also be used to front-end an ICE. Some debugger vendors provide this feature for specific ICEs, though it's not common. If you plan to use an ICE, see whether you can choose tools, including a debugger, that explicitly support the ICE — you'll have a much nicer debugging setup.

Another hitch to using an in-circuit emulator is that its capability to correctly disassemble execution traces may be hindered on high-end processors that prefetch instructions and cache memory. In an attempt to achieve faster processing speeds, some processors prefetch instructions from memory when they have free bus cycles. In the process, if the program branches, the processor discards any unused instructions. Unfortunately, an ICE sees only part of a processor's actions. The ICE sees which instructions the processor read from memory, but it doesn't know which instructions the CPU executed and which it discarded. The ICE must figure that out on its own. Needless to say, some ICEs do a better job than others, and no ICE gets it right all the time. You have to keep this in mind, and sometimes do your own analysis, when reviewing trace disassemblies.

An ICE's capability to gather information is hindered also if a processor has an on-chip memory cache: memory reads that hit the cache won't even appear on the address bus, which is what an ICE monitors to gather most of its information. One solution to this problem is to disable the on-chip cache, enabling the ICE to see all memory accesses. Unfortunately, this changes the timing characteristics of the system and can make some timing-dependent bugs hard to reproduce.

Finally, ICEs can be expensive. According to *Embedded Systems Programming 1998 Buyer's Guide Issue,* an ICE can cost as little as $150 or as much as $30,000, depending on the capabilities you need.

Note: The full version of ToolSuite includes built-in support for ICEs from Microtek and Applied Microsystems. This allows you to debug your application program at the source-code level, and debug ETS Monitor at the assembly-language level.

An ICE Alternative

ICE hardware can be expensive. In addition, ICE speeds lag available processor speeds typically by a year or more. Because of that lag, if you want to use the latest (and fastest) processor, an ICE that can debug it is probably unavailable.

A variation on the ICE is a technology referred to as BDM — background debug mode. BDM consists of hardware that a designer adds to a microprocessor to allow developers to perform ICE-like debugging on the chip. (Motorola's 683xx microprocessor family includes BDM capabilities.) Additional pins on the chip provide designers with a back door into the chip, with only a little additional board hardware.

Some BDM systems require little more than software and an adapter cable that links the BDM edge connectors to your computer's parallel ports. Others involve the purchase of a plug-in board that goes into your PC and acts as the interface. Admittedly, using BDM is slower than using an ICE, but it's a great deal cheaper. High-end BDM systems are usually no more than $2000.

ROM EMULATORS

The name really says it all: a ROM emulator *emulates ROM.* A ROM emulator is a box with two cables. One cable connects to the serial port on your development system. You use this serial connection to download new executables to the ROM emulator. The other cable plugs into the ROM socket on your target system. The target hardware thinks it's accessing ROM, but it's seeing the memory in the ROM emulator, which contains the program you've downloaded for testing. Usually, a particular ROM emulator will support two or three ROM sizes and configurations.

A ROM emulator buys you turnaround time in the edit-compile-download-debug cycle. When you're debugging your program in ROM, the usual cycle is to pop out the old PROMs, drop them in a PROM burner, burn in the new software, and then put the chips back in your target system. That can get old pretty quickly. With a ROM emulator, you can build your program, download it to the target using the ROM emulator, run it, make alterations to the program on the host based on how well or poorly the program worked, and download it again. This can save you a lot of time if you have to debug much of your program in ROM.

ROM emulators are priced more reasonably than in-circuit emulators. According to *Embedded Systems Programming 1998 Buyer's Guide Issue,* prices for ROM emulators can run from $100 to $6000.

SOFTWARE SIMULATORS

A *software simulator* imitates all or part of the target hardware in a software environment. Depending on what and how much is being simulated, software simulators can be large and elaborate, because they have to make an application *think* that it's running on hardware (and sometimes with other software) that isn't there. Each instruction executed in the application must be faithfully fake-executed by the simulator.

On the low end, a software simulator may simply mimic the behavior of a chip and memory. For example, simulators targeted at the 8051 8-bit microcontroller — available from companies such as ChipTools and Archimedes Software — not only simulate the 8051 chip and memory but also feign most of the 8051's on-chip peripherals, including a serial port, parallel I/O lines, and timers. Although this is low end in the sense that the hardware is 8 bit, it is by no means trivial. A software simulator for the 8051 must not only execute an application's instructions so that all the effects that a given instruction has on the state of the 8051's internal registers are properly mimicked, but must also replicate the behavior of the peripheral hardware. Each execution of an instruction, which occurs in lockstep with the cycles of the chip's clock crystal, must be accompanied by an appropriate advancing of the simulator's hypothetical timer. And the timer must be advanced according to the simulated clock speed. The 8051 can be operated over a range of system clock frequencies. From the perspective of executing code, the timer appears to advance at a slower rate on a simulated 10-MHz system than on a simulated 8-MHz system.

High-end simulators allow you to create a model of large real-time systems. Using the ObjecTime system (from the company of the same name), designers of large real-time systems can build models of substantial complexity. ObjecTime can even simulate the actions of nonexistent hardware. So a developer can exercise an as-yet-undeployed application and verify that it works according to specification (presuming the final hardware is built according to specification).

The advantage of software simulators lies in how they enable engineers and programmers to do serious development work before they see actual hardware. Errors in application logic can be quickly revealed and addressed with a software simulator. And depending on the capabilities of the simulator, even some hardware-related faults can be corrected. For example, some software simulators supply input stimulus files; a capability that allows you to script a set of inputs to play through the simulator. You can tell the simulator to deliver an interrupt 10 ms after your application starts, another interrupt 20 ms later, and so on. In this way, you can exercise your application in a precisely controlled fashion that would be otherwise impossible or prohibitively expensive using hardware.

A disadvantage to simulators is that they run much slower than actual hardware, typically between 10 to 100 times slower. So you shouldn't use them to find timing-related errors. Simulators are also not available for all processors, particularly high-end processors that are prohibitively complex to simulate.

DEBUGGING WITH TOOLSUITE

In Chapter 3, "Software Installation and Setup," we said that we would be debugging applications using a combination of Microsoft Developer Studio and Embedded StudioExpress, an add-in that comes with ToolSuite. We also showed you how to install Embedded StudioExpress. Now we illustrate how to use these tools to cross-debug software on a *target* system. In case you're unfamiliar with Microsoft's tools, we begin by debugging a simple program using just Developer Studio. (In 6.0, Microsoft refers to VC++ and Developer Studio as VC++. We refer to each separately.) Then we show you how to use the extensions in StudioExpress by debugging a multithreaded program.

A BUGGY CALCULATION

A Buggy Calculation is a simple program with a simple bug. Actually, it's more accurate to describe the program as having the potential for a simple bug. You'll understand when you look through the source code, which follows:

```c
#include <stdio.h>

void main(void)
{
    int   distance, time, speed;
    char *t1="Thank you for your input\n";
    char *t2=NULL;
    printf("Enter the distance traveled, in miles:\n");
    scanf("%d", &distance);
    printf("Enter the elapsed time, in minutes\n");
    scanf("%d", &time);
    speed = (60 * distance) / time;
    printf("The effective speed in miles per hour: %d\n", speed);
    // t2 = t1;
    printf(t2);
}
```

As you can see, this program merely accepts a value for distance and a value for elapsed time, and from those inputs calculates the average speed in miles per hour. It then displays a final thank you message.

Nothing about this application is — or needs to be — inherently embedded or real-time. Its sole purpose is to get you started debugging ETS Kernel programs with Developer Studio.

As you've probably noticed, the program has a couple of obvious bugs. First, it doesn't check to see whether a user entered a value of zero for time, which will cause a divide-by-zero exception. Second, it inadvertently passes a null pointer to the C library `printf()` function. When `printf()` attempts to dereference the pointer, it causes a general protection fault (GPF) because of the null pointer detection feature in ETS Kernel, which was described in Chapter 3. As we explained there, a common programming error is accessing memory through an uninitialized pointer variable. Because uninitialized variables often are zero, ETS Kernel traps accesses to lower memory.

DEBUGGING THE APPLICATION

The source code for the Buggy Calculation project is in the \TSLITE\PROJECTS\DIVBUG direc-tory. The program is small and consists of a single source code file, DIVBUG.C.

Note: If you're using Visual C++ 5.*x*, rebuild DIVBUG.EXE before debugging it. The exe-cutable on the CD-ROM was built with Visual C++ 6.0, and contains symbol information not compatible with Visual C++ 5.*x*.

Boot ETS Monitor on the embedded target, run Developer Studio, and open the DIVBUG workspace, as described in Chapter 3. Then start a Developer Studio debugging session by choosing Start Debug|Step Into from the Build menu.

At this point, StudioExpress looks at DIVBUG.EXE for the ETS Kernel signature. It finds it and not only starts up the debugger, but also creates a Windows DOS box for the program and downloads the application to the target. The download happens exactly as we described in Chapter 3. If you have problems getting the download to work, go back to the "Programming Projects" section in Chapter 3 and make sure you can get the Hello World project to download and run.

When the application has finished downloading, you see the window in Figure 4-1, which is the same Developer Studio debugger screen you use for Windows programs. The source window contains the C code for DIVBUG, with the instruction pointer waiting at the begin-ning of main().

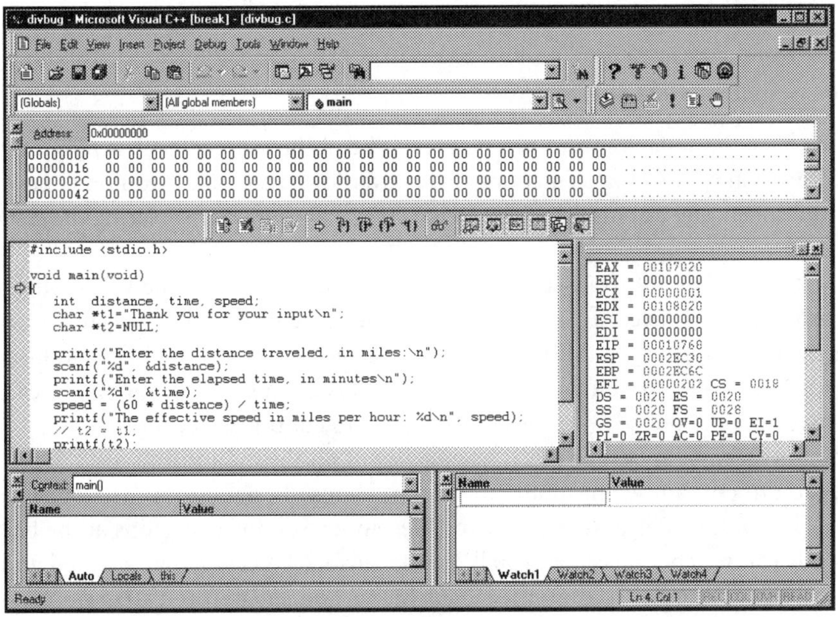

Figure 4-1: We ran this program with the debugger configured to display memory, registers, variables, and watch windows. You can use the windows you find most useful.

Before you go on, note that the last button on the taskbar is for the DOS box associated with DIVBUG running on your embedded target.

Now it's time to execute the program and watch what happens. Select Go from the Debug menu to run the program. In response to the prompts for distance and time, enter 30 and 0, respectively. The console I/O appears in the DOS box shown in Figure 4-2.

When you press Enter after entering 0, Developer Studio displays the message, "Unhandled exception in divbug.exe: 0xC0000094: Integer Divide by Zero."

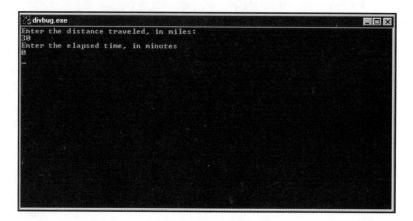

Figure 4-2: Entering the values 30 and 0 will cause a bug to surface.

Click OK and Developer Studio shows us that the instruction pointer is on this line of code:

```
speed = (60 * distance) / time;
```

We see from the variables window in Figure 4-3 that the value of time is zero, and it's the attempted division by zero that caused the divide overflow exception. If you don't have a variables window open, you can display the current value of the variable by placing the cursor over the variable.

Ultimately, you'd want to insert a check in the code for a zero time value, but to verify that the program runs successfully if a nonzero time value is entered, try again with a value of 10 for the time. You can do this in two ways. The easiest way to continue is to just change the value of time in the variables window to 0x0A, press Enter so the debugger stores the new value in memory, and press F5 (or select Debug|Go) to continue execution.

Sometimes it's not as easy as this to change input on the fly, and you need to restart the debug session to enter different input. To do this, choose Restart from the Debug menu. A new copy of DIVBUG.EXE is downloaded, and Developer Studio again stops at the beginning of main(). If you watch the taskbar, you'll see the current DOS window is closed and a new window is opened. Choose Go from the Debug menu, and enter 30 and 10 in response to the prompts for distance and time, respectively.

Before you have time to look at the output in the DOS box, Developer Studio tells you that another error has occurred by displaying the message, "Unhandled exception in divbug.exe: 0xC0000005: Access Violation."

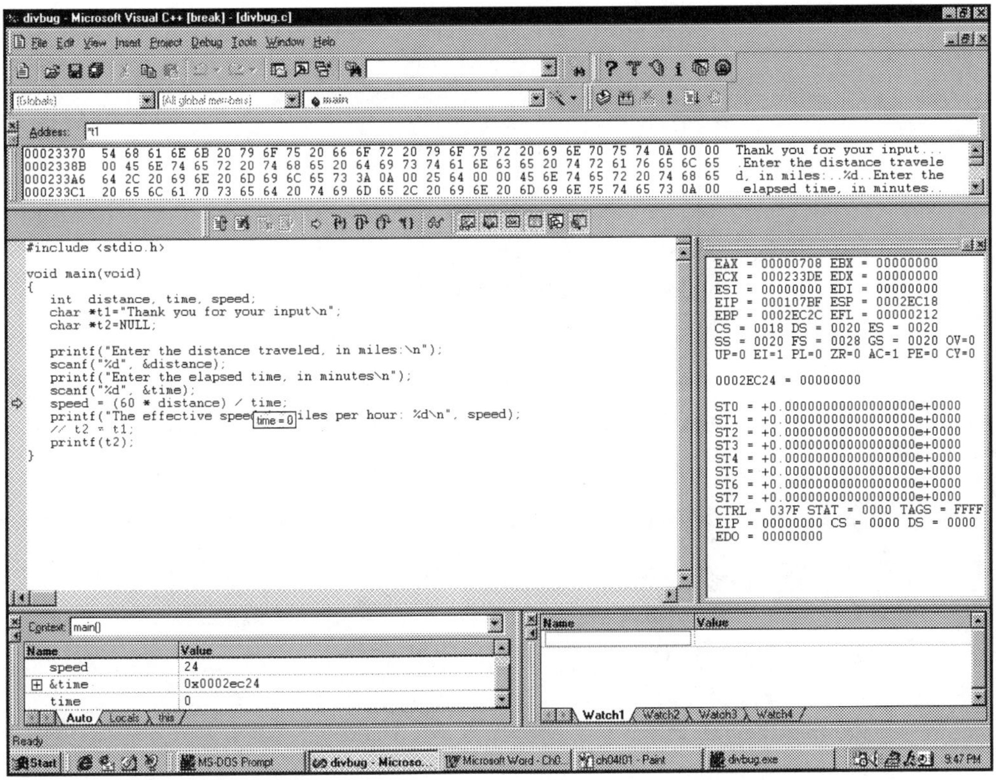

Figure 4-3: The bug in this program is that it accepts zero for a time value, which causes a divide-by-zero exception.

Click OK to close the dialog box. Because DIVBUG is linked with the debug version of the C run-time library, Developer Studio tries to display the source code for the C library function that received the exception. If you didn't install source code for the run-time library, or Developer Studio doesn't have the directory for the run-time source, Developer Studio displays the dialog box in Figure 4-4, prompting you to enter the directory where C run-time source is located.

If Developer Studio finds the source code, however, it displays it in the source window, as shown in Figure 4-5.

Before you track down this access violation, you should make sure that the calculation was correct. As you can see in Figure 4-6, when we entered 30 for distance and 10 for time, the program correctly calculated the speed in miles per hour.

Shift your attention back to finding the access violation, and scroll up in the source window. You see that you're inside a function called _output(), which the comments say performs printf() style output to a stream. Position the mouse pointer over the format variable on the source line that received the exception, and you can see that this pointer variable is zero (null). The source instruction is attempting to dereference the pointer, which caused an exception because of the null pointer detection feature of ETS Kernel.

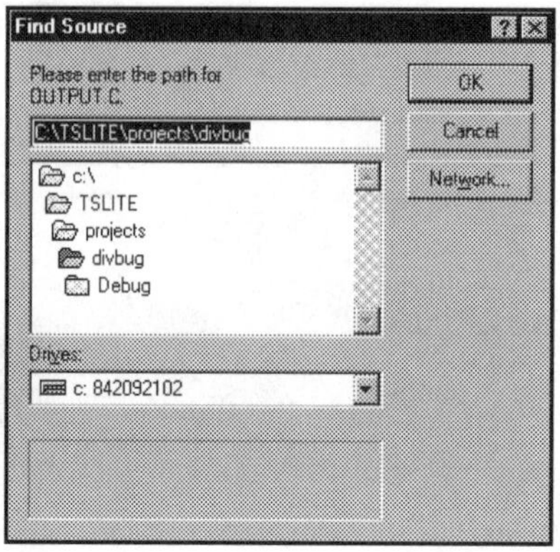

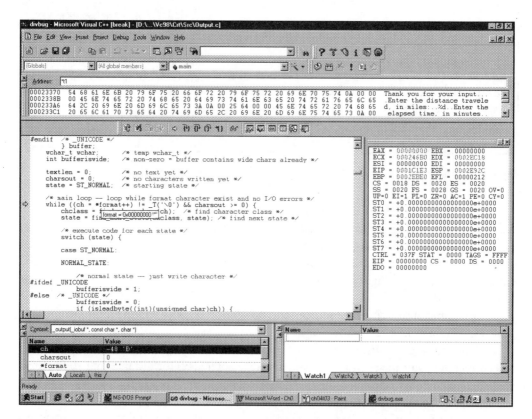

Figure 4-4: Enter the correct C run-time library source code directory, or click Cancel to debug without source code in assembly language.

Figure 4-5: The source for the C Library function that received the access violation error. Notice that the format pointer variable is null.

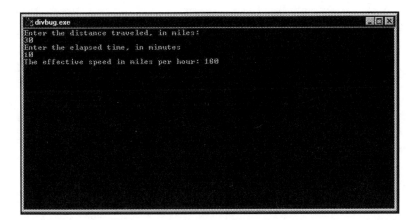

Figure 4-6: By substituting another value for 0, we confirm that the bug is a divide-by-zero error and not a general calculation error.

Because `format` is one of the function parameters passed to `_output()`, let's bring up the call stack window in Figure 4-7 to see who called `_output()`. Close the registers window to make room.

You can see that `_output()` was called by `printf()`, which was called by `main()`, and that `printf()` was passed a null pointer as an argument. Clearly, the offending code is in `main()`. Double-click `main()` in the call stack window to display the source for the offending `printf()` call, as shown in Figure 4-8.

Looking at the source code, you see that we forgot to store a pointer to a valid string in variable `t2` before passing `t2` to `printf()`. Now you can do one of two things. One, you can fix the source code. Or two, if you want to check first to see whether fixing this bug will let the program complete correctly, you can select Debug|Restart, set a breakpoint on the call to `printf()`, and store the value for the `t1` pointer in `t2`.

Symbol Table

As you work with the Developer Studio debugger, you may find yourself wondering how the debugger switches so easily between source code and executable machine instructions. And how does the debugger know what location in physical memory corresponds to a variable in the source-code program?

The answer is a *symbol table*, an elaborate kind of data structure generated during compilation that lists all symbols, their locations in the program, and their attributes. The linker then attaches the table to the executable when it builds the executable file. You tell the Visual C++ compiler to generate a symbol table with the /Z7 switch, and you tell the linker to hook the table into the executable file with the −cvsym switch. At run time, the debugger consults this table to determine the locations of variables, functions, and even the executable instruction that corresponds to the start of a particular line in the source code file.

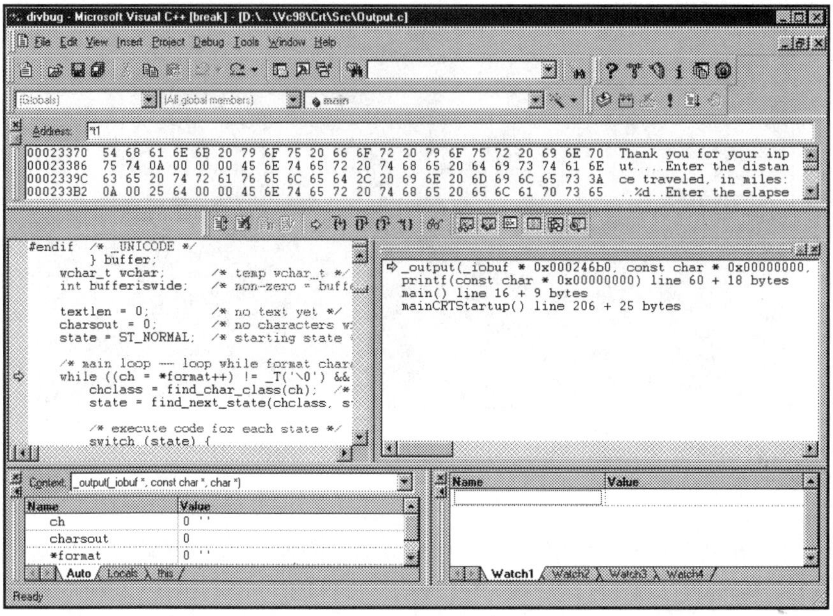

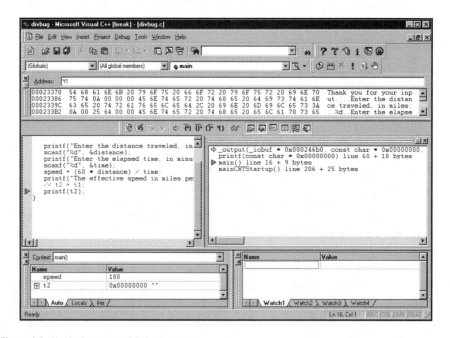

Figure 4-7: The call stack window lets us trace the sequence of instructions.

Figure 4-8: Here's the access violation bug.

EMBEDDED STUDIOEXPRESS EXTENSIONS

As you've just seen, the full functionality of the Developer Studio debugger is available to you when debugging ETS Kernel applications. To thoroughly debug true real-time embedded applications, however, you may find that you need more information than the Developer Studio debugger can provide. For example, you may need to peek inside the operating system for information on program threads or poke around the hardware on the target system to see what interrupts are currently active.

Embedded StudioExpress has two features for this purpose: Target Port Input/Output and Target System Information.

TARGET PORT INPUT/OUTPUT

Target Port Input/Output allows input from and output to hardware ports on the target system. The capability to read and write hardware registers can be extremely useful when debugging device drivers or other software components that directly access hardware, because it allows you to see the state of the hardware device.

In this section, you try it out. To read the interrupt mask register on the master 8259A programmable interrupt controller, port number 0x21, select the Target Port Input/Output icon on the StudioExpress toolbar, enter 21 as the hexadecimal port number, and click the Input button. As Figure 4-9 shows, Target Port Input/Output returns a value of hexadecimal FA. This indicates that all interrupts except IRQ0 (the timer tick interrupt) and IRQ2 (used to daisy-chain the slave interrupt controller) are currently masked or disabled in the master interrupt controller. The other interrupts are masked because the only hardware driver linked into this program is the timer driver; all unused interrupts are masked by default.

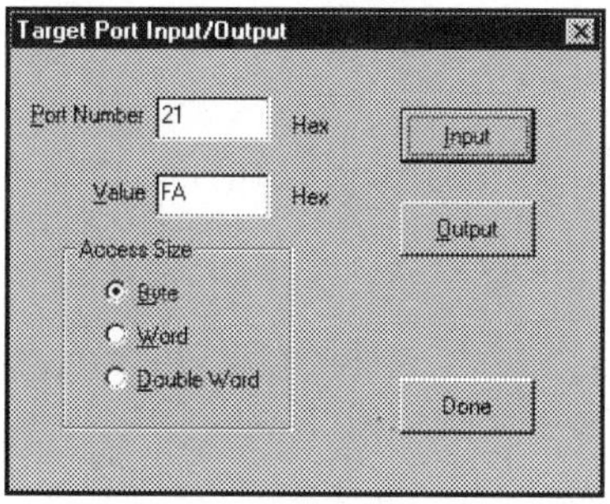

Figure 4-9: To read an I/O port, enter a port number and click Input.

When performing port I/O, make sure the correct access size for the hardware port is selected. Most hardware ports read and write 8-bit values, but occasionally you'll encounter a device with a 16-bit or 32-bit I/O port.

Target System Information

Clicking the Target System Information icon displays a window that lets you view just about anything that has to do with your embedded target. We take you through these items of

interest, shortly. First, to show the full capabilities of this feature, we debug the real-time multithreaded application RTHELLO.C, shown in Listing 4-1.

Listing 4-1: RTHELLO.C

```
// RTHELLO.C — Multithreaded (real-time) hello world program
// Copyright (c) 1998 Phar Lap Software, Inc.  All rights reserved.

#define WIN32_LEAN_AND_MEAN
#include <windows.h>
#include <stdio.h>
#include <process.h>
#include <embkern.h>

#define STACK_SIZE (16 * 1024)

void OneHello(void *id);

volatile DWORD alive;
int num_threads = 5;
void main()
{
    int i;
    int id = 0;
    HANDLE hThread;
    char ThreadName[32];
    // start threads
    for (i = 0 ; i < num_threads ; i++)
    {
        hThread = (HANDLE) _beginthread(OneHello, STACK_SIZE,
                                        (void *) id);
        if (hThread != (HANDLE)-1)
        {
            sprintf(ThreadName, "OneHello %c", 'A' + id);
            EtsSetThreadDebugName(hThread, ThreadName);
            ++id;
            InterlockedIncrement((LPLONG)&alive);
        }
    }
    while (alive)
        Sleep(50);
    printf("main thread terminates\n");
    exit(0);
}
void OneHello(void *id)
```

```
{
    int i;
    for(i = 0; i < 5; ++i)
        printf("Hello From Thread %c\n", 'A' + (int)id);
    InterlockedDecrement((LPLONG)&alive);
    _endthread();
}
```

As you can see, it's a simple application that starts five independent threads. Each thread loops five times, prints a "Hello from thread *x*" message each time, and then exits. The threads are A, B, C, D, and E. When all threads have completed, the main thread terminates execution.

Note: If you're using Visual C++ 5.*x*, rebuild RTHELLO.EXE before debugging it. The executable on the CD-ROM was built with Visual C++ 6.0, and contains symbol information not compatible with Visual C++ 5.*x*.

From Developer Studio, open the RTHELLO workspace that you'll find located in \TSLITE\PROJECTS\RTHELLO. As shown in Figure 4-10, set a breakpoint on the call to printf() in the OneHello() function, and press F5 (Debug|Go) a few times to allow all the threads to get spawned. A few "Hello…" messages are printed in the DOS box. Because the threads don't attempt to synchronize with each other, the messages may appear in any order, and one or more threads may complete their processing before all the threads start running.

Now click the Target System Information icon on the toolbar. StudioExpress displays a list of topics for which additional information is available in a window, as shown in Figure 4-11.

Clicking the name of any topic displays detailed information about that subsystem. You can then save this information to a file by clicking the Save button. You can also save the information for all topics to a file by highlighting Embedded Target, the first item in the hierarchical list, and then clicking Save. In either case, the file you save is immediately opened in the main debugger window, as shown in Figure 4-12.

Next, we'll look at some of the information that's available, choosing a few of the more interesting topics to give you an idea of the capabilities of Target System Information. You might want to look at some of the other information on your own.

Kernel Information

The Kernel topic includes information about ETS Kernel, an example of which is given in Figure 4-13. The specific items listed at this level of detail vary depending on which kernel components and kernel options have been selected.

For this particular program, information is available for six features:

- **System Tables** allows you to see the content of the Global Descriptor and Interrupt Descriptor Tables; each IDT entry includes the address at which the interrupt handler has been installed.

- **Boot Method** lists the method used to boot the embedded target and the kernel run mode.

- **Display Interface** describes the target screen driver, including the assigned I/O and memory addresses, as well as the current contents of screen memory.

- **BIOS Information** describes the BIOS on the embedded target.

- **Target Hardware Information** displays basic information about the target system including the type of CPU, display, timer, clock, interrupt controller, and numeric coprocessor.

- **ETS Kernel Startup Settings** is a list of the configuration information passed to ETS Kernel from CFIGKERN.

Different levels of information are available for the different subsystems. As long as there's a plus sign (+) in the box next to some text, you can click the box to get more information. Conversely, click on a box with a minus sign (-) to hide information.

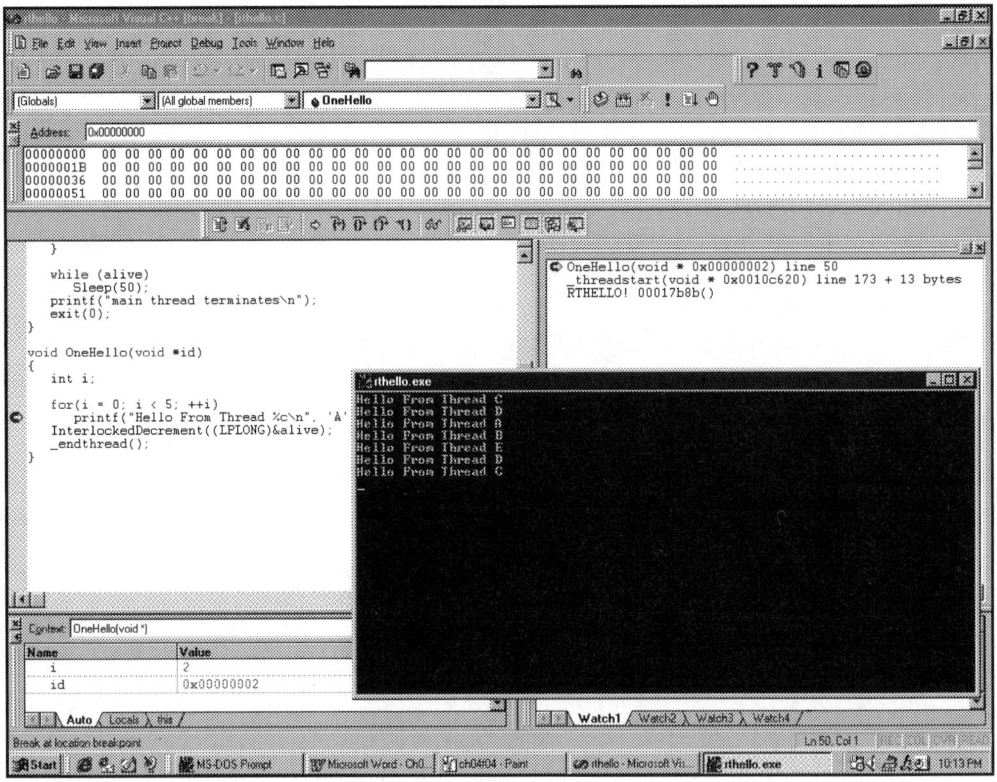

Figure 4-10: The real-time Hello program is spawning threads on the target machine.

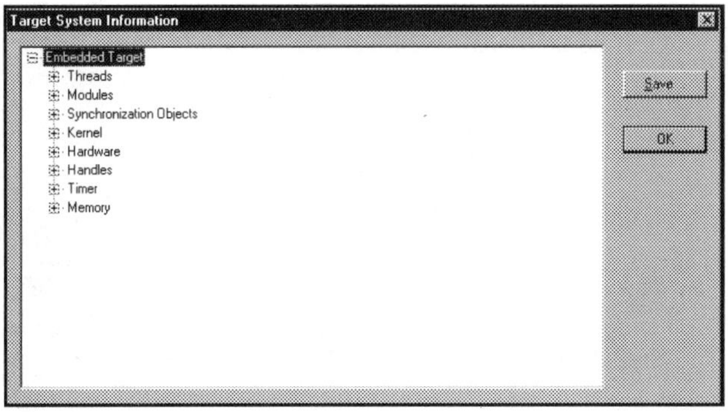

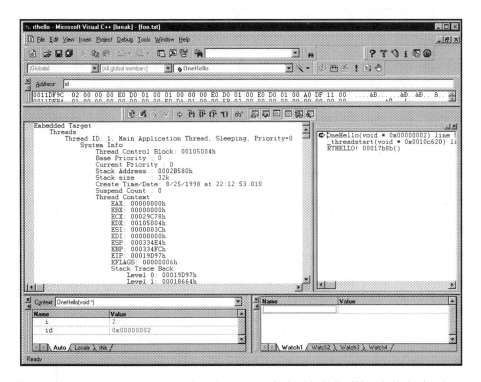

Figure 4-11: The Target System Information icon displays a window that allows you to view information on various components of the embedded system.

Figure 4-12: You can save all information from the various topics in a single file. Although this is a lot of information, it can be handy to have it all in one place for perusal.

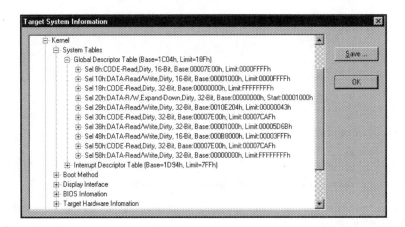

Figure 4-13: The Global Descriptor Table maintained by ETS Kernel has 10 segments defined.

Hardware Information

The Hardware topic displays settings for the interrupt controllers on the system. You'll use it to examine the settings for the master 8259A controller, the same one you read the interrupt mask register from earlier. The results are displayed in Figure 4-14.

Of particular interest here are the interrupts currently in service and the interrupts with requests pending. Notice that IRQ0, the timer interrupt, has a request pending. When you're stopped in the debugger, interrupts are disabled on the embedded target, so you'll often see pending interrupts waiting to be processed when you start the application running again.

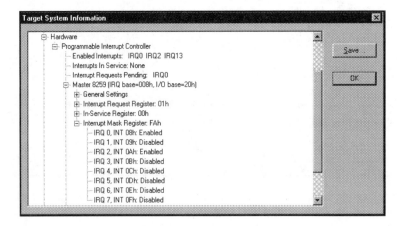

Figure 4-14: The interrupt mask register value is the same value you obtained earlier using the Target Input/Output tool to read I/O port 0x21 on the master 8259A.

Memory Information

The Memory topic displays information about the amount of memory on the target system and its usage by ETS Kernel. Information about memory usage by the application program is supplied under the Modules topic.

Thread Information

Next, you look at some of the information available to help track down problems in multi-threaded applications. The Threads, Synchronization Objects, and Handles topics are all of interest when debugging multithreaded programs.

In Figure 4-15, you see some of the information available on Thread ID 4, which is also named OneHello A. (We set this name with the call to `EtsSetThreadDebugName()` after creating the thread.) OneHello A is currently blocked on an unnamed critical section owned by OneHello B.

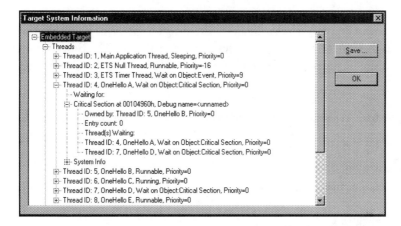

Figure 4-15: Multithreaded programs are a frequent source of timing errors. You can debug them using the thread details provided by the Target System Information tool.

It's interesting to note that OneHello D is also blocked on this critical section. Because the threads only call `printf()` in a loop, it's easy to guess that they're blocked on a critical section that the thread-aware C run-time library uses to control access to part or all of the `printf()` code.

If you were to explore the System Info available about thread OneHello A, you would learn the thread's stack size and location, its priority, the address of the thread control block maintained by the OS for this thread, its creation time, and its context. You'd also see a function call traceback for this thread.

Another way to spelunk around the threads in the system is to look at the synchronization objects in the system. Some of the ones on our target system are shown in Figure 4-16. You could look at the unnamed critical section that OneHello A is waiting on (identifying it by its address, because it doesn't have a name). But let's look instead at a synchronization object owned by the operating system: an event used by the timer driver.

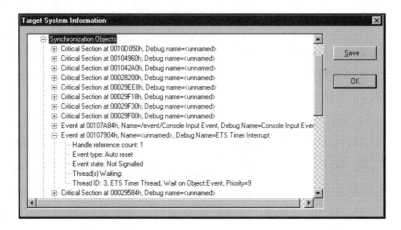

Figure 4-16: A synchronization object is used by threads to coordinate access to shared resources.

You can see in Figure 4-16 that the ETS Timer Interrupt event is an auto reset event that currently has one thread waiting on it, the ETS timer thread. The timer driver signals this event to wake up the timer thread (which advances time in the system) each time a timer tick interrupt occurs.

Handles are another way to look at multithreaded applications. A *handle* is an opaque value assigned for referencing objects managed by the operating system. Although Win32 handles are created for all sorts of objects in a system, such as open files, handles exist also for all threads and synchronization objects. In Figure 4-17, you can again look at the critical section on which OneHello A is blocked, this time finding it by its handle.

As you've seen, the Target System Information tool gives you another way to view the details of a target system. It's an extension of Embedded StudioExpress that's quite helpful for debugging applications.

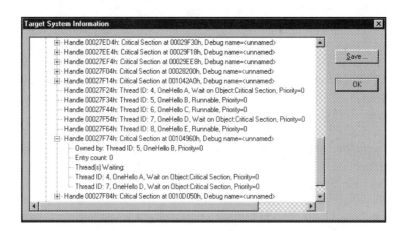

Figure 4-17: Often an object handle is the quickest way to look up information on the object.

Debugging ROM Applications

When we compiled and linked DIVBUG, we used command-line switches that created symbolic information that the debugger uses to associate locations in the executable file with variable and function names. (See the "Symbol Table" sidebar.) This symbolic information is written into the DIVBUG executable file. We compiled and linked this program as we would any desktop application because we were going to download and debug DIVBUG in the target's RAM.

However, many embedded applications execute from in ROM. If you plan to put an application in ROM, the executable you create (actually, an image of what will be burned into ROM) shouldn't carry this additional symbolic information — you don't want it to take up valuable space in ROM.

The version of LinkLoc in the full TNT Embedded ToolSuite product recognizes special switches that cause it to create a separate symbol file. The result of a compile and link is therefore two files — a copy of the executable ready for burning into ROM and an associated symbol file. At debug time, you point the debugger at this symbol file rather than at the executable file. The debugger makes all the connections between symbols and ROM locations, and debugging proceeds as though you were working with a program in RAM.

The only limitation to debugging a ROM application (other than the fact that if you find an error, you have to rebuild the application and re-burn the ROM) is the number of breakpoints you can have active at a time. For RAM applications, the debugger can create a breakpoint by overwriting the appropriate code location with a special instruction (a software interrupt). Because that's impossible after an application is in ROM, the debugger uses breakpoint registers in the processor. (Intel-compatible 32-bit processors have four such registers.)

We discuss working with applications in ROM more in Chapter 21, "ROMing an Application."

SUMMARY

Certain debugging challenges in the embedded real-time world are not present in the desktop development realm. Nevertheless, you can use your good ol' software cross-debugger as your primary debugging instrument. However, you may also need to use hardware and software tools devised to aid developers of embedded real-time systems in this unique and often unenviable task. We gave an overview of a few of the more frequently used tools, including ICEs, ROM emulators, and software simulators. We also introduced you to Embedded StudioExpress, a tool on the CD-ROM that adds the capabilities of an embedded software debugger to Microsoft's Developer Studio.

The projects coming up are far more elaborate than the Hello World and DIVBUG applications we used in this chapter to demonstrate debugging with Developer Studio and StudioExpress. Still, the basic compiling, linking, and debugging steps remain the same.

5

A Point-of-Sale Terminal

The project in this chapter is a simulation of a smart cash register. Such a device is called a POS (point-of-sale) terminal. A POS terminal is a smart cash register in the sense that it has not only the features you would expect of a traditional cash register, but also possesses capabilities found in computer-based systems. You've probably seen such terminals in action. Whether you're buying a Coke or a couch, many stores use POS terminals to process sales. Like cash registers, POS terminals keep track of all the items entered, total the sale, and control access to a cash drawer. Like the computers they are, however, POS terminals usually have some kind of connection to a store-wide database server. Typically, a product is identified by entering its Universal Product Code (UPC), or bar code, with a scanner attached to the terminal or by entering the corresponding number on the keypad. The terminal can then look up the bar code in the database to obtain a product description, an accurate price, the sale price if the item is on sale, whether or not the item is subject to sales tax, and so on. The terminal can also update inventory information in the database as products are sold. These features result in many benefits, including reducing the possibility of operator error, speeding up the checkout procedure, improving inventory tracking and sales tax reporting, and making the task of updating product prices less error-prone.

We start this chapter by describing the functionality of the POS we want to simulate. Then we explain how we'll simulate the POS on a PC target computer, rather than on actual POS hardware, and describe the software design process for the simulation. As we mentioned in Chapter 2, "Designing and Developing Your Real-Time System," creating a simulation is a good way to begin development before you have the hardware. Not all projects call for creating a simulation, but for many it's a useful way to begin writing and testing code apart from the hardware. It's useful to us in this book because it lets us demonstrate how to build embedded systems without requiring you to have any hardware beyond two desktop systems and a LapLink-compatible cable. It's important to keep in mind, however, that a simulation isn't a perfect imitation of a project. The purpose of a simulation is to build and test a subset of functions. To explain how to migrate from the simulation to a real embedded system, then, we include a sidebar, "Beyond Simulation."

Finally, we step you through building and running the application and then give you an overview of the source code for the project. We look at the source code more closely in the two chapters that follow, where we examine the two topics for which this project serves as an introduction:

- **Writing to the display and reading from the keyboard.** Although these seem like separate topics, we place them together because, when combined, they constitute the user interface. Consequently, this makes an excellent starting point for exploring I/O to peripheral devices in embedded systems.

- **Using file systems in embedded systems.** As embedded systems get larger and more complex, they often need some kind of persistent data storage and a method for storing and retrieving the data — in other words, a file system. We look at file systems from the perspective of an embedded systems developer.

In each of these topic chapters, we first cover the topic generally, as it applies to all embedded systems. Then we use excerpts from the POS terminal's source code as illustration. We repeat this pattern throughout the book: Excerpts from a project's source code illustrate a theoretical topic.

HOW THE POS PROJECT WORKS

The POS system we plan to build provides much of the functionality you normally find in a modern, intelligent cash register. The POS system controls access to the system, allows the cashier to enter items by scanning the bar code or entering the corresponding number on the keypad, communicates over a network with a store's central database server to obtain product description and pricing information, and updates the inventory database on the server as products are sold. A video display shows the current sale status, and a built-in printer generates customer receipts. Because the central database server is often under a heavy load, the POS terminal includes local disk storage, where it keeps a copy of the product information database that is updated daily and stores transactions for later transmission to the database server. This reduces network traffic to the central server and also allows the POS terminal to operate if the central server is down. The POS system includes a cash drawer that can be opened only by inserting a key in a lock or under system control when a sale is completed.

To work as described, the POS system will consist of the following components:

- A system controller, consisting of a CPU, memory, and a power supply
- A video monitor for displaying output and echoing user input
- A bar code scanner for scanning product labels
- A keypad for entering products and quantities
- A printer for printing customer receipts
- A local disk storage system and its associated file system to store the local copy of the inventory database and to cache transaction records for later transmission to the store's central database server
- A network interface card for communications with the central database server
- A cash drawer

The components of the POS system are shown in Figure 5-1.

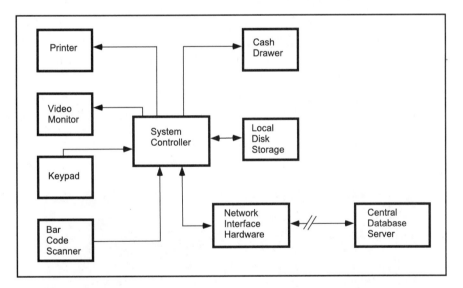

Figure 5-1: This high-level diagram shows the major hardware components of the POS system.

To access the system, an operator or cashier logs on to the system with a user ID and a password. The POS terminal verifies the validity of the user and password against an encrypted database on the central database server. If the entry doesn't have a match, the person isn't given access. This prevents an unauthorized person from operating the POS terminal. The POS terminal will not respond to any input until a user has logged on.

After logging on, the cashier begins a sale by pressing the Start Sale key. The operator enters the items a customer wants to purchase by scanning the item's bar code or by typing the bar code number on the keypad. The system then looks for the bar code number in the local copy of the inventory database. This lookup normally succeeds because the local database on each POS terminal is updated daily from the store's central database. If the bar code number is not found, however, the system queries the central database over the network. If either lookup succeeds, the item's price, description, and whether it is subject to sales tax are displayed. If both lookups fail, an error message is displayed. The operator then has the option to enter the item simply by entering a price.

After an item is entered in the system, the cashier enters a quantity for the item. After all items have been entered, the cashier presses the Total key to obtain the sale total. After entering the amount of money received from the customer, the cashier presses the End Sale key to open the cash drawer, print a customer receipt, and see the change owed to the customer.

When a sale is completed, the central inventory database is updated to reflect the items sold. If the store database server is down, the POS terminal caches the sale information on its local hard disk for later transmission to the central database.

DESIGNING THE SIMULATION

For our POS simulation, we simplify the system so that we can focus on the topics we're demonstrating with this project, namely keyboard and screen I/O and file systems. We start by removing the bar code scanner, the printer, and the cash drawer from the simulation. Other, more localized simplifications are noted in this section.

To start the simulation design, we'll create an interface. Figure 5-2 shows a mockup of the POS display. It consists of two windows, one above the other. The upper window — called the banner window — includes a title line, a system status line that indicates whether the POS system is logged on or off, and two lines used to display valid commands and error messages and prompt for input. These bottom two lines change depending on the state of the system.

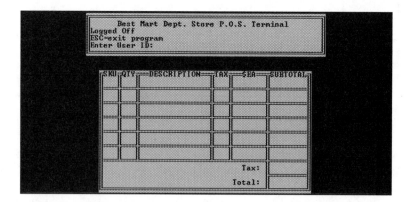

Figure 5-2: The POS terminal display has a dual-window structure. Log-on and status information are in the upper window; line-item entry takes place in the lower window.

The lower window — called the sale window — is the site of line-item entry when the POS system is active and a sale is in progress. This window is arranged as a grid, allowing the operator to enter up to six items. (Each item comprises a row of the grid.) User entry occurs in the first two columns of each row of the grid. The first column accepts a SKU (Stock Keeping Unit) number; the second accepts a quantity. When the user enters a SKU number, the system looks up the item's description, taxable flag, and unit price, and displays these items in the appropriate columns. When the user enters an associated quantity, the POS system calculates and displays the line-item subtotal, as well as the current tax total and sale total.

The design of the sale window in the simulation differs from the actual POS in three ways. First, for the SKU, we use a number that can have a maximum of three digits rather than a typical 12-digit bar code number. The advantage for the simulation (which has no scanner) is that you don't have to type as many digits. To the software, there's not much difference between a 3-digit number and a 12-digit number, other than the width of the field on the display.

Second, the cashier must enter a SKU number that exists in the database; if the SKU lookup fails, the cashier does not have the option of simply entering a price instead. In the real POS, the cashier has to be able to enter any item a customer finds in the store, even if it was inadvertently left out of the database. Finally, the simulation limits the number of sales items per customer to six; the actual POS will have no upper bound on the number of items purchased. We made these last two simplifications to minimize the complexity of our sample project so we could focus on the topics we want to illustrate. If you were building a simulation as a first step toward building a real POS system, you would want your user interface to look exactly as it would in the final system, rather than taking the shortcuts we're using here.

You can navigate the interface with just a few keys:

- The Backspace key clears the most recent entered keystroke.
- The Enter key indicates data entry.
- The F1 function key initiates a sale.
- The F2 function key clears the current entry.
- The F3 function key clears the current line item.
- The F4 function key clears an entire sale.
- The ESC key closes the current sale, logs off the current user, or shuts down the terminal (terminating the program), depending on the system state.

If an invalid key is pressed, the system beeps. If a SKU lookup fails or a user ID lookup fails, the system beeps and displays an error message in the banner window.

After we have a mockup of the interface, the next step is to design the databases. The real POS system would access a relational database using SQL (Structured Query Language) or some other database access method. For a simulation in an actual product design, you might choose to completely implement your database access code and create actual databases; then, when the hardware was ready, you could port the completed code to the final hardware. Or, depending on your hardware design schedule, you might decide to use the simulation to focus on the user interface, and just write some quick throwaway code to simulate the database until you move the code onto the hardware.

Using a Local and a Remote Database

The POS terminal project uses a local and a remote database. The local database on the POS terminal is a subset of the central database on the host. When a SKU is entered, the POS terminal references its local database first. If the SKU is found, processing proceeds. Otherwise, the POS terminal queries the host database.

For many situations, designing a database system that keeps all the data at the central server is suitable. If the demands on the central server will be great, however, because a large number of computers will be requesting data from the server or because the central system will also be handling other functions while processing requests from the computers, you should consider another design.

The alternative we use for the POS system is to keep a copy of the inventory database on the POS terminals. This is a viable option due to the rapidly declining cost of hard disk storage (as well as the shrinking footprint of disk drives). Even if the entire inventory cannot fit in the POS terminal's local storage space, you could cache the most frequently requested items locally. In that case, the POS terminal would query the central server only when the clerk recorded the sale of an item not in the local database. (After the query, the local database could be updated to hold the record of the inventory item.)

This arrangement has several advantages. Traffic between the terminals and server is reduced. Response time will always be quick and never suffer because of heavy load conditions. The local file system of a given register can be optimized for its department. Less expensive, slower networking technologies such as infrared links can be used, allowing the store to save money yet adapt to peak shopping times by quickly setting up temporary checkout lanes to service customers. And last but not least, the terminals can continue to operate if the central server goes down.

For this project, we've chosen to simulate the database with ASCII files in a simple format rather than interfacing to a relational database. This choice was made for several reasons. For our purpose of illustrating file systems, ASCII files work as well as relational database files. Also, interfacing to relational databases is beyond the scope of this book, and in any case is not particularly different in embedded software than in, say, a Windows application. Finally, if we designed databases for a specific relational database product, you would have to have that database product to run the POS simulation.

The local product database is kept on local disk storage in an MS-DOS-compatible FAT file system, in a single file named LSKUPOS.DAT (for local SKU POS database). The LSKUPOS.DAT file is stored in the root directory of the ETS Kernel boot disk. We get to the format of the database file in a moment.

The remote database consists of three files stored on the host computer in the \ETSLITE\PROJECTS\POS directory. The remote database files are accessed with standard

C library file I/O routines, using the host file system feature of ETS Kernel. We chose to use the host file system support rather than network I/O, as we specified for the actual POS terminal, because we're using this project to examine file systems; networking is covered in a later project. The RSKUPOS.DAT (remote SKU POS database) file is the store product database file. The USRPOS.DAT (user POS database) file contains the database of authorized users of the POS terminals. The SYSPOS.DAT (system POS database) file contains any necessary system information.

The format of the product database files (LSKUPOS.DAT and RSKUPOS.DAT) is simple, consisting of a series of ASCII records, each terminated by a carriage return and a line feed. In turn, each record consists of four fields:

- **SKU number.** This is an integer and can be up to three digits. Each item must have a different SKU number.

- **Product description.** This is an alphanumeric field that may be up to 15 characters long. The field can contain blanks, but commas are not permitted.

- **Taxable flag.** This field will contain either a Y or an N, indicating whether the item is taxable.

- **Product's unit price.** This is a free-form numeric field in the sense that no restriction is placed on the location of the decimal point. The system will read 12.34 as easily as 0.2. (The latter is understood by the system to mean 20 cents.) Also, the absence of a decimal point indicates a cost in whole dollars; an entry of 12 is read as 12.00.

The fields within each record are comma-delimited; that is, the software recognizes a comma as a field separator. So, for example, the following record:

```
100, Chewing Gum, Y, 2.00
```

is understood by the software to define a taxable item called Chewing Gum with a SKU of 100 and a unit price of $2.00. We've provided sample LSKUPOS.DAT and RSKUPOS.DAT files that the CD-ROM installation copies to the POS project subdirectory. You can examine these files to see the format.

Our specification for the POS terminal includes the automatic update of inventory information on the store's central database server at the conclusion of each sale. This requires additional fields in each record of the product database, to include at a minimum a product count. We chose to not implement this feature in our simulation, to minimize the size and complexity of the project.

Recall that product SKUs are first looked up in the local database, and then in the remote database if the local lookup fails. In a store, the local database would be updated daily in an attempt to ensure that the POS terminal almost never needs to access the remote database. To illustrate the system's capability to perform a remote database lookup when necessary, LSKUPOS.DAT intentionally does not contain all the records in RSKUPOS.DAT.

The format of USRPOS.DAT, the personnel roster file, is the same as the inventory files. USRPOS.DAT is composed of a list of records, each delimited by a carriage return and a line feed. Each record has only two fields:

- **Two-character alphanumeric user ID code.** Each ID code must be unique.
- **User's name.** This is a 14-character alphanumeric field.

Before an operator can use a POS terminal, the operator must log on to the system. The logon process involves entering a valid two-character ID code, which the terminal verifies by querying USRPOS.DAT.

Finally, the last remote file, SYSPOS.DAT, contains a single record, the content of which is an integer that specifies the tax percentage that will be applied to taxable items. For example, a 10 in this record indicates a tax of 10 percent. The value currently stored in the SYSPOS.DAT file sets the tax rate at 7 percent.

SOFTWARE SUBSYSTEMS

Now that we've designed the user interface and the database structure for our simulation, we're ready to break the POS project down into subsystems. We chose to split the POS system's software into three major subsystems:

- **User interface subsystem.** This is the heart of the system and includes all the keyboard input and display management functions, as well as the associated business logic behind them. In other words, the user interface subsystem handles sales processing (item entry, calculation, and so on). It also handles user logon and logoff.
- **Database subsystem.** These are the routines that provide access to all the data used by the POS software. Other subsystems call into the database subsystem to look up user IDs and product SKUs and read the associated information.
- **Windowing subsystem.** This is a collection of routines to handle creating windows on the display and writing text and attributes to the windows. The windowing subsystem is called by the user interface subsystem to handle all display updates.

SOFTWARE INTERFACES

Having specified the functionality performed by each software subsystem, we now need to define the interface each subsystem will provide. We don't want to bog you down with the specifics of designing too many software interfaces. Often the interfaces are straightforward, and documenting all of them would become repetitive. As a compromise, we document selected subsystems within each project. (The header files for each project clearly identify all subsystem interfaces, so you can easily examine on your own the ones we don't cover.) Because the projects are written in C, we use the C programming language's data structures and function prototypes to document the software interfaces.

For the POS system project, we look at the user interface and database subsystems. As we've mentioned, the user interface subsystem is responsible for managing all keyboard input and display update and for processing the sale. We defined the following interface functions for this subsystem:

- **BOOL InitializeUserIface(void).** The InitializeUserIface() function must be called by the system at start-up. It initializes the windowing subsystem, and then makes calls to the windowing subsystem to draw the two windows on the display. If an error occurs, FALSE is returned.

- **void CleanupUserIface(void).** The CleanupUserIface() function is called at system shutdown to restore the original display contents.

- **BOOL UserLogon(void).** UserLogon() is called when the system is waiting for a cashier to log on to the POS terminal. It prompts the operator for a user ID. If a valid ID is entered, the function records the cashier's identity, and then returns TRUE. If the operator presses the ESC key to exit the simulation program, FALSE is returned.

- **BOOL StartSale(void).** StartSale() is called when the system is ready for a sale to be initiated. It displays the valid keystrokes in the banner window, and then returns TRUE if the cashier presses the F1 key to begin a sale or FALSE if ESC is pressed to log the current cashier off the POS terminal.

- **void ProcessSale(void).** The system calls ProcessSale() when a sale is initiated to handle the entry of all items to be purchased. As the cashier enters each item, ProcessSale() updates the display and allows the cashier to edit or reenter the information on the current item. When the operator closes the sale, ProcessSale() returns, leaving the sale items displayed in the sale window.

- **void ClearSalesWindow(void).** ClearSalesWindow() is called to erase the contents of the sale window before starting a new sale or whenever the cashier logs off the system.

Routines in the database subsystem are called into service in two situations. First, whenever an operator logs on, the POS software reads the USRPOS.DAT file to determine whether the logon ID is valid. Second, whenever the operator enters a SKU number (in the process of adding line items to a sale), the system looks up the SKU in the database to obtain the item's price and description. Given these requirements, we've defined a database subsystem interface consisting of the following functions:

- **BOOL InitializeDatabase(void).** InitializeDatabase() must be called by the system at start-up to perform any necessary initialization of the database subsystem (primarily opening database files). This function returns TRUE if the subsystem initializes successfully or FALSE if an error occurs.

- **void CleanupDatabase(void).** CleanupDatabase() must be called at system shutdown to allow the database subsystem to close open files and shut down in an orderly fashion.

Beyond Simulation

Whenever you write a simulation, you need to think about how the simulation code will differ from the actual production code and what you'll have to add, delete, and rewrite when you move the simulation onto the real hardware. You need that analysis to provide accurate schedules, showing how long you need to move from the simulation step to a final product. So in each of our project chapters, we include a sidebar called "Beyond Simulation" that summarizes how the simulation code on the CD-ROM differs from the code needed to build the embedded system we've described.

We start by describing how the existing code would need to change for the three software subsystems.

From a software point of view, the display on the POS hardware would look similar to a PC display. You might need to make some minor changes to the ETS Kernel display driver to accommodate the differences. As we noted in the section on designing the simulation, we took some shortcuts in the user interface design because the purpose of our simulation was to illustrate keyboard and screen I/O, rather than be the first step in an actual POS product. Those shortcuts were: using SKUs rather than bar code numbers; requiring a valid SKU rather than allowing the cashier to enter a price without a SKU; and limiting a sale to six items. Since your goal would be building a real POS rather than an book example, you wouldn't take those shortcuts in your simulation, and the display code in your simulation (in both the user interface subsystem and the windowing subsystem) would be identical to the display code in the production system.

The POS keypad would look, to the software, a lot like a standard PC keyboard. You might have to tweak the ETS Kernel keyboard driver to handle any hardware differences. One big difference between the simulation and the actual POS, however, is that the POS terminal must accept input from a scanner in addition to the keyboard. That difference means that calling _getch(), which blocks (does not return) until a key is pressed, is not a viable option in the final system. Instead, you would have to write a keyboard driver callback that could handle keyboard input asynchronously, a technique we illustrate in our next project, described in Chapter 8, "A Simple UPS."

You would have to rewrite the database subsystem. In the simulation, we chose to use ASCII files for the product database so that we could illustrate file I/O in an embedded system. In the POS terminal, you would want to talk over a network to a database server running on another computer. In addition to looking up items in the database, you would have to add code to update the inventory database after each sale is complete, to cache sale information locally if the network is down, and to accept a download to update the local copy of the product database.

Finally, you would need to add some functionality to handle the hardware we ignored in our simulation. You have to be able to accept input from the bar code scanner. Like the keyboard input for the final system, this would need to be interrupt-driven so that the input could be handled asynchronously, while the terminal was busy performing some other task. You would have to add the functionality of opening the cash drawer when the sale is complete; that would require only a small piece of code that writes a value to a hardware I/O port. And you would need to print a sales receipt for the customer at the conclusion of the sale.

- **BOOL LookupID(char *pUserID).** The `LookupID()` routine looks up a user ID in the remote database. It takes as input a null-terminated user ID string, and returns TRUE if the user ID is found in the database or FALSE for an invalid user ID. The other output of this function, the user's name, is needed throughout the system and is therefore stored in a global variable.

- **BOOL LookupSku(SALES_ENTRY *pEntry).** A SALES_ENTRY structure is defined as follows:

```
typedef struct {
    DWORD  Sku;                // Stock Keeping Unit
    DWORD  Quantity;           // number of items
    DWORD  Price;              // unit price, in cents
    BOOL   fTaxable;           // T ==> item is taxable
    char   Description[16];    // item description
} SALES_ENTRY;
```

The `LookupSku()` routine looks up a SKU, first in the local database and then, if necessary, in the remote database. It returns TRUE if the SKU is found or FALSE for an invalid SKU. The caller of `LookupSku()` must fill in the `Sku` field of the SALES_ENTRY structure as inputs to the function. If the lookup succeeds, `LookupSku` fills in the `Price`, `fTaxable`, and `Description` fields.

START-UP AND SHUTDOWN PROCESSES

At system start-up, the three software subsystems must be initialized. The database and user interface subsystems may be initialized in any order. The windowing subsystem initialization function is called by the user interface subsystem, because only the user interface subsystem uses the windowing subsystem. In addition to initializing any hardware it controls, each subsystem must perform the following:

- The database subsystem must open the local and remote database files and must read the tax percentage from the remote database and store it in a global variable.

- The user interface subsystem must initialize the windowing subsystem, and must then create and display an empty sales window (with all the fixed headings and lines drawn, but no entries) and a blank banner window.

- The windowing subsystem must identify the display hardware and clear the display.

At shutdown, each subsystem must perform the following operations:

- The database subsystem must close all open files.

- The user interface subsystem must shut down the windowing subsystem.

- The windowing subsystem must free up any memory it allocated to manage windows and restore the original contents of the display.

ERROR HANDLING

POS errors fall into the following general categories:

- **Initialization errors.** Any errors during start-up are reported with an informative error message. The system then terminates.

- **User input errors.** Any user input errors are reported with an informative error message in the banner window, and the system continues to wait for input.

- **Illegal key errors.** If the user presses an illegal key, the POS system beeps the speaker and ignores the key.

BUILDING THE POS PROJECT

When you ran the setup program on the CD-ROM, the source code and data files for the POS project were installed on the host in the \ETSLITE\PROJECTS\POS directory. A prebuilt executable, POS.EXE, was installed in the RELEASE subdirectory. You can build the POS.EXE executable by opening the POS.DSW workspace file from Microsoft Developer Studio and selecting Build|Rebuild All. Chapter 3, "Software Installation and Setup," contains complete details on building the programming projects.

RUNNING THE POS PROJECT

The POS program reads data files on both the host and target systems. The data files for the host system are already in place. You have to copy the target system's data file to the ETS Monitor boot disk, manually. From your host system, copy the LSKUPOS.DAT file in \ETSLITE\PROJECTS\POS to the root directory of the ETS Monitor boot disk.

> **Note:** The data files you've copied from the CD-ROM are preloaded with dummy data. Because the data is simple ASCII, you can modify them with your favorite word processor. If you do, be sure to preserve the format. (Each file includes embedded comments that remind you of the proper format.) Also, if you modify the LSKUPOS.DAT file on your host system, you need to copy it to the ETS Monitor boot disk for the POS terminal system to see those changes.

With the executable built and all data files in place, you're ready to run the POS application. Let's step through a sample session.

First, put the ETS Monitor boot disk in the target's floppy drive and turn on your target system. ETS Monitor should load, report its presence, and wait for action from the host system.

Download and execute the POS application from Microsoft Developer Studio by opening the POS.DSW workspace and clicking Build|Execute pos.exe.

If you prefer to run the program directly, open a DOS box on the host computer and set the current directory to \ETSLITE\PROJECTS\POS. The POS program attempts to open remote database files in the current directory on the host, so the appropriate current directory setting is required for this project. Run the program by entering

```
runemb release\pos
```

RUNEMB is a host program that downloads a program to the target and executes it.

After the application is initialized, the POS terminal prompts you to enter a user ID. Because we seeded the database, we know that MT is a valid ID. So type MT and press Enter. As shown in Figure 5-3, the ID MT corresponds to user Mark Twain, whose name is displayed in the lower-right corner. The system is now in the logged-on state.

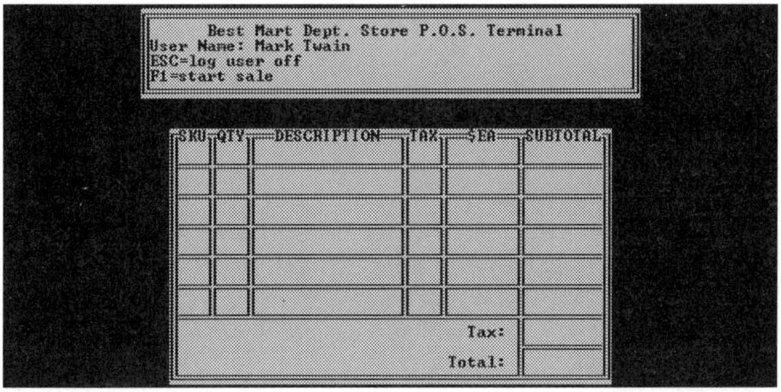

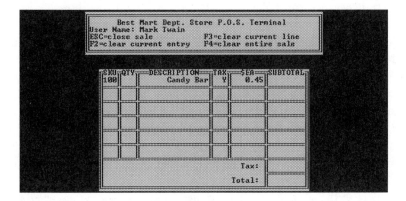

Figure 5-3: User Mark Twain has logged on to the POS terminal. The user's name is displayed, as is the current mode of the terminal. From this point, Mark could either begin entering a sale or log off.

Begin a new sale by pressing the F1 key. Notice that the cursor is positioned in the first line item's SKU entry field, ready for a SKU number. As with the user database, the inventory database files (LSKUPOS.DAT and RSKUPOS.DAT) are preloaded with test data.

For the first SKU number, type 100 and press Enter. The system retrieves the information for inventory item 100 and, as shown in Figure 5-4, displays the item's description, taxable flag, and unit price in the appropriate columns.

Figure 5-4: After Mark enters a line item, the POS system fetches the item's description, taxable flag, and unit price. It also positions the cursor in the quantity (Qty) field.

Type 1 for the quantity of candy bars sold and press Enter. The POS terminal calculates the subtotal for the line item, as well as the current total for the sale. The system then positions the cursor in the entry field for the next line item's SKU number.

Enter 102 for the second SKU number and enter 2 for the quantity (of tweed jackets). The display should look like Figure 5-5.

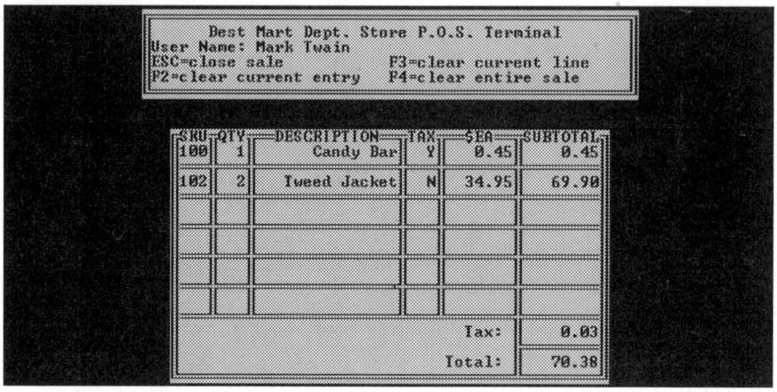

Figure 5-5: As the sale progresses, the POS system continually calculates and updates the amount of tax, line-item subtotals, and the current sale total.

At this point, you could proceed in one of three ways:

- Enter another line item, or
- Press the ESC key and close the sale, or
- Press the F4 key and clear (abort) the current sale.

Let's enter another line item, but this time we will select a SKU in the remote database, 101. We put it there when we seeded the database, to demonstrate how the POS software responds when it doesn't find an entry in the local database.

Enter SKU 101. You'll notice that the floppy disk on the POS terminal is being accessed. The software is first searching the local database, just as it did for the previous SKUs. When it doesn't find the number, the software accesses the host and searches the remote database. Shortly, it finds the item — a pound of cheddar cheese that costs $3.40 — in the remote file and displays it on-screen, just as though it were a local database item. If you had entered a SKU that was not in the local or the remote databases, the system would respond with an error message.

The cursor is now in the quantity field. Type 1 and press Enter. As shown in Figure 5-6, the POS terminal displays the subtotal for the cheddar cheese, as well as the current grand total for the sale.

Finally, let's close the sale and log off. Press the ESC key, and the system reverts to the state of waiting for the operator to start a new sale. The results of the previous sale continue to be displayed in the sale window until a new sale is initiated. Press the ESC key again to log Mark Twain off the system. In this state, you or another user can log on to the system or shut the POS software down by pressing ESC a third time.

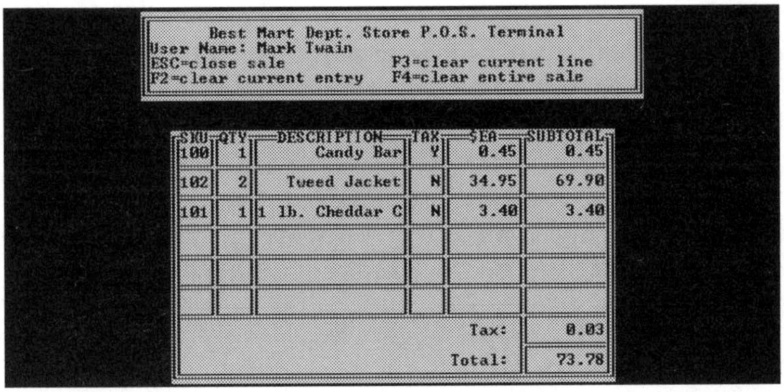

Figure 5-6: The information for the last item entered was fetched from the database file on the remote (host) system.

A QUICK TOUR OF THE SOURCE

Each subsystem for the POS project is placed in a separate source file. The main loop for the program is in the POS.C file. The main loop includes the main() function, the InitializePos() function (which calls the initialization function for each subsystem), and the CleanupPos() function (which shuts down each subsystem). The main() routine controls the system state:

```
void main(void)
{
    if (!InitializePos())
        return;
//
// Just loop through our three states:
// 1. Log on a user
// 2. Start a sale
// 3. Process a sale
//
    while (UserLogon())
    {
        while (StartSale())
        {
            ClearSalesWindow();
            ProcessSale();
        }
        ClearSalesWindow();
    }

    CleanupPos();
    return;
}
```

After initializing the system, the main() routine sits in two nested while() loops, calling the user interface subsystem to change system states. The outer loop calls UserLogon() to either log on a new cashier or exit the system. When a cashier is logged on, the inner loop calls

StartSale() to wait for the user to either press F1 to start a new sale or press ESC to log off. Each time a new sale is initiated, the sale window is cleared of the previous sale by calling ClearSalesWindow(), and ProcessSale() is called to accept the entry of items until the cashier presses ESC to close the sale.

The user interface subsystem is in USERIFC.C. This subsystem is responsible for accepting all operator input from the keyboard and formatting and writing the display contents. Because this is a single-tasking application completely driven by operator input (it does something only when the cashier presses a key), the GetKey() keyboard input routine is simple:

```
//
// Get the next character from the keyboard.  This function
// blocks until a key is pressed.
//
int GetKey(void)
{
    int ch;

    ch = _getch();

//
// For a function key or cursor key, _getch() returns either
// 0 or 0xE0 with the next call returning the key code for
// the extended key.  We just combine the two values and set
// bit 16 to mark it as an extended keycode.
//
    if (ch == 0 || ch == 0xE0)
        ch = 0x10000 | (ch << 8) | _getch();

    return ch;
}
```

The GetKey() routine calls the C library _getch() routine to obtain the next keystroke. Although _getch() blocks (does not return) until the next time the operator presses a key, this is acceptable because the system doesn't need to do anything between keystrokes. Because the simulation uses some keys (function keys and cursor keys) that aren't in the ASCII character set, the function calls _getch() a second time if it returns a value indicating that an extended key (a non-ASCII key) was pressed.

The bulk of the code in USERIFC.C is devoted to updating the display. It makes calls into the windowing subsystem to handle low-level output of text and attributes to the banner and sale windows. Rather than examine all the code in USERIFC.C, which would get repetitive, let's look at one representative function. A good illustration of the user interface code is in UserLogon() in Listing 5-1. The UserLogon() routine waits for the operator to either enter a valid user ID to log on to the terminal or press the ESC key to exit the program.

Listing 5-1: The UserLogon() routine

```
//
// In logon user state.
// Wait for a valid user ID to be typed or for the user to
// press ESC to exit the program.
//
// Returns:        TRUE  if user successfully logged on
//                 FALSE if ESC pressed; terminate program
//
BOOL UserLogon(void)
{
    int  Key;           // current keystroke
    char UserID[3];     // current contents of ID field
    int  nch;           // # chars in UserID

//
// Initialize the contents of the banner window
//
    ClearWindow(hBannerWin);
    SetWindowTextPos(hBannerWin, 0, 0);
    WriteWindowText(hBannerWin, STORE_NAME);
    SetWindowTextPos(hBannerWin, 0, 1);
    WriteWindowText(hBannerWin, "Logged Off");
    SetWindowTextPos(hBannerWin, 0, 2);
    WriteWindowText(hBannerWin, "ESC=exit program");
    SetWindowTextPos(hBannerWin, 0, 3);
    WriteWindowText(hBannerWin, "Enter User ID:");

//
// Process the user entering the user ID.  Besides printable
// keys, we recognize Backspace to delete the last character,
// Enter to indicate the ID is entered, and ESC to exit
// the program.
//
ENTER_ID:
    UserID[0] = UserID[1] = ' ';
    UserID[2] = 0;
    nch = 0;
    while (TRUE)
    {
//
// Update the ID field to reflect what happened the last
// time thru the loop, and get the next keystroke.
//
        SetWindowCursorPos(hBannerWin, 15 + nch, 3);
        SetWindowTextPos(hBannerWin, 15, 3);
        WriteWindowText(hBannerWin, UserID);
        Key = GetKey();
```

```
//
// Process the key appropriately.
//
        if (isgraph(Key))
        {
            if (nch < 2)
                UserID[nch++] = (char) Key;
            else
                UnusedKey();
        }
        else if (Key == '\b')   // Backspace
        {
            if (nch > 0)
                UserID[--nch] = ' ';
            else
                UnusedKey();
        }
        else if (Key == ESC)    // Escape
        {
            HideCursor();
            return FALSE;
        }
        else if (Key == '\r')   // Return
            break;
        else
            UnusedKey();
    }
    HideCursor();

//
// Lookup the user ID that was entered.
//
    UserID[nch] = 0;
    if (!LookupID(UserID))
    {
        SetWindowTextPos(hBannerWin, 0, 1);
        WriteWindowText(hBannerWin, "User ID: %s not found.   ",
                        UserID);
        goto ENTER_ID;
    }
    return TRUE;
}
```

The first section of code displays the user prompts in the banner window; this is just a sequence of calls to the windowing subsystem to output text at the appropriate window locations.

Next, the function enters a loop to allow the operator to enter a user ID code. Each time through the loop, we call the windowing subsystem to update the contents of the user ID input field on the screen and then call GetKey() to get the next keystroke. The keystroke is processed appropriately; if an invalid key is pressed, the keystroke is ignored and we call UnusedKey() to beep the speaker.

After the Enter key is pressed, the database subsystem function LookupID() is called to validate the entered ID against the list of valid users in the database. If the lookup fails, the ID input field is cleared and the function waits for more input.

The DATABASE.C file contains the source code for the database subsystem, which consists of initialization and shutdown routines that open and close the database files and the interface functions previously documented. We take a closer look at this code in Chapter 7, "File Systems."

The windowing subsystem source code is in the \ETSLITE\PROJECTS\UTILS\WINSYS.C file. It's placed in a separate directory because it's shared by more than one programming project. The object code for the windowing subsystem, along with some utility routines for beeping the speaker, are placed in the UTILS.LIB library, which is linked in when POS.EXE is built. The windowing subsystem contains functions for creating, destroying, and managing windows on the display.

SUMMARY

In this chapter, we constructed a point-of-sale (POS) terminal simulation that mimics the intelligent cash registers in many stores. We created a brief specification for a POS system, and then designed a simulation that could run on standard PC hardware. After walking through an example sale on the simulation program, we looked at the source for the simulation program, examining the main program loop, keyboard input, and one of the user interface routines that accepts operator input and updates the display.

In the next chapter, we talk about keyboard and screen I/O in embedded systems, looking at the user interface code in the POS simulation as an illustration. Then in Chapter 7, "File Systems," we cover the topic of file systems, using the database subsystem code in our POS project as an example.

6

Keyboard and Screen I/O

Keyboard input and screen output form the basic user interface of desktop systems. We are all familiar with the ubiquitous desktop keyboard and CRT (cathode ray tube) or monitor; these are the primary devices by which we enter information into and receive information from a computer.

An embedded system, however, is less likely than its desktop cousin to use a keyboard and a monitor. User interface devices in embedded systems vary so greatly that some can't accurately be called displays or keyboards; *input and output devices* is the only classification broad enough to cover them all. Small, deeply embedded devices may use nothing more than one or two LEDs as indicator lights. Larger devices may employ seven-segment LEDs (capable of displaying numbers and some characters, like a calculator display) or equivalent LCD alphanumeric displays. Portable or handheld embedded systems might use LCDs that can display graphics as well as text. Finally, large embedded systems such as those used in medical settings, scientific research, and military applications may use high-resolution monitors as good or better than anything found on the desktop. Likewise, input devices may be as humble as a single pushbutton or as proud as a 100-key-plus PC keyboard.

You don't have to dig much deeper to find even more variation. LCDs alone, for example, come in a wide range of shapes, sizes, and capabilities. You can find LCDs that are monochrome, color, and backlit, as small as a watchface or as big as a 17-inch CRT, and used in everything from home thermostats and digital watches to laboratory and industrial equipment.

Why so many devices? Constraints and demands placed on embedded systems dictate specific solutions. When taken together, requirements such as size, weight, power consumption, and cost often leave little room to choose anything but a particular device. In fact, the guiding rule for selecting input and output devices is to keep your system's requirements foremost and match them to the hardware's capabilities. For example, does your application need an alphanumeric display, or can you get away with a simple LED output? If you do need to display alphanumeric data, would a small LCD character module with a display of, say, four lines by 40 characters be sufficient? In other words, resist the tendency to provide more capabilities than the system needs.

This conventional wisdom is not without justification. And it's such an important point that we'll digress for a moment. Unnecessary features often bear hidden requirements. Pushbuttons and small keypads require minimal hardware. (If your project calls for a pushbutton interface, investigate using a CPU with on-chip parallel ports. Beyond that, the only additional hardware you'll need are the pushbuttons and a few resistors.) Larger keypads (greater than about 16 keys) and small, customized keyboards (such as you find on handheld computers) may need a keyboard controller chip. If your application needs a full QWERTY keyboard, you'll definitely have to incorporate a keyboard controller in your design.

Including extra features can also tax system and programming resources. Including high-resolution pixel graphics, for example, requires several times the video memory needed for an alphanumeric display. A modest 640 x 480 screen of 256 colors (standard VGA) requires more than 300K of graphics memory, whereas an 80 x 25 character alphanumeric display needs only about 4K of graphics memory. In addition, software support for pixel graphics can be daunting, because it can involve libraries for windowing, two-dimensional graphics, and possibly three-dimensional graphics. If you can't purchase such libraries, they must be written.

So, as you can see, although it's tempting to choose a device with more capabilities, the price of those extra features may be something you can't afford by the time the project is finished.

The good news is that powerful new chips are making it easier and cheaper to include more capabilities. Although it's always important to match requirements with capabilities, at the time of this writing, integrated CPUs are coming to market that mitigate some of the tradeoffs. Embedded processors from companies such as NEC, Philips, and AMD include a graphics controller. Most of these on-chip controllers are designed to interface directly to LCDs. Using such a chip may make additional external graphics hardware unnecessary. The chip manufacturers can supply you with sample device-driver software that can give you a jump on writing your video device driver. These integrated processors usually also have on-chip keyboard controllers, providing you with further savings in external hardware.

To get back to our discussion, though, desktop and embedded input and output devices have a second major difference: standardization. Whether you're a PC, Macintosh, or UNIX user, graduating from a 15-inch to a 17-inch or larger monitor is easy. Switching from a traditional-style keyboard to an ergonomic one is something we do without much thought. The reason for this ease in changing hardware is compatibility: compatibility within a particular vendor's product line and, more often than not, compatibility among products from various vendors. Although each device varies in features such as cost, size, and resolution, fundamental standardization of device categories within platforms is a huge benefit to users, manufacturers, sellers, and programmers alike.

Unfortunately, in this respect, too, the embedded world is different. The huge range of diversity in embedded systems works against standardization. Devices are rarely compatible within or across vendors' product lines or with the standards of their desktop counterparts. Although this is slowly changing, as more embedded systems migrate to 32 bits and use processors and peripherals found also in desktop systems, the capability to interchange devices on an embedded system is still the exception rather than the rule.

The diversity of embedded systems often leaves programmers and project managers with the prospect that someone will have to either write device drivers for the screen and keyboard (and other peripherals in the system) from scratch or adapt existing drivers written for a different platform. If your application is a deeply embedded system with minimal user I/O requirements — a few buttons and LEDs, for example — the task of writing your own drivers won't consume much development time. If your system is larger and demands more complex user I/O capabilities, writing your own device drivers can be a significant drain on programming resources. In the May 1997 issue of *Embedded Systems Programming*, Shaul Gal-Oz and Avi Cohen noted in their article, "The Hazards of Device Driver Design," that "writing device drivers on more complex systems may require 30% of the development time." That's a sizeable chunk of time.

Fortunately, the growing availability of embeddable off-the-shelf single-board computers containing CPUs, memory, and widely used peripheral controllers offers designers of embedded systems the ability to utilize a wide variety of third-party keyboard and screen hardware. This eliminates the hardware tasks of designing, building, and interfacing custom keyboard and screen circuitry. These single-board computers also alleviate the software burden of writing device drivers. Most are available with standard BIOSes in onboard ROM. The BIOS provides the necessary drivers for controlling keyboard and screen. And if you do need to write your own drivers, the fact that these systems use popular peripheral controllers means there are usually device drivers available that you can fairly easily port to your particular embedded system.

BUTTONS, KEYPADS, AND KEYBOARDS

Because of the tremendous variety of input devices used in embedded systems, it's difficult to include specifics when writing about the embedded market as a whole. You'll see some code in the second half of the chapter, when you look at the POS project's use of the keyboard and screen. For now, we describe the spectrum of input devices from buttons to keyboards, and identify some of the software and hardware issues you might encounter.

Some embedded systems don't need entire keyboards. Just a few buttons suffice for the application. Let's look at how you'd build a pushbutton interface for such a system.

Recall that the CPU for small embedded systems is often a microcontroller — a microprocessor whose primary job is to control the hardware to which it's attached. Many modern microcontrollers have on-chip parallel I/O ports. Pins on the CPU are mapped to specific processor registers or memory locations. If a particular pin is an input port, digital data sent to that pin appears at an associated bit location in the CPU's register or memory location.

Your program can simply read the bit to determine the data value at the input pin. Similarly, if a pin is an output port, writing to the specific bit in the CPU register will set the CPU pin to the corresponding binary value.

Depending on the microcontroller, some I/O pins may be strictly input, others strictly output, and still others programmable (bidirectional). The I/O direction of a programmable pin is usually governed by a specific bit in a direction register on the processor. For example, setting the bit to a 1 will make that microcontroller pin an output pin; setting the bit to a 0 will make it an input pin. (The correspondence between bit value and direction will vary from processor to processor, but you get the idea.)

With this information in hand, it's easy to see how you could build a simple pushbutton interface. An example is shown in Figure 6-1. One pole of the pushbutton is connected to ground. The other is connected to a digital input pin. (The pin can be on the CPU or, if the processor doesn't have parallel I/O pins on-chip, the pin can be on a parallel I/O chip connected to the processor.) The input pin is also connected to the positive supply voltage with a pullup resistor, so the input pin will read as a logic 1 rather than float to an unpredictable level, when the button is open (released). When the pushbutton is closed (depressed), the input pin is connected to ground and reads as a logic 0.

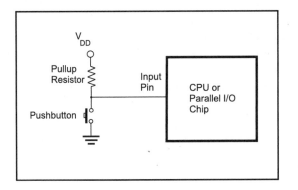

Figure 6-1: You can connect a simple pushbutton to an embedded system with the help of a single pullup resistor. Some microcontrollers and parallel I/O chips have internal pullup resistors built into certain input pins, so the external resistor is unnecessary.

Software for such a circuit has to perform what's known as *debouncing*. Whenever a switch closes or opens, it never does so cleanly. It bounces — opening and closing contact rapidly until it settles into being completely closed or completely open. Unfortunately, a computer can see this bouncing, and software that doesn't take it into account might interpret bouncing as the user rapidly pressing the button. Because this is a well-understood problem with solutions described in numerous texts, we won't go into the details here. One good book on the subject is *The 80x86 IBM PC & Compatible Computers: Assembly Language, Design, and Interfacing,* by Muhammad Ali Mazidi and Janice Gillespie Mazidi (Prentice-Hall, 1995). It contains sample code that shows how to deal with debouncing. For now, realize that writing software to handle pushbuttons is more than just looking for a 0 bit or a 1 bit.

For user inputs that require more keys, you can connect a small keypad to an embedded system using the I/O pins of a CPU (or parallel I/O chip). Figure 6-2 illustrates this arrangement. The keys are organized in a matrix. One set of I/O pins are designated as outputs, and drive the columns of the matrix. Another set of I/O pins are designated as inputs, and become the rows of the matrix. Each key has one pole connected to a column rail and the other pole connected to a row rail.

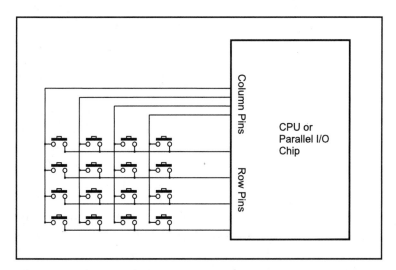

Figure 6-2: The keys on a keypad or keyboard are arranged in a matrix. This layout is a 4 by 4 key matrix. To see if a key has been pressed, the microcontroller scans the rows and columns.

The CPU determines whether a key is pressed by executing software that scans the matrix. An outer loop cycles through, writing a logic 0 on one of the column pins (keeping all other column pins at logic 1). Then an inner loop cycles through reading each row pin. If a key at a row and column intersection is pressed, the input reads a 0 (because closing the key has connected the output to the input). If a key is not pressed, the input pin reads a logic 1. (The digital logic used by most microprocessors and peripheral circuitry sees an open or floating connection as being at a logic 1 state.)

The software scanning the key matrix also has to perform debouncing. And unless the microcontroller is dedicated to controlling the keyboard (for instance, if the embedded system you're building is a keyboard for a desktop computer) and has no other work to perform, you have to put the scanning code into a driver that runs on a regular basis and can signal the rest of the system after a key is pressed. The details of programming the key hardware are straightforward, however.

For many small embedded systems, using I/O pins to directly drive a key matrix is a cheap way to provide keypad input. You can minimize chip count if you choose for your system CPU a microcontroller chip with enough I/O pins on-chip to support the size keypad you'll need.

For further information on connecting pushbuttons and keypads to your embedded system, the book we recommended earlier, *The 80x86 IBM PC & Compatible Computers: Assembly Language, Design, and Interfacing,* is an excellent choice.

If your application requires a full keyboard, you'll almost certainly choose to use a keyboard controller to interface the keyboard to the CPU. The keyboard itself has a microcontroller that scans the matrix rows and columns to detect keypresses. It debounces the keys and delivers information about keypresses and key releases over a serial interface to the system motherboard. Keys are identified by a scan code or the matrix coordinates of the key. At the system CPU, this serial data has to be read and buffered as bytes; usually this task is performed by a dedicated keyboard controller, either on a separate IC or on-chip on the processor. The keyboard controller normally interrupts the CPU whenever a key is pressed or released. A keyboard driver, through its interrupt handler, handles interrupts from the keyboard controller.

A keyboard driver performs a number of tasks. It reads an I/O port on the keyboard controller to determine which key caused the interrupt. Then it translates scan codes to virtual key codes and buffers this information, making the key codes available to the rest of the system when they are requested. Because scan-code-to-key-code mapping is performed in software by the device driver, support for keyboards for different languages is possible by simply changing the key mapping table used by the driver. If a key is held down, the driver determines whether it's a key that should be repeated or used to modify other keystrokes (such as Ctrl and Alt). Processing both keypresses and key releases lets the driver make this determination. The driver is also responsible for automatic echoing of keystrokes to the display device if requested, and possibly beeping a speaker or triggering some other alarm if its internal key buffer is full because no application is consuming the keystrokes.

Although a keyboard driver is a relatively small and straightforward piece of code, it does include an interrupt service routine (ISR) to handle keyboard controller interrupts. As always when writing interrupt handlers, you must carefully craft the keyboard ISR to ensure that it does its job quickly and reliably without affecting responsiveness in other areas of the system. We examine the problems often encountered when writing ISRs in Chapter 9, "Interrupts."

LEDS, LCDS, AND DISPLAYS

At the very low end of devices for what we would call user output is the light-emitting diode (LED). An LED is often used to make a user aware of a condition. For example, an LED might be turned on or off to indicate that the power is on or off or that a button is pressed or released. A blinking LED might indicate an abnormal condition.

Typically, you connect an LED to a parallel output pin either on the CPU or on a parallel I/O chip. In most cases, a parallel output pin provides enough current to drive an LED directly, and will need only a current-limiting resistor between the LED and ground. Such an arrangement is shown in Figure 6-3. (The value for the current-limiting resistor varies depending on the LED type and the current supplied by the output port.)

A device driver (if you can call it that) for LED output is trivial. Sending a logic 1 to the output pin turns the LED on. A logic 0 at the output pin turns the LED off.

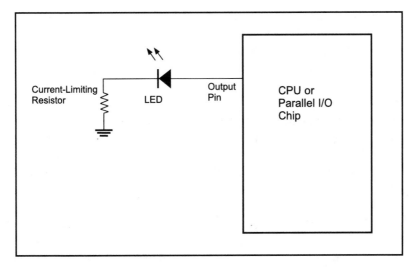

Figure 6-3: Connecting an LED to an embedded system is straightforward and requires little more than a parallel output pin and a current-limiting resistor.

Slightly up the display food-chain, you'll find the seven-segment LED, so named for the seven lines used to digitally display the number 8, as depicted in Figure 6-4. Seven-segment LEDs are mainly used to display numbers, but they can display also some letters as block characters. (The letter *K,* for example, is impossible to represent on a seven-segment LED.)

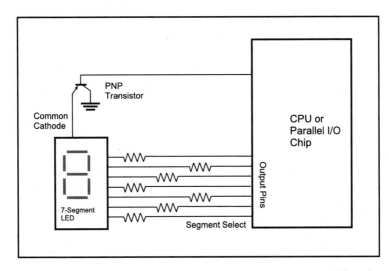

Figure 6-4: Shown here is the connection for a single device. Driving a seven-segment LED requires more components than driving a simple LED.

Each segment select line shown in Figure 6-4 is driven by output pins on the CPU or parallel I/O chip, and controls one of the LED's seven segments. To illuminate a segment, you send a logic 0 to the output pin connected to the PNP transistor's base. This turns the transistor on, providing a conduction path for the common cathode to which all the LEDs are internally connected. Writing a logic 1 on the appropriate segment select line illuminates the chosen segment.

Because one seven-segment LED displays only one number at a time (or possibly a letter), gangs of seven-segment LEDs often make up the displays for digital timers and clocks, readouts for digital voltmeters, calculator displays, and so on. Multiple seven-segment LEDs are driven simply by adding separate connections (and transistors) to the common cathode on each of the LEDs. The segment select lines are multiplexed to all seven-segment LEDs. So to activate a particular segment on a particular LED the software first turns on that LED's transistor and then activates the correct segment select line.

However, because an LED doesn't have memory, the moment that software proceeds to illuminate a different segment on the LED or any segment on a different LED, the segment that was just illuminated turns off. To drive multiple seven-segment LEDs, the driver software simply cycles periodically through all the segments, turning on each that must be illuminated for only a fraction of a second. The human eye is fooled by this and sees segments that — though not as bright as if current were continuously applied to the segment — still appear to be continuously turned on. (If human eyes were more sensitive, they would see the flickering of the LED segments being turned on and off.)

In place of seven-segment LEDs, many applications now use LCD character modules. Like LEDs, LCDs are ideal for embedded systems that require limited alphanumeric display capabilities (such as digital clocks, digital thermometers, and small handheld systems). But that's where the likeness between LEDs and LCDs ends.

LCDs are lightweight and consume little power. Most LCD modules attach to a CPU or a parallel I/O chip by means of a parallel interface; some use a serial interface. The CPU displays alphanumeric characters on the LCD screen by sending a combination of commands and data through the interface. The LCD, in turn, interprets the commands and displays the data using either segments or pixels, depending on the LCD module chosen. LCD modules have onboard memory so that the screen drivers needn't continuously send output to maintain the display.

The toughest programming chore required for communicating with an LCD module is creating a driver that implements the precise timing required for the control signals. To complicate matters further, timing specifications vary from device to device.

An example of an LCD module is Hitachi's LM032, which is illustrated in Figure 6-5. This device is capable of displaying two 40-character lines of alphanumeric information. You connect an LM032 to an embedded system through parallel I/O signals. The module requires four control signals and a data bus. The data bus can be either 4 or 8 bits wide. An 8-bit data bus provides faster communication to the LCD module than the 4-bit bus, but a 4-bit data bus takes less board space. In addition, the 4-bit interface allows designers of super-small embedded systems to conserve parallel I/O pins.

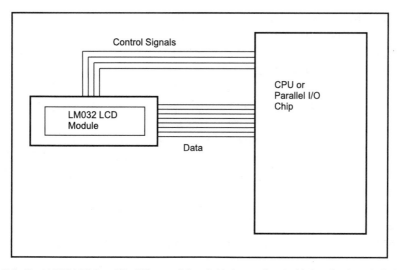

Figure 6-5: The LM032 LCD from Hitachi is a module suitable for small embedded applications. It displays alphanumeric characters on two 40-character lines.

Software displays information on the LM032 by sending a combination of command bytes and data bytes. The LCD distinguishes between command and data bytes by examining the most significant bit (MSB): command bytes have the MSB set to 1; data bytes have the MSB set to 0. A command byte tells the LCD where on the screen the following data byte should be displayed.

To speed transfers, you can program the LM032 so that it automatically increments the display location after it receives each data byte. In this way, each data byte needn't be preceded by a command byte; the embedded system can send a single command byte, followed by a string of data bytes. Each data byte is placed in the LM032's on-chip graphics memory at sequentially higher address locations. The mapping between graphics memory and onscreen locations is such that the characters are displayed in left-to-right, top-down fashion.

Finally, high-end embedded systems often require a full-size high-resolution display similar to the monitor you use on your desktop system. These displays are driven by video display adapter hardware that includes display memory and hardware to translate the memory contents into video signals. The display memory is part of the system's memory space, so the system CPU can directly write to (and read) display memory rather than using a custom serial or parallel interface, as we saw earlier with the LCD modules. The video adapter typically also includes I/O ports used for setting video modes, sending graphics drawing commands, and so on.

Typically, for an alphanumeric display, the display memory is organized as rows of ASCII characters and attributes. Graphics display memory has no standard organization, although two organizations are common. The first is an array of bytes, in which each byte holds the color information for a single pixel. The second is an array of bit planes, in which each bit plane contains the values for one bit of the set of bits that hold all the information for a pixel on the display. The number of bit planes per pixel determines the number of colors available to a pixel. For example, 4-bit planes provide for 16 colors, 8-bit planes provide for 256 colors, and so on.

Some graphics video adapters also include a graphics engine that accepts graphics commands, such as draw line or draw circle, from an application. In turn, the graphics engine executes these commands and updates the display memory accordingly. Unfortunately, graphics engines have no standard industry interface, so systems that want to take advantage of the enhanced performance provided by these graphics engines typically need to include a separate graphics display driver for each supported video adapter.

Writing a video driver for an alphanumeric display is almost trivial; all you have to do is write characters and attributes directly into the display memory; the hardware takes care of the rest. Graphics drivers and libraries, on the other hand, are extremely complex, and are beyond the scope of this book. If you're interested in graphics programming, a good resource is *Michael Abrash's Graphics Programming Black Book,* by Michael Abrash (The Coriolis Group, 1997).

ETS KERNEL SUPPORT OF KEYBOARD AND SCREEN I/O

We've combined two components of ETS Kernel in this chapter: keyboard and screen capabilities. In a moment, we go over these two areas separately. But first, let's group them together as a single unit called console I/O. ToolSuite uses the term *console I/O* to be consistent with Win32. A Win32 character-mode application uses an I/O interface called a console, because it mimics computer consoles of old. Those terminals consisted of a CRT and a keyboard, and could display only characters with limited attributes, such as underline, reverse video, or bold. The user interfaces for Win32 character-mode applications must operate within these same limitations. The benefit, for applications that don't require a graphical user interface, is reduced size and complexity.

A Windows character-mode application performs high-level I/O using C or C++ run-time library support (for example, C++ input and output streams, or the C library printf() and scanf() functions). If the application needs more control than that provided by the C/C++ library, it can perform I/O at a lower level by calling Win32 console APIs. ETS Kernel provides this same functionality at the C/C++ run-time library level and for keyboard input at the Win32 level. ETS Kernel support for Win32 screen output functions, however, is limited to enough functionality to make the C run-time library work; it lacks the low-level support needed for such operations as positioning the cursor, writing to arbitrary locations on the display, and controlling character attributes. As a result, when you look at the code for the windowing subsystem used in the POS project, you'll see that the subsystem, rather than making Win32 calls to write to the display, writes directly to video memory on the display adapter.

Host Console I/O

In addition to console I/O on the target embedded system, ETS Kernel supports transparently redirecting console I/O to the host computer, communicating over the same cable used for downloading and debugging the application. As long as the application restricts itself to C/C++ run-time library console I/O function calls and Win32 keyboard API function calls, it can call the `EtsSelectConsole()` routine to direct console I/O to either the host or the target system. This feature can be useful for such things as sending debug output to the host without disturbing the contents of the embedded target's display or performing I/O on the host as part of an automated regression test for the application. (The output of the windowing subsystem used in the POS project cannot be redirected to the host computer because the windowing subsystem writes to the display memory directly.)

The syntax for `EtsSelectConsole()` is

```
int EtsSelectConsole(int Type);
```

where the input argument *Type* can take one of four constant values:

- `ETS_CO_LOCAL`
- `ETS_CO_HOST`
- `ETS_CO_NONE`
- `ETS_CO_QUERY`

Setting *Type* to `ETS_CO_LOCAL` directs console I/O to the target system. Setting *Type* to `ETS_CO_HOST` directs console I/O to the host. The value `ETS_CO_NONE` disables console I/O, which is useful in debugging. For example, if you've peppered the code with `printf()` statements to help during development but you don't want to remove the `printf()` statements just yet, you can disable them for the time being using `ETS_CO_NONE`. Finally, `ETS_CO_QUERY` queries the console setting without altering it. The `EtsSelectConsole()` function returns the previous console I/O setting.

By default, console I/O is directed to the target if the screen and keyboard drivers are linked in; otherwise it's directed to the host. If you direct console I/O to a nonexistent location (for example, if you direct it locally but your application doesn't have a screen or keyboard driver, or if you direct it to the host but there is no host connection), screen output is just discarded, and any calls to get keyboard input return immediately with no input and with an error if the function has an error return value.

ETS Kernel Keyboard Driver

The keyboard driver included with ToolSuite is written for a PC or compatible 8042 keyboard controller. As for all ETS Kernel drivers, the full ToolSuite product (but not the Lite version on the CD-ROM) includes complete source code for the keyboard driver, which you can use as a starting point when writing a driver for a different keyboard controller. The driver handles interrupts from the controller, translates scan codes to virtual key codes, stores information about the keystrokes in a buffer, and provides keystrokes to the Win32 APIs (which in turn provide keystrokes to the C run-time library).

In addition to providing keystrokes to applications through Win32 and C run-time library functions, the keyboard driver allows applications to install a callback function that the driver calls each time a keyboard interrupt occurs. The data structure in Listing 6-1 is passed as an argument to the callback function. It contains detailed information about the interrupt.

Listing 6-1: The data structure for a callback function

```
typedef struct _ETS_KEY_EVENT_RECORD {
    BOOL bKeyDown;                      // 1->key down, 0->key up
    WORD wRepeatCount;                  // always 1
    WORD wVirtualKeyCode;              // as defined by windows.h VK_*
    WORD wVirtualScanCode;            // hardware kbd scan code
    union {
        unsigned short Unused;
        CHAR     AsciiChar;            // 0 if non-ascii key code
    } uChar;
    DWORD dwControlKeyState;           // bits defined below
} ETS_KEY_EVENT_RECORD;

//
// ControlKeyState flags
//
#define RIGHT_ALT_PRESSED       0x0001 // the right alt key is pressed.
#define LEFT_ALT_PRESSED        0x0002 // the left alt key is pressed.
#define RIGHT_CTRL_PRESSED      0x0004 // the right ctrl key is pressed.
#define LEFT_CTRL_PRESSED       0x0008 // the left ctrl key is pressed.
#define SHIFT_PRESSED           0x0010 // the shift key is pressed.
#define NUMLOCK_ON              0x0020 // the numlock light is on.
#define SCROLLLOCK_ON           0x0040 // the scrolllock light is on.
#define CAPSLOCK_ON             0x0080 // the capslock light is on.
#define ENHANCED_KEY            0x0100 // the key is enhanced.
```

From the information contained in the ETS_KEY_EVENT_RECORD structure, your application can determine, for example, whether the Shift, Alt, and/or Ctrl keys have been pressed. It can even determine which Shift key — left or right — was pressed. In this chapter, we use a C run-time library function to get keystrokes. In Chapter 9, "Interrupts," we show you how to create a keyboard callback routine for an application that needs low-level control of the keyboard.

ETS KERNEL SCREEN DRIVER

The screen driver for ETS Kernel supports alphanumeric video modes on standard PC video adapters. In addition to initializing the display, the screen driver provides only enough support — basically positioning the cursor, writing text at the current cursor position, and scrolling the screen — to provide for the requirements of the C run-time library display output functions. To do anything more elaborate, you must write directly to the display adapter, either in the application itself or by replacing the ETS Kernel screen driver with your own driver.

ETS Kernel Replaceable Device Drivers

Every program doesn't need every device driver. Some real-time programs, for example, may not need keyboard input. Others may not need to perform screen output. By implementing optional device drivers, ToolSuite lets you remove the drivers whose functionality you don't need so you can keep your application's memory consumption to a minimum.

In addition to being optional, ETS Kernel drivers are replaceable. Custom hardware often requires custom drivers. ToolSuite lets you replace the ETS Kernel device drivers with your own as the situation requires. For example, suppose you determine that your application will use a special keypad for user input. However, you want to continue to use the same function calls in your embedded program. (Perhaps you'll be doing your development work on a PC system with a full-blown keyboard, and you intend on migrating to the embedded system with the keypad later in the development cycle.) You can write your own keyboard device driver so that the embedded application sees the same keyboard services as before, but is unaware that the attached keyboard is something other than a standard PC keyboard.

Documentation and source code for writing replacement device drivers for the keyboard, the screen, timers, disk drives, network adapters, and so on are available in the full product.

The ETS Kernel screen driver supports two display adapters: the MDA (monochrome display adapter) and the CGA (color graphics adapter). Long-time PC users will recognize these acronyms from the first days of the IBM PC. The MDA was the early monochrome system employed by the first 8088-driven PC; the CGA was the first color display adapter.

The MDA supports a single video mode — mode 7 (although you don't need to know that to use ETS Kernel or an MDA system, for that matter). This mode is referred to as an alphanumeric mode because it can display only alphanumeric characters. You can't draw lines or circles or anything graphic on an MDA system.

You can, however, draw graphics on a CGA system, which supports seven video modes. Four of those video modes are alphanumeric modes (as on the MDA); three are graphics modes. The different modes of the CGA afford varying resolutions. For example, in video mode 1, your program can display 40 x 25 characters on the screen in one of 16 colors. In video mode 4, your program can draw graphics on the screen with a resolution of 320 x 200 pixels, using a palette of four colors (actually, two palettes of four colors, but only one palette is available at a time).

Note: PC display adapters can display information in one of several modes. If you run Windows, you are insulated from this knowledge by the Control Panel, which depicts the variety of modes by presenting you with a pick-list from which you can select your screen's configuration. So, for example, if you use the Control Panel to change your screen's resolution from 640 x 480 pixels in 256 colors to 1024 x 768 pixels in 256 colors, you're actually changing your adapter's video mode.

To strike the proper balance between space and usability, the graphics driver supplied with ETS Kernel supports one mode each for MDA and CGA systems. That is to say, regardless of the graphics adapter in your target system, a single video mode is available. In particular, ETS Kernel supports the equivalent of video mode 7 for MDA systems and video mode 3 for CGA systems. (Mode 7 is 80 x 25 characters with black-and-white text, while mode 3 is 80 x 25 characters with 16 foreground and 8 background colors.)

As mentioned, this limitation represents a calculated tradeoff between space and capability. Had the designers of ETS Kernel chosen to support all CGA graphics modes, it would have resulted in a larger video device driver. Support for a single mode on the MDA and the CGA minimizes the size of the driver while providing the widest coverage of hardware platforms. Virtually every 386 or better system with a graphics controller can support CGA text mode. (Most systems have a VGA-compatible controller, which supports CGA as a subset.)

CODE FROM THE POS PROJECT

You've seen that the POS project uses a standard keyboard to simulate the keypad on the POS terminal, and a desktop monitor to imitate the terminal's display. In this section, you look at the code that accomplishes these tasks. Let's start with the keyboard.

KEYBOARD INPUT

You already know how an application uses the standard C library routines to perform keyboard input. Besides the capability to switch console I/O between host and target — through the `EtsSelectConsole()` call — nothing is unusual about using such standard C I/O routines in ToolSuite applications. In the POS project, we chose to use the C library for keyboard input because it's the simplest method and sufficient to illustrate our points. In Chapter 9, "Interrupts," we examine the code for a project that reads keyboard input using keyboard callbacks, a more powerful but more complicated technique; the requirements for that project couldn't be satisfied by C library routines.

The keyboard input subsystem of the POS project uses the input routine `_getch()`, and it does so for two reasons. First, the `_getch()` routine reads keystrokes one at a time. This is in contrast to routines such as `scanf()`, which reads whole strings at a time. Because user input to the POS system might — at any time — be a function key to which the system must respond, the `_getch()` routine's character-at-a-time response is just what we need. Second, the `_getch()` routine reads function keys.

When the ASCII standard was first developed back in 1968, it assigned numeric values 0 through 127 (where 0 is the null character) to a set of characters, numerals, and symbols. By the time the PC was being designed years later, however, 128 values were no longer enough. The designers of the PC skirted this problem by expanding the number of ASCII codes available for keystrokes and assigning them to keys and key combinations for which there were no ASCII equivalents. For example, no ASCII codes were assigned to function keys or to the Home, End, PgUp, and PgDn keys. These additional codes are known on the PC as extended character codes.

To make sure there was no possibility of confusing a standard ASCII character with an extended one, the designers used 2 bytes for the extended codes, with the first byte always 0 or 128. Because no keys on the keyboard return a single-byte code of either 0 or 128, there was no confusion. The second byte contains the key code for the extended key, which can assume any value from 0 to 255.

The ANSI standard Visual C++ routine getchar() reads only keys that have an ASCII code. Hence, we use the non-ANSI standard Visual C++ routine _getch() because it accepts extended keys such as function keys. The POS software calls _getch() when it's expecting keyboard input. When the user presses a key, _getch() returns with an integer corresponding to the ASCII or extended code of the key that was pressed. The syntax for _getch() is

```
int _getch(void);
```

You can see how all this works if you examine the code in Listing 6-2.

Listing 6-2: The GetKey() routine

```
//
// Get the next character from the keyboard.   This function
// blocks until a key is pressed.
//
int GetKey(void)
{
    int ch;

    ch = _getch();

//
// For a function key or cursor key, _getch() returns either
// 0 or 0xE0 with the next call returning the key code for
// the extended key.  We just combine the two values and set
// bit 16 to mark it as an extended keycode.
//
    if (ch == 0 || ch == 0xE0)
        ch = 0x10000 | (ch << 8) | _getch();

    return ch;
}
```

The GetKey() routine is the bedrock function for the POS software's keyboard input: all keyboard input routines in the software call GetKey().

Notice that GetKey() potentially calls _getch() twice. After the first call, GetKey() examines the value returned by _getch(). If that value is not 0 or 128 (hexadecimal E0), GetKey() knows that the keystroke corresponded to a standard ASCII character and returns that character's value.

If the returned value is 0 or 128 (hexadecimal 0 or E0), however, GetKey() knows that the user pressed a key that corresponds to an extended key code sequence. In that case, GetKey() calls _getch() to get the second half of the sequence.

Polling

Some embedded applications that use a keypad or a keyboard enjoy enough processor power that the processor can simply watch the device to see whether the user has pressed a key. To watch a keyboard or a keypad, a program executes a tight loop that repeatedly tests a bit at a given I/O or memory address. When the monitored bit changes, the program processes the event. This kind of I/O management is referred to as *polling*. It isn't restricted to keyboards and keypads. A serial port, for example, signals the arrival of a character by setting a bit in a register. A serial port's receive routine might enter a tight loop, watching that register's bit and reading each character as it arrives. In many small applications, using a polling technique to service input and output works perfectly well. Routines that use polling are easy to write, understand, and maintain.

Polling, however, has a potential pitfall. You have to explicitly make processor time available to whatever other operations need servicing. Otherwise, the rest of your application will experience what is referred to as *starvation*. If the processor is spending too much time looking for, say, keyboard input, it may be unable to service another device quickly enough. Some hardware devices must be serviced on a precise and regular basis or they fail. For example, stepper motors — used in moving an armature a precise distance — must receive a pulse train of a specific frequency and with a specific duty cycle to work properly. Some embedded systems — for the sake of reduced cost — use the processor to control the stepper motor directly. A system using a polling technique to handle I/O while controlling a stepper motor would have to be carefully written so as to properly interweave handling the stepper motor with servicing other I/O devices.

To avoid having your application suffer from the sit-and-wait phenomenon that _getch() exhibits, you can use the _kbhit() function to poll the keyboard. Like _getch(), _kbhit() is not an ANSI C standard function, although it is supported by most compilers, including Visual C++.

The _kbhit() routine returns immediately (so there's no waiting) with a value indicating whether or not the user has pressed a key. It's a simple matter to write a loop that examines _kbhit() and, if a key has been pressed, calls _getch() to determine the ASCII or extended key code. If a key has not been pressed, the routine does other processing for the program, returning later to call _kbhit() to check for a keystroke again.

Polling tends to be used only in simple embedded systems. In systems with real-time requirements, it's almost always better to use interrupts to ensure timely responses to external events and avoid consuming CPU cycles with repeated polling.

So that calling routines can recognize an extended key, GetKey() concatenates the two characters returned by _getch(). GetKey() sets bit 16 to guarantee that the resulting value won't fall in the ASCII character set, places the first character of the extended key code sequence in bits 0 through 7, and places the second character in bits 8 through 15. (Note that because integers are defined as 32-bit values, plenty of room is available to store this concatenated version of extended key codes.)

One final remark concerning the _getch() function: it's a blocking call. That is, _getch() will not return from being called until the user has pressed a key. In the POS system, we can tolerate this behavior because no background activities can occur while the system waits for the user to press a key. Some embedded systems, however, must respond to external events that happen unpredictably; the systems must be built to respond to those events whenever they occur. If a system is blocked — waiting for the user to press a key — it might miss handling one of those unpredictable events (the arrival of a character at a serial port, perhaps) and consequently lose information or otherwise fail. This is the case in our future projects, so we choose a different way to manage keyboard input. Specifically, in Chapter 9, "Interrupts," keyboard callbacks provide a nonblocking means of handling keyboard input.

SCREEN OUTPUT

The user interface we designed for the POS project includes a display with two text windows: the banner window, used to display operator prompts and error messages, and the sale window, used to enter and display items for the current sale. The POS interface software, as you might imagine, must be able to create and destroy windows, control the text and attributes in the title bar and status lines, write text and attributes to a specific window, and so on. To accomplish these tasks, the software needs to be able to write text to arbitrary locations on the screen and manipulate character attributes.

We wrote a windowing subsystem that provides this functionality for the interface software. You'll find it in the WINSYS.C file, in the \TSLITE\PROJECTS\UTILS directory. We won't examine the code that manages the text windows; that's relatively straightforward and easy to understand. We will, however, look at the code that writes to the screen and manipulates attributes. These two operations are interesting because we couldn't implement them using the C run-time library — its output routines are too simple. And we couldn't use the Win32 APIs because ETS Kernel doesn't support them for screen output. So we wrote directly to video memory.

Directly accessing video memory requires two steps. First, your program must determine what sort of display hardware is available on the system. It must do this because it accesses display memory through a pointer variable, and the characteristics of display memory — where it is located in the system's memory map, the way in which the display hardware interprets the contents of that memory, and so on — are directly dependent on the display type. If you want a truly portable application, it must do some initialization work to determine these characteristics.

> **Note:** If you are certain that your application will always be run on systems with a particular kind of display hardware, you could dispense determining what display hardware is available and simply hardcode everything.

Second, and more importantly, your application must map memory locations to onscreen positions. This amounts to having a routine that answers the question: "I want to place a character at row x and column y on the screen. What memory address is that?" After you have that memory address in a pointer, putting characters where you want them on the display is straightforward.

Let's look at the hardware determination code first.

Initializing the Screen

Before the POS application can output anything to the screen, it must first call the windowing subsystem's initialization routine, InitWinsys(). The source code for InitWinsys() appears in Listing 6-3.

Listing 6-3: The InitWinsys() routine

```
//
// Initialize windowing subsystem.
// Returns FALSE for error; TRUE for success.
//
BOOL InitWinsys(void)
{
    EK_KERNELINFO KernInf;
    int    len;
//
// Get local screen parameters.
// Save the current contents of the local screen so we can
// restore it when we're finished.
//
    EtsGetSystemInfo(&KernInf, NULL);
    pScrnInf = (SCREENINFO *)KernInf.pScreenInfo;
    if (pScrnInf == NULL || pScrnInf->InitFlag != 1 ||
            pScrnInf->Height < 25 || pScrnInf->Width < 80 ||
            pScrnInf->Width > MAX_COLS ||
            !(KernInf.PCATCompat & (EK_PER_MDA | EK_PER_CGA)))
        return FALSE;
    fMonochrome = (KernInf.PCATCompat & EK_PER_CGA) ? FALSE : TRUE;8.
    pScreen = (char *)
            (fMonochrome ? KernInf.MemMono : KernInf.MemCga);
    nConLines = pScrnInf->Height;
    nConCols = pScrnInf->Width;
    len = pScrnInf->Width * pScrnInf->Height*pScrnInf->BytesPerCell;
    pSaveScreenData = malloc(len);
    if (pSaveScreenData == NULL)
        return FALSE;
    memcpy(pSaveScreenData, pScreen, len);
//
// Init the rest of the globals.
//
    pFirstWin = NULL;
//
// Make the cursor disappear by moving it past the end of
// the screen, and blank the screen.
//
    SetCursorPosition(pScrnInf->Height + 2, 0);
    EraseConsole();
    return TRUE;
}
```

The InitWinsys() routine first calls EtsGetSystemInfo(). EtsGetSystemInfo() returns a data structure rich with information about the target system. InitWinsys() is interested in the members of the data structure that describe characteristics of the display hardware. InitWinsys() can use this information to adjust itself to the particulars of the current environment.

Just after the call to EtsGetSystemInfo(), InitWinsys() copies the pointer identified by the pScreenInfo member of the KernInf structure into the pScrnInf variable. This variable is of data type SCREENINFO, which is defined in Listing 6-4. You'll want to refer to this structure as you examine the InitWinsys() routine.

Listing 6-4: The SCREENINFO structure

```
typedef struct tagSCREENINFO
    {
    SHORT  InitFlag;      // 0 if screen has not been initialized
                          // 1 if screen has been initialized
                          // -1 if no screen was found to initialize
    WORD   Unused;        // Keep things aligned
    USHORT RealSeg;       // Segment of screen memory in real mode
    USHORT ProtSeg;       // Segment of screen memory in protected mode
    DWORD  Base;          // Screen address for the current PutChar
    WORD   CRTCAddr;      // Address of CRTC for updating cursor position
    USHORT Width;         // # of characters per line
    USHORT Height;        // # of lines on the screen
    USHORT BytesPerCell;  // Flag if attribute byte is required.
    USHORT Attribute;     // Attribute byte for screen characters
    USHORT CurRow;        // Current cursor row
    USHORT CurCol;        // Current cursor column
    } SCREENINFO;
```

The InitWinsys() routine must perform a train of elaborate comparisons on the data structure given by pScrnInf to verify that the display parameters are compatible with the requirements of the windowing subsystem. To wit:

```
if (pScrnInf == NULL || pScrnInf->InitFlag != 1 ||
        pScrnInf->Height < 25 || pScrnInf->Width < 80 ||
        pScrnInf->Width > MAX_COLS ||
        !(KernInf.PCATCompat & (EK_PER_MDA | EK_PER_CGA)))
    return FALSE;
```

This massive if() statement verifies the following:

- The pointer to the screen information data is not null. If it is, a screen driver is not available.

- The screen has been initialized. This initialization is performed by hardware-specific code in ETS Monitor.

- The screen height is greater than or equal to 25 characters, and the screen width is greater than or equal to 80 characters.

- The width parameter does not exceed the MAX_COLS constant.
- The display is either MDA or CGA compatible.

Of these comparisons, we should explain why the program verifies the screen size and the width parameter. The program checks for a minimum screen size of 80 x 25 characters to ensure that the screen is large enough for a useable user interface. The size of 80 x 25 was chosen only because that's the smallest size found on a standard PC computer. The windowing subsystem software can work fine with smaller screen sizes, if needed.

The program compares the width parameter to MAX_COLS to ensure a buffer size. Elsewhere, the software allocates a buffer to hold lines of text or character attributes. Those allocations are performed based on the constant MAX_COLS. The inclusion of the comparison with MAX_COLS here guarantees that the buffers will be of adequate size.

Next, InitWinsys() selects the screen memory's base address, and places that in the pScreen pointer. This is easily accomplished by moving the correct member of the KernInf structure — either MemMono or MemCga, depending on the display type — into pScreen.

The InitWinsys() routine then sets a number of flags (for example, whether the display is monochrome or color) and stores some values (screen width and height) in global variables so that they can be accessed more quickly by other routines in the WINSYS library. If InitWinsys() had left those flags and variables in the SCREENINFO structure, other routines would have been forced to access them through a pointer. Pointer access is slower than the direct access of a global variable. Also, the programmer would have to type the additional characters required to specify a member of a referenced structure rather than simply typing the much shorter global variable's name.

So that the initial display (that is, whatever was on screen before the application started) can be restored when the application terminates, InitWinsys() creates a holding buffer referenced by pSaveScreenData and copies to it the contents of the current screen. CleanupWinsys() — called when the application terminates — copies the contents of that buffer back to screen memory. This is a case of programmatic politeness. When the application terminates, the WINSYS subsystem puts things back the way it found them.

Next, InitWinsys() sets the console to the host. If an error involving screen mismanagement occurs, this setting permits WINSYS to send error messages to the host with printf() statements. Because all WINSYS output is written directly to video memory, the POS output still appears on the embedded target's display. Also, if you're trying to debug your application, setting the console to host lets you print debug messages to the host without messing up the target display.

Finally, InitWinsys() moves the cursor off screen, which makes the cursor disappear, and clears the display.

Calculating a Character's Position and Displaying a String

Before your application can write characters to — or read them from — display memory, you must calculate the memory location corresponding to a given screen position. You need some

Display Memory

The video adapter board on a PC system includes a block of RAM referred to as the *video buffer*, or *display memory*. To the CPU, this memory acts like ordinary memory. The CPU can read or write to display memory as easily as it reads and writes to other RAM in the system.

However, display memory is also attached to video display circuitry, which reads the memory repeatedly to refresh (update) the display. So, whatever is in display memory determines what is displayed. When your program must display something on the screen, the CPU writes to display memory. In most cases, lower-level routines handle the interaction with display memory; all you need to use in your programs are `printf()` and `putchar()` statements and so on. If you know where display memory is located and how data in it corresponds to what's shown on the screen, however, your program can directly manipulate display memory. This allows your program to utilize the full potential of the video hardware attached to your system. Later in this chapter, we show you the correspondence between addresses in display memory and onscreen locations (at least for the video systems supported by ETS Kernel).

The amount of display memory in a given system varies depending on the type and capabilities of the video adapter, as well as the video mode it is programmed to use. Consult the documentation of your video hardware for details.

macro or function that can convert row-column screen coordinates to a memory location. WINSYS tackles this conversion with a scary-looking macro:

```
//
// Macro to calculate the offset of a cell in the video refresh
// buffer for a particular row/column position
//
#define CellOffset(r, c) ((((r) * pScrnInf->Width) + (c)) * \
                    pScrnInf->BytesPerCell)
```

Given a row and column position (`r` and `c`), the `CellOffset` macro calculates the byte offset from the beginning of the screen memory buffer. Although this macro is lengthy, it's easy to see how it works. First, `CellOffset` multiplies the row coordinate by the screen width (`pScrnInf->Width`) and then adds the column coordinate. At this point, the macro has calculated the number of character positions (or cells) from the start of screen memory to the targeted coordinate. `CellOffset` then multiplies that value by the number of bytes per cell (bytes per character position) to produce the number of bytes from the start of screen memory to the targeted position.

Notice that this macro works regardless of screen resolution, provided that the mapping of memory position to onscreen character location is identical to the mapping shown in Figure 6-6.

You can see the `CellOffset` macro in action if you examine the following routine, `myWriteConsoleOutputCharacter()`, whose job it is to write a string of characters to the

Character Attributes

Each character on a PC text-mode screen is controlled by 2 bytes in video memory: a character byte and an attribute byte. This is illustrated in Figure 6-6.

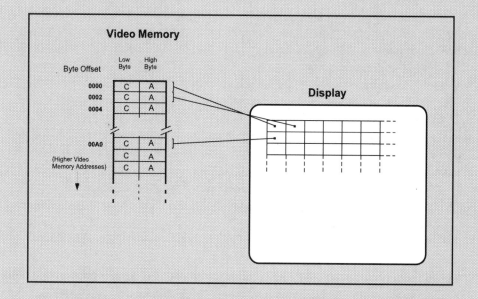

Figure 6-6: Each character location on a display is controlled by a pair of bytes in video memory. The low byte of the pair (shown here with a C) selects the character to be displayed. The high byte (shown here with an A) sets the character's attributes. Notice that, as you proceed from low to high video memory addresses, the corresponding screen location advances from left to right, top to bottom. So, the 0th byte-pair corresponds to the upper leftmost character on the display. The 80th byte pair (hexadecimal 00A0) corresponds to the first character on the second row, and so on.

The character byte determines what symbol — a letter, a number, a punctuation mark, and so on — appears on the screen. What's the purpose of the attribute byte?

A character's attribute byte determines *how* the onscreen symbol looks. The attribute byte's effect varies depending on whether you have CGA or MDA hardware. On CGA systems, the attribute byte controls a character's foreground and background color. On MDA systems, the attribute byte controls intensity, reverse video (whether the character or its background is white or black), and whether the character is underlined. Also, on both CGA and MDA systems, a special bit in the attribute byte can determine whether a character blinks.

For a CGA-compatible system, the low-order nibble (bits 0–3) determines the character's foreground attributes, and the high-order nibble (bits 4–7) determines the character's background attributes. The foreground attribute values correspond to colors as shown next. Notice that the low 3 bits of the nibble select a color, and the high bit (bit 3) is an intensity bit.

Nibble value (hexadecimal)	Color
00	Black
01	Blue
02	Green
03	Cyan
04	Red
05	Violet
06	Yellow
07	White
08	Gray
09	Intense blue
0A	Intense green
0B	Intense cyan
0C	Intense red
0D	Intense violet
0E	Intense yellow
0F	Intense white

Background attributes work almost the same way, but with a twist. When the system is initialized, a special bit in the video hardware is set so that setting the high-order bit in the nibble, bit 7, causes the character to blink. (This differs from foreground attributes, where the high-order bit in the nibble, bit 3, is an intensity bit.) If you know how to program the video adapter hardware, however, you can modify the way the system interprets bit 7 so that background attributes follow the same pattern as shown in the table; that is, bit 7 becomes an intensity control bit rather than a blink bit. (We suggest you consult a good book on programming PC graphics hardware for the details on how to do this.)

If you're using an MDA graphics system, only four values produce distinct results when stored in the attribute byte:

- Hexadecimal 07 produces a normal white character on a black background.

- Hexadecimal 70 produces a reverse-video character (that is, a black character on a white background).

- Hexadecimal 01 produces an underlined character.

- Hexadecimal 00 produces an invisible character (that is, a black character on a black background).

In addition, an MDA-compatible system will recognize bit 7 of the attribute byte as being either a blink bit or an intensity bit (as on the CGA). Most PC systems will, at boot time, initialize the video controller hardware to interpret bit 7 as a blink bit.

screen. This code is from the WINSYS.C file, and demonstrates not only the use of the CellOffset() macro but also how to perform direct screen output:

```
BOOL WINAPI myWriteConsoleOutputCharacter(
    HANDLE hConsoleOutput,
    LPSTR lpCharacter,
    DWORD nLength,
    COORD dwWriteCoord,
    LPDWORD lpNumberOfCharsWritten
    )
{
    char    *pChar;      // current screen address
    char    *pEnd;       // end of screen
    int     i, len;

    pChar = pScreen + CellOffset(dwWriteCoord.Y, dwWriteCoord.X);
    pEnd = pScreen + CellOffset(pScrnInf->Height-1,pScrnInf->Width);
    len = (pEnd - pChar)/ pScrnInf->BytesPerCell;
    if (len > nLength)
        len = nLength;
    for (i = 0; i < len; ++i, ++lpCharacter,
                        pChar += pScrnInf->BytesPerCell)
        *pChar = *lpCharacter;
    *lpNumberOfCharsWritten = len;
    return TRUE;
}
```

The lpCharacter argument is a pointer to the buffer holding the string to be displayed. The nLength argument holds the length of that string. The dwWriteCoord data structure consists of two members: the two screen coordinates where the first character in the string will be displayed. Finally, myWriteConsoleOutputCharacter() returns the number of characters that were displayed by means of the pointer lpNumberOfCharsWritten.

> **Note:** myWriteConsoleOutputCharacter() returns lpNumberOfCharsWritten because it's possible that the caller might request the routine to display more characters than can fit on the screen (given the starting coordinates and the length of the string). As you'll see, myWriteConsoleOutputCharacter() determines how many characters it can actually write, and returns that value so the caller can be made aware of any characters that fell off the end of the display.

The routine begins by calculating two memory locations: the address corresponding to the screen coordinates given by the caller and the address of the end of the display (the lowest, rightmost character position). The difference between these two addresses is the space within which the displayed string must fit. The routine calculates this difference, and it becomes the upper limit of the number of characters to be displayed.

Next, myWriteConsoleOutputCharacter() enters a for() loop, copying each character from the address given by lpCharacter (the source) to the address given by pChar (the destination). Notice that with each step through the loop, the lpCharacter pointer advances by one character (1 byte), while the `pChar` pointer strides ahead by the value given by `pScrnInf->BytesPerCell`. The discrepancy is because `lpCharacter` points to the source string, whereas `pChar` points to the location in memory where the string is being stored. If the application is running on a system with a CGA display, each character position on the screen is defined by 2 bytes: the first byte holds the character and the second holds the display attribute. If the routine advanced `pChar` by 1 byte for each pass through the loop, some of the characters would be stored at attribute locations. We're not sure what the result would look like, but it wouldn't be pretty. The `BytesPerCell` member of the `pScrnInf` structure holds the number of bytes for each character position on the screen, regardless of the screen hardware. So, incrementing `pChar` by that amount each time through the loop stores the string at the proper locations in screen memory for both MDA and CGA displays.

When `myWriteConsoleOutputCharacter()` exits the loop, it sets the returned value associated with the `lpNumberOfCharsWritten` pointer argument, and then exits.

SUMMARY

The demands placed on embedded systems often require developers to consider a wide range of input and output devices. After taking a look at the hardware interfaces for some of these devices, as well as some of the software issues that surface in implementing them, you can see why virtually no standardization exists in embedded systems.

As more and more embedded systems are built using standard 32-bit processors and peripherals, though, this will change. In the POS project, we used the standard keyboard and display hardware found in PC platforms, which we programmed with standard C library calls and Win32 console APIs. We introduced rudimentary, character-at-a-time keyboard input routines, and showed how an application can process keyboard input in a fashion that takes into account the extended key codes that may be returned by some keys on the PC keyboard.

The screen output in the POS project is performed by writing directly to the display memory, a technique that permits the fastest possible display update times. We showed how the windowing subsystem determines the characteristics of the screen hardware and initializes that hardware. You also learned how ETS Kernel allows your application to access screen memory directly, which provides greater control over the characteristics of screen output than would be available with simple console-I/O calls.

7

File Systems

You might not think of a file system as an ingredient of an embedded system. Deeply embedded systems comprised chiefly of a CPU, memory, and user-interface hardware have little need — or room — for anything as complex as a file system. Embedded systems that must manage and transfer persistent data (data retained even after a system is turned off), however, require a file system.

You're already familiar with file systems on desktop systems. A file system provides a structure for naming, storing, accessing, sharing, updating, and protecting persistent data on a permanent storage medium. To organize persistent data logically, a file system uses a named, hierarchical directory structure. This capability, to organize data logically, enables a file system to support random access, both to files in the directory structure and to data in individual files. Random access lets a user or a system find information easily and quickly, without having to scan through large amounts of data.

Equally important in managing data is a file system's capability to provide *device independence,* where an application's file manipulations are independent of the storage medium. A device-independent file system makes sure that a given operation performed by an application, such as saving, copying, and finding a file, produces the same result on every device it supports. The advantage to device independence is that you can choose from a range of devices.

Finally, a file system enables you to easily transfer data between systems with the same file storage structure. For example, suppose your embedded system is a remote data collection device. After the system gathers data, it has to be transferred to your lab for analysis by a desktop system. Unfortunately, your budget doesn't cover the cost of having a connection between the remote device and your data analysis system. (The remote device is on a mountaintop, so you can't run a network cable to it, and you can't afford a wireless modem.) One solution is to equip the embedded system with an inexpensive 3½" floppy disk drive and store the collected data on a disk. You can retrieve the disk at some regular interval, take it back to the lab, pop it into your system, and — provided that both the remote and desktop systems use the same file storage structure — copy the data to your desktop machine.

You may need to transfer data *to* an embedded system, as well. For example, consider a medical instrument that gathers information on a patient and then produces a list of possible diagnoses by looking up similar case histories in a medical database. The medical database is large and is stored in a file system. Updates to the database are issued quarterly. To update this system on site, you could include flash memory chips or a flash memory PC Card when you build the system. Then, when an update to the database is released, you can download the database to the flash memory device or save the database to a new card and ship it to each site.

After you decide to use a file system, two tasks await: choosing a file system and choosing a storage medium.

CHOOSING A FILE SYSTEM

In most cases, the file system you use in your embedded application is simply a component of whatever RTOS you've chosen. You must select a file system as a standalone component only rarely — if you're writing your own RTOS or the RTOS you've selected doesn't include a file system. If you do have to choose a file system and integrate it with your RTOS, you should consider a several criteria. You should compare the cost, code size, and ease of portability of the file systems you are considering. If you need the ability to transfer files to other systems, you'll want to choose a file storage format that's compatible with the file systems used on those systems. Check the API provided by the file system; it should be easy to use, and ideally should look similar (or identical) to well-known, standardized file I/O interfaces such as the ANSI C run-time library, POSIX, or Win32. Finally, in the sections below, we discuss three very important features of real-time file systems: performance, reliability, and multitasking and multiuser capabilities.

PERFORMANCE

Performance is typically an issue if your application will be using storage media with slow access times, such as floppy and hard disk drives. File system software can compensate for slow access using *caching*. Whenever software performs a disk-read operation, the system reads not only the data requested, but the entire disk sector on which the data resides (and possibly the next higher adjacent sectors). In that way, future read requests can be served by reading memory rather than the disk drive.

Similarly, the file system might buffer write operations, which means the data is initially written into a memory buffer. With buffering, the write request returns more quickly, and the application software doesn't have to wait for the write access operation to complete. The file system software writes the data to disk at a later time, when the system is in an idle state.

Write buffering is risky if the system is in an environment that could cause it to crash. If the system goes down before the buffer is written to disk, the file system and data could become corrupted. Consequently, many systems use write-through caching, in which the write buffer is simply part of the caching, and data is written not only to the cache but also directly to the disk. Because the data remains in the cache, a subsequent read operation does not have to go to the disk.

RELIABILITY

Corrupted data files are bad enough; a corrupted file system is even worse. When evaluating a file system, find out how it or the operating system ensures file system reliability and consistency:

- A file system is *reliable* if the file data and the directory structure are unlikely to become corrupted in a system crash.
- A file system is *consistent* if the data structures used to organize the directory structure and file storage are internally consistent, that is, if all possible ways to access a specific file or data in a file result in the same outcome.

We've already mentioned one measure a file system can take to protect your files and itself against inconsistency and corruption should the system crash: using a write-through cache. A write-through cache immediately writes modified blocks out to disk — whether they are data blocks or file system blocks.

Most file systems mark bad blocks to improve reliability. This method removes the bad blocks from the list of free blocks so they are not used.

In addition to finding out what's built into the file system to ensure reliability and consistency, find out whether the operating system includes a program to verify that the file system isn't corrupted and attempt to correct any problems encountered. After a system crash, such a program can sometimes recover data that would otherwise be lost.

MULTITASKING AND MULTIUSER CAPABILITIES

If you're designing a multitasking or multiuser system, in which more than one task needs to perform file I/O, make sure the file system allows multiple tasks efficient access. More than one task should be able to perform file I/O simultaneously. That is, one task shouldn't block another for the entire time that it's executing within the file system. A task should block another only to avoid performing the same operation simultaneously, such as simultaneously writing to the same file or updating the same directory data structure. In addition, the file system should have built-in file-sharing capabilities. Multiple users or tasks should be permitted to read a single file simultaneously, but only one user or task should be permitted to write to a file at one time.

CHOOSING A STORAGE DEVICE

You can choose from several types of storage devices: RAM disks, flash disks, ROM disks, trusty floppy and hard disks, CD-ROM drives, and magnetic tape. Which device you use depends on the project's constraints and the customer's requirements.

RAM DISKS

A *RAM disk* is a block of RAM that the file system reserves for file operations. The file system performs direct memory reads and writes instead of accessing an external disk drive, with its attendant latencies. RAM disks are typically used when you need fast access to data organized in files and hierarchical directories.

RAM disks are the one solution discussed here that can't be used for persistent data storage; a RAM disk can be used only for temporary storage because you lose the data in a RAM disk when you turn off power to the system. The big advantage of RAM disks is access speed. Some applications organize temporary data using the hierarchical structure of a file system; others copy heavily used files from persistent storage to a RAM disk at run time to boost system performance. It's uncommon to keep important data in a RAM disk, however, because all the data would be lost in a system crash or a power failure.

FLASH DISKS

Flash disks contain *flash memory,* a type of memory that retains its contents permanently, like ROM, but can be written to without using special hardware write circuitry, like RAM. These characteristics make flash memory particularly suitable for storing data.

Flash memory has some drawbacks, however. First, flash memory costs more than RAM or ROM. Second, although its read access times are typically better than ROM, flash memory cannot match the speed of RAM. Third, flash memory cells have a limited lifetime: writing to the cells causes them to wear out and lose their ability to retain information. File systems that interface to flash disks must perform both *bad block management,* which detects bad memory and stops using it, and *wear leveling,* which attempts to spread write operations evenly across the flash device to maximize the memory's lifetime.

By far the worst problem with flash memory, though, is that write operations take a long time (on the order of milliseconds), and no read access is permitted while the write is in progress. As a result, flash memory is often used for applications that require only read access to a storage device. Flash memory is more costly than ROM for such applications, but updating software is simply a matter of downloading to flash memory rather than turning off the system and physically replacing chips. Fortunately, some new flash memory devices are dramatically reducing the latencies associated with write operations.

Even with large write latencies, flash memory is still viable for some applications that need to store data. The access times for writing to a flash disk, although slower than other memory-based storage solutions, are on the same order of magnitude as a very fast hard disk.

The two common configurations for flash memory are dual in-line packages (DIPs) and PC Cards. DIPs look like linear memory to the system, like a ROM or RAM chip. Flash memory PC Cards can be inserted in any standard PC Card socket. Some PC Card flash devices look like linear memory to the system. A second kind of PC Card device, called an ATA (for AT Attachment) flash disk, contains hardware and software that present a PC standard IDE disk interface to the file system and perform bad block management and wear leveling inside the PC Card device. Although ATA flash disks are more expensive than other flash PC Cards, they are attractive because they work with a file system's standard IDE disk driver; you don't need a special flash memory disk driver. Linear flash memory, by contrast, requires specialized flash file system software, which can perform bad block management and wear leveling, operations standard file systems are not prepared to handle.

ATA flash disks are a popular storage medium not only because they're removable but also because they're small and use less power than a floppy or hard disk. They're rugged, too: they have no moving parts to wear out or break, and no heads to crash if the system receives a blow or other impact. As long as both target and host systems have PC Card slots, moving data from one to the other can be as easy with a flash disk as with a floppy.

Nothing is spurring the use of flash disks in embedded devices more than the improvements in flash technology. Intel now offers a flash memory PC card with 64MB of memory, and individual chips with 64Mbits of storage. In addition, companies such as Intel have announced multi-level encoding (MLE) flash memory. Whereas typical flash memory chips store a single bit per memory cell (as do standard RAM and ROM devices), MLE chips, such as Intel's StrataFlash, can store two bits per cell — twice the density in the same silicon space of typical flash memory chips.

ROM DISKS

If your application needs to only read data, consider using a *ROM disk,* which is simply a block of ROM. A ROM disk has several advantages. It has very fast access times relative to a disk drive, takes no additional space, and ensures that your read-only data won't be inadvertently modified. ROM chips are inexpensive compared to any kind of disk drive and to flash memory. And, as with flash disks, ROM disks are rugged and consume little power.

On the downside, updating the contents of ROM is difficult. You must burn new PROMs, pop out the old chips, and insert the new chips on the circuit board. If you have to do this often, you'll start to wish you used flash memory, which can be updated in place with a simple software download. In addition, ROM isn't suitable for storing large amounts of information; memory chips are practical for data storage on the order of tens of megabytes, as opposed to gigabytes on hard disk drives.

Read-only data stored on ROM and flash disks is sometimes stored in a compressed format; the data must be uncompressed and copied into RAM memory to be used. This feature is sometimes used, for example, with code that is copied to RAM for execution because of the faster access times offered by RAM memory. Using a compressed format allows more code to be stored on the ROM or flash disk. This technique is particularly useful for systems that use code overlays or dynamic link libraries to load code dynamically, in response to user input or specific events. Such dynamically configurable systems sometimes have quite large quantities of loadable code modules, making compressed storage an attractive feature. Traditionally, compression has been handled above the file system level, by application software or by the overlay or DLL loader. However, some file systems offer a compression feature built into the file system.

Hard Disk Drives

If your embedded system needs the capability to store large amounts of data, as is the case with systems that save data for later analysis or serve data to other computers over a network, the choice for storage is a hard disk. If you need to store huge amounts of data, you can get almost unlimited storage capacities with very large hard disks or disk arrays. And although an individual hard drive can cost several hundred dollars, that same hard drive has gigabytes of storage capacity, making its cost per megabyte far lower than any other file system storage media.

Other factors to consider for including a hard disk in your system are cost, space, power, and data access times. After you decide that the data storage requirements of your system dictate a hard disk, you've increased your system cost by a few hundred dollars and added a new box that needs to be shoehorned into the system. You have to determine whether your budget and your system chassis can accommodate a disk drive. In addition, you may need a larger and more expensive power supply to meet the additional power requirements of the hard disk. Some drives have power-saving features; you can program them to spin down if they haven't been accessed after a certain period of time. The next time an application requests data from the drive, however, you have to take into account a spinup time.

Data access times and data transfer rates with hard disks are far slower than they are with RAM or ROM disks, and far slower than read transfers to a flash disk. (Write transfer times of hard disks and flash disks are comparable.) Before data is read from or written to a hard disk, the disk heads must physically seek to the appropriate track on the disk, and then the desired sector must spin around to the disk heads. In addition, data transfer rates are dictated by how fast the disk spins. On the positive side, as disks get smaller and data is stored more densely, both access times and transfer rates improve.

Floppy Disk Drives

Floppy disk drives have, by far, the lowest data storage capacities and the slowest access times and data transfer rates of any data storage devices. So why would anyone use a floppy drive in an embedded system? Floppy drives are an inexpensive, ubiquitous read/write removable media — a combination that's tough to beat. The PC Card ATA flash disk is also a read/write removable device, but it is an order of magnitude more expensive than a floppy disk (though it also provides an order of magnitude more storage capacity than the 1.4MB of a standard floppy disk). In addition, floppy disk drives are almost universal on desktop computers, but PC Card slots are typically available only on laptop computers, again making floppies more attractive than ATA flash disks as a data transfer medium.

Occasionally, floppy drives are used in embedded systems as a boot device. If the embedded application (or even part of the application) is loaded off a floppy, it's easy to upgrade the application in the field and to boot a different application (if, for example, a field service engineer wants to run some test software). Still, because a floppy drive is slow and less durable than other boot options, such as a ROM, few embedded systems boot from a floppy.

CD-ROM Drives

CD-ROM drives are another choice for storing read-only data. They have relatively large data capacities (about 750MB) and access rates close to the speeds offered by a hard disk. CD-ROMS have some of the same disadvantages as hard disks, namely, cost, power consumption, and space. But like floppies and ATA flash disks, CD-ROMs are removable media and, as with floppies, the media cost is low. CD-ROMs are a good choice for systems that need access to large read-only databases, especially if the databases are updated frequently or the system uses multiple databases.

Magnetic Tape

Magnetic tape drives are not random-access devices; the data on a tape cartridge must be read or written serially. They're also relatively slow devices, reading or writing on the order of one to three megabytes per second. These characteristics make them best suited for backing up data from disk drives, or for collecting and storing large quantities of data for later processing elsewhere. Tape drives require their own (relatively simple) file systems; because the data is stored sequentially rather than randomly accessed, they are fundamentally different from the other storage devices discussed above. There are a wide variety of tape formats, sizes, and densities available. Currently, the most widely used tape format is the ½-inch data cartridge, defined by IBM publication GA 32-0048. Data is typically stored on these cartridges in 32 tracks, with a cartridge capacity of more than 2GB. (Siemens has recently announced a 128-track cartridge with an uncompressed data capacity of 10GB.)

ETS KERNEL FILE SYSTEM

ETS Kernel includes an MS-DOS-compatible file system. The file system is programmed by calling either the standard C library file I/O functions or the Win32 APIs for file I/O. As well as supporting file I/O on the embedded target system, ETS Kernel allows applications to perform remote file I/O on the host computer.

Local File System

The term *local file system* refers to the software that performs file I/O on the embedded target computer. Programs that need file I/O must link in the optional file system component of ETS Kernel.

ETS Kernel supports MS-DOS-compatible FAT16 and FAT32 file systems. At first, that might not seem like much, given that every Windows-based system in the world has the same capability. But that ubiquity is what makes ToolSuite's support of an MS-DOS file system so worthwhile. As we mentioned, a file system provides an element of portability among machines that recognize the file system's format. And the MS-DOS file system format is easily the most widely used file system in the desktop computer world. Hence, data stored using an MS-DOS-compatible file system can be moved easily among several hardware platforms.

ETS Kernel supports floppy drives, IDE hard drives, RAM and ROM disks, PC Card ATA flash disks, and M-Systems flash disks. (The Lite version of ETS Kernel included with this book supports only floppy drives. The full version of TNT Embedded ToolSuite includes source code for all drivers and documentation for creating your own drivers, should you need to write a new device driver, such as a SCSI driver.)

REMOTE FILE SYSTEM

ETS Kernel has an innovative feature, called the *remote file system,* that allows an embedded application to perform file I/O on the host system. The application accesses the host's file system through the same LapLink-compatible cable that serves as a connection for downloading and debugging programs. A single function call (which we cover later in this chapter) redirects the file open calls to either the remote or local file system. Beyond that, an application simply employs standard C I/O library routines to manage data files. An application may simultaneously perform file I/O on both local and remote files. After the file is opened, the file system knows whether the file is local or remote from its file handle.

The ETS Kernel file system's remote capability is particularly worthwhile during application development. For example, you could use the remote file system to log data from the embedded application on the target to the hard disk on the host. Perhaps your program is complex enough that it thwarts even the best debugger. You could build your own trace utility that records a program's execution to a file on the host system, and peruse this file later for post-mortem debugging.

Another use for the remote file system is to access a repository of data on the host and use it as input to your embedded application on the target. Rather than hardcoding test data into your application, you store the data in a file on the host and have the application read the data at start-up. You could keep a collection of test data files on the host, thereby providing different data conditions to which you can expose the application. You could even use this approach to maintain regression tests for new releases of your application.

Finally, you can use the remote file system capability to debug a program that will ultimately use the local file system. It's usually easier to create and modify files on your host system because that's where all your familiar editing tools are located. If you want to try out an embedded application that will eventually use the local file system, it's a simple matter (a single function call) to redirect the embedded application's file system calls so that they access the remote system. When you're satisfied that the application is functioning properly, modify that one function call, and all remote file I/O becomes local file I/O.

FILE I/O IN THE POS PROJECT

To illustrate using a file system in an embedded application, let's look at the code from the POS project. The most striking feature of this code is that it looks like file I/O code in a desktop application. The standard C library calls, `fopen()`, `fclose()`, `fread()`, and `fwrite()`, are used to manipulate files. That's exactly what you want; the file system in your embedded OS should be fully integrated, so you can use standard methods for file I/O and not have to learn a new interface.

Let's start by recapping the role that file systems play in the POS project. The POS project accesses both local and remote data files. The data file in the local file system, LSKUPOS.DAT, holds a subset of the store's overall inventory. In a real application, this local data set might act either as a kind of cache — storing information for frequently accessed items — or as a subset partitioned according to the particular terminal's location. (For example, a POS terminal in the sporting goods department could have only sports products' data in its local data file.)

> **Note:** Remember, our simulation uses the target's floppy disk as the storage medium for the local data file. In a real application, the local data file would probably be copied to either a RAM disk or a flash memory disk, thereby providing faster access and reducing the system cost for the terminal by removing the disk drive and probably using a smaller power supply.

We use the remote file system to simulate the kind of network that might exist in a real-world department store. The host system plays the role of the central server for our simulated network. It holds three data files used by the POS terminal: SYSPOS.DAT has the system-wide tax rate, USRPOS.DAT contains the user logon IDs, and RSKUPOS.DAT has the remote inventory database. Using the remote file system to access a database on the host lets us set up our simulation quickly because we don't have to implement networking and database access code.

The POS file I/O code is in the DATABASE.C file. We'll look at the POS project's file system handling code by examining the InitializeDatabase() routine in Listing 7-1. This routine does all the up-front work of opening and reading both local and remote data files.

Listing 7-1: The InitializeDatabase() routine

```
//
// Initialize the database subsystem
//
// Returns:   TRUE    if success
//            FALSE   if error
//
BOOL InitializeDatabase(void)
{
    FILE *hRemoteSysFile;  // handle for SYSPOS.DAT on host

//
// Open the system database file (SYSPOS.DAT) on the host
// system, extract the data in it (the tax percentage),
// and then close the file.
//
    if (EtsSelectFileSystem(ETS_FS_HOST) < 0)
    {
        printf("Unable to select host file system\n");
        return FALSE;
    }
```

```
    hRemoteSysFile = fopen("syspos.dat", "rt");
    if (hRemoteSysFile == NULL)
    {
       printf("Unable to open SYSPOS.DAT on host system\n");
       return FALSE;
    }
    if (!LookupTaxPercent(hRemoteSysFile))
    {
       printf("Unable to read tax percentage from SYSPOS.DAT\n");
       return FALSE;
    }
    fclose(hRemoteSysFile);

//
// Open the user database file (USRPOS.DAT) and remote SKU
// database file (RSKUPOS.DAT) on the host system.  We will
// keep these files open for the duration of the program.
//
    hRemoteUserFile = fopen("usrpos.dat", "rt");
    if (hRemoteUserFile == NULL)
    {
       printf("Unable to open USRPOS.DAT on host system\n");
       return FALSE;
    }
    hRemoteSkuFile = fopen("rskupos.dat", "rt");
    if (hRemoteSkuFile == NULL)
    {
       printf("Unable to open RSKUPOS.DAT on host system\n");
       goto CLOSE_USR;
    }

//
// Open the local SKU database file (LSKUPOS.DAT) on the A:
// diskette drive on the local system.  We will keep this file
// open for the duration of the program.
//
    if (EtsSelectFileSystem(ETS_FS_LOCAL) < 0)
    {
       printf("Unable to select local file system\n");
       goto CLOSE_RSKU;
    }
    hLocalSkuFile = fopen("a:\\lskupos.dat", "rt");
    if (hLocalSkuFile == NULL)
    {
       printf("Unable to open A:\\LSKUPOS.DAT on local system\n");
       goto CLOSE_RSKU;
    }

    return TRUE;
```

```
//
// Error returns — clean up before returning
//
CLOSE_LSKU:
    fclose(hLocalSkuFile);
CLOSE_RSKU:
    fclose(hRemoteUserFile);
CLOSE_USR:
    fclose(hRemoteSkuFile);
    return FALSE;
}
```

The first chore of `InitializeDatabase()` is to open the `SYSPOS.DAT` file and read the tax percentage amount. This file is stored on the remote system, so `IntializeDatabase()` must redirect file open calls accordingly. It does this by calling `EtsSelectFileSystem()`. `EtsSelectFileSystem()` is the routine we hinted at previously; its job is to redirect upcoming file open calls to either the local or remote file system. This routine accepts a single argument that can have one of four values:

- `ETS_FS_LOCAL`

- `ETS_FS_HOST`

- `ETS_FS_NONE`

- `ETS_FS_QUERY`

These arguments function similarly to those we saw for console I/O in Chapter 6, "Keyboard and Screen I/O." Use the `ETS_FS_LOCAL` argument to select the local (target) file system and `ETS_FS_HOST` to select the remote (host) file system. To disable the file system, use `ETS_FS_NONE`. (You're unlikely to want to disable the file system, but this value is useful as a return value from `EtsSelectConsole()`.) Lastly, use the `ETS_FS_QUERY` value to query the file system setting without changing it. The `EtsSelectConsole()` function returns the previous file system setting.

In this case, the argument is `ETS_FS_HOST`, so the effect of this call is to declare that any subsequent file open calls will be aimed at the remote file system.

Note: The `ETS_FS_HOST` value is defined in the `EMBKERN.H` file. This file was stored in the `\TSLITE\INCLUDE` subdirectory when you installed ToolSuite Lite from the CD-ROM.

Notice that `EtsSelectFileSystem()` returns a value that the program can use to determine whether the call succeeded. This return value also indicates whether communication with the remote file system is even possible. A return value of `ETS_FS_LOCAL`, `ETS_FS_HOST`, or `ETS_FS_NONE` indicates that the file system is selected as stated a few paragraphs back. A return value less than 0 denotes an error condition; either a system failure has occurred or the program has attempted to access an unavailable file system. This can happen, for example, if the application is running on a system with no connection to a host computer, and attempts a call of the form `EtsSelectFileSystem(ETS_FS_HOST)`.

Given that the call to `EtsSelectFileSystem()` succeeds, the program proceeds to open the `SYSPOS.DAT` data file with the standard C library `fopen()` routine.

Remember that, after a file is open, the file pointer is unaffected by subsequent calls to `EtsSelectFileSystem()`. In other words, if a program calls `EtsSelectFileSystem()` to access the remote file system, opens a file (call it file A), and then calls `EtsSelectFileSystem()` again to access the local file system and open another file (call it file B), the file pointers associated with files A and B will function properly. Each pointer knows where its file is located and makes sure the program reads from and writes to the correct file system.

The program then calls `LookupTaxPercent()` in Listing 7-2 to read the tax amount from the `SYSPOS.DAT` file.

Listing 7-2: The LookupTaxPercent() routine

```
//
// Reads the tax percentage from the system database file.
//
// Returns:   TRUE  if success
//            FALSE if SKU not found
//
BOOL LookupTaxPercent(FILE *hFile)
{
    char   Buf[256];      // buffers a line from database file
    int    nField;        // number of fields read by sscanf
//
// Loop, reading lines from the file until
// (a) we get a non-comment line, which should contain the
//     tax percentage, or
// (b) we hit end of file
//
    while (TRUE)
    {
//
// Read the next line.  If end-of-file, exit loop.
//
        if (fgets(Buf, sizeof(Buf), hFile) == NULL)
            break;
//
// Any line starting with a '#' is a comment;  skip it.
//
        if (Buf[0] == '#')
            continue;
//
// This line should just contain a single field, the tax
// percentage.  Anything else is an error.
//
        nField = sscanf(Buf, " %lu", &TaxPercent);
        if (nField != 1)
            break;
        return TRUE;
    }
```

```
//
// We didn't find the tax percentage.
//
    return FALSE;
}
```

LookupTaxPercent() is simple; it uses the fgets() C library call to read lines one at a time from the SYSPOS.DAT file, and then uses sscanf() to convert the tax percentage from ASCII to an integer value. The unremarkable-ness of LookupTaxPercent() reveals the ease with which you can program file I/O with ETS Kernel. File system calls — local or remote — are vanilla C library calls.

InitializeDatabase() closes the SYSPOS.DAT file and then proceeds to open the other two remote data files: USRPOS.DAT and RSKUPOS.DAT. These files are kept open for the duration of the program's execution, because they are used repeatedly to look up user IDs as cashiers log on to the terminal and to look up product SKUs as items are entered during a sale. We won't bother to look at the routines that read the USRPOS.DAT and RSKUPOS.DAT files; the file I/O they perform is as straightforward as that in the LookupTaxPercent() routine we just examined.

Next, InitializeDatabase() switches to the local file system:

```
if (EtsSelectFileSystem(ETS_FS_LOCAL) < 0)
{
    printf("Unable to select local file system\n");
    goto CLOSE_RSKU;
}
hLocalSkuFile = fopen("a:\\lskupos.dat", "rt");
if (hLocalSkuFile == NULL)
{
    printf("Unable to open A:\\LSKUPOS.DAT on local system\n");
    goto CLOSE_RSKU;
}
```

This time, notice that the argument to EtsSelectFileSystem() is ETS_FS_LOCAL. After the local file system has been selected, the InitializeDatabase() routine opens the local file LSKUPOS.DAT. Once more, it's important to repeat that the remote file pointers are unaffected by the EtsSelectFileSystem(ETS_FS_LOCAL) call.

If a problem occurs while the InitializeDatabase() routine is executing, several error exits are available. You've probably already seen the forbidden goto statements throughout the routine. This is one of the few cases in which using a goto statement is practical. First, it allows us to gather the error cleanup code in a single place. Second, it makes for shorter — and easier to read — code. We would otherwise have to place repeated fclose() statements throughout the routine to handle the file closings.

SUMMARY

In this chapter, we introduced you to the idea of using a file system in your embedded application: Sometimes an embedded system can benefit from the persistent storage support and file portability capabilities that a file system provides. After we discussed how to choose a file system and various storage solutions, we presented the file system capabilities of the TNT Embedded ToolSuite system. As you've seen, adding such capabilities to your application is remarkably easy. With the exception of a single function call (to toggle between the local and remote file systems), file I/O with ETS Kernel uses the same library routines with which any moderately accomplished C programmer is familiar.

A Simple UPS

I n this next project, we build an uninterruptible power supply (UPS). More accurately, we build the brains for a UPS. A UPS makes sure that the flow of electricity to electronic equipment such as a computer system isn't interrupted by a brownout or a power outage. To prevent interruption, UPS devices usually operate in one of two ways. A UPS that's a standby power system (SPS) provides AC power to equipment while continuously monitoring the AC power line. When it detects a change in the AC voltage that's unacceptably high or low, it switches to the battery. An online UPS, on the other hand, continuously provides power from the battery, which in turn draws AC current to keep fully charged. When the AC voltage goes outside the acceptable range, the UPS disconnects AC power from the battery charger until the power returns to a tolerable level.

How long a UPS provides power depends on the size of its battery. Some UPS devices are designed to give you just enough time to save your work and properly shut down a single system or a small network; the batteries often last for only 5 to 10 minutes. Others can power large mission-critical systems, such as network file servers that must be available around the clock, for up to several hours.

In addition to supplying power, a UPS also protects equipment from electrical fluctuations that could be potentially damaging. Some parts of the world — including areas of the U.S. — have unreliable AC power and frequently experience brownouts, power surges, and other types of power fluctuations. A *brownout* occurs when AC voltage drops below a certain threshold for an extended period of time. Most UPS manufacturers consider a brownout to occur when the voltage drops more than 8 or 10 percent below the baseline voltage. A brownout can be damaging because its effect on a computer system is unpredictable. Some computer systems can survive a brownout; others either shut down or perform a system reset, which can result in lost data and even a corrupted disk, if the shutdown or reset occurs when a disk-write operation is in progress.

Note: Old, transformer-based power supplies are particularly susceptible to brownouts, as are appliances and electrical motors. Ironically, low voltage into such electrical devices can actually burn them out.

A *power surge* occurs when AC voltage becomes unacceptably high (usually 10 percent over the baseline voltage) for a short or long period of time. Numerous conditions can lead to power surges. Mild surges, for example, can take place in industrial areas where large pieces of electrical and electromechanical equipment are turning on and off. More severe surges can result from lightning strikes. Surges can fry the circuitry of electronic components.

A UPS provides a buffer between a computer system and uncertain wall-outlet power. It deals with reduced, fluctuating power by providing AC power delivered from the battery. To handle mild voltage surges, some UPS devices use switching transformers; others will (as in the case of reduced power) deliver power from the battery. To manage large surges, most use surge protection circuitry.

Why did we choose a UPS as our project in this and subsequent chapters? The hardware and operation of a UPS is generally simple and straightforward. In addition, you're probably familiar with the concept — if not the specifics — of how a UPS works, so you'll be able to quickly grasp the background details and move on to the software discussions. This is important because the purpose of this book is to show you how to write embedded applications. It would be an unnecessary distraction if we chose an example that was too complex; instead of focusing on understanding topics fundamental to all embedded systems, you'd be preoccupied with example details that have no application beyond this book.

Another reason we chose a UPS is because it's extensible. In upcoming chapters, we upgrade the simple UPS in this chapter to handle multitasking, serial I/O, and finally, networking, including accessing the UPS through the Web. This strategy harkens back to our notion of keeping the examples in a supporting rather than a leading role. By building on previous projects, you can focus on new topics, technologies, and techniques rather than on a new piece of hardware. More importantly, we've found that it's often instructive to watch a project progress through various stages of development and enhancement.

Finally, as did the POS system, a UPS lends itself to simulation: It's relatively easy to build a program that mimics the operations and functions of a UPS. Then, using your target and desktop systems, you can run the program and see how it works. You can also make changes to the program, recompile it, and run it again with your enhancements.

The program we present in this chapter is for a standby power system, and we use it to introduce two topics: interrupts and timers. An *interrupt* is a signal generated by hardware or software and sent to the processor or generated directly by the processor. When an interrupt occurs, the processor transfers control to a software routine known as an *interrupt handler,* or an *interrupt service routine* (ISR). The interrupt handler then executes its set of instructions and returns control to the processor. As you'll see, embedded systems use interrupts to respond quickly to external events.

Two kinds of timers are used in computer systems. A *count-up timer* tracks elapsed time; this allows the system to keep an accurate time-of-day clock. A *count-down timer* is similar to an egg timer; it counts down a specific period of time and then notifies the system (usually with an interrupt) that the period has elapsed. Although it's possible to implement timers entirely in software, at least the counting part of a timer is almost always implemented in hardware. The hardware timer has I/O ports that allow software to set its initial values, start it, stop it, read the current count, and so on. Count-up timers often have the capability to periodically interrupt the system, so that software doesn't have to remember to poll the timer to keep track of elapsed time.

Rather than having two timer chips in a system, count-down timers are sometimes implemented in software; the software uses the interrupts from a count-up timer to period-ically decrement the value of the count-down timer. In the UPS program, we use the periodic interrupts from the PC 8254 Programmable Interval Timer chip to track elapsed time and drive UPS activities that must be performed at regular intervals.

HOW THE UPS PROJECT WORKS

The specifications for our UPS calls for a system that, on a day-to-day basis, provides AC power to a load that's connected to it. A *load* is one or more devices, such as a computer, that draw power. The most important function of our UPS is to monitor the AC power and detect changes in voltage. If the UPS determines that the power has fallen too low or surged too high for safe operation, it switches from AC to battery power and sounds an audible alarm. This alarm notifies the user that the load is being battery powered.

While the battery is online, the UPS continues to monitor the AC power. If the AC voltage returns to an acceptable level before the battery runs down, the UPS takes the battery offline and returns to supplying the computer with AC power. The switch from AC to battery power, and vice versa, is performed without interrupting the flow of current to the load.

In addition to monitoring the voltage, the UPS detects the presence or absence of a load and monitors the charge in the battery, recharging it when necessary.

> **Note:** If the AC power remains in a state unsuitable for recharging the battery (that is, the AC voltage is too high or too low), ultimately, the battery will discharge. Most UPS devices signal the battery's impending depletion with an audible alarm. Our second version of the UPS pro-ject will simulate completely draining the battery, and provide a distinct alarm for the onset of that event.

To work as described, our UPS should be built using the following hardware:

- **A battery.** This is a lead-acid battery like the one in a car.
- **A battery monitor.** This is a device that measures the charge in a battery.
- **A battery charger.** This device converts AC to DC and supplies a current to the bat-tery to recharge it.
- **An AC line monitor.** This is an isolated A/D converter that provides an instantaneous AC line voltage reading.
- **An inverter.** This is a device that converts DC to AC to supply AC power to the load.

- **Switching circuitry.** The system will have two computer-controlled switches. One turns power to the connected loads on and off; the other changes the source of power either from the battery to AC or from AC to the battery.

- **A system controller.** The brains of the UPS will be a microcomputer. But to provide any worthwhile control functions, the microcomputer must consist of more than a CPU. A system controller is a hardware module that consists of a CPU, ROM, RAM, I/O ports, and a power supply.

- **A load monitor.** This is an analog/digital circuit that detects a draw on the current.

- **Indicator lights and speaker.** Four indicator lights and a speaker inform a user of the status of the UPS.

- **A pushbutton.** The pushbutton controls the power to the load, not to the UPS.

The top-level block diagram in Figure 8-1 shows all the hardware components of the UPS. Refer to this diagram as we describe how the UPS performs its tasks. The AC line monitor watches the AC power line. If it detects an unacceptable change in voltage, the monitor signals the CPU. The CPU toggles the battery/AC switch to switch to the battery as the power source. When the battery is used as the power source, it powers the UPS itself in addition to

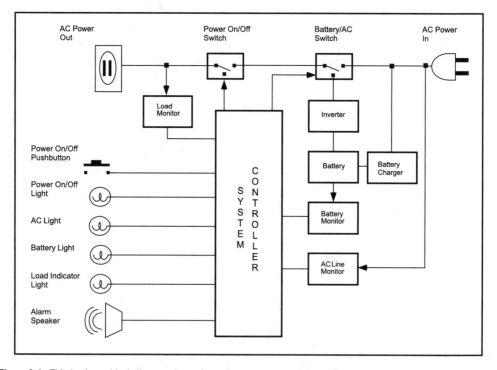

Figure 8-1: This hardware block diagram shows the major components of the UPS and their interconnections. The system controller consists of a CPU, memory, I/O, and a power supply.

any load. When the AC line monitor signals that AC power is back in the acceptable range, the CPU switches back to AC as the power source.

AC power is acceptable or good when the voltage is between 110 to 130 volts. We regard AC power as unacceptable or bad at any other voltage levels, which can damage a PC or other device.

Note: The low and high voltage levels we've selected are approximate. Real UPS systems may tolerate a wider — or narrower — range of low and high voltages.

The lead-acid battery uses and delivers DC, so we must include an electronic device called an *inverter*. When the battery is online, the inverter converts the battery's DC power to AC before making it available through the UPS to the load. The load monitor watches the line that feeds into the AC power-out socket for a load. The system controller uses this information to decide whether to illuminate the load indicator light. The power on/off switch controls power to the load, not to the UPS, and is normally set to the same state as the user-controlled power on/off pushbutton, with one exception: If the AC power is bad and the battery is discharged, the system controller will always turn off the power on/off switch to prevent unacceptable power from being distributed to the load. A user controls the power to the load by pressing the power on/off pushbutton.

Switching time is critical, particularly for the battery/AC switch. If it switches too slowly, the load connected to the UPS could be affected by line noise that may be introduced during the transition from AC to battery power and back again.

The four indicator lights and a speaker on the front panel of the UPS inform the user of the status of the UPS. The power on/off light indicates if power is being supplied to the AC power-out socket; the battery light indicates if the battery is online or offline; the load indicator light shows if a load is present or absent; and the AC light indicates if AC is good or bad. The speaker sounds a warning when the AC power is bad and the battery is put online, reminding the user that the load will continue to receive power only as long as the battery has a charge.

DESIGNING THE SIMULATION

We design the software simulation of the UPS in the same way we design the software in any embedded system, using the design steps described in Chapter 2, "Designing and Developing Your Real-Time System." A simulation, however, has one additional step; we must define the user interface that the simulation will present in place of the hardware components in the actual UPS. Figure 8-2 shows a mock-up of the screen display for the UPS simulation.

The simulation screen is divided into two sections. Each window in the upper section represents one of the four status lights on the UPS. If the Power window says Off, the Load window displays Absent, the AC Power window says Bad, or the Battery window displays Offline, the corresponding indicator lights on the UPS panel would be off. Conversely, if the Power window says On, the Load window says Present, the AC Power window displays Good, or the Battery window displays Online, the corresponding indicator lights on the UPS panel would be on. The background color of the window changes to indicate that the state of any one of the lights has changed.

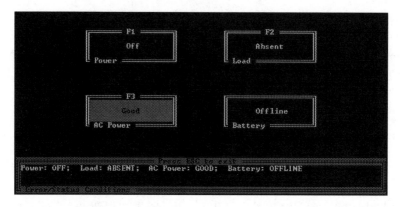

Figure 8-2: The interface of the UPS simulation. Each rectangular window simulates an indicator light by changing its background color. You simulate input by pressing the function keys shown above each window.

You can simulate inputs to the UPS by pressing the corresponding function key. The F1 key simulates the power on/off pushbutton, which controls power to the load, not to the UPS. The F2 key simulates the sensing capability provided by the load monitor; pressing F2 adds or removes the load from the UPS. The F3 key simulates the sensing capability provided by the AC line monitor; pressing F3 toggles between AC power good and bad. As you change the inputs, the battery will be put online and taken offline as appropriate. In addition, the text in each window changes, indicating that the state of the UPS system has changed. Pressing the ESC key ends the simulation program.

The lower section of the display is a small status window. It provides a parallel view into the state of the system, and displays error messages if keys that aren't used in the simulation are pressed.

SOFTWARE SUBSYSTEMS

When partitioning the simulation into software subsystems, remember that one of the goals is to make moving the simulation software onto the actual hardware, when it's ready, as painless as possible. We try to isolate software that's used only for the simulation into separate subsystems, so that when we migrate the system to the real hardware, we can easily replace the simulation subsystems with new subsystems that manipulate the UPS hardware components. Because subsystems are accessed only by well-defined interfaces, it's easier to remove an entire subsystem than it is to hunt down and remove or replace dozens of individual functions scattered throughout the program.

The event subsystem forms the core of the UPS. As various events of interest to the UPS occur, other subsystems notice the events and pass them to the event subsystem for processing. The event subsystem is responsible for changing the UPS state appropriately and performing any other required actions. In the simulation, the event subsystem updates the display; in a real UPS, it would update the status lights on the front panel, switch between battery and AC power, and so on. Because events occur asynchronously in real time, the event subsystem must be capable of receiving events and queuing them for later processing when it's performing other actions. In other words, the interface function that accepts events and queues them must run at interrupt time (when an interrupt occurs) and must guarantee that data structures accessed by the function won't be corrupted, even if the function is executing on behalf of two or more interrupts simultaneously.

The windowing subsystem is responsible for writing to and updating the simulation's display. Because these are the same functions that the windowing subsystem performed for the POS simulation, we use the same collection of routines here.

The key processing subsystem provides low-level key-input processing. These routines receive a user's keystroke, map the key to a UPS event, and pass the event code to the event subsystem for processing. Unlike the POS project, we can't obtain keystrokes by calling the C run-time library because that call blocks waiting for a keystroke, which is unacceptable in a system that must be able to respond simultaneously to multiple inputs. This simulation has two possible inputs: the timer and the keyboard. A real UPS has additional inputs from the various hardware monitors in the system. If we were building a multithreaded application (which we do in later versions of the UPS), we could create a separate thread to read keystrokes; that thread would be able to block without stopping the rest of the system. But in this single-threaded version of the UPS, we must read keystrokes and pass them to the event subsystem at interrupt time.

The timer subsystem generates periodic (in this simulation, every 500 milliseconds) timer events and passes them to the event subsystem. These timer events provide the mechanism for implementing an activity that repeats as scheduled. In this simulation, the timer events are used to blink the AC light at half-second intervals when the AC power is bad. Because this program is single-threaded, we generate timer events by hooking the hardware timer interrupt.

SOFTWARE INTERFACES

The next step in the design process is to define the interfaces that the software subsystems will use to communicate with each other. Most of the subsystem interfaces are simple and clearly documented in the code. We examine the most interesting interface, the interface to the event subsystem. You can find prototypes for the interface functions for all subsystems in the UPS.H file.

The event subsystem consists of four interface functions:

- **BOOL InitEventsys(void).** The system must call the InitEventsys() function at startup to initialize the event queue. InitEventsys() also simulates the initial state of the UPS (battery offline, power off, no load, and AC power good). It returns TRUE if the initialization succeeded; FALSE otherwise.

- **void CleanupEventsys(void).** The system must call the CleanupEventsys() function at shutdown to provide an orderly termination of event processing.

- **void EventLoop(void).** Except during start-up and shutdown, the EventLoop() function is always executing while the UPS is running. It is called once after initialization is complete; when it returns, the simulation program cleans up and terminates. The `EventLoop()` function repeatedly examines the event queue to see whether a new event has arrived. When `EventLoop()` finds an event at the front of the queue, it removes the event and calls the proper event handler.

- **void AddEvent(int Event, DWORD ControlKeyState, WORD VirtualKeyCode, CHAR AsciiChar)**. This function is called by other subsystems when an event occurs. `AddEvent()` just adds the event to the event queue to be processed by the main event loop. Because `AddEvent()` is called at interrupt time, it has to ensure that the event queue data structures are not corrupted, even if it is called by two or more interrupt handlers simultaneously. The primary argument to `AddEvent()` is an integer identifying the event that occurred:

```
#define EVENT_POWER    0        // power on/off key pressed
#define EVENT_LOAD     1        // load present/absent key pressed
#define EVENT_AC       2        // AC good/bad key pressed
#define EVENT_EXIT     -1       // exit the program
#define EVENT_TIMER    -2       // timer event signaled every 500 ms.
#define EVENT_UNUSED_KEY -3     // unused key pressed
```

The other three arguments to `AddEvent()` are used only for the `EVENT_UNUSED_KEY` event, and enable the event subsystem to display an informative error message. The final system will not have a keyboard, and therefore no key processing subsystem or unused key event, so these three arguments to `AddEvent()` will be removed.

START-UP AND SHUTDOWN PROCESSES

At system start-up, the initialization routines for each of the four software subsystems must be called. The windowing subsystem must be initialized first, because it is used by the event subsystem. The event subsystem must be initialized before the timer and key processing subsystems, because they make calls into the event subsystem as events occur. The event subsystem initializes the internal data structures used to manage the queue of events waiting to be processed. In addition, the event subsystem initializes the UPS state and the user interface (the contents of the display).

The key processing subsystem registers the keyboard interrupt callback routine with the keyboard driver during initialization, and the timer subsystem registers the timer interrupt callback routine with the timer driver. The windowing subsystem is the only one that initializes hardware as part of its start-up routine. It identifies and clears the display.

With the exception of the event subsystem, each subsystem performs certain shutdown operations. The key processing and timer subsystems unhook their respective callback routines, which they registered during initialization. And the windowing subsystem frees any memory it allocated for managing windows. It also restores the original contents of the display.

Beyond Simulation

How does our simulation differ from the software you would write for an actual UPS system? As you might expect, you have to replace code wherever we simulate a hardware input or output.

Recall that our simulation has four subsystems: the event subsystem, the timer subsystem, the key processing subsystem, and the windowing subsystem. The key processing and windowing subsystems are used entirely to simulate UPS inputs and outputs; these subsystems would not exist on a real UPS.

The timer subsystem just generates periodic timer events and could operate unmodified on UPS hardware. The timer subsystem uses the ETS Kernel timer driver to hook timer interrupts; if the UPS hardware doesn't use a PC-compatible timer, you'd have to modify the timer driver code appropriately.

In the event subsystem, the event loop processing would be unchanged. You would need to replace the code that changes the simulation display as a result of a state change with code that toggles the status lights on the UPS front panel and brings the battery online or offline, as necessary. Toggling lights is so simple that you could do it inline in the event subsystem; to manipulate the battery, you'd make calls to a battery subsystem you'd have to write.

You would need several additional subsystems:

- A battery subsystem to bring the battery online or offline, to monitor the battery charge, and have the battery charger recharge the battery when needed

- A load subsystem to monitor when a load is added or removed, and generate load events to be processed by the event subsystem

- An AC power subsystem to monitor the AC power quality and generate AC power events when the AC power transitions from good to bad or vice versa

You would need to change the start-up code as well. Rather than assuming a hardwired initial UPS state like the simulation does, you'd have to check the AC power and load status and construct the initial UPS state from those inputs.

Finally, the simulation fatal error routine exits the simulation program. For an actual UPS, it should shut down the software subsystems and run the start-up code again to restart the UPS. The fatal error routine gets called in a panic situation, when the software detects an impossible condition and doesn't know what else to do. On a critical system like a UPS, it's obviously unacceptable to shut down when an error occurs.

ERROR HANDLING

As with the POS system, the UPS system reports initialization errors by displaying an error message and terminating the system. If a user presses an illegal key, the system beeps the speaker and ignores the key. If the system detects an error condition that indicates a bug in the system, it prints a fatal error message and shuts down the system. In a critical system like a UPS, it's better to reinitialize the system and continue operation when an error occurs. We build a version of the UPS that restarts when an error occurs in Chapter 20, "C++ Exceptions and Structured Exceptions."

BUILDING THE UPS PROJECT

The files for this first UPS project are in the \TSLITE\PROJECTS\UPS1 directory. If you just want to run the program, you can use the prebuilt executable, UPS1.EXE. To build the executable from Visual C++ Developer Studio, open the UPS1.DSW workspace file and click Build|Rebuild All. More details on building the projects are provided in Chapter 3, "Software Installation and Setup."

RUNNING THE UPS PROJECT

Download and execute the UPS application from Visual C++ Developer Studio by clicking Build|Execute ups1.exe. Or if you prefer to run the program from a DOS box, set the current directory to \TSLITE\PROJECTS\UPS1 and enter the following command:

```
runemb release\ups1
```

When the UPS simulation starts, it is in its initial state: the power to the load is off, AC power is good, the battery is offline, and no load is attached.

After you have the simulation running, the first step is to supply power to the AC power-out socket by pressing F1. (This is in preparation for attaching a load to the UPS.) As shown in Figure 8-3, the background and text in the Power window changes to On, and the status window is updated.

Figure 8-3: When you press the Power on/off button and the text changes to On, the UPS is ready to deliver power to a load.

Now press F2. As shown in Figure 8-4, the background color of the Load window changes, and its text switches to read Present. Again, the status window changes to reflect the state of the UPS.

To simulate a power fault, press F3. As Figure 8-5 illustrates, the AC Power window now indicates that the power is bad, and the Battery window indicates that the battery is online,

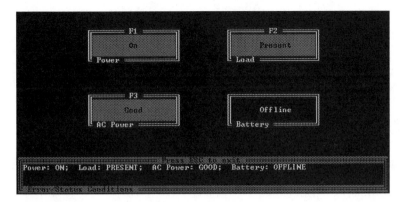

Figure 8-4: This is the normal operating state of the UPS: Power is applied to the AC power-out socket — into which we have plugged some device — and the AC power is good. Because AC power is being delivered to the load, the battery is offline.

showing that the UPS is now delivering power from the battery. Unfortunately, what we can't show you with screen shots is that the AC Power indicator is also flashing, simulating the alarm that would sound when the power is bad and the battery is put online.

Press the F3 key again and the outage is terminated, AC power returns to good, and the system takes the battery offline.

Note: If this were an actual system rather than a simulation, the UPS would now check the level of the battery and determine whether it needs recharging. In a later version of the UPS simulation, we simulate the battery discharging and recharging.

Finally, you can remove the load by pressing F2, and turn off the power to AC power out by pressing F1.

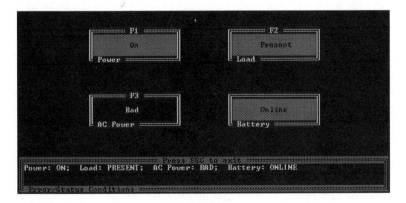

Figure 8-5: Pressing the F3 key simulates a power outage. The system automatically puts the battery online and the AC Power window flashes on and off, simulating an alarm.

A QUICK TOUR OF THE SOURCE

The source files for the UPS system are divided along subsystem lines. You'll find the outermost routines in the UPS.C file. These include main(), InitializeUps() (which calls each subsystem's initialization routine), and CleanupUps() (which calls each subsystem's cleanup routine).

The main() routine for the simulation is straightforward:

```
void main(void)
{
//
// Initialize the system
//
    if (!InitializeUps())
        return;
//
// Process events until the user exits
//
    EventLoop();
//
// Cleanup and exit
//
    CleanupUps();
    return;
}
```

It initializes all the software subsystems, and then calls the event loop interface routine in the event subsystem. When the event loop returns, the program shuts down all the subsystems and terminates.

The event subsystem code is in EVENT.C. The event subsystem is responsible for changing the state of the UPS as external events occur. In addition to changing the state of the UPS, the event subsystem must take any actions necessary to respond to the event. In our simulation, this means updating the user interface on the display to reflect the change in the UPS state. Because the event subsystem is responsible for updating the display, it also initializes the display by calling the windowing subsystem from its initialization function.

The event loop in EVENT.C was written using a state machine concept. A state machine's response to input is determined by what happened before the input or, in other words, what state the system is in when it receives the input. So a state machine may receive identical input and yet respond differently. For example, suppose that the AC is good, the battery is offline, no load is present, and you plug in a PC to the UPS. The system responds by indicating that a load is now present. Now suppose that the next time you plug in a PC, the AC is bad (and everything else is the same). This time, the system responds by indicating that a load is present and putting the battery online. Same input, different responses.

Figure 8-6 is a state diagram for our simulated UPS system. If you create such a diagram when you're writing this type of software, it will help ensure that you account for every state the system could be in and every state's response to all inputs it could receive.

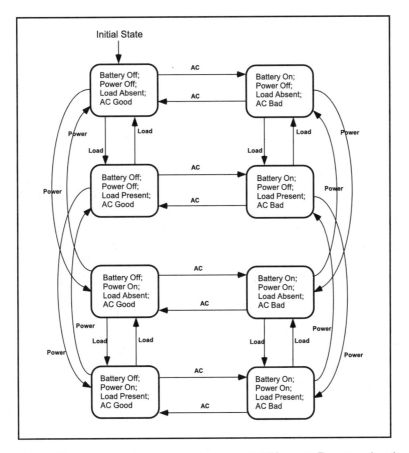

Figure 8-6: The UPS state diagram shows the possible states of the UPS system. The arrows show the state transitions that results as events occur.

The usual way to implement a state machine in software is a next state table. This is a two-dimensional matrix that is indexed by the current state and an event. The table entry gives the new state that results from the occurrence of the event. There are two benefits to using a table lookup for state transitions: the code to implement state transitions is very efficient, and it's trivial to implement changes to the state diagram.

The number of possible states in the system is two to the *n*th power, where *n* is the number of conditions that make up the system state. In the UPS, the system state has four components: the battery state, the load state, the power state, and the AC state. In the UPS.H header file, we assign a bit to each component, and logically OR the bits together to obtain the system state value. Since there are four components, there are 2^4, or 16, possible state values.

```
//
// Bit definitions for UPS system state dword
// In this simulation, the AC state and the battery state always
// change in lockstep (if AC is bad, the battery is online, and vice
// versa), which implies we could combine them into one bit.  But in
```

```
// the real system the AC state and the battery state will be
// separately monitored by hardware, so it makes sense to keep
// separate state bits.
//
#define STATE_AC_BAD      0x00000001    // 1 ==> AC bad, 0 ==> good
#define STATE_LOAD_PRESENT 0x00000002   // 1 ==> load present,
                                        // 0 ==> absent
#define STATE_POWER_ON    0x00000004    // 1 ==> power on, 0 ==> off
#define STATE_BATT_ON     0x00000008    // 1 ==> battery on, 0 ==> off
#define NSTATES           16            // number of states = 2**4
```

But why does the state diagram in Figure 8-6 show only 8 states if there are 16 possible states in the system? Because 8 of the possible states are illegal. Specifically, you will never get to a state where the battery is on and AC power is good, or where the battery is off and AC power is bad. If the battery and AC power states are mirror images, why not combine them into one state bit and reduce the number of states to 8? The reason is that when you migrate the system to actual UPS hardware, the state of AC power and the battery will be detected by hardware circuits rather than dictated by the simulation software, and it will be possible, for example, for the AC power to be bad and the battery to be offline (although only for an extremely brief period, unless the UPS has a system failure). Therefore, in the actual UPS, you need all 16 states in the state table.

The state table for the UPS is at the top of the EVENT.C file and shown below. The table is a 16 by 3 array, indexed by the 16 possible system states, and the three possible events (a change in AC status, load status, or power to the load).

```
//
// Next state table, indexed by current state and event
// Note there are a number of invalid states.  You can't have:
//    battery off and AC bad
//    battery on and AC good
//
DWORD NextState[NSTATES][NEVENTS] = {
{4, 2, 9},     // 0: battery off, power off, load absent, AC good
{0, 0, 0},     // invalid: batt off, power off, load absent, AC bad
{6, 0, 11},    // 2: battery off, power off, load present, AC good
{0, 0, 0},     // invalid: batt off, power off, load present, AC bad
{0, 6, 13},    // 4: battery off, power on, load absent, AC good
{0, 0, 0},     // invalid: batt off, power on, load absent, AC bad
{2, 4, 15},    // 6: battery off, power on, load present, AC good
{0, 0, 0},     // invalid: batt off, power on, load present, AC bad
{0, 0, 0},     // invalid: battery on, power off, load absent, AC good
{13, 11, 0},   // 9: battery on, power off, load absent, AC bad
{0, 0, 0},     // invalid: batt on, power off, load present, AC good
{15, 9, 2},    // 11: battery on, power off, load present, AC bad
{0, 0, 0},     // invalid: battery on, power on, load absent, AC good
{9, 15, 4},    // 13: battery on, power on, load absent, AC bad
{0, 0, 0},     // invalid: battery on, power on, load present, AC good
{11, 13, 6}    // 15: battery on, power on, load present, AC bad
};
```

Next, look at the event loop code, where the table lookup for the state transitions is implemented:

```
//
// Main event loop.  Just loops, waiting for events to occur
// and processing them, and exits when the user types ESC.
//
void EventLoop(void)
{
    UPS_EVENT NextEvent;      // next event to process
    DWORD  PrevState;         // previous system state

    while (TRUE)
    {
        GetEvent(&NextEvent);
        if (NextEvent.Event >= 0 && NextEvent.Event < NEVENTS)
        {
            // event that can cause state change occurred
            PrevState = CurrState;
            CurrState = NextState[CurrState][NextEvent.Event];
            if (PrevState == CurrState)
                FatalErr("Event %d didn't cause a state change from "
                        "state %02Xh\n", NextEvent.Event, PrevState);
            ProcessState(PrevState);
        }
        else if (NextEvent.Event == EVENT_EXIT)
            break;
        else if (NextEvent.Event == EVENT_UNUSED_KEY)
            UnusedKey(&NextEvent);
        else
            FatalErr("GetEvent() returned an invalid event "
                    "code: %d\n", NextEvent.Event);
    }
}
```

`EventLoop()` loops continuously, calling `GetEvent()` each time through the loop to retrieve the next event in the event queue. `GetEvent()` just waits for an event to occur if the queue is empty; this is where the simulation program will spend most of its time. The event structure filled in by `GetEvent()` has the following contents:

```
//
// UPS event queue entry
//
typedef struct _UPS_EVENT {
    struct _UPS_EVENT *pNext;   // next event in queue
    int    Event;               // event that occurred
    DWORD  ControlKeyState;     // only for UNUSED_KEY event
    WORD   VirtualKeyCode;      // only for UNUSED_KEY event
    CHAR   AsciiChar;           // only for UNUSED_KEY event
} UPS_EVENT;
```

and the `Event` member of the structure can assume the following values:

```
//
// Events that can occur to change the system state.  In this
// program, all events are simulated by the user pressing a key.
// These event values are used to index the next state table.
//
#define EVENT_POWER   0        // power on/off key pressed
#define EVENT_LOAD    1        // load present/absent key pressed
#define EVENT_AC      2        // AC good/bad key pressed
#define NEVENTS       3        // number of possible events


//
// Events that don't change the system state, but which
// require some action.
//
#define EVENT_EXIT        -1   // exit the program
#define EVENT_TIMER       -2   // timer event signaled every 500 ms.
#define EVENT_UNUSED_KEY  -3   // unused key pressed
```

Notice that events are divided into two categories. Positive events can change the system state; negative events don't change the state of the system but do require that the UPS take some kind of action. For positive events, the event loop looks up the next state in the state transition table, and then calls `ProcessState()` to take any action required by the state change. For an exit event, the code breaks out of the loop to return to the `main()` routine. When a timer event occurs, `ProcessTimers()` is called to perform any time-dependent actions. If an unused keystroke occurs, `UnusedKey()` is called to display an error message in the status window and beep the speaker. If anything unexpected happens, `FatalErr()` is called to print an error message and terminate the program. As we noted previously, in a real UPS (and in the version of the UPS simulation you encounter in Chapter 20, "C++ Exceptions and Structured Exceptions"), the `FatalErr()` routine would restart the UPS to ensure uninterrupted power to the load.

In this simulation, all `ProcessState()` has to do is update the display. (A real UPS would need to control external hardware such as switches and lights in response to a state change.) `ProcessState()` changes the color and text on each window that has changed state, and updates the status window to the new UPS status. The following code fragment, for the AC Power window, shows the calls `ProcessState()` makes to the windowing subsystem to update the display:

```
//
// For any components of the system state which have changed,
// update the display and do any other necessary processing.
//
    ChangedStates = PrevState ^ CurrState;
```

```
    if (ChangedStates & STATE_POWER_ON)
    {
        ClearWindow(hPowerWin);
        if (CurrState & STATE_POWER_ON)
        {
            SetWindowColors(hPowerWin, WH_ON_BLUE, BLK_ON_YEL);
            WriteWindowText(hPowerWin, "\n        On");
        }
        else
        {
            SetWindowColors(hPowerWin, WH_ON_BLUE, WH_ON_BLK);
            WriteWindowText(hPowerWin, "\n        Off");
        }
    }
```

If the state of AC power has changed, `ProcessState()` clears the AC Power window and then sets the window colors and text to reflect the new state.

`ProcessTimers()` performs little processing in this version of the UPS project. The only time-dependent operation in this simulation is the blinking of the background on the AC Power window that is performed (to alert the user) when the AC power is bad and the UPS is operating on battery:

```
//
// This function is called when a timer event occurs (every 500 ms.)
// to process any time-dependent display or state changes.
//
void ProcessTimers(void)
{
    if (CurrState & STATE_AC_BAD)
    {
//
// AC is bad.  Toggle the AC window background between black and red.
//
        if (fRedACBad)
        {
            SetWindowColors(hACWin, WH_ON_BLUE, WH_ON_BLK);
            fRedACBad = FALSE;
        }
        else
        {
            SetWindowColors(hACWin, WH_ON_BLUE, WH_ON_RED);
            fRedACBad = TRUE;
        }
    }
    return;
}
```

If the AC power is good, `ProcessTimers()` returns immediately without doing anything. If AC power is bad, the background color on the AC Power window is toggled.

The other responsibility of the event subsystem is maintaining a queue of events that have occurred. A queue is needed so that if two (or more) events occur in quick succession, they can be queued for processing as they are received. This allows the subsystem generating the event to hand the event off and go back to its duties without waiting for the event subsystem to be ready to process the event. You already looked at the prototype for `AddEvent()`, the interface function for adding events to the queue. The event subsystem includes a corresponding function, `GetEvent()`, for removing events from the queue. `GetEvent()` is not an interface function because it's used only by the event subsystem itself; no other subsystem needs to consume events. Because events are generated when hardware interrupts occur, we examine the code for `AddEvent()` and `GetEvent()` in Chapter 9, "Interrupts."

The `KEY.C` file is the source code for the key processing subsystem, which consists of the initialization and shutdown routines specific to that subsystem, as well as the keyboard interrupt callback routine. Similarly, the `TIMER.C` file is the source code for the timer subsystem's initialization and shutdown routines and the timer interrupt callback routine. You look at the keyboard code in Chapter 9, "Interrupts," and the timer code in Chapter 10, "Timers."

The windowing subsystem is shared with the POS project and was described in Chapters 5 and 6; its source code is found in the `\ETSLITE\PROJECTS\UTILS\WINSYS.C` directory.

SUMMARY

This wraps up our overview of the second project, a simulation of a bare-bones UPS. In the next chapter, we discuss interrupts in embedded systems and show how the driver callbacks used in the project give your application high-level control over some of the more common interrupts such as keyboard I/O and timer interrupts. Then in Chapter 10, "Timers," you look closely at the different types of hardware and software timers used in embedded systems and examine the timer code in the UPS project.

9

Interrupts

I n previous chapters, we discussed various input mechanisms used in embedded systems and how a system must respond, often in real time, to the input it receives through one of these devices. Interrupts, the subject of this chapter, enable a system to respond instantaneously to the push of a button or the press of a key. An interrupt is a request to the CPU for service; it is also a way to pass control from one area of the system to another.

When writing programs for a desktop system, you usually don't think about interrupts because the system uses a standard set of devices and the device drivers included with the operating system handle all interrupt processing. When writing embedded applications, however, you must understand how interrupts work because your system often includes one or more pieces of special-purpose hardware. You usually have to write a device driver from scratch or adapt a generic device driver. For most hardware devices, you use interrupts to get the attention of the CPU instead of requiring the CPU to periodically poll the device to see whether it needs servicing. Why? Using interrupts instead of polling yields faster response times and lower overhead. So as a developer of embedded systems, you need to understand how interrupts work and how to write reliable and efficient interrupt handlers.

The three kinds, or categories, of interrupts are hardware interrupts, software interrupts, and exceptions. The terms *hardware interrupt* and *interrupt* are often used synonymously. In a nutshell, a hardware interrupt is a signal generated by a peripheral device and sent to the CPU. This signal tells the CPU that something has happened that the CPU ought to know about. In turn, the CPU executes an interrupt service routine (ISR), which takes action in response to the interrupt. Each interrupt has a corresponding ISR.

A device doesn't have to be managed by a hardware interrupt. You can connect a device to the CPU and program the CPU to poll the device. In other words, write a tight loop that repeatedly checks the device to see whether its status has changed. When the device's status does change, the CPU responds appropriately; otherwise, the loop checks the device again.

Using interrupts, however, is usually more efficient than polling. In an interrupt-driven arrangement, the CPU turns its attention to the device only when required. In this way, the CPU's computing resources can be used to perform other tasks — or conserved — when the CPU is not servicing the interrupt. In some situations, using interrupts allows the designer to build a system that goes to sleep when no devices need servicing. Such systems can be used in battery-powered devices. The CPU, when not responding to an interrupt, goes into a low-power mode and thereby extends battery life.

A *software interrupt* is similar to a hardware interrupt in that it is a request to the CPU for service, and it causes one code module to pass control to another. The two interrupts are similar from the CPU's point of view, too. The CPU responds to both hardware and software interrupts by executing an ISR. The difference between hardware and software interrupts is the trigger mechanism. The trigger of a hardware interrupt is an electrical signal from an external device. The trigger of a software interrupt is the execution of a machine-language instruction.

Note: Different processors have different mnemonics for the software interrupt instruction. On the 80x86 processor, for example, the software interrupt instruction is the INT instruction. On the 68000-processor family, it's the TRAP instruction. Some processors don't even have software interrupt instructions.

A software interrupt is unlike a hardware interrupt in that its execution is planned — it's an instruction that the programmer deliberately wrote into the software at a specific point. By contrast, a hardware interrupt takes place asynchronously. Because a hardware interrupt comes from outside the CPU, its execution is an unplanned event. For example, there's no telling when you'll press the next key on the keyboard and generate a keyboard interrupt.

The third type of interrupt is an exception. An *exception* (often called a *processor exception*) is an interrupt that is internal to the CPU and triggered by a software program's attempt to perform an unexpected or illegal operation. As with hardware and software interrupts, exceptions cause a transfer of control, and the CPU responds to the exception by executing an ISR.

You've already seen an exception in action, back in Chapter 4, "Debugging." Remember the DIVBUG program? Its bug was an attempted division by zero, which generates a processor exception. A program can cause an exception in other ways, as you see later in the chapter.

All three interrupt flavors cause the CPU to jump (transfer execution) to a known location and then execute an ISR. The CPU transfers execution to an ISR in much the same way that it calls a subroutine. When the CPU executes a subroutine call instruction, it first pushes the return location onto the stack. When the subroutine is finished, it issues a return statement that pops the stack into the instruction pointer and returns control to the instruction following the call location. When the CPU invokes an ISR, the return location is placed on the stack. As a consequence, the ISR can return to the code that was executing when the interrupt occurred.

This capability — to return to the code that was interrupted after processing the interrupt — is important, particularly for hardware interrupts and exceptions, which occur outside the program's control. Remember that a hardware interrupt is asynchronous. The CPU can be in the middle of doing. . . well . . . anything when a hardware interrupt happens. Because an ISR returns control to whatever code was executing when the interrupt occurred, however, the interruption is not a problem. The interrupted code continues with whatever task it was performing, unaware that the interrupt ever occurred. Exceptions are similarly unexpected. This subroutine quality of an ISR enables it to clean up whatever conditions caused the exception, and then return control to the instruction following the offending instruction. The executing program is unaware that the exception ISR stepped in, corrected things, and then bowed out.

Some exceptions can be severe enough that they are beyond recovery, and the current application must be aborted. An attempted division-by-zero exception might be deemed fatal, for example, in a missile launch initialization sequence. But even in that circumstance, the fact that an ISR acts like a subroutine is useful. Here's why: Because the CPU pushes the return location on the stack, the exception-handling ISR can inspect the stack to locate the instruction that caused the exception in the first place. Then the ISR can examine that instruction and make an informed decision as to whether or not the application must be stopped — perhaps even relaying information to the user or operator describing why the application was halted.

As a developer of embedded systems, you're unlikely to be called on to write software interrupts or exception handlers, unless you're writing an operating system or a debugger. But you are likely to encounter hardware interrupts. For example, suppose your embedded system includes a proprietary piece of hardware that must interrupt the processor occasionally. You have to write a device driver for your hardware that includes an ISR to respond to the hardware interrupt. More commonly, perhaps your system incorporates a chip (such as an Ethernet chip) or a board (such as a disk controller) that uses hardware interrupts. The chip or board manufacturer provides a sample interrupt handler written for some other hardware and operating system platform. Your job is to port this sample code to your own embedded system. To do that successfully, you need to understand the material presented in this chapter.

HOW INTERRUPTS WORK

Now that we've briefly described the different kinds of interrupts, let's look at how interrupts work and what each is suited for.

HARDWARE INTERRUPTS

Almost all processors have at least one pin designated as an interrupt input pin. Similarly, many peripheral device controller chips have a pin designated as an interrupt output pin. Connect one to the other, and when something occurs on the peripheral device, its controller chip informs the processor by generating a hardware interrupt. Figure 9-1 shows the hardware connection for a simple system consisting of a single peripheral controller that generates an interrupt to the CPU. The interrupt request line connects the interrupt output pin on the controller to the interrupt input pin on the CPU.

When an event occurs on the hardware device managed by the peripheral controller, the controller sends a signal down the interrupt request line to the CPU. The controller is requesting service from the CPU. The CPU responds by transferring control to an ISR, which services the request by reading data from or writing data to the peripheral controller through the data bus.

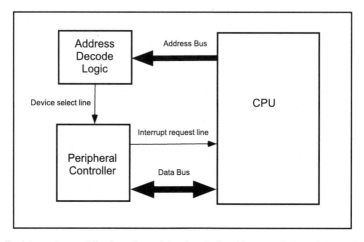

Figure 9-1: The interrupt request line from the peripheral controller chip connects to an interrupt input pin on the CPU. When the controller needs servicing from the CPU, the controller sends a signal down the interrupt request line. In response, the CPU transfers control to an ISR that executes and, through the data bus, reads data from the peripheral controller, or writes data to the peripheral controller, or both. When the CPU reads data from (or writes data to) the peripheral controller chip, the CPU first places the controller's address on the address bus. The decode logic interprets that address and enables I/O to the controller through the device select line.

Here's an example. Suppose you have a keyboard controller chip designed to connect to a standard keyboard, just like the one you use on your desktop system. You connect the controller chip's interrupt output pin to the CPU's interrupt input pin. When someone presses a key on the keyboard, the controller chip reads the key value and stores it in an internal register. The controller then sends an interrupt to the CPU, which transfers control to a keyboard-handling ISR. The ISR reads the key value from the controller's register by means of the data bus, and stores the key value in a keystroke buffer maintained by the keyboard device driver. Application programs read a user's key input using an operating system call that queries the keyboard device driver.

This one-peripheral controller design is sufficient for very small systems. However, it's rare for a computer system to have only a single peripheral device attached. Most CPUs at work today cope with multiple peripheral devices and, therefore, multiple controllers. You can build a system to handle multiple controllers in two ways: use a processor that has multiple interrupt input pins or include an interrupt controller chip in your design.

A processor with multiple interrupt input pins replicates the hardware connection depicted in Figure 9-1. That is, the interrupt output pin of each peripheral controller is connected to a separate interrupt input pin on the CPU. When the CPU receives an interrupt request on any one of its interrupt input pins, the CPU transfers control to the associated ISR that, in turn, reads data from or writes data to the peripheral controller using the data bus. The CPU transfers control to the corresponding ISR using a process known as *vectoring*. We describe interrupt vectors shortly.

An interrupt controller chip, on the other hand, assists a CPU by doing the work required to handle multiple peripheral controllers. Figure 9-2 illustrates a design using an external interrupt controller. The interrupt output pins of the peripheral controller chips are connected to interrupt input pins on an interrupt controller chip. The interrupt controller accommodates multiple interrupts, usually in a power of 2. A typical interrupt controller chip might support 8 or 16 peripheral devices.

The interrupt controller chip is, in turn, connected to the processor's interrupt input pin and data bus. When an interrupt triggered by one of the peripheral devices arrives at the interrupt controller, the interrupt controller interrupts the CPU. The CPU completes its current instruction and then acknowledges the receipt of the interrupt by sending a signal down the interrupt acknowledge line. In response to the acknowledgement, the interrupt controller

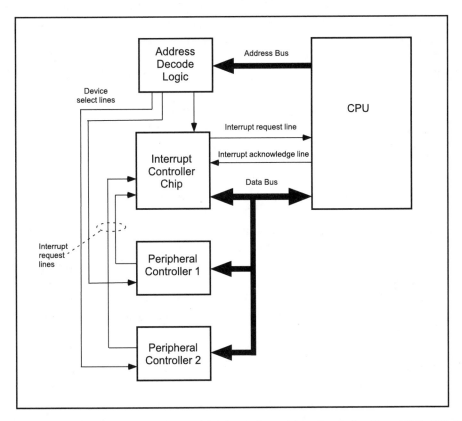

Figure 9-2: In systems with more than one peripheral controller, an interrupt controller chip assists the CPU. On some systems, the interrupt controller chip is integrated onto the CPU. The interrupt request lines from the peripheral controllers go to the interrupt controller chip. The interrupt controller chip acts as a kind of demultiplexor, intelligently combining two or more interrupt request lines into one interrupt request line that goes to the CPU.

places on the CPU's data bus a binary value that tells the CPU which interrupt needs servicing. This value is the interrupt number.

Most interrupt controllers can be cascaded in master-slave fashion. In other words, you can designate one master controller and one or more slave controllers. One interrupt input is used on the master controller for each cascaded slave controller. When an interrupt arrives at one of the slave interrupt controllers, the slave interrupts the master controller, which in turn interrupts the CPU. In this way, the interrupt hardware is extensible. A designer can build a system using as many interrupt controllers — and therefore supporting as many devices — as required.

Priorities

The presence of multiple hardware devices leads to a question: How does a system respond when more than one device generates an interrupt at the same time? The answer is: by processing interrupts with the highest priority levels first.

Each hardware interrupt is assigned a unique priority. On CPUs with multiple interrupt input pins, the priority of each interrupt is usually hardwired into the processor. For systems that use an interrupt controller, whether the controller is on-chip or external, the priorities are programmed into the controller by software, usually when the system is initialized. When two or more interrupts happen simultaneously, one will have the highest priority. That interrupt will be serviced first. The lower-priority interrupts are put on hold and dealt with in order of priority.

In systems that support multiple interrupts, something must keep track of pending interrupts — lower-priority interrupts that are waiting for higher-priority interrupts to be serviced. CPUs with multiple interrupt input pins have the equivalent of an on-chip interrupt controller, and it is the job of the on-chip controller to keep track of pending interrupts. On systems that have an external interrupt controller, the interrupt controller keeps track of pending interrupts, and presents them to the CPU in order of their priority.

Interrupt priorities also play a role while an interrupt is being serviced. That is, a higher-priority interrupt can interrupt the execution of a lower-priority interrupt's ISR. For example, suppose you have a simple application in which you've designated interrupt A as having a higher priority than interrupt B. During your application's execution, interrupt B occurs, thus causing ISR B to be executed. However, before ISR B completes execution, interrupt A occurs. Because you've set interrupt A's priority as higher than B's, the interrupt controller passes interrupt A along to the CPU immediately, rather than waiting until ISR B completes. In turn, the CPU puts ISR B on hold and runs ISR A; ISR A is given priority over ISR B. When ISR A completes, the CPU returns to and finishes executing ISR B.

Had the priorities been reversed — had interrupt B had a higher priority than interrupt A — interrupt A would have had to wait. The CPU would not have been informed that interrupt A occurred until ISR B completed.

You may be wondering how the interrupt controller knows when the ISR for a particular interrupt has finished executing. In most systems, the interrupt controller (whether it is external or integrated on the CPU) responds to a given interrupt by — among other things — setting a bit in an internal register to indicate that the interrupt is being serviced. Consequently, the interrupt controller knows when a particular ISR is active. Then, at the conclusion of processing the interrupt, the ISR executes an instruction that tells the interrupt controller that the ISR has completed. The interrupt controller clears the appropriate bit in the internal register, marking the conclusion of the ISR. This allows the interrupt controller to properly manage interrupt priorities.

Interrupt Vectors

Earlier we said that when the CPU receives an interrupt, it executes the appropriate ISR. This happens regardless of whether a peripheral device is connected directly to a pin on the CPU or to an on-chip or external interrupt controller. But how does the CPU know which ISR to run? The answer is that every interrupt has a number. When the CPU acknowledges the interrupt request, the interrupt controller places the interrupt number on the data bus. The CPU uses this interrupt number to vector to the correct ISR. Let's examine the process.

Figure 9-3 illustrates what happens when an interrupt first arrives: the CPU saves the current instruction pointer register and flags register on the stack.

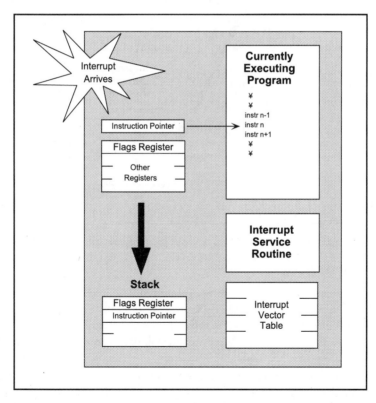

Figure 9-3: An interrupt arrives while the CPU is executing instruction n. In response to the interrupt, the system saves the current instruction pointer and flags register on the stack. Note that the system will complete its execution of the current instruction before dealing with the interrupt.

Then, as shown in Figure 9-4, the CPU uses the interrupt number to determine an offset into the interrupt vector table. The *interrupt vector table* is a collection of pointers to ISRs. Each pointer corresponds to one of the interrupt numbers that the processor supports. Also, each entry in the table is a fixed number of bytes long, just long enough to store a full memory address.

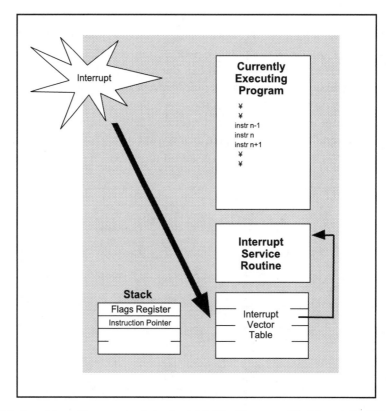

Figure 9-4: Every interrupt has a number that uniquely identifies the source of the interrupt. The CPU, possibly with an interrupt controller chip, uses the interrupt number to determine an offset into the interrupt vector table, which is a collection of pointers to interrupt service routines.

The CPU loads the instruction pointer register with the offset to the ISR for a particular interrupt, as shown in Figure 9-5, and the ISR begins executing. Before the ISR services the interrupt, it saves on the stack any CPU registers it will use. These are shown in the diagram as "Other Registers."

When the ISR is finished, it restores the registers from the stack, as shown in Figure 9-6. It also restores the flags register and instruction pointer register. This last operation returns control to the interrupted program. The act of the CPU transferring control to one of the memory locations that contains an ISR is often called *vectoring*.

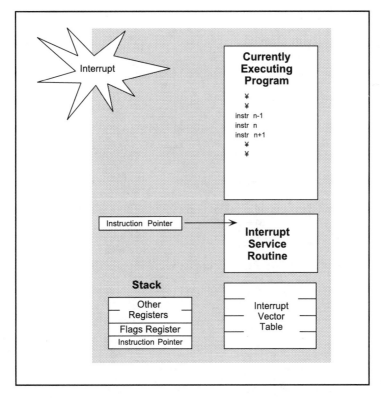

Figure 9-5: The CPU loads the instruction pointer with the offset to the ISR for this particular interrupt. The ISR begins executing. Notice that the ISR should, as one of its first jobs, save any CPU registers that it will use. These will be the "other registers" that the program was using at the time it was interrupted.

Some processors use a jump table in place of an interrupt vector table. Each entry in the table is just long enough to allow the storage of a jump instruction. Instead of looking up the vector in the table, the processor jumps to a table entry. Because the table entry is itself a jump instruction, the CPU literally hopscotches to the ISR.

Maskable Interrupts

Some hardware interrupts can be *masked,* or disabled; that is, the CPU is told to ignore them. This is usually accomplished in one of two ways. With most processors, executing a special machine instruction tells the CPU to disable all maskable interrupts; this is typically referred to as disabling interrupts. In addition, the interrupt controller normally has the capability to mask individual — rather than all — interrupts.

When should you disable interrupts? When the CPU must perform an activity that must not be interrupted. This is sometimes referred to as an *atomic activity.* A good example of such an activity is when the operating system needs to update system data structures, such as the page tables used to implement virtual memory or the queues of blocked tasks maintained by the scheduler in a multitasking system. If an interrupt occurred while one of these critical

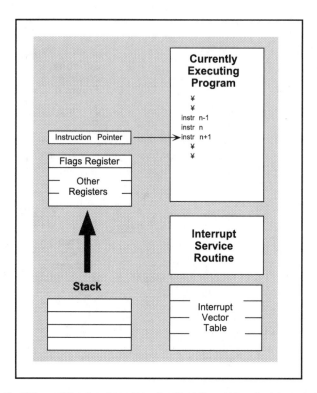

Figure 9-6: When the ISR completes, it restores (from the stack) the registers the interrupted program was using. It also restores the flags register and instruction pointer. This last operation effectively returns control to the interrupted program, which is unaware that it has been interrupted because all the registers it was using have been returned to their original state. Note that the popping of the flags and instruction pointer is usually handled by a single instruction — the last one the ISR executes.

data structures was in a partially updated state — for example, with a dangling pointer or an out-of-date entry — the ISR might inadvertently execute some code that references the invalid data structure, causing a system crash. Disabling interrupts for the duration of the code that modifies the data structure protects against such crashes.

When should you mask a specific interrupt, rather than disabling all interrupts? One reason to mask a specific interrupt is if it is not in use, to prevent any possibility of a spurious interrupt occurring. Most operating systems mask any unused interrupts during initialization. An ISR might also mask its corresponding interrupt to prevent reentrancy, and then unmask it when it has completed processing. This has the advantage of disabling only that specific interrupt, while allowing other interrupts to be processed. (ISR reentrancy and strategies to prevent being reentered are covered in more detail later in this chapter.)

One final note: processors that support maskable interrupts will usually include a single interrupt input pin defined as a non-maskable interrupt pin. (The acronym NMI is almost always used to refer to this interrupt.) The processor cannot be programmed to ignore the NMI input. System designers connect the NMI pin to some device that — if it interrupts the processor — must not be ignored under any circumstances. For example, in many processors, the NMI input pin is attached to the circuitry that detects memory parity errors. This makes perfect sense: the occurrence of a memory parity error indicates memory failure. Should this happen, the NMI's ISR could alert the operator and then halt the system.

SOFTWARE INTERRUPTS

As we said previously, a software interrupt works like a hardware interrupt, only it isn't triggered by some external device. Instead, a software interrupt is generated by the CPU itself when it executes a specific instruction in either application or system code. Another difference is that software interrupts, unlike hardware interrupts, cannot be disabled on most processors.

It's also interesting to compare a software interrupt to a procedure call. When a software interrupt is issued, the corresponding ISR executes and then returns to the code that issued the interrupt. This is similar to a procedure executing and then returning to the code that called it. However, software interrupts and procedure calls have three differences. As you saw previously, an interrupt automatically preserves the processor flags; that doesn't happen in a procedure call. Second, to invoke an ISR, you need to know only its interrupt number, not the memory location of the ISR; a procedure call instruction includes the memory address of the procedure. Finally, on processors that support privileged (or system) and unprivileged (or application) modes of execution, an interrupt can automatically switch the CPU to a more privileged level, possibly also switching to a secure system-level stack. Normal procedure calls can't call across privilege levels, although often a special procedure call instruction is provided specifically for calling from application code to system code.

These differences between software interrupts and procedure calls provide clues to the utility of software interrupts. The capability to call something without knowing its address and to switch privilege levels make software interrupts ideal for calling from application level code to system code. Hence, some popular operating systems use a software interrupt as the gateway into operating system services. If you've ever written any substantial MS-DOS programs, you are probably familiar with the INT 21H instruction, which is the software interrupt that calls into the high-level MS-DOS system services. Similarly, the 68000-version of Apple's Mac OS used a TRAP instruction to call into the operating system.

Some operating systems (such as Windows) support dynamic, or load-time, linking, which makes it possible for programs to directly call procedures in other programs or in the operating system. On systems providing dynamic linking capabilities, software interrupts aren't used for system calls.

Debuggers also use software interrupts, usually a specific reserved interrupt number, to implement debugger breakpoints. Because the interrupt is on a special, reserved interrupt number, the software interrupt can be generated by a 1-byte (no need for a second byte to specify the number of the interrupt) instruction opcode often called a *breakpoint instruction*. Debuggers use this breakpoint instruction to overwrite instructions in a program being debugged. When the breakpoint instruction is executed, control vectors to the ISR that the debugger has installed, allowing the debugger to stop the application and pop up a debugger window. Because the breakpoint instruction is only 1 byte long, inserting a breakpoint can never overwrite more than one opcode in the application program.

Finally, application programs sometimes use software interrupts to provide services to or communicate with other applications. Application A, for example, installs an ISR on a particular agreed-upon interrupt number. Application B can then call into application A by issuing that software interrupt, without needing to know the memory address of any procedures in application A. Because most multitasking operating systems provide other, better ways for interapplication communications, software interrupts are not frequently used. But it does deserve mention because it was widely used in the single-tasking MS-DOS by the class of programs known as terminate-and-stay-resident (TSR) programs, which installed themselves in memory and then provided services to subsequently run applications.

EXCEPTIONS

An *exception* is a processor-triggered interrupt that indicates something bad has happened, or that a condition that needs immediate attention has occurred. You can think of it as a kind of asynchronous software interrupt; it's triggered by software, but it's unintentional — that is, the software doesn't know beforehand that a particular instruction will cause an exception to occur. As with hardware and software interrupts, an exception causes the CPU to transfer control to the appropriate ISR. Exceptions are given higher priority than either hardware or software interrupts and can't be masked.

As we said previously, you've already seen an exception in action with the DIVBUG program back in Chapter 4, "Debugging." In that situation, the processor triggered an exception when an instruction attempted division by zero. The variety of exceptions recognized and responded to by a CPU varies from processor to processor. Example situations that can raise an exception include the attempt to execute an unknown instruction, a reference to a virtual memory page that is currently swapped to disk, the attempt to execute a math coprocessor instruction when no math coprocessor is available, and the execution of an instruction that causes numeric overflow. Notice that some of these conditions are due to program errors, and some signal events that need immediate attention. For example, in an operating system with virtual memory support, the system handles a page fault by swapping in the referenced page and allowing the program to continue. Similarly, if the system includes a floating-point emulator rather than a hardware coprocessor, the emulator would use the math coprocessor exception to gain control and emulate floating-point instructions. In other circumstances, these same exceptions might indicate error conditions: for example, a reference to an unmapped page, or executing a floating-point instruction on a system with neither a math coprocessor nor an emulator.

Hardwired into a processor is circuitry that recognizes exceptions. When an exception occurs, the CPU transfers control to the specific ISR associated with that exception. Therefore, in response to a division-by-zero exception, the processor executes one ISR; in response to the attempt to execute an unknown instruction, the processor executes a different ISR; and so on. (The situation is analogous to the CPU vectoring to a specific ISR in response to its associated hardware interrupt number.)

Another example of an exception can occur in a protected operating system. An operating system is said to be *protected* if applications running on that OS are loaded into specific memory regions, and the CPU includes mechanisms that allow the OS to set boundaries on those applications. In short, if an application attempts to read or write to a memory address outside the bounds the OS has set for it, that attempt triggers an exception. The operating system can then take action to terminate the application (because such an attempt invariably indicates a fatal bug in the application), and do so in a way that protects other applications that may be running concurrently.

An operating system always installs ISRs for all possible processor exceptions. When an exception occurs, the OS will either terminate the application or take some action (such as swapping a referenced virtual page into memory) that allows the application to continue to execute.

A debugger also installs ISRs for all processor exceptions. When an exception occurs in a program being debugged, the debugger pops up and allows you to examine memory and registers to determine the reason the program caused an exception.

In Chapter 20, "C++ Exceptions and Structured Exceptions," we cover exceptions in greater detail and show you how to use some of the Win32 structured exception-handling capability provided by ETS Kernel, which enables you to easily handle exceptions in an application program.

ISR FUNDAMENTALS

When writing an interrupt service routine, the most important fact to keep in mind is that interrupts are asynchronous. An interrupt can happen at any time; you can't predict what program will be running, or where that program will be in its execution, when the interrupt occurs. That program will get put on hold while the processor invokes the ISR.

Because you can't know the state of the system when an interrupt occurs, you need to write an ISR so that it first saves the contents of all the registers it will be using, and then restores those registers before exiting. Otherwise, when the ISR completes and returns control, the interrupted application — which has no idea it had been interrupted — will find oddball values sitting in CPU registers. Your system will start to crash in strange ways that can't be replicated, because each time your ISR runs and corrupts the registers, a different section of application code will be executing, and the resulting crash scenario will be unique.

To be more precise, an ISR must preserve the CPU state; when the ISR returns, it must look to the interrupted code as if nothing has occurred. On most processors, the *CPU state* consists of general registers and the processor flags. Usually, the processor flags are saved on the stack along with the address of the interrupted code, and the return-from-interrupt instruction executed at the end of the ISR automatically restores the flags and returns control to the interrupted application. On processors with privilege levels or a system/user mode, a stack switch may also automatically occur as part of the process of entering and returning from an ISR. For the processor you have selected, make sure you understand what constitutes the CPU state, and whether ISRs must preserve anything in addition to general registers.

In addition to preserving the CPU state, an ISR must carefully control access to shared resources. A *shared resource* is a hardware device or memory location that can be accessed by different applications (or by different routines in the same application). If the programmer isn't careful, one piece of code might step on the toes of another. Access to a shared resource must be coordinated so that the integrity of the resource is maintained. Otherwise, data may be incorrectly read from or written to the resource, with erroneous results.

Usually, a shared resource is used by both the ISR and the application to communicate with each other. The most common example of a shared resource is a memory buffer. One piece of code generates data, and the other piece consumes the data. If both the ISR and the application attempt to update the data structures simultaneously, the outcome is typically a corrupted data structure, resulting in either lost data or a system crash.

Access to resources shared with an ISR is usually controlled by disabling interrupts in the application around any code that reads or writes to the resource. Other synchronization mechanisms, such as critical sections, semaphores, and so on, can't be used in an ISR because it's usually not possible for an ISR to block indefinitely, waiting for a resource to be available. An ISR must complete its processing and return quickly, to keep data from backing up and potentially overflowing on the interrupting device. (We cover synchronization objects in detail in Chapter 12, "Multitasking.") By disabling interrupts, the application ensures that the ISR cannot run until the application has completed accessing the resource. In the code for the ISR, you don't need to do anything to prevent the application from running; on most systems, an ISR can be preempted only by another ISR.

Be careful when disabling interrupts, however. When you disable interrupts, you close down the system's capability to receive stimuli from the outside world. System responsiveness can be affected. Keep critical sections of code in which you disable interrupts as short as possible. We discuss this process in more detail in the "Interrupt Latency" section, later in this chapter. If you absolutely must access a shared resource for a long time, rather than disabling all interrupts, you should mask only the interrupt for the particular ISR that shares the resource, to allow the rest of the system to respond to external events.

Because each ISR handles interrupts from a different device, it's unusual to share resources between ISRs. If your system does share resources between two or more ISRs, however, the lower-priority ISR will need to disable interrupts whenever it accesses the shared resource to prevent the higher-priority ISR from running. As with interrupt disabling in application code, you'll want to keep any such critical sections as short as possible to avoid affecting system response times adversely. As you'll see in the upcoming "Reentrancy" and "Interrupt Latency" sections, it's desirable for an ISR to reenable interrupts as soon as it begins to run, and leave them enabled during most of (ideally, all) its execution.

Another desirable characteristic of an ISR is brevity. An ISR should do only what it needs to do, and no more, for several reasons. If the ISR takes too long to process an interrupt, the external device may be kept waiting too long before its next interrupt is serviced, with a resulting loss of data. The responsiveness of currently running applications may suffer if an ISR takes too long to execute. Because ISRs are difficult to debug effectively, keeping them short will simplify the job of making the system reliable. And in a multitasking system, ISRs can't use the synchronization primitives (which we describe in Chapter 12, "Multitasking") that make sharing resources easy, so you want to limit the number of resources accessed by the ISR. Let's illustrate this with an extreme example of how *not* to write an ISR.

Assume that your system includes an ISR that reads data from a handheld data collection device attached to a host computer through the serial port. The data coming in represents temperature values. An application reads the temperature data and displays it in the form of a bar graph on the screen. Should you write the ISR so that when it fetches a byte from the serial port, it converts that byte to a numerical value corresponding to the temperature, and then draws the appropriately sized bar graph on the screen?

No. The data conversion and graph drawing should be performed elsewhere in the application. If the ISR is spending its time converting numbers and drawing graphs, it might not be able to keep up with the flow of data coming in from the serial port. Better to put the incoming data on a queue. The ISR fills the queue with data at one end, and the higher-level application takes the data off the queue at the other end, converts the data, and graphs it.

Finally, bugs in ISRs can be difficult to find. Because of the asynchronous nature of ISRs, a bug rarely manifests itself in the same way twice — the crash or corrupted data that is the result of the bug often depends on what was running when the interrupt occurred. Bugs in ISRs tend to occur only under specific timing conditions, so sometimes the system will run for minutes, hours, or days, and then suddenly crash inexplicably. Because the ISR may run successfully thousands (or hundreds of thousands) of times before the bug occurs, setting a breakpoint in the relevant invocation of the ISR can be next to impossible. And even if you do successfully set a breakpoint in the ISR, stepping the code may change the timing of the interaction between the CPU and external devices such that the bug doesn't occur.

So what do you do? Most importantly, program defensively. Spend a lot of time reviewing the code you write for the ISR to try to ferret out bugs during development. It's really worth the extra effort up front to avoid the frustration later of spending days chasing a single bug in an ISR. Writing short ISRs helps; it's easier to keep bugs out of a small piece of code than a large piece of code.

And when your system does start to crash in nonreproducible ways, stop and think before you start debugging. Keep track of the different ways it crashes and see whether you can discern a pattern. After you come up with a theory, try to prove or disprove the theory as efficiently as you can, so that you don't waste time following false leads. Sometimes you can simplify (or remove) a suspect ISR in an attempt to prove (or disprove) that it contains the problem. Often you may need to insert special debugging code that checks for a suspected buggy condition; then you can put a breakpoint on the code that runs when the condition occurs, and you won't hit the breakpoint when the ISR is operating correctly. Sometimes you can use an emulator or another hardware debugging aid that allows you to trigger on a known problem condition and then look backward in a trace buffer to see the last several hundred instructions that executed before the crash.

USING HIGH-LEVEL LANGUAGES

It's often desirable to write an ISR in a high-level language, such as C, for the same reasons you write applications in a high-level language: it's faster and easier, and the code is more understandable and maintainable. But several differences exist between writing a normal function in a high-level language and writing an ISR. An ISR must not have the standard function prologue and epilogue that the compiler normally inserts automatically. Instead, an ISR prologue must save the machine state, and the epilogue must restore the machine state, inform the interrupt controller that the ISR has completed, and execute the return-from-interrupt instruction. Finally, any assumptions the compiler makes about the machine state must be adhered to by the ISR. Compiler run-time initialization code often sets particular processor flags — and sometimes even one or more of the general registers — to specific values; the compiler assumes that those conditions will remain true to generate more optimized code. Depending on the processor and system architecture, the ISR may even need to switch stacks if the compiler makes the assumption that the stack is in the application's address space.

Very few compilers provide built-in support for writing an ISR directly in a high-level language. Usually, you have to write an assembly language wrapper function that saves the machine state, sets up the language assumptions, calls a high-level language function to do the work for the ISR, and then restores the machine state and returns from the interrupt. That may seem like a lot of work, but you usually have to do it only once; the same assembly language wrapper can often be used for all interrupts in the system. And many real-time operating systems provide APIs to install ISRs written in a high-level language (which means the OS vendor has written the assembly language wrapper for you).

REENTRANCY

Code that is *reentrant* can execute simultaneously in two or more contexts. Reentrant code is most familiar in multitasking systems, in which two or more processes or threads are executing simultaneously. We talk about reentrancy in Chapter 12, "Multitasking." But even in a single-tasking application, reentrancy is a consideration with ISRs because they occur asynchronously.

You should consider two types of reentrancy with ISRs:

- Functions that are shared by multiple ISRs, or by an ISR and the application, must be reentrant.

- An entire ISR may be reentrant.

Reentrant Functions

You'll most commonly encounter reentrancy in functions used by more than one ISR. For example, suppose you've written an ISR that calls function X. Later, you write another ISR that also calls function X. What happens if the first ISR executes, calls function X, but is then interrupted by the second ISR? Ultimately, function X will be called again — it will be reentered. (In a sense, two copies of function X are in play. One is inactive, having been placed on hold by the second interrupt; the other is active.)

For multiple ISRs to use one function, write the function so that it is reentrant. That is, write the function so that more than one ISR can call it simultaneously. If the function is simple enough — it accesses no hardware and calls no other functions — you can make it reentrant by using only local variables.

If, however, the function accesses data or hardware that is available globally (that is, accessible from other parts of the application or other applications running on the system), you must control the function's access to that data or hardware by carefully disabling interrupts around all code that uses global data or hardware. The *synchronization mechanisms* used by multitasking applications to resolve this problem (as you shall see in Chapter 12) are not normally available to interrupt handlers because they require that the code be able to block (stop running) until a resource is available. ISRs cannot block because of the requirement that they do their work and return quickly; when code blocks, the time until it runs again is unpredictable.

The concept of reentrancy can be confusing, so here's a simple example to illustrate what can go wrong when two ISRs call a function that isn't reentrant.

Suppose you have a routine that accesses a global memory location, and that location is being used as a counter. It counts the number of times hardware interrupts have occurred. Consequently, any hardware ISR that executes will call this routine to update that counter. To update the counter, the routine must read the memory location, increment it, and write it back out. If the routine is interrupted in the process of reading and incrementing the counter, it might miss a count. Suppose ISR A calls the routine. The routine reads the value of 3 from the location, and increments it to 4. But before ISR A writes it back out, ISR B interrupts and calls the routine. This second instance of the routine reads the value of 3, increments it, and writes a 4 back to memory. Then, when ISR A's instance of the routine resumes execution, it stores a 4 as well, instead of storing a 5.

The solution is to disable interrupts at the beginning of the routine that updates the counter, and restore the original interrupt state at the end of the routine. In addition, any code in the main application that uses the counter must disable interrupts around its use of the counter.

Figuring out whether all or part of an ISR must be reentrant requires a clear understanding of the entire system. You must determine whether the ISR accesses globally available data or hardware in such a way that, should the ISR itself be interrupted, the data or hardware *might* be in an inconsistent state from the perspective of the ISR. If so, you must either rewrite the ISR to use only local data or carefully disable interrupts around critical sections of code.

When you examine the interrupt code in the UPS project later in this chapter, you'll see an example of a reentrant function: the AddEvent() function, which is called by both the timer and keyboard ISRs.

Reentrant ISRs

An ISR is reentrant if, while the ISR is handling an interrupt, the same interrupt can occur again and the ISR can process the second occurrence of the interrupt before it has completed processing the first.

Software ISRs are often written to be reentrant. Consider the case of a multitasking OS that provides operating system services through a software interrupt mechanism. A reentrant ISR would be desirable because more than one task could call the OS at the same time.

Hardware ISRs, on the other hand, are almost never reentrant. Unlike a software ISR, a hardware ISR has to perform I/O with a peripheral device; to have two such operations being conducted simultaneously is an almost certain recipe for disaster.

A hardware ISR can prevent reentrancy by leaving interrupts disabled. But as noted previously, it's desirable to reenable interrupts to allow ISRs for other hardware interrupts to run. Therefore, an ISR usually protects itself from being reentered either by not telling the interrupt controller to allow more interrupts of that type until processing is complete or by programming the peripheral device to not issue any more interrupts until the ISR completes its processing.

Sometimes, to avoid the overhead of having a second interrupt occur immediately after completing processing of the first interrupt, hardware ISRs perform their processing in a loop. Each time through the loop, the ISR checks whether the peripheral wants to interrupt again. If no interrupt is pending, the ISR completes its processing by programming the device or the interrupt controller to allow interrupts again, and returns to the interrupted code. If the device has another interrupt pending, the ISR just loops back to the beginning of the routine and processes the second request immediately.

If, for some unusual reason, you need to write a reentrant hardware ISR, the same principles outlined for writing reentrant functions apply: protect access to global variables and hardware by carefully disabling interrupts around critical sections of code.

INTERRUPT LATENCY

Interrupt latency is the amount of time that elapses between the time a device requests an interrupt and the time the first instruction for the hardware ISR executes. The two components of interrupt latency are:

- The time it takes the CPU to recognize and process an interrupt request
- The dispatch time (if any) needed by the operating system before it transfers control to your ISR

The dispatch time in a real-time OS is normally a small, constant value. It's typically either zero, if your ISR is vectored to directly by the processor, or the amount of time required by the assembly language wrapper to save the machine state and set up the high-level language environment, if the OS allows you to install ISRs written in a high-level language. (By way of contrast, in a non-real-time OS such as Windows, dispatch time is not a constant value and can be quite large because, when an interrupt occurs, the OS may choose to do some unrelated bookkeeping task before it invokes your ISR.)

The time required for the CPU to begin processing an interrupt request is more variable and can become unacceptably large under certain circumstances if you're not careful. When an interrupt request is raised, the CPU might not acknowledge it for three reasons:

- If all interrupts are disabled.
- If the particular interrupt is masked.
- If a higher-priority ISR is executing (the interrupt controller typically masks all lower-priority interrupts until the higher-priority ISR completes).

If you're building a real-time system, one of your goals is to ensure that both the CPU response time and the OS dispatch time have upper bounds that are acceptably small.

All interrupts are normally disabled when an ISR is entered. It's important for your ISR to reenable interrupts as soon as possible so that the CPU can respond to other interrupt requests. Likewise, you should try to keep any critical sections of code that disable interrupts (inside shared reentrant functions, for example) as short as possible. If your system has strict real-time requirements, remember that your OS will also have critical sections with interrupts disabled (inside the scheduler, for example); insofar as you can, try to ensure that the real-time OS you select has reasonable upper limits on the length of time that interrupts can be disabled.

A specific interrupt is normally masked in the interrupt controller for the duration of the ISR, to protect against reentrancy. This is desirable, but you need to make sure the ISR completes its job as quickly as possible so that a second interrupt by the same device won't be unacceptably delayed.

With most interrupt controllers, all lower-priority interrupts may be masked for the duration of a higher-priority interrupt. This is usually desirable to ensure that higher-priority ISRs can run to completion without being interrupted by lower-priority interrupts. But again, make sure your ISR finishes quickly. When lower-priority interrupts are masked, not only additional interrupts by the same device, but also all interrupts by lower-priority devices, will have to wait. If a high-priority ISR runs too long, you may choose to acknowledge the interrupt to the interrupt controller (thus allowing interrupts by both lower-priority devices and additional interrupts by the interrupting device), but still prevent reentrancy by programming the device itself not to request another interrupt.

What if two or more devices request interrupts simultaneously? In this case, the interrupt controller selects the highest-priority device to interrupt the CPU first, and the length of time the other device(s) will have to wait is determined by the factors just discussed — namely, how long interrupts are disabled and how long the waiting interrupts are masked in the interrupt controller.

In the design of a real-time system, you should consider what your worst-case interrupt latency might be. Typically, it will occur when all possible interrupts in the system are requested almost simultaneously. For example, suppose your system has interrupts A, B, and C, with A being the highest-priority device and C the lowest. Your worst case for device A is where device C interrupts, then B, and then A. You have to look at the ISRs for B and C to see how long they leave interrupts disabled, to determine how long A will have to wait for its interrupt request to get processed. Similarly, for device C, the worst case is when all three devices interrupt simultaneously (because A and B, having a higher priority, are processed before C). In this case, you need to consider not only how long interrupts are disabled by the

ISRs for A and B, but also how long C is masked in the interrupt controller; C may have to wait for the ISRs for A and B to run to completion, even if interrupts are reenabled.

Another factor in worst-case latency may be the number of threads or processes in your system. The scheduler for the real-time OS normally needs to disable interrupts while it's processing lists of blocked or waiting threads, to protect the list structures from being corrupted if the scheduler is reentered. If the design of your system requires large numbers of threads or processes, you may need to perform some latency measurements to check that the scheduler isn't disabling interrupts for unacceptably long periods.

To summarize, in any real-time system with strict response time requirements, you should:

- Make sure your ISRs are as short as possible. Make the ISR do the minimum amount of work needed to allow the device to continue operating, and complete the work (processing data, for example) inside one of the application threads or processes.

- Keep the length of time interrupts are disabled, both inside ISRs and in the application, as short as possible.

- Try not to let any individual interrupt be masked in the interrupt controller for a long period of time.

- Choose device priorities carefully, remembering that interrupt latencies for lower-priority devices will typically be longer than those for higher-priority devices.

- Keep the number of threads or processes in your system from growing unreasonably large.

- Construct worst-case scenarios and do ballpark calculations on what the interrupt latencies will be in those situations. If you can, try to actually make those worst-case scenarios happen and then measure the latencies. The sooner you discover you have a problem, the more time you'll have to reengineer your software design or, in the worst case, redesign your hardware to use a faster processor.

CHAINING ISRS

When the same interrupt has two or more ISRs, you must chain the ISRs; that is, after the first ISR completes its processing, it must invoke the second ISR, and so on. The last ISR in the chain returns to the interrupted code in the application. If this chaining did not occur, only the last ISR installed would be run. Chaining interrupts is not normally required in an embedded system, which typically has a single, dedicated application and no need to install multiple ISRs for a single interrupt. However, embedded systems built around simple, single-tasking operating systems such as MS-DOS sometimes need to run multiple programs, and the problem of separate programs needing to hook the same interrupt does occur.

Usually, you need to worry about chaining ISRs only if your ISR is installed at the hardware level (vectored to directly by the processor when the interrupt occurs). If you use an OS service to install an interrupt handler, the OS should take care of ensuring that all installed interrupt handlers for a particular interrupt are invoked. (In other words, the OS does the chaining for you.) And for many devices, chaining isn't something you have to worry about; it doesn't make sense to have more than one ISR for a disk device, for example. But if you're writing an ISR for a device (such as a timer) for which more than one piece of code may want to process interrupts, your ISR must be capable of chaining to any previously installed ISRs.

Chaining ISRs is similar to returning to the originally interrupted code. You have to make sure the machine state is identical to what it was when the interrupt originally occurred. But instead of returning to the originally interrupted code, you jump to the entry point of the next ISR in the chain. When you chain to another ISR, you have to leave the interrupt context (the information needed to return to the originally interrupted code, usually kept on the stack) intact, so that the last ISR in the chain can complete normally. Usually, only the last ISR in the chain will unmask the interrupt in the interrupt controller to allow the device to interrupt again, and only the last ISR will do any programming or resetting of the device.

MULTITASKING CONSIDERATIONS

Finally, writing ISRs in a multithreading or multiprocessing environment involves additional requirements or considerations. We won't go into these in detail until Chapter 12, "Multitasking," because we need to use the multitasking concepts discussed in that chapter. For the moment, just bear in mind that you must take additional care writing your ISRs in a multitasking system.

INTERRUPTS ON THE PC ARCHITECTURE

Because ETS Kernel runs on PC hardware, let's examine that platform's support of interrupts. We focus on hardware interrupts, given their importance to the developer of embedded systems.

Processors in the x86 family can support up to 256 interrupts, and use an interrupt vector table as the means of associating each interrupt with the location of the ISR to handle it. In real mode (in which the processor executes as though it is an 8086), the interrupt vector table begins at memory location 0. Each vector table entry is 32 bits long and holds the address of an ISR.

In protected mode (in which ETS Kernel executes), the interrupt vector table is replaced by the analogous interrupt descriptor table (IDT), also containing 256 entries. The IDT can be located anywhere in memory; a dedicated CPU register called IDTR contains the address of the IDT. Each entry in the IDT contains an interrupt gate, a trap gate, or a task gate. Interrupt gates and trap gates contain the address of an ISR; the only difference between them is that interrupt gates disable interrupts before entering the ISR, and trap gates do not. Task gates save the CPU state and switch to a new CPU state before entering the ISR. Most x86 operating systems use interrupt gates for all IDT entries. Task gates are very rarely used, because they slow down processing of interrupts too much.

PC systems use an external interrupt controller chip, the 8259A. The 8259A has connections for up to 8 hardware interrupts, numbered IR0 – IR7. Multiple 8259As can be connected in cascading fashion to allow control of up to 64 hardware interrupts. The 8259A is connected to the CPU by means of the INTR (interrupt request) line.

A peripheral device connected to the 8259A can signal an interrupt by setting one of the 8259A's interrupt input pins from LOW to HIGH. This causes the 8259A to send an interrupt request signal to the CPU through INTR. The CPU responds with an interrupt acknowledge signal, INTA, and then expects the 8259A to place on the data bus a value between 0 and 255. That value is the interrupt number; each interrupt in the system is assigned a unique number. On the 80x86 processor, the interrupt number identifies the location in the interrupt vector table (or IDT, depending on whether the processor is executing in real or protected mode) that gives the location of the ISR associated with this hardware interrupt. The CPU transfers control to the ISR, which services the interrupt.

If more than one interrupt arrives at the interrupt controller at the same time, the 8259A can be programmed to prioritize interrupts; higher-priority interrupts are serviced before lower-priority interrupts, which are put on hold. The 8259A allows several prioritization modes; their details are beyond the scope of this book. We describe only the mode used on the PC. (A good discussion of prioritization modes can be found in *The 80x86 IBM PC & Compatible Computers: Assembly Language, Design, and Interfacing*, by Muhammad Ali Mazidi and Janice Gillispie Mazidi, Prentice Hall, 1995.)

On a PC, two 8259A interrupt controllers are cascaded, with interrupt request line 2 (IR2) on the master controller used as the cascade connection for the slave controller. The master controller thus has seven possible interrupts, numbered IRQ0, IRQ1, and IRQ3 – 7, and the slave controller has eight possible interrupts numbered IRQ8 – 15. The interrupt priority is assigned such that, on each controller, the lowest numbered interrupt has the highest priority. Because the slave controller is cascaded on IR2, the eight interrupts from the slave (IRQ8 – 15) are all higher priority than interrupts IRQ3 – 7 on the master controller. Table 9-1 lists PC interrupts in priority order, showing their interrupt vector assignments and device assignments.

Table 9-1: PC Hardware Interrupts

Hardware Interrupt	Vector	Device	Priority
IRQ0	08h	Timer tick	Highest
IRQ1	09h	Keyboard	
IRQ2	0Ah	Slave cascade connection	
IRQ8	70h	Real-time clock	
IRQ9	71h	Unassigned	
IRQ10	72h	Unassigned	
IRQ11	73h	Unassigned	
IRQ12	74h	Unassigned	
IRQ13	75h	Floating-point coprocessor	
IRQ14	76h	Hard disk controller	
IRQ15	77h	Unassigned	
IRQ3	0Bh	COM2 serial port	
IRQ4	0Ch	COM1 serial port	
IRQ5	0Dh	LPT2 parallel port	
IRQ6	0Eh	Floppy disk controller	
IRQ7	0Fh	LPT1 parallel port	Lowest

The 8259A has three registers that control which devices can interrupt at any given time: the interrupt mask register (IMR), the interrupt request register (IRR), and the in-service register (ISR), not to be confused with interrupt service routine, which is the meaning of ISR throughout this book, except for this section. Each of these registers has 8 bits, with bit 0 corresponding to IR0 for that interrupt controller, bit 1 to IR1, and so on.

The interrupt mask register (IMR) allows software to mask (disable) individual interrupts. Writing a 1 bit to the IMR masks the corresponding interrupt. For example, writing 20h to the slave controller IMR masks the floating-point coprocessor interrupt (IRQ13, or IR5 on the slave controller).

When a device generates an interrupt, but the interrupt has not yet been passed through to the CPU, the bit corresponding to that interrupt is set in the interrupt request register (IRR). After the 8259A has requested the CPU to acknowledge that interrupt, it clears the bit in the IRR and sets the bit for that interrupt in the in-service register (ISR). The bit in the ISR stays set until the interrupt handler explicitly clears the bit by issuing an end of interrupt (EOI) command to the interrupt controller. Interrupt handlers for devices that interrupt through the slave controller must issue an EOI both to the slave controller for the device's interrupt line and to the master controller for IR2, the cascade connection to the slave controller.

As long as a bit is set in the in-service register, the interrupt corresponding to that bit and all lower-priority interrupts are disabled (requests will not be passed through to the CPU), regardless of whether they are unmasked in the IMR. Higher-priority interrupts are still serviced as they come in.

Normally, an interrupt handler will not issue the EOI command until it has completed its processing and is ready to return to the interrupted application. As you might recall, this prevents the handler from being reentered. Notice that with the 8259A (as with many interrupt controllers), preventing reentrancy has the side effect (usually desirable) of also preventing all lower-priority interrupts from being serviced. For example, if the system is processing a keyboard interrupt, interrupts from the hard disk controller have to wait until the keyboard interrupt handler completes its processing, but timer tick interrupts are processed immediately, preempting the keyboard handler.

If you have a particular interrupt handler that takes too long to run, causing unacceptable latencies for lower-priority interrupts, you have a couple of options. You can rewrite your interrupt handler to complete more quickly (always the best choice). Or you can issue the EOI command at the beginning of the interrupt handler, to allow lower-priority interrupts to be serviced before your handler completes. To prevent your handler from being reentered, before issuing the EOI command you can either mask your interrupt in the IMR or program the device to not interrupt. At the end of the handler, instead of issuing the EOI command, you would unmask it in the IMR or program the device to start interrupting again.

INTERRUPT HANDLING UNDER ETS KERNEL

ETS Kernel maintains an IDT with interrupt gates for all 256 interrupts. By default, each IDT entry points to an assembly language wrapper (called the *umbrella interrupt handler* in the TNT Embedded ToolSuite documentation) that saves registers, sets up a C/C++ environment, and calls a C/C++ function to handle the interrupt. ETS Kernel maintains an internal, parallel, interrupt vector table that contains the address of the C/C++ interrupt functions. For all unused interrupts, the default C/C++ interrupt function just returns.

Application programs can either install C/C++ interrupt handlers (the usual case) or install interrupt handlers directly in the IDT, in which case the ETS Kernel assembly language wrapper does not execute and the application's handler is responsible for saving and restoring the machine state.

ETS Kernel always installs handlers for all processor exceptions (interrupts 00h – 0Eh); these are used for debugging the program and for structured exception handling support (see Chapter 20, "C++ Exceptions and Structured Exceptions"). Software interrupts FEh and FFh are used internally by ETS Kernel for communications between kernel components. Depending on which optional kernel components your application uses, the kernel may install handlers for several hardware interrupts. For example, the timer driver uses IRQ0 (interrupt 08h), the keyboard driver uses IRQ1 (interrupt 09h), and the file system uses IRQ6 and IRQ14 (interrupts 0Eh and 76h).

You may have noticed that the PC has a conflict between processor exceptions and hardware interrupts; interrupt numbers 08h – 0Eh are used for both processor exceptions and hardware interrupts IRQ0 – IRQ6. The assembly language wrapper handler in ETS Kernel can distinguish between processor exceptions and hardware interrupts, and will correctly invoke either the exception handler or the interrupt handler, as appropriate. If you install an IDT handler for one of these interrupts, you are responsible for determining whether the interrupt is a processor exception or a hardware interrupt.

C INTERRUPT HANDLERS

ETS Kernel provides APIs for installing C hardware and software interrupt handlers, and for saving and restoring the original interrupt vectors. These functions accept CPU interrupt numbers from 0 to 255 as arguments, so for hardware interrupts there is an additional step: mapping a hardware interrupt number to a CPU interrupt number. In Table 9-1, we showed the standard mapping for hardware interrupts. If ETS Kernel is used on a non-PC architecture, the interrupt mappings may differ, so an API is provided for application software to determine which CPU interrupts are used for hardware interrupts.

To install a C hardware interrupt handler under ETS Kernel, your code would look like this:

```
ETSHANDLER SavedVector;
int IntNumber;

// get CPU interrupt number for this hardware interrupt
IntNumber = EtsPicGetIRQIntNumber(IRQNumber);

// save original interrupt vector and install C handler
EtsSaveInterruptHandler(IntNumber, &SavedVector);
EtsSetInterruptHandler(IntNumber, MyCInterruptHandler);
```

If your application needs to remove its interrupt handler at some point, you would restore the original interrupt vector with this call:

```
EtsRestoreInterruptHandler(IntNumber, &SavedVector);
```

The interrupt handler itself is called with a pointer to a structure containing the contents of all the CPU registers at the time the interrupt occurred. This register structure is placed on the stack by the ETS Kernel assembly language wrapper. The C interrupt handler can examine these registers, and if necessary, modify the register contents to change register values on the return to the interrupted code. Only a software interrupt handler would ever change register values; because of the asynchronous nature of hardware interrupts, hardware interrupt handlers must *never* modify the CPU state when they return.

The interrupt handler is entered with interrupts disabled. Normally, the interrupt handler would immediately reenable interrupts to allow higher-priority interrupts to be processed, minimizing system interrupt latency. For hardware interrupts, after the handler completes its processing of the interrupt, the handler would normally issue an end of interrupt (EOI) command to the interrupt controller so that additional interrupts by this device and lower-priority interrupts could be processed. Depending on how you choose to handle reentrancy and latency issues in your system, you may choose a different structure for your interrupt handler. The structure of a typical hardware interrupt handler looks like the following:

```
void __cdecl MyCIntHandler(ETSINTREGS *pRegs)
{
    // enable interrupts
    EtsSetInterruptFlag(ETS_ENABLEINTS);

    // perform device I/O to process the interrupt

    // issue EOI to 8259A interrupt controller
    EtsPicEOI(IRQNumber);
    return;
}
```

In a multithreaded application, the interrupt handler may need some additional logic to control reentrancy and latency; Chapter 12 expands this sample interrupt handler to illustrate the additional complexities introduced by multithreading.

In addition to C hardware and software interrupt handlers, you can also install C processor exception handlers, using the EtsSaveExceptionVector(), EtsSetExceptionHandler(), and EtsRestoreExceptionHandler() APIs. However, if you do need to handle processor exceptions, it's strongly recommended that you use structured exception handling rather than installing ISRs for processor exceptions. Structured exception handling, which is covered in Chapter 20, allows your application to cooperate with debuggers, making it easier to debug your application.

The first UPS project, which we call the "Simple UPS," does not contain any C interrupt handlers, so we won't be looking at any examples in this chapter. However, the second UPS project, dubbed the "Smart UPS," has a C interrupt handler for the serial port hardware interrupt, and Chapter 12, "Multitasking," examines the code in the serial port interrupt handler.

IDT INTERRUPT HANDLERS

The ETS Kernel APIs that install interrupt handlers directly in the IDT are called `EtsSaveIDTHandler()`, `EtsSetIDTHandler()`, and `EtsRestoreIDTHandler()`. You may want to install an IDT handler for interrupts that have simple processing requirements and need high-speed processing. By eliminating the saving and restoring of all CPU registers performed by the ETS Kernel umbrella handler, interrupts can be processed more efficiently.

This speed advantage, however, must be weighed against the loss of the convenience and reliability that writing a C interrupt handler confers. IDT interrupt handlers must be written in assembly language so that they can correctly save and restore the CPU state and return by executing an IRETD (protected-mode return-from-interrupt instruction). An IDT handler must restore all CPU registers it modifies. Unless the interrupt handler is very simple, you'll probably end up doing almost as much saving and restoring as is performed by the ETS Kernel umbrella handler, losing most of your performance advantage.

Because of the strong advantages of writing handlers in C, none of the code projects in this book use IDT interrupt handlers.

TIMER AND KEYBOARD CALLBACKS

Most hardware interrupts never need more than one interrupt handler. For example, if you are using a hard disk, you'll either use the disk driver provided with the ToolSuite file system or replace it with your own disk driver; you won't use both of them.

The timer and keyboard interrupts are unique, however, in that they are not only used by ETS Kernel (to provide time-of-day and multithreading services and to support C run-time library keyboard services), but also are needed by many applications with requirements that can't be fulfilled by C run-time or Win32 APIs. You could write your own interrupt handler that performed whatever processing was needed, and then chain to the ETS Kernel interrupt handler, allowing the timer or keyboard driver to do its processing of the interrupt. But that seems like an onerous requirement for the application's author.

The ETS Kernel timer and keyboard drivers therefore support a generalized callback facility. (The same callback mechanism is used elsewhere in ETS Kernel, to notify the application of events such as the scheduling of threads.) Applications can install callbacks that are called by the driver whenever a timer or keyboard interrupt occurs. Applications can install multiple callbacks for either interrupt; whenever the interrupt occurs, all installed callbacks are invoked, unless one of them returns a value telling the driver to terminate early, skipping the rest of the callbacks in the chain.

In addition to the advantages of easy cooperation with the ETS Kernel drivers, callbacks are also easier to write than ISRs. Because the driver handles the details of reentrancy and latency control and performing I/O with the hardware device, the callback doesn't need to concern itself with talking to the hardware. The callback is invoked with interrupts enabled, and is passed a pointer to a structure containing detailed hardware information.

For example, if you install a keyboard callback, whenever the user presses a key (which generates an interrupt), a handler in the keyboard driver packages information regarding the keystroke into a structure and transfers control to your callback routine (handing your routine the structure). Pressing the key on the keyboard is referred to as an *event;* the callback routine is an *event handler.* In this particular example, the event is generated by a keyboard interrupt, so the callback routine is really a high-level interrupt service routine.

Let's see what's involved in writing callback routines, regardless of what event the callback routine is supposed to handle. When you're writing a callback, you need to think about three tasks:

- Registering the callback

- Writing the callback routine itself

- Removing the callback

Registering the callback is simple. You register your callback to tell ETS Kernel everything it needs to call the routine. The `EtsRegisterCallback()` function accomplishes this. When your program calls `EtsRegisterCallback()`, it passes a pointer to your callback function, and tells ETS Kernel to place that pointer in an internal data structure that associates the callback with the event. When the event occurs, the kernel knows who to call.

Here's the format of the `EtsRegisterCallback()` function:

```
BOOL EtsRegisterCallback(WORD Type,
    ETS_CALLBACK pCallback,
    DWORD ulOpaque,
    BOOL bAdd);
```

The first argument, *Type*, identifies the device driver that this callback is associated with. Hence, *Type* determines which events will trigger the kernel calling the callback routine. The kernel recognizes eight possible values for *Type*. (`EMBKERN.H` defines constants for each of the eight types.) In this chapter, we are interested in two types of callbacks: timer and keyboard. The ToolSuite-defined constant for *Type* that specifies a timer callback is `ETS_CB_TIMER`. The ToolSuite-defined constant that specifies a keyboard callback is `ETS_CB_KEYBOARD`.

The second argument, *pCallback*, is a pointer to the callback function itself. We'll show the syntax for a callback function in a moment. Let's finish with the arguments for `EtsRegisterCallback()` first.

The third argument, *ulOpaque*, is a double word. The value of *ulOpaque* is passed to the callback function by ETS Kernel when the kernel calls the callback.

The final argument, *bAdd*, determines whether the call to `EtsRegisterCallback()` registers or removes the callback function pointed to by *pCallback*. Setting *bAdd* to the value `ETS_CB_ADD` registers the callback; setting it to `ETS_CB_DELETE` removes the callback.

`EtsRegisterCallback()` returns a boolean result. If the result is TRUE, the operation has succeeded. If the result is FALSE, something went wrong. You can find out what went wrong by calling the Win32 function `GetLastError()`. This function returns a code number corresponding to the error most recently generated by your application.

Let's skip to removing the callback, which is simple also because it's the reverse of registering the callback. You use the same kernel function to remove the callback as you did to register the callback, `EtsRegisterCallback()`.

Recall that the fourth argument to `EtsRegisterCallback()`, *bAdd*, can assume one of two values: `ETS_CB_ADD` and `ETS_CB_DELETE`. Setting *bAdd* to `ETS_CB_ADD` registers the callback. Setting it to `ETS_CB_DELETE` removes the callback.

When removing a callback, the third argument, *ulOpaque*, is ignored. The first two arguments, *Type* and *pCallback*, are required. `EtsRegisterCallback()` needs the first to know the callback's type and the second to know which particular callback you're removing.

The callback routine itself is where all the work takes place. The syntax for a callback function looks like this:

```
int callback_routine_name(ETS_INPUT_RECORD *pEvent, DWORD ulOpaque);
```

As you can see, the function takes two arguments. Let's look at the second argument first, *ulOpaque*. This argument corresponds to the argument of the same name in the `EtsRegisterCallback()` function. It's intended to be used by the application developer as needed; the application specifies the value to be passed to the callback at the time the callback is installed. Most callbacks won't need to use this argument.

The first argument, *pEvent*, is a pointer to a structure of type `ETS_INPUT_RECORD`. This is a moderately complex union of event record data structures:

```
typedef struct _ETS_INPUT_RECORD {
  WORD EventType;
  WORD pad;
  union {
    ETS_TIMER_EVENT_RECORD TimerEvent;
    ETS_KEY_EVENT_RECORD KeyEvent;
    ETS_EXIT_EVENT_RECORD ExitEvent;
    ETS_TASK_EVENT_RECORD TaskSwitchEvent;
  } Event;
} ETS_INPUT_RECORD;
```

An event record carries data associated with the event that triggered ETS Kernel calling the callback routine. For example, when a timer event occurs, the driver fills the `TimerEvent` member data structure with information about the timer event. It then sets the `EventType` member to indicate that the `ETS_INPUT_RECORD` contains an event of type timer, and passes this `ETS_INPUT_RECORD` union into the callback routine as the first argument. Hence, the callback routine can examine the `EventType` member of the `ETS_INPUT_RECORD` to determine which member of the event union is the appropriate event record structure, and then read the information from that event record.

Note: Because you normally install a separate callback routine for each event of interest, a callback rarely needs to examine the `EventType` member; the callback already knows what kind of events will be passed to it. A keyboard callback, for example, will always be passed key events and will therefore use the `KeyEvent` member of the union; a timer callback will always be passed timer events and will therefore use the `TimerEvent` member; and so on. You need to examine `EventType` only if you write a generalized callback routine that you installed to handle multiple events.

We look at the details of the `KeyEvent` structure in a moment, when we discuss the keyboard callback in the UPS project. We examine the `TimerEvent` structure in Chapter 10, "Timers," which covers the UPS timer callback. We won't look at the structures for the other types of events and callbacks supported by ETS Kernel because we limit our discussion of ToolSuite features to those that help illustrate the general embedded programming concepts covered in this book.

Finally, notice that a callback routine returns an `int`, which can be one of two values: `ETS_CB_STOP` or `ETS_CB_CONTINUE`. This return value allows the callback to control how the kernel chains multiple callbacks installed for a single event. For example, suppose you had an application that needed one timer callback to read the status of an input port once every half second, and another callback to flash a light every 5 seconds to let the operator know that the computer system was still functioning. You might find it programmatically easier to create two timer callbacks, rather than attempt to weave both functions into one.

This is where the callback's return value comes in. If a callback returns with a value of `ETS_CB_STOP`, it's telling ETS Kernel: Don't call any more callbacks of my type for this event. On the other hand, a return value of `ETS_CB_CONTINUE` tells ETS Kernel: Call the next callback in the chain (if there is one).

INTERRUPTS IN THE UPS PROJECT

The UPS project needs to perform processing when timer tick interrupts and keyboard interrupts occur. It uses the ETS Kernel callback mechanism to install timer and keyboard callbacks, rather than writing ISRs to handle the interrupts. We'll look at the source for both callbacks.

KEYBOARD CALLBACKS

User input in the UPS project is built atop a keyboard callback. Are you wondering why we didn't use the simple keyboard routine from the POS project? You may recall that the POS keyboard routine used the C library function `_getch()`, which is a blocking call. A blocking call doesn't let a program return from the call until the appropriate condition exists. In the case of the POS program, the program doesn't return from the call until a user presses a key. Considering the design of the POS program, this was appropriate. However, the UPS program — under certain circumstances — has to perform multiple activities simultaneously. For example, when the AC power is bad, the UPS application needs to be able to flash the AC power button as an alarm, even while it is waiting for the user to enter the next command on the keyboard. In a multithreaded program, we could put the blocking call to `_getch()` in a separate thread, allowing the main application thread to continue doing other processing. But this is a single-tasking program. Because we need a feature not provided by the C run-time library (namely, nonblocking keyboard input), we need to process keystrokes at the interrupt level instead.

The routine that initializes the keyboard handler for the UPS system is simple and consists of not much more than a call to `EtsRegisterCallback()` wrapped in an `if()` statement:

```
//
// Initializes the key processing subsystem
//
// Returns:   TRUE if success
//            FALSE if error
//
BOOL InitKeysys(void)
{
//
// install keyboard callback
//
    if (!EtsRegisterCallback(ETS_CB_KEYBOARD, KeyHandler, 0, ETS_CB_ADD))
        return FALSE;
    return TRUE;
}
```

This routine registers the callback routine, KeyHandler, returning a TRUE value if the registration succeeded and FALSE otherwise. Notice that our keyboard callback has no real use for the *ulOpaque* argument, so we set that to 0.

Removing the callback is even simpler:

```
//
// Cleans up the key processing subsystem for exit
//
void CleanupKeysys(void)
{
//
// Unhook keyboard callback
//
    EtsRegisterCallback(ETS_CB_KEYBOARD, KeyHandler, 0, ETS_CB_DELETE);
    return;
}
```

This routine, CleanupKeysys(), is called as part of the shutdown processing of the UPS system. It's not much more than a wrapper around a call to EtsRegisterCallback(). Notice that the *bAdd* argument is set to ETS_CB_DELETE to remove the callback. In the InitKeysys() routine, that same argument was ETS_CB_ADD.

The keyboard callback routine itself is more interesting:

```
//
// Registered keyboard interrupt callback called by the keyboard
// driver when a keyboard interrupt occurs.
//
int __cdecl KeyHandler(ETS_INPUT_RECORD *pInpRec, DWORD dmy)
{
    ETS_KEY_EVENT_RECORD *pKey;
    WORD      VKey;
    BOOL      fCtrl,fAlt,fShift;
    int       Event;       // event corresponding to pressed key
    pKey = &pInpRec->Event.KeyEvent;
```

```
    if (!pKey->bKeyDown)
        return ETS_CB_STOP;     // process keys on make, not break
    VKey = pKey->wVirtualKeyCode;
    if (VKey == VK_SHIFT || VKey == VK_CONTROL || VKey == VK_MENU)
        return ETS_CB_STOP;     // ignore special keys
//
// Process any keys we recognize (F1, F2, F3, F4, ESC).  We just
// discard all other keystrokes.
//
    fCtrl = (pKey->dwControlKeyState & RIGHT_CTRL_PRESSED)
            || (pKey->dwControlKeyState & LEFT_CTRL_PRESSED);
    fAlt = (pKey->dwControlKeyState & RIGHT_ALT_PRESSED)
            || (pKey->dwControlKeyState & LEFT_ALT_PRESSED);
    fShift = (pKey->dwControlKeyState & SHIFT_PRESSED);
    if (fCtrl || fAlt || fShift)
    {
        Event = EVENT_UNUSED_KEY;
        goto ADD_EVENT;
    }

    switch (VKey)
    {
    case VK_F1:
        Event = EVENT_POWER;
        break;
    case VK_F2:
        Event = EVENT_LOAD;
        break;
    case VK_F3:
        Event = EVENT_AC;
        break;
    case VK_ESCAPE:
        Event = EVENT_EXIT;
        break;
default:
        Event = EVENT_UNUSED_KEY;
        break;
    }

ADD_EVENT:
//
// Add the event to the end of the event queue.
//
    AddEvent(Event, pKey->dwControlKeyState, VKey,
             pKey->uChar.AsciiChar);
    return ETS_CB_STOP;
}
```

Notice that the routine is defined with the __cdecl prefix. ETS Kernel requires you to use this prefix for all callback functions for two reasons. First, the __cdecl prefix overrides inap-

propriate compiler optimizations. In some cases, you can optimize your application's performance by requesting that the compiler pass arguments through registers rather than the stack.
ETS Kernel, however, expects arguments to be pushed onto the stack. If the compiler uses register passing for any callback functions, the callback functions will look for data in registers
that the kernel has put onto the stack. To ensure that the callback's interface is what the kernel
expects, you are required to use the __cdecl prefix, which overrides such optimizations.

The second reason ETS Kernel requires __cdecl is to ensure that a callback adheres to C's
calling conventions. If you put your callback in a C++ source file because the rest of your application is written in C++, __cdecl will force the compiler to use C calling conventions — which
is what the kernel expects — rather than C++ calling conventions.

The callback routine begins by examining the contents of the event record. It does
this by loading a local pointer, pKey, with the address of the KeyEvent member of the
ETS_INPUT_RECORD that was passed in by ETS Kernel.

```
pKey = &pInpRec->Event.KeyEvent;
```

The KeyEvent structure has the following format:

```
typedef struct _ETS_KEY_EVENT_RECORD
{ BOOL bKeyDown;              // 1=key down, 0=key up
  WORD wRepeatCount;          // Always 1
  WORD wVirtualKeyCode;       // Defined in Windows.h
  WORD wVirtualScanCode;      // Hardware scan code
  union
  {    unsigned short Unused;
       CHAR AsciiChar;
  } uChar;
  DWORD dwControlKeyState; // State of control keys
}
```

The first member of the event record that the callback routine inspects is bKeyDown. Pressing
a key on the keyboard generates two events: one associated with pushing the key (a key down
event) and another associated with releasing the key (a key up event). We don't want the
application to respond to the release of a key; we want it to respond to the press of a key. If
it responded to a key release and you pressed a key and held it down, the system would not
respond until you released the key.

The following if() statement essentially casts out key up events:

```
if (!pKey->bKeyDown)
    return ETS_CB_STOP;    // process keys on make, not break
```

Notice that every return statement in the callback returns a value of ETS_CB_STOP rather than
ETS_CB_CONTINUE. This tells ETS Kernel not to call any more keyboard callbacks; in particular, the kernel callback that arranges to pass keystrokes up to the C run-time library level will
not get called. Because this program consumes all keystrokes at the driver callback level, not
at the C run-time library level, we return ETS_CB_STOP to prevent keystrokes from accumu-
lating, unused, in the C run-time library.

Next, the keyboard callback begins a kind of sifting process. It filters keys that the program will be ignoring. For example, the following code snippet ignores special keys, such as Shift and Ctrl:

```
VKey = pKey->wVirtualKeyCode;
if (VKey == VK_SHIFT || VKey == VK_CONTROL || VKey == VK_MENU)
    return ETS_CB_STOP;    // ignore special keys
```

The callback ignores the key by simply issuing a `return` statement. Ignored keys never go in the UPS application's event queue. Shift and Ctrl are ignored because they are used to modify other keys (for example, Ctrl-C and Shift-F1), not as keystrokes that have meaning on their own. They generate key down and key up events so that the driver can track whether they are held down when another key is pressed. But because the information passed to the callback by the driver includes flags specifying which special keys, if any, are held down, the callback is freed from doing the tracking itself and can just discard the key down event for special keys.

Next, the callback looks at the actual key code to decide what event to generate. If a key that is not used by the UPS program is pressed, an unused key event is generated so that the event loop can display an error message. Because none of the recognized keys use the Shift, Ctrl, or Alt modifiers, the code discards any such keystrokes:

```
fCtrl = (pKey->dwControlKeyState & RIGHT_CTRL_PRESSED)
        || (pKey->dwControlKeyState & LEFT_CTRL_PRESSED);
fAlt = (pKey->dwControlKeyState & RIGHT_ALT_PRESSED)
        || (pKey->dwControlKeyState & LEFT_ALT_PRESSED);
fShift = (pKey->dwControlKeyState & SHIFT_PRESSED);
if (fCtrl || fAlt || fShift)
{
    Event = EVENT_UNUSED_KEY;
    goto ADD_EVENT;
}

switch (VKey)
{
case VK_F1:
    Event = EVENT_POWER;
    break;
case VK_F2:
    Event = EVENT_LOAD;
    break;
case VK_F3:
    Event = EVENT_AC;
    break;
case VK_ESCAPE:
    Event = EVENT_EXIT;
    break;
default:
    Event = EVENT_UNUSED_KEY;
    break;
}
```

Reentrant Functions

The `AddEvent()` routine is called in both the keyboard and timer callback functions. Recall that functions called by more than one ISR must be reentrant. Because `AddEvent()` is a reentrant function, let's take a close look at it.

First, a warning. We use the word *event* in more than one context, and that overloading of the word's meaning could get confusing. In one case, we use it to describe the message structures within which ETS Kernel bundles descriptions of system activities that trigger keyboard and timer callbacks. Those message structures are called *event records*. (They are the members of the `ETS_INPUT_RECORD` union.)

In another case, we use *event* when we discuss the internals of the UPS application. Recall that the UPS application uses an event loop to ferry information arriving from the keyboard and timer callbacks to the various routines that do the work in the program. That information is stored in what the UPS software refers to as an *event structure*. Event structures are linked in an event queue.

Right now, let's focus on this latter case — events in the UPS. First, the event queue; this is a singly linked list of event structures. As a new event occurs (the user presses a key, a timer tick occurs), the driver triggers the appropriate callback, which places information about that event into an event structure, and attaches that structure to the end of the event queue. As the event loop runs, it pulls event structures from the front of the queue and calls the appropriate routine to respond to the event. New events arrive at the tail of the queue; older events are removed from the front. Note that the queue works in FIFO (first in, first out) fashion, so the relative ordering of events in time is preserved. It's the job of `AddEvent()` to place new event structures in the queue.

Now, before we go on, let's ask a question: Where do those event structures come from? The answer, it turns out, is yet another queue. We call this second queue the *free list*. When the UPS application starts up, it allocates a set of empty event structures, and links them to create a free list of event structures. (Note that `AddEvent()` does not call `malloc()` directly to create the free list. That's because `AddEvent()` is called at interrupt time, and you cannot call `malloc()` — or most other C run-time library functions — from an interrupt routine. The `malloc()` call is not reentrant.)

`AddEvent()`, therefore, takes an unused event structure off the free list, fills it with data, and places it in the event queue. (The event loop in the main part of the program takes the event structure from the queue, extracts the data from it, and places the used up structure back on the free list where it can be reused. We take a brief look at the extraction process in a moment.)

`AddEvent()` must be careful in how it handles these queues. To see why, look at the code:

```
//
// Allocates an event structure and adds it to the event
// queue. If there are no free event structures, the event
// is just discarded.
//
void AddEvent(int Event, DWORD ControlKeyState,
              WORD VirtualKeyCode, CHAR AsciiChar)
```

```
{
    UPS_EVENT *pEvent;          // allocated event record
    UPS_EVENT *pLastEvent;      // last event in queue

//
// Disable interrupts while modifying event lists so
// the keyboard and timer interrupt handlers can't step
// on each other.
//
    _asm pushfd
    _asm cli

//
// allocate and initialize an event structure
//
    if (pFreeEvent == NULL)
    {
        _asm popfd
        return;
    }
    pEvent = (UPS_EVENT *) pFreeEvent;
    pFreeEvent = pFreeEvent->pNext;
    pEvent->Event = Event;
    pEvent->ControlKeyState = ControlKeyState;
    pEvent->VirtualKeyCode = VirtualKeyCode;
    pEvent->AsciiChar = AsciiChar;

//
// insert it in the list
//
    for (pLastEvent = (UPS_EVENT *) pFirstEvent;
            pLastEvent != NULL && pLastEvent->pNext != NULL;
            pLastEvent = pLastEvent->pNext)
        ;
    if (pLastEvent == NULL)
        pFirstEvent = pEvent;
    else
        pLastEvent->pNext = pEvent;
    pEvent->pNext = NULL;

//
// Re-enable interrupts and exit
//
    _asm popfd
    return;
}
```

You can see that `AddEvent()` does something unconventional and executes a pair of assembly language instructions. First is the `pushfd` instruction, which pushes the x86 processor's flags register onto the stack. `AddEvent()` pushes the flags register to preserve the interrupt flag because the second of the assembly language instructions is `cli` (clear interrupt flag), which causes the processor to ignore all but non-maskable interrupts. (The `cli` instruction clears the interrupt flag, so, without the preceding `pushfd` instruction, `AddEvent()` wouldn't know what state the interrupt flag was in before the execution of `cli`.)

Now, jump quickly to the end of the routine and notice the assembly language `popfd` instruction just before the `return` statement. The `popfd` instruction undoes what `pushfd` did; `popfd` pops the flags register from the stack. This has the effect of restoring the interrupt enable flag (remember, the flags register was pushed before the `cli` instruction) and therefore reenabling interrupts.

The result, then, is that the code between `cli` and `popfd` is uninterruptible. No other code in the application can execute until it completes. Why is this important?

The reason: `AddEvent()` must protect shared resources, which are the free list and the event queue. Remember, both the keyboard and timer callback routines call `AddEvent()`. Suppose for a moment that you remove the assembly instructions. Consider what might happen if the user presses a key, and shortly thereafter (in the computer's notion of shortly) a timer interrupt occurs. First, the keyboard callback is called, and it calls `AddEvent()`. `AddEvent()` goes to remove an event structure from the free list and obtains a pointer to the first member of that list:

```
pEvent = (UPS_EVENT *) pFreeEvent;
```

But, just then, the timer interrupt occurs. Because the timer interrupt has a higher priority than the keyboard interrupt, the timer interrupt is serviced immediately, rather than waiting for the keyboard ISR to complete. The timer callback wakes up, calls `AddEvent()`, and the timer callback's invocation of `AddEvent()` also obtains a pointer to the first item on the free list. Unfortunately, it's the same pointer that the keyboard callback had obtained. So, the first invocation of `AddEvent()` completes, filling the event structure with information about a timer event. Then, when the keyboard callback's invocation of `AddEvent()` resumes, it overwrites the event structure that the timer callback had just filled.

You get the idea. The free list and the event queue, because they may be accessed by routines that can interrupt one another, must be protected so that any operations on either queue are indivisible — uninterruptible.

The reverse operation is performed by the `GetEvent()` function, which is called by the main event loop in the application. The job of `GetEvent()` is to extract the first event from the queue and return the freed structure to the free list. `GetEvent()` must also disable interrupts, and for the same reason `AddEvent()` does. Although `GetEvent()` is called in the main application — and not at interrupt time — it must still protect access to the event queue. If it didn't, a callback might be triggered while `GetEvent()` was executing, potentially corrupting the queue structure.

The actual work performed by `AddEvent()` should be easy to follow now. It's basically in two parts. The first pulls an empty event structure off the free list and fills it in:

```
//
// allocate and initialize an event structure
//
    if (pFreeEvent == NULL)
    {
        _asm popfd
        return;
    }
    pEvent = (UPS_EVENT *) pFreeEvent;
    pFreeEvent = pFreeEvent->pNext;
    pEvent->Event = Event;
    pEvent->ControlKeyState = ControlKeyState;
    pEvent->VirtualKeyCode = VirtualKeyCode;
    pEvent->AsciiChar = AsciiChar;
```

Notice that if the free list is empty, the routine restores the interrupt flag and exits. Otherwise, the program removes the allocated event structure from the front of the free list. AddEvent() then places the current event and keystroke information in the members of the newly obtained event structure.

The second half of the routine searches for the end of the list, and attaches the new event structure to the queue's last member.

```
//
// insert it in the list
//
    for (pLastEvent = (UPS_EVENT *) pFirstEvent;
            pLastEvent != NULL && pLastEvent->pNext != NULL;
            pLastEvent = pLastEvent->pNext)
        ;
    if (pLastEvent == NULL)
        pFirstEvent = pEvent;
    else
        pLastEvent->pNext = pEvent;
    pEvent->pNext = NULL;
```

The routine must account for the possibility that the event queue is empty, in which case the current event becomes the first event. Otherwise, the current event is linked to the end and becomes the new last event.

The keyboard callback concludes by adding the key event to the UPS software's event queue:

```
// Add the event to the end of the event queue.
    AddEvent(Event, pKey->dwControlKeyState, VKey,
            pKey->uChar.AsciiChar);
```

It does this first with a call to the AddEvent() function, which creates an entry in the event queue and fills it in. The key code information passed to AddEvent() is used only for an unused key event, in which case the event loop uses it to generate an error message.

TIMER CALLBACKS

As you know, when the UPS detects an improper AC line level, it — among other things — flashes the AC Power window. This simulates flashing an LED at some repeated interval. If we had wanted to get simple, we could have written a loop that turns the light on, kills some time in an empty inner loop, turns the light off, turns the light on, and so on forever.

However, whenever the application requested the alarm to be sounded, the CPU would have ended up spending its entire time running a loop, flashing a simulated lightbulb. Adding support for other UPS activities during the alarm signal would have been a complicated, error-prone, and ugly programming chore. We would have found it difficult, for example, to insert into the middle of that loop a call to the keyboard handler to watch for user input.

A looped alarm also would have wasted CPU resources. The CPU need only turn its attention to the alarm signal when the simulated light must be changed (from on to off, or off to on). We don't need our program chewing up processor cycles waiting for the proper time to elapse to switch the state of the alarm signal.

Consequently, we used a timer callback to manage the changing of the alarm signal state. The CPU pays attention to the alarm when it must.

We go into timers in more detail in the next chapter. For now, we want to focus on the details of the timer callback. All you need to know right now about a timer is that it provides a way for your application to set a future wake-up signal for itself (similar to how you set your alarm clock to wake yourself up in the morning).

The initialization code for the timer callback is similar to the analogous code for initializing the keyboard callback:

```
//
// Initializes the timer subsystem
//
// Returns: TRUE if success
//          FALSE if error
//
BOOL InitTimersys(void)
{
//
// Initialize timer globals
//
    elapsedWhole = elapsedFrac = 0;
//
// install timer callback
//
    if (!EtsRegisterCallback(ETS_CB_TIMER, TimerHandler, 0, ETS_CB_ADD))
        return FALSE;
    return TRUE;
}
```

The initialization routines for the timer and the keyboard differ in only two noteworthy ways. First, the timer routine initializes a pair of global variables, elapsedWhole and elapsedFrac. As you see in the next chapter, the timer callback will use these variables to accumulate elapsed time.

The second, and more important, difference is in the call to `EtsRegisterCallback()`. The *Type* argument is set to `ETS_CB_TIMER`, and the *pCallBack* argument is `TimerHandler`. Hence, ETS Kernel is told to register the `TimerHandler()` routine as a timer callback.

The routine to remove the timer callback is straightforward:

```
//
// Cleans up the timer subsystem for exit
//
void CleanupTimersys(void)
{
//
// unhook timer callback
//
    EtsRegisterCallback(ETS_CB_TIMER, TimerHandler, 0, ETS_CB_DELETE);
    return;
}
```

As with the keyboard callback, the `CleanupTimersys()` routine is nothing more than a wrapper around the `EtsRegisterCallback()` function call.

Finally, there's the timer callback itself:

```
//
// Registered timer interrupt callback called by the timer
// driver when a timer interrupt occurs.  Every time 500 ms
// elapses, we stuff a timer event in the event queue.
//
int __cdecl TimerHandler(ETS_INPUT_RECORD *pInpRec, DWORD dmy)
{
//
// Update our elapsed time counters.
//
    elapsedWhole += pInpRec->Event.TimerEvent.elapsedWhole;
    elapsedFrac += pInpRec->Event.TimerEvent.elapsedFrac;
    if (elapsedFrac < pInpRec->Event.TimerEvent.elapsedFrac)
        // carry out
        ++ elapsedWhole;
//
// Generate timer event if 500 ms has elapsed.  If the
// event queue gets full, just ignore the event.
//
    if (elapsedWhole >= 500)
    {
        AddEvent(EVENT_TIMER);
        elapsedWhole -= 500;
    }
//
// Let the rest of the timer callback functions run
//
    return ETS_CB_CONTINUE;
}
```

The callback simply accumulates elapsed time in the two globals, `elapsedWhole` and `elapsedFrac`. It then examines `elapsedWhole` to determine if 500 ms has elapsed and — if so — places a timer tick event in the event queue.

SUMMARY

In this chapter, we introduced interrupts, discussing briefly the different kinds of interrupts supported by most CPUs: hardware interrupts, software interrupts, and exceptions. We looked at how interrupts work, at how peripheral devices are connected to the CPU to build a system that supports interrupts, and at how the CPU reacts internally to the arrival of an interrupt. We discussed the use of an interrupt controller to support interrupts from multiple devices, and talked about criteria for selecting interrupt priorities on systems with multiple interrupts, and why the capability to mask individual interrupts is important. Then we examined the process of writing interrupt service routines. After giving some general pointers on how to write ISRs, we took a close look at the problems of reentrancy and interrupt latency.

To illustrate some of the general concepts that we discussed, we looked at the specific example of how interrupts work on a PC hardware platform, and how the 8259A interrupt controller used on the PC operates. This led to a discussion of the support for interrupts provided by ETS Kernel. The preferred method for writing an ISR is to use the kernel support for installing an ISR written in C. If you prefer, you can go right to the hardware level and install an assembly language ISR vectored to directly by the processor. And for the special case of timer and keyboard interrupts, the kernel drivers support a generalized interrupt callback mechanism that is simpler than writing an ISR.

Finally, we focused on the interrupt processing performed by the UPS project when timer and keyboard interrupts occur. We looked at the keyboard and timer callback routines: how to install them, how they worked, and how to remove them. And we dissected the `AddEvent()` function, a reentrant routine used by both the timer and keyboard callbacks.

10

Timers

A *timer* is circuitry that a computer system uses to measure the passage of time. You can think of a timer as providing the CPU with the equivalent of a digital watch. Some timers are inside CPUs and referred to as *on-chip timers*; others are external timer hardware — usually a single chip connected to the CPU by interrupt, data, and address lines.

On-chip timers are more common than external timers in embedded systems. One reason for this is a developer's ever-present goal to use the fewest number of chips. Using a CPU with a built-in timer means one less chip a developer needs to use. A second reason is that a wide range of processors have on-chip timers. Virtually all 16- and 32-bit embedded processors include built-in timers, as do many 8-bit embedded processors. Even tiny 4-bit processors include timers, which is hardly surprising when you consider that the largest market served by 4-bit processors is the digital watch market.

The components, configurations, and features of on-chip and external hardware timers vary. What you choose depends on the needs of your system. For some simple requirements, the system clock can function as the timer. Most embedded applications, however, require more sophisticated timers that have more extensive capabilities. Usually such timers consist of a circuit that includes a crystal oscillator and a counter or register. They have some I/O ports that allow software to control the timer, and are attached to an interrupt pin on the processor. The crystal generates a signal at a fixed frequency. The signal is fed into the clock input on the counter and causes it to count either up or down.

Count-down timers are normally used to drive periodic actions performed by the system. The operating system initializes the counter value and starts it counting down. When the counter reaches zero, the timer generates an interrupt (unless the operating system has programmed it not to interrupt because it wants to poll the timer rather than have it interrupt). The operating system then performs whatever actions are required, reprograms the timer with a new counter value, and starts it counting down for the next periodic event.

Count-up timers are typically used to measure elapsed time or provide very accurate tracking of the time of day. The operating system initializes the timer, either to zero or (more commonly) to a value relative to a fixed date and time, and starts the timer counting up. The system can then read the counter value to get a very accurate time reading. If the timer is allowed to reach its maximum count, the counter wraps to zero and continues to count up. It's the job of software to either reset the counter before it wraps or to detect the wrapping and factor it into the elapsed time calculations. Some count-up timers have the capability to generate periodic interrupts.

Most hardware timers are programmable. That is, you can write software to control a hardware timer and alter its characteristics. Precisely which characteristics of a timer can be changed varies with the timer hardware itself. Most programmable timers, however, permit software to perform such functions as turning the timer on and off, telling the timer's counter to either count in base 2 or base 10 (that is, operate in binary or binary-coded decimal, BCD), and reading and writing the counter. Most chips that have two or three timers, whether they're a CPU or a separate timer chip, permit software to exercise additional control. For example, one of the three timers on the PC timer chip is connected to the system's speaker. That timer lets software control the output frequency to the speaker, which is what causes the speaker to emit different pitches. Hence, the timer permits the software to control that device.

TIMER APPLICATIONS

There are many uses for a timer's capability to measure time intervals and generate interrupts at a predetermined moment. Some of the more common applications include the following:

- **Implementing a real-time clock.** A real-time clock is a count-up timer powered by a battery that allows it to continue to run when the system is turned off. Real-time clocks usually allow software to directly read and write the current year, month, day, hour, minute, second, and sometimes microsecond. Some real-time clocks just keep a counter containing a value relative to a fixed date in the past (for example, the number of microseconds since midnight on January 1, 1900). When the system is restarted, the operating system reads the timer to determine the correct date and time.

- **Producing a repeating output at a fixed frequency.** This can be as simple as flashing a light or as complicated as producing a pulsed waveform (often used in controlling stepper motors).

- **Polling the status of a device at regular intervals.** Suppose your application is measuring temperature, but the analog-to-digital converter (ADC) hardware requires a certain amount of time to "settle" between each measurement. You can use a timer-generated interrupt to trigger an ISR that polls the ADC at a rate to provide a steady stream of temperature measurements while remaining within the sampling rate tolerances.

- **Setting an alarm clock; that is, setting a time by which certain events must occur.** Suppose you're writing software for an ATM. Most ATMs are programmed to eat a card if no additional user input on the keypad occurs in the middle of a transaction, or if the user doesn't withdraw the card within a certain amount of time after it's been returned to the user. This feature protects a card from being stolen; the assumption is that if a user doesn't respond within a certain period of time, he or she has either walked off and forgotten the card or something is wrong. The ATM takes the card for safekeeping.

  You write your software, then, so that when a user activates an ATM by putting a card in the slot, the software sets an alarm by programming a timer to generate an interrupt at some predetermined moment. Suppose you set the alarm for one minute. Hence, the timer generates an interrupt every minute from now until the card is removed from the slot. When the timer generates an interrupt, it triggers an ISR that checks the slot for a card. If the ISR finds one, it checks to see when the last user input occurred. If user input has occurred since the previous invocation of the ISR, the current ISR simply returns. If user input hasn't occurred since it checked 1 minute ago, the ISR invokes the card-eating routine and the ATM keeps the card.

- **Maintaining the system time of day.** A common technique for updating the time of day kept by the OS is to program a count-down timer to interrupt at a specific frequency — for example, every 100 milliseconds. (On a PC, the BIOS initializes the programmable interval timer to interrupt every 54.93 milliseconds.) Each time this periodic, or timer tick, interrupt occurs, the operating system updates the system's time of day, either by adding the time interval measured since the previous interrupt to the previous time-of-day value, or by reading a separate real-time clock. The time of day is often kept internally by the operating system in units of, say, milliseconds since a specific date and time. When an application requests the current time, that raw number is converted into the current date, hour, minutes, and seconds.

  A timer tick interrupt is useful also for driving anything else that needs to occur on a periodic basis — either in the operating system or in the application. For example, the scheduler in a real-time operating system is responsible for preempting a task when its time slice has expired, and scheduling another runnable task to get the next time slice. To notice that a task's time slice has expired, the scheduler needs to check the current time periodically. Invoking the scheduler each time a timer tick interrupt occurs is the easiest way to implement time slicing with the lowest overhead. Other examples of common periodic operations are performing memory refresh and updating memory page reference counts for a virtual memory system.

- **Providing a watchdog timer.** A watchdog timer is a special kind of timer used as a fail-safe mechanism. In some embedded systems, using a watchdog timer may be a matter of convenience, such as when it's implemented to prevent a system from getting stuck in a loop, locking up, or for any reason becoming unresponsive to user input. In other systems where malfunctioning software can result in damage or injury, however, using a watchdog timer is a necessity.

On the hardware side, a watchdog timer's interrupt output line is connected to the RESET line of the processor. On the software side, a programmer implements a watchdog timer by periodically resetting the watchdog timer's counter to its initial value if the system is still functioning normally. As long as the application executes properly, the instructions that restart the watchdog timer are called before the timer reaches zero. If the software malfunctions, the code that restarts the timer fails to execute, the timer counts down to zero, and the watchdog timer reboots the system.

Many systems that include a watchdog timer provide mechanisms that allow the initialization code — the code called during bootup — to determine whether the system is being powered up or rebooted; the latter indicates a software malfunction. If the reboot was caused by a watchdog timer, the software can examine the hardware, ascertain whether the system is still operational, and either restart the system or attempt to shut it down gracefully so that nothing gets broken and no one gets hurt.

SELECTING TIMER HARDWARE

How do you know whether you need a timer? If the software in your system needs to know the time of day, measure intervals, or generate events at predetermined moments, you need one or more timers. Both CPUs and external timer chips are available with up to two to three timers per chip. To determine how many timers your application will need, identify all the activities in your system that will require a timer. Then ascertain which activities can share a timer and which ones require a dedicated timer. Several periodic activities can often be serviced by a single periodic count-down timer. A watchdog timer, on the other hand, requires a dedicated timer (because when it counts down to zero, it resets the system rather than generating an interrupt). A time-of-day clock that tracks time even when the system is off requires a dedicated timer. If you can get the current date and time when the system starts (possibly over a network connection, for example), however, you can keep track of time using an interval timer that also services other timing needs in the system.

If you've determined that a timer is required, the next step is choosing its capabilities. These generally fall into three categories: resolution, programmability, and integration.

Your first task is to accurately assess the resolution or fineness of time measurements, such as milliseconds or microseconds, that your application requires. Again, your assessment depends on your project constraints and requirements. You should determine the kind of resolution required for time-of-day information and task time slices, and the resolution requirements of other periodic activities performed by the system. Assessing resolution is important for two reasons. First, high-resolution timers are more expensive than low-resolution timers. You don't want to spend money for a timer that measures microseconds when all you need is time measured to a tenth of a second. Second, the circuitry required to support a timer demands tighter tolerances as the timer's base frequency increases. So you don't want to commit yourself to more than you need.

When it comes to programmability, the question isn't whether to choose a programmable timer or not, but which programmable features to select. You may want to choose a timer that counts in both binary and BCD, or that has multiple counting modes (for example, a mode that stops after counting to zero or automatically resets after counting to zero). You also may want a count-up or a count-down timer, and one that can generate interrupts. It's well worth the time to compare the programmable features of various timers in addition to analyzing your software's requirements before making this decision.

As we indicated previously, many CPUs have timers integrated directly on chip. In fact, CPUs often have two or three timers on chip. Obviously, taking only timers into consideration, you're better off choosing a processor with integrated timers because you'll have fewer chips in your design. That advantage, however, has to be weighed against all the other considerations that go into choosing a processor. And if the on-chip timers don't have the features you require, you'll have to add an external timer into your system anyway.

Finally, if you're building a really low-cost system in which you're counting pennies, you can build a timer with just a hardware divisor that reduces the system clock frequency and feeds into one of the interrupt input pins on the processor. This design generates an interrupt at a fixed frequency, and relies on an interrupt service routine to measure passage of time. With this approach, you don't need a timer chip, but there are some drawbacks. The maximum resolution of such a "mostly software" timer is far less than a hardware timer, simply because there are practical limits to how often you can interrupt the processor without taking up most (or a significant percentage) of the CPU's time. The software counter in the ISR is also not as accurate as the hardware counter on a timer chip. And any time you use software rather than hardware to do something, you're consuming a bit more of the CPU's time, which can be a problem if processor utilization is already close to 100 percent.

SOFTWARE CONSIDERATIONS

After you've determined a timer's hardware capabilities, it's time to select software that fully exploits the capabilities of your hardware. First, make sure the APIs of any third-party run-time software (RTOS, run-time kernel, or run-time library) let you measure time at the same resolution as the hardware timer. In fact, it's a good idea to run a test and verify that the software delivers, rather than accept what the specs say. Some operating systems deployed on multiple hardware platforms provide timer-related routines capable of high resolution, but the actual resolution at run time depends on the current hardware. In other words, although an OS runs on platform A and B, the resolution provided by the timer routines may be higher when run on platform A than when run on platform B. Other operating systems simply don't deliver the full capabilities of the underlying timer hardware. Whereas the timer hardware may measure intervals in milliseconds, an operating system may measure time to only a tenth of a second.

Second, if you've chosen a programmable timer, make sure your RTOS or kernel includes an API for programming it. Otherwise, you'll probably be forced to write assembly language routines to program the timer.

Finally, if your application requires OS services that are unrelated to determining the time of day or utilizing periodic timer interrupts but are nonetheless dependent on a timer, verify that the OS you've chosen provides those services. One such service is support for a watchdog timer.

ETS KERNEL TIMERS

ETS Kernel includes a timer driver for the PC 8254 Programmable Interrupt Timer chip and the PC MC146818 real-time clock chip to provide timer-related functions that fall into two categories:

- Time-of-day services
- Timer interrupt services

As we've noted for other drivers, the full ToolSuite product includes the source code to the timer driver. This allows you to easily port the driver to other timer chips or to program the chip hardware, if your system specifications call for it.

ETS Kernel lets you use all the functions defined in the standard ANSI C TIME.H header file to access the time-of-day services. Some examples of these functions are clock(), difftime(), and time(). ETS Kernel also supports Win32-compatible time routines. These include functions for converting among various time formats, such as the Win32 64-bit file time format, the UTC (Universal Time Code) or GMT (Greenwich mean time) format, and the DOS time format; reading and setting time zone information; and accessing the Win32 high-resolution performance counter. The performance counter can measure time durations well into the milliseconds. Its resolution depends on the capabilities of the hardware.

To provide time-of-day services, the timer driver reads the MC146818 real-time clock chip at startup, gets the initial date and time, and writes a new date and time to the real-time clock whenever an application calls the SetLocalTime() function.

To provide timer interrupt services, the timer driver performs two functions: It programs the timer hardware to trigger timer interrupts at a fixed frequency, and it allows an application to install one or more timer callbacks that the timer driver calls when an interrupt occurs.

The timer driver programs the hardware to trigger timer interrupts at a fixed frequency of once every 10 milliseconds. This is the default because it provides good performance on low-end processors. For example, at this interrupt rate, servicing timer interrupts consumes only 5 percent of the processor time on a 20MHz 386SX machine.

Although ETS Kernel programs the timer to generate interrupts at 10-ms intervals, you can alter this timer interrupt period by calling the EtsSetTimerPeriod() function. If your application is controlling a device that needs servicing once every 9 ms, for example, call EtsSetTimerPeriod() and set the timer interrupt to 9 ms. Be aware, however, that there's a practical lower limit to which you can set the timer period. That lower limit depends on your processor's clock speed and the time taken by your timer interrupt handlers. If you set the period to a value that's too small, your application could spend all its time in the timer interrupt handler, with no free CPU time left over to do anything else. There's also a fixed limit: the lowest value that `EtsSetTimerPeriod()` will accept is 1 ms.

Note: If you suspect that the setting for the timer interrupt is too high or too low for your particular application, the full product of the TNT Embedded ToolSuite includes a sample program that measures the overhead of the timer driver. You can execute the program, changing the setting each time, and determine how much processor time is being consumed by the timer driver.

In addition to facilitating interrupts to occur at a fixed frequency, the timer driver provides timer interrupt services using callbacks. Several applications we mentioned at the beginning of this chapter require interrupt services. Callbacks would work for implementing most of these. We show you how by looking at the code for the UPS project.

TIMERS IN THE UPS PROJECT

We covered registering and removing the timer callback in the preceding chapter, so we'll skip directly to reviewing the code for the timer callback.

The UPS software uses a timer callback to trigger the UPS's alarm signal. Once every 500 ms (one-half second), the timer callback places a timer event on the UPS application's event queue. The UPS event processing loop receives this event and decides whether to turn the alarm signal on or off.

While the callback places an event on the queue every 500 ms, the timer driver has programmed the hardware to trigger an interrupt every 10 ms. Hence, the callback shouldn't place an event on the queue every time an interrupt is generated. To determine when it should place an event on the queue, the timer callback must keep track of the time since it last did so. As shown in Listing 10-1, the timer callback keeps track using two global variables: `elapsedWhole` and `elapsedFrac`.

Listing 10-1: Timer callback

```
//
// Registered timer interrupt callback called by the timer
// driver when a timer interrupt occurs.  Every time 500ms
// elapses, we stuff a timer event on the event queue.
//
int __cdecl TimerHandler(ETS_INPUT_RECORD *pInpRec, DWORD dmy)
{
//
// Update our elapsed time counters.
//
    elapsedWhole += pInpRec->Event.TimerEvent.elapsedWhole;
    elapsedFrac += pInpRec->Event.TimerEvent.elapsedFrac;
    if (elapsedFrac < pInpRec->Event.TimerEvent.elapsedFrac)
       // carry out
       ++ elapsedWhole;
```

```
//
// Generate timer event if 500ms has elapsed.  If the
// event queue gets full, just ignore the event.
//
    if (elapsedWhole >= 500)
    {
        AddEvent(EVENT_TIMER);
        elapsedWhole -= 500;
    }


//
// Let the rest of the timer callback functions run
//
    return ETS_CB_CONTINUE;
}
```

The elapsedWhole and elapsedFrac global variables are updated at the beginning of the callback routine and contain the elapsed time — in whole and fractional milliseconds — since the callback routine last added a timer event to the event queue. (In case you're wondering about initialization, these two global variables are initialized by the InitTimersys() routine. The callback and InitTimersys() routines are in the TIMER.C file.)

The callback routine is able to update the elapsed time globals thanks to the timer record passed to the callback by the driver. This record is a simple data structure, consisting of two double-word (32-bit) members:

```
typedef struct _ETS_TIMER_EVENT_RECORD
{   DWORD elapsedWhole;    // whole # of milliseconds
    DWORD elapsedFrac;     // fractional ms * 2^32
}
ETS_TIMER_EVENT_RECORD;
```

The two members of this structure carry the whole and fractional milliseconds that have elapsed since the last timer tick (which is also the time since the callback was last called). The callback first adds the whole milliseconds elapsed to the elapsedWhole global variable. Then the callback adds the fractional milliseconds elapsed to the elapsedFrac global variable.

Finally, the callback uses an if() statement to deal with any carry-out of the fractional milliseconds :

```
if(elapsedFrac < pInpRec->Event.TimerEvent.elapsedFrac)
    ++elapsedWhole;
```

Because the global variables and data structure members that hold whole and fractional milliseconds are defined as unsigned, the callback routine can verify that a carry has occurred by comparing the elapsedFrac global variable to the elapsedFrac data structure member. If the global variable is less, the accumulation of the fractional seconds must have resulted in a rollover. In that case, the carry must be added into the elapsedWhole global variable.

The 8254 Timer

The timer circuit used on PC-compatible computers is the 8254 Programmable Interval Timer (PIT). A diagram of the 8254 (and how it is connected to other components on a PC system) is shown in Figure 10-1. (Note: The variety of timer chips available to the developer of embedded systems is too vast to even list. We focus on the 8254 simply because it's the timer used by the PC system.)

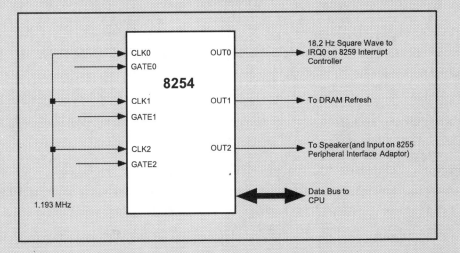

Figure 10-1: The 8254 Programmable Interval Timer (PIT) is the core of the PC's timer hardware. It consists of three counters. Each counter is served by two inputs: a CLK input that sets the counter's frequency and a GATE input that allows external hardware to enable or disable the counter. Also, each counter has an output line that can be used to send timer-controlled pulses, or square waves, to connected hardware.

Inside the 8254 are three independent 16-bit counters. Each can be programmed to operate in one of six modes. Also, each counter has two inputs and one output. One input is a CLK line; the other is a GATE. The CLK input expects a fixed-frequency clock signal (pulse train). The frequency of the CLK input sets the base frequency of the corresponding counter. The GATE input enables or disables the associated counter.

The shape (duty cycle) and frequency of the output signal (OUT) of a counter depends on how you program the counter (the counter's mode, as well as the setting of the counter's initial count). A counter can be programmed to generate single pulses or a train of pulses.

The CPU can access the 8254's counters through the data bus. On the PC, the PIT appears at four I/O addresses. Three addresses provide access to the value in each counter. The fourth is a control register. Software can program the functions of the PIT's counters by first writing to the control register (which sets the mode for the counter), and then initializing the specific counter's value. The counter then begins decrementing the count value at the frequency of the signal at that counter's CLK input (one decrement per tick of the CLK). As mentioned, the frequency and shape of the signal on the OUT line depends on how the counter has been programmed.

Here's an example: Look again at Figure 10-1. Notice that the input to all three PIT counters is a 1.193-MHz pulse train (generated by a crystal circuit elsewhere on the PC motherboard). Upon power up, the PC firmware programs counter 0 to mode 3 — this mode causes the counter to emit a square wave whose frequency is based on both the CLK frequency of the counter and the counter's initial value. The firmware then initializes the counter with a value of 65536. (Actually, the initial value is 0, which the counter — having only 16 bits — treats as an initial value of 65536.) The counter then begins counting down at a rate of 1.193 MHz (the CLK input frequency), decrementing the count by 1 for each tick on the CLK line. Through half the countdown (32768 steps), the OUT0 line is high. Through the remaining half, the output is low, thus generating a square wave of 18.2 Hz. When the counter counts back to 0, it restarts (setting its output high) and counting down again from 65536. (Not shown in the figure is the fact that the GATE input on counter 0 is tied to 5V; consequently, the counter is permanently enabled.)

The output of counter zero is connected to IRQ0 on the PC's 8259 interrupt controller. IRQ0 is the timer interrupt for the PC system. Therefore, the output of the 8259's counter zero is the source of the PC's 18.2-times-per-second timer interrupt. This interrupt awakens an ISR that provides the time-of-day services for the system.

As you can see in Figure 10-1, the other counters are connected to other devices on the PC system. The details of their function (as well as the programming details) are beyond the scope of this book. A good description of the 8254 — how it's wired into the PC, as well as how it's programmed — can be found in *The 80x86 IBM PC & Compatible Computers: Assembly Language, Design, and Interfacing*, by Muhammad and Janice Mazidi (Prentice Hall, 1995).

The remainder of the code is straightforward: When 500 ms have elapsed, the callback calls AddEvent(EVENT_TIMER) to place a timer event on the UPS queue, and then resets the elapsedWhole global variable by subtracting 500 ms.

It's worth reiterating that a timer callback is really an interrupt service routine. Therefore, it should do as little processing as possible. In this case, the callback only measures duration, and — when the proper time for switching the alarm has elapsed — places a timer event on the event queue. The response to the event (the modifying of the display) is handled elsewhere in the application.

Although the UPS software uses a single timer callback, your application can register more than one timer callback with the timer driver. You could, as your application dictates, assign different duties to each callback. (For example, you might have one callback service an on-screen time-of-day clock, while another callback monitors an attached peripheral.) The overhead associated with a timer callback is minimal, so the decision to install multiple callbacks or a single callback function that performs multiple actions is largely a matter of taste. You do, however, need to keep some details in mind.

First, callbacks are called in the reverse order in which they were registered. So if your program registers timer callback A and later registers timer callback B, when a timer tick occurs, B is called first and A is called second (after B returns).

Second, you do have some control over whether the timer driver calls multiple callbacks. Notice that the UPS timer callback returns with a value of ETS_CB_CONTINUE. This tells the driver callback management system to continue calling other timer callbacks (should they exist). If the callback returns with a value of ETS_CB_STOP, any remaining callbacks will not be invoked. Under normal circumstances, a timer callback should never return ETS_CB_STOP. The reason is that the first callback installed (and therefore the last one invoked) is the callback in the timer driver itself that maintains the system time of day. So if you install a timer callback that returns ETS_CB_STOP, time will cease to pass as far as the Win32 functions, the C run-time library functions, or the real-time scheduler are concerned.

SUMMARY

Timers are at the core of real-time embedded systems, so you should examine their components, configurations, and features closely and carefully to ensure that they match the constraints and requirements of your project.

We discussed a few types of timers, specifically, count-up, count-down, and programmable timers, and some common applications for them. When selecting timer hardware, remember to first determine the number of timers you need, and then assess the timer capabilities your project requires in terms of resolution, programmability, and integration. The most important criteria for choosing timer software is to make sure it exploits your hardware and provides a level of abstraction so you can program the timer without writing assembly routines. To illustrate this, we used ETS Kernel. It provides access to time-of-day functions using standard C library routines and Win32-compatible routines. To provide interrupt-driven timers, you can write an ISR, but ETS supports callback functions that are easier to write and use.

Multitasking and serial I/O are next on the list of embedded topics to discuss. But before we endeavor to explain them, we enhance our UPS project in the next chapter so we can use the project as an implementation example.

A Smart UPS

W e've seen that delivering real-time performance depends on a number of hardware and software solutions. We're about to add two more to the software list: multitasking and serial I/O.

Multitasking is a system's capability to work on more than one task at a time. It is particularly useful in real-time systems not only because it lets a system handle more than one activity at a time, but also because it lets the developer prioritize activities, so that critical system inputs and requirements are always serviced first.

Serial I/O is a method for transferring data. It is fundamental to the development of real-time applications because it's inexpensive in terms of hardware costs, well understood, and widely used. Serial I/O is used to send and receive data within a system, to send and receive data between a system and its peripherals, and for communicating among systems.

To illustrate how to implement multitasking and serial I/O in an embedded system, we add these capabilities to the Simple UPS project presented in Chapter 8. The Smart UPS we introduce in this chapter is a real-time multitasking application that uses serial I/O. We show you how using multitasking simplifies the job of managing multiple activities. We use serial I/O to allow a remote computer to connect to the UPS and monitor its activity.

Our implementation of serial I/O in this project means that you need that second cable connection discussed in Chapter 3, "Software Installation and Setup." As before, you download the embedded application to the target using your existing connection. You use the second cable for serial communications between the host and the target. Remember that for serial I/O, the second cable must be a serial cable.

HOW THE SMART UPS PROJECT WORKS

The specification for this second UPS project is the same as the one presented in Chapter 8, "A Simple UPS," with one addition: It must be capable of being operated remotely. Remote control is a particularly useful feature. It means that the UPS can be off-site, on another floor, or in some other out-of-the-way location — such as under a desk. A user can monitor UPS activity and control the power on/off switch without leaving the office or crawling around on the floor.

To build this UPS, we begin with the same hardware components as before: a system controller, a battery and a charger, battery and load monitors, an AC line monitor, an inverter, switches, a pushbutton, indicator lights, and a speaker. To these we add a host PC and a serial cable. Figure 11-1 shows the new configuration.

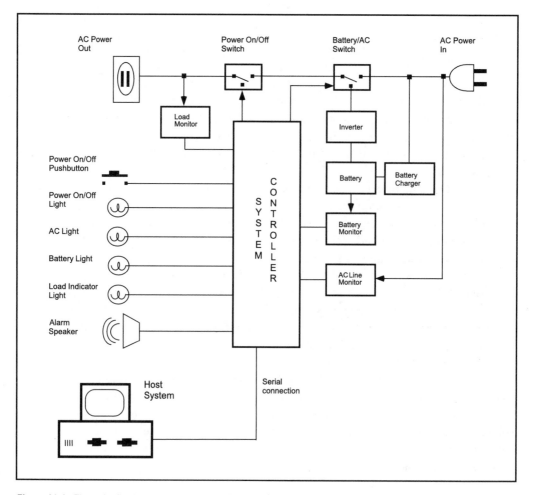

Figure 11-1: The major hardware components of a UPS that is operated remotely.

On its system controller, the UPS has a bidirectional serial I/O port. We use the serial cable to connect the serial I/O port on the target to a serial port on the host monitoring system. This host system is a standard PC-compatible computer running Windows 95, 98, or NT.

The host system communicates with the UPS over the serial connection. It continuously requests status information from the UPS system and displays it in a window on the host computer. The UPS status information includes the presence or absence of a load, the AC power status, the battery status, and whether or not power is supplied to the load, all of which are also shown by the LEDs on the UPS hardware. The UPS status information includes additional information about the remaining battery life that cannot be ascertained from the physical UPS panel lights. In addition to simulating hardware inputs, the host program can send commands to the UPS to turn the power to the load on or off. This feature relieves a user from crawling under a desk to locate and push the Power On/Off pushbutton.

DESIGNING THE SIMULATION

The software simulation for the Smart UPS is divided into two programs. WINUPS.EXE is a user-interface program that runs on the host, displaying UPS status and simulating UPS inputs; UPS2.EXE simulates the underlying UPS hardware and runs on the target. The two programs communicate over a serial connection. We discuss the user interface first.

WINUPS serves two purposes. First, it displays the current status of the UPS system, as described for the system requirements. Second, in addition to providing a Power On/Off input to the UPS system, it can also simulate the two hardware inputs — the AC Line Monitor and the Load Monitor — needed by the UPS simulation. Because we're building a remote user-interface program as part of the system requirements, it's an obvious choice to use that same program to simulate hardware inputs, rather than using a keyboard on the target system as we did for the Simple UPS. A screen shot of the main window of WINUPS is shown in Figure 11-2.

The WINUPS main window is divided into three sections. The uppermost section, Simulate UPS Inputs, contains the same input options as the original UPS project. Clicking any one of the buttons in this section causes WINUPS to send the corresponding command to the target through the serial port. Clicking the Power On button instructs the target to supply power to a load, an alternative to walking over to the system and pressing the Power On/Off pushbutton. Clicking the AC Power Bad button commands the target to simulate the AC line monitor detecting AC power going bad. Finally, clicking the Add Load button tells the target to simulate adding a load to the system. The text for the buttons changes depending on the UPS state. Specifically, the Power button text reads Power On if no power is being supplied to the load, and reads Power Off if power is being supplied to the load. The AC Power button reads AC Power Bad if the AC power is good, or AC Power Good if it is bad. The Load button reads Add Load if no load is on the system, and Remove Load if a load is present.

UPS2, the simulation running on the target, processes the commands it receives from WINUPS; that is, it simulates the hardware input and changes the UPS state accordingly. After UPS2 executes each command, it sends the current UPS state information to WINUPS. In

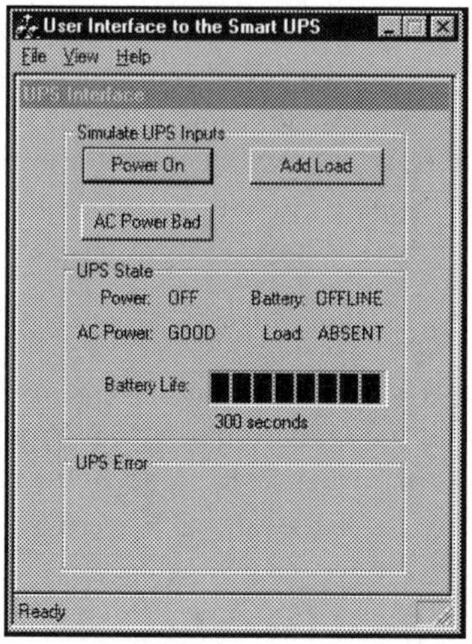

Figure 11-2: This UPS project uses a Windows interface rather than a character-based one to simulate the hardware's input and output controls.

addition to the commands to simulate hardware inputs, UPS2 recognizes a command that just requests the current UPS state, without changing any hardware inputs. The command that requests the UPS state is used by WINUPS to continuously update the UPS state display on the host computer.

The middle section, UPS State, shows the current status of the power to the load (on or off), AC power (good or bad), battery (online or offline), and load (present or absent). Notice that we added a Battery Life indicator. It provides a bar chart that graphically depicts the remaining battery life and an associated numeric field that shows the corresponding time in seconds.

The Smart UPS simulates the battery discharging when a load is run off the battery, and simulates the battery recharging when AC power returns. The maximum battery life is 300 seconds (5 minutes). The battery recharge rate is 50 percent (that is, the battery gains 1 second of life for every 2 seconds of recharge time). During battery discharge, UPS2 beeps the speaker once every 5 seconds. During the last 30 seconds of battery life, the software increases the frequency, beeping the speaker once every 2 seconds. This implementation more closely reflects a battery's operation and a UPS's response.

The WINUPS program automatically requests new state information from the UPS system every 3 seconds. This allows WINUPS to continuously update the battery life indicator (and other state information) to reflect the current UPS state.

Finally, the bottom section, UPS Error, displays error messages from the UPS.

We won't explore WINUPS further, because our focus here is embedded applications. Nevertheless, fully commented source code is available in the \TSLITE\PROJECTS\UPS2\WIN-UPS directory. You can compile the code or simply run the precompiled application, WIN-UPS.EXE. We go over the steps for building and running the project later in the chapter.

SOFTWARE SUBSYSTEMS

As before, we designed the software subsystems for the Smart UPS so that migration from the simulation to the actual system is as simple as possible. The block diagram in Figure 11-3 provides a good bird's-eye view of the software architecture. We'll use the figure as a guide for describing how each of the subsystems work separately and together. There are five subsystems in the Smart UPS:

- Serial I/O subsystem
- Command receive subsystem
- Timer subsystem
- Messaging subsystem
- Event subsystem

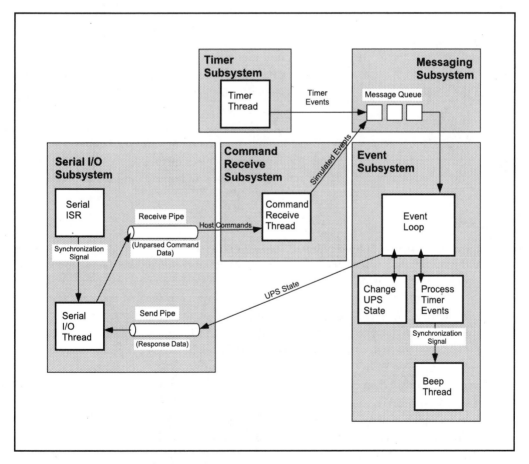

Figure 11-3: There are five subsystems within the Smart UPS that work together to simulate the UPS hardware.

Serial I/O Subsystem

The serial I/O subsystem is responsible for writing characters to and reading characters from the serial port. It consists of an ISR that handles serial port interrupts and wakes up a thread to perform the actual serial I/O. The interface to the subsystem consists of read-characters and write-characters functions, which use pipes to exchange data with the serial I/O thread.

Command Receive Subsystem

Information arriving at the serial port from the host consists of commands from WINUPS. The command receive subsystem receives incoming data by calling the read-characters function in the serial I/O subsystem. Then the command receive subsystem parses the byte stream into commands, packages the commands as simulated events, and passes the events to the event subsystem using the message queue. Unrecognized commands are simply discarded — the communications protocol has no provision for requesting that a command be resent.

Timer Subsystem

The timer subsystem consists of a single timer thread that serves the same purpose as the timer callback in Chapter 10, "Timers." The timer thread awakens at regular intervals and injects timer events on the message queue. These timer events provide a steady heartbeat that enables the Smart UPS to perform time-related activities.

Messaging Subsystem

The messaging subsystem manages the message queue, which is the data conduit into the event loop for the timer and command receive subsystems. The messaging subsystem allows multiple threads to add messages to the tail of the queue and remove messages from the head of the queue.

Event Subsystem

The job of the event subsystem is to take incoming events off the message queue and dispatch them to their proper handlers. This project has two types of events: simulated hardware input events, generated by commands received from WINUPS, and timer events, generated by the timer thread. Simulated input events are handled by calling a routine that updates the current UPS state and then, for most events, sends the new UPS state to WINUPS.

Timer events are used to decrement a counter when the battery is online and discharging. Fully charged, the battery has a life of 5 minutes. When the battery is put online, the event subsystem begins performing a 5-minute countdown, during which time it beeps the speaker once every 5 seconds. When the subsystem recognizes that the battery life is less than 30 seconds, it beeps the speaker once every 2 seconds.

The event subsystem also uses these timer events to increment a counter when the battery is offline and charging. If the battery life is less than 5 minutes and AC power is set to good, the event subsystem begins incrementing the counter. The subsystem charges the battery one-half second for every second of elapsed time, simulating the fact that charge time is always longer than the battery's discharge time.

SOFTWARE INTERFACES

Defining software interfaces is the next step in the design process. We'll examine the interfaces for the serial I/O subsystem (by far the most interesting), the command receive subsystem, and the messaging subsystem. As with the Simple UPS, prototypes for the interface functions for all subsystems are in the UPS.H file.

Serial I/O Subsystem

The serial I/O subsystem consists of four interface functions:

- **BOOL InitSerialsys(BOOL fCom1)**. UPS2 calls InitSerialsys() at start-up to initialize the serial I/O subsystem. The fCom1 argument specifies the COM port (TRUE for COM1 or FALSE for COM2) that the target system will use for serial communications. The default is COM1. The InitSerialsys() function first verifies that the port is available (that is, it exists and is not being used by ETS Kernel for host communications). InitSerialsys() then creates the send and receive pipes that will be used to transfer serial I/O data between the serial I/O thread and the SerialRead() and SerialWrite() functions called by the other subsystems. Next, InitSerialsys() launches the serial I/O thread that will act as the serial I/O device driver. Finally, InitSerialsys() installs the serial ISR and programs the serial port hardware to the proper bit rates, bits-per-character, and so on. A return value of TRUE indicates success; FALSE indicates failure.

- **void CleanupSerialsys(void)**. At shutdown, UPS2 must call CleanupSerialsys() to provide an orderly termination of the serial I/O subsystem. The CleanupSerialsys() function unhooks the serial ISR and terminates the serial I/O thread. In addition, CleanupSerialsys() closes the send and receive pipes.

- **BOOL SerialWrite(void *pBuf, DWORD nChar, BOOL fWait)**. UPS2 writes data to the serial port by calling the SerialWrite() function. The pBuf argument is a pointer to the buffer holding the characters that will be written to the serial port. The nChar argument specifies the number of characters to be written. Finally, the fWait argument allows the caller to specify whether SerialWrite() will wait until all the characters are written, or return immediately (with an error) if the characters cannot be written immediately. A return value of TRUE indicates success, FALSE indicates failure.

- **DWORD SerialRead(void *pBuf, DWORD nChar, BOOL fWait)**. The SerialRead() function is the converse of SerialWrite(). UPS2 reads bytes from the serial port by calling SerialRead(). The pBuf argument is a pointer to the buffer that the bytes will be read into. The nChar argument indicates the number of bytes that are to be read from the serial port. The caller sets the fWait argument to TRUE if SerialRead() is to wait for the requested number of bytes (nChar) to arrive. If fWait is set to FALSE, SerialRead() always returns immediately. The return value is equal to nChar if the read succeeds, and otherwise indicates the number of bytes currently available to be read.

Command Receive Subsystem

The command receive subsystem runs as a separate thread in the background. UPS2 makes only two explicit calls into this subsystem:

- **BOOL InitCmdsys(void)**. This routine initializes the command receive subsystem. It requires no arguments, and returns a Boolean value of TRUE if it is successful, FALSE if it fails. InitCmdsys() creates the command receive thread.

- **void CleanupCmdsys(void)**. This routine shuts down the command receive subsystem. It signals the command receive thread to terminate, waits for acknowledgement from the thread that termination was successful, and then exits.

Messaging Subsystem

The messaging subsystem interface consists of four functions:

- **HANDLE MsgQueueCreate(DWORD MsgSize, DWORD nMsgs)**. This function creates a message queue. The parameter MsgSize specifies the size of a message, and the parameter nMsgs specifies how many messages the queue holds at a time. This function returns a handle — a unique value by which the queue can be referenced. The MsgQueueCreate() function returns NULL if not enough space is available to create the queue.

- **BOOL MsgQueueDelete(HANDLE hQueue)**. This function deletes a message queue that's been created by MsgQueueCreate(). The hQueue argument is the handle (returned by MsgQueueCreate()) that identifies the queue to be deleted. If the handle given by hQueue is invalid, MsgQueueDelete() returns FALSE; otherwise it returns TRUE.

- **int MsgWrite(HANDLE hQueue, void *pMsg, BOOL fWait)**. MsgWrite() writes a message to the message queue. (This function is analogous to the AddEvent() function described back in Chapter 8, "A Simple UPS.") The hQueue argument specifies the queue to which the message will be written, and the pMsg argument is a pointer to the buffer holding the message to be written. (Note that the caller needn't identify the size of the message. All messages are required to conform to the MsgSize argument specified in the MsgQueueCreate() call.) If the caller sets fWait to TRUE and the queue is full, MsgWrite() waits until a slot frees up (into which it can deposit the message) before returning. If fWait is set to FALSE and the queue is full, MsgWrite() returns immediately. MsgWrite() returns a 1 if it is successful in writing a message to the queue, a 0 if the queue is full and MsgWrite() returns without depositing a message in the queue, and a -1 if an invalid handle was specified.

- **int MsgRead(HANDLE hQueue, void *pMsg, BOOL fWait)**. MsgRead() reads a message from the queue identified by the handle hQueue. The message is read into the buffer pointed to by pMsg. If the caller has set fWait to TRUE and the queue is empty, MsgRead() waits until an item arrives in the queue. If fWait is FALSE and the queue is empty, MsgRead() returns immediately. The MsgRead() function returns a 1 if it successfully reads a message from the queue, a 0 if the queue is empty and it returns without reading a message from the queue, and a -1 if an invalid handle was specified.

START-UP AND SHUTDOWN PROCESSES

The start-up and shutdown processes are more involved than their equivalents in the Simple UPS. At system start-up, because UPS2 is a multitasking application that uses multiple threads, the initialization routines must launch each thread.

First, the UPS2 initialization code calls the messaging subsystem to create the message queue used to send events to the event subsystem. Because several subsystems use this queue, it must be created before initializing the subsystems.

Next, the subsystem initialization routines are called. The event subsystem initializes the UPS state and creates the beep thread, which is signaled to beep the speaker when the battery is discharging. The serial I/O subsystem creates the serial I/O thread for sending and receiving characters over the serial port, and then installs an ISR to handle interrupts from the serial port. The command receive subsystem creates a command receive thread that waits for commands to arrive from WINUPS. The timer subsystem creates the timer thread that generates periodic timer events for processing by the event subsystem.

Beyond Simulation

A number of modifications and additions to the WINUPS and UPS2 simulations have to be made to turn the Smart UPS project into a real UPS system.

If this were a real application, the WINUPS program would be without the Add Load and AC Power Bad buttons, because they were implemented only to control aspects of the simulation. The only button left would be Power On, so that you could operate the UPS remotely. The UPS State section of WINUPS would be unchanged.

Within UPS2, the serial, timer, and messaging subsystems would remain unchanged. You would recode the command receive subsystem to recognize fewer commands than it does now. Because the WINUPS system would no longer send commands to the UPS to set AC power to good or bad, for example, the command receive subsystem would no longer need to recognize them.

You would remove the battery simulation code in the event subsystem. The event subsystem would instead call into a new battery subsystem, which would provide function calls to control putting the battery online or offline and monitoring the battery charge level.

A real UPS would have front-panel status lights, and the event subsystem would be modified to control the status lights in addition to sending the UPS status through the serial subsystem to the WINUPS program.

You'd have to create a load subsystem, whose job would be to monitor the load on the UPS. Whenever the load changed, the load subsystem would call the messaging subsystem to send load-changed events to the event subsystem.

Finally, you'd add an AC power monitoring subsystem. This subsystem would watch the quality of the incoming AC power. If the quality should change, the subsystem would call the messaging subsystem and pass it events indicating that the AC power is either good or bad.

At system shutdown, the individual shutdown routines for each subsystem are called. These routines terminate the threads they created at initialization and free up any other resources they have allocated. In particular, the serial I/O subsystem must restore the original serial interrupt vector (which probably points to an ISR that does nothing). Otherwise, subsequent serial interrupts will trigger (or attempt to trigger) an ISR that's part of a now-terminated application; the result would be anyone's guess.

ERROR HANDLING

Fatal errors and initialization errors are handled in this project as they were in the previous UPS project.

New to this version is an error condition that occurs if a user attempts to attach a load when the battery is completely discharged and AC is still bad. In this situation, the event subsystem sends WINUPS a message containing an error string, and WINUPS displays it in the UPS Error portion of its main window.

BUILDING THE SMART UPS PROJECT

The source code files for UPS2 are in the \TSLITE\PROJECTS\UPS2\UPS2 directory; the source files for WINUPS are in the \TSLITE\PROJECTS\UPS2\WINUPS directory. Within each of these directories, you'll notice a RELEASE subdirectory that contains a prebuilt executable for the respective program. If you want to only run the programs, you can use the prebuilt executables. To build either executable from Visual C++ Developer Studio, open the UPS2.DSW or WINUPS.DSW workspace file, and then click Build|Rebuild All. More details on building the projects are provided in Chapter 3, "Software Installation and Setup."

RUNNING THE SMART UPS PROJECT

Before we run the programs in this project, UPS2.EXE and WINUPS.EXE, make sure you have correctly connected the target system to the host computer. Figure 11-4 shows the recommended configuration.

The serial communications connection is over a LapLink-compatible serial cable that connects the COM1 serial ports on the host and the target. The downloading and debugging connection is over a LapLink-compatible parallel cable connecting the LPT1 parallel ports on the host and the target.

> **Note:** What if you don't have a parallel port on both computers, or you don't have a parallel cable? If both computers each have two serial ports, you can use two serial cables, one for the downloading/debugging connection and the other for the serial communications connection. We recommend you connect COM1 to COM1 and COM2 to COM2, to keep your sanity intact. Chapter 3, "Software Installation and Setup," tells you how to configure ETS Kernel and the host side software to use a serial connection for downloading anddebugging. If you choose to use the COM2-to-COM2 cable for the serial communications connection, you have to instruct both WINUPS and UPS2 to use COM2. We show you how to do this next.

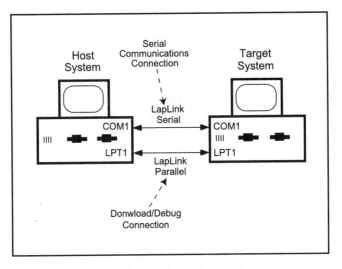

Figure 11-4: The recommended system configuration for the Smart UPS.

With the cable configuration set up, begin by downloading and running UPS2, although it doesn't matter which application you launch first. From Developer Studio, click Build|Execute ups2.exe. If the serial connection is made to COM2 rather than COM1, select Project|Settings, select the Debug tab, and enter com2 in the box for Program arguments; then click Build|Execute ups2.exe.

If you prefer to run the program from a DOS box, set the current directory to \TSLITE\PROJECTS\UPS2\UPS2 and then enter the following command:

```
runemb release\ups2
```

If the serial connection is made to COM2 rather than the default COM1 on your target system, enter the com2 parameter on the command line:

```
runemb release\ups2 com2
```

Execute the host application from Developer Studio by clicking Build|Execute winups.exe. Alternatively, at the DOS prompt, set the current directory to \TSLITE\PROJECTS\UPS2 \WINUPS\RELEASE and type:

```
winups
```

Because this is a Windows program, you could execute it also from the Windows Start menu or from Windows Explorer.

The next step is to configure WINUPS to communicate with UPS2. From the WINUPS File menu, select Port Settings. This displays the dialog box shown in Figure 11-5. Select COM port 1 or 2 on the host that WINUPS will use to communicate with the target, and then click OK.

Now select File|Connect To UPS. WINUPS should display the current status of the UPS, as shown in Figure 11-6. If WINUPS reports that it's unable to connect to the UPS through the chosen serial port, you can either abort the program or ignore the error. Choose Ignore if

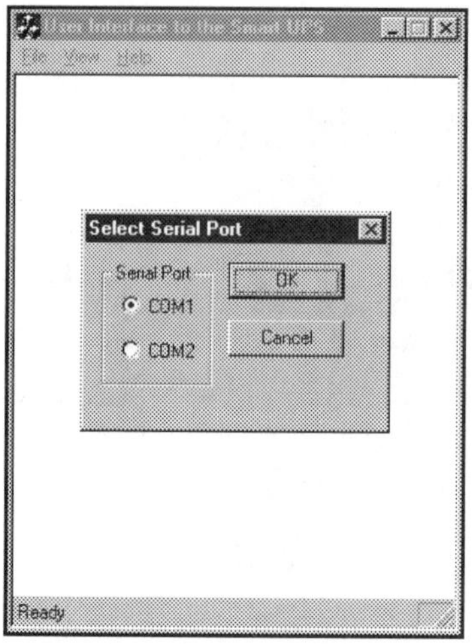

Figure 11-5: Configure WINUPS to use the correct serial port setting.

you think you may have selected the wrong COM port. Return to the dialog box shown in Figure 11-5, choose the proper COM port, and retry File|Connect To UPS. Otherwise, choose Abort, check your cable connections, and verify that you started UPS2 on the target and that you selected the correct target serial port when you launched UPS2. If your cable connections and port selections look correct, try another communications program, such as LapLink, to see whether it will work over the cable connection you've made. If not, check to make sure your null modem cable has the correct wiring. The cabling for a null modem is described in Appendix C, "Configuring Serial Networking Connections for Windows."

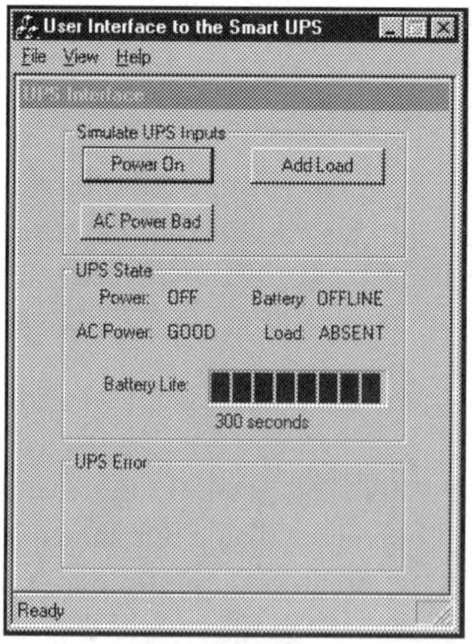

Figure 11-6: WINUPS reports the initial state of the UPS.

Note: How do you shut down the target program (without rebooting) if you're unable to establish a serial connection? Simply make the DOS box used to download UPS2 (either the DOS box automatically created by Developer Studio when you ran the program or the DOS box you used to enter the RUNEMB download command) the current window. Then press Ctrl-Break to kill the UPS2 program on the target.

Notice that the initial state of the UPS is the same as it was in Chapter 8: the power to the load is off, the battery is offline, AC power is good, and no load is present. Also notice that the battery is at 100 percent capacity, with 300 seconds of life remaining.

Let's put the UPS in its normal state by adding a load. Click the Power On button. Notice that its label changes to Power Off and that the Power field in the UPS State section changes to ON. Click the Add Load button. Its label changes to Remove Load, and the Load field reports PRESENT. The UPS is now delivering power to a load. Because AC power is still good, the battery is offline and at full capacity.

Now simulate a power failure. Press the AC Power Bad button. Several things happen at once, as Figure 11-7 shows: the button's label changes to AC Power Good, the AC Power field changes to BAD, and the Battery Life bar graph and seconds indicator decrease in real time to reflect the declining battery capacity. What we can't depict here is that the target's speaker is beeping.

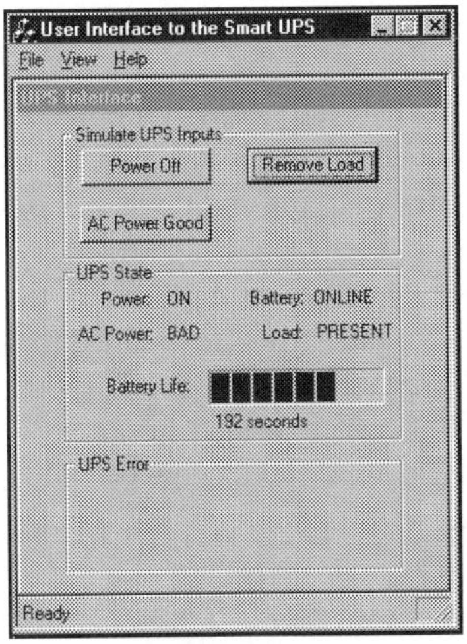

Figure 11-7: Triggering a power failure puts the battery online so that it can supply power to the load.

If you keep the AC power bad long enough for the battery life to drop to 30 seconds, you'll hear that the beeping picks up tempo. Ordinarily, when the battery is online, beeps occur once every 5 seconds. When the battery is in its last 30 seconds of life, however, the beep frequency increases to once every 2 seconds.

If you completely discharge the battery, the load is automatically disconnected. The system does not let you reconnect the load until the AC power is good.

If you don't completely discharge the battery, and instead return the AC power to good, you'll notice that not only does the beeping stop, but the battery begins to recharge. As mentioned earlier, the recharging rate is half the discharge rate (the battery gains a half-second of life for each second of charge time).

Experiment with the UPS system. Try discharging the battery to 0 and connecting a load to see the error message. Also try discharging the battery until the Battery Life indicator reads less than 30 seconds, briefly returning the AC power to good, and then setting AC power to bad again. The UPS should correctly detect the less-than-30-second battery life and beep the speaker at the proper rate. You can even disconnect the serial cable while the UPS2 and WIN-UPS simulations are running. Neither application fails; both continue executing in whatever state they were at the time the cable was disconnected. Reconnect the cable, and you can pick up where you left off.

When you finish experimenting, exit both programs by either selecting File|Exit in WIN-UPS or closing the WINUPS window. Before WINUPS exits, it sends a command to UPS2 instructing it to terminate.

A QUICK TOUR OF THE SOURCE

The source files for UPS2 are divided along subsystem lines. The outermost routines are in UPS.C. These include main() (identical to the code for the Simple UPS), InitializeUps() (which calls each subsystem's initialization routine), and CleanupUps() (which calls each subsystem's cleanup routine).

The event subsystem is in EVENT.C. The event loop and state machine are substantially the same as in the Simple UPS. What's new is the code to send the UPS state back to WIN-UPS, the simulation of the battery charging and discharging, and the addition of a thread to beep the speaker.

In the event loop, after each event has been processed, the event subsystem packages the UPS state into a UPS_RESPONSE data structure (defined in UPSIFACE.H), and then calls the serial I/O subsystem to send the data structure to WINUPS. UPSIFACE.H also contains defines for commands sent by WINUPS, and is located in the \TSLITE\PROJECTS\UPS2 directory, because it needs to be included by both UPS2 and WINUPS. The UPS_RESPONSE structure contains the following data:

```
//
// Response structure sent by UPS to WINUPS program. All non-BYTE values
// are packed in network byte order (MS byte first).
//
typedef struct {
    BYTE UpsID;              // ID, defined below
    DWORD State;            // UPS state DWORD
    DWORD msBatteryLife;   // Battery life, in milliseconds
    DWORD msMaxLife;       // Maximum battery life, in milliseconds
    BYTE ErrLen;           // Length (including terminating 0)
                           //   of error string following struct
} UPS_RESPONSE;
#define UPS_ID      0xA5
```

The structure contains an ID byte (used for error detection by the communications code), the UPS state DWORD, the number of milliseconds of battery life remaining, the maximum battery life (so WINUPS can calculate battery life remaining as a percentage), and an optional error message.

Notice that all variables longer than a byte are packed in big endian byte order (most significant byte first). Although for this application we know that both host and target use the same byte ordering (little endian, because they're both x86 machines), it's good practice when writing communications code to pack all data in a machine-independent byte order, so that the application will work even if the two communicating machines use a different byte order. We chose big endian as the communications byte order because that's the byte ordering used in most network stacks. The SendResponse() function in Listing 11-1 loads the UPS_RESPONSE structure and sends it to WINUPS.

Listing 11-1: The SendResponse() function

```
//
// Sends a response to the WINUPS program.
//
void SendResponse(char *pErrMsg)
{
    UPS_RESPONSE Response;
//
// Build the response structure.  All values larger than a byte are
// packed in a machine-independent order. (We use a MS-byte-first order
// because that is the same order used by network applications.) Packing
// and unpacking data values sent between two machines protects you from
// differences in byte ordering on different computer architectures.
// While it's not strictly necessary for this application (because we
// know that both UPS.EXE and WINUPS.EXE will run on x86 machines), we
// do it here to show what you'd need to do when building a distributed
// application that runs on different computer architectures.
//
    Response.UpsID = UPS_ID;
    Response.State = PackDword(CurrState);
    Response.msBatteryLife = PackDword(msBatteryLife);
    Response.msMaxLife = PackDword(MAX_BATTERY_LIFE);
    Response.ErrLen = (BYTE) strlen(pErrMsg);
    if (Response.ErrLen > 0)
        ++Response.ErrLen;
//
// Send the response structure and error message string if any.
// Since we wait to send chars, no need to check for an error return.
//
    SerialWrite(&Response, sizeof(Response), TRUE);
    if (Response.ErrLen > 0)
        SerialWrite(pErrMsg, Response.ErrLen, TRUE);
    return;
}
```

The code to load the structure is straightforward. The packing routines are in X86PACK.C, which is in the \TSLITE\PROJECTS\UPS2 directory so that the routines can be used by both UPS2 and WINUPS. To send the structure to WINUPS, we just call SerialWrite(), with a second call to send the error message if one is present. Notice that, to avoid having to cope with partial sends, we request SerialWrite() to block until it is able to buffer all the data to be sent. In other words, if the serial I/O subsystem is currently sending a lot of data, and its internal buffer (the send pipe in Figure 11-3) doesn't have enough room for the new data, the calling thread (the event loop) goes to sleep until the serial I/O subsystem has sent enough data to free up some space in the buffer. You see how the blocking code in the serial I/O subsystem is implemented in Chapter 12, "Multitasking."

The most important addition to the event subsystem is its handling of the battery simulation. The event subsystem has been modified to this end in several places. For example, in the GetNextState() routine, which handles the transition of the system from the current state to the next state, you find the following code, which deals with how the system reacts when the user attempts to attach a load to a discharged battery:

```
//
// Pick up the new state from the state table.  However, if the new
//. state will cause a drain on the battery, but the battery is dead,
// then we have to ignore the event if the user is trying to supply
// power to a load, or turn the power off if the AC just went bad, and
// generate an error.
//
    NewState = NextState[CurrState][Event];
    if ((NewState & STATE_AC_BAD) && (NewState & STATE_POWER_ON) &&
        (NewState & STATE_LOAD_PRESENT) && msBatteryLife == 0)
    {
        if (Event == EVENT_AC)
           CurrState = NextState[NewState][EVENT_POWER];
        fBeep = TRUE;
        strcpy(pErrMsg, "Can't supply power to a load because "
             "the AC is bad and the battery life is zero");
    }
```

In the preceding code snippet, the event subsystem sets the new state, and then examines the status of the AC power, the status of the power to the load, whether a load is present, and the current battery level. If the user is attempting to supply power to a load using the battery and the battery's charge level is zero, the system generates an error message.

Also, notice the second inner if() statement. That checks to see whether the AC power has just gone bad. If that's true (and the battery level is zero — a condition tested by the outer if() statement), the code simulates the arrival of an EVENT_POWER event, which has the effect of turning off the power to the load.

Further on in GetNextState(), you encounter the code that simulates the discharging and charging of the battery:

```
//
// Update the battery charging/discharging status
//
      if (!(CurrState & STATE_AC_BAD))
      {
          // AC good--battery is charging
          fBatteryCharging = TRUE;
          fBatteryDischarging = FALSE;
      }
      else
      {
          // AC bad--we're not charging
          fBatteryCharging = FALSE;
          if ((CurrState & STATE_POWER_ON) &&
             (CurrState & STATE_LOAD_PRESENT))
          {
              // power on and load present--we're discharging the battery
              if (!fBatteryDischarging)
              {
                  fBatteryDischarging = TRUE;
                  msSinceLastDischargeBeep = 0;
                  fBeep = TRUE;
              }
          }
          else
              // we're not discharging the battery
              fBatteryDischarging = FALSE;
      }
  }
```

First, notice in this code that two Boolean variables are associated with battery charging and discharging: fBatteryCharging and fBatteryDischarging. It would seem that the two conditions (charging and discharging) would be mutually exclusive, but they aren't. Note that the battery could be neither charging nor discharging — it could be either fully charged or fully discharged.

In any case, the code first examines the status of AC power. If AC power is good, the battery is set to the charging state. If AC power is bad, the battery is not charging — but it might not be discharging, either. It could be that no load is attached, which is the next condition the code checks for. If AC power is bad, the power to the load is on, and a load is attached, the battery is discharging. (Notice that the code also sets the msSinceLastDischargeBeep variable to zero. This variable keeps track of the time since the last speaker beep. Because this is the point in the code where the simulated discharge begins, this variable must be initialized to zero.)

The remainder of the code that handles battery charging and discharging is in the ProcessTimers() function in Listing 11-2. ProcessTimers() is called whenever the event loop receives a timer event.

Listing 11-2: The ProcessTimers() function

```
//
// This function is called when a timer event occurs (approx.
// every TIMER_PERIOD ms.) to process any time-dependent changes to
// the UPS system.
//
void ProcessTimers(DWORD Msecs)
{
//
// If battery is currently recharging, increase its life
// appropriately.
//
    if (fBatteryCharging)
    {
        msBatteryLife += Msecs * BATT_RECH_PERCENT / 100;
        if (msBatteryLife > MAX_BATTERY_LIFE)
            msBatteryLife = MAX_BATTERY_LIFE;
    }
//
// If battery is currently discharging, decrease its life
// and beep if necessary.  If battery life goes down to zero,
// we have to turn off the power and stop discharging.
//
    else if (fBatteryDischarging)
    {
        if (msBatteryLife >= Msecs)
            msBatteryLife -= Msecs;
        else
        {
            msBatteryLife = 0;
            if (CurrState & STATE_POWER_ON)
                CurrState = NextState[CurrState][EVENT_POWER];
            fBatteryDischarging = FALSE;
        }
        msSinceLastDischargeBeep += Msecs;
        if (msSinceLastDischargeBeep >= BATT_BEEP_PERIOD ||
            (msBatteryLife <= BATT_BEEP_PANIC &&
             msSinceLastDischargeBeep >= BATT_PANIC_PERIOD))
        {
            SetEvent(hBeepEvent);
            msSinceLastDischargeBeep = 0;
        }
    }
    return;
}
```

If the battery is currently charging, we increment the battery life by the number of milliseconds since the last timer event times the recharge rate. If the battery is discharging, we decrement the battery life. In addition, if the time since the last beep used to warn the user when the battery is discharging exceeds the beep period (5 seconds for the first 4 minutes of battery life, and 2 seconds for the last 30 seconds of life), we call SetEvent() to signal the beep thread. We describe how Win32 events and other synchronization objects used in multithreaded programs work in Chapter 12, "Multitasking."

The code to beep the speaker is placed in a separate thread, because the speaker is beeped by turning it on, waiting a specific period of time and then turning the speaker off again. The event subsystem can't afford to wait while the speaker is beeped; it has to be constantly checking for new events arriving in the message queue. We solve that problem by putting the code to beep the speaker in a separate thread that doesn't have any other responsibilities.

In this version of the UPS system, we factored out the queue mechanism that the event subsystem used to ferry event information to different parts of the application. We created a generic message queue that coordinates the passing of messages among different threads in UPS2. The messaging subsystem is in MESSAGE.C, and we examine it in Chapter 12, "Multitasking."

The command receive subsystem (in CMDRECV.C) creates a thread that sits in a loop waiting for commands to arrive over the serial connection. It converts the commands to simulated events and adds them to the message queue. The timer subsystem (in TIMER.C) creates a thread that wakes up periodically and adds a timer event to the message queue. We look at the code for the command receive and timer subsystems in Chapter 12 also.

The serial I/O subsystem is in SERIAL.C. It consists of an ISR, a thread, and two interface functions to read and write characters over the serial port. The ISR just signals the serial I/O thread when an interrupt occurs; it's the job of the thread to perform all the serial port I/O to send and receive characters over the wire. The read and write functions communicate with the serial I/O thread through send and receive pipes, which also serve to buffer received characters and characters waiting to be sent. We cover the serial I/O subsystem code in Chapter 13, "Serial I/O."

SUMMARY

This concludes our introduction to the smart UPS. In this version, we built the UPS as a multithreaded program, which greatly simplifies the process of responding to inputs from multiple sources. We also added a serial communications capability to a Windows program used to simulate UPS inputs and display UPS state information. In the next chapter, we explore the important topic of multitasking. A closer examination of the source code for UPS2 will allow us to put our theoretical discussions of multitasking to practice. Following that, in Chapter 13, we discuss serial I/O and use the code in the serial I/O subsystem to demonstrate a working example of low-level serial I/O routines.

12

Multitasking

W hat is a task? A *task* is a generic term that refers to an activity carried out by software that occurs independently from other activities in the system. For example, if you run two programs, such as a word processor and a spreadsheet, on your desktop system, each of those executing programs is a task. You can perform a recalculation in your spreadsheet and edit a letter simultaneously. Similarly, the word processing application itself might be internally divided into three separate tasks; the formatting and justification engine, the display task, and the printing task. The word processor can let you edit a document, automatically flow the new text and repaginate the document, and print a second document in the background, all at the same time.

Tasks that are separate executing programs, called *processes*, and tasks that execute in the context of a single program, called *threads*, may appear to be different animals. As you'll see in this chapter, however, they have as many similarities as they have differences. When we use the word *task* in this chapter, we mean that the concept being discussed applies to both processes and threads.

Multitasking is probably most often described as a computer's capability to perform more than one task at the same time. Sometimes this definition is taken literally and thought to mean that the CPU is executing multiple instructions simultaneously. But the correct interpretation of this description is that the multitasking operating system is an adept juggler, switching from task to task quickly and seamlessly. Although the CPU appears to be performing its tasks simultaneously, it is processing only one instruction at a time.

Using a multitasking operating system has two important benefits: the capability to accomplish more work in the same amount of time, and the capability to handle multiple tasks simultaneously.

In most cases, a multitasking OS gets work done faster than a single-tasking system, even though the underlying CPU processes instructions one at a time. This is because a multitasking OS isn't stymied by the inevitable delays encountered in executing a task. If it can't continue executing a task, it turns its attention to another task. Suppose an OS has to run two tasks, A and B. Task A runs to a point in its execution where it must stop and wait for input (perhaps user input from a keyboard). In a single-tasking system, the system waits to complete task A before going to task B. In a multitasking system, it doesn't wait. The system turns its attention to task B, helping task B do its work while task A is waiting for input. When task A receives input, the system stops working on task B and returns to task A.

Getting more work accomplished in less time is always good no matter what computer system you're using. But for embedded systems in particular, a multitasking operating system's capability to handle multiple tasks is a second and crucial benefit.

We've said that a real-time embedded system must respond immediately to input. The fact is that it often must respond immediately to *multiple* inputs. That is, it must be able to receive input from more than one source at a time, and it must be able to respond by sending output to more than one recipient at a time.

Similarly, some embedded applications are effective only if they're built to handle multiple tasks — they would be useless if written as single-tasking applications. Consider a heart monitoring application that monitors the heartbeat of a patient, issues a warning when it becomes irregular, saves all its recordings to a file, and prints a summary report on demand. It's useless if it has to stop monitoring a patient to print a report.

So in this chapter, we focus on using a multitasking OS and building multitasking applications. We start by describing processes and threads, and discussing when to choose threads or processes (or both) in a real-time system. Then we cover how an OS schedules tasks, in particular the scheduling algorithms most desirable for real-time programming. Task synchronization and intertask communications are next; these are the methods tasks use to interact with each other. Then we discuss what kind of multitasking features to look for in an RTOS, and techniques for debugging multitasking applications. We conclude the chapter by examining the code for the various threads in the Smart UPS project.

PROCESSES AND MULTIPROCESSING

A process is most commonly defined as an executing program. A program consists of algorithms expressed in the program's code. A process is an activity, performing work in accordance with the program's algorithms. As illustrated in Figure 12-1, a process consists of a collection of memory areas allocated to the process by the operating system, plus the current CPU state. When a program is launched, the operating system creates a process, and allocates a collection of memory areas. This collection consists of the following:

- A code area that contains the process's executable code.
- A stack area that holds local variables and function return pointers.
- A data area where the process stores its global variables.

- A heap area that holds dynamically allocated memory (as is returned by the `malloc()` C run-time library call, for example).

- A system area that contains information maintained by the operating system on behalf of the process. The system area includes information about resources allocated to the process, such as data structures for open files or for network connections. The system area includes information also about the process itself, such as the location of its memory regions and the process's saved CPU state if it is not currently running.

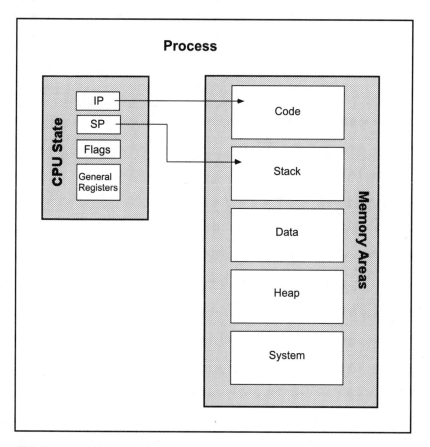

Figure 12-1: A process is defined by the CPU state (the contents of specific registers) as well as a number of memory areas that the operating system allocates and assigns to the process.

From the perspective of the operating system, a process owns its memory areas. A running process is defined also by the current CPU state. The CPU state consists of the general processor registers, the instruction pointer (IP) and the stack pointer (SP), processor flags, and any other CPU registers that can be modified by an application program. When a process is not running, its CPU state is saved in the process's system memory area.

The contents of the IP register point to the location of the current executing instruction in the process's code space. The contents of the SP register point to the location of the current stack frame in the process's stack area. A *stack frame* is a section in a process's stack area that holds the local variables of the currently executing function, plus information needed to return to the calling function when the current function executes a `return` statement.

The flags register holds the status of the CPU. On many processors, a bit in the flags register is used to enable or disable interrupts. Other bits in the flags register may indicate the current process's privilege level. (Some processes in the system have higher privilege levels than others. For example, in many systems, a high privilege level is needed before the CPU will allow a process to directly access I/O hardware. Only OS kernel processes are permitted to have such a high privilege level. This requirement reduces the likelihood that a poorly written application program will inadvertently manipulate the hardware in some destructive fashion. Only the operating system can directly access hardware.) Still other bits in the flags register are set as the result of compare instructions and are subsequently used by conditional branch instructions.

Finally, the general registers support process execution. Accumulators hold operands for logical and mathematical functions, pointer registers hold addresses for indirect addressing operations, and so on.

Note: For 32-bit members of the 80x86 family, general registers include registers that point to the starting addresses of the process's memory areas. For example, the CS register points to the start of the code area, and the SS register points to the start of the stack area.

Running more than one process at the same time is called *multiprocessing*. An operating system runs multiple processes by constantly switching from one process's context to another or, more simply, by context switching.

A process's context consists of its memory areas and CPU state. An operating system switches contexts by suspending the execution of the current process, saving its CPU state, and loading the context of the next process to run. Loading the new process's context consists of making the memory areas accessible and loading the CPU registers. Making memory areas accessible may involve switching to new memory management data structures in a system with hardware memory management, or it may involve no work if all processes are always accessible in system memory.

The operating system lets each process run for up to a specific maximum time, called a *time slice*. When a process's time slice expires, the OS selects another process (using a scheduling algorithm) and switches to that process's context. Although at any given instant only one process is running, all processes make forward progress if viewed over a long enough time interval.

Although all processes (or some portion of all processes, in a virtual memory system) are in system memory at the same time, only the memory areas owned by the current process are accessible. In systems with memory management hardware, the operating system can usually protect the memory areas of nonactive processes so that any attempt to access them results in a memory protection fault. In systems without hardware memory protection, an errant pointer can accidentally read or write to another process's memory area, but there is no way to intentionally read or write to another process's memory area because you can't obtain information about where other processes are located in memory.

If processes cannot directly access each other's memory areas, how do they exchange data or interact with each other? The operating system provides communication mechanisms, such as shared memory and pipes, for processes that need to cooperate. We discuss intertask communications later in this chapter.

Processes using communication mechanisms such as shared memory, however, need techniques for controlling access to shared resources. Because a process doesn't know when its time slice might expire and another process might be scheduled, it needs a way to protect access to a shared resource. If the process is preempted (the OS switches to another process) in the middle of accessing a resource, this protection prevents the newly scheduled process from also accessing the resource and potentially corrupting data. Processes use synchronization objects to prevent corruption of shared data; we describe how that works shortly.

Processes are normally created when programs are launched, either by a user of the system or by another process calling the operating system. In either case, the operating system allocates memory for the process, loads it into memory, and initializes the data structures in the system memory area. In some operating systems, processes can also clone themselves to create a new process; for instance, the UNIX `fork()` call does this. Processes created in this way often share the same code memory area to conserve on memory use, but they each get their own stack, data, heap, and system data areas. Processes created by cloning may sound like threads (which are covered in the next section), because they are running the same program code. They are actually processes, however, because they each have their own, separate global data, unlike threads.

THREADS AND MULTITHREADING

A thread is an independent flow of execution in a process. In a multithreaded operating system, a process consists of one or more threads. All threads in a process share the code, data, heap, and system memory areas of that process, as shown in Figure 12-2. Each thread has a separate CPU state and a separate stack, a block of memory allocated out of the process's stack memory area.

Because all threads of a process share the same data and heap memory areas, all global data in the process can be accessed by any of the threads. Because each thread has its own stack, all local variables and function arguments are unique (private) to a specific thread.

Because threads share the same code and global data, they are tied much more closely than processes, and they tend to interact much more than separate processes do. For this reason, synchronization objects are likely to be used more frequently in multithreaded applications than they are in multiprocessing applications. The ways in which synchronization objects and intertask communications are used, however, is identical between processes and between threads. It's easier for threads to interact because they automatically have some shared memory for communication: the process's global data. But the principles of interaction are the same, regardless of whether you are programming threads or processes.

Because threads share the same system area, resources that the operating system allocates to a program are available to all threads in that process, just as global data is available to all threads. That means, for example, that if Thread #1 were to open a file, Thread #2 could access the file without having to open it. However, just as processes must control access to shared resources, so too must threads: Information in the system area is potentially available to all threads, so you must carefully control access to that information using synchronization objects.

> ### Thread-Specific Data
>
> In multithreaded applications, global, or static, data is shared by all threads, and local, or temporary, data is private to each thread. Most multithreading operating systems implement a third kind of data: static data that is private to a thread. This kind of data is often called thread-specific data. (In Win32 systems, it's called thread local storage.)
>
> Thread-specific data is useful because it provides a way for a thread to have private data that is persistent (doesn't go away when a function returns, like local variables) and can be accessed by any function in the program.
>
> Because global data defined with the standard syntax of the programming language is shared by all threads, most operating systems implement thread-specific data with APIs that the application calls. For instance, Win32 systems have four APIs to implement thread local storage. `TlsAlloc()` is used to allocate an index to a slot in thread local storage. `TlsSetValue()` and `TlsGetValue()` are used to store and retrieve a DWORD value in the allocated slot; a separate value is kept for each thread in the system. Normally, the value stored is a pointer to an arbitrary block of memory used by the thread as it wants. Finally, `TlsFree()` is called to free the thread local storage slot.

Context switching between threads in the same process involves simply saving the CPU state for the current thread and loading the CPU state for the new thread. Memory management data structures do not need to be changed, because the threads share the same memory areas. (If the context switch is between threads of different processes, the memory management data structures must also be updated.) Because less work is required for context switching between threads than between processes, you'll sometimes see threads called *lightweight processes*. In Figure 12-2, when the operating system switches from Thread #1 to Thread #2, all it needs to do is save the CPU registers for Thread #1 in the system memory area and then reload the CPU registers with the values saved for Thread #2. Because IP and SP are reloaded as part of the CPU state, after the context switch, the processor is executing at the code location for Thread #2 and using the stack allocated to Thread #2.

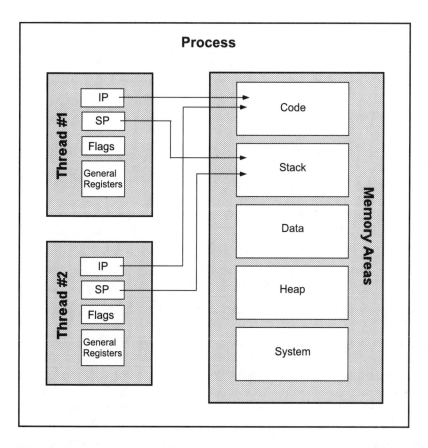

Figure 12-2: In a multithreaded system, a process can be composed of more than one thread. Each thread is a separate flow of execution. Notice that Thread #1 and Thread #2 are executing at different points in the code area.

Reentrancy

In Chapter 9, "Interrupts," we described reentrant routines used in interrupt processing. Reentrancy is important also when writing multithreaded applications. Because threads share the same code, two different threads can easily be executing in the same function simultaneously. For this to occur reliably, the function must be written to be reentrant.

Functions that use only local variables are automatically reentrant. Because all the data for the function is on the stack, each thread has unique values for all variables, and threads cannot interfere with each other.

You have to be more careful, however, with functions that use global data or shared resources such as open files or network connections. You need to synchronize access to the shared data or resources to ensure that one thread can't corrupt the results of another thread that is simultaneously executing in the function.

For example, consider a simple function, `ExtendBuffer()`, that extends the size of a memory buffer allocated from the heap. The function uses two global variables, a pointer to the buffer and the current buffer size. The function also protects against being passed a new size smaller than the current buffer size; it never wants to reduce the buffer size.

```c
int BufSize;
char *pBuf;
void ExtendBuffer(int NewSize)
{
    if (NewSize <= BufSize)
        return;
    BufSize = NewSize;
    pBuf = realloc(pBuf, NewSize);
    return;
}
```

Suppose the current buffer size is 100 bytes, and Thread A calls `ExtendBuffer()` with `NewSize` equal to 200. `ExtendBuffer()` updates the `BufSize` global variable to 200, but just before it calls `realloc()`, its time slice expires, and the OS preempts Thread A and schedules Thread B. Thread B immediately calls `ExtendBuffer()` with `NewSize` equal to 300. `BufSize` is updated to 300, and the buffer is extended to 300 bytes. You can see what's about to happen. The next time the OS schedules Thread A, it will erroneously shrink the buffer from 300 bytes to 200 bytes. Not only has the buffer size been reduced, which is never supposed to happen, but also the `BufSize` global variable now claims that 300 bytes are in the buffer when in fact it has only 200.

To make `ExtendBuffer()` reentrant, we have to use a synchronization object to control access to the shared global variables, `BufSize` and `pBuf`, and the shared memory buffer resource. We see various types of synchronization objects later in this chapter. For now, let's use a mutual exclusion (mutex) object. Only one thread at a time can acquire a mutex; any others are blocked (put on a list of waiting threads) by the OS until the first thread releases the mutex. Using two functions provided by an imaginary OS to acquire and release a mutex object, we'll recode the function to make it reentrant:

```c
int BufSize;
char *pBuf;
Mutex BufMutex;
void ExtendBuffer(int NewSize)
{
    if (NewSize <= BufSize)
        return;
    AcquireMutex(BufMutex);
    BufSize = NewSize;
    pBuf = realloc(pBuf, NewSize);
    ReleaseMutex(BufMutex);
    return;
}
```

Now when Thread B calls `ExtendBuffer()`, it will block on the `BufMutex` mutex before it attempts to update `BufSize` or resize the buffer. Eventually, the OS will schedule Thread A again, which will finish resizing the buffer to 200 bytes and release the mutex. Thread B then acquires the mutex and becomes runnable again; the next time it is scheduled, it can correctly resize the buffer to 300 bytes.

When building a multithreaded application, you don't have to make all your functions reentrant. If a function is called by only one thread, there's no need to make it reentrant (though you still have to synchronize access to global data or resources also used by other functions in other threads). Usually, most of the code for each thread is unique to that thread; we see this when we look at the threads of the Smart UPS later in this chapter. Utility routines, such as those in the C run-time library or the messaging subsystem of the Smart UPS, tend to be used by multiple threads. When writing a function, just remember to consider whether it will be called by more than one thread.

PROCESSES VERSUS THREADS

Most operating systems of the past (even multiprocessing ones) were single-threaded. Most simple programs, when they're executing, are single-threaded. More and more, however, both multiprocessing and single-processing operating systems are embracing multithreading.

We can therefore identify three categories of multitasking operating systems:

- **Multiprocessing/single-threading.** This kind of operating system supports multiple, simultaneously executing processes. Each process, however, consists of only a single thread of execution. Most early multitasking operating systems were of this type; examples include OS/386, VAX/VMS, Windows 3.1, and the old versions of UNIX before the introduction of POSIX threads.

- **Single-processing/multithreading.** This sort of multitasking operating system runs only one process. Within this process, however, multiple threads of execution can occur. ETS Kernel is a single-processing/multithreading operating system.

- **Multiprocessing/multithreading.** Finally, this sort of operating system allows both multiple processes and multiple threads within each process. The Windows 95, 98, and NT operating systems and UNIX systems with POSIX threads support are multiprocessing/multithreading operating systems.

You have the same three choices when designing the architecture of your multitasking embedded system. (You have to select an RTOS that supports the multitasking architecture you plan to use.) Let's look first at why — and how — you'd want to use multithreading in an embedded system.

Many embedded systems, such as a printer, a cell telephone, or a cable modem, are designed to perform one primary activity. In such systems, all actions performed by the code tend to be interrelated. This means the various code subsystems need the capability to easily communicate with each other. For this sort of system, a multithreaded, single-process application is usually the best approach. Putting all the code in one process lets all the threads share global data and other system resources, making communication between different parts of the system straightforward.

In deciding how to split an application into threads, try to identify activities that would benefit from being performed in parallel. In particular, you can often simplify your design by creating a separate thread for each kind of I/O in the system. Then each I/O thread can block whenever necessary to wait for I/O to complete, without having any effect on the responsiveness of the rest of the system. This is the approach taken in the Smart UPS, as you see later in this chapter. Another approach is to identify different kinds of processing that can be performed independently. For example, a printer might have one thread that accepts new jobs over a network connection and queues them for printing, a second thread that crunches PostScript and converts it into a stream of bits, and a third thread that sends the bits to the printer hardware. To identify potential threads in your system, a good place to start is the subsystems you've defined. Because subsystems are designed to perform well-defined jobs with simple, clear interfaces to the rest of the system, they are often good candidates for threads.

Other embedded systems perform a wider variety of operations, some of which require only minimal (or no) interaction. For example, a factory automation system may include several different programs to communicate with several different stations on the factory floor, a spreadsheet application for presenting a graphical summary of factory operations, and a database application for viewing personnel information, job assignments, and work schedules. Similarly, a handheld PDA (Personal Digital Assistant) might run calendar, address book, email, and spreadsheet applications. Such systems are much more easily implemented as multiprocessing systems. Each application can be designed, implemented, and debugged as a separate program, and run as a separate process. Breaking a system that performs several different, minimally related activities into separate processes makes the system easier to understand and easier to implement. In multiprocessing systems, it's usually obvious how to divide the system into processes.

Another reason for using multiprocessing is that, as we've already stated, processes are protected from one another by the operating system (with the help of hardware). The failure of one process does not necessarily mean the failure of the whole system. More importantly, an errant process cannot inadvertently write into the memory space of another process (and thereby corrupt the victim process). Consequently, processes are good for embedded systems that must be kept running even if one or more processes fail.

Some operating systems are composed of cooperating processes. An example is the QNX real-time operating system, within which most operating system services — file system management, device management, network management — are provided by processes. The protection offered by processes means that components of the operating system can be updated on the fly, without having to stop the operating system. In addition, if one portion of the system — for example, the file system manager — crashes, the protection inherent in the processes means you can restart the crashed manager without a complete system reboot.

Finally, a decision to use both multithreading and multiprocessing should be made only after you've decided to implement a multiprocessing system. Evaluate each of the processes in your system; if any would benefit from multithreading — using the criteria we described here — you should select an RTOS that is both multithreading and multiprocessing.

Multiprocessor Systems

We've been talking about multiprocess*ing* systems; multiprocess*or* systems are also available.

A multiprocessor system is a computer system composed of more than one CPU. Tasks are distributed across the CPUs; precisely how they are distributed depends on the hardware, the operating system, and how the programmer chooses to dole out the task load. In some systems, each processor runs the same program, but is handed a different piece of the overall data. Such systems are referred to as *parallel processing systems*. These systems are often applied in scene-rendering applications, such as creating special effects in movies. Each processor in the system is given a different piece of the overall scene to render. When all the processors are finished, the pieces are assembled to create the complete scene.

In other systems, a task may run several time slices on one processor, then several on another, and so on. Furthermore, while one task runs on processor A, a different task runs on processor B.

A multiprocessor system is more than a collection of independent CPUs, all of which happen to be running at the same time. Some means of allowing the CPUs to communicate with one another must be provided (so that tasks in the system can communicate). A variety of schemes have been concocted for this. One such scheme was the now-defunct Inmos Transputer CPU. It was equipped with between two and four (depending on the model) high-speed serial links. Processor-to-processor communications were accomplished by wiring the processors together through the serial links. (Many Transputer boards came with little wires with special connectors for stringing the processors together.) All sorts of topologies were possible — rings, trees, lattices — each more suitable than others for particular algorithms. (Analog Devices' SHARC digital signal processor uses high-speed links that provide a processor-to-processor communications scheme similar to the Transputer's.)

Another interprocessor communications medium that some multiprocessor systems use is a kind of shared bus. Each processor has its own local cache and memory, but specific memory addresses are mapped to nonlocal memory (the local memory of other processors). Special hardware decodes nonlocal memory requests, and automatically builds and transmits request packets along the shared bus, thus invisibly turning a memory request into a bus message. When the message arrives, hardware at the destination decodes it, fetches the requested data, and sends it back.

SMP, symmetric multiprocessing, is a third scheme. In SMP desktop systems, each processor has its own local high-speed cache memory, but all processors share access to system memory. Special circuitry manages access to the shared memory bus in such a way that each processor is (as much as possible) guaranteed equal access to system memory. Hence the term *symmetric multiprocessing;* no one processor is given preferential access to memory and system resources.

Programming multiprocessor systems can be complex. Debugging such systems can be nightmarish. A developer debugging a multiprocessor application must somehow herd a collection of multiple tasks running on multiple CPUs, all talking to one another. Simply put, because so many simultaneous activities are taking place, it's difficult to track down the precise source of a problem when it occurs.

In systems such as multi-Transputer (or multi-SHARC) arrangements, interprocessor communications time is a concern. Because the processors themselves participate in the transfer of data, the time it takes for a piece of information to travel from one processor to another can be nondeterministic if no direct route exists between source and destination. (An intervening processor may be occupied with a particularly devilish computation, delaying the passing of the message.)

Task synchronization is tough enough on a single-processor system; it's even worse on multiprocessor systems. Architects of multiprocessor systems must provide hardware and software functions that provide some kind of guaranteed synchronization feature so that tasks have a reliable means of coordinating their activities. For example, Mercury Computer System's RACEway bus, a high-speed multiprocessor bus used for implementation in real-time multiprocessing systems, implements an atomic test-and write-operation. This allows one processor in the system to test the value of a bit in another processor's local memory and — depending on the value of the bit — either alter the bit and return success, or return failure. Because the operation is atomic, it can be used by programmers to create a host of higher-level synchronization objects (semaphores, mutexes, and so forth).

Multiprocessor systems are usually used in only high-end embedded systems that require intense computational capabilities. Examples of such applications include radar, sonar, and image processing systems. If you're interested in the topic, you can find more information in *Real-Time Multicomputer Systems*, by Richard M. Stein (Ellis Horwood Ltd, 1992) and *Distributed Real-Time Systems*, by J. Tsai, Y. Bi, S. Yang, and R. Smith (John Wiley & Sons, 1996).

SCHEDULING

We've said that the way a multitasking operating system works is by running a task and then switching to another task. The amount of time an OS lets a task execute — called a *time slice*, or *quantum* — is of a fixed duration. The operating system doles out a time slice to each task, one after the other.

When the time slice for a running task ends, the portion of the operating system called the *scheduler* determines which task will have the next time slice.

Note: Remember, *task* is a generic term. It can refer to either a process or a thread. Throughout this chapter, when we use the word *task*, the concepts apply to both processes and threads.

A task can be in one of three states:

- **Running.** In this state, the task is executing.

- **Ready.** Tasks in the ready state are waiting their turn for the CPU. Nothing is keeping a ready task from executing, other than the fact that the task must wait its turn for the CPU.

- **Blocked (or suspended).** A blocked task is waiting for something to happen. Usually, a blocked task is waiting for a synchronization object to change state. However, the task may have been purposefully placed in a suspended state for a period of time. For example, a task that needs to execute intermittently can request to be put to sleep for a fixed period of time. (A *synchronization object* is an operating system service that tasks can use to coordinate access to shared resources. One task, for example, may use a synchronization object to lock access to a file. Other tasks wanting to open the file will be blocked by the synchronization object guarding the file.)

A scheduler maintains one or more internal lists for keeping track of the state of each task. Typically, it has one ready list and a separate blocked list for each synchronization object on which tasks are waiting. The task at the head of the ready list is the next one to run. Tasks on any of the blocked lists are suspended. They are waiting for some event: input from a device, a message from another task, the change in state of a synchronization object, and so on. Whenever an event occurs for which a task on a blocked list is waiting, the task is removed from the blocked list and placed on the ready list, where it waits its turn for execution.

When a running task blocks on a synchronization object, or when its time slice expires, the operating system needs to perform a context switch to another task. We summarized this earlier, but let's go through it step by step. A context switch involves the following:

1. **Saving the active context for the current task.** The scheduler saves the active context in an in-memory data structure called the *task control block* (TCB). The precise structure of a TCB varies from OS to OS and depends on whether the task is a process or a thread. At a minimum, the TCB includes the saved CPU state for the task and, if the task is a process, information on each of the memory areas allocated for the process. The TCB is then placed on the ready list or the appropriate blocked list.

2. **Selecting the next task.** The scheduler determines which task will run next and removes it from the ready list.

3. **Loading the next task's context.** If the task is a process, the scheduler loads any memory management data structures needed to enable access to the memory areas for the incoming task. Then it loads the task's saved CPU state, except for the stack pointer and instruction pointer registers.

4. **Transferring control to the next task.** As a final step, the operating system loads the task's values for the stack pointer and instruction pointer registers. The loading of the instruction pointer register results in the transfer of control to the task. The task resumes execution at the point where it was last made inactive.

Although the preceding explains how context switching works, it leaves us with a question: How does a scheduler determine which task runs next? The answer depends on the scheduling algorithm used. Many scheduling algorithms are available, such as first in, first out (FIFO), round robin, shortest job first, and shortest remaining time. For real-time systems, it's critical that the scheduling algorithm be deterministic; that is, it's always possible to predict which task will run next. Many RTOSs use round robin scheduling because it's simple and predictable, so we'll describe that algorithm here. For other scheduling algorithms, refer to any good book on operating systems, such as *Operating Systems: Design and Implementation,* by Andrew S. Tanenbaum (Prentice Hall, 1997).

Cooperative versus Preemptive Multitasking

Multitasking operating systems can be divided into two categories: cooperative and preemptive.

In a cooperative multitasking operating system, tasks cooperate (hence the name) in terms of sharing processor time. Specifically, each task gives up its use of the processor by making a call into the OS's task scheduler.

A programmer writing an application for a cooperative multitasking operating system must write into the application the calls that perform task switching. The programmer must be aware of the time between those calls and must guard against placing those calls so that the task hogs processor time. For example, if an application must sort a large list, the calls must be inserted into the sort algorithm so that other tasks aren't starved while the application is sorting the list.

The drawback of a cooperative multitasking operating system is that the failure of any task to make the task switch call affects all other tasks in the system. Consequently, an error in a task could cause the task to monopolize CPU time. More importantly, if a task fails (crashes), the call to the scheduler is never made, and the system locks up.

Microsoft's Windows 3.x and the Mac OS are examples of a cooperative multitasking operating system.

In a preemptive multitasking operating system, tasks are preempted by a portion of the operating system called the scheduler. This preemption is accomplished with the aid of a timer interrupt. Here's how it works.

Tasks in a preemptive OS are allowed to run for a fixed length of time, called a time slice, or quantum. At the end of the time slice, a timer interrupt awakens an ISR that, in turn, transfers control to the operating system's scheduler. The scheduler saves the state of the current task and then determines which task will run next, according to whatever scheduling algorithm it's using. The scheduler transfers control to this new task, which is allowed to run for a time slice. At the end of that time slice, the scheduler kicks in again, saves the task state, selects a new task, and the process repeats.

In a preemptive multitasking operating system, an errant task has less chance of affecting other parts of the system. The timer interrupt, which drives the system, is immune to the failure of an individual task. As long as the timer interrupt ISR and task switching kernel of the operating system remain intact, the system can continue to run, even if a task crashes completely. (Most modern preemptive operating systems use the memory protection mechanisms of their host processors to protect the operating system kernel from deranged tasks. This makes it even less likely that an application's failure will adversely affect the entire system.)

Preemptive multitasking operating systems are more common than cooperative multitasking operating systems. Windows 95, 98 and NT, OS/2, and virtually all UNIX variants use preemptive multitasking. Virtually all commercial RTOSs use preemptive multitasking.

ROUND-ROBIN SCHEDULING

The scheduling scheme you'll find at the heart of most real-time operating systems is round-robin scheduling. We've illustrated how it works in Figure 12-3. The contexts for the tasks that are ready to run are kept on the ready list, which is implemented as a linked list of task control blocks. Assuming all tasks have equal priority, the scheduler removes the TCB at the head of the ready list, and makes its associated task the current executing task. This is often referred to as *switching in the task's context*. That task runs for a time slice, at the end of which the scheduler (awakened by the timer interrupt) saves the state of the task (often referred to as *switching out the task's context*), places its TCB at the end of the list, pulls the next TCB off the head of the list, and runs that task. The scheduler continues to repeat the process, with each task running for an equal time slice, by proceeding through the list, taking the next task off the head of the list and tacking the task that just ran onto the tail of the list.

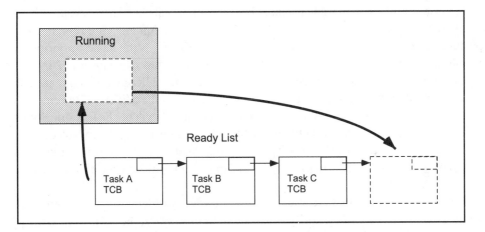

Figure 12-3: In round-robin scheduling, the scheduler maintains a linked list of tasks to run. Each task gets its turn to run. The task at the head of the list goes first; when its time slice is over, it is moved to the end of the list.

You'll notice that we're not showing any blocked lists in this illustration. If, for example, a running task makes an I/O request that causes it to wait for a response from an I/O device, the scheduler places that task on the blocked list for that device and runs the task at the head of the ready list. When the I/O response arrives, the scheduler moves the blocked task to the end of the ready list, and the task reenters the cycle.

TASK PRIORITIES

We've been describing the scheduling process as if all tasks were equal, but this is rarely the case. More often than not, some tasks are more important than other tasks. In this case, the programmer assigns each task in the system a priority — a numeric value that assigns a level of importance to the task. When it's time for the scheduler to choose the next task to run, it selects the task from the ready list that has the highest priority.

Implementing task priorities are an important distinguishing characteristic of real-time scheduling algorithms. An RTOS has to implement deterministic scheduling, so that the programmer can, given any circumstance, always identify which task in the application will run. Therefore, a scheduler in an RTOS always selects the highest-priority ready task as the next task to run. If the outgoing task has a higher priority than any task on the ready list, it is immediately scheduled again and gets the next time slice, as well. By contrast, desktop operating systems such as Windows occasionally boost the priorities of low-priority tasks to ensure they get some CPU time. This is anathema in a real-time system: To guarantee that the system meets its real-time deadlines, the programmer has to have complete control over which task or tasks are eligible to run.

What happens if several tasks are assigned the same level of importance? The answer is that tasks within the same priority level are serviced in accordance with the scheduling algorithm used by the RTOS.

For instance, in a system using round-robin scheduling, equal priority tasks are serviced in the round-robin fashion we just described. Look at the illustration in Figure 12-4. It depicts an operating system that defines three priority levels: 1 – 3. Level 1 is the highest priority; level 3, the lowest. A snapshot of the ready list shows three priority 1 tasks, two priority 2 tasks, and a single priority 3 task. Notice the ordering of tasks on the list. Higher-priority tasks are grouped toward the head of the list, and lower-priority tasks are toward the tail. This is *priority ordering*. The next task to run — the task at the head of the ready list — will be the first priority 1 task.

The scheduler will cycle through the priority 1 tasks using its round-robin algorithm, giving each a time slice in turn. The priority 2 tasks must wait until all priority 1 tasks are either blocked or terminated. Similarly, priority 3 tasks must wait until all priority 1 and 2 tasks are blocked or terminated.

The system's blocked lists are also organized in priority order, just like the ready list. For example, if a priority 2 and a priority 3 task are both blocked on the same mutex, the priority 2 task is always at the head of the blocked list, regardless of which task blocked on the mutex first. When the mutex is released, the priority 2 task is unblocked, given ownership of the mutex, and placed on the ready list.

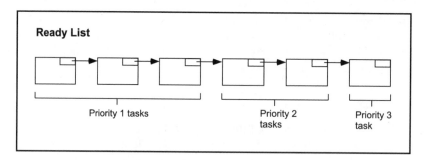

Figure 12-4: In a round-robin scheduler with priorities, TCBs are ordered on the ready list according to their priorities. Higher-priority tasks are toward the head of the list and are the first to be given CPU time; lower-priority tasks are toward the end of the ready list.

What happens if a low priority task is running (because all high-priority tasks are blocked), and one of the high-priority tasks becomes unblocked, perhaps because the low-priority task released the mutex on which the high-priority task was blocked? In that case, the scheduler *immediately* switches out the context of the low-priority task and places it back on the ready list, and switches in the context of the high-priority task. This context switch is performed even though the low-priority task's time slice has not yet expired. In other words, time slicing is a way to share the CPU between tasks of equal priority. For tasks of unequal priority, time slicing is irrelevant; *the highest priority runnable thread always runs.*

PRIORITY INVERSION

A pitfall associated with task prioritization is referred to as *priority inversion*. Priority inversion is a situation where a low-priority task acts as though it has a higher priority than a high-priority task. The system won't behave as the programmer planned.

For priority inversion to occur, the system must have at least three tasks. Here's an example. Suppose a system is running three tasks: T1, T2, and T3. T1 has the highest priority, T2 lower, and T3 the lowest. At some point, tasks T1 and T2 are blocked, so the OS runs task T3. T3 requests access to a shared resource — a file, say — and obtains an exclusive access lock on that file (which means no other tasks may open the file until the file is unlocked). T3 begins processing the data in the file, but in the midst of the processing, T1 becomes unblocked and preempts T3. T1 tries to open the same file that T3 has opened, but T1 is blocked due to T3's exclusive lock on the file. In the meantime, task T2 has become unblocked. So, the OS schedules and runs T2.

Priority inversion has occurred; a lower-priority task is executing as if it were the highest-priority task. Task T1 cannot run because the resource it needs is locked. Task T3 needs to run to complete its processing of the file, unlock the file, and make it available to T1. But T3 can't run because T2 is unblocked and has a higher priority than T3. T2 has effectively acquired a higher priority than T1 because the entire system is at the mercy of task T2; T3 and — as a consequence — T1 cannot run until T2 is either blocked or terminates.

Most operating systems solve priority inversion using a technique called *priority inheritance*, in which a low-priority task that locks a resource temporarily inherits the priority of the highest-priority task blocked by that resource. In the example, an OS providing priority inheritance would boost the priority of task T3 to the priority of task T1. T3 — having a higher priority than T2 — would be allowed to run, would complete its processing on the file, and would unlock it. After the resource was released, the operating system would return T3 to its original priority level. With the file now available, T1 would be unblocked and could resume processing.

Priority inversion is particularly detrimental when it occurs in hard real-time systems. Recall that an important aspect of hard real-time systems is determinacy, which means the system is guaranteed to behave in a predictable way with regards to task scheduling. Priority inversion can make the system unpredictable — a low-priority task will behave like a high-priority one, and a high-priority task will behave like a low-priority one.

The Martian Chronicles: Priority Inversion on Another World

Priority inversion is not simply a theoretical subject described in books. It happens in the real world. In fact, it happened on the Mars Pathfinder. Several days into the mission — after the spacecraft was on Mars and had begun to gather meteorological and other data — the Pathfinder's computer system began experiencing system resets. Each time the reset occurred, the remainder of the activities scheduled for that day were not accomplished; they would be delayed until the next day.

The spacecraft's computer system featured a shared memory area that allowed different components of the spacecraft to communicate with one another. Several tasks were involved: A high-priority bus distribution task that moved certain important data in and out of the shared memory area, a low-priority meteorological task that used the shared memory area to publish its data, and several medium-priority tasks that performed other spacecraft functions. Add to the mix a mutex that governed access to the shared memory area. If either the bus distribution or the meteorological task wanted access to the shared memory area, the task would first have to acquire the mutex. Doing so would block the other task until the mutex was released.

Sometimes the meteorological task would acquire the mutex and then get preempted by one of the medium-priority tasks in the system. The bus distribution task would block on the mutex that the meteorological task could not release, because its priority was lower than the medium-priority tasks. This was a classic priority inversion. Usually, the medium-priority tasks would finish their work, the meteorological task would run and release the mutex, and the system would function correctly.

Occasionally, however, the medium-priority tasks had enough work to do that the meteorological task was prevented from running for a long time. At least, it was blocked long enough that another high-priority task, a scheduling task that periodically scheduled activities for the next bus cycle, ran and noticed that the bus distribution task had failed to complete its work in the previous cycle. Because this was a hard deadline in the system, the scheduling task signaled an error that caused a system reset.

It took engineers back on the earth hours and hours of running simulations on a replica of the spacecraft to locate the problem. The version of the VxWorks operating system used on the Pathfinder had priority inheritance turned off by default, for optimum performance. Individual synchronization objects could be created with priority inheritance enabled, but this particular mutex had slipped through the cracks and was created with priority inheritance disabled.

Luckily, the Pathfinder engineers had included a program that could patch the software on the spacecraft. They could transmit data identifying the differences between the software on the spacecraft and the desired software, and the patch program would apply the patch. The patch they finally decided to use was to modify a global variable that would change the default creation parameters of a certain class of synchronization objects, including the mutex that was causing the problem, to enable priority inheritance. There was some concern that this would have side effects, because it would add extra processing overhead in the operating system and also change the behavior of some of the other synchronization objects in the system. After extensive analysis of the system code and testing the patched code on the earth before transmitting the patch to Pathfinder, however, the engineers concluded that the modification was safe.

Problem solved.

DEADLOCK

Deadlock occurs when tasks prevent each other from running because of a cyclic locking and requesting of resources. By resources, we mean any shared resource that the task may have to wait to acquire; for example, a lock on a file, or ownership of a mutex or other synchronization object. One task locks Resource 1 and requests Resource 2; another task has already locked Resource 2 and requests Resource 1. Each task is stalled, waiting for a resource to become available, and in the meantime has blocked access to one or more resource(s) that — once released — will unblock the other task. This situation is illustrated in Figure 12-5.

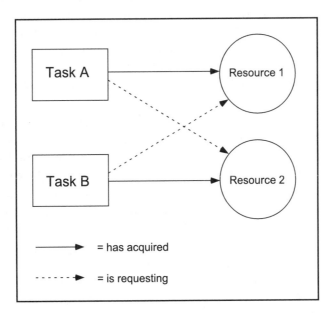

Figure 12-5: In deadlock, each task owns a resource that the other wants, and each task wants a resource that the other owns.

Note that what we've described is the simplest form of deadlock — involving two tasks. Elaborate interactions of tasks and shared resources can also create deadlock: for example, Task A waiting for Resource 1, locking Resource 2; Task B waiting for Resource 2, locking Resource 3; Task C waiting for Resource 3, locking Resource 1; and so on for arbitrarily large numbers of tasks.

The tools for detecting and solving such complex deadlock scenarios involve a branch of mathematics called graph theory (which we won't go into here). You can, however, prevent deadlock by imposing rules on how tasks acquire resources. One simple technique that is frequently used is to impose a linear ordering on the resources that tasks might be vying for. In other words, if you have several tasks that will access resources A, B, and C, construct your application so that tasks acquire and release the resources in the same order. Make sure all tasks acquire A before they try to acquire B, and acquire B before they try to acquire C. This eliminates the possibility of one task acquiring A and B, while another has acquired B and is trying to get A. Other alternatives are to require a task to request all its required resources at once, or to require tasks denied a resource to immediately release all other resources they are holding and then start acquiring resources again.

Also, be aware of the simplest mistake: programming a task so that it acquires a resource and never releases it. If a task locks a file for exclusive access, don't forget to have the task release the lock. Otherwise, other tasks in the system may simply go to sleep forever.

Computer scientists have tried to develop workable algorithms for *deadlock avoidance,* in which an operating system detects and denies a resource request that might lead to deadlock, and *deadlock detection,* in which an operating system detects a deadlock and recovers by terminating one or more tasks. These techniques are not useful in real-time systems, however, because of the overhead in implementing the algorithms, and because recovering from a deadlock by arbitrarily terminating tasks is usually not acceptable. For now, it's up to application developers to prevent deadlock with careful coding.

STARVATION

A task is *starved,* or indefinitely postponed, when the scheduler gives it little or no CPU time. Imagine a system that supports two priority levels, low and high. And, as usual in a real-time system, the scheduling algorithm is such that a low-priority task runs only if no high-priority tasks are ready to run. If high-priority Task A begins executing and then enters an infinite loop, the low-priority tasks will be starved. They will never be scheduled to run, and will never get CPU time. Other high-priority tasks, however, will round-robin with Task A. But, unless the operating system terminates Task A — perhaps by user intervention — all low-priority tasks will be starved.

Little can be said in regard to preventing task starvation, other than to examine the priorities you assign to each task while you're designing the application. Make sure you don't create a high-priority task that is always executing and thus starves other tasks in the system.

SYNCHRONIZATION

In a multitasking system, tasks can interact. Sometimes they interact directly with each other; other times they interact indirectly through shared resources. These interactions must be coordinated, or *synchronized,* to prevent what's called a race condition.

A *race condition* occurs when the outcome of the computation of two or more tasks depends on how quickly the tasks execute. More rigorously, given tasks A and B, and a location in the execution of A called a1, and a location in the execution of B called b1, a race condition exists if A's reaching a1 before B gets to b1 causes a different computational result than if B reaches b1 before A gets to a1. The tasks are in a race, so to speak.

Here's a down-to-the-assembly-language look at what happens to make a race condition. Suppose Task A and Task B access a counter variable. Each task increments the counter variable using the following code:

```
counter+=1;
```

which, when the compiler is finished with it, generates processor instructions that look like this (we'll use pseudocode):

```
LOADA      counter
INCRA
STOREA     counter
```

The first instruction loads the value of counter into the CPU's accumulator. The next instruction adds 1. The final instruction stores the result back into counter.

So Task A reaches this series of instructions when the counter has a value of 3. It executes LOADA and loads a 3 into the accumulator. Before Task A can execute the INCRA instruction, however, the task's time slice ends, and the scheduler switches it out. Because a task's context includes CPU registers, the contents of the accumulator (a value of 3) is stored with Task A's context.

The scheduler starts Task B. Task B reaches these instructions and executes LOADA. Because Task A didn't store a result in counter, Task B fetches 3 into the accumulator also. Task B then executes INCRA, executes STOREA, and continues with whatever instructions follow. The contents of counter is 4.

At some later time, Task A is rescheduled. The scheduler reloads Task A's context and places 3 back in the accumulator. You can begin to see the problem. Task A restarts, executes INCRA, executes STOREA, and proceeds to the next instruction. The contents of counter is 4 — again.

Had Task A not been preempted at the moment it was, had it managed to execute the INCRA and STOREA instructions, the value of counter would be 5 — which is what it should be. Because neither task guarded its access to the counter variable, a race condition occurred.

Every task has sections of code that perform internal computations that do not lead to races. Every task has code that also accesses shared memory or other shared resources that can result in a race condition. The code section that accesses the shared resource is called a *critical section*; in our example, the critical section is just one C statement, or three assembly language instructions. To avoid race conditions, we need *mutual exclusion*, a means of ensuring that only one task can be executing in a critical section at any moment.

Most operating systems have a variety of *synchronization objects* that you can use to synchronize the use of shared resources and prevent race conditions. We cover several common types of synchronization objects in the following sections. Different synchronization objects are tuned to provide optimal solutions to different problems and are provided by operating systems as a matter of convenience; any one kind of synchronization object can be used to derive the other types.

MUTEX OBJECTS

A *mutex object,* sometimes called a *critical section object,* derives its name from its use in coordinating mutually exclusive access to a shared resource. A mutex object can be in one of two states: owned or free. A mutex object can be owned by only one task at a time.

Operating systems that support mutexes provide two function calls for manipulating them: a wait call and a release call. When a task wants to acquire a mutex, it issues a wait call. If the mutex is free, the wait call returns immediately and the calling task has acquired ownership of the mutex. If the mutex is already owned, the wait call doesn't return, and the calling task is blocked. A task waiting on a mutex becomes unblocked (the wait call returns) when the owner of the mutex issues a release call on the mutex.

A mutex is similar to a room built around a critical section of code. The room has one door in and one door out. Furthermore, a guard at the door admits only one person (task) into the room (critical section) at any given time. Tasks that arrive at the entrance while the room is occupied must wait at the door until the room becomes empty. Also, the guard (the operating system) sees to it that those waiting at the door are admitted in task priority order (VIPs first) and, within the same priority, in the order in which they arrived (no breaking lines, so to speak).

It's easy to see how to use a mutex. You wait on the mutex at the beginning of a critical section of code. When you've finished accessing the shared resource (you reach the end of the critical section), you release the mutex so that other tasks can acquire the mutex and access the shared resource. Ideally, you try to keep your critical sections of code as short as possible, to avoid making other tasks wait for a long time.

> **Note:** The Win32 API provides separate mutex and critical section objects. They both provide the same service; the difference is that a critical section object can be shared among threads only within the same process, but a mutex object can be shared among threads of different processes. Critical section objects are implemented with less overhead than mutex objects in Windows, so it's preferable to use critical section objects in a single-process, multi-threaded application.

SEMAPHORE OBJECTS

Another synchronization object, introduced to the computer world in 1965 by E.W. Dijkstra (at that time, at the Technical University of Eindhoven in the Netherlands) is the semaphore. A *semaphore* consists of a data item, which we'll call a count, and a pair of operations, wait and release, which are implemented as OS APIs. A task requesting access to whatever resource the semaphore guards, performs a wait operation on the semaphore. When a task is finished with that resource, it performs a release.

The semaphore's count determines what happens when a wait or a release operation executes. When your program creates a semaphore, it sets the semaphore's count to an initial value that is a positive number. This value indicates the number of tasks the semaphore will let pass before closing the door. Whenever a task performs a wait call on the semaphore, the operating system first checks to see whether the semaphore's count is greater than 0. If so, the call succeeds (the task is allowed to continue), and the count is decremented by 1. If the count is 0, however, the task is blocked.

When a task has finished using whatever resource the semaphore is guarding, the task issues a release call on the semaphore. The release call causes the operating system to increment the semaphore's count by 1.

For example, suppose you've written an application that communicates with other software across a network. You determine that your operating system supports up to five simultaneous network connections. You could guard the network access portion of your application with a semaphore whose initial count is set to 5. Such a semaphore would allow five tasks to access the network. If a sixth task attempted to access the network, it would be blocked (the semaphore's count would be 0) until one of the tasks using the network closed its network connection and performed a release call on the semaphore.

Semaphores created with an initial count of 1 are commonly called *binary semaphores,* because they can assume a value of only 0 or 1; they allow only one task at a time access to the shared resource. Semaphores with an initial count greater than 1 are called *counting semaphores.*

Unlike a mutex, a semaphore is not owned by a specific task, because a semaphore can give multiple tasks simultaneous access to a shared resource. This means priority inheritance cannot be implemented for semaphores; it's up to you to ensure that priority inversion does not occur in any code that uses semaphores. Also, because a semaphore is not owned, the operating system can't check whether a task releasing a semaphore ever waited on it. Therefore, any task can increment a semaphore's count by releasing it, even if the task never waited on the semaphore. It's up to the application program to use the semaphore consistently.

EVENT OBJECTS

Event objects are typically used for synchronizing task processing rather than for controlling access to shared resources. An event object is analogous in function to an on-off switch. It's a mechanism that lets a task sleep until, for example, some data is ready for it to process or a request is ready for it to service.

Operating system functions allow tasks to set to signaled (turn on) as well as reset to nonsignaled (turn off) an event object. Event objects can be created in either the signaled or the nonsignaled state. When a task waits on a nonsignaled event object, the task blocks until another thread sets the event object. When a task waits on a signaled event object, the task does not block. A common use of an event object is to notify a task when a pending I/O operation has been completed. For example, a task that processes data acquired by an A/D board might wait on an event object that is set when an A/D driver task fills a buffer with data.

The two types of event objects are auto reset events and manual reset events. Auto reset events are automatically reset to nonsignaled when a single waiting task is released (unblocked). If multiple tasks are waiting on the event, only the highest-priority waiting task (and, within the same priority, the task that has been waiting the longest) is released. The next time a running task sets the event, another waiting task is released, and so on.

Manual reset events remain set to signaled after a task sets them. If multiple tasks are waiting on the event, they are all released when another task sets the event. Subsequent tasks that wait on the event object proceed immediately, without blocking. To cause tasks to block on the event again, a task must explicitly reset the event object to its nonsignaled state.

Like semaphores, events are not associated with task ownership. Any task may set or reset an event at any time.

You see some examples of the use of event objects when you examine the Smart UPS code.

> ### To Signal or Not to Signal
>
> We've used several terms for the states of the various synchronization objects. For example, we've said that event objects are either set or reset; mutex objects are either owned or free.
>
> The states of synchronization objects have formal names, regardless of whether an object is a semaphore, a mutex, an event object, and so on. A given synchronization object can be in one of two states:
>
> - **Nonsignaled.** In this state, a task issuing a wait call on a synchronization object is blocked. This state corresponds to the event object's reset state and to the mutex object's owned state. It corresponds also to a semaphore's count being 0.
>
> - **Signaled.** In this state, a task issuing a wait call on the synchronization object is not blocked. This corresponds to the event object's set state, to the mutex object's free state, and to the semaphore's count being 1 or greater.

INTERLOCKED VARIABLE ACCESS

Interlocked variable access is the name given to a set of functions that help tasks synchronize access to a global variable. Interlocked variable access is used primarily by threads, because all threads can directly access the global variables of a process. Processes, however, can use interlocked variable access to obtain synchronized access to a variable in a shared memory block.

The synchronization provided by interlocked variable access is through atomic operations: actions performed indivisibly. In other words, while a task is performing these actions, the operating system guarantees that no other task can access the variable. Typical operations provided include increment the variable and return the new value; decrement the variable and return the new value; and exchange the contents of two variables.

Interlocked variable access provides more efficient access to individual shared variables than is possible using synchronization objects. For example, consider a section of code that needs to increment a shared counter and copy the result to a local variable. Using a mutex to synchronize access to the counter, and using some generic API names, we would write:

```
Wait(CounterMutex);
LocalCounter = ++Counter;
Release(CounterMutex);
```

Using interlocked variable access, we would instead write:

```
LocalCounter = InterlockedIncrement(Counter);
```

The `InterlockedIncrement()` call has less operating system overhead than the `Wait()` and `Release()` calls. In addition, we don't have to create the `CounterMutex` synchronization object just to control access to the `Counter` variable, or alternatively create one mutex that controls access to many different global variables, which would increase the likelihood of blocking because the mutex would be used more frequently.

INTERTASK COMMUNICATION

Multitasking operating systems provide several mechanisms to facilitate intertask communication. This is usually called *interprocess communication* (IPC); the name was invented before multithreaded operating systems existed. Although processes have a greater need for IPC than do threads, which can communicate through shared global data, some IPC mechanisms, such as pipes and message queues, can be — and often are — used by threads as well as processes. IPC sits at the heart of such diverse features as cutting and pasting from one application to another, embedding a graph from a spreadsheet inside a word processing document, and allowing the components of complex applications, such as integrated development environments, to seamlessly exchange data.

PIPES

A *pipe* (sometimes called a *pipeline*) is a simple communications channel that can be used to send data from one task to another. This channel is implemented in software and managed by the operating system. Application software sees a pipe as being similar to a data file. The pipe can be opened, closed, written to, and read from using the C standard library file I/O functions. Unlike a file, however, a pipe is unidirectional: It has a source end and a destination (or sink) end. The task at the source end can only write to the pipe; the task at the destination end can only read from it.

Pipes transfer *streamed data*, that is, data in the form of a series, or stream, of bytes. Accessing a pipe, therefore, looks a lot like accessing a sequential file.

A task at the source end writes data to the pipe using the same system calls that a task uses to write bytes to a file. At the destination end, the receiving task can read that data, again using the same system calls that a task would use to read a file. Each end of a pipe can be used by only one task. In other words, you can't have multiple tasks write to a pipe or multiple tasks read from a pipe.

A pipe also acts like a queue. Depending on the pipe's length (how many bytes it can hold before it must be emptied by a read operation), the task on the source end can continue to write data into the pipe until the pipe fills up. When the task on the destination end finally begins reading data from the pipe, the data will be delivered in the order in which it was fed into the pipe.

If a task attempts to write to a full pipe, it is blocked until the receiving task reads enough data from the other end of the pipe to make room for the new data. Similarly, an attempt to read from an empty pipe will block until enough data to satisfy the read request has been written to the pipe.

MESSAGE QUEUES

Whereas a pipe allows the transmission of streamed data from task to task, a message queue allows the transmission of arbitrary structures (messages) from task to task. Also, message queues are not unidirectional; after a task creates (or obtains access to) a message queue, that task can send messages to or receive messages in the queue. As with pipes, tasks using message queues must be prepared for the possibility of blocking when attempting to write to a full queue or read from an empty queue.

In contrast to the mechanisms for reading and writing data through pipes (standard file read/write calls), I/O on message queues uses special message send and message receive calls. These calls are designed to handle the transfer of data structures of arbitrary size.

Some message queue implementations support the notion of *message type*. When a task places a message in the queue, it can associate a *type* identifier (an integer) with the message. The task receiving the message can determine the nature of the message's contents by examining the *type* field rather than having to look inside the message. For example, suppose that one task is sending text and graphical data to another through a message queue. Text messages could be identified by a *type* value of 1, and image messages could be identified by a *type* value of 2. The receiver would then know how to process each message by looking at the *type* field. Tasks can implement their own method of message identification in the content of the message. But having a standardized identification method imposed by the message queue service simplifies message identification and improves reliability.

SHARED MEMORY

Shared memory: The name says it all. Shared memory is a region of memory shared by multiple processes; each process that accesses shared memory sees the memory as though it were part of that process's private memory space. Shared memory is provided for interprocess communications rather than interthread communications; after all, threads in a process already share all their global data.

Here's how shared memory works. First, a process must create the shared memory region. It does this by making a call to the operating system, specifying the size of the region and a symbolic name. The operating system creates the region, maps it into the process's data area, and returns a pointer to the shared memory's starting address. The process can use the pointer to read from and write to the shared memory.

Any other process that wants to access the shared memory must make an operating system call to attach the shared memory to its address space. This call to the attach routine must include the symbolic name, so that the operating system can identify the desired shared memory region. (More than one shared memory region may be active at a given time.) The operating system maps the shared memory region into the process's data area, and returns a pointer containing the memory's starting address.

A programmer writing applications that will use shared memory must select the symbolic name and use it in calls to create and attach shared memory. It's also up to the programmer to decide how many processes may attach the shared memory region to their address spaces.

Shared memory is the fastest and most dangerous of all IPC mechanisms. It's fast because transfers occur at memory access speeds. It's dangerous because it can have the same problems that can plague multithreaded access to global variables. Namely, mismanaged shared memory can result in race conditions. Processes should therefore use a synchronization object, such as a mutex, to control access to shared memory.

REMOTE PROCEDURE CALLS

A remote procedure call (RPC) is another mechanism provided for only interprocess, not interthread, communications. (Threads share all the code within a process.) As its name suggests, a remote procedure call allows a procedure in one process to directly call a procedure in another process. The two processes may be running in the same computer, or they may be running on two different computers connected by a network.

The goal of an RPC is to make it as easy to call a procedure in another process as it is to call a procedure within the local process. In practice, this goal is difficult to achieve. You normally have to define all procedures that can be called remotely using a metalanguage to define procedure names, data types, and which direction data needs to be passed (in to the callee, returned to the caller, or both). An RPC generator program compiles these procedure definitions into stubs that package the procedure parameters in a machine-independent format and invoke the remote procedure, using RPC services provided by the operating system. When you call a remote procedure, your compiler generates a call to a stub function created by the RPC generator. While the actual procedure call in your source code is as easy to write as a call to a local procedure, you have to do a lot of work defining all the remote procedure interfaces first.

RPC mechanisms are powerful but also complex. To give you an idea of just how complex, the specification for the Open Software Foundation's Distributed Computing Environment (DCE), which is implemented by Windows and other operating systems, is many hundreds of pages long. Because of its complexity, remote procedure calling is not yet widely used in embedded systems.

INTERRUPT HANDLING

Writing an interrupt service routine (ISR) is slightly more complicated in a multitasking application. First, you have to consider whether it's possible that an ISR can be preempted for another task. Some operating systems always know when an ISR is running and don't allow other (noninterrupt) tasks to be scheduled. Other operating systems run an ISR in the context of the task that was executing when the interrupt occurred; on those systems, if the scheduler runs, it might decide to switch contexts to another, higher-priority, task. Because it's almost always undesirable for a task switch to occur when an ISR is running, you have to take additional steps (what steps, exactly, depends on the operating system) to prevent preemption inside an ISR.

Second, in a multitasking system, an ISR can usually signal a synchronization object to wake up a task to perform the I/O to the hardware device. In other words, the code to service the interrupt is moved out of the ISR and into a device driver task. This technique has three advantages: you can keep your ISRs short; you can call any operating system or run-time library that you want in a task (something you cannot do in an ISR); and you can use task priorities to control which interrupts get serviced first when multiple interrupts occur simultaneously.

It's difficult to generalize about these issues because the details can be quite different depending on the operating system. When we discuss the code in the Smart UPS later in this chapter, we describe in detail how to write ISRs for a multitasking system under ETS Kernel. Seeing the options and tradeoffs involved for a particular operating system should help to clarify these points.

CHOOSING AN RTOS

Multitasking features are only one of many factors in your choice of an RTOS. But multitasking is an important enough part of the OS that it's worthwhile to put together a checklist of features you need for your application; this section helps you create that list. First, you have to decide whether you need multithreading capability, multiprocessing, or both; we covered that decision in an earlier section. Then, using the following questions as a guide, create a list of features required to successfully build your application.

- **Is the number of tasks that can be created at run time limited?** Your application determines the upper limit, and you want an estimate of this limit before you settle on an operating system.

- **What types of interprocess communication mechanisms are supported?** Be sure that the IPC mechanism you've selected for your application is available in your selected operating system. For example, if you determine that your application needs the throughput offered by shared memory, you don't want an operating system that supports only message queues.

- **Is the time slice adjustable?** If the time slice is too small, an unacceptably large percentage of overall processor time will be spent in context switching. If the time slice is too large, you lose responsiveness. Unless the operating system provides some sort of debugging mechanism that lets you measure context switch time and application run time, determining the best time slice value for a given application is more a matter of trial-and-error than anything else. You run the application, measure its performance, alter the time slice, run the application again, and see whether the performance is better, worse, or unchanged. Repeat this process until you've reached an optimum. But for this to work, you need to be able to adjust the time slice.

- **Does the operating system support priority inheritance or some other safeguard to protect against priority inversion?** (Remember the Mars Pathfinder mission.)

- **Does the operating system support the synchronization object(s) you've chosen for your application?** Perhaps you've settled on your favorite synchronization object, or you're moving an existing application to a new platform and the source code already presumes one or more specific synchronization objects. Regardless of the reason, if your application will be using interlocked variable access, for example, make sure the operating system supports it.

- **Does the operating system allow you to select the scheduling algorithm?** Some operating systems actually allow you to choose from more than one scheduling algorithm (round-robin; first-come, first-served; and so on). This lets you experiment with different algorithms and select which is best for your particular application. In addition, although it should be automatic for any operating system called an RTOS, verify that the scheduling algorithm is deterministic.

- **Are the task switching times provided by the RTOS acceptable?** The switching times for different operating systems usually don't differ much, and for most embedded systems, switching times is not a critical factor. But if your system requires large numbers of tasks or has stringent timing requirements, you may need to compare timings from different operating systems.

- **Does the operating system's performance scale acceptably as you add more tasks (be they threads or processes)?** This may or may not be important to your application. It could be that your application will require only a fixed number of tasks throughout its lifetime. If not — if your application may grow over time to consist of more simultaneous tasks — it's important to know how well the operating system can handle the growth. As you add more tasks, the number of internal data structures — task control blocks, synchronization objects, and lists of blocked tasks — that the OS needs to manage grows. As a result, OS processing overhead will start to consume a larger percentage of total CPU time. In addition, *interrupt latencies* (the maximum time between when an interrupt occurs and when your application starts processing it) may increase because the scheduler may need to disable interrupts for longer periods of time as it processes the greater number of data structures. Unfortunately, such OS scalability is not easy to measure. You may need to write a benchmark program that lets you set the number of tasks to be created and measures the overall performance degradation as more and more tasks are created. Even if you can create such a benchmark, you'll need to obtain an evaluation copy of the operating system to run the benchmark. Provided you can do this, running the test on all your candidate operating systems will help you choose the best one.

  Note: The May 1996 issue of *Dr. Dobb's Journal* featured the article "Benchmarking Real-Time Operating Systems," by Eric McRae, which describes a benchmark program (and attendant hardware) that the author used to measure various operating system characteristics, including context switch times, message passing performance, and task priority management. Source code is included with the article.

- **Finally, what tools support does the operating system offer?** Are good, well-tested, multitasking-aware compilers and debuggers available for the operating system? If you're going to be building a multithreaded application, is the compiler's run-time library thread-safe? Debugging a multiprocessing or multithreaded application can be a challenge. Can you set breakpoints in selected processes or threads? Can you examine the states of synchronization objects? The development tools — especially the debugger — need to be well integrated with the operating system.

DEBUGGING

Debugging a multitasking application is more challenging than debugging a single-tasking application for the simple reason that, in a multitasking application, more than one thing is happening at a time. Tasks interact with one another — reading and writing global memory, acquiring and releasing synchronization objects — and sometimes, in those places where the activity of one task affects the activity of another, the two tasks can trip one another up. Add more tasks to the mixture, and you have more opportunity for trip-ups.

Making matters worse, bugs in multitasking applications are often timing related and can appear intermittently. The proper sequence of events needed to trigger the bug may happen only occasionally. Furthermore, the environment itself can affect the ordering of task execution. The mere act of using a debugger may change the program timing sufficiently to make the problem disappear!

When you debug a multithreaded application, by definition you are debugging all threads at once because they all share the same code and global data. This suggests that your debugger will need to be multithread-aware, or provide additional features to aid you in examining and controlling the threads in your program. We'll list some features a good debugger should have, in a moment.

In a multiprocessing system, you'll often debug just one process, or program, at a time. All other processes in the system will be running and interacting with the process you're debugging, but you won't be able to examine or control the other processes. In some ways, that's a simpler scenario; it's similar to debugging a single-tasking program. You just debug your process's interactions with other processes the same way you'd debug any other outside interaction, such as file or network I/O. This is often acceptable because processes tend to be more loosely coupled (have less interaction) than threads. In a tightly coupled multiprocessing system, however, you may need the capability to set breakpoints and examine memory in more than one process at a time. If so, you'll want to find a multiprocessing OS with a debugger that lets you run multiple debug sessions (one per process to be debugged) simultaneously. Each debug session will allow you to view and control only one process, but whenever you hit a breakpoint in one debug session, all processes are stopped and you can switch between debug sessions to examine each process of interest.

In a good multitasking debugger (for either a multithreading or multiprocessing system), you should be able to examine the state of all synchronization objects. You should be able to see which synchronization objects are signaled and nonsignaled, which objects are owned by which tasks, which tasks are blocked on which objects, and so on. The debugger should be able to freeze individual threads or processes, so you can simplify the interactions that can occur while you're homing in on a particular bug.

In a multithreading debugger, you need to be able to easily see which thread you're stopped in when you hit a breakpoint. You need also to be able to easily select a different thread context, so that you can view the local data and get a stack traceback for each thread in the system. If the OS allows you to associate ASCII names with threads, the debugger should be able to display the thread name as well as the thread ID to make it easier for you to identify threads.

Here are a few suggestions that might help in your next debugging assault on a multitasking application:

- **If two or more tasks simply stop, it's probably caused by a deadlock.** We described how to avoid deadlock in an earlier part of this chapter. Use the debugger to inspect synchronization objects to see which tasks are blocked on which objects, and which tasks own which objects. That information should allow you to determine the source of the deadlock.

- **If one task simply stops, it's probably waiting for some event that hasn't occurred.** Again, use the debugger to find out which synchronization object the task is blocked on; that will tell you what it's waiting for.

- **If the problem is a piece of shared data that is being mysteriously corrupted, suspect a race condition.** Most debuggers allow you to set a breakpoint that halts execution when a location has changed; you can use that feature to home in on the corrupted data element and freeze the application when it changes. That might allow you to identify which combination of tasks has caused the problem.

- **For timing problems that occur intermittently or that go away when you use the debugger, you'll sometimes be forced to instrument your application with trace statements.** Often, you can't print the trace information to a display device or write it to a file because that changes the timing characteristics of the program too much and makes the problem disappear. Your best bet is to store the trace information in a data structure in memory, and then run a post-mortem program that retrieves the data and prints it or saves it to a file for analysis. Many RTOSs, including ETS Kernel, provide a tracing capability that lets you log events of interest performed by both the operating system and your application. Make sure your trace information includes information identifying the task as well as the event.

- **If you don't want other tasks to run while you're debugging a particular piece of code, tell the debugger to suspend those tasks.** Don't forget to release the tasks when you're ready to let the application run normally again.

- **Finally, remember that most problems in multitasking applications occur from the misuse of shared resources — global memory, files, synchronization objects, and so on.** Consequently, you'll reduce the number of potential problems if you can minimize shared resources. Seek out the redundant use of synchronization objects and eliminate it. For example, don't guard a global variable with two synchronization objects when one will do.

Here are a few additional suggestions that apply only to multithreaded applications:

- **During debugging, if you set a breakpoint and the program stops on the breakpoint, know what thread you're stopped in.** If the breakpoint is on a line of code that can be executed by more than one thread, don't assume you know which thread was executing when the breakpoint was reached — check it.

- Every time you let the application run — even just a single step — one or more threads may run and do arbitrary amounts of work before the thread you're debugging gets scheduled, and you get control in the debugger again. And if you're debugging a shared piece of code, you may even be in a different thread when you get control again. Because the debugger implements single steps by setting a temporary breakpoint, another thread might reach the temporary breakpoint before the thread through which you were single-stepping.

- If you hit a permanent breakpoint in some other thread before you hit the temporary breakpoint for your single-step, that temporary breakpoint is gone. If you still want to stop at the temporary breakpoint (where you would have been had the single-step succeeded), you have to select the original thread in the debugger and set a permanent breakpoint at the desired location.

THREADS IN THE SMART UPS PROJECT

In the Smart UPS project, the work performed by the program is distributed across five threads (including the main application thread). We distributed the work by identifying the independent control activities in the project and assigning each to a separate thread. As you'll see, this distribution of work makes the entire application easier to understand and simpler to implement.

In addition, in the serial I/O subsystem, we used multithreading to help the system be more responsive to interrupts. A thread (rather than an interrupt handler) manages the work of moving data into and out of the system. Because the bulk of the communications work takes place in a thread, interrupts are disabled for a minimal amount of time.

Before we look at the source code, let's go over some general programming practices, or techniques, for programming threads in ETS Kernel. You'll be seeing these techniques throughout the examples, so it's important that you become familiar with them up front. Because ETS Kernel implements Win32 multithreading APIs, you may also find the following reference helpful: *Win32 Multithreaded Programming,* by Aaron Cohen and Mike Woodring (O'Reilly & Associates, 1998).

STARTING A THREAD

Remember that a thread is a flow of execution within a process. When a process begins, it contains a single thread. Additional threads within that process must be started explicitly. A thread is started by a call to `_beginthreadex()`, a C run-time library routine. You may wonder why we use a run-time library function rather than the corresponding Win32 API, `StartThread()`. The reason is that calling `_beginthreadex()` allows the multithreaded C run-time library to perform any per-thread initialization that it needs. The `_beginthreadex()` function calls `StartThread()` for us.

The _beginthreadex() function's prototype is

```
unsigned long _beginthreadex(
    void *security,
    unsigned stack_size,
    unsigned (__stdcall *start_address)(void *),
    void *arglist,
    unsigned create_flags,
    unsigned *thread_id);
```

The first argument is an optional pointer to a SECURITY_ATTRIBUTES structure, and should always be NULL under ETS Kernel.

The second argument — stack_size — specifies the number of bytes to allocate to the stack. The value you stipulate for this argument will vary depending on the complexity of the thread. Unfortunately, there are no real guidelines for a recommended size, beyond the fact that the more arguments a thread uses and the more heavily nested its function calls, the more stack space it will need. You can specify 0 for this argument, in which case the operating system sets the size of the thread stack equal to that of the main thread.

The third argument — start_address — is the address of the thread function. Note that it's defined to have an unsigned integer return value. Note also that it accepts a single argument of type pointer-to-void (void *). Consequently, you can pass to the thread function a pointer to an arbitrarily large and complex data structure (which is another way of saying you can pass the thread just about anything you need to).

The thread function must be defined with a __stdcall calling convention. Win32 defines a standardized calling convention, rather than the default calling convention for the language you're programming in (C, C++, or some other language such as Pascal), so that the operating system will know how to pass arguments to the thread function.

The fourth argument — arglist — is the arbitrary pointer passed to the thread function as its input argument. You must provide some sort of input value for this argument, even if it's simply a NULL to act as a placeholder.

The fifth argument, create_flags, should be 0 to have the thread start running immediately after it is created, or CREATE_SUSPENDED to create the thread in a suspended state. Finally, the thread_id argument is a pointer to an unsigned integer that receives the thread ID for the created thread. The operating system assigns a unique, non-reused thread ID as each thread is created.

The call to _beginthreadex() causes ETS Kernel to set up the necessary stack space and other storage space needed to maintain the context of the thread, and begin executing the thread unless CREATE_SUSPENDED was specified. The _beginthreadex() function returns a -1 if an error has occurred. Otherwise, it returns a handle to the created thread. The application uses this handle to identify the created thread in subsequent calls to the operating system. (The thread handle is analogous to a file handle returned by the fopen() routine.) With a thread handle, the application can perform such operations as altering a thread's priority or even terminating the thread. You'll see ETS Kernel calls for these operations shortly.

Note: The C run-time library provides two pairs of thread create and exit functions: _beginthreadex() and _endthreadex(), and _beginthread() and _endthread(). The extended version, _beginthreadex() and _endthreadex(), closely models the functionality of the underlying Win32 APIs, StartThread() and ExitThread(), and is the recommended pair of functions for that reason. The _beginthread() and _endthread() function pair provides a simplified interface that does not support thread exit codes, cannot create threads in a suspended state, and does not return a thread ID (though _beginthread() does return a thread handle, which is more useful than a thread ID). Another difference is that _endthread() closes the thread handle returned by _beginthread(); _endthreadex() does not close the handle returned by beginthreadex(). So, if you use _beginthread(), you must *not* close the returned thread handle. If you use _beginthreadex(), on the other hand, you *must* close the thread handle, either immediately or after the thread terminates, to allow the operating system to reclaim the thread resources that can't be freed until the last handle to the thread is closed.

CONTROLLING THREAD PRIORITY

To set the priority of threads in your application, and thereby fine-tune each thread's responsiveness to the task it performs, call the SetThreadPriority() function. Threads executing background activities can be given low priorities; threads performing important jobs that must be given preference over other activities can be assigned high priorities.

ETS Kernel recognizes a range of 31 thread priorities, extending from -15 (the lowest) to +15 (the highest). When you create a thread with the _beginthreadex() function, that thread starts life with a priority of 0 — in the middle, so to speak. (That value is defined as a constant in the Win32 header files included with Visual C++, THREAD_PRIORITY_NORMAL.)

Although you may use any values in the -15 to +15 range, note that some threads that handle device drivers inside ETS Kernel are assigned priorities above +8. Consequently, any application threads set to a priority above +8 should need to do only minimal processing each time they run; otherwise, they could hamper the responsiveness of the ETS Kernel's device drivers.

The SetThreadPriority() function has the following syntax:

```
BOOL SetThreadPriority(HANDLE hThread, int Priority);
```

where hThread is the handle of the thread whose priority you want to alter, and Priority is the new priority value. SetThreadPriority() returns a Boolean TRUE if the function succeeds, or FALSE if it fails.

In addition, a thread can change its own priority. (This capability is useful if the environment is changing such that the thread needs more or less CPU attention. For example, suppose a thread is processing incoming data that's being written into a memory buffer. The thread may notice that the buffer is filling too rapidly, boost its priority temporarily so that it has more CPU time to process the data, and then reduce its priority when the processing is finished.) The GetCurrentThread() routine allows a thread to obtain its own handle:

```
HANDLE GetCurrentThread();
```

For example, to change its priority level to 4, a thread could execute the following:

```
SetThreadPriority(GetCurrentThread(),4);
```

If you want to determine a thread's priority, you can call the GetThreadPriority() function. The syntax of GetThreadPriority() is

```
int GetThreadPriority(HANDLE hThread);
```

This function takes a single argument — the thread's handle — and returns the priority level as an integer.

TERMINATING A THREAD

Under normal circumstances, a thread terminates when the thread function (the one referenced in the _beginthreadex() call) executes a return statement. In this case, the thread terminates itself. ETS Kernel automatically releases any memory allocated to the thread for the stack and context, and automatically releases any synchronization objects held by the thread.

Alternatively, a thread can terminate itself at any point by calling the _endthreadex() function. The prototype for _endthreadex() is

```
void _endthreadex(unsigned exit_code);
```

The _endthreadex() function has no return value (because, after _endthreadex() is called, there's no caller for the thread to return anything to). The call to _endthreadex() causes ETS Kernel to release resources that were allocated to the thread. A single argument, the thread exit code that the operating system associates with the terminated thread, is passed to _endthreadex().

> **Note:** When a thread terminates by returning from the function given as an argument in the _beginthreadex() function (the first way to terminate a thread, which we just described), the thread is actually making an implicit call to _endthreadex().

Finally, one thread can kill another thread. All that is required for Thread A to kill Thread B is for Thread A to have Thread B's handle. Thread A can then call TerminateThread(), whose prototype is

```
BOOL TerminateThread(HANDLE hThread, DWORD dwExitCode);
```

The TerminateThread() function returns a single Boolean value that indicates success or failure. The function's first argument is the handle of the thread that is to be terminated. The second argument is the thread exit code that the operating system associates with the terminated thread.

> **Note:** Win32 supports a thread exit code, which allows a thread to indicate why it terminated. The exit code is the value returned by the thread function, the argument to _endthreadex(), or the argument to TerminateThread(). Some other part of the application can read that exit code with the GetExitCodeThread() function and determine whether the thread terminated normally or terminated itself due to an error condition.

Suspending a Thread

Another operation can be performed on a thread. We won't describe it in detail, because it's not used in the UPS project, but it is useful enough to be mentioned. This operation is called suspending a thread. Basically, an application can tell a thread to go to sleep. It will remain in that state until the application calls the resume function.

Two functions are involved: SuspendThread() and ResumeThread(). The syntax for SuspendThread() is

    DWORD SuspendThread(HANDLE hThread);

Given a thread's handle, an application can call SuspendThread() and put that thread to sleep. The thread won't wake up until the application calls ResumeThread(). The syntax for ResumeThread() is

    DWORD ResumeThread(HANDLE hThread);

Each call to SuspendThread() increases a thread's suspend count. Each call to ResumeThread() decreases that count. As a result, if an application calls SuspendThread() three times, for example, it has to call ResumeThread() three times before the thread wakes up.

SuspendThread() can be useful when urgent processing must take place and all low-priority threads need to be put on hold to make sure that they don't tie up system resources.

Be careful, however. Don't suspend a thread that holds a lock on a resource or a synchronization object. Otherwise, you could cause other threads in the system — threads you wanted to keep active — to block, waiting for access to resources held prisoner by the suspended thread.

WRITING ISRS

In Chapter 9, "Interrupts," we described the way an interrupt handler in a single-tasking application should be structured under ETS Kernel. Let's review that code again here:

```
void __cdecl MyCIntHandler(ETSINTREGS *pRegs)
{
    // enable interrupts
    EtsSetInterruptFlag(ETS_ENABLEINTS);

    // perform device I/O to process the interrupt

    // issue EOI to 8259A interrupt controller
    EtsPicEOI(IRQNumber);
    return;
}
```

On entry to the interrupt handler, we reenable interrupts to minimize system latency. The handler won't get reentered because we haven't yet issued the end-of-interrupt command to the 8259A interrupt controller. After doing all the work of processing the interrupt, we issue the EOI to the 8259A immediately before exiting the handler.

Now let's modify this sample handler for a multithreaded application. The goal is to prevent the kernel scheduler from running and performing a context switch to another thread before the ISR has completed. An ISR runs in the context of whatever thread was executing when the hardware interrupt occurred. That means an interrupt handler doesn't know what thread priority it runs at; the priority varies depending on the priority of the thread executing at the time of the interrupt. (Remember that thread priority is unrelated to interrupt priority, which was covered in Chapter 9, "Interrupts." Interrupt priority is determined by how the interrupt controller is programmed, and an ISR does know its interrupt priority.) If the scheduler runs, it might preempt the ISR and run another thread. This is undesirable, because unless we know the thread priority when the ISR is executing, we can't predict when that thread will be scheduled again and the ISR can complete its processing. So we have to prevent preemption in an ISR.

```
void __cdecl MyCIntHandler(ETSINTREGS *pRegs)
{
    // lock the scheduler to prevent preemption
    EtsSetISRPriority();

    // enable interrupts
    EtsSetInterruptFlag(ETS_ENABLEINTS);

// perform device I/O to process the interrupt

    // disable interrupts
    EtsSetInterruptFlag(ETS_DISABLEINTS);

    // issue EOI to 8259A interrupt controller
    EtsPicEOI(IRQNumber);

    // unlock the scheduler to allow preemption
    EtsClearISRPriority();

    return;
}
```

The scheduler runs and might decide to schedule another thread under two circumstances. The first is whenever a timer tick interrupt occurs. The second is whenever an API call is made to either signal or wait on a synchronization object. If you need to enable interrupts or signal a synchronization object (you can't wait on a synchronization object in an ISR), you must first disable the scheduler. The EtsSetISRPriority() API locks the scheduler to prevent preemption. This function must be called before enabling interrupts. At the end of the ISR, we disable interrupts again and call EtsClearISRPriority() to unlock the scheduler.

We disable interrupts before calling EtsClearISRPriority() to protect against an unlikely scenario. The ISR may be executing in the context of the system null, or idle, thread, which has the lowest thread priority (-15). If the ISR uses a strategy (which we describe in a moment) of signaling a thread to let it perform the I/O to the device, a higher-priority runnable thread (the one we signaled) will always exist when EtsClearISRPriority() is called, and so the scheduler will preempt the ISR running in the context of the idle thread immediately. This leaves the interrupt stack frame (the saved registers and data pushed by the system umbrella interrupt handler, which totals close to 100 bytes) on the idle thread's stack. Everything's fine so far. Because interrupts are enabled, however, the next time the idle thread is scheduled, another interrupt could occur immediately before the umbrella handler gets a chance to run and pop off the old interrupt stack frame. When the second ISR calls EtsClearISRPriority() and gets preempted, we have two interrupt stack frames on the idle thread's stack. If this happens enough times in succession, the stack for the idle thread (which is 2K in size) could overflow, causing the scheduler to flag a fatal error and kill the application. By disabling interrupts before calling EtsClearISRPriority(), each time the idle task is scheduled again, the umbrella handler gets to run and clean up the interrupt stack frame; only when it returns from the original interrupt, reenabling interrupts, will the new interrupt be processed.

Three good strategies are available for writing ISRs in a multithreaded system. The first strategy is appropriate when the ISR has little processing to perform. In that case, you can simply perform all the I/O in the ISR, without ever reenabling interrupts. Because interrupts stay disabled, the scheduler can't run and it isn't necessary to call EtsSetISRPriority() to prevent preemption.

The second strategy is to perform all the work in the ISR, but to enable interrupts because the processing is lengthy enough that leaving interrupts disabled would adversely affect overall system latency. In this case, you must call EtsSetISRPriority() as shown in the sample code, so that a timer tick interrupt can't result in the ISR being preempted.

The third strategy is to not perform the device I/O in the ISR; instead, you signal a device thread to wake up and service the interrupt. In that case, even if you don't reenable interrupts, you must call EtsSetISRPriority() to prevent preemption when you call the API to signal the synchronization object.

Let's explore this third strategy, signaling a separate device thread to service the interrupt. This approach is attractive for two reasons. First, a thread can make any system or run-time library calls it wants; an ISR is restricted to a handful of Win32 APIs (GetCurrentThreadId(), GetTickCount(), PulseEvent(), QueryPerformanceCounter(), ReleaseSemaphore(), ResetEvent(), ResumeThread(), and SetEvent()) and the small subset of C run-time library functions that are reentrant, such as string manipulation functions. In particular, a thread can make system calls that might block, which an ISR can never do. Second, by handling interrupts in threads, you can select driver thread priorities carefully to reflect the relative importance of servicing each interrupt. Then, when multiple interrupts occur simultaneously, the ISRs all execute and complete quickly, and the ETS Kernel's thread priority mechanism arbitrates which device thread runs first. The serial port interrupt handler in the Smart UPS project uses this strategy.

Keep in mind, however, that using device threads to service interrupts complicates system latency considerations. The latency to process an interrupt now has two components; the time between the occurrence of the interrupt and the execution of the first instruction of the

ISR (which we discussed in Chapter 9, "Interrupts"), plus the time it takes for the scheduler to dispatch the device thread. This second component of latency, the thread dispatch time, is affected by the relative priorities of the threads in the system and by how long the scheduler is locked by a call to EtsSetISRPriority(). To minimize latencies in a multithreaded system, you should minimize not only the length of time that interrupts are disabled, but also the length of time the scheduler is locked. You must also carefully choose device thread priorities to ensure that higher-priority interrupts get precedence; but be careful to avoid lengthy processing in high-priority threads to prevent unacceptable latencies for lower-priority device threads.

THE SMART UPS CODE

Next, we turn our attention to the source code in the Smart UPS project. We examine the source code for the various threads in the system:

- **Serial I/O thread.** Handles the low-level serial I/O (the transmission and reception of individual bytes).

- **Command receive thread.** Receives commands the host system sends down the serial cable to the target, and uses them to generate simulated UPS events, which are sent to the event subsystem for processing.

- **Beep thread.** Beeps the speaker whenever a particular event object is signaled.

- **Timer thread.** Generates timer events and sends them to the UPS's event subsystem, taking the place of the timer callback in the first UPS project.

We examine also the code in the messaging subsystem and the event subsystem. The messaging subsystem is a collection of thread-safe (reentrant) routines for managing message queues. The event subsystem executes in the context of the main program thread; we show how it interacts with the other threads in the system.

Serial I/O Thread

You look at the most interesting subsystem first: the serial I/O subsystem, which handles serial communications for the Smart UPS. This subsystem contains an ISR for handling interrupts from the serial port, a serial I/O thread for performing the I/O to the UART, and two interface functions for reading bytes from and writing bytes to the serial port. The source code for the serial I/O subsystem is in the SERIAL.C file. You'll see this code again in the next chapter, where we focus on those aspects of it that have to do with controlling the serial port. Here, however, you look at the multithreading aspects of the code.

Let's start by examining Listing 12-1, which is the code related to multithreading in the InitSerialsys() routine that initializes the subsystem. InitSerialsys() also initializes the UART hardware and installs the interrupt service routine; you look at the code that controls the UART in Chapter 13, "Serial I/O," and you saw how to install an ISR in Chapter 9, "Interrupts." Here, we reproduce the code that creates the pipes used for interthread communications, the event objects used for synchronization, and the serial I/O thread itself.

Listing 12-1: Serial I/O subsystem initialization

```
//
// Create receive and send pipes.
//
    if (!CreatePipe(&hComRcvRead,&hComRcvWrite,NULL,SER_PIPE_SIZE))
    {
        printf("Can't create COM receive pipe\n");
        return FALSE;
    }
    if (!CreatePipe(&hComSendRead,&hComSendWrite,NULL,SER_PIPE_SIZE))
    {
        printf("Can't create COM send pipe\n");
        goto CLOSE_RCV_PIPE;
    }
    InitializeCriticalSection(&SerCritSec);
    nComRcvPipeBytes = 0;
    nComSendPipeBytes = 0;
//
// Create auto-reset events used by the serial interrupt
// handler to signal the serial I/O thread to process an interrupt,
// and used for thread termination.
//
    hComEvent = CreateEvent(NULL, FALSE, FALSE, "ComEvent");
    hComExitEvent = CreateEvent(NULL, FALSE, FALSE, "ComExitEvent");
    if (hComEvent == NULL || hComExitEvent == NULL)
    {
        printf("Error creating events for serial I/O thread\n");
        goto CLOSE_SEND_PIPE;
    }

//
// Create the serial I/O thread and hook the interrupt.  Since we
// know the thread doesn't need much stack, we'll limit its
// stack size to save memory. We also set the thread priority to
// 1, so it's higher priority than the other threads in the
// application (which all get the default priority of 0).  This
// ensures we are responsive to serial interrupts; we also know
// the serial I/O thread completes its work quickly, so it won't
// hog CPU time.
//
    hComThread = (HANDLE) _beginthreadex(NULL, 0x1000, ComThread,
                                         NULL, 0, &idComThread);
    if (hComThread == (HANDLE) -1)
    {
        printf("Error %d creating serial I/O thread\n",
               GetLastError());
        goto CLOSE_EVENTS;
    }
    EtsSetThreadDebugName(hComThread, "COM Thread");
    SetThreadPriority(hComThread, 1);
```

The receive pipe is used to buffer data received over the serial link; the send pipe buffers data waiting to be sent over the wire. You see how these pipes are used shortly. We call `CreatePipe()` twice to create the two pipes. The first two arguments to `CreatePipe()` are pointers to variables that receive the read and write handles for the created pipe. The third argument is an optional pointer to a security attributes structure, which is not used by ETS Kernel. The last argument specifies the pipe buffer size in bytes; if you pass 0 for the size, ETS Kernel uses a default size of 1K. The serial I/O subsystem uses a pipe size of 512 bytes. We also call `InitializeCriticalSection()` to create a critical section object that we will use to synchronize access to the `nComRcvPipeBytes` and `nComSendPipeBytes` variables, which track the amount of data in each pipe.

Next, we create the two event objects used for thread synchronization in the communications subsystem. The `CreateEvent()` function takes four arguments: an optional pointer to a security attributes structure; a flag that is TRUE to specify a manual-reset event object or FALSE for auto reset; a flag that is TRUE to make the initial state of the event be signaled or FALSE for nonsignaled; and an optional pointer to an event name. Specifying an event name allows you to easily identify event objects when viewing them in the debugger. Using event names also allows programs to obtain a handle to a previously created event object. Each event object is created with an initial state of nonsignaled and as an auto-reset event, so it is automatically reset to nonsignaled each time a thread waiting on the event is released. We use `hComEvent` to signal the serial I/O thread that a serial port interrupt has occurred, and `hComExitEvent` to signal the serial I/O thread to terminate.

Finally, we call `_beginthreadex()` to create the serial I/O thread. This function takes six parameters: a NULL pointer to a security structure; the size of the stack in bytes; the name of the top-level function (`ComThread()`) in the thread; the argument to pass to `ComThread()`; a flag (0) that means run the thread immediately after creating it; and a pointer to a variable that receives the thread ID. Because we know `ComThread()` needs very little stack space (as you'll see shortly, the entire thread is just one function), we give it a 4K stack rather than passing in 0 to give it a stack as large as the main program thread. We have no need to pass an argument to `ComThread()`, so we pass in NULL. We use `EtsSetThreadDebugName()` to give the thread an ASCII name, so that it's easy to identify in the debugger. We also call `SetThreadPriority()` to set the thread's priority to 1. All the other application threads in the Smart UPS are assigned the default priority of 0; we give the serial I/O thread a higher priority because we want it to be responsive to interrupts from the serial port; that is, we want it to be scheduled as soon as possible after the interrupt occurs. Because this thread consumes little CPU time when it runs (it just does some quick I/O to the UART and then blocks again), it's an ideal candidate for a high-priority thread.

Note: ETS Kernel provides a function, `EtsDumpThreads()`, that can be used to diagnose program bugs in multithreaded applications. `EtsDumpThreads()` outputs a variety of information associated with each active thread in the system, including each thread's priority and any synchronization objects (such as a mutex or a critical section object) that the thread is waiting on. By calling `EtsSetThreadDebugName()`, you can associate a name with each thread, thus making the output of `EtsDumpThreads()` easier to read. In Chapter 4, "Debugging," you saw how to display this same information from the Microsoft Developer Studio debugger.

Now that you've seen the initialization code, let's look at how work is accomplished in this subsystem. Serial I/O is driven by interrupts from the UART for the serial communications port. As you can see from the source code for the interrupt handler in Listing 12-2, however, the ISR doesn't do much work at all.

Listing 12-2: A serial I/O interrupt handler

```
//
// COM interrupt handler.  All it does is signal the serial I/O
// thread which will wake up and perform the I/O to the UART.
//

void __cdecl ComHandler(ETSINTREGS *pRegs)
{
    int    Mask;

//
// Disable the scheduler so no other threads can run, and
// re-enable interrupts.
//
    EtsSetISRPriority();
    _asm sti;

//
// Mask this interrupt, and then issue EOI so we can't get this
// interrupt again but all other ISRs can run.  Then signal the
// thread which will do the real work.  That thread will unmask
// the COM interrupt again when it's done processing this interrupt.
//
    Mask = _inp(PIC_1_A1);
    _outp(PIC_1_A1, Mask | UartIntMask);
    _outp(PIC_1_A0, PIC_EOI);
    SetEvent(hComEvent);

//
// Ok, the thread is ready to run.  We can release the scheduler,
// and return, which will re-enable interrupts.
//
    _asm cli;
    EtsClearISRPriority();
    return;
}
```

As usual in an ISR, ComHandler() almost immediately reenables interrupts so that higher-priority interrupts can be processed by the system. Notice, however, that ComHandler() calls EtsSetISRPriority() first to lock the scheduler so that it won't run any other threads. As we noted earlier in this chapter, this is important because the ISR is running in the context of whatever thread was active when the interrupt occurred; we have no idea how low (or high) the priority of that thread is. If we hadn't called EtsSetISRPriority()

and a timer tick occurred after we reenabled interrupts, the scheduler could preempt us and run another thread.

Next, we mask the serial port interrupt in the 8259A interrupt controller, so that we can't get any more interrupts until the interrupt is unmasked again. (You see the code that does this later, in the serial I/O thread.) Then we issue the EOI command to the interrupt controller. This is a slight variation on the generic interrupt handler we showed earlier, in which the EOI command wasn't sent until processing was complete, to prevent reentrancy if another serial interrupt occurred. Here, we instead prevent reentrancy by masking the serial interrupt in the interrupt controller. The difference is that by issuing the EOI command at the beginning of the interrupt handler, we can allow the processing of all other interrupts, rather than just higher-priority interrupts. As we noted in Chapter 9, "Interrupts," it's sometimes desirable and sometimes not desirable to allow lower-priority interrupts to be processed before your ISR completes. In the Smart UPS, it's irrelevant, because the only other interrupt in the system is the timer, which has a higher priority anyway. We did it this way to demonstrate alternatives.

Once the interrupt is safely masked, we signal the hComEvent event object to wake up the serial I/O thread to process the interrupt. Here, again, it's important that we've disabled the scheduler. If we hadn't disabled the scheduler, when we make the SetEvent() call into the scheduler, it might decide to run another, higher-priority thread; we want to make sure the ISR is able to exit before any other threads can run.

And that's it. The ISR just unlocks the scheduler by calling EtsClearISRPriority() (after first disabling interrupts), and exits.

Now let's look at the code for the serial I/O thread (the ComThread() function), which does the work of reading bytes from and writing bytes to the UART. We'll just reproduce interesting sections of code here; you look at the entire thread in Chapter 13, "Serial I/O." First, look at the code that waits for serial port interrupts to be signaled:

```
//
// Sit in an infinite loop waking up every time we get signaled by
// the interrupt handler.  Whenever we wake up we'll do as much I/O
// as we can, and then go to sleep again.
//
    WaitEvents[0] = hComEvent;
    WaitEvents[1] = hComExitEvent;
    while (TRUE)
    {
//
// Wait until interrupt event or exit event is signaled
//
        if (WaitForMultipleObjects(2, WaitEvents, FALSE, INFINITE)
              != WAIT_OBJECT_0)
            break;
```

The WaitForMultipleObjects() call blocks the thread until one of the event objects passed in the call, hComEvent and hComExitEvent, is signaled. The first two arguments to WaitForMultipleObjects() are the number of handles in the handle array and a pointer to the handle array. The third argument is a flag that is TRUE to wait until all synchronization objects in the array are signaled, or FALSE to return when any one of the objects is signaled. The last argument is a timeout value, in milliseconds. In this case, we are waiting until either hComEvent (the event signaled when an interrupt occurs) or hComExitEvent (which is signaled to tell the thread to exit) is signaled and there is no timeout. WaitForMultipleObjects() returns one of the following values:

- WAIT_OBJECT_0 to (WAIT_OBJECT_0 + nObjects - 1). The return value minus WAIT_OBJECT_0 is the array index of the signaled object.

- WAIT_TIMEOUT. The timeout interval elapsed before any objects were signaled.

- WAIT_ABANDONED_0 to (WAIT_ABANDONED_0 + nObjects - 1). This is returned when one of the objects is a mutex, and the thread that owns it has terminated. The thread calling WaitForMultipleObjects() becomes the new owner of the mutex.

Because we have no timeout, and no mutex objects are in the array, the only possible return values are WAIT_OBJECT_0 and WAIT_OBJECT_0+1. The if() statement checks whether the return value is not WAIT_OBJECT_0, in which case the signaled object must have been hComExitEvent, so we break out of the loop and exit the thread by calling _endthreadex(). Otherwise, the hComEvent object was signaled, so we continue with code that processes the interrupt and sends and receives characters over the UART; after all pending communications have been performed, the code loops back up to the WaitForMultipleObjects() call to go back to sleep until the next time there's work to do.

We talk about the I/O to the UART in Chapter 13. For now, keep in mind that each time the thread wakes up, it sits in a loop performing I/O to the UART until there are both no more incoming characters to read and no more data to send, or the UART has no more buffer space for data. Let's look next at the code that reads characters from the UART, which shows the use of the receive pipe:

```
case SIO_IDRCVD:  // received data available
    // read until the FIFO is empty (this works also
    // for 8250/16450, which have a 1-char "FIFO"),
    // and stuff the chars read into the pipe.  If pipe
    // is full, just discard chars.  Reading a char
    // clears SIO_IDRCVD.
    EnterCriticalSection(&SerCritSec);
    do
    {
      ch = (BYTE) _inp((USHORT)(UartPort + SIO_RECVR));
      if (nComRcvPipeBytes + 1 <= SER_PIPE_SIZE)
      {
          WriteFile(hComRcvWrite, &ch, 1, &dwTemp, NULL);
          ++ nComRcvPipeBytes;
      }
    } while (_inp((USHORT)(UartPort + SIO_LSR)) & SIO_LSRCV);
    LeaveCriticalSection(&SerCritSec);
    break;
```

The do loop in this case statement handles reading bytes of data from the receiver buffer register in the UART until the receiver buffer register is empty. If the UART has a FIFO buffer for received data, we may be able to read multiple bytes. After calling _inp() to read each byte, we call WriteFile() to write the byte to the receive pipe. Notice, however, that we enter a critical section to write the pipe, and we maintain a count (nComRcvPipeBytes) of the number of bytes of data in the receive pipe. What's that all about?

Recall that the WaitForMultipleObjects() call has a timeout parameter; if you want to, you can use a zero timeout to simply check whether a synchronization object is signaled, without blocking. Pipes, however, have no timeout. The WriteFile() call blocks on a full pipe until some data is read from the other end of the pipe; checking whether the pipe is empty is impossible. Similarly, ReadFile() blocks on an empty pipe until someone writes data into the other end; checking for that condition is impossible, too.

In the serial I/O thread, we can't afford to block on a pipe because we have to keep pumping data through the UART, in both directions, as fast as possible. The only time we want to block in this thread is when any pending I/O is finished and the thread can go back to sleep until the next serial port interrupt occurs.

So, we keep a count of the number of characters in each pipe so we can detect pipe full and pipe empty conditions. Because nComRecvPipeBytes is a shared global variable, we must enter a critical section to safely access the variable. After we read a received byte of data from the UART, we check nComRecvPipeBytes before attempting to write a byte to the receive pipe. If the pipe is full, we just discard the byte we obtained from the UART, rather than blocking on the WriteFile() call. If we blocked while we owned the critical section object, that would create a deadlock condition, because the code that reads data from the other end of the receive pipe (which you see in a moment) wouldn't be able to acquire the critical section object to read data from the pipe. We don't expect to ever have to discard data; the pipe size (512 bytes) is large enough that a pipe full condition almost certainly means something else is drastically wrong somewhere in the system. After determining that the pipe is not full, we write the byte to the pipe and increment the global byte count. When the receiver FIFO buffer is empty and we no longer need to access the receive pipe, we exit the critical section.

Now let's look at the other end of the receive pipe, which is accessed by the SerialRead() function that is part of the interface to the serial I/O subsystem. Because this function, which is shown is Listing 12-3, is called by code outside the subsystem, it executes in the context of whatever thread called it.

Listing 12-3: The SerialRead() function

```
//
// Reads characters from the serial port.  If fWait is
// TRUE, will wait for the requested number of characters
// to be received before returning.  If fWait is FALSE, will
// return immediately with an error if there are less than
// the requested number of characters available.
//
```

```
// This function is non-reentrant; it may only be called
// by one thread in the system.
//
// Returns: nChar if success
//          if error, number of available characters
//
DWORD SerialRead(char *pBuf, DWORD nChar, BOOL fWait)
{
    DWORD dwTemp;
    DWORD nToRead;
    DWORD nRead;

    EnterCriticalSection(&SerCritSec);
    if (nComRcvPipeBytes >= nChar)
    {
        // enough chars are available in pipe
        ReadFile(hComRcvRead, pBuf, nChar, &dwTemp, NULL);
        nComRcvPipeBytes -= nChar;
        LeaveCriticalSection(&SerCritSec);
        return nChar;
    }
    else
    {
        // we'll have to wait for chars to arrive
        nToRead = nComRcvPipeBytes;
        LeaveCriticalSection(&SerCritSec);
        if (!fWait)
            return nToRead;
        for (nRead = 0; nRead < nChar;
             pBuf += nToRead, nRead += nToRead)
        {
            nToRead = min(nChar - nRead, SER_PIPE_SIZE);
            ReadFile(hComRcvRead, pBuf, nToRead, &dwTemp, NULL);
            EnterCriticalSection(&SerCritSec);
            nComRcvPipeBytes -= nToRead;
            LeaveCriticalSection(&SerCritSec);
        }
        return nChar;
    }
}
```

SerialRead() takes a buffer pointer and a character count as arguments. It also takes a flag that specifies whether the caller wants to wait or get an immediate error return when the pipe has insufficient data to satisfy the read immediately.

SerialRead() first acquires the critical section object and checks the shared global variable to see whether the pipe has enough bytes to satisfy the read request. If so, the ReadFile() call won't block and we read bytes from the pipe into the caller's buffer, decrement the global byte count, exit the critical section, and return.

If the read request can't be satisfied immediately, we copy the global byte count to a local variable and exit the critical section. Then, if the caller doesn't want to wait, we return the number of bytes available.

If the caller does want to wait, we call `ReadFile()`; that call blocks until enough data is in the pipe to satisfy the request. Notice that `SerialRead()` supports read requests larger than the pipe size; if necessary, it makes multiple calls to `ReadFile()` to read the requested data.

The `ReadFile()` call we expect to block is made without acquiring the critical section object, because we don't want to block in a critical section. After the read call returns, we enter a critical section to update the `nComRcvPipeBytes` shared global variable. But doesn't that mean a small window of time exists during which the shared global variable doesn't have the correct value? The answer is yes; but we've written the code in such a way that it won't cause any problems. When the global variable is inaccurate, it always states that more data is in the pipe than is actually present. This doesn't cause a problem in the serial I/O thread code; the worst that could happen is the code throws away a byte unnecessarily if it thinks the pipe is full when it isn't. No problem results in this instance of the `SerialRead()` function either, because the next thing we do after calling `ReadFile()` is acquire the critical section object and update the global variable.

But what if two threads were in `SerialRead()` at the same time; in other words, what if `SerialRead()` needs to be reentrant? Then this *would* be a problem: Another thread calling `SerialRead()` might think data is in the pipe when it isn't, and inadvertently block on the first `ReadFile()` call in the function, which is inside a critical section of code.

It turns out we don't need to make `SerialRead()` reentrant; in the Smart UPS, only one thread (the command receive thread) calls `SerialRead()`. If you think about it, having multiple threads reading a single serial port wouldn't make much sense, because there would be no easy way to guarantee that one thread wouldn't read data intended for another.

We could make a reentrant version of `SerialRead()`, if necessary, but only at the cost of additional complexity. We wouldn't be able to use the `ReadFile()` call to implement the blocking functionality required when `fWait` is TRUE. Instead, we would have to create an additional synchronization object — an event object — that `SerialRead()` could block on. The serial I/O thread would signal the event when it added new data to the pipe; the thread inside `SerialRead()` would wake up, read the new data inside a critical section, and then block on the event again if the read request was not yet satisfied. This would be fairly straightforward to implement; you might want to try making `SerialRead()` (and `SerialWrite()`) reentrant as an exercise.

Now look at the code that handles sending data out over the serial connection. You look first at the code in the serial I/O thread that writes data to the UART:

```
case SIO_IDXMTE: // transmit holding register empty
    // if there's chars to send in the pipe, write
    // up to MaxXmitChars to the transmit FIFO. Whether
    // or not we write a char, SIO_IDXMTE was already
    // cleared by reading the interrupt identification
    // register.  After entering the critical section,
    // double-check that xmit holding register is still
```

```
        // empty, in case SerialWrite() ran inbetween us
        // reading the ID register and entering the critical
        // section.
        EnterCriticalSection(&SerCritSec);
        if (_inp((USHORT)(UartPort + SIO_LSR)) & SIO_LSXHRE)
        {
            for (i = 0; i<MaxXmitChars && nComSendPipeBytes>0;
                ++ i, - nComSendPipeBytes)
            {
                ReadFile(hComSendRead, &ch, 1, &dwTemp, NULL);
                _outp((USHORT)(UartPort + SIO_XMITR), (int)ch);
            }
        }
        LeaveCriticalSection(&SerCritSec);
        break;
```

Notice that the entire block of code, including the I/O to the UART, is inside a critical section. The reason the I/O is in a critical section is that SerialWrite(), which you see in a moment, also needs to write characters to the UART. The UART registers are a shared resource just like the global data counts; because multiple threads need to write to the transmit holding register in the UART, we have to synchronize the register writes by placing them inside critical sections of code.

After entering the critical section, we check whether the transmitter holding register is empty. It might not be empty if a thread calling SerialWrite() got scheduled after we read the interrupt ID register but before we entered the critical section. Since SerialWrite() also writes to the transmitter holding register, it might no longer be empty. In the Smart UPS, the serial I/O thread is the highest priority application thread in the system, so it can't get pre-empted by a thread calling SerialWrite(). We wrote the serial I/O subsystem so it can also work in other applications with higher priority threads calling SerialWrite().

If the transmitter holding register is empty (as is normally the case), we enter a loop to read bytes from the serial pipe and write them to the transmitter holding register. Each time through the loop, we read 1 byte from the send pipe, write it to the UART, and decrement the shared global variable nComSendPipeBytes. Because the loop terminates when the send pipe is empty, we know the call to ReadFile() will return immediately without blocking. We write more than 1 byte if the UART contains a FIFO buffer for send data; programming the FIFOs is covered in Chapter 13. The MaxXmitChars variable that controls how many bytes are written to the UART is set when the UART is initialized.

Notice that we use the same critical section object for both sending data and receiving data. Because the resources used for sending and receiving data (the global variables, the pipes, and the UART registers) are distinct, we could use two critical section objects, one for send resources and the other for receive resources. This technique would have the advantage of reducing the likelihood that an attempt to acquire the critical section object would block, because each critical section object would be used only half as often. So why didn't we use two synchronization objects?

Because we were careful to keep each critical section of code short and ensure that we can't block inside a critical section, we made the judgment that blocking would be infrequent, even if a single critical section object was used for both sending and receiving data. All else being equal, it's a good idea to minimize the number of synchronization objects in the system. It simplifies your code, reducing the likelihood that you might make a coding mistake that could result in deadlock or some other problem. Minimizing the number of synchronization objects also reduces the amount of data the scheduler has to manage, thereby reducing overall operating system overhead.

Let's look at Listing 12-4, the `SerialWrite()` interface function for sending data out over the serial connection, which writes to the other end of the send pipe.

Listing 12-4: The SerialWrite() function

```
//
// Writes characters to the serial port.  If fWait is TRUE, will wait
// for sufficient buffer space.  If fWait is FALSE, will write as many
// characters as possible to the buffer and then return immediately.
//
// This function is non-reentrant; it may only be called by one thread
// in the system.
//
// Returns: nChar       if success
//          otherwise   number of chars written
//
DWORD SerialWrite(char *pBuf, DWORD nChar, BOOL fWait)
{
    DWORD nSent;
    DWORD nToSend;
    int   i;
    DWORD dwTemp;
    BYTE  chTemp;

//
// Initialize the number of bytes sent, and enter the
// critical section that controls access to the pipe.
//
    nSent = 0;
    EnterCriticalSection(&SerCritSec);

//
// If the write pipe is empty and the transmit holding register is also
// empty, then writing the bytes to the pipe won't work; the UART won't
// signal a transmit register empty interrupt, so the serial I/O thread
// will never read the bytes out of the pipe and write them to the UART.
//
// So, in that case, we write up to MaxXmitChars bytes directly to the
// UART, and then write any leftover bytes to the pipe. When the byte(s)
// we wrote to the UART get sent, it will issue the THRE interrupt, and
// the serial I/O thread can send the rest of the bytes.
//
```

```
WRITE_UART:
    if (nComSendPipeBytes == 0 &&
        (_inp((USHORT)(UartPort+SIO_LSR)) & SIO_LSXHRE))
    {
        for (i = 0; i < MaxXmitChars && nSent < nChar;
            ++ i, ++ pBuf, ++ nSent)
        {
            _outp((USHORT)(UartPort + SIO_XMITR), (int) *pBuf);
        }
    }
//
// Write as many characters as will fit in the pipe without  blocking,
// and leave the critical section.  If we've written all the characters,
//  or the caller doesn't want to wait, return the number of bytes sent.
//
WRITE_PIPE:
    nToSend = min(SER_PIPE_SIZE - nComSendPipeBytes, nChar - nSent);
    if (nToSend > 0)
    {
        WriteFile(hComSendWrite, pBuf, nToSend, &dwTemp, NULL);
        nComSendPipeBytes += nToSend;
        pBuf += nToSend;
        nSent += nToSend;
    }
    LeaveCriticalSection(&SerCritSec);
    if (nSent >= nChar || !fWait)
        return nSent;
//
// OK, we didn't write all the data, and the caller wants to block. So,
// block till we can write one char into the pipe. Then re-acquire the
// critical section, and check if the pipe is empty (except for the byte
// we just wrote to it). If so, get that byte back out of the pipe, and
// jump back to the start of the function to try to write the UART
// directly again, in case the serial I/O thread is sleeping. If there
// are bytes in the pipe, there's no danger of data not getting sent, so
// leave the byte in the pipe (updating the variables accordingly), and
// jump back to try to write the remainder of the data to the pipe.
//
    WriteFile(hComSendWrite, pBuf, 1, &dwTemp, NULL);
    EnterCriticalSection(&SerCritSec);
    if (nComSendPipeBytes == 0)
    {
        ReadFile(hComSendRead, &chTemp, 1, &dwTemp, NULL);
        goto WRITE_UART;
    }
    ++ nComSendPipeBytes;
    ++ pBuf;
    ++ nSent;
    goto WRITE_PIPE;
}
```

SerialWrite() takes a buffer pointer and a character count as arguments. It also takes a flag that specifies whether the caller wants to wait or get an immediate error return, if the pipe has insufficient buffer space to satisfy the write immediately. In the event of an error return, SerialWrite() writes as much data as it can to the pipe and returns the number of characters written.

The first thing SerialWrite() does is acquire the critical section object. Next, if the send pipe is empty, SerialWrite() writes up to MaxXmitChars characters directly to the UART transmit holding register; just as the serial I/O thread does when it gets a transmit register empty interrupt. This is done because the serial I/O thread wakes up only when a serial port interrupt occurs. If data is in the pipe, the serial I/O thread either is currently executing, sucking data out of the pipe, or has filled the UART's transmit buffer and gone back to sleep; after the UART empties the transmit buffer, it will interrupt again, waking up the serial I/O thread. If no data is in the pipe, on the other hand, the UART may have emptied its transmit buffer long ago, so it won't interrupt again to say it's ready for more transmit data. If no receive data is arriving over the serial connection (the other activity that would cause the UART to interrupt) as well, the serial I/O thread might never wake up to process the new data in the pipe! So we have to write the data directly to the UART until its transmit FIFO buffer fills up. The need to write to the transmit holding register in SerialWrite() is also why we need to synchronize access to the transmit holding register both here and in the serial I/O thread.

After we've finished any I/O to the UART, we write as much data as we can to the pipe, update the nComSendPipeBytes shared global count, and release the critical section object. If we've sent all the data or the caller doesn't want to wait, we then return.

If we have more data to send and the caller wants to wait, we call WriteFile() to write a single byte to the file. Because we expect this call to block, we make it outside a critical section of code. When WriteFile() returns, we acquire the critical section object again. If the pipe is now empty (except for the byte we've just written), once again the serial I/O thread might be sleeping, so we empty the pipe again and jump back up to the code that writes to the UART directly. If the pipe already has data, we increment the global count variable to account for the new byte we've added, update our buffer pointer, and jump back up to the code that attempts to write more data to the pipe.

As was the case with SerialRead(), this call to write the pipe from outside a critical section means the global count variable might temporarily get out of sync with the pipe, which makes SerialWrite() non-reentrant. However, SerialWrite() is called by only one thread — the main thread executing in the event subsystem — so it's acceptable for SerialWrite() to be non-reentrant. When the global variable is incorrect, it says there's less data in the pipe than is actually there, which doesn't cause a problem in the serial I/O thread. The serial I/O thread might think there's no data to transmit and go back to sleep when in fact a byte is in the pipe; but in that case the SerialWrite() function takes care of reading the byte back out of the pipe and writing to the UART directly.

Finally, let's look at the CleanupSerialsys() function, which is called to shut down the serial I/O subsystem when the program exits. We leave the code that interacts with the UART for Chapter 13, and just reproduce here the code that relates to multithreading:

```
//
// Unhook the interrupt and kill the thread
//
    EtsRestoreInterruptHandler(UartIntNum, &ComSaveHand);
    if (SetEvent(hComExitEvent))
        WaitForSingleObject(hComThread, INFINITE);
    CloseHandle(hComThread);
//
// Close the event and pipe handles
//
    CloseHandle(hComEvent);
    CloseHandle(hComExitEvent);
    DeleteCriticalSection(&SerCritSec);
    CloseHandle(hComSendRead);
    CloseHandle(hComSendWrite);
    CloseHandle(hComRcvRead);
    CloseHandle(hComRcvWrite);
```

The code first restores the original serial port interrupt handler, and then tells the serial I/O thread to exit. This is accomplished by signaling the hComExitEvent event object, which as you saw earlier will cause the serial I/O thread to call _endthreadex(). We need to wait for the serial I/O thread to exit before we proceed, however; otherwise, we might close handles (such as event handles and pipe handles) that the serial I/O thread is still using! We just wait on the thread handle for the serial I/O thread; when ETS Kernel terminates the thread, it signals the handle, which allows us to proceed. After the thread has terminated, we close the thread handle, which allows ETS Kernel to free up all operating system data structures allocated for that thread.

After the serial I/O thread has terminated, the rest is easy. We just close the handles to all the synchronization objects and pipes we created, to allow the operating system to free up the resources allocated to them.

Command Receive Thread

The source to the command receive subsystem is in the CMDRECV.C file. The job of the command receive thread is to read commands sent by the host system. These commands are packets of bytes sent through the serial cable each time the user clicks one of the buttons in the GUI. Each action a user can perform on the host GUI corresponds to a command: set the AC power good, set the UPS power off, and so on. The command receive thread dispatches these commands to the UPS system's event queue. We placed this code in a separate thread because the work performed by this code is an independent activity.

> **Note:** Potential for confusion exists because we have two kinds of events: simulated UPS events, such as AC power going bad or a load being added, and Win32 event objects, which are synchronization objects. We try to make it clear which we're talking about by calling them *UPS events* and *event objects,* respectively.

Data arrives at the serial port as a stream, a series of consecutive bytes. Commands, however, are encoded as packets. That is, a command from the host is a series of one or more bytes that have a beginning and an end. Another task that the command receive thread must perform is the extraction of command packets from the stream of incoming bytes. (It's not unlike a ham radio operator listening to a stream of letters in Morse code. The operator's job is to decode the letters and put them together into words, or packets.)

The command receive subsystem consists of the initialize and cleanup interface routines and the command receive thread itself. We create and exit the thread as we did for the serial I/O thread, so we won't bother to look at the initialize and cleanup routines for this subsystem. Let's look at the code for the command receive thread, which is shown in Listing12-5.

Listing 12-5: The command receive thread

```
//
// The command receive thread loops checking for data to arrive
// over the serial port, and checking if has been told to exit.
// We need to synchronize with the exit of the command receive
// thread to make sure it doesn't try to call into the serial
// subsystem to attempt to read the serial port after the serial
// subsystem has shut down.
//
unsigned __stdcall RecvThread(void *pUnused)
{
    int         nRead;
    WINUPS_CMD Cmd;
    UPS_EVENT  Event;

    while (TRUE)
    {
//
// If a command has arrived over the serial line, read it and
// send an event message to the event subsystem.
// If we get a bad command, just discard it and try to re-sync
// by reading bytes one at a time until we get an ID byte or
// all characters are drained from the serial receive queue.
//
        if (SerialRead(&Cmd, 1, FALSE) == 1)
        {
            if (Cmd.WinupsID != WINUPS_ID)
                continue;
            // Read the rest of the command;  if not yet there,
            // give it time to arrive (1 msec/char should be
            // plenty of time at 19200 baud).
            nRead = SerialRead(((char *)&Cmd)+1, sizeof(Cmd)-1, FALSE);
            if (nRead < sizeof(Cmd) - 1)
            {
                Sleep(sizeof(Cmd) - 1 - nRead);
                if (SerialRead(((char *)&Cmd) + 1 + nRead,
                            sizeof(Cmd) - 1 - nRead, FALSE) !=
                    sizeof(Cmd) - 1 - nRead)
                continue;
            }
```

```
                  // send the event message
                  switch(Cmd.Command)
                  {
                  case CMD_STATUS:
                     Event.Event = EVENT_STATUS;
                     break;
                  case CMD_POWER:
                     Event.Event = EVENT_POWER;
                     break;
                  case CMD_ACPOWER:
                     Event.Event = EVENT_AC;
                     break;
                  case CMD_LOAD:
                     Event.Event = EVENT_LOAD;
                     break;
                  case CMD_EXIT:
                     Event.Event = EVENT_EXIT;
                     break;
                  default:  // bad command
                     continue;
                  }
                  MsgWrite(hEventQueue, &Event, TRUE);
            }
      // Check if we've been told to exit.
            if (WaitForSingleObject(hRecvExitEvent, 0) != WAIT_TIMEOUT)
               break;
      //
      // Give up the rest of our time slice to other runnable threads,
      // so we don't hog the CPU just checking for incoming serial data.
      // Sleep(0) only allows the same or higher priority threads to run,
      // so use Sleep(10) so we will also yield to lower priority threads.
      //
            Sleep(10);
         }


      //
      // Terminate the thread.
      //
         _endthreadex(0);
      }
```

The `RecvThread()` routine is a single, eternal `while` loop. At the head of the loop, the thread calls the `SerialRead()` function to read the next command packet from the serial I/O subsystem. The command structure is shown next and defined in the UPSIFACE.H header file, which is shared by UPS2.EXE and WINUPS.EXE.

```
//
// Pack all structures sent over the wire to ensure no problems due to
// different structure alignment in the two programs.
//
```

```
#pragma pack(1)
//
// Command structure sent from WINUPS program to UPS
//
typedef struct {
    BYTE WinupsID;       // ID, defined below
    BYTE Command;        // command code
} WINUPS_CMD;
#define WINUPS_ID 0xF0
```

The members of the structure are packed on byte boundaries with the compiler pack() pragma; this ensures that we won't have any problems due to different default structure packing on the two systems.

The command structure is simple: It consists of an ID byte, defined as 0xF0, and the command byte. Using an ID byte at the beginning of data structures sent over a communications link is useful for detecting lost data bytes and for resynchronizing when data is lost.

Recall that the SerialRead() function in the serial I/O subsystem has a wait functionality. Why not just request an entire command packet at once, and have SerialRead() wait until it arrives?

We don't do this for two reasons. First, we also need to respond to the hRecvExitEvent event object being signaled to tell the thread to terminate. If we're blocked inside a call to SerialRead(), we can't check the event object. Second, we want to provide a means of recovering from lost or corrupted data. By reading bytes one at a time until we see the ID byte that marks the start of a command structure, we can resynchronize with the command structures in the data stream.

So, all our calls to SerialRead() specify to return immediately if data is not present. If we're able to read a byte of data, we keep reading data until no more is available or we see an ID byte; when we get an ID byte, we read the rest of the command structure.

After we obtain a valid command packet, we process the command to generate a UPS event structure to add to the UPS event queue. The UPS event structure shown here is defined in the UPS.H header file.

```
//
// UPS event queue entry
//
typedef struct _UPS_EVENT {
    int    Event;        // event that occurred
    DWORD  Msecs;        // for timer event, number of milliseconds
                         // since last timer event.
} UPS_EVENT;
```

Because UPS timer events are not generated by this subsystem, we need to fill out only the Event member of the structure; we do this in the switch() statement that maps command bytes to simulated UPS events, as shown in Listing 12-5. The UPS event structure is then added to the UPS event queue by calling MsgWrite(), one of the interface functions to the messaging subsystem.

Each time through the loop, whether or not a command packet must be processed, we call `WaitForSingleObject()` to check whether the `hRecvExitEvent` event object has been signaled. In previous wait calls, we always specified a timeout value of `INFINITE`. This time, we use a zero timeout, so `WaitForSingleObject()` will always return immediately. If the return value is `WAIT_TIMEOUT`, the event object is nonsignaled, so we stay in the loop. Otherwise, the event object was signaled, so we break out of the loop, and then exit the thread by calling `_endthreadex()`.

At the bottom of the loop is a `Sleep(10)` call, which suspends the thread for at least 10 milliseconds. Because we didn't use any blocking calls in the receive loop, we want to give up the rest of our current time slice each time through the loop. Otherwise, we'd be wasting precious CPU time to constantly check whether any receive data is available. That checking is unnecessary: At 19200 baud, the maximum data rate is about one character every half a millisecond. A `Sleep(0)` call yields to threads with the same or higher priority. By sleeping for a specific number of milliseconds, we can also allow lower-priority threads to run.

Beep Thread

The beep thread is created by the event subsystem; its source code is in the `EVENT.C` file. The thread create and exit code is the same as you've seen for the serial I/O thread, so we won't reproduce it here.

The beep thread's task is simple: Every time the `hBeepEvent` event object is signaled, it beeps the speaker. Beeping the speaker is an activity that can take place separate from other actions in the system. It is therefore an ideal candidate for a thread. Take a look at the code for the thread, which is shown in Listing 12-6.

Listing 12-6: The beep thread

```
//
// The Beep thread spends most of its time blocked on two events.
// hBeepEvent is signaled to tell it to beep, and hBeepExitEvent is
// signaled to tell it to exit. We need to synchronize with the exit of
// the Beep thread to make sure it isn't in the middle of a beep when
// the program exits — if it were, it would never turn off the speaker
// hardware, with the annoying result that the machine would keep
// whining at you after the program had terminated!
//
unsigned __stdcall BeepThread(void *pUnused){
    HANDLE WaitEvents[2];
    WaitEvents[0] = hBeepEvent;
    WaitEvents[1] = hBeepExitEvent;
    while (TRUE)
    {
        if (WaitForMultipleObjects(2, WaitEvents, FALSE, INFINITE)
                != WAIT_OBJECT_0)
            break;
        SpeakerTone(880, 250);
    }
    _endthreadex(0);
}
```

BeepThread() spends most of its time blocked inside WaitForMultipleObjects(). If hBeepExitEvent is signaled, it exits by calling _endthreadex(). Otherwise, hBeepEvent was signaled, so it calls SpeakerTone() to beep the speaker, and then loops back to block again on WaitForMultipleObjects().

SpeakerTone() is pulled in from the UTILSMT.LIB library; the source code is in \TSLITE\PROJECTS\UTILS\SPEAKER.C. SpeakerTone() doesn't return for the duration of the beep, in this case 250 milliseconds. It turns the speaker on, calls Sleep() for the beep duration, turns the speaker off, and then returns. Because SpeakerTone() suspends the calling thread for the duration of the beep, it's an ideal candidate to put in a separate thread; you certainly wouldn't want to call it in any thread with any real-time deadlines.

Timer Thread

The timer subsystem code is in the TIMER.C file. The timer thread replaces the timer callback that we used in the Simple UPS project. Because the timer thread's jobs are to simply keep track of elapsed time and to place timer events in the UPS system's message queue, the timer thread is short.

Listing 12-7: The timer thread

```
//
// Timer thread.  Wakes up approximately every TIMER_PERIOD
// milliseconds and sends a timer event to the event subsystem.
//
unsigned __stdcall TimerThread(void *pUnused)
{
    DWORD msUsed;
    DWORD LastTickCount;
    DWORD NewTickCount;
    UPS_EVENT Event;

    Event.Event = EVENT_TIMER;
    LastTickCount = GetTickCount();
    while (TRUE)
    {
        msUsed = GetTickCount() - LastTickCount;
        if (msUsed < TIMER_PERIOD)
            Sleep(TIMER_PERIOD - msUsed);
        NewTickCount = GetTickCount();
        Event.Msecs = NewTickCount - LastTickCount;
        LastTickCount = NewTickCount;
        MsgWrite(hEventQueue, &Event, TRUE);
    }
}
```

As with the other threads we've shown, the timer thread's body is simply a while() loop. Aided by the GetTickCount() routine (which returns the number of millisecond clock ticks since the system was started), each time through the loop, the timer thread measures the elapsed time since the last timer event was deposited in the message queue.

The timer thread uses the `LastTickCount` variable to hold the time (in clock ticks) that the last timer event was put in the message queue. The thread calculates the number of milliseconds that must elapse before the next timer event can go in the message queue, and puts itself to sleep for that amount of time. Each time the thread wakes up, it records the current tick count, and places a timer event in the message queue.

The timer thread shows, among other things, that there's often more than one way to accomplish the same job. In the Simple UPS system, we used a timer callback to do what the timer thread does here. Note, however, that this version of the timer subsystem is simpler than the callback version — because we've used a thread, no register and unregister calls are necessary.

In general, it's always better to do something with a thread than with an ISR routine (or a callback, which actually runs as part of an ISR). As you've seen, ISR routines require more care: They affect the interrupt hardware of the system, it's difficult to control their priority, you have to think about how long they will execute, and you have to worry about which system calls you can and cannot make from within an ISR.

> **Note:** The other threads we showed in this chapter are notified of impending system shutdown through synchronization objects (event objects). The main thread would notify the subordinate thread of the intent to shut the system down, and the subordinate thread would acknowledge before terminating. Note, however, that the timer thread uses no such signaling system. That's because the timer thread uses no system resources. There are no handles to close or memory blocks to free. We just leave the timer thread running right up until system shutdown. When the application terminates, the timer thread is terminated with it.

Messaging Subsystem

In the Smart UPS, we need a mechanism for multiple threads to send simulated UPS events to the event subsystem. We used pipes for interthread communications in the serial I/O subsystem, but pipes are designed to have just one writer and one reader, so they aren't suitable for our needs this time.

The messaging subsystem, which is in the MESSAGE.C file, is a collection of utility routines that manage general-purpose message queues. Each queue can have multiple writers and multiple readers, if desired. Messages are added (written) to the tail of the queue and removed (read) from the head of the queue. All functions in the messaging subsystem are reentrant, so they can be called simultaneously by multiple threads. To keep this example code simple, the messages in each message queue must all be the same size. This suits the needs of the Smart UPS, which always places the same structure — the UPS event structure — in the event message queue. For a more generalized messaging subsystem, you'd want an individual message queue to support messages of different sizes; that exercise is left to the reader.

In the Smart UPS, we create one message queue, the UPS event message queue. The call that creates the queue is in the `InitializeUps()` function in the UPS.C file:

```
//
// Create the message queue used by the command and timer subsystems to
// send events to the event subsystem. We have to do this first, since
// all the subsystems need to use these globals.
//
```

```
    hEventQueue = MsgQueueCreate(sizeof(UPS_EVENT), 10);
    if (hEventQueue == NULL)
    {
        printf("Insufficient memory to create event queue\n");
        return FALSE;
    }
```

The `MsgQueueCreate()` call creates a message queue that holds up to ten messages, each the size of a `UPS_EVENT` structure. It returns a handle, `hEventQueue`, which is used to identify the queue in subsequent calls to the messaging subsystem. Take a look at the source for `MsgQueueCreate()`, which is shown in Listing 12-8.

Listing 12-8: The MsgQueueCreate() function

```
//
// Creates a message queue capable of holding up to
// nMsgs fixed-size messages of MsgSize bytes.
// Returns NULL if insufficient memory to create queue.
//
HANDLE MsgQueueCreate(DWORD MsgSize, DWORD nMsgs)
{
    MSG_QUEUE_HDR   *pHdr;
    pHdr = malloc(sizeof(MSG_QUEUE_HDR) + MsgSize*(nMsgs+1));
    if (pHdr == NULL)
        goto ERR;
    pHdr->Sig = MSG_QUEUE_SIG;
    pHdr->MsgSize = MsgSize;
    pHdr->pStartQueue = ((char *)pHdr) + sizeof(MSG_QUEUE_HDR);
    pHdr->pEndQueue = pHdr->pStartQueue + MsgSize*(nMsgs+1);
    pHdr->pFirstMsg = pHdr->pNextFree = pHdr->pStartQueue;
    pHdr->hWriteEvent = CreateEvent(NULL, FALSE, FALSE,
                        "Message Queue Write Event");
    if (pHdr->hWriteEvent == NULL)
        goto FREE_HDR;
    pHdr->hReadEvent = CreateEvent(NULL, FALSE, FALSE,
                        "Message Queue Read Event");
    if (pHdr->hReadEvent == NULL)
        goto CLOSE_WRITE;
    InitializeCriticalSection(&pHdr->CritSec);
    EtsSetCritSecDebugName(&pHdr->CritSec, "Message Queue "
            "Critical Section");
    return (HANDLE) pHdr;
CLOSE_WRITE:
    CloseHandle(pHdr->hWriteEvent);
FREE_HDR:
    free(pHdr);
ERR:
    return NULL;
}
```

MsgQueueCreate() allocates a block of memory that contains a queue header structure and enough memory to hold the requested number of messages. It then initializes the header structure and returns a pointer to the queue header as a handle. The messaging subsystem has no global variables, which simplifies the job of making all its functions reentrant.

But why does MsgQueueCreate() preallocate enough memory for the maximum number of messages? Wouldn't it be nicer if the queue could just grow dynamically as needed when new messages are added? The reason MsgQueueCreate() preallocates memory for a fixed-size queue is to avoid having to perform a memory allocate operation when messages are added to the queue. This makes the MsgWrite() function that adds a message to a queue execute faster, and it also avoids the need to deal with running out of memory when adding a message.

Let's look at the contents of the queue header structure:

```
//
// Message queue header.  Queue is empty when  pFirstMsg == pNextFree,
// full when pNextFree points to the slot before pFirstMsg
//
typedef struct {
    DWORD Sig;                  // structure signature, defined below
    DWORD MsgSize;              // size, in bytes, of each message
    char *pStartQueue;         // ptr to start of queue array
    char *pEndQueue;           // ptr to one past end of queue array
    char *pFirstMsg;           // ptr to first message in queue
    char *pNextFree;           // ptr to next free message slot in queue
    HANDLE hWriteEvent;        // writers block here on full queue
    HANDLE hReadEvent;         // readers block here on empty queue
    CRITICAL_SECTION CritSec;  // gates access to queue
} MSG_QUEUE_HDR;
#define MSG_QUEUE_SIG 0x5147534D  // 'MSGQ' ASCII signature
#define FREE_QUEUE_SIG 0x51475346 // 'FSGQ' sig for freed queue
```

The first structure member is a signature, used by the messaging subsystem to validate queue handles passed in by callers. When a queue is deleted, the signature changes to FREE_QUEUE_SIG before the memory block is freed. This ensures that programs can't use stale handles to queues that have been deleted but whose memory hasn't been reused yet. Using ASCII signatures for active and deleted queue headers is also a debugging trick that helps you easily identify data structures when viewing memory from a debugger.

Next come the four pointers that track the data in the circular queue. The start and end pointers are fixed and identify the memory block allocated to hold the queue data (which immediately follows the queue header). As messages are added to the queue, pNextFree advances until the queue is full (when pNextFree is one entry before pFirstMsg). As messages are removed from the queue, pFirstMsg advances until the queue is empty (when pFirstMsg reaches pNextFree). To distinguish between the queue full and queue empty conditions, we waste one message entry in the queue: When the queue is full, the entry pointed to by `pFirstMsg` is not used. That's why `MsgQueueCreate()` allocates memory for one more message entry than the number requested by the caller.

Finally, three synchronization objects are used to control access to the queue. Two event objects are used by writers to block when the queue is full and by readers to block when the queue is empty, respectively. The event objects are auto-reset events that start in the nonsignaled state. A critical section object controls access to all data (pointers and message entries) in the queue.

Looking at Listing 12-9, let's examine how these synchronization objects are used when adding (writing) a new entry to the queue.

Listing 12-9: The MsgWrite() function

```
//
// Writes a message to a fixed-size message queue.
// If queue is full, optionally waits if fWait is TRUE.
//
// Returns:  1     if success
//           0     if queue full and fWait FALSE
//          -1     if invalid handle
//
int MsgWrite(HANDLE hQueue, void *pMsg, BOOL fWait)
{
    MSG_QUEUE_HDR    *pHdr;
    char             *pNextFree;

    pHdr = (MSG_QUEUE_HDR *) hQueue;
    if (pHdr->Sig != MSG_QUEUE_SIG)
        return -1;

//
// If the queue is full, either return an error or block until
// there is a free slot.
//
RESTART:
    EnterCriticalSection(&pHdr->CritSec);
    pNextFree = pHdr->pNextFree + pHdr->MsgSize;
    if (pNextFree >= pHdr->pEndQueue)
        pNextFree = pHdr->pStartQueue;
    if (pNextFree == pHdr->pFirstMsg)
    {
        LeaveCriticalSection(&pHdr->CritSec);
        if (!fWait)
            return 0;
        WaitForSingleObject(pHdr->hWriteEvent, INFINITE);
        goto RESTART;
    }
```

```
//
// Write the message to the queue, update the next free message
// slot pointer, and wake up any blocked readers.
//
    memcpy(pHdr->pNextFree, pMsg, pHdr->MsgSize);
    pHdr->pNextFree = pNextFree;
    LeaveCriticalSection(&pHdr->CritSec);
    SetEvent(pHdr->hReadEvent);
    return 1;
}
```

MsgWrite() first validates the queue handle (the pointer to the queue header structure) by checking the header signature. It then acquires the critical section object so it can access the queue data. Then it calculates what the free pointer will be after the insert operation is performed. If the new free pointer will be equal to the first message pointer, the queue is already full and we have to either wait or return a queue full error.

To block, we first release the critical section so that other threads (in particular, readers) will be able to access the queue. Then we block on the write event object. When the write event is signaled, we wake up and jump back to the beginning of the function, where we acquire the critical section and try again. If multiple threads are blocked on the write event, only one will wake up, because we're using auto-reset events. We'll see where the write event object gets signaled in a moment.

If room is available in the queue, we add the new message at the tail of the queue and update the free pointer. Because we're now finished with the queue data, we release the critical section object. Finally, we signal the read event to wake one blocked reading thread.

Now let's examine the code in Listing 12-10 to remove (read) a message from a queue, to see the other side of the thread synchronization.

Listing 12-10: The MsgRead() function

```
//
// Reads a message from a fixed-size message queue.
// If queue is empty, optionally waits if fWait is TRUE.
//
// Returns:  1     if success
//           0     if queue empty and fWait FALSE
//          -1     if invalid handle
//
int MsgRead(HANDLE hQueue, void *pMsg, BOOL fWait)
{
    MSG_QUEUE_HDR   *pHdr;
    pHdr = (MSG_QUEUE_HDR *) hQueue;
    if (pHdr->Sig != MSG_QUEUE_SIG)
        return -1;
//
// If the queue is empty, either return an error or block until
// there is a message.
//
```

```
RESTART:
    EnterCriticalSection(&pHdr->CritSec);
    if (pHdr->pFirstMsg == pHdr->pNextFree)
    {
        LeaveCriticalSection(&pHdr->CritSec);
        if (!fWait)
            return 0;
        WaitForSingleObject(pHdr->hReadEvent, INFINITE);
        goto RESTART;
    }
//
// Read the message from the queue, update the first message
// pointer, and wake up any blocked writers.
//
    memcpy(pMsg, pHdr->pFirstMsg, pHdr->MsgSize);
    pHdr->pFirstMsg += pHdr->MsgSize;
    if (pHdr->pFirstMsg >= pHdr->pEndQueue)
        pHdr->pFirstMsg = pHdr->pStartQueue;
    LeaveCriticalSection(&pHdr->CritSec);
    SetEvent(pHdr->hWriteEvent);
    return 1;
}
```

After validating the handle, `MsgRead()` acquires the critical section object and checks whether any messages are in the queue. If not, it releases the critical section and, if requested to wait, blocks on the queue read event object.

Because we've seen the code that signals the read event object — in the `MsgWrite()` function — let's think about how this synchronization works. Suppose the first thing that happens after queue creation is a call to `MsgRead()`. Then we'll block on the read event. When a second thread calls `MsgWrite()` and adds a message to the queue, it signals the read event, and the first thread wakes up and removes the message from the queue.

Suppose, instead, that two messages are added to the queue before any calls to `MsgRead()` occur. The first two calls to `MsgRead()` successfully read the two messages in the queue. The third `MsgRead()` call should block...but wait, the read event is in a signaled state because each of the calls to `MsgWrite()` signaled the read event object! We don't block on the first call to `WaitForSingleObject()`, but the code still works; now that we've waited on the event object once, it's reset back to nonsignaled. We'll immediately discover that the queue is still empty, call `WaitForSingleObject()` again, and this time we'll block correctly.

Finally, consider the case in which two threads have called `MsgRead()` when the queue is empty, so two threads are blocked on the read event object. When a third thread calls `MsgWrite()`, adds a message to the queue, and signals the read event, one of the two blocked threads wakes up (either the highest priority thread or, if they're the same priority, the one that blocked first). The other thread remains blocked; because we're using an auto-reset event, when the first thread wakes up, the event object is reset to the nonsignaled state.

After `MsgRead()` has determined that at least one message is in the queue, it copies the message at the head of the queue to the caller's buffer, updates `pFirstMsg` to remove the message from the queue, and leaves the critical section. Then it signals the write event object to wake up any writers who blocked when the queue was full.

Now that we've seen how the write event object is used in `MsgRead()`, we can see how the thread synchronization works for full message queues. It's substantially similar to the synchronization we just described for empty queues, so we'll leave it as an exercise for the reader.

Event Subsystem

We conclude our examination of the multithreading code in the Smart UPS project with a look at the event subsystem, found in the `EVENT.C` file. We described the event subsystem thoroughly in Chapter 11; we add a few details here.

The event subsystem (with the exception of the beep thread, which we already discussed) executes in the context of the main thread — that is, the thread created by the operating system when the `UPS2.EXE` program was launched. The event subsystem interacts with threads other than the main thread in three ways: by reading the UPS event queue (which, you'll recall, is written by other threads); by calling the serial I/O subsystem to send responses over the serial connection to the WINUPS program; and by signaling the beep thread to beep the speaker.

Let's look first at the code that reads a UPS event structure from the event queue. This call is in the `EventLoop()` function, inside the loop that gets events and processes them:

```
    //
    // Read the next event from the event queue.  This call blocks until
    // there is an event to read.
    //
        if (MsgRead(hEventQueue, &NextEvent, TRUE) != 1)
            FatalErr("Unexpected error while reading event queue\n");
```

As you can see, we request `MsgRead()` to block if no messages are in the queue. This means the event subsystem is going to spend most of its time blocked inside the `MsgRead()` function; that's okay because the event subsystem doesn't have to respond to anything except simulated events, all of which arrive through the event message queue.

The code that sends a response to the WINUPS program is also inside `EventLoop()`, after we process the simulated event:

```
    //
    // Any event except a timer event was from a command sent
    // by the remote WINUPS front-end program.  Send a response
    // to WINUPS.
    //
        if (NextEvent.Event != EVENT_TIMER)
            SendResponse(ErrMsg);
    }
```

Timer events aren't the result of a command sent from the WINUPS program, so the event subsystem won't be sending a response. The other events (power on/off, load add/remove, AC power good/bad, report UPS status), however, all require that a response be sent to the

WINUPS program. The only command that doesn't require a response is the exit command; we processed that one before we got to the `SendResponse()` call by exiting from the event loop.

The code for the `SendResponse()` function is in Listing 12-11.

Listing 12-11: The SendResponse() function

```
//
// Sends a response to the WINUPS program.
//
void SendResponse(char *pErrMsg)
{
    UPS_RESPONSE Response;

    //
    // Build the response structure.  All values larger than a
    // byte are packed in a machine-independent order. (We use
    // a MS-byte-first order, because that is the same order
    // used by network applications.)  Packing and unpacking
    // data values sent between two machines protects you from
    // differences in byte ordering on different computer
    // architectures. Although it's not strictly necessary for
    // this application (because we know that both UPS.EXE and
    // WINUPS.EXE will run on x86 machines), we do it here to
    // show what you'd need to do when building a distributed
    // application that runs on different computer architectures.
    //
    Response.UpsID = UPS_ID;
    Response.State = PackDword(CurrState);
    Response.msBatteryLife = PackDword(msBatteryLife);
    Response.msMaxLife = PackDword(MAX_BATTERY_LIFE);
    Response.ErrLen = (BYTE) strlen(pErrMsg);
    if (Response.ErrLen > 0)
        ++Response.ErrLen;

    //
    // send the response structure and error message string if any.
    // Since we wait to send chars, no need to check for an
    // error return.
    //
    SerialWrite(&Response, sizeof(Response), TRUE);
    if (Response.ErrLen > 0)
        SerialWrite(pErrMsg, Response.ErrLen, TRUE);

    return;
}
```

This function loads up a UPS_RESPONSE structure and calls `SerialWrite()` to send it out over the serial connection. If there's an error message, the string is sent immediately following the structure. Notice that we request `SerialWrite()` to wait if the send pipe is full. We don't expect to ever have to wait, because we're not sending a lot of data in this application, and we have a good-sized (512 bytes) pipe to buffer the data. But worst case, if the pipe is full, we might have to wait for enough characters to be sent to free up buffer space for the structure (14 bytes) and an error message (255 bytes maximum, but typically 20–40 bytes). Still, at 19200 baud, or approximately half a millisecond per character, sending even 14 bytes takes several milliseconds, a long time in a real-time system. In our simulation, it's not a problem, because the command from WINUPS and the response sent back to WINUPS are synchronous; WINUPS won't send another command until it gets a response. In a real UPS, which would get events in real time from hardware interrupts, the possibility of blocking inside the `SerialWrite()` call would be unacceptable. We'd have to move the code that sends the response to WINUPS into a separate thread, just as we did with the beep code. Then the only time the event loop would block would be when it's waiting for new UPS events to appear in the event queue.

Like the `WINUPS_CMD` structure you saw earlier, the members of the `UPS_RESPONSE` structure are packed on byte boundaries with the compiler `pack()` pragma. We force structure packing in case the compilers used to build the `UPS2.EXE` and `WINUPS.EXE` programs had different default structure alignments. We saw the `UPS_RESPONSE` structure and described how (and why) data in it is packed in a machine-independent byte order in Chapter 11, so we won't describe that again here.

Finally, you've already seen the code in the event subsystem that signals the beep event object to wake up the beep thread. It's in the code that handles the simulation of battery charging and discharging, which we described in Chapter 11.

SUMMARY

Multitasking is an important feature of real-time operating systems, and critical for implementing real-time responses to external stimuli and for efficient utilization of the CPU. In this chapter, we described processes and threads, and gave some guidelines for when you'd want to use processes, threads, or both in a real-time multitasking application. We described how the operating system schedules tasks, and covered important topics such as deterministic scheduling, task priorities, priority inversion, and deadlock. Task synchronization is an important part of developing a real-time system; we described mutex, semaphore, and event synchronization objects, and when and how you'd want to use each of them. Intertask communications is another important topic; tasks have to be able to communicate to cooperate effectively. We covered pipes, message queues, shared memory, and remote procedure calls. We also gave you some guidelines for choosing a multitasking RTOS and for debugging your multitasking applications.

Finally, we went into detail describing the multithreading aspects of the code in the Smart UPS project. Although wading through a lot of code can be tedious, multitasking problems are more complex and subtle than other programming problems. The Smart UPS illustrates many of the general concepts we covered in the first part of the chapter, so we hope you took the time to examine the code.

13

Serial I/O

A computer can send data from one point to another in one of two ways: serial transmission or parallel transmission. If data is sent in parallel fashion, multiple bits are transferred simultaneously. Cables designed to transfer parallel data have multiple data-carrying signal wires.

By comparison, data sent in serial fashion is transferred 1 bit at a time down a single signal wire. Data is broken apart into its constituent bits, and each bit is sent through the signal wire — one after the other. The device at the receiving end reassembles the bits into their original aggregates (bytes, words, double words, and so on).

The differences between serial and parallel transfers can be seen in Figure 13-1, in which the data byte 11001110 (in binary) is being transferred from transmitter to receiver. The parallel connection provides a signal wire for each bit of the byte, and the byte is sent all in one shot. The serial connection consists of a single wire that carries each bit — one at a time — from source to destination.

Parallel communication has a speed advantage over serial communication, because multiple bits are transferred simultaneously. So why is serial communication so popular? The reason is, mostly because serial transmission is cheaper. Less hardware in transmitters and receivers is required for serial versus parallel transmission. The real cost savings with serial transmission, however, are in the cabling. Wires carrying digital (or analog) signals are prone to picking up noise from the environment, especially over long runs. The presence of several signal wires in a single cable aggravates this problem, because of crosstalk (interference) between the wires. For reliable data transmission, especially over long cable runs, it's necessary to shield (insulate) the wires. Parallel cables are much more costly, both because there are more signal wires and because better shielding is required for parallel cables because of crosstalk.

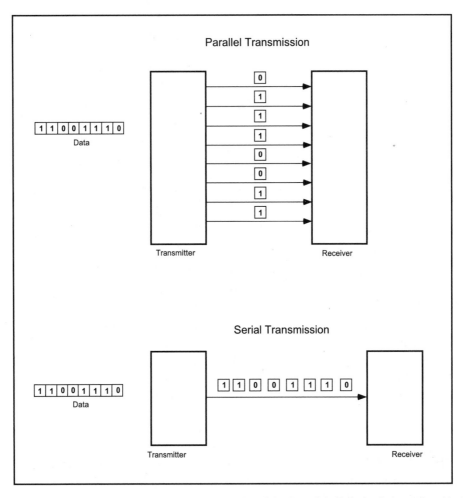

Figure 13-1: In a parallel transfer, each bit of data is transferred simultaneously. Each signal wire carries a bit of the original byte from transmitter to receiver. In a serial transfer, the original byte is taken apart into individual bits, which are sent down a single wire one after the other.

Another reason why serial communication is so popular is because serial cables are easier to work with — more flexible and less bulky — than parallel cables with their multiple wires. That's why parallel communication is used mostly for very short cable runs; for example, a cable to a printer or to a SCSI peripheral device. Connections over medium to long distances, such as telephone, cable television, and local area networks, virtually all use serial communication.

Finally, serial communication is almost universally used for connecting systems to low-to-medium-speed peripheral devices, such as keyboards, mice, and modems. Since these devices don't need the ultra-high data rates possible with parallel communications, cost savings dictate the use of serial communications hardware and cabling.

Serial communication can involve either unidirectional or bidirectional data transfers. A one-way serial connection between two computers requires only two wires: a signal wire for the data and a ground wire. If one computer always transmits and the other always receives, this is referred to as *simplex* transmission. If the system is built so that sometimes one computer and sometimes the other transmit over the data wire, the transmission is *half-duplex*. (Only one computer can be transmitting at any given time in a half-duplex arrangement.) A *full-duplex* arrangement has two signal wires and one ground wire. One signal wire carries data from Computer A to Computer B; the other signal wire carries data from Computer B to Computer A. Both computers can be simultaneously transmitting and receiving over a full-duplex connection.

In this chapter, you examine the use of serial communication, or serial I/O, in the Smart UPS project. You also look at some of the many uses of serial communications in computer systems. Serial communication is not restricted to an RS-232 cable between a computer and a modem.

To begin, then, we present some of the basic terminology and concepts used in serial communications. We briefly describe a few of the more popular electrical standards and communications protocols for serial communication, present an overview of the function of a UART (universal asynchronous receiver-transmitter), and provide some guidelines for writing ISRs to service serial port interrupts. We follow that with a deeper look into RS-232, the most popular serial communications standard. Serial buses are the next topic; we describe some of the standards defined for peripheral serial buses, which connect multiple devices to a single serial port on a computer, and chip serial buses, which connect multiple IC chips to a CPU. Finally, we explore the code in the serial I/O subsystem of the Smart UPS project and describe the operation of the 8250/16x50 family of UARTs used in the PC architecture.

FUNDAMENTALS OF SERIAL I/O

Before delving into a topic, we often find it useful to brief ourselves on the terms and concepts we'll encounter. In the following sections, we describe some of the essentials of serial I/O, including definitions of terminology, popular communication standards, and the UART chip.

BAUD RATE VERSUS BITS PER SECOND

Baud rate means the number of signal changes of a communications channel per second; that is, it is the frequency at which electrical signals are sent down the communications line. Baud rate is an electrical unit of measure, not necessarily a measure of the data transfer rate on the line.

The data transfer rate for serial communications is normally expressed in bits per second (bps). The bit transfer rate is equal to the baud rate only when 1 data bit is encoded in one electrical signaling period. If compression or an encoding algorithm is used, the bit transfer rate exceeds the underlying baud rate.

A UART deals only with receiving and transmitting electrical signals; you therefore program a UART to transmit and receive at a specific baud rate. A modem (modulator/demodulator), on the other hand, typically uses an encoding algorithm (such as phase shift keying), often in conjunction with a compression algorithm, to increase bit transfer rates, whether the modem communicates using telephone lines, radio waves, or a direct cable connection. So you normally speak of the bit transfer rate, or bits per second, when discussing communications using a modem. For a direct serial connection without a modem (a null modem connection, such as we use in our Smart UPS system), the bps rate is equal to the baud rate, because the two UARTs are directly connected and no signal encoding occurs.

The character transfer rate is derived from the bps rate. To perform the calculation, you need to know how many data bits are used to encode one character and the overhead (that is, the synchronization bits and the parity or other error-checking bits) of the serial communications protocol. For example, if you are using an RS-232 link programmed for 8 data bits per character, 1 start bit, 1 stop bit, and no parity, then 10 bits must be transferred for each character sent. Therefore, in this example, you convert from bps to characters per second by dividing by 10.

ASYNCHRONOUS VERSUS SYNCHRONOUS COMMUNICATIONS

You'll see the words *asynchronous* and *synchronous* used frequently in discussions of serial communications. In *asynchronous serial communication,* data bits are transmitted as a series of pulses, with each pulse a fixed width (in time). The width of each bit is determined by the transmission frequency. Both the sender and the receiver must be using the same frequency for communication to occur; no clock signal or other information about frequency is included in the transmission. Asynchronous data bits are grouped in characters (usually, a character is a byte — though you'll see shortly that such is not always the case), and all the bits that make up a character are framed between a start bit and a stop bit.

In most cases, the amount of data transmitted between start and stop bits is a byte, but asynchronous data can be transmitted in 5-, 6-, 7-, or 8-bit characters. (In the old days, when serial ports were used primarily to send printable data between a user I/O device and a computer, 7 bits were sufficient to encode all ASCII characters. In the really old days, Baudot, an officer in the French Telegraph Service from whom we get the term *baud rate*, invented the 5-bit code used to transmit uppercase characters, numbers, and a few symbols over telegraph lines. These days, serial communication devices routinely send more than just ASCII data, so 8-bit characters are the norm.)

The start bit serves to alert the receiver that a character is on its way. The stop bit informs the receiver that it has received the last bit of a character. So, start and stop bits serve to synchronize sender and receiver. In effect, the sender and receiver resynchronize with each character transmitted.

Optionally, the transmitted character can be accompanied by a parity bit transmitted just before the stop bit. The parity bit provides error detection. Its value depends on two things: the number of 1 bits in the character (counting the parity bit itself, but not counting the start and stop bits), and whether the transmitting circuitry is set to generate an even or an odd parity bit. If the transmitter is set to even parity, the parity bit is set so that the data bits plus the parity bit have an even number of 1 bits. If the transmitter is set to odd parity, the parity bit is set so that the data bits plus the parity bit contain an odd number of 1 bits. For example, if the transmitter is set to generate even parity, the 8-bit character 00010001 would have a parity bit of 0.

The transmitter and receiver must be set to the same parity (even or odd) for clean communication. When the receiver gets a character containing the wrong parity bit, it indicates that the transmission has become garbled (from a faulty connection, noise on the line, and so on).

In asynchronous communication, data is transferred in small packets, usually consisting of a single byte or character, as shown in Figure 13-2. The packets are framed by start and stop bits, with an optional parity bit. Each packet is called a *serial data unit* (SDU).

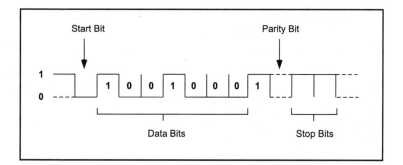

Figure 13-2: This figure shows an SDU (serial data unit) for the binary character 10001001. Notice that the low bit is sent first (after the start bit, which is a binary 0). The parity bit would be set high or low depending on the transmitting device's parity mode (odd, even, mark, or space). This particular protocol uses a binary one for the 2 stop bits. If another packet were hot on the heels of this one, the stop bits would be followed immediately by the next start bit (in which case the signal would drop to a binary 0). Otherwise, the signal on the serial line would go to the idle state (indicated by a binary 1).

In *synchronous serial communication,* data is transferred in large streams called *packets,* or *frames,* that each consist of hundreds or thousands of bits depending on the protocol used. In most synchronous protocols, packets start and end with synchronization characters (unique bit patterns that signal the start and end of the packet).

Synchronous serial communication protocols can be either bit synchronous or byte synchronous, as shown in Figure 13-3. A frame in a bit synchronous protocol consists of an arbitrary number of bits, framed by the start and end bit sequences, or flags; HDLC (High-level Data Link Control) is an example of a bit synchronous protocol. A frame in a byte synchronous protocol always contains data that is a multiple of bytes, framed by starting and ending byte sequences. IBM's Binary Synchronous Communication (BISYNC) protocol, used for communication with IBM mainframes, is an example of a byte synchronous protocol.

Because such large packets are involved, some sort of shared clock signal is needed to keep the sender and receiver synchronized. In some cases, this clock signal is transmitted between sender and receiver on a separate wire. In other cases, the clock signal is embedded in the data signal. How this is accomplished is beyond the scope of this book. A good explanation is given in *Data and Computer Communications,* by William Stallings (Macmillan Publishing, 1991).

Synchronous protocols can transmit more information per unit time than asynchronous protocols, primarily because synchronous protocols have a lower overhead in terms of the total number of bits required to transfer a given amount of data. Each character transmitted

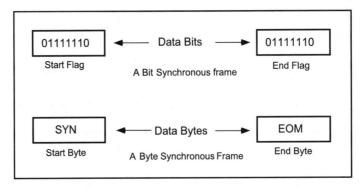

Figure 13-3: Synchronous protocols transmit a frame of data at a time, delimited by start and end flags. Bit synchronous protocols transmit frames with an arbitrary number of bits, delimited by flag bytes such as 01111110, the 0x7E flag used by the HDLC protocol. Byte synchronous protocols transmit data as bytes, with frames delimited by special byte characters such as the SYN (synchronize) and EOM (end-of-message) bytes shown here. Synchronous protocols often include additional header or trailer fields containing the message type, flow control information, and an error checksum.

using an asynchronous protocol must be framed by start and stop bits and carry an optional parity bit. By contrast, synchronous protocols use two synchronization characters to frame a large or small number of bits. (In other words, the ratio of non-data bits to data bits is much lower in synchronous protocols.)

Synchronous protocols are suitable when the transmission of data is likely to be continuous (in which case, large packets make sense), as in, for example, a computer network. Asynchronous protocols are useful when the transmission is likely to be intermittent, as in, for example, a computer mouse.

ERROR DETECTION

Serial communication errors occur for many reasons, such as signal attenuation over long lines, line noise introduced by radio frequency interference, and poor quality telephone lines. The acceptability of communication errors depends on the application. For example, if you're dialing into a mainframe to type a few commands and read the responses by eye, occasional errors may be acceptable because a human (you) is present to notice the problem and reenter the command. On the other hand, data processed by a program (such as data sent over a networking connection) usually requires some kind of error detection capability to operate properly.

The most common form of error detection in asynchronous serial communication is the addition of a parity bit to each character sent. The parity bit is set to either 0 or 1 to make the number of 1 bits in the character plus the parity bit either even or odd. (Mark parity, a parity bit that is always 1, and space parity, which is always 0, also exist but aren't particularly useful, because the receiver can detect errors only in the parity bit, not in the data bits.) Using parity, the receiver can detect errors in odd numbers of bits but not in even numbers of bits. This makes parity a notoriously unreliable technique for detecting errors.

At a higher level, error detection is performed at a packet (a block of data) level, using a checksum calculated by adding the values of all the bytes in the packet. This has the virtue of being easy to implement and quick to calculate. A 16-bit checksum detects a much higher percentage of possible errors than can be found with a parity check, but a checksum is not completely reliable. For example, if two characters have opposite bits (0 and 1) in the same bit position, and the bit in each character is corrupted, the checksum will be the same and the error will not be detected. Nevertheless, checksums are commonly used in higher-level protocols, such as networking protocols. The checksum allows packets with errors to be detected and discarded, and the receiver then requests retransmission of the corrupted packets. The use of checksums in network protocols is why you usually disable parity in an asynchronous serial communication protocol used over a networking connection; because the higher-level networking protocol is handling error detection and the resending of data, you have no need to slow down character transmission rates with the extra overhead of a parity bit, which offers unreliable error detection anyway.

An extremely powerful error detection algorithm is a cyclic redundancy check (CRC). CRCs, like checksums, are calculated on a block of bytes. A 16-bit CRC offers error detection of 100 percent for burst errors of 16 bits or less, and 99.99 percent for longer burst errors. For even higher reliability (but with more overhead), you can use a 32-bit CRC. CRCs are often used in synchronous serial communication protocols such as HDLC, and in higher-level protocols such as some networking protocols. You can find a good description of CRC calculations in *C Programmer's Guide to Serial Communications,* by Joe Campbell (Howard W. Sams & Company, 1993).

Flow Control

Serial communications usually use some kind of *flow control*, mechanisms that prevent receivers from being overwhelmed with data they are not prepared to process. The receiver must be able to tell the transmitter when to stop sending data and when it is okay to resume sending. Without flow control, data overruns result in unexpected errors or in lower throughput due to the need to retransmit data. You can implement flow control in hardware or software.

Hardware flow control takes the form of separate signals, or wires, in the serial cable. For example, the RS-232 standard includes the Request to Send (RTS) and Clear to Send (CTS) pair of handshaking signals for flow control. Hardware signals are usually turned on and off by software; the technique is called hardware flow control because it requires additional hardware in the form of wires and pins.

Software flow control is necessary when a physical connection between the two communicating devices is impossible (such as two modems talking over a phone line) or when hardware flow control is not supported by the electrical standard. Software flow control consists of handshaking information embedded in the data stream.

Asynchronous communication protocols must assign special meaning to two specific characters used to stop and start the flow of data. The most common pair of characters is XON/XOFF, usually assigned to Ctrl-Q and Ctrl-S, respectively, in the ASCII character set. Using special characters for flow control has an obvious drawback: those two characters cannot appear in the data stream. That works if, for example, only printable ASCII data is transmitted, such as for a dial-up remote logon connection to a computer. If arbitrary binary data is being sent, either flow control must be implemented at a higher level, where data is processed in packets, or a mechanism must exist to escape special characters (the flow control characters and the escape character itself) when they occur in the data stream.

Synchronous communication protocols typically perform flow control at frame boundaries because the flow control can be included with the framing characters. The most common technique is automatic repeat request (ARQ), which uses ACK/NAK (acknowledgment/negative acknowledgment) for the flow control characters. After the sender sends the framing character that ends the frame, it waits for the receiver to reply with an ACK character before continuing with the next frame. If the receiver detects an error, it responds with a NAK instead, in which case the sender retransmits the entire frame.

Finally, higher-level protocols, such as networking protocols, perform flow control at the packet level. Typically, protocol information is included in a header with each packet. The header contains flow control information for acknowledging receipt of packets or requesting retransmission of packets if an error occurs or a packet is lost. You see an example of this in Chapter 15, "Networking," when you examine the TCP protocol in the TCP/IP networking stack.

ELECTRICAL STANDARDS AND COMMUNICATION PROTOCOLS

Dozens of serial communication standards exist. It's useful to divide standards into two categories: electrical standards and communication protocols. An *electrical standard* specifies the electrical characteristics of the signals used to carry information (voltages, waveforms, impedance, maximum line length, and so on). A *communication protocol* describes how data is encoded and decoded and any additional information required by the protocol for synchronization and error detection. Some standards specify both an electrical standard and a communication protocol; others specify only one. In general, you can use the communication protocol of your choice over any connection, regardless of the underlying electrical standard. We summarize a few of the more popular serial standards in this section.

RS-232

RS-232 is both an electrical standard and a communications protocol. You can, however, use the RS-232 electrical standard with a different communication protocol; for example, the HDLC protocol is often used over an RS-232 link.

The RS-232C standard (the RS-232 standard, Revision C, usually just referred to as RS-232) is published by the Electronic Industries Association (EIA) and is the most widely used serial communication standard worldwide. The electrical standard specifies bidirectional communication on an unbalanced line (a single wire), with a voltage between 5 and 15V considered a 1 bit, and a voltage between -5 and -15V a 0 bit. Separate wires are also specified for hardware flow control signals and for modem control signals.

The communication protocol specifies an SDU that consists of 1 start bit at logic 0, followed by 5, 6, 7, or 8 data bits, followed by an optional parity bit, and terminated by 1 or 2 stop bits at logic 1. When the line is idle, it is kept at a logic-1 level.

You look at RS-232 in more detail later in this chapter.

RS-422 and RS-423

The RS-422 standard was created to correct some of the electrical shortcomings of RS-232. First, the RS-232 interface assumes a common ground between the two ends of the connection. Over long distances, this assumption is not always valid. Second, a signal on a single line can't be effectively screened for noise. By manufacturing a well-screened cable, one can minimize the influence of outside noise, but internally generated noise remains a problem. Crosstalk introduced by capacitance between the lines in the cable increases as baud rate and line length increase, until eventually the data is unreadable.

Because RS-422 was created to solve problems in the electrical standard, it uses the same communication protocol as RS-232. The RS-422 electrical standard uses a balanced transmission scheme in which two conductors transmit the data signals. Four signal wires are therefore needed to allow bidirectional simultaneous communication. Signals are transmitted as voltage differences between the two conductors. As a differential voltage, the signal is not affected by differences in ground voltage between sender and receiver. This design also has a high immunity to noise, because signal noise likely appears equally on both conductors, especially if both wires are twisted together to ensure that neither line is permanently closer to a noise source than the other. Because signals appear as voltage differences, the noise on both conductors is canceled out at the receiver. RS-422 is rated at 100 Kbaud at up to 1200 meters (higher over shorter distances). RS-232, on the other hand, is rated at only 20 Kbaud at 15 meters. (In practice, however, RS-232 is often run at 100 to 200 Kbaud over cables up to 10 meters.)

Another member of the RS-232 family is RS-423. RS-423 also uses unbalanced transmission but has improved electrical characteristics compared to RS-232. Specifically, the voltage difference between logic 0 and logic 1 is smaller in RS-423. The smaller voltage swing allows higher throughput. For example, RS-423 can sustain a 300 Kbaud transmission speed at up to 10 meters.

In spite of the technical advantages, RS-422 and RS-423 have not made inroads on the popularity of RS-232. RS-232 is simple, well understood, and supported everywhere. To date, these advantages have outweighed the higher data rates allowed by using RS-422 or RS-423.

HDLC

High-level Data Link Control (HDLC) is a popular bit synchronous communication protocol published by the ISO (International Standards Organization). HDLC is often used as the data link layer in a network stack, and for modem-to-modem and fax-to-fax communications. For example, HDLC is specified as the data link layer on X.25 networks. X.25 defines additional header and trailer fields in the standard HDLC frame, and calls the enhanced HDLC protocol Link Access Procedure Balanced (LAPB). HDLC is sometimes used as the data link layer for serial TCP/IP network connections, although SLIP (Serial Line Internet Protocol) and PPP (Point-to-Point Protocol) are more common. HDLC is also specified as part of the V.42 error detection and data compression standard used by modems. V.42 adds a 16- or 32-bit CRC, a sequence number, and other fields to the standard HDLC frame, and calls the resulting protocol Link Access Procedure for Modems (LAPM).

HDLC is used for both point-to-point (with just two connected computers) and multidrop (with multiple connected computers) data links. Two configurations, unbalanced and balanced, are supported. An unbalanced configuration consists of one primary station (a node on the data link) and one or more secondary stations. Two operational modes are available for unbalanced configurations. In normal response mode (NRM), a secondary station can transmit a frame (a *response*) only in response to a frame (a *command*) sent by the primary station. In asynchronous response mode (ARM), a secondary station is permitted to initiate a transmission under certain conditions (such as error conditions).

A balanced HDLC configuration is used in point-to-point connections, where the two stations at either end of the connection have equal status and perform both primary and secondary functions as the situation dictates. Either station may initiate transmission at any time. Balanced configurations always use asynchronous balanced mode (ABM) as the operational mode.

The standard HDLC frame, shown in Figure 13-4, uses a unique 8-bit sequence called a flag, 01111110 (0x7E), to delimit the start and end of a frame. The HDLC transmitter ensures that the flag never occurs within the frame data by preventing six 1 bits from occurring in a row. This is accomplished by inserting a 0 bit after any sequence of five consecutive 1 bits in the frame data, a process known as *zero bit insertion,* or *bit stuffing.* The HDLC receiver removes the inserted 0 bits.

Start Flag	Address	Control	Data	CRC	End Flag
01111110	8 bits	8 bits	Variable	16 bits	01111110

Figure 13-4: The standard frame format for HDLC is delimited by unique 8-bit starting and ending flags, and in addition to the application data contains an address field, a control field, and a 16-bit CRC field for error detection.

In addition to the start and end flags, the standard frame includes three fields plus the application data: the address field, the CRC field, and the control field. The address field is used in unbalanced configurations. Every secondary station is assigned a unique address. In frames (commands) transmitted by the primary station, the address field contains the address of the receiving secondary station. In frames (responses) transmitted by a secondary station, the address field contains the address of the transmitting station. Addresses are also assigned as group addresses, which are received by all secondary stations in the group, and as broadcast addresses, which are received by all secondary stations on the link.

The CRC field (also called the frame check sequence, or FCS, field) contains a 16-bit cyclic redundancy checksum for the complete frame contents, excluding the start and end flags. The receiver uses the CRC to detect errors; the frame is discarded if errors are detected.

The control field marks frames as unnumbered frames, information frames, or supervisory frames. Unnumbered frames are used to set up and disconnect links. An information frame carries application data. The control field in an information frame includes two numbers: Ns, the send number of the information frame, and Nr, the receive number of the next expected information frame. Nr is an acknowledgment that the sending station has received information frames numbered up to Nr-1. The send and receive numbers are used by the protocol software to track messages and detect lost messages.

A supervisory frame is used to carry protocol control information. Because it never carries application data, no Ns is in the control field. Instead, the control field includes Nr and 4 flag bits. The receive ready flag acknowledges receipt of information frames up to Nr-1 and requests transmission of the next information frame. The receive not ready flag acknowledges frames through Nr-1 but indicates the station is temporarily not ready to receive another frame. The reject flag indicates an error condition and requests that retransmission should start with frame number Nr. The selective reject flag specifies that only a single frame has been discarded, and requests retransmission of frame Nr only.

HDLC also defines an aborted frame, shown in Figure 13-5. If an error occurs during transmission or the sender wants to preempt a frame with a higher priority frame, the transmitter terminates the frame early and uses the bit pattern 01111111 (0x7F) as the ending flag. The receiver discards any frames received with the abort flag.

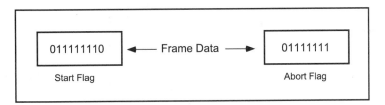

Figure 13-5: An aborted HDLC frame is marked with an ending flag value of 0x7F rather than the normal flag value 0x7E.

THE UART

The low-level dirty work of serial communication — which bits are transmitted when, and how fast — is handled by an integrated circuit called a UART (universal asynchronous receiver-transmitter). The UART's job is to perform all the mundane tasks involved in converting parallel data (that is, a byte) to serial data and transmitting that serial data to another UART.

This means the UART also receives serial data, upon which the UART performs the reverse transformation of turning serial bits back into a byte. Hence, the *RT* part of the UART's acronym: the UART both sends and receives. The UART can send and receive simultaneously, if it's connected to a transmission line that can handle bidirectional data.

> **Note:** A serial communication IC related to the UART is the USART, which stands for universal synchronous/asynchronous receiver-transmitter. A USART can be programmed to handle both synchronous and asynchronous serial protocols. An example of a USART is the Zilog Z8530 Serial Communications Controller (SCC), used in the Macintosh computer.

A simplified block diagram of a UART, showing how it fits into a computer system, is shown in Figure 13-6. The CPU sends data to and receives data from the UART through the data bus. The data bus connects to the UART's two internal registers.

To send data, the CPU writes the data byte into the UART's parallel-in, serial-out shift register. This register sends the parallel data out the UART, 1 bit at a time; the transmission speed is governed by the baud rate to which the UART has been programmed by the CPU. (To keep the diagram simple, we haven't shown other registers in the UART. These other registers — among other things — allow the CPU to program the UART to a range of baud rates. The external clock circuit, shown in the diagram, provides the base clock signal from which the baud rates are derived.)

On the receiving end, bits arriving at the UART's input line are deposited into the serial-in, parallel-out shift register. This register reassembles the serial bits into a single byte, which the CPU reads through the data bus. Again, the bit speed of the received bytes depends on the

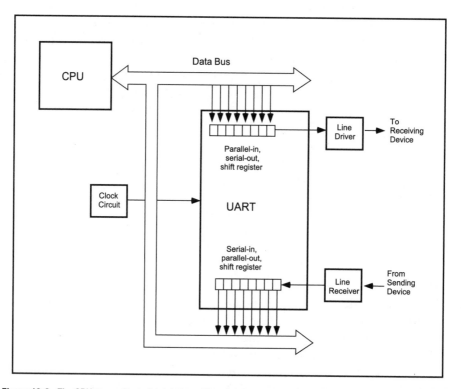

Figure 13-6: The CPU transmits serial data by writing the data to a UART. The data goes into a special register — a parallel-in, serial-out shift register — whose job is to turn the byte into a stream of bits. The speed of the process is governed by an external clock circuit, which provides a stable pulse train at a fixed frequency. (UARTs have built-in divisor circuits that allow the device to derive a variety of baud rates from the single clock signal.) The output of the UART passes through a line driver circuit, which provides the necessary power and voltage conversions to drive the wire of the serial cable. The receiving side of the system is a mirror-image of the sending side. Serial data passes through a line receiver circuit, which conditions it to levels acceptable to the UART. The data is shifted into a serial-in, parallel-out shift register, which the CPU reads using the system data bus.

baud rate of the UART. Consequently, the transmitting and receiving UARTs must be programmed to the same baud rate for communications to work.

Notice the line driver and line receiver blocks in Figure 13-6. These represent circuits that sit between the UART and whatever transmission medium is being used. The voltages and currents at which a UART operates — usually +/- 5V for TTL-level (transistor-transistor logic) UARTs, +/-3V for the newer CMOS-based (complementary metal-oxide silicon) UARTs — are incompatible with the signal requirements of most transmission media. For example, recall that RS-232 requires voltages that ranged from -15V to +15V.

The line drivers and line receivers convert the electrical levels that the UART can tolerate to the levels the transmission medium requires. An example of a popular line driver and receiver combination is the 1488/1489 line driver/receiver, which converts between TTL (+/- 5V) levels and RS-232 levels.

WRITING SERIAL PORT ISRS

After you've decided that your application will use a serial interface and you've selected the hardware, you need to think about software issues. If your application will use the serial port for input, an ISR (interrupt service routine) is a necessary component of your serial device driver. Probably the biggest problem with writing an ISR for a serial port is the potential high frequency of the interrupts. For example, at 115,200 baud, your serial port ISR could be faced with handling over 10,000 interrupts per second, presuming that an interrupt occurs with each incoming character. (And note that we're considering interrupts generated by only incoming characters. Serial devices can be programmed to generate interrupts when they are ready to send the next character. If you write your system to use interrupts to signal readiness to transmit as well, the number of interrupts per second goes beyond the 10,000 figure.)

If your application needs to handle such high data rates, it's a good idea to use a UART with a buffer. In that way, an interrupt is generated only when the buffer nears being filled, and a single call to the ISR retrieves multiple characters. Also (as we mentioned in Chapter 9, "Interrupts"), keep your ISR small; do the minimum amount of work in the ISR and leave the rest for the application. Finally, maximize the number of characters transferred per call to the ISR. For example, if the ISR is handling the reception of characters, write it so that before the ISR exits, it checks to see whether additional characters have arrived (and if they have, reads them).

THE RS-232C SERIAL STANDARD

RS-232C is a serial interface standard and likely the most popular interface standard for serial communication. Because it is an interface standard, RS-232C consists of mechanical, electrical, functional, and procedural specifications. The mechanical specification defines the pin assignments used to connect two RS-232-compliant systems together. The electrical specification defines the characteristics of the signals that carry the data. The functional specification defines the duties of each of the signal wires given in the mechanical specification. Finally, the procedural specification defines how each circuit carries out its duties.

RS-232 was designed to connect Data Terminal Equipment (DTE), or computers and terminals, with Data Communications Equipment (DCE), or modems. In the real world, RS-232 is used also to connect computers directly to computers and to connect non-modem devices such as printers directly to computers.

MECHANICAL SPECIFICATION

RS-232-compliant connectors can be found on the back of virtually every desktop computer in use today. The RS-232 standard itself specifies only the pin assignments for a 25-pin connector, and that a male connector should be used for the DTE (Data Terminal Equipment) end of the connection and a female connector for the DCE (Data Communications Equipment) connection. The standard is silent on any mechanical characteristics of the connectors, but de facto standards have evolved. On PC computers, the RS-232 connectors are the COM ports, which are either 9-pin or 25-pin connectors (DB-9 and DB-25 connectors, respectively).

How can a 9-pin connector be used for a standard that specifies 25 signals? Many signals defined by RS-232 are designed for synchronous data transmission. RS-232 is used far more often for asynchronous communication than for synchronous communication, so we'll discuss only the asynchronous signals here. Table 13-1 shows the signals defined for asynchronous communication and their assignments to 25-pin connectors (in accordance with the RS-232 standard) and 9-pin connectors (in accordance with the de facto standard). The two signals omitted on the DB-9 connector, protective ground and DSRD, are not needed for reliable communication.

Table 13-1: RS-232 Asynchronous I/O Signals

25 Pin	9 Pin	Signal	Direction	Description
1	-	protective ground	none	chassis ground
2	3	TD	from DTE	Transmitted Data
3	2	RD	to DTE	Received Data
4	7	RTS	from DTE	Request to Send; DTE wants to transmit data
5	8	CTS	to DTE	Clear to Send; DCE is ready to receive data
6	6	DSR	to DTE	Data Set Ready; DCE is initialized and ready to communicate
7	5	signal ground	none	common line for data circuit
8	1	DCD	to DTE	Data Carrier Detect; DCE has detected a carrier signal from the transmission target
20	4	DTR	from DTE	Data Terminal Ready; DTE is initialized and ready to communicate
22	9	RI	to DTE	Ring Indicator; indicates incoming call
23	-	DSRD	bidirectional	Data Signal Rate Detector; selects the higher of two data rates

ELECTRICAL SPECIFICATION

RS-232 transmits signals on what is known as an *unbalanced line*. This means the electrical signal that carries data from source to destination travels along a single wire. Signals on that wire are referenced to a ground wire, which acts as an electrical return path. RS-232 is unbalanced because although two wires are needed to create an electrical circuit, a signal wire and a ground wire, only one of the two wires carries the data. An RS-232 cable, therefore, has two signal wires allowing simultaneous bidirectional communication. RD and TD each carry data in one direction and use the ground wire as the signal reference.

At any output pin of an RS-232-compliant port, a logic 1 is signified by any voltage between +5V and +15V; a logic 0 is any voltage between -5V and -15V. At any input pin of an RS-232-compliant port, a logic 1 is any voltage between +3V and +15 V; a logic 0 is anything between -3V and -15V. Because digital signal levels inside a computer are 0V to +5V for TTL circuits (0V to +3V on some newer systems that use all CMOS logic), a system implementing RS-232 communications must include some type of level conversion circuitry. For conversion from RS-232 levels to TTL levels (or to CMOS levels), the system uses a line receiver circuit. For conversion from TLL (or from CMOS) logic levels to RS-232 levels (sending), the system uses a line driver circuit. Note that the receiver uses a wider span of acceptable voltages than the transmitter to account for voltage drops through the cable. A variety of integrated circuits are available that incorporate both line drivers and line receivers on a single chip. Probably the most popular is the MAX232 IC, available from sources such as TI and Dallas Semiconductor.

Because RS-232 uses unbalanced transmission, RS-232 cables are susceptible to the adverse effects of electrical noise over long distances (though they are more immune than a parallel cable). Such noise causes spurious erroneous signals on the line; the upshot is that the receiver receives something other than what the sender has sent. These limitations restrict an RS-232's cable length to 50 feet (about 15 meters).

FUNCTIONAL SPECIFICATION

Table 13-1 gives you a bird's-eye view of the functional specification for the RS-232 signals. Notice that only two of the signals carry data: TD and RD. The other signals are handshaking signals and are used to coordinate the flow of information between devices.

RS-232 was originally designed for use in telecommunications equipment, and much of its nomenclature carries hints of that origin. For example, the classic RS-232 arrangement was a computer system connected to a modem. In fact, that's still one of the most popular uses of RS-232 today. The computer is referred to as the Data Terminal Equipment (DTE). The modem attached to the DTE is referred to as the Data Communications Equipment (DCE). (The modem was called the Data Communications Equipment because it communicated with the outside world.)

Because the computer was the device the user operated directly, all RS-232 signal functions are defined from the perspective of the DTE. Hence, TD (transmit data) is defined as data transmitted from DTE to DCE.

PROCEDURAL SPECIFICATION

Keeping the definitions of DTE and DCE in mind, and referring to Table 13-1, we can see how the more important RS-232 signals were used to coordinate communication between DTE and DCE.

- The DTE device activates DTR (Data Terminal Ready) to indicate that it is operating correctly and ready to communicate with the DCE.

- The DCE device's counterpart to DTR is DSR (Data Set Ready). The DCE device activates DSR when it is ready to communicate with the DTE device.

- The DTE device asserts RTS (Request to Send) when it has data that it's ready to transmit to the DCE device.

- In response to RTS, the DCE device asserts CTS (Clear to Send). The DTE device takes this signal as the go-ahead to begin transmitting data.

- When a modem that is a DCE device detects a carrier (indicating that it has established contact with another modem at the other end of the line), the DCE asserts the DCD (Data Carrier Detect) signal.

- Similarly, a modem asserts the RI (Ring Indicator) signal when it detects a ring signal. This is used for systems that allow users to dial in (using a modem) from an outside line. When a caller dials in and causes the modem to activate the RI signal, software on the host system commands the modem to answer the phone and begin communication.

RS-232 always requires one end of the connection to be a DCE connection, even if you're connecting two DTE devices (two computers) directly, without going through modems. This problem is solved with the use of a null modem cable, which allows both ends of the connection to think that they are the DTE and the other end of the cable is the DCE. To accomplish this, the TD and RD wires are crossed in the cable, so that transmitted data from each end goes to received data at the other end. The handshaking signals are either cross-wired or hardwired so they are always asserted or de-asserted, as appropriate. Appendix C shows the cabling required for a null modem connection.

PERIPHERAL SERIAL BUSES

Peripheral serial buses offer a way for a hardware designer to connect peripheral devices to a computer system using a serial connection that provides throughput competitive with a parallel connection, well into the megabyte-per-second range. Peripheral serial buses can be used in place of bulkier parallel buses (such as SCSI) to reduce board size as well as electrical emissions. Some hard disk drives are already available with peripheral serial interfaces.

The advantages of peripheral serial buses over parallel buses are cost, convenience, and increased cable length. A serial connection requires fewer wires than a parallel connection; hence, a serial cable is more flexible and easier to work with than a parallel cable and can fit in tighter places. Because a serial cable is smaller, it's easier to shield and is therefore simultaneously less noisy and more noise-immune than a parallel connection; this means you can use longer cables than are possible with, for example, SCSI. In addition, the amount of silicon needed to drive a serial bus is less than is required to drive a parallel bus, so power consumption is reduced.

Two popular peripheral serial bus standards are USB (universal serial bus) and Firewire (more formally known as IEEE 1394). Another, less popular, peripheral serial bus standard is SSA (Serial Storage Architecture), which began life as a proprietary IBM standard and is not (at this time) gaining popularity. We look at only USB and Firewire here.

The universal serial bus is a high-speed serial bus. It was designed for connecting PCs and peripherals, such as keyboards and mice, and has become popular as a means of connecting PCs and embedded consumer devices such as digital camcorders, digital still cameras, and digital audio devices. A USB system can be built using a tree-style or daisy-chain configuration. In a tree-style configuration, a root bus connects to a hub device, which provides multiple connections for other devices in much the same way that an extension cord provides multiple outlets. In a daisy-chain configuration, each peripheral device provides two USB connectors, so that each device can connect to two other devices. For example, device A connects to device B, which also connects to device C, and so on. A single USB channel can support up to 27 devices. A *channel* is a series of USB devices connected through a common bus.

USB was developed by a consortium that included Compaq, DEC, IBM, Intel, Microsoft, and Northern Telecom. It supports two levels of transfer speed: 12 Mbps for high-speed devices (digital video and audio), and 1.5 Mbps for low-speed devices (keyboards, joysticks, and so on). USB supports hot-plugging; that is, you can attach or remove a device to an active USB cable. You don't have to turn off the power, attach the device, and reboot the system.

Note: Intel manufactures a variety of USB controller chips and USB-compatible microprocessors. You can find piles of USB-related information at Intel's developer site at `http://developer.intel.com`.

Firewire was developed by Apple Computer as the potential replacement for the SCSI bus on its Macintosh computers. Firewire is less expensive to implement than SCSI, mainly because Firewire cables require fewer conductors than SCSI; Firewire cables use 6 wires, and SCSI requires a minimum of 25.

Like USB, Firewire supports hot-plugging. Also like USB, Firewire connections can be either tree-like or daisy-chained. A single Firewire bus can support up to 63 devices. The Firewire protocol recognizes three transfer rates: 98.3 Mbps, 196.6 Mbps, and 393.2 Mbps. At the time of this writing, Firewire is used in some digital video consumer devices such as the camcorders from Sony and Matsushita. You can find more information on Firewire at the DV and Firewire Central web site at `http://www.dvcentral.org`.

Note: The transfer rates shown are approximate; we rounded to the first decimal place. For example, the 98.3 Mbps rate we quoted is actually 98.304 Mbps. So that you don't have to remember lots of numbers, the IEEE 1394 specification calls the three rates S100, S200, and S400 (lowest to highest).

MIDI

MIDI is an acronym for Musical Instrument Digital Interface. MIDI is a serial interface standard that appeared in 1983 on electronic synthesizer equipment from manufacturers such as Oberheim, Roland, and Sequential Circuits. MIDI provides a way to connect electronic musical instruments so that they can communicate with one another. Because the electronic music industry has adopted MIDI across the board, musicians have the comfort of knowing that any MIDI-compatible device can communicate with any other MIDI-compatible device.

MIDI devices can control one another. For example, a single MIDI-equipped keyboard (musical keyboard, that is) can control multiple MIDI-equipped sound-generating devices, allowing a musician playing a single electronic keyboard to control multiple sound-generating devices (which can be from different manufacturers). As the musician plays the keyboard, data is sent through the MIDI connection that carries information about the musician's performance: which keys have been pressed, how hard they were pressed, which keys have been released, and so on. The receiving sound generators receive that MIDI information, decode it, and emit the proper sounds at the proper time and the proper velocity.

MIDI interfaces are also available for most personal computers. With the appropriate software, a musician can play a tune on a MIDI-compatible instrument, and the performance will be captured by the computer software. This allows a performer to have a small but extremely capable recording studio right inside the computer. Just as one might edit, cut, and paste words in a word processor, the musician can edit, cut, and paste notes in a musical score. After the score is complete, the musician can instruct the computer to transmit the MIDI data to the synthesizer; in effect, the computer flawlessly plays the synthesizer.

The MIDI specification defines physical characteristics (cable length, connector pin assignments) and electrical characteristics (voltage levels, bit rate, character length), as well as the encodings for MIDI commands that can be transmitted along the cable.

A MIDI cable transmits data in unidirectional (simplex) fashion. A MIDI-equipped device can have up to three types of MIDI connectors: MIDI OUT, MIDI IN, and MIDI THRU. A device transmits information through its MIDI OUT port. (When a musician plays a MIDI-equipped keyboard, MIDI information about the performance is sent out the MIDI OUT port.) A device receives information through its MIDI IN port. The MIDI THRU connector is a pass-through connection; data arriving at the MIDI IN port is echoed through the MIDI THRU port. This allows you to daisy-chain MIDI devices.

Consequently, a typical MIDI setup includes a single master device (usually a musical keyboard instrument) whose MIDI OUT port is connected to another instrument's MIDI IN port. That instrument's MIDI THRU port is connected to the next instrument's MIDI IN port, whose MIDI THRU port is connected to the *next* instrument's MIDI IN port, and so on through the daisy chain.

The MIDI specification allows you to have up to 16 devices in a daisy chain. Each device can be programmed to have a unique 4-bit identifier (called a *channel*). MIDI's electrical specification, however, allows a single MIDI OUT port to drive only four or five daisy-chained devices. MIDI repeater boxes, which are available from a number of manufacturers, provide the necessary electrical boost to allow you to interconnect as many MIDI devices as your budget can stand.

MIDI is not a particularly fast serial interface. It runs at 31.250 Kbps, which is generally adequate for the nature of data it is transporting (musical performance data). Some specialized electronic instrument controllers, such as pitch bend wheels, can tax the bandwidth of a MIDI connection; an improved MIDI specification, which may be available by the time you read this, will solve any current bandwidth problems.

You can get more information about the MIDI specification from *MIDI: A Comprehensive Introduction,* by Joseph Rothstein (A-R Editions, Inc., 1992).

CHIP-TO-CHIP SERIAL BUSES

Some chip manufacturers have devised chip-to-chip serial buses for interfacing their peripheral chips — mainly, EEPROMs, flash memory, and ADCs (analog-to-digital converters) — to microprocessors. As compared to a typical parallel system bus, which requires multiple address and data lines, serial buses require only one or two data lines, a clock line, and a ground. Because fewer circuit traces are needed between chips, a system using a serial bus is much smaller than one using a parallel bus. In addition, the power needed to drive a serial bus is less than that required to drive a parallel bus (for the simple reason that a serial bus has fewer lines), which makes a serial bus a likely contender for chip interconnections in low-power applications.

A serial bus between the CPU and a peripheral chip means that access to that chip is slower than access through a parallel bus. Consequently, chips that interface to the CPU with a serial connection should be used only in situations where size or power matters, and speed doesn't. Serial buses can transfer data at speeds from tens of kilobits per second to megabits per second (depending on the technology). Parallel system buses typically transfer at speeds from tens of megabits per second to megabytes per second.

Most chip-to-chip serial buses operate using a master/slave scheme. The master — almost always the CPU — initiates all data transfers by sending a command to the slave (or slaves). Supported commands vary with the implementation, but all chip-to-chip serial buses support data-read and data-write commands. And because chip-to-chip serial buses are often used to connect the CPU to EEPROM and flash memory devices, most support an erase command.

So, for example, a CPU reading data from a memory chip through a serial bus first transmits a read command to the chip through the data line. The CPU follows the command with the address of the data item to be read. The target memory device decodes the command and subsequent address, fetches the data requested, and transmits that to the CPU. (All signals that pass along the data line are synchronized to the clock signal on the clock line.)

The three popular serial chip-to-chip interfaces are I2C (Inter-IC connect), Microwire, and SPI (serial peripheral interface). I2C was developed by Philips Semiconductor for interfacing peripheral chips to its line of 8051-variant embedded processors. More devices are available that support I2C than either Microwire or SPI, because I2C has a few advantages over Microwire and

SPI. First, it requires only three wires between a CPU and the peripheral chips: a bidirectional data line, a clock line, and a ground. Microwire requires a minimum of four, and SPI requires five. Second, it is more immune to noise than SPI or Microwire. I2C's noise immunity makes it a good choice in electrically noisy environments such as under the hood of a car. Finally, I2C is a multidrop bus. That is, similar to a small Ethernet network, device addresses are transmitted along the I2C signal wires, so you can attach multiple devices to an I2C bus without having to run a chip select line to each device. Again, the advantage is fewer wires.

I2C does have several disadvantages, however. First, it's slower than the other chip-to-chip serial buses. Also, the specification allows for only 8 slave devices. (Microchip is proposing an updated version of the I2C specification, however, that would raise the number of devices on the bus to 256). Finally, using a bidirectional data line means multiple devices may attempt to transmit on the bus simultaneously. This, in turn, could result in data collisions and corrupt data. I2C interfaces, therefore, require extra logic to detect collisions and retransmit data.

Microwire was developed by National Semiconductor and has been in use longer than either I2C or SPI. It requires a minimum of four wires: a bidirectional data line, a chip select line, a clock line, and a ground. Unlike I2C, Microwire uses a separate chip select line and doesn't pass device addresses on the data line. While this design requires Microwire to use more wires than I2C, there's no upper limit (at least theoretically) to the number of chips you can put on a Microwire bus. Microwire is limited only by the amount of current each chip can supply to the Microwire bus. I2C, on the other hand, is limited to the number of address-able destinations built into the protocol. In terms of transfer speeds, Microwire is faster than I2C but slower than SPI.

Note that we said Microwire requires a *minimum* of four wires. Chips that support Microwire have two pins for transferring data: a data-in pin and a data-out pin. These pins can be wired together, thus resulting in a single, bidirectional data line between a chip and a CPU. These pins also can be connected to independent data-in and data-out lines, resulting in a more robust bidirectional design. (Articles on Microwire note that if the data-in and data-out lines are combined, bus contention can occur in some instances, possibly resulting in corrupted data. One such article is Brian Dipert's in the January 15, 1998, issue of *EDN Magazine*, titled "EEPROMs: Survival of the Fittest.")

Microwire's greatest disadvantage is the fact that its data and chip select lines can float to a logic 1 state when no active device is driving them. This can occur when the CPU is reset. The potential problem occurs if the clock line is active and devices read the bus while the CPU is being reset. Because the erase command is a stream of 1 bits, some devices might think they're being instructed to erase one (or more) of their memory locations. The only solution to this problem is a careful hardware design that guarantees that the clock signal will not be present when the data and chip-select lines are not being driven by any device.

SPI, the third interface in this discussion, was developed by Motorola and is available on many of its embedded processors. It is the fastest-growing chip-to-chip serial bus. SPI's growth in popularity is due largely to its high throughput. Currently, SPI transfers data at clock speeds up to 5 MHz. This is faster than IC2 and Microwire. New versions (at the time we were writing this) were promising speeds double that.

Functionally, SPI looks similar to Microwire. The five signal lines that make up an SPI bus have a one-to-one correspondence with the signal lines in a robust configuration of the Microwire bus: a line each for data out, data in, chip select, clock, and ground. SPI addresses Microwire's misinterpreted command error by defining commands so that no command is all ones or all zeros. Its only disadvantage is that few devices provide an SPI interface, but that's likely to improve.

SERIAL I/O IN THE SMART UPS

In the Smart UPS, the system communicates with a host computer through a serial connection. This allows the UPS to report status information to the host; it also allows the host system to provide simulated inputs to the UPS. The serial I/O subsystem in the UPS application uses an ISR to handle low-level serial I/O. Using interrupts rather than polling to drive serial I/O allows us to keep the software responsive to serial transfers without consuming so much CPU time that it retards the performance of the rest of the system. Interrupts drive both incoming and outgoing serial data. The serial I/O subsystem in this example would make an excellent starting point for a serial subsystem in your own applications. The code is in SERIAL.C in the \TSLITE\PROJECTS\UPS2\UPS2 subdirectory. Constants and bit assignments for the 8250 and 16550 UART registers are in PCIO.H in the \TSLITE\INCLUDE subdirectory.

We've used a thread to help us keep the serial ISR small. (We covered threads and the role they played in the serial I/O subsystem in the preceding chapter.) Using a serial I/O thread to handle the transfer of data reduces the ISR to a routine that simply signals the thread that an interrupt has taken place. The other threads in the system transfer serial I/O data to and from the serial I/O thread through pipes. We described how the thread synchronization in the serial I/O subsystem worked in Chapter 12; in this chapter, we focus on the code that programs the UART to perform the data transfers.

A block diagram of the components of the serial I/O subsystem and how they interoperate is shown in Figure 13-7. The figure excludes the initialization and shutdown routines; we're showing only those components that are active during the application's normal run time.

When the Smart UPS application wants to write bytes to the serial port, threads in the application call SerialWrite(). The SerialWrite() routine first attempts to send bytes directly to the UART's transmitter holding register. If that's not possible because the register is full, SerialWrite() writes the bytes to the send pipe. The send pipe buffers the data being sent out. At some later time, the UART generates a transmitter-holding-register-empty interrupt. This interrupt causes the Serial ISR to signal the serial I/O thread to wake up and transfer the bytes out of the send pipe and into the transmitter holding register.

Reading bytes from the UART is entirely interrupt driven. When a byte arrives, the Serial ISR wakes the serial I/O thread, which reads the byte from the UART and places it in the receive pipe. The receive pipe buffers data coming in. When the application calls SerialRead(), the function simply reads the byte(s) out of the pipe.

Before we get into the code in the serial I/O subsystem, let's take a brief look at how the 8250/16x50 UART family works.

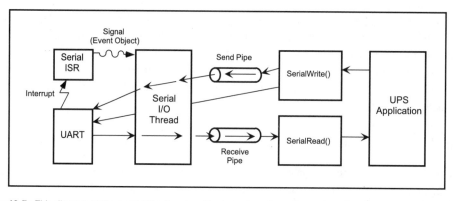

Figure 13-7: This diagram of the serial I/O subsystem illustrates how its component routines interoperate. The rest of the system interfaces to the serial I/O subsystem by calling the SerialWrite() and SerialRead() routines. Data is buffered between these routines and the serial ISR thread (which performs the actual hardware I/O) using two pipes: one for sending data and one for receiving. Notice that SerialWrite() also communicates directly with the UART.

THE 8250/16X50 UART FAMILY

Most PC-compatible systems use a UART that's either in a separate IC or on-chip, and that's a derivative of the original 8250 UART that appeared on the first IBM PC/XT. The 386EX is an example of an embedded chip with a UART on-chip. The 8250 allowed transfer speeds up to only 9600 baud. It was replaced by the faster 16450 UART, which allows transfer speeds up to 115200 baud while maintaining software compatibility with its 8250 ancestor.

In these days of high serial throughput, however, the 16450 is inadequate because it (like the 8250) has only a single input register for receiving bytes. At 9600 baud, a byte arrives approximately once per millisecond. At 115200 baud, you get a byte about every 87 microseconds! Although in some circumstances it may be possible to service an interrupt every 87 microseconds, if interrupts occurred at that frequency, many embedded systems would consume so much CPU time that very little other work would get accomplished.

Consequently, the 16450 has pretty much been replaced by either the 16550, 16650, or 16750 UARTs. Each of these newer UARTs include on-chip FIFO buffers (16 bytes for the 16550, 32 bytes for the 16650, 64 bytes for the 16750) that allow the UART to accumulate multiple incoming bytes before interrupting the CPU, and buffer multiple outgoing bytes waiting to be sent. Depending on how the serial driver uses the FIFO buffers and how constant the stream of serial data is, this can reduce the number of serial interrupts received by the CPU by a factor of ten or more. This frees the CPU for other processing.

Note: The 16550, 16650, and 16750 maintain programming compatibility with the original 8250. The only substantial difference is that a single interrupt on an 8250 signals the arrival of a single byte. On the 16550 and later, a single interrupt means software should read multiple bytes from the UART's input FIFO buffer. The serial driver has to enable the use of the FIFO buffers, however; if the serial driver doesn't enable the FIFO buffers, the chip behaves just like an 8250.

The software for the serial I/O subsystem, which we present shortly, makes heavy use of the UART registers. Let's look at those registers, so you'll have a clearer idea of what's taking place in the source code.

The 8250 has 9 registers, the 16450 has 10, and the 16550 and later have 11. These registers are accessed at 8 consecutive I/O addresses, starting at the base address assigned to the UART. On the PC architecture, serial port COM1 is assigned a base address of 0x3F8, and COM2 is assigned 0x2F8. Some registers are read-only, some are write-only, and others can be read and written (we'll identify which is which). Also, some address sharing takes place at the lowest two I/O addresses. Specifically, the divisor latch register is actually a 16-bit register that sits at offsets 0 and 1 from the base address, a location it shares with the character transmitter and character receiver registers (both at offset 0) and the interrupt enable register (at offset 1). Which register has ownership of that location is determined by the state of the DLAB (divisor latch access bit), bit 7 of the line control register.

The registers and their I/O offsets from the UART's base address follow:

- **Transmitter holding register (offset 0).** This write-only register is accessed when the DLAB bit is 0. To send a character out the serial port, the CPU writes the character to this register. On the 16550 and later UARTs, this register is used to write characters to the back of the transmitter FIFO buffer.

- **Receiver buffer register (offset 0).** This read-only register is accessed when the DLAB bit is 0. When the UART receives a character through the serial line, it places the character in this register. Note that start, stop, and parity bits are removed from the character; only data bits are deposited in this register. On the 16550 and later UARTs, this register is used to read characters from the front of the receiver FIFO buffer.

- **Interrupt enable register (offset 1).** This read/write register allows you to select which events will cause the UART to generate interrupts, as follows:

Bit	Meaning
0	Received data ready. Setting this bit causes the UART to interrupt when data is in the receiver buffer register. For the 16550 and later UARTs, this interrupt is generated when 1, 4, 8, or 14 bytes are in the receiver FIFO buffer, depending on how the FIFO control register is programmed.
1	Transmitter holding register empty. Setting this bit causes the UART to interrupt when the transmitter holding register (the transmitter FIFO buffer for the 16550 and later) becomes empty.
2	Receiver error or break. Setting this bit causes the UART to interrupt when a receiver error or a break condition occurs. The specific error is reported in the line status register.
3	RS-232 status signal change. Setting this bit causes the UART to interrupt when the state of one of the RS-232 status signals (available by reading the modem status register) changes.
4–7	Unused.

- **Interrupt identification register (offset 2).** This read-only register allows software to determine the reason for the highest priority pending UART interrupt. An interrupt remains pending until software clears it by performing the appropriate action, as follows:

Bit	Meaning
0	No pending interrupt. If this bit is set, no interrupt is pending. If this bit is clear, the highest priority pending interrupt is identified by bits 1 and 2.
1–2	Interrupt identity. This 2-bit field identifies the highest priority pending interrupt.
3–7	Unused.

The interrupt identity bits have the following meaning, where higher values in the interrupt bits correspond to a higher-priority interrupt:

Identity Bits	Meaning
00	RS-232 status signal changed (lowest priority). This condition is cleared by reading the modem status register.
01	Transmitter holding register empty. This condition is cleared either by reading the interrupt identification register or by writing a byte to the transmitter holding register.
10	Received data available. This condition is cleared by reading the receiver buffer register (for the 16550 and later, by reading enough characters from the receiver FIFO buffer to drop it below the threshold set for generating an interrupt).
11	Receiver error or break (highest priority). This condition is cleared by reading the line status register.

- **FIFO control register (offset 2).** This write-only register appears on only the 16550 and later UARTs, and is used to enable the receiver and transmitter FIFO buffers and control their use, as follows:

Bit	Meaning
0	FIFO enable. Setting this bit enables the use of the transmitter and receiver FIFO buffers instead of the 1-byte transmitter holding register and receiver buffer register.
1	Receiver FIFO reset. Setting this bit clears all data from the receiver FIFO buffer.
2	Transmitter FIFO reset. Setting this bit clears all data from the transmitter FIFO buffer.

Bit	Meaning
3	DMA mode select. Setting this bit selects a DMA (direct memory access) mode, which transfers the entire contents of the FIFO buffers to or from memory in one I/O operation. A computer with PC-compatible architecture does not support this mode.
4–5	Reserved. Should always be written as zeros.
6–7	Receiver FIFO trigger level. The value in this field controls the character threshold in the FIFO buffer at which the UART generates an interrupt. A 0 in this field causes an interrupt to be generated when 1 character is in the receiver FIFO buffer. A value of 1 selects a threshold of 4 characters, 2 selects 8 characters, and 3 selects 14 characters.

- **Line control register (offset 3).** The primary use of this register is to set the format of transmitted and received data, as follows:

Bit	Meaning
0–1	Number of data bits per character. Setting this field to 0 selects 5 data bits per character, 1 selects 6 data bits, 2 selects 7 data bits, and 3 selects 8 data bits
2	Number of stop bits. Setting this bit selects 2 stop bits; clearing it selects 1 stop bit.
3–5	Parity select. Set this field to one of the following values: 000 — No parity 001 — Odd parity 011 — Even parity 101 — Mark parity (the parity bit is always 1) 111 — Space parity (the parity bit is always 0)
6	Break control bit. When set to 1, the serial output of the UART is forced to logical 0. (A break character is a low signal — a space — on the serial line for a period equal to 1 character transfer; that is the period of time that would be required to send a start bit, data bits, a parity bit, and stop bits). You must clear this bit again before you can resume sending data.
7	Divisor latch access bit. When this bit is set, I/O offsets 0 and 1 access the divisor latch register. When this bit is cleared, offset 0 reads the receiver buffer register and writes the transmitter holding register, and offset 1 accesses the interrupt enable register.

- **Modem control register (offset 4).** This read/write register allows software to control the RS-232 status lines DTR and RTS, as follows:

Bit	Meaning
0	Data Terminal Ready (DTR). Setting this bit asserts the RS-232 DTR signal; clearing it de-asserts DTR.
1	Request to Send (RTS). Setting this bit asserts the RS-232 RTS signal; clearing it de-asserts RTS.
2	Output 1 pin. This bit drives the OUT1 pin on the UART, which is not used for RS-232 connections.
3	Output 2 pin. This bit drives the OUT2 pin on the UART, which is not used for RS-232 connections.
4	Loopback check. Setting this bit enables a loopback feature for testing the UART.
5–7	Unused.

- **Line status register (offset 5).** Bits in this read-only register record a variety of status conditions. In general, when the UART generates a receiver error interrupt, software can consult this register to determine the interrupt's cause, as follows:

Bit	Meaning
0	Received data ready. This bit is set if data is in the receiver buffer register (or the receiver FIFO buffer has exceeded the programmed threshold on the 16550 and later UARTs).
1	Overrun error. This bit is set if the data in the receiver buffer register has been overwritten (because the serial driver isn't reading it fast enough to keep up with incoming data).
2	Parity error. This bit is set if a parity error was detected in incoming data.
3	Framing error. This bit is set if an incoming character did not have a valid stop bit.
4	Break indicator. This bit is set if the receive data line is held in the space (logic 0) state for longer than one character time. This bit is cleared whenever this register is read.
5	Transmitter holding register empty. This bit is set if the transmitter holding register (or the transmitter FIFO buffer, for 16550 and later UARTs) is empty.
6	Transmitter empty. This bit is set if both the transmitter holding register (or FIFO buffer) and the transmitter shift register used to serialize and send the currently transmitting character are empty.
7	FIFO data error. If the FIFO buffers are enabled, this bit is set if at least one of the characters in the FIFO buffer had a parity or framing error. Reading the line status register clears this bit.

- **Modem status register (offset 6)**. This read-only register provides access to the RS-232 status signals DCD, RI, DSR, and CTS, as follows:

Bit	Meaning
0	Change in Clear to Send (CTS). This bit is set if the sense of CTS has changed since the last time the register was read.
1	Change in Data Set Ready (DSR). This bit is set if the sense of DSR has changed since the last time the register was read.
2	Change in Ring Indicator (RI). This bit is set if the sense of RI has changed since the last time the register was read.
3	Change in Data Carrier Detect (DCD). This bit is set if the sense of DCD has changed since the last time the register was read.
4	CTS. This bit is set if CTS is asserted, and cleared if CTS is de-asserted.
5	DSR. This bit is set if DSR is asserted, and cleared if DSR is de-asserted.
6	RI. This bit is set if RI is asserted, and cleared if RI is de-asserted.
7	DCD. This bit is set if DCD is asserted, and cleared if DCD is de-asserted.

- **Scratch pad register (offset 7)**. The CPU may use this register as a storage element. This register appears on only the 16450 and later UARTs.
- **Divisor latch register (offsets 0 and 1)**. This read/write register shares its I/O locations with the receiver buffer register/transmitter holding register, and the interrupt enable register. The divisor latch is accessible when the DLAB bit in the line control register is set to 1. The other registers are accessible when DLAB is set to 0.

The divisor latch is a 16-bit register. I/O offset 0 holds its low 8 bits; offset 1 holds its high 8 bits. The value in the divisor latch register determines the baud rate of the UART, using the following formula:

```
value in divisor latch = clock frequency / (baud rate x 16)
```

where clock frequency is the frequency of the clock signal into the UART. (For PC systems, the clock signal is 1.8432 MHz). Table 13-2 shows divisor latch register values for baud rates supported by PC computers.

Table 13-2: Divisor Register Values

Baud rate	Divisor (decimal)
110	1047
300	384
600	192
1200	96

continues

Table 13-2: Divisor Register Values (continued)

Baud rate	Divisor (decimal)
2400	48
4800	24
9600	12
19200	6
38400	3
57600	2
115200	1

INITIALIZING THE SERIAL I/O SUBSYSTEM

The InitSerialsys() routine has many jobs to do — nine to be specific. In this section, we step through them one at a time.

First, InitSerialsys() determines which serial port (COM1 or COM2) will be used by the target embedded application to communicate with the host system. It does this using the following instructions:

```
BOOL InitSerialsys(BOOL fCom1)
{
    int        mask;
    VSB_VARS *pVsbVars;
    EK_KERNELINFO ki;
    unsigned idComThread;
```

Second, as shown in Listing 13-1, InitSerialsys() sets several global variables based on which serial port has been selected, and determines whether that port is in use by ETS Kernel's target-to-host communications system.

Listing 13-1: Setting global variables

```
//
// Set up globals for serial port, and make sure the desired
// port is not being used by the ETS Kernel for host
// communications.
//

    if (fCom1)
    {
        UartPort = SIO_COM1_BASE;
        // COM1 interrupts on IRQ4
        UartIntNum = 8 + 4;
        UartIntMask = PIC_MASK_IR4;
    }
```

```
    else
    {
        UartPort = SIO_COM2_BASE;
        // COM2 interrupts on IRQ3
        UartIntNum = 8 + 3;
        UartIntMask = PIC_MASK_IR3;
    }

    pVsbVars = EtsGetVsbVarsPointer();
    EtsGetSystemInfo(&ki, NULL);
    if (!ki.fRunMode && pVsbVars->fSerComPresent &&
        ((fCom1 && pVsbVars->ComPortNumber == 1) ||
         (!fCom1 && pVsbVars->ComPortNumber == 2)))
    {
        printf("Serial port COM%s is already in use by the "
               "ETS Kernel for host communications\n",
               fCom1 ? "1" : "2");
        return FALSE;
    }
```

The global variables are used throughout the serial port routines. Three global variables must be initialized:

- **UartPort.** Holds the value of the base I/O address. As we showed earlier, the UART registers on the PC reside at a series of contiguous I/O addresses. The `UartPort` variable holds the base (starting) I/O address of those registers.

- **UartIntNum.** Holds the interrupt number for the serial port being used. The serial I/O routines need this to know which interrupt to hook the ISR to.

- **UartIntMask.** Holds the interrupt mask for the serial port interrupt in the peripheral interrupt controller. This mask is used to temporarily prevent serial port interrupts from occurring, as we saw in the discussion of the serial ISR in Chapter 12, "Multitasking."

If `InitSerialsys()` determines that the selected serial port is in use, the routine issues an error message and returns FALSE to indicate that the subsystem was unable to initialize. If it is not in use, the serial I/O subsystem programs the 8259 interrupt controller (which you saw in Chapter 9, "Interrupts") to mask off the interrupt associated with the UART, as follows:

```
    //
    // Make sure the serial port interrupt is masked off
    // in the 8259 until we're done initializing.
    //
    mask = _inp(PIC_1_A1);
    _outp(PIC_1_A1, mask | UartIntMask);
```

While the software is initializing the serial port, we don't want any serial port interrupts to occur. Otherwise, the system may attempt to execute an ISR with the hardware incompletely configured.

Third, the initialization routine creates the serial I/O thread, the synchronization objects, and the pipes used for interthread communication. We examined that code in Chapter 12, "Multitasking," so we won't revisit it here.

Fourth, InitSerialsys() saves the vector to the current serial ISR and then installs the new ISR handler. The routine must save the vector so it can restore the ISR when the serial I/O subsystem shuts down. (In most cases, the vector to the current ISR will be an empty routine. But we wrote the code so that it will execute regardless of what state the system is in before application startup.) Here's the code snippet that performs this task:

```
if(!EtsSaveInterruptHandler(UartIntNum, &ComSaveHand))
{
    printf("Can't save COM interrupt vector\n");
    goto EXIT_THREAD;
}
if(!EtsSetInterruptHandler(UartIntNum, ComHandler))
{
    printf("Can't set COM interrupt vector\n");
    goto EXIT_THREAD;
}
```

Fifth, the serial I/O subsystem configures the serial port hardware by determining whether the UART is a 16550 or later and, if it is, enabling the FIFO buffers for better performance. Listing 13-2 show the code excerpt from the InitSerialsys() routine that completes this task.

Listing 13-2: Configuring the serial port

```
//
// If this is a 16550 or later, enable the FIFOs in the
// transmit and receive buffers.  We set the UART to
// interrupt when the receive FIFO queue has 8 characters
// (it interrupts anyway if there are characters in the
// FIFO and no new characters is received for one character
// time).  We set the maximum number of characters to write
// to the transmit FIFO when we get a transmitter buffer
// register empty interrupt to 16, the size of the FIFO.
//
// We detect a 16550 or later by attempting to enable the
// FIFOs and then checking if the two FIFO enable bits get
// turned on in the ID register.
//
    _outp((USHORT)(UartPort + SIO_FIFO), SIO_FCRENB);
    if ((_inp((USHORT)(UartPort + SIO_INTID)) & SIO_IDFENB)
        == SIO_IDFENB)
    {
        // Some 16550-compatible chipsets have a bug where they
        // will get stuck with a line status interrupt if you
        // attempt to clear the FIFO and enable it at the same
        // time if data is present. To work around this, we
```

```
        // (1) turn off the FIFO and read a byte first, then
        // (2) enable the FIFO and reset the FIFOs in two steps
        // rather than 1.
        _outp((USHORT)(UartPort + SIO_FIFO), 0);
        _inp((USHORT)(UartPort + SIO_RECVR));
        _outp((USHORT)(UartPort + SIO_FIFO), SIO_FCRENB|SIO_FCRR08);
        _outp((USHORT)(UartPort + SIO_FIFO),
              SIO_FCRENB | SIO_FCRRR | SIO_FCRXR | SIO_FCRR08);
        MaxXmitChars = 16;
    }
    else
    {
        // 8250/16450 have no FIFOs.
        _outp((USHORT)(UartPort + SIO_FIFO), 0);
        MaxXmitChars = 1;
    }
```

If the UART is a 16550 or later, it can be set to generate an interrupt when the receiver FIFO buffer contains 1, 4, 8, or 14 characters. Generally, you want to set this number high, to reduce the number of interrupts and therefore reduce overhead, which should improve overall program performance. If you set it to 14, however, remember that you have only two character times (less than 200 microseconds at 115200 baud) to respond to the interrupt and read data out of the FIFO buffer before a receive overrun occurs. We were conservative and set it to 8, to minimize the chance of overruns. If receive data is less than 8 characters (which is the case in the Smart UPS, which receives 2-byte command packets from WINUPS), the UART generates an interrupt anyway if data is in the FIFO buffer and no new characters are received for one character time.

We also set the MaxXmitChars global variable, which controls how many characters we will attempt to write to the transmitter FIFO buffer when we get a transmitter-holding-register-empty interrupt (which is signaled when the FIFO buffer is emptied). We set this value to 16, the size of the FIFO buffer, or to 1 if the UART does not have FIFO buffers. Here too, the more characters you write to the FIFO buffer at one time, the fewer the number of interrupts you have to process. The tradeoff is that you can't prevent the transmission of characters after they are in the FIFO buffer. If your application uses RS-232 hardware flow control signals (we don't in the Smart UPS), it's often desirable to write fewer characters to the FIFO buffer so that you can minimize the number of characters that are sent after the Clear to Send or Data Set Ready signal is de-asserted.

Sixth, with the 16550-specific initialization completed, we program the UART register to set values for the bit rate, the number of stop and start bits, and the parity using these instructions:

```
//
// Set port parameters to:
//    19200 baud   (set UART divisor to 6)
//    8 data, 1 stop, no parity
//
```

```
    _outp((USHORT)(UartPort + SIO_LCR), SIO_LCRDLA);
    _outp(UartPort, 6);                 // LSB of divisor is 6
    _outp((USHORT)(UartPort + 1), 0);   // MSB of divisor is 0
    _outp((USHORT)(UartPort + SIO_LCR), SIO_LCR8NP1S);
```

Notice that the port number for each UART register is relative to UartPort — the base address of the UART's I/O registers. Using the constant SIO_LCRDLA, the code sets the proper bit in the line control register to activate access to the divisor register. Next, the code stores the clock divisor — 6 — in the divisor register, thus setting the bit rate to 19200. Writing another predefined constant, SIO_LCR8NP1S, to the line control register sets the character length to 8 bits, and specifies a single stop bit and no parity.

Seventh, we set the interrupts to which the UART will respond as follows:

```
//
// Program the COMM port to request interrupts for all events,
// bring up DTR, RTS and enable interrupts.
//
    _outp((USHORT)(UartPort + SIO_INTEN), SIO_INTSON);
    _outp((USHORT)(UartPort + SIO_MCR), SIO_MCRON);
```

The interrupt enable register is loaded with a value that configures the UART to generate an interrupt when a character is received, when the transmitter holding register is emptied, when an error is detected on the transmission line, and when any of the RS-232 status signals change state. Then we write the modem control register to enable the DTR and RTS status signals.

Note: Bytes don't go out a serial port as fast as the computer can deliver them to the serial port. The CPU places a byte in the UART's transmitter holding register, and the UART begins the job of sending that byte down the serial line, 1 bit at a time. From the CPU's perspective, that can take a while. The UART can be programmed to trigger an interrupt when the transmitter holding register is empty. In that way, the CPU can do something else instead of wasting time waiting for the UART to send a byte. When the interrupt is triggered, the ISR routine wakes up, stuffs another byte in the transmitter holding register, and then exits; the CPU can again go off and do something else while the next byte is transmitted, and so on. Some UARTs have internal multibyte buffers, so the ISR can stuff several bytes into the UART, giving the CPU even more free time to do something else while the UART is busy sending a bunch of characters down the wire.

Eighth, at this point, we're ready to unmask the UART interrupt in the peripheral interrupt controller. Before we do this, however, we must clear any pending interrupts in the UART. Anything pending now is due to some stale condition that occurred before we started programming the UART and was never cleared; this step is part of initializing the UART to a clean state. As the following code shows, we clear all possible pending interrupts by reading all the registers used to report interrupts:

```
//
// Read the Line Status Register, Receiver Buffer Register,
// the interrupt ID Register, and the Modem Status Register
// to clear any interrupts which might be pending.
//
```

```
    _inp((USHORT)(UartPort + SIO_LSR));
    _inp((USHORT)(UartPort + SIO_RECVR));
    _inp((USHORT)(UartPort + SIO_INTID));
    _inp((USHORT)(UartPort + SIO_MSR));
```

Ninth, and last, this code clears the mask bit for the UART in the 8259's interrupt mask register:

```
//
// Enable serial port interrupts in the 8259
//
    mask = _inp(PIC_1_A1);
    _outp(PIC_1_A1, mask & ~UartIntMask);
    return TRUE;
```

This allows the 8259 to interrupt the CPU when the UART requests an interrupt.

CLEANING UP

When the Smart UPS program terminates, the CleanupSerialsys() routine is called to shut down the serial I/O subsystem; this is the reverse of initialization. It's simpler, though, because it amounts to turning off and closing things.

First, as you see in the following, the CleanupSerialsys() routine turns off all sources of interrupts from the UART, and turns off the modem control signals:

```
//
// Cleans up the serial I/O subsystem for exit
//
void CleanupSerialsys(void)
{
    int mask;

//
// Shut down the UART and turn off its interrupts
//
    _outp((USHORT)(UartPort + SIO_INTEN), SIO_INTSOFF);
    _outp((USHORT)(UartPort + SIO_MCR), SIO_MCROFF);
```

De-asserting the DTR and RTS signals coming from the UART has the effect of telling whatever device is connected to the PC's serial port: "I'm not accepting serial I/O right now."

Next, the CleanupSerialsys() routine uses these instructions to mask off the UART interrupt in the PIC:

```
//
// Mask off serial port interrupts in the 8259
//
    mask = _inp(PIC_1_A1);
    _outp(PIC_1_A1, mask | UartIntMask);
```

This follows the convention used by ETS Kernel: interrupts for any device not being used by the system are masked in the 8259. Although we have already programmed the UART not to generate interrupts, this step makes absolutely sure the CPU won't receive interrupts from devices without device drivers.

With interrupts disabled, the shutdown routine is now free to restore the previous ISR vector, as this snippet shows:

```
//
// Unhook the interrupt and kill the thread
//
    EtsRestoreInterruptHandler(UartIntNum, &ComSaveHand);
    if (SetEvent(hComExitEvent))
        WaitForSingleObject(hComThread, INFINITE);
    CloseHandle(hComThread);
```

This code also signals the serial I/O thread to exit using the hComExitEvent object. Notice that this code waits on the thread handle for the thread to terminate before proceeding. We do this because the serial I/O thread code uses several synchronization objects we are about to delete.

Finally, the shutdown routine closes all Win32 event objects, deletes the critical section object, and closes the send and receive pipes, as shown here:

```
//
// Close the event and pipe handles
//
    CloseHandle(hComEvent);
    CloseHandle(hComExitEvent);
    DeleteCriticalSection(&SerCritSec);
    CloseHandle(hComSendRead);
    CloseHandle(hComSendWrite);
    CloseHandle(hComRcvRead);
    CloseHandle(hComRcvWrite);

    return;
}
```

The cleanup is complete.

THE SERIAL I/O THREAD

The ComThread() routine is the serial I/O thread — the true workhorse of the serial interrupt system. It reads characters from and writes characters to serial port registers. Consequently, it responds to interrupts for both sending and receiving characters.

> **Note:** ComThread() also responds to interrupts generated by other parts of the serial I/O hardware, such as interrupts caused by parity errors or transmission overruns. However, the portion of the code that would handle such errors merely clears the interrupt condition and takes no other action. If you're interested in creating a more robust serial I/O system, feel free to add whatever code you think is warranted.

ComThread() consists of the infinite loop in Listing 13-3. At the top of the loop, the thread blocks until an interrupt occurs and the ISR signals the hComEvent synchronization object.

After processing the source(s) of the interrupt, ComThread() goes back to sleep again at the top of the loop. Take a look at the loop, with all UART processing code stripped out.

Listing 13-3: The ComThread() loop

```
//
// Serial I/O thread that gets scheduled when a COM interrupt
// occurs.  This thread handles both reading and writing the UART.
//
unsigned __stdcall ComThread(void *pUnused)
{
    int    Mask;            // 8259 interrupt mask
    int    id;             // interrupt ID
    BYTE   ch;             // character received/sent
    DWORD  dwTemp;
    HANDLE WaitEvents[2];

//
// Sit in an infinite loop waking up every time we get signaled by
// the interrupt handler.  Whenever we wake up we'll do as much I/O
// as we can, and then go to sleep again.
//
    WaitEvents[0] = hComEvent;
    WaitEvents[1] = hComExitEvent;
    while (TRUE)
    {
//
// Wait until interrupt event or exit event is signaled
//
        if (WaitForMultipleObjects(2, WaitEvents, FALSE, INFINITE)
                != WAIT_OBJECT_0)
            break;

//
// OK, an interrupt occurred.  Read the interrupt ID port of
// the 8250 to determine the cause of the interrupt then take
// appropriate action.  If multiple interrupt conditions
// exist simultaneously, the highest priority condition is
// reported (highest is serialization error, then receive,
// then transmit, lowest is RS-232 status signal change). We loop,
// processing and clearing interrupt conditions,
// until there are no more pending interrupts.
//
        while (TRUE)
        {
            id = _inp((USHORT)(UartPort + SIO_INTID));
            if(id & SIO_IPEND)
            {
                // no more interrupts are pending
                break;
            }
```

```
            switch(id & SIO_IDMSK)
            {
                ... code to perform UART I/O removed ...
            }
        }

    //
    // OK, no more we can do for now.  Unmask the serial port  interrupt in
    // the 8259 and loop back up to block until the next interrupt occurs.
    //
        Mask = _inp(PIC_1_A1);
        _outp(PIC_1_A1, Mask & ~UartIntMask);
    }

    // Exit event was signaled.
    _endthreadex(0);
}
```

We discussed the `WaitForMultipleObjects()` function in Chapter 12, "Multitasking." If `hComExitEvent` is signaled by the cleanup routine, we break out of the loop and exit the thread. Otherwise, `hComEvent` must have been signaled by the ISR, so we perform I/O to the UART until there is no more work left to do. Notice that the I/O is performed in an inner loop that keeps iterating, reading the interrupt identification register and processing interrupt requests, until there are no more pending interrupt requests from the UART to process. The technique of checking for multiple interrupt requests in the processing for a single interrupt (whether performed in the ISR or, as in this case, in a separate thread) helps reduce the interrupt overhead when writing the driver for a device (such as a UART) that can potentially generate interrupts at very high rates.

After processing is complete, we unmask the UART interrupt in the PIC and loop back to block on the synchronization objects again. The code to unmask the UART interrupt is necessary because, as we saw in Chapter 12, the ISR leaves the interrupt masked; there's no benefit to receiving additional hardware interrupts until we've finished all the processing we can perform and are ready to go back to sleep.

The UART reports the highest priority pending interrupt request in the interrupt identification register. Interrupt request priorities are, from highest to lowest, serialization errors (reported in the line status register), data received, transmitter buffer empty, and change of an RS-232 status signal (reported in the modem status register). The code to handle UART I/O consists of a large `switch()` statement on the contents of the interrupt identification register. Each case of the `switch()` statement takes the appropriate action based on the reason for the interrupt, and clears the interrupt condition at the UART. Let's look at the cases of the `switch()` statement one at a time, starting with the following clause for receiving characters:

```
case SIO_IDRCVD:  // received data available
    // read until the FIFO is empty (this works also for 8250/16450,
    // which have a 1-char "FIFO"), and stuff the chars read into the
    // pipe.  If pipe is full, just discard chars.  Reading a char
    // clears SIO_IDRCVD.
```

```
EnterCriticalSection(&SerCritSec);
do
{
    ch = (BYTE) _inp((USHORT)(UartPort + SIO_RECVR));
    if (nComRcvPipeBytes + 1 <= SER_PIPE_SIZE)
    {
        WriteFile(hComRcvWrite, &ch, 1, &dwTemp, NULL);
        ++ nComRcvPipeBytes;
    }
} while (_inp((USHORT)(UartPort + SIO_LSR)) & SIO_LSRCV);
LeaveCriticalSection(&SerCritSec);
break;
```

The receive data bit is set in the interrupt identification register if one or more characters are in the receiver FIFO buffer. We simply read bytes from the receiver buffer register until the FIFO buffer is empty. Reading the receiver buffer register clears the receive data interrupt condition in the ID register. As we read each byte from the UART, we write it to the receive data pipe, discarding the byte in the extremely unlikely event that the pipe is full.

The other end of the receive data pipe is read by the SerialRead() interface function, which is called by other threads in the Smart UPS program. We examined the code in SerialRead() and discussed how the thread synchronization worked in Chapter 12.

The sending of data is triggered by the transmitter-holding-register-empty interrupt, as shown here:

```
case SIO_IDXMTE: // transmit holding register empty
    // if there's chars to send in the pipe, write
    // up to MaxXmitChars to the transmit FIFO. Whether
    // or not we write a char, SIO_IDXMTE was already
    // cleared by reading the interrupt identification
    // register.  After entering the critical section,
    // double-check that xmit holding register is still
    // empty, in case SerialWrite() ran inbetween us
    // reading the ID register and entering the critical
    // section.
    EnterCriticalSection(&SerCritSec);
    if (_inp((USHORT)(UartPort + SIO_LSR)) & SIO_LSXHRE)
    {
        for (i = 0; i<MaxXmitChars && nComSendPipeBytes>0;
            ++ i, − nComSendPipeBytes)
        {
            ReadFile(hComSendRead, &ch, 1, &dwTemp, NULL);
            _outp((USHORT)(UartPort + SIO_XMITR), (int)ch);
        }
    }
    LeaveCriticalSection(&SerCritSec);
    break;
```

Notice that the I/O to the UART and the access to the send pipe are in a critical section of code. We do this because SerialWrite() also writes characters to the transmitter holding register (as you saw in Chapter 12), and we have to make sure that both the serial I/O thread and the thread that called `SerialWrite()` don't attempt to write to the transmit holding register at the same time. After acquiring the critical section object, we check whether the transmitter holding register is still empty. That happens only if a thread calling `SerialWrite()` runs after `ComThread()` reads the interrupt ID register but before ComThread() enters the critical section. That situation isn't possible in the Smart UPS, because we've made `ComThread()` the highest priority thread in the system (except for the ETS Kernel timer driver thread). But we've also designed the serial I/O subsystem as a general-purpose serial port driver; this check ensures that the code can run correctly in systems where higher priority threads call `SerialWrite()`.

Having verified that the transmitter holding register is empty and data is in the pipe, we read bytes from the pipe and write them to the transmitter holding register until either the pipe is empty or we have written the maximum number of bytes to the transmitter FIFO buffer. The transmitter register empty bit in the interrupt ID register has already been cleared by the act of reading the ID register, so this code doesn't need to do anything to clear the source of the interrupt. Let's look at the code in Listing 13-4 that performs I/O to the UART in the `SerialWrite()` routine.

Listing 13-4: The SerialWrite() function

```
DWORD SerialWrite(char *pBuf, DWORD nChar, BOOL fWait)
{
    DWORD nSent;
    DWORD nToSend;
    int   i;
    DWORD dwTemp;
    BYTE  chTemp;
//
// Initialize the number of bytes sent, and enter the
// critical section that controls access to the pipe.
//
    nSent = 0;
    EnterCriticalSection(&SerCritSec);

//
// If the write pipe is empty and the transmit holding register is
// also empty, then writing the bytes to the pipe won't work;
// the UART won't signal a transmit register empty interrupt, so
// the serial I/O thread will never read the bytes out of the
// pipe and write them to the UART.
//
// So, in that case, we write up to MaxXmitChars bytes directly
// to the UART, and then write any leftover bytes to the pipe.
// When the byte(s) we wrote to the UART get sent, it will
// issue the THRE interrupt, and the serial I/O thread can
// send the rest of the bytes.
//
```

```
WRITE_UART:
    if (nComSendPipeBytes == 0 &&
        (_inp((USHORT)(UartPort+SIO_LSR)) & SIO_LSXHRE))
    {
        for (i = 0; i < MaxXmitChars && nSent < nChar;
             ++ i, ++ pBuf, ++ nSent)
        {
            _outp((USHORT)(UartPort + SIO_XMITR), (int) *pBuf);
        }
    }

//
// Write as many characters as will fit in the pipe without blocking,
// and leave the critical section.  If we've written all the characters,
// or the caller doesn't want to wait, return the number of bytes sent.
//
WRITE_PIPE:
    nToSend = min(SER_PIPE_SIZE - nComSendPipeBytes, nChar - nSent);
    if (nToSend > 0)
    {
        WriteFile(hComSendWrite, pBuf, nToSend, &dwTemp, NULL);
        nComSendPipeBytes += nToSend;
        pBuf += nToSend;
        nSent += nToSend;
    }
    LeaveCriticalSection(&SerCritSec);
    if (nSent >= nChar || !fWait)
        return nSent;
//
// OK, we didn't write all the data, and the caller wants to block. So,
// block till we can write one char into the pipe.Then re-acquire the
// critical section, and check if the pipe is empty (except for the byte
// we just wrote to it). If so, get that byte back out of the pipe, and
// jump back to the start of the function to try to write the UART
// directly again, in case the serial I/O thread is sleeping. If there
// are bytes in the pipe, there's no danger of data not getting sent, so
// leave the byte in the pipe (updating the variables accordingly), and
// jump back to try to write the remainder of the data to the pipe.
//
    WriteFile(hComSendWrite, pBuf, 1, &dwTemp, NULL);
    EnterCriticalSection(&SerCritSec);
    if (nComSendPipeBytes == 0)
    {
        ReadFile(hComSendRead, &chTemp, 1, &dwTemp, NULL);
        goto WRITE_UART;
    }
    ++ nComSendPipeBytes;
    ++ pBuf;
    ++ nSent;
    goto WRITE_PIPE;
}
```

`SerialWrite()` acquires the critical section object before attempting any UART I/O; this is necessary to prevent interference with the code in the serial I/O thread that also writes to the UART transmitter holding register. If the send pipe is currently empty and the transmitter holding register is also empty, the serial I/O thread isn't trying to send data and isn't going to get a transmitter-holding-register-empty interrupt, so if we just add bytes to the send pipe, they will never get sent! Therefore, if both the pipe and the transmitter holding register are empty, `SerialWrite()` writes up to `MaxXmitChars` bytes directly to the transmitter FIFO buffer (recall that `MaxXmitChars` is set to 1 for the 8250 and 16450, which have no FIFO buffer). Then `SerialWrite()` writes the rest of the data to the send pipe to be processed by the serial I/O thread, which wakes up because of the interrupt when the bytes in the transmitter FIFO buffer get sent. We've already discussed (in Chapter 12) the synchronization logic in `SerialWrite()` for writing the pipe and blocking when the pipe is full.

The next `case` clause handles interrupts generated by changes in the state of the RS-232 handshaking signals:

```
case SIO_IDMSR:  // modem status register changed
    // Read MSR to clear it
    _inp((USHORT)(UartPort + SIO_MSR));
    break;
```

The code in this clause reads the modem status register. Reading the register clears the source of the interrupt and provides information on why the interrupt occurred. We've left the remainder of this clause empty because our application doesn't require it. The code skeleton has been left in place for you in case you want to modify the code for a more elaborate serial I/O subsystem.

> **Note:** You might want to enhance the serial I/O subsystem to use the signals in the modem status register. For example, a modem sets the Data Carrier Detect (DCD) line active if the modem detects a carrier signal on the phone line (meaning that it has established a connection with the remote modem on the other end of the phone line). If the Data Carrier Detect signal becomes inactive, that could indicate that the other modem has hung up or somehow the phone connection has been lost. The change in DCD triggers an interrupt. A more elaborate serial I/O handler, responding to the interrupt, could determine when the interrupt was caused by a lost carrier detect signal and close the connection or take other appropriate action.

Similarly, the following clause, introduced by `SIO_IDRLS`, responds to interrupts that involve the line status register:

```
case SIO_IDRLS:  // received line state register changed
    // Read LSR to clear it
    _inp((USHORT)(UartPort + SIO_LSR));
    break;
```

Events that could trigger this interrupt are generated by error conditions: parity errors, framing errors, or overrun errors. As in the preceding clause, we must read the register to clear the register's contents so that any future interrupt won't be misinterpreted as having been generated by the line status register. Also, this application doesn't perform any error handling, so the clause is immediately exited (with the `break` statement). We've left this skeleton in case you want to modify the code for your own serial I/O subsystem. For example, you could add code that responds to the detection of a parity error by informing the user or perhaps sending a request to the transmitting computer asking that it resend the bad character.

SUMMARY

Serial communication is everywhere. It's used for wide area network connections over telephone lines or radio links, to connect peripherals to your desktop computer, and to transfer data between two computers sitting next to each other. It's even used for buses to connect chips to a CPU. Chip-to-chip serial buses and peripheral serial buses offer two attractive advantages to the developer of embedded systems: They provide lower power consumption and smaller space requirements than parallel buses used in the same capacity.

In this chapter, we introduced you to some fundamental concepts in serial communications. We looked at the details of RS-232, the most widely used standard for serial communications. We examined the 8250/16x50 family of UARTs (the de facto UART standard for embedded and desktop PC computers). Finally, we concluded our exploration of the Smart UPS project's serial I/O subsystem. To implement efficient serial I/O, you need a combination of software tools you've already met. In Chapter 12, "Multitasking," you saw how ISRs, synchronization objects, and intertask communications objects are used in the serial I/O subsystem. In this chapter, we concentrated on the code that performs the I/O to the UART, controlling the actual transmission and reception of characters on the serial line.

CHAPTER

14

A Network-Aware UPS

In the past, networking capabilities were included only in embedded products — such as printers, fax machines, and routers — that were designed to be accessed over a network to perform their primary function. Now as network access and, even more importantly, Internet access in the workplace becomes more the rule than the exception, it's crucial to consider whether your embedded products should be accessible over a network or the Internet. One of the most important benefits to including network and Internet support is remote access.

Being able to remotely access an embedded system makes many tasks not only possible but convenient. Remote data collection is a good example. If an embedded system is on a network or the Internet, a user can schedule regular automatic data downloads, receive up-to-the-minute data updates on demand, route data so that output from one system is input to another system, and so on, regardless of whether the embedded system is down the hall or thousands of miles away.

Remote device configuration and maintenance are two other examples. Embedded systems that can be remotely accessed over a network or the Internet are easier to configure, maintain, upgrade, and monitor than standalone systems. Much can be reconfigured, corrected, patched, added, and watched by dialing in or logging on. And the relative ease with which you can accomplish these tasks over a network or an Internet connection often results in your performing them more frequently and more quickly. The benefit of frequent maintenance, upgrades, and monitoring is preventing problems; the benefit of speed is less downtime when problems do occur.

You can't do everything over a network or the Internet; sometimes only an on-site visit will do. But even then, you experience the benefits of a networked system, because you can understand the status of the system before heading out to the field, rather than after you arrive. By knowing the situation in advance, you can bring the proper tools and equipment: the part that needs to be replaced or the software that needs to patched, for example. You arrive knowing — rather than hoping — that you have what you need to work on the system.

Undoubtedly, the use of networking in embedded systems has been spurred by the Internet and the World Wide Web. Their growth and popularity have resulted in the following:

- **Worldwide connections.** Using the Internet, you can connect to an embedded system that's practically anywhere in the world, and you can do so through a local connection to an Internet service provider (ISP).

- **Standard protocols.** Specific networking technologies have become standard, not only for the Internet and the Web, but also for networks. TCP/IP, PPP, SLIP, Ethernet, and HTTP are the protocols used for Internet and intranet communications.

- **A platform-independent interface.** The web browser has been called the universal GUI. This is because, using HTML, you can create an interactive interface that runs on any platform using an Internet-compliant web browser.

Developers of embedded systems can use networking capabilities to add new product features and to realize programming efficiencies. For example, standard protocols and a web browser make it feasible to include online documentation and configuration information in some embedded systems. Licensing standardized networking software packages for use in your system enables quicker product development cycles — an important feature in a world where time to market often determines a product's success.

To demonstrate the benefits of connectivity, as well as how to implement networking using standard Internet and Web protocols, this chapter presents a Network-Aware UPS. This UPS is accessible over a TCP/IP network connection and uses a standard Internet web browser as its interface. By incorporating these widely accepted standards into our application, we made our application compatible with most company networks and jettisoned our proprietary host side and communications software from the Smart UPS. In addition, using components (TCP/IP, web servers, and web browser) available from a number of sources, rather than writing code from scratch, we built our product quickly. We also improved product usability; rather than requiring users to install and use a proprietary front-end program to communicate with the UPS, we allow them to use their familiar web browser.

As you might anticipate, this product specification contains many networking terms. If you're not familiar with them, bear with us; they are explained in subsequent chapters. Specifically, in Chapter 15, "Networking," we discuss networking and various protocols; and in Chapter 16, "Connecting to the Web," we explore web servers and their respective protocols as well as HTML.

HOW THE NETWORK-AWARE UPS PROJECT WORKS

The network-aware version of our UPS is an enhancement of the Smart UPS we specified in Chapter 11. The goal for this project is the same as it was for Chapter 11: to build a UPS capable of being accessed remotely. What's different is the solution. Recall that the Smart UPS talked to a remote host over a dedicated serial connection, using a proprietary communications protocol to converse with a proprietary. GUI application. Our Network-Aware UPS communicates to a remote host over an industry-standard TCP/IP network connection, and converses with any Internet-compliant web browser.

To build this UPS, we use the same hardware components as specified in Chapter 11: a system controller, a battery, a battery charger, battery and load monitors, an AC line monitor, an inverter, switches, a pushbutton, indicator lights, a speaker, a host PC, and a serial cable. In addition, we need to make sure we have the hardware for a network connection.

Because different customers have different networking requirements, we build this UPS with the hardware necessary for one of three network-connection configurations. The first configuration uses the serial I/O port already on the system controller for the UPS. This enables users to connect from a host to the UPS using either a direct serial connection or an external modem and phone line. The second configuration includes an internal modem, for users who know they want to make a phone connection to the UPS. The third configuration includes an Ethernet card. This enables users to connect from an intranet, a network within a company or organization.

No matter which communications configuration a customer chooses, the UPS works the same. The UPS software uses an Internet-compliant web server to send status information to and receive configuration information from a web browser, such as Microsoft Internet Explorer or Netscape Navigator, running on a host. The web server does this by embedding the information in HTML (Hypertext Markup Language) commands, and transferring the HTML page to a web browser using HTTP (Hypertext Transfer Protocol). The browser on the host interprets the HTML code and displays a web page showing the UPS status information, as well as buttons that, if clicked, send configuration commands back to the UPS.

The underlying network stack uses TCP/IP (Transmission Control Protocol/Internet Protocol), which we selected because it's the most popular worldwide networking protocol. For the serial connection, we selected the PPP (Point-to-Point Protocol) network interface protocol rather than SLIP (Serial Line Internet Protocol), because PPP is more flexible and popular. For the Ethernet connection, we use the Ethernet network interface protocol.

DESIGNING THE SIMULATION

For our simulation of the Network-Aware UPS, we chose the direct serial connection configuration for two reasons. First, ToolSuite Lite does not include Ethernet drivers in its networking support; you have to purchase the full version of ToolSuite for Ethernet capability. Second, we didn't want to require you to have two modems and two phone lines (one each for the host and the embedded target) to run the simulation. As in the Smart UPS project, we use a LapLink-compatible null modem cable to connect the target machine running the UPS simulation to the host computer.

Note: The host computer for the network connection doesn't have to be the same as the Windows host computer you use to build, download, and debug programs. It can be any computer that runs a web browser and supports PPP network connections over a direct serial link.

As usual, we start the simulation design by creating the user interface. In this project, a web browser displays the user interface by processing the HTML commands in the web page created by the UPS system. As you can see in Figure 14-1, our interface design is similar to the proprietary GUI interface we built for the Smart UPS.

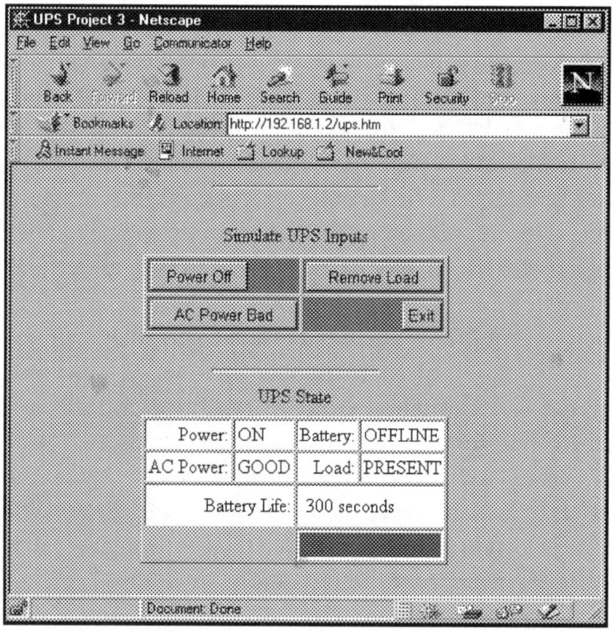

Figure 14-1: The user interface for the Network-Aware UPS runs under any compliant web browser, such as Netscape Navigator (shown here) or Microsoft Internet Explorer.

The upper section of the user interface contains pushbuttons to simulate inputs to the UPS. Clicking a button sends a request for a new web page; encoded in the request is information identifying the button. The UPS system simulates the input specified by the button and then returns a new page containing the updated system status.

Notice that this interface contains the Exit button, which didn't exist in the Smart UPS. Because the user interface for the Smart UPS is a dedicated program, it knows to tell the UPS simulation to exit when the user closes the program. A web browser, however, is a general-purpose application that can access any web site; you don't necessarily want to exit the web browser when you have finished accessing the UPS; even if you did want to exit, the web browser wouldn't inform the UPS that it was terminating. Because no implicit termination is present, we have to add an explicit button to tell the UPS simulation to exit.

The lower section of the user interface consists of a table containing text entries showing the state of the simulated lights on the UPS, plus a bar graph showing the battery life remaining. The HTTP response returned by the web server contains a header field that instructs the web browser to automatically request a refresh of the web page every 5 seconds. This automatic update allows the battery life indicator to track the current state of the UPS system.

When the battery is discharging (because the AC is bad and a load is present), the UPS system beeps the speaker every 5 seconds. When the battery life is below 30 seconds, the UPS beeps every 2 seconds to warn the user that the battery is about to run out. When the AC power changes to good again, the battery recharges at a 50 percent rate (that is, for every 2 seconds it recharges, the battery life increases by 1 second).

Finally, if users select an invalid input (for example, they attempt to add a load when the AC power is bad and the battery life has run down to zero), the server adds a third section to the web page containing the text of an error message.

SOFTWARE SUBSYSTEMS

By now, you're familiar with the core subsystems in the UPS projects. A block diagram showing the subsystems in the Network-Aware UPS is depicted in Figure 14-2. The diagram is similar to the subsystem diagram for the Smart UPS project because it includes a few of the same subsystems — specifically, the timer, messaging, and event subsystems.

The timer and messaging subsystems are implemented exactly as they were in the Smart UPS. The event subsystem is almost the same. In the Smart UPS, the event subsystem sends a response back to the host computer by calling the serial I/O subsystem. Here, the event subsystem pipes the UPS status to the web server subsystem, which has replaced the serial I/O and command receive subsystems.

The job of the web server subsystem is to handle HTTP requests that come over the network, add simulated events specified by the button press encoded in the HTTP request to the message queue, package into an HTML page the UPS status piped from the event subsystem, and send the HTML page to the browser. If you think the web server subsystem has a lot to do, you're right. However, the TCP/IP support and the HTTP server are software components supplied with ETS Kernel. All the web server subsystem has to do itself is handle the communications with the messaging and event subsystems, and create the HTML page when requested. Here, again, it has help. ETS Kernel includes HTML-on-the-Fly, a library that assists in building the HTML page. So, although the web server subsystem has a lot of work to do, we have to write only a small amount of code to implement the necessary functionality.

SOFTWARE INTERFACES

You've seen in previous UPS projects the software interfaces for all the subsystems except the web server subsystem, so we look at the web server subsystem here. As before, UPS.H contains prototypes for the interface functions for all subsystems.

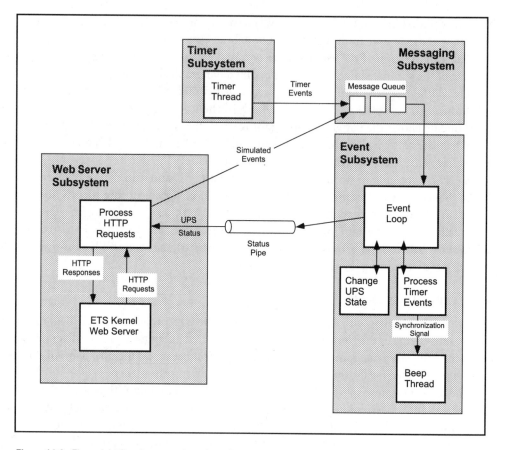

Figure 14-2: The serial I/O and command receive subsystems in the Smart UPS are replaced by the web server subsystem in the Network-Aware UPS.

The web server subsystem provides two interface functions to the rest of UPS3.EXE, the Network-Aware UPS program:

- **BOOL InitWebsys(BOOL fCom1)**. UPS3 calls InitWebsys() at start-up to initialize the PPP and serial drivers and start the HTTP server. It returns TRUE if initialization succeeds or FALSE otherwise.

- **void CleanupWebsys(void)**. UPS3 calls the CleanupWebsys() function at shutdown to shut down the HTTP server and clean up allocated resources.

In addition, the web server subsystem implements functions required by the HTTP server component of ETS Kernel. You can find prototypes for these functions in \TSLITE\INCLUDE\HTTPSERV.H:

- **void GetURI(REQ_INPUTS *pInp, REQ_OUTPUTS *pOutp)**. The HTTP server calls GetURI() when it receives an HTTP request for the document at a URI (Uniform Resource

Beyond Simulation

The differences between the simulation and an actual UPS system are similar to the differences we noted for the Smart UPS simulation.

The timer and messaging subsystems would be unchanged. In the web server subsystem, you'd need to modify the HTML page to have only one button, the Power On/Off button. This would allow a user to turn off power to the load from a remote location, without walking over to the UPS box. The buttons to add or remove a load and to simulate good or bad AC power would disappear, because those are hardware inputs on a real UPS. The UPS state information in the HTML page would be unchanged.

The remaining differences are those we describe in previous UPS projects: namely, adding software subsystems that handle the hardware I/O and generate events for the battery, load, and AC power; and modifying the event subsystem to control the status lights on the UPS box, in addition to sending UPS status to the web browser.

Identifier) from the web browser. This function processes any parameters (such as buttons that were pushed) that arrive as part of the request, and returns an HTML document that is sent to the browser. You look at the REQ_INPUTS and REQ_OUTPUTS structures (also found in HTTPSERV.H) later when you examine the code for this subsystem.

- **void WebServerError(BOOL fFatal, char *pErrMsg)**. When an error occurs, the HTTP server calls WebServerError(). The web server subsystem prints the error message and, if it's flagged as a fatal error, calls the FatalErr() function to shut down the program.

Note: A Universal Resource Locator (URL) is the fully qualified name of a page on the Internet; it includes a protocol name, a host computer name, and a page name on that host. A Uniform Resource Identifier (URI) is the page name on the host computer. You type the full URL into the Location, Address, or URL field on your browser. The browser connects to the specified host computer using the specified protocol and sends a request for a web page at the specified URI to that host. For example, http://developer.intel.com/sites /developer/index.htm is a URL; /sites/developer/index.htm is the web page your browser would request from the HTTP server running on the developer.intel.com host.

START-UP AND SHUTDOWN PROCESSES

Start-up and shutdown for the Network-Aware UPS resembles that performed for the Smart UPS project. All new code is in the web server subsystem. At start-up, the web server subsystem initializes the configuration information needed by the PPP driver to accept connections from a Windows host. The subsystem then starts the HTTP server, which creates a thread to listen for HTTP connections from a web browser. At shutdown, the web server subsystem stops the HTTP server and cleans up any resources it allocated.

ERROR HANDLING

Error handling in the Network-Aware UPS is the same as in the previous UPS projects. Initialization errors are handled by printing an error message and terminating the program. Fatal errors during program execution are handled by printing an error message, shutting down each subsystem, and exiting. In Chapter 20, "C++ Exceptions and Structured Exceptions," you see a version of the UPS project that restarts the system when a fatal error occurs.

BUILDING THE NETWORK-AWARE UPS PROJECT

The Network-Aware UPS project is in TSLITE\PROJECTS\UPS3. A prebuilt executable, UPS3.EXE, is provided if you want to skip the build step. To build the executable from Visual C++ Developer Studio, open the workspace file (UPS3.DSW) and click Build|Rebuild All. Chapter 3, "Software Installation and Setup," contains complete details on building the projects.

RUNNING THE NETWORK-AWARE UPS PROJECT

Before executing UPS3.EXE, make sure you have correctly connected the target system to the host computer. Figure 14-3 shows the recommended configuration.

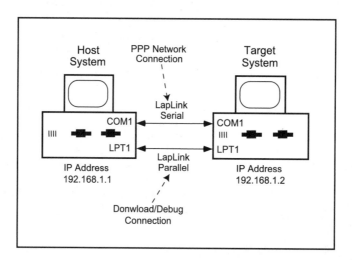

Figure 14-3: The host and target are connected by two cables: a parallel cable used for downloading and debugging, and a serial cable used for the network connection.

The network connection is over a LapLink-compatible serial cable that connects the COM1 ports on the host and target. The download and debug connection is over a LapLink-compatible parallel cable that connects the LPT1 ports on the host and target.

Unlike the connection diagram in Figure 11-4 of Chapter 11, Figure 14-3 includes the IP addresses of the host and target systems, 192.168.1.1 and 192.168.1.2, respectively. We've selected IP addresses from a block of IP addresses reserved for testing; that is, these IP addresses will never occur in a real network. This is important, because it prevents any possibility of conflict with other networks to which your Windows host computer may be connected. We explain IP test addresses in much more detail in Chapter 15, "Networking."

The next step before running the program is to create a new connection entry in the Dial-Up Networking program on your Windows host computer. Appendix C, "Configuring Serial Networking Connections for Windows," contains step-by-step instructions for doing this under Windows 95, 98, and NT. When you're finished, the Dial-Up Networking phone book will have a new connection icon as shown in Figure 14-4. We name ours UPS Connection.

> **Note:** If you have two serial ports on each computer, you can use two serial cables, one for downloading and debugging and the other for the network connection. Connect COM1 to COM1, and COM2 to COM2. Chapter 3, "Software Installation and Setup," tells you how to configure ETS Kernel and the host side software for downloading and debugging using a serial connection. If you choose to use the COM2 ports for the network connection, you have to instruct both the host and the target UPS program to use COM2. On the host system, right-click your Dial-Up Networking connection icon, choose Properties, under the General tab click Configure, and then select port COM2. On the target system, give the UPS program the parameter com2 on the command line. From Developer Studio, choose Project|Settings, choose the Debug tab, and enter com2 in the Program arguments box. From the DOS command prompt, set the current directory to \TSLITE\PROJECTS\UPS3, and type the command runemb release\ups3 com2.

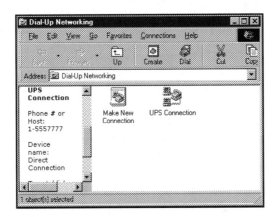

Figure 14-4: We created a dial-up connection from the host to the UPS.

> **Note:** If you use Windows NT, you have to make a small change to the project source code. For direct (non-modem) connections initiated by all versions of Windows, the Windows host sends an ASCII prompt as part of the connection setup process. This prompt is different for Windows 95/98 and Windows NT. The code for the Network-Aware UPS project assumes the prompt used by Windows 95 and 98 (the telephone number you configured in the Dial-Up Networking connection). If you use Windows NT as your host, you must edit the WEBMEM.C

file and rebuild the UPS application to get your network connection to work. In the function `SetupSerialConnection()`, change the line

```
SEArray[0].Expect = "5557777\x0D";
```

to read

```
SEArray[0].Expect = "CLIENT";
```

You're finally ready to run the Network-Aware UPS program. From Developer Studio, download and execute the UPS application by selecting Build|Execute ups3.exe. Or if you prefer, from a DOS command prompt set the current directory to \TSLITE\PROJECTS\UPS3 and type:

```
runemb release\ups3
```

After UPS3.EXE has been downloaded to the target system, double-click the UPS Connection icon in your Dial-Up Networking window on the host. The Connect To dialog box shown in Figure 14-5 appears.

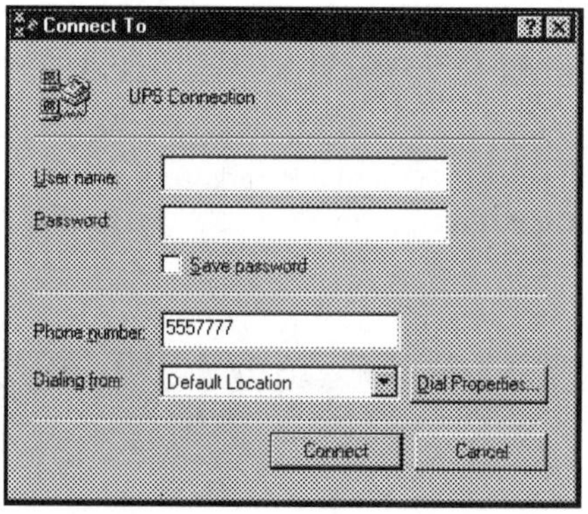

Figure 14-5: You connect to the UPS system as you would to the Web.

Click the Connect button to initiate the connection with the UPS target system. You should see the series of windows shown in Figure 14-6 as the connection is established.

Now that you've established a network connection between the Windows host and the embedded target, the next step is to start your favorite web browser on your host computer. In the Address, Location, or URL box, enter `http://192.168.1.2/` as the destination URL (Universal Resource Locator). Recall that 192.168.1.2 is the IP address of the embedded target. Because we've just set up a temporary network using test IP addresses, no name is associated with these IP addresses, and we have to enter the IP address rather than a host name. The browser will connect to the HTTP server on the target at IP address 192.168.1.2 (the UPS machine) and request the page at URI /. (The forward slash indicates a request for the top level, or home, page.) After the Network-Aware UPS returns the web page, your browser displays the information shown in Figure 14-7.

The home page shows two links. Click the "About this UPS system" link to display the web page, shown in Figure 14-8, which has a short description.

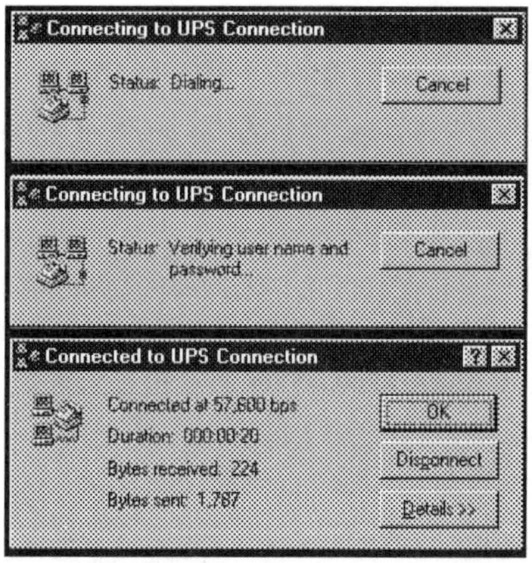

Figure 14-6: These dialog boxes are displayed in succession when you connect to the target. After the connection is established, you can use your web browser to interact with the UPS system.

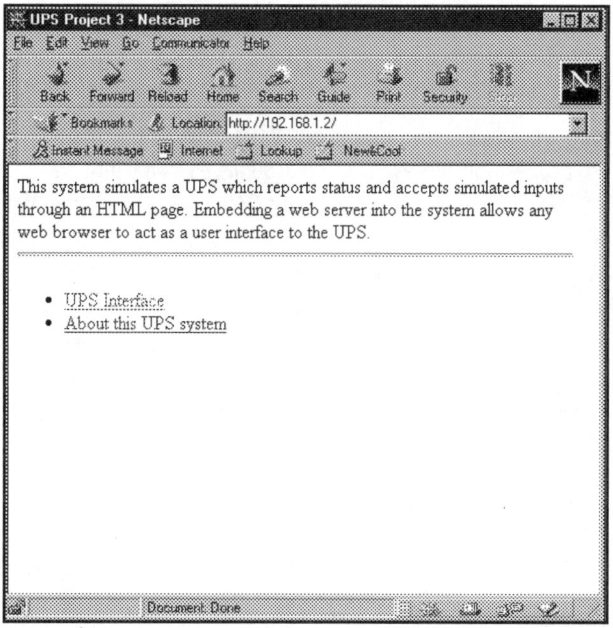

Figure 14-7: The home page for the Network-Aware UPS project.

We included the "About this UPS system" link to point out another benefit to networking embedded systems: having online help and documentation. Online documentation is useful, especially for users not physically located in the same building as the device (which is where the paper documentation is likely to be). Also, documentation in paper form is easily lost. By having a networked device store its own documentation, the documentation is always available.

Troubleshooting the Network Connection

If you can't establish a network connection, it's probably due to a setup or configuration problem. Try the following suggestions to track down the source of the problem:

- **Check the cable.** Check your null modem cable connection to make sure the cable is plugged into the correct ports. Try to run another communications program, such as LapLink, over the cable connection. If it doesn't work, you probably have a bad cable. Try another cable, and verify that the cable wiring conforms to the specifications listed in Appendix C.

- **Check the software configuration.** If you've verified that the cable connection works, the next item to check is the software configuration. Check your Dial-Up Networking connection Properties on the host computer to make sure you've selected the correct COM port and direct cable connection serial driver, as described in Appendix C. If you're using COM2 on the target computer, make sure you correctly entered com2 as a command-line parameter when you ran the UPS3.EXE program. If your software configuration is correct, reduce the baud rate as described next. If you're running under Windows NT, make sure you've made the code change to WEBMEM.C described in an earlier note. Finally, if you've made any changes to the UPS source code, make sure you remembered to rebuild the executable file.

- **Try a slower baud rate.** The serial port parameters used for the UPS project are 57600 baud with RTS/CTS hardware handshaking enabled, 8 data bits, no parity, and 1 stop bit. If either the host or the target computer does not have a UART with a data buffer (the 16550 UART has a buffer, but the 16450 and 8250 do not), characters may occasionally be lost at such a high baud rate. This is because even with hardware handshaking, the data flow may not be turned off quickly enough. If you can't establish a network connection, try using 38400 or even 19200 baud. You have to edit WEBMEM.C to change the hardwired baud rate in the SetupSerialConnection() function. In addition, you have to change the baud rate for the Dial-Up Networking connection you set up on the host. (In the Dial-Up Networking dialog box, choose File|Properties. Click the Configure button, and change the Maximum speed setting.)

- **Check the connection log file.** Open the Properties for the Dial-Up Networking connection, under the General tab click Configure, under the Connection tab click Advanced, and click View Log. The information saved by the Windows serial driver in the log file may assist you in determining the source of the problem.

- **Abort the UPS application.** How do you shut down the target program without rebooting if you're unable to establish a network connection? Simply make the DOS box used to download the UPS program (either the DOS box automatically created by Developer Studio when you ran the program or the DOS box you used to enter the RUNEMB download command) the current window. Then press Ctrl-Break simultaneously to kill the UPS application program.

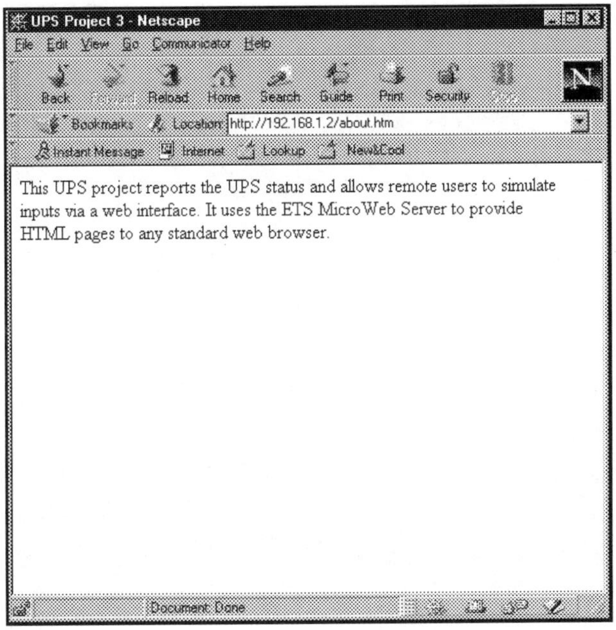

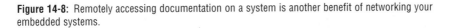

Figure 14-8: Remotely accessing documentation on a system is another benefit of networking your embedded systems.

Moreover, if a system implements a web server and has local file system storage, you can store an HTML manual on your embedded system, complete with indexes and links.

Now go back to the home page of the UPS and click the "UPS Interface" link. The user interface to the UPS, shown in Figure 14-9, is displayed.

As noted, this page contains two sections implemented as HTML tables. The top table consists of four pushbuttons used to simulate UPS inputs. The bottom table displays the current UPS status. You will notice that the display keeps refreshing. Each web page sent to the browser includes a header field that instructs the browser to request an update in 5 seconds. We inspect the HTML code for this web page in Chapter 16.

Although it's not apparent from the display, the generation of the HTML page is dynamic. That is, when the web server receives a request, it constructs the HTML page in memory, providing up-to-the-microsecond information about the device. The capability to generate HTML on demand is key to using the Internet for viewing and controlling a real-time system.

The Network-Aware UPS responds to simulated inputs in the same way as the Smart UPS. For example, add a load, turn on power to the load, and set the AC power to bad. The battery starts discharging, and the UPS machine beeps every 5 seconds to indicate the AC power bad condition. The web browser updates the host display approximately every 5 seconds as it automatically requests new web pages from the UPS system. This allows the user to see the battery discharging, as shown in Figure 14-10.

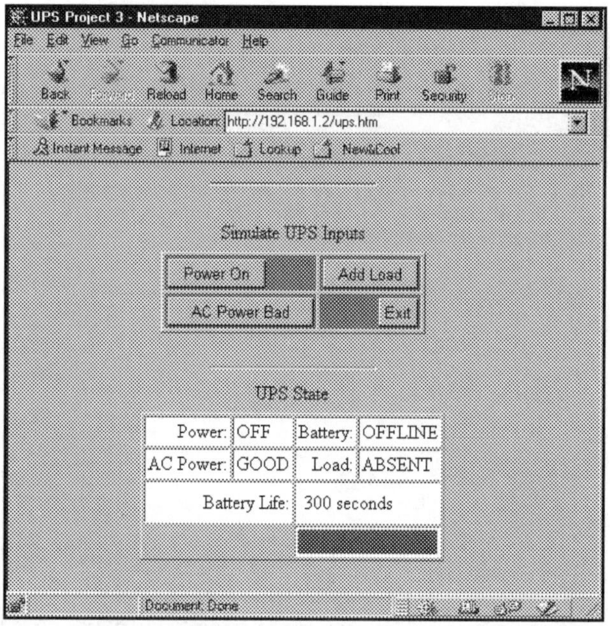

Figure 14-9: The user interface for the Network-Aware UPS system.

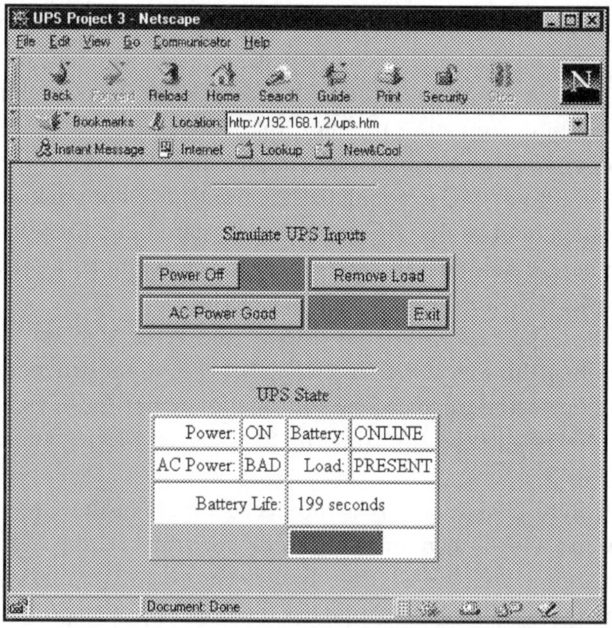

Figure 14-10. The user can see the UPS battery continuously discharging when the AC power is bad.

Note: The bar graph for the battery life indicator uses a relatively obscure HTML feature that allows a GIF file (in this case, a single pixel) to be replicated as many times as necessary to fill a percentage of a table cell. We tested this feature on Netscape Navigator 4.0 and Microsoft Internet Explorer 4.0; it's possible the bar graph may not display correctly on other web browsers.

If you click the Exit button to exit the application, the UPS returns a status page as shown in Figure 14-11. The status page notifies the browser that the UPS application is exiting. The UPS then shuts down the network connection and terminates.

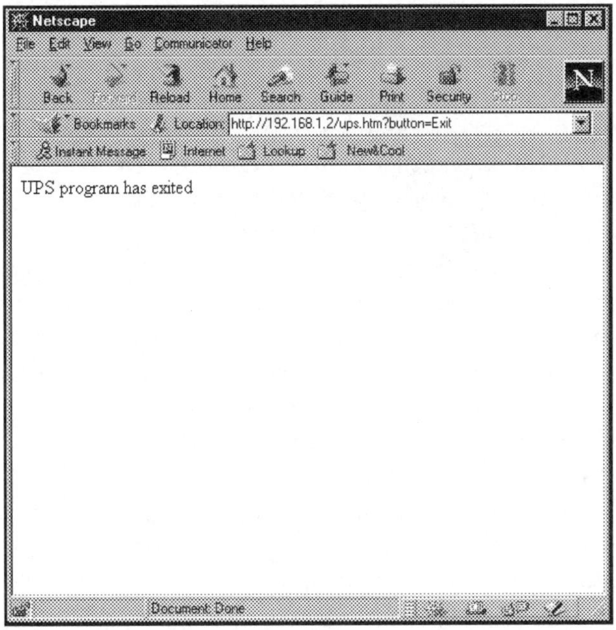

Figure 14-11: The UPS tells the web browser it's exiting by sending it a status page.

The Dial-Up Networking connection then detects that the PPP connection has terminated and displays the dialog box in Figure 14-12.

Click Cancel to terminate the Dial-Up Networking connection on the host side. You can't reestablish the connection after the target program has exited. To reconnect, you must restart the UPS program and then click Connect from the Dial-Up Networking Connect To window, which is shown in Figure 14-5.

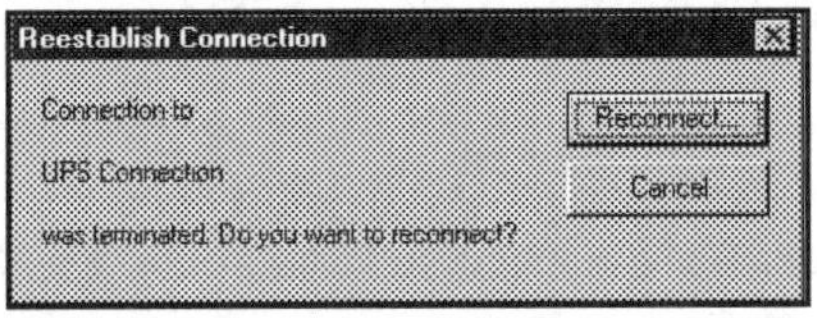

Figure 14-12: If you're using a direct serial connection, you can't reestablish a connection after the UPS program has terminated.

Other Network Configurations

We chose the simplest network configuration we could find for this project to make it easy for you to get this program running. Other network configurations, however, are supported under ToolSuite.

As mentioned, the full version of ToolSuite (but not ToolSuite Lite) supports Ethernet network connections. On an Ethernet network, you can directly communicate with any other host on your local intranet, and if your local network is connected to the Internet, you can communicate with any host on it. Communication with hosts on other networks is transparent to the application program. The TCP/IP software automatically sends traffic destined for other networks to a gateway computer (also called a router) on the local intranet; the gateway forwards the traffic (perhaps through several other gateways) to its final destination. We describe this in more detail in Chapter 15, "Networking."

With a serial connection, by definition you are directly connected to only one other host. However, serial connections also support gateways. For example, when you dial an ISP (Internet service provider) from home, the ISP acts as a gateway that forwards your computer's network traffic to other hosts on the Internet. In this UPS project, we configured the PPP driver to assume that no gateway is present. In fact, Windows 95 and 98 cannot act as a gateway for another machine connected through a serial connection (now you know for sure that your ISP doesn't run Windows 95 or 98). Windows NT can act as a gateway, but not in the configuration used for this project, in which the embedded target waits for the connection and the Windows machine initiates the connection. If we turned it around and had Windows NT wait for the connection and the embedded target dial in over a phone line (not over a direct null modem connection), we'd be able to use the routing capabilities of Windows NT.

Another limitation of this UPS project is that only one network connection can be made for the duration of the ETS Kernel program. This is a limitation of direct null modem connections under ToolSuite. If a connection was made over a modem, multiple network connections would be possible during a single run of the UPS application. For example, after starting the UPS program on the target, Computer A could dial in, connect to the embedded target, and check the UPS status and simulate some inputs. After the user on Computer A is finished and disconnects (by clicking Disconnect in the Dial-Up Networking connection window), Computer B could then dial in to talk to the UPS.

Networking connections are flexible and therefore complicated. In the full version of ToolSuite, an entire manual is devoted to how to configure, establish, and debug different kinds of network connections. In this book, we want to explain the basics of networking rather than all the possible configuration options and their details, so we show you only one way to set up the connection.

A QUICK TOUR OF THE SOURCE

With the exception of the source code for the web server subsystem in WEBMEM.C, you've seen all the source code in the Network-Aware UPS from the previous UPS projects. We examine the code for the interface between the event subsystem and the web server subsystem here, and look at the web server subsystem in detail in Chapter 16.

The web server subsystem interfaces with the event subsystem in two ways. First, it sends events to the event subsystem that result from a user clicking buttons in the web browser to simulate UPS inputs. These events are sent using the event message queue, the same mechanism used by the Smart UPS in Chapter 11.

Second, the web server subsystem needs to get the current UPS status from the event subsystem after it has finished processing a simulated event. We chose to send this information using a pipe, which is designed for one-way transfer of information between two threads. Using a pipe is suitable also because we can block on an empty pipe. The web server subsystem has to wait for the event subsystem to process a simulated event; it's much better to write the code so the web server subsystem blocks and doesn't consume any CPU cycles, rather than have it spin in a busy loop waiting for the event subsystem to complete.

We'll examine code from two files: WEBMEM.C and EVENT.C. WEBMEM.C contains the UpsInterface() function, which is invoked to generate the UPS interface (the web page containing the UPS status and the simulated input buttons). At the top of this function is code to interact with the event subsystem. UpsInterface() queues a command (either a simulated input, if the user clicked a button, or a request for UPS status, if the browser is refreshing the web page) for the event subsystem to process. UpsInterface() then waits for the event subsystem to send UPS status information through the status pipe. After UpsInterface() has the status information, it generates the web page (we see this code in Chapter 16) and returns it to the browser. EVENT.C contains the SendStatus() function, which sends UPS status information through the pipe. We won't revisit the code that reads simulated events from the event message queue and processes them, because we described it for the Smart UPS.

Let's look first at the code in UpsInterface() that sends a simulated input or a status request to the event subsystem. The function has already determined which button was clicked or if no button was clicked (in which case we simply request the status without simulating an input); you see this code in Chapter 16.

```
//
// Send the command to the event subsystem, and wait for the
// response.  If we time out on the communication, we just
// return an error message for our HTML page.
//
    StartTime = GetTickCount();
    while (TRUE)
    {
        if (MsgWrite(hEventQueue, &Event, FALSE) == 1)
            break;
        Sleep(10);
        if (GetTickCount() - StartTime > EVENT_TIMEOUT)
        {
            html_text("Server error: timeout sending to event thread\n");
            goto DONE_NO_REFRESH;
        }
    }
```

```
if (Event.Event == EVENT_EXIT)
{
    html_text("UPS program has exited\n");
    goto DONE_NO_REFRESH;
}
```

We call MsgWrite() to write the simulated event or status request to the event queue maintained by the messaging subsystem. We want to be able to time out if the queue is full and isn't being emptied by the event subsystem for some reason (that is, the program has a bug), so we instruct MsgWrite() not to wait if the queue is full. We keep calling MsgWrite() in a loop, calling Sleep() between calls so we don't consume too much CPU time, until the write succeeds or we exceed the timeout.

If the simulated event received is EVENT_EXIT (the user clicked the Exit button in the browser window), we create a simple web page that notifies the user that the UPS system is terminating and exit from the UpsInterface() function, without waiting for the event subsystem to send back the UPS status (it won't anyway, because it and the rest of the system are shutting down).

If the simulated event received is something other than EVENT_EXIT, the event subsystem calls SendStatus() to send the status of the UPS to the web server subsystem, as shown here:

```
//
// Sends status to the web server thread.
//
void SendStatus(char *pErrMsg)
{
    UPS_STATUS Status;
    DWORD      dwTemp;

// Build the status structure.
    Status.State = CurrState;
    Status.msBatteryLife = msBatteryLife;
    Status.msMaxLife = MAX_BATTERY_LIFE;
    Status.ErrLen = strlen(pErrMsg);
    if (Status.ErrLen > 0)
        ++Status.ErrLen;

//
// Write the status structure, and error message string if any,
// to the UPS status pipe.
//
    WriteFile(hStatusPipeWrite, &Status, sizeof(Status), &dwTemp, NULL);
    if (Status.ErrLen > 0)
        WriteFile(hStatusPipeWrite, pErrMsg, Status.ErrLen, &dwTemp, NULL);

    return;
}
```

This straightforward function packages the information about the UPS status in a structure, and sends it through the status pipe by calling WriteFile(), a Win32 function. If the event subsystem sends an error message string with the status, the string (including the terminating zero character) is written to the pipe immediately after the structure. The length of the error message string is included in the status structure, so the web server subsystem knows whether an error message is present and, if so, its length.

We return now to the `UpsInterface()` function. The next order of business is to get the UPS status from the event subsystem. To do this, we call `WaitForSingleObject()` on the status pipe, passing it the time remaining until our timeout is exceeded. `WaitForSingleObject()` blocks until data to read is in the pipe or until the timeout value is reached. If data is in the pipe before the timeout is reached, `ReadFile()` is called to read the status structure from the pipe. If an error message string is associated with the status, we call `WaitForSingleObject()` and then call `ReadFile()` a second time to read the error message, as follows:

```
ElapsedTime = GetTickCount() - StartTime;
if (ElapsedTime > EVENT_TIMEOUT ||
    WaitForSingleObject(hStatusPipeRead,
            EVENT_TIMEOUT - ElapsedTime) != WAIT_OBJECT_0)
{
    html_text("Server error: timeout receiving from event thread\n");
    goto DONE_NO_REFRESH;
}
if (!ReadFile(hStatusPipeRead, &Status, sizeof(Status), &Len,
            NULL) || Len != sizeof(Status))
{
    html_text("Server error: read error receiving from "
            "event thread\n");
    goto DONE_NO_REFRESH;
}
if (Status.ErrLen > 0)
{
    ElapsedTime = GetTickCount() - StartTime;
    if (ElapsedTime > EVENT_TIMEOUT ||
        WaitForSingleObject(hStatusPipeRead,
                EVENT_TIMEOUT - ElapsedTime) != WAIT_OBJECT_0)
    {
        html_text("Server error: timeout receiving from "
                "event thread\n");
        goto DONE_NO_REFRESH;
    }
    if (!ReadFile(hStatusPipeRead, ErrMsg, Status.ErrLen, &Len,
                NULL) || Len != Status.ErrLen)
    {
        html_text("Server error: read error receiving from "
                "event thread\n");
        goto DONE_NO_REFRESH;
    }
}
```

As you can see, checks throughout this code determine whether more than EVENT_TIME-OUT milliseconds (#defined in WEBMEM.C as 1000 milliseconds) have elapsed since we started processing the request. If we exceed the timeout, the function gives up and returns an error message to the browser in an HTML page. Unless the program has a bug, we should never come close to exceeding this timeout. The checks ensure that we send a response to the web browser and don't block forever if we do encounter a bug.

`UpsInterface()` then goes on to construct the web page it will send to the web browser. You look at that code, too, in Chapter 16.

SUMMARY

Implementing networking in an embedded system allows remote access to the system, which has many advantages. This remote access capability enables you to maintain, upgrade, and monitor systems easily, frequently, and quickly, which in turn goes a long way toward preventing problems. Although these advantages may not eliminate field visits, networked systems can provide the information you need in advance so you can be more productive on-site.

We used Internet protocols to make our UPS system network-aware, and we used a web browser for our user interface. We chose to use Internet-compatible technologies in the networking software for two reasons. First, these technologies are widely accepted standards used not only for Internet communications but also for intranet communications. Second, because Internet protocols are so widely used, you can find many sources for networking technology components and compatible user programs. By using existing products for the TCP/IP network stack, the HTTP server, and the web browser, we were able to jettison our proprietary communications software from the Smart UPS, implement new features, and speed our time to market.

Although networking isn't appropriate for all embedded systems, benefits such as those just listed make it worthwhile to assess the advantages of networking. In the next two chapters, we describe important networking technologies and discuss incorporating them into embedded projects.

15

Networking

Networking is a subject that lives up to the truism that the more you learn, the more there is to learn. If that seems a bit discouraging, we can promise you this: The more you learn, the more solutions you'll discover. The possibilities networking offers developers of embedded systems — whether your job is to design, build, or maintain these systems — are numerous, practical, and affordable. That said, arriving at real-world solutions requires an understanding of the project's requirements and the technology. We leave the former to you. In this chapter, we address the latter by introducing you to networking.

We begin with an overview of some basic networking concepts, technologies, and connection methods. One technology that is especially suited for networking embedded systems — and for more reasons than just the popularity of the Internet — is TCP/IP. We tell you why and then delve into the details of the TCP/IP protocol stack. Finally, we demonstrate what's involved in adding networking capabilities to an embedded application.

Keep in mind that this chapter is an introduction. To cover networking in-depth requires an entire book. An excellent reference on networking is *Computer Networks,* by Andrew S. Tanenbaum (Prentice Hall, 1996). The definitive reference on TCP/IP is the three-volume set *Internetworking with TCP/IP,* by Douglas E. Comer and David L. Stevens (Prentice Hall, 1995).

NETWORKING CONCEPTS

We start by defining some fundamental terms and concepts used when talking about networking. This will give you the groundwork you need to understand networking in more depth.

WHAT IS A NETWORK?

A *network* is two or more computers, or *hosts*, that can communicate with each other. So whenever you connect two or more computers, even with a null-modem cable, they are considered to be networked. In Chapter 14, you did exactly this. You connected your desktop PC to a system that was running the UPS simulation. After bootup, each system could run by itself and use the network link, the null-modem cable, to communicate with the other.

Networked computers don't need to be physically close to be networked. As long as your computer can communicate with another computer, it doesn't matter whether the other computer is across the room, in the building across the street, on the other side of the world, or in a satellite orbiting the earth — the two computers still constitute a network.

Networks are often divided into two groups: local area networks and wide area networks. A *local area network* (LAN) is a collection of connected computers and devices located relatively close together, usually in the same building or group of buildings. A *wide area network* (WAN) is a group of connected computers and devices geographically distant, such as a computer in a truck cab that communicates through a satellite link to a computer at a company's headquarters.

INTERNETWORKS AND THE INTERNET

An *internet,* or more precisely an *internetwork,* is two or more networks that are connected so that a host on one network can communicate with a host on another network. Each network on an internet does not need to be implemented with the same network technology. The computer at the connection point between the networks translates between the protocols used by two different network technologies.

The Internet is the largest internetwork in the world and is based on the TCP/IP protocol stack, although you can access the Internet from networks using other protocols. The Internet began in the late 1970s and early 1980s as a worldwide network of military and university computers funded primarily by the United States government. Today, the Internet consists of public and private computers and has grown to encompass millions of computers and tens of millions of users in every country in the world. (According to Tony Rutkowski of General Magic, Inc., `http://www.genmagic.com/Internet/Trends/slide-3.html`, as of January 1997, 16 million hosts (computers) were on the Internet, up from 9.5 million in 1996 and 4.9 million in 1995. According to Euro-Marketing, `http://www.euromktg.com/globstats/`, as of August 1998, 133 million people had access to the Internet.)

NETWORK TECHNOLOGIES

A *network technology* defines a hardware implementation for transferring data from a computer to a network medium. In particular, a network technology defines (among other things) how data is packaged on the wire and how data collisions are handled. Two popular LAN technologies are Ethernet and IBM Token Ring. Ethernet is a technology developed at the Xerox Palo Alto Research Center (PARC) in the 1970s for connecting computers in a bus or a star topology. The data is packaged in packets with an Ethernet header that is added and removed by hardware on each network host. Collisions are handled by a collision detection algorithm that allows the network hardware on each host to notice the collision and resend the packet.

IBM Token Ring, on the other hand, uses token passing for bus arbitration, to avoid the possibility of data collisions. Networks based on IBM Token Ring technology are connected in either a ring or a star topology, so that the token can be passed in a well-defined path from host to host around the network.

One technology used for WANs is Asynchronous Transfer Mode (ATM). ATM is used over very high-speed telephone connections (usually T1 or T3 lines) to send fixed-sized (128-byte) packets of data. ATM has features for easily multiplexing voice and video with data, so that available bandwidth can be utilized more effectively. Other technologies used for WANs are frame relay and time-division multiplexing (TDM).

PROTOCOLS

A *protocol* is a set of conventions, or rules, used to enable communication between two computers. A protocol defines how communication is initiated and terminated, what data structures, formats, and sequences are used to exchange data, and so on. A protocol can be so simple that it can be described in a page or two, such as the Internet ECHO protocol that's used to test connections. Or it may be complex and require hundreds of pages of specification, such as the Hypertext Transfer Protocol (HTTP) used for browsing the Internet. By adhering to well-defined protocols, applications running on different network hosts can communicate easily.

THE ISO/OSI NETWORK DESIGN MODEL

The International Standards Organization (ISO) created a network design model called the Reference Model of Open Systems Interconnection (OSI) in the late 1970s and early 1980s. This model, depicted in Figure 15-1, defines a network implementation consisting of seven distinct layers for transferring data over a network. Each layer is assigned a specific, well-defined function to perform and interfaces only to the layer directly above or below. The layers are stacked, one on top of the other, which is why network software (layers 2–6 in the ISO/OSI model) is often referred to as a *network stack* or simply a *stack*, as in "I need to port a TCP/IP stack to my embedded system."

The ISO/OSI model is a design guide for how network software in general should be built; it isn't a specification for a particular network architecture. Most network architectures use some kind of layering model, though the specific layers may not be an exact match with the layers defined in the ISO/OSI model. You can usually, however, define a mapping between any network architecture and the ISO/OSI model; you see an example of this later in the chapter when you take a close look at the TCP/IP protocol stack.

Figure 15-1 shows not just the layers in a network stack, but also how two network hosts, A and B, communicate using the model. The solid arrows show actual communication; the dotted arrows show virtual communication. Within a network stack on a host, then, actual

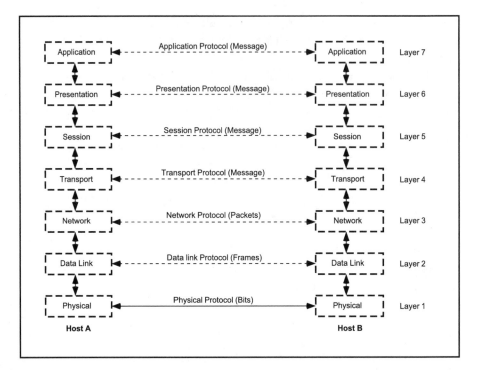

Figure 15-1: Each layer in the ISO/OSI model carries on a virtual conversation with the same layer on another network host and interfaces directly with the layers above and below it.

communication occurs between adjacent layers. Between network stacks, virtual communication occurs with a corresponding layer. Typically, each layer in a network stack uses a specific protocol (or protocols) to communicate with a corresponding layer on a remote host.

For example, a web browser application on host A might communicate with a web server application on host B using HTTP. When the application on host A wants to send data to the application on host B, it formats the data in accordance with HTTP and then calls the next layer down, the presentation layer. The presentation layer might modify the data or add a new wrapper around the data; it then calls the next layer down, the session layer. You can see the pattern: the data gets passed down the stack, layer by layer, until it reaches the physical layer and is transmitted to host B. When the data is received by host B, it is passed up the stack, with each layer removing the wrapper or undoing the data modification performed by the corresponding layer on host A. When the data arrives at the web server at the application layer, everything except the structure imposed by HTTP on host A has been removed. So actual communication occurred between each layer on each stack, and virtual communication occurred between the corresponding application layers using HTTP. We explain further why this is known as virtual communication in a moment. Right now, take a closer look at the functionality performed by each layer in the ISO/OSI networking model.

Physical Layer

The *physical layer* is responsible for transmitting data from one host to another. The physical layer defines the electrical signals for data, control, and timing, the cable requirements, and mechanical details of connectors. An example of standards in this layer are Ethernet, RS-232, and modem standards such as V.22.

Data Link Layer

The *data link layer's* primary responsibility is ensuring data integrity by detecting and correcting corrupted data. When an application on a host transmits data, the data link layer accepts an array of bytes from the network layer and packages the data into a *data frame*. When the data link layer creates the frame, it adds the hardware addresses for the source and destination hosts and a cyclic redundancy check (CRC) or similar error-checking mechanism. Then the data link layer passes the frame as a sequence of bits to the physical layer for transmission. The network layer is required to pass chunks of data that conform to the maximum size of a data frame; that is, the upper layers, not the data link layer, are responsible for breaking the data into units small enough for transmission.

When a host receives data, the data link layer receives a sequence of bits from the physical layer and stores them in memory as frames. After performing error detection and, if necessary, correction, the hardware addresses added by the transmitting data link layer are stripped and the original data is passed up to the network layer. If an uncorrectable error is detected, the frame is discarded. The data link layer does not request retransmission of uncorrectable frames. As you'll see, that's the job of the transport layer.

The data link protocol defines the format of the data frames and the technique used for error correction. Depending on the network technology, one standard or two standards specify the physical layer's requirements and the data link protocol. For example, the Ethernet and Token Ring standards both specify the physical layer's electrical and physical requirements and the structure of data frames. By contrast, RS-232, RS-422, and HDLC are physical layer standards that don't specify the data link layer protocol. In combination with these standards, then, you commonly find SLIP (Serial Line Internet Protocol) and PPP (Point-to-Point Protocol) as the data link protocols.

Network Layer

The *network layer's* job is to control the flow of data between two hosts by selecting the route, or path, that data follows from source host to destination host. When the network layer receives data from the transport layer, the network layer encapsulates it in units called *packets*. The network layer adds to each packet a header that contains the network address (which is different from the hardware address the data link layer adds) of the source and destination hosts, and any additional data, such as routing information, needed for the network layer to do its job. Then the network layer sends the packets to the data link layer. On the receiving host, the network layer strips the packet wrapper and passes the data up to the transport layer.

The network layer commonly uses routing tables to identify the best route or routes to a particular destination. Routing tables may be static or dynamic. Static routing tables are manually set up by network administrators whenever they change the network configuration, and are never modified by software. Dynamic routing tables are automatically updated by the network layer software as hosts begin and end network sessions. Nevertheless, whether static or dynamic routing tables are used, the network layer monitors the network traffic and selects routes that minimize traffic congestion. It also maintains traffic counts of packets sent to and received by specific hosts; these counts can be used for billing customers for service or for tracking congestion.

The network layer protocol defines the structure and contents of a packet, and defines the operations performed by the network layer. An example of a network layer protocol is the Internet Protocol (IP) in the TCP/IP protocol stack.

Transport Layer

The *transport layer* is responsible for transporting data to and from the correct application on a host and for ensuring that the data arrives intact and in sequence. Let's look at these functions one at a time. To deliver data to the correct program, the transport layer accepts session messages of arbitrary length from the session layer. If a message exceeds the maximum size of a data frame, the transport layer breaks the session message, using a process called *fragmentation,* into two or more transport messages that are small enough for transmission by the data link layer. Then, to each transport message, the transport layer adds a header with information on reassembling the fragments in the correct sequence. The header also identifies the source and destination applications on the two hosts. On the receiving host, the transport layer is responsible for stripping the header added by the sending transport layer, reassembling the transport messages into session messages, and passing them along to the session layer.

To ensure that the data arrives intact, the transport layers on both hosts maintain an end-to-end conversation, or connection. The information used to maintain the connection is passed in the transport message header. If the transport layer needs to communicate with its counterpart about the connection and no session layer data needs to be sent, it sends a transport message that contains only the transport layer header, with no data to pass to the layer above. As you saw, when layers below the transport layer send packets or frames to the corresponding layer on the other host, they never know whether the packets arrived intact. The transport layers, by contrast, maintain a virtual connection that includes acknowledging the receipt of data and requesting data to be resent if expected data never arrives or is corrupted on receipt.

The transport layer is also responsible for implementing flow control to ensure that messages or fragments aren't sent faster than the receiving transport layer can handle them. Like fragmentation, addressing, and connection information, the flow control information is stored in the message header.

The transport layer protocol defines the fragmentation, connection, and flow control mechanisms, as well as the structure and contents of the messages created by the transport layer. Examples of transport layer protocols are the Transmission Control Protocol (TCP) and User Datagram Protocol (UDP) in the TCP/IP protocol stack.

Messages, Packets, and Frames

It's important to note that the terms message, packet, and frame have different meanings. A *message* is a data stream passed between layers that maintains a virtual connection. Referring back to Figure 15-1, you can see that the transport layers on two network hosts exchange messages over a virtual connection, as do the layers above the transport layer (the session, presentation, and application layers).

A *packet* is a self-contained unit of data passed between connectionless layers. The network layer on a host sends packets to the network layer on another host. A *frame* (also called a *data frame*) is a self-contained unit of data sent and received by the data link layer.

Session Layer

On many networks, users have to log on to a network session to use network services. The *session layer* is responsible for negotiating the connections for a network session, handling account names and passwords, and authorizing users.

Presentation Layer

The *presentation layer* provides the application layer with an abstract interface to other devices on the network, taking care of the details of transforming data or sending specific commands to specific devices. It performs general-purpose functions or data transformations that are required by applications during network communications. For example, the presentation layer could handle the interface to a network printer, provide communications with a network file server, and perform EBCDIC-to-ASCII data conversion for video terminals attached to the network.

Application Layer

The application layer contains all the functionality specific to a particular network application. In many cases, network applications use existing, well-defined application protocols to communicate. On the other hand, if you're writing a special-purpose proprietary network application, you might decide to design a proprietary protocol that suits the needs of your application. Examples of well-known Internet application protocols are Simple Mail Transfer Protocol (SMTP) for email, Hypertext Transfer Protocol (HTTP) for transferring web pages between web servers and browsers, and File Transfer Protocol (FTP) for downloading and uploading files.

REPEATERS, BRIDGES, AND ROUTERS

A *repeater* amplifies and retransmits electrical signals so that the signals can travel longer distances. For example, if you need a very long cable for an Ethernet bus, you may have to place several repeaters along the cable so that the signal isn't too attenuated after traveling the length of the cable. The maximum cable length before a repeater is needed varies depending on the network technology. A repeater operates at the physical layer of the ISO/OSI model.

A *bridge* is a device that connects two networks that use the same network technology (such as Ethernet). A bridge reads the destination address of a frame on a network and retransmits it to the appropriate network. Bridges enable you to set up several small networks rather than one large, sprawling network. You should consider dividing up a network into two or more if a network's throughput, reliability, or security are poor.

Heavy traffic on a large network often results in frequent data collisions and slows throughput. By splitting one network into two or more and connecting them using a bridge, each resulting network sees less traffic, because each sees only frames that either originate on or are destined for it. Network failures are hard to prevent, but you can improve overall network reliability by containing them. If you divide a network into two or more networks with each having fewer hosts, a glitch will cause only the hosts on that particular network to fail rather than the entire system. Security is usually a serious concern on networks. You can improve security by using a bridge to restrict the types of traffic allowed to flow on and off a particular network. Bridges operate at the data link layer of the ISO/OSI model.

A *router* (also called a *gateway*) transfers, or routes, data between networks of the same or different technologies. In addition, a router has a network address on each network to which it is connected, and packets are addressed to it as well as to the host. Suppose a host on network A needs to transmit a packet to a host on network B. Network A encapsulates the packet to the host on network B inside a frame addressed to the router host. The router host retransmits the packet encapsulated in a frame addressed to the destination host if the router has a direct connection to network B. If the router does not have a direct connection to network B, it forwards the packet to another router that is "closer" to network B, and so on. In addition to forwarding packets, a router can translate (read and write frames in different formats used by different network technologies) from one network technology to another (for example, from Ethernet to Token Ring). Routers are what make huge networks of networks, such as the Internet, possible. A router operates at the network layer in the ISO/OSI model.

Virtual Communication

As you saw earlier, in the ISO/OSI model, the network layer on host A communicates with the corresponding network layer on host B. That conversation is called *virtual communication,* because the actual data flow is down the layers of host A, across the physical connection to host B, and up the layers of host B until it reaches the target layer. Because of the layer abstraction in the model, each layer can ignore the actual data flow in the layers below and concentrate on the virtual conversation with its peer. This concept of virtual communication between peer layers is used in network programming because it makes programs easier to write, maintain, and understand.

Virtual communication does not necessarily imply a connection. The data sent between peer layers always takes the form of discrete messages, packets, or frames. Whether or not a virtual connection is made depends on the protocol used by that network layer. For a virtual connection to occur, the protocol must include mechanisms for establishing, maintaining, and closing the connection between the peer layers on the two network hosts.

Virtual connections are, in essence, agreements between corresponding network layers on two network stacks to respond to any communication they receive from the other until one of the layers terminates the connection. Specifically, virtual connections occur at the transport and higher layers of the network stack. A virtual connection simulates a physical circuit, like an analog telephone call that makes a physical connection with relays and switches.

COMPARING CONNECTION-ORIENTED AND CONNECTIONLESS PROTOCOLS

Connection-oriented protocols implement a two-way virtual connection with the peer network layer on the remote host. After the connection is established, application software can send and receive streams of data without worrying about discrete packets or messages. The connection is maintained until one of the applications terminates the connection, at which time the other application is notified that disconnection is in progress. The disconnect is not completed until the second application terminates its end of the connection. Examples of connection-oriented protocols are TCP (in the transport layer) and HTTP (in the application layer), both from the TCP/IP network standard. You can compare a connection-oriented protocol with a telephone call. One person (application) initiates the call; when the other person (application) picks up the phone, the connection is established. The connection is continuously maintained until one of the parties hangs up the phone.

Connectionless protocols, on the other hand, do not establish or maintain a virtual connection. Instead, a connectionless protocol is used to send discrete packets to and receive discrete packets from the peer layer on the remote host. Because no connection is maintained, packets may arrive in a different order from the order in which they were sent. Using a connectionless protocol to transmit data is similar to using the United States Post Office to send a letter: a unit of information, essentially whatever fits in the envelope, is addressed and sent to a destination or a recipient. There is no way to know whether the information was received or lost in transit. Examples of connectionless protocols are UDP (in the transport layer) and ECHO (in the application layer), both from the TCP/IP network standard.

COMPARING RELIABLE AND UNRELIABLE PROTOCOLS

Reliable protocols allow applications to send and receive data without being concerned about whether data is corrupted, lost, or arrives out of sequence. The work of providing this reliable communication abstraction is the responsibility of the protocol implementation. *Unreliable protocols*, on the other hand, do not provide the application with any indication that anything might have gone wrong; instead, data integrity becomes the responsibility of the application. As you will see when you look at TCP/IP later in this chapter, network stacks are often constructed using unreliable protocols in the lower layers and reliable protocols in the upper layers.

THE CLIENT/SERVER MODEL

Most connection-oriented protocols use a client/server model. One side of the connection is designated as the server, and the other side is designated as the client. The server provides information, data, or resources to the client. Typically, a server is always listening for clients to make connections. After a connection is made, the client makes a request of the server. The server responds with the requested data or with an error. Of course, the client could be requesting to send data to the server, in which case the server's response would be "go ahead, start sending" or an error. The conversation continues until one side, usually the client, decides it wants to disconnect, at which time the session is terminated. In the client/server model, a single server often services requests from many clients. Common examples of programs that use the client/server model are database servers, file servers, and web servers.

Not all connection-oriented protocols use the client/server model; some use the peer-to-peer model. Communications using a peer-to-peer protocol is one-on-one; each host carries on a conversation with only one other host at a time. This is in contrast to the client/server model in which one server responds to multiple clients simultaneously. The client/server model is the more popular of the two and works well for the majority of network communication implementations.

NETWORKING IN EMBEDDED SYSTEMS

Now that you have the basic concepts under your belt, how do you go about building a network-aware embedded system? Although the details depend on your application, we can give you some guidelines.

SELECTING THE PROTOCOL STACK

Which protocol stack you choose is usually dictated by the systems your embedded system will communicate with and what network technologies those systems use. For example, if you're building a network-based fax machine that will be accessible from a Novell server, you must select a protocol stack that implements NetWare printing protocols. If, on the other hand, you're building a fax machine that will be accessible from the largest number of networks possible, you could select TCP/IP, which is the most widely used protocol due to the growth of the Internet. Or you could choose to support both TCP/IP and NetWare in your fax machine, making it accessible from both TCP/IP and NetWare local area networks.

As part of the process of choosing a network stack, or weighing the costs versus the benefits of adding networking capability to your system, you should estimate the resource requirements of the stack. First, what are the memory requirements of your protocol stack? Adding more software will make your system bigger. How much bigger depends on the protocol stack implementation and the features you implement. This may not be a big issue when memory prices are low.

Second, what hardware resources are required to network your product? You may need an Ethernet card, or a UART and a serial connector, or a radio transceiver. These costs should be factored into your decision.

Finally, consider the overhead that the protocol stack will impose on CPU requirements. Adding networking support might introduce additional latency into the real-time response of your system. If you need to add a faster CPU because of the overhead of networking support, your system costs will increase. This factor can be difficult to analyze before you build and test your system. If you buy your protocol stack from your RTOS vendor, however, the stack will be well integrated and your vendor will be able to provide you with the realistic real-time characteristics of their system.

SELECTING A NETWORK TECHNOLOGY

To select a network technology, consider how users will want to connect this system to a network. You may need to offer more than one option to broaden your potential market. For LAN connections, Ethernet is probably the most popular technology. Token Ring is still fairly widely used. For serial connections, RS-232 plus a modem is most common. For long, direct cable connections or high baud rates, choose RS-422 or RS-485, which use balanced transmission lines and are, therefore, less sensitive to line noise. If your systems will be mobile, you may need to support a radio frequency serial connection.

SELECTING AN EXISTING IMPLEMENTATION

If possible, choose the protocol stack implementation provided by your RTOS vendor. This should ensure that the stack is well integrated with the RTOS. In addition, your vendor will be able to provide technical support for both the RTOS and the protocol stack. If you can't find a vendor that provides both the RTOS and stack you need, you have to purchase them from two separate vendors. This is less desirable, because you'll have to spend time porting the stack to the RTOS. If this is your only choice, try to choose a stack that has been ported to many different platforms, because the more times a stack has been ported, the more streamlined the porting process usually becomes. Make sure both the network stack vendor and the RTOS vendor will be able to give you technical support during the porting process.

We strongly recommend that you don't write your own protocol stack. Writing a protocol stack is very complicated; unless you really understand networking, it's likely that you'll spend an inordinate amount of time debugging subtle networking problems. Instead, find a vendor with a debugged and working stack, so that you can concentrate on writing the application-specific code for your system.

USING STANDARD APPLICATION PROTOCOLS

By using standard protocols at the application layer, you can leverage standard tools that have already been written and are widely available. In Chapter 14, "A Network-Aware UPS," we saw that by using HTML and HTTP, which are standard application data formats and protocols, we did not have to write a custom application program for the desktop system. This saves a lot of time. Also, if you use a standard application protocol that has a broad application base, you don't need to distribute the tool. For example, almost anyone connected to the Internet already has a web browser, so you don't have to install a browser on every system that needs to access your embedded system.

POPULAR NETWORK ARCHITECTURES

A *network architecture* is the modular format and design structure of a computer network. All of the popular network architectures we discuss here are based on the ISO/OSI layered model of network design. The most important part of designing the network architecture is designing the protocols to be used by the different layers of network software. Because the protocols are an integral part of each layer — in fact, most of the code in a network layer is devoted to implementing the protocol or protocols used by that layer — a network architecture is often also called a *protocol stack*, or sometimes a *protocol suite*.

Over the years, a variety of network protocol stacks have been implemented. Most of these are vendor specific and provide a solution for some specific type of applications. One of the earliest standard protocol stacks is NetBIOS. It was specified by IBM and Microsoft in the early 1980s to provide a standard programming interface that enabled PCs to communicate with mainframe applications, such as databases. But in addition to specifying PC-to-mainframe communications, NetBIOS also included protocols for communicating with other NetBIOS machines, making networks of PCs possible. Initially, NetBIOS supported only DOS, but implementations were added for OS/2, UNIX, and Windows as those operating systems became popular.

Novell developed the IPX/SPX (Internetwork Packet Exchange/Sequenced Packet Exchange) protocol stack as part of an overall networking architecture called NetWare. NetWare is a network operating system that runs on a dedicated machine and implements network server functions, such as remote file storage and printing. IPX operates at the network layer and offers an unreliable datagram delivery and routing service, similar to IP in the TCP/IP stack. SPX operates at the transport layer and offers a reliable connection-oriented service, similar to TCP. Novell initially provided an IPX/SPX stack for DOS machines, and later added implementations that run under Windows, UNIX, and OS/2.

Another vendor-based network architecture is AppleTalk. AppleTalk was designed by Apple in the mid 1980s, for use with their Macintosh line of desktop computers. One of the major goals of AppleTalk was to allow network access to laser printers, which at the time cost more than the computer. Eventually, AppleTalk was implemented on other operating systems, such as DOS, Windows, and UNIX, mainly so computers running these operating systems could access Apple laser printers.

The TCP/IP network architecture development was funded by the Advanced Research Projects Agency (ARPA) of the United States government, beginning in the mid 1970s. By the late 1970s, a worldwide network of military and university computers were based on the TCP/IP protocol stack; this was the beginning of the Internet. TCP/IP standards and protocols are in the public domain and are maintained by the Internet Engineering Task Force (IETF). TCP/IP was developed to give military and university staff a fast and easy method of exchanging information. For this reason, among the earliest application layer protocols developed for TCP/IP were the File Transfer Protocol (FTP) for exchanging files and the Simple Mail Transfer Protocol (SMTP) for sending email messages. As the advantages of sharing devices over a network became apparent, additional protocols were quickly added to support other networking features, such as file servers and print servers.

Each of these network architectures was developed to solve a specific problem: NetBIOS enabled access to mainframe services; IPX/SPX enabled a non-mainframe — specifically, a LAN — server architecture; AppleTalk provided access to printers; and TCP/IP enabled the easy exchange of information. Over the years, these networking protocols have been extended and generalized, so that they all provide similar access, such as remote file, database, printer, and email access. In addition, implementations can be found for most desktop and mini-computer operating systems. Protocol stacks for these network architectures are available for use in embedded systems. However, unless you are developing an embedded device that must communicate with computers that implement a particular network architecture, the best choice for compatibility with the widest range of networks and devices is the TCP/IP stack.

ADVANTAGES OF THE **TCP/IP** PROTOCOL STACK

You should look at TCP/IP in detail and consider it as an architecture for embedded systems for several reasons:

- **Free standards.** The TCP/IP standards are free. The standards development is carried out in the public domain, and the current organization that maintains the protocols, the Internet Engineering Task Force (IETF), is sponsored by industry and research organizations. All the standards that have been developed are publicly disseminated over the Internet free of charge.

  This open design philosophy is one factor that has encouraged many vendors to implement TCP/IP in their operating system software and develop new application layer protocols that run on top of TCP/IP. Another factor is the availability of a reference implementation, which was developed by the University of California at Berkeley. The reference implementation is part of the BSD UNIX operating system and can be used in commercial products, as long as credit is given to the developers.

- **Robust.** The original motivation for developing the TCP/IP networking protocols was to implement a government defense network. Two of the many criteria for a defense network are that it must be easily deployed and it must be robust — that is, it must function under unexpected conditions and even if it is partially crippled. Hence, the TCP/IP protocols are easily deployed and robust. No better testimony to this fact can be found than in the quick growth and consistent reliability of the Internet.

- **Heterogeneous.** TCP/IP was intended to network computers from different vendors. Here, too, the current implementation of the Internet with its variety of equipment connecting through a variety of network links — from standard phone lines to satellite and fiber-optic links — attests to the developers having achieved their goal. TCP/IP defines the network byte order (big endian, or most significant byte first) for data structures (such as packet headers) that need to be readable by any network host. This permits TCP/IP implementations on computers with different byte order architectures to communicate easily. Although the specific byte order used is not important, agreeing to one is important.

- **Infrastructure.** In short, and to turn a phrase, the Internet is the network. It provides a global network infrastructure that you can use to make your system accessible worldwide. For example, suppose you design and deploy an embedded device with a modem interface, and then connect it to the Internet through your local Internet service provider (ISP). You could then access the device from a computer located anywhere in the world, and the device could also download data and software updates.

- **Lightweight Stack.** The TCP/IP protocol suite is relatively small for the functionality it provides. The basic TCP/IP protocol stack can be implemented in as little as 30K including a simple application-level protocol such as FTP (although full implementations are more typically in the 75 to 150K range). The Network-Aware UPS, which includes ETS Kernel, the TCP/IP stack, and an embedded web server, weighs in at less than 300K. This makes it possible to cheaply build basic Internet applications in ROM for embedded systems. TCP/IP implementations exist for personal digital assistants (PDAs) that enable users to do email and web browsing from their PDA. Expect to see communications devices, such as cellular telephones, embed TCP/IP-based applications soon.

Downloading TCP/IP Standards

The TCP/IP specifications are available for downloading as documents called Request for Comments (RFCs). Each document is assigned a number and is referenced with the letters *RFC* and its number. For example, the document that describes FTP is called RFC 959. You can review an overview of all available RFCs by referencing the RFC index, which lists the RFC number and title. The index also provides the current status of the document. Not all RFC documents define a protocol. Some RFCs may give only information or overviews, and other are drafts for new ideas or protocols. The current status in the index identifies which files contain standards, drafts, or information only.

When reviewing the index, keep in mind that RFCs describing a protocol might be obsolete due to newer documents. Working groups that develop RFCs are organized by the IETF. Typically, a draft of a proposed standard, or a draft of a revision to a current standard, is made available and the general public is invited to comment on the document. The working group then meets and revises the standard. When the standard is complete, it is published with a new RFC number.

RFCs are available at various FTP and Web sites. One such FTP site is `ftp://ftp.uu.net/inet/rfc`. A good Web site is `http://www.internic.net/ds/`, which contains a page full of links to various resources for RFCs and IETF documents.

On the FTP site, the document that contains the RFC index is named `rfc-index`. The RFCs themselves are stored as individual files and in different file formats. ASCII versions of RFCs are given names in the format `rfcnnnn`, where *nnnn* is the RFC number. Copies of RFCs stored in UNIX *compress* file format are given names in the format `rfcnnnn.Z`.

THE TCP/IP NETWORK IMPLEMENTATION

Now you're ready to look at the TCP/IP protocol stack. We present an overview of the layers and protocols that the TCP/IP protocol stack uses. Then we dive in and examine how some of the protocols work. As before, we start at the bottom of the stack and work our way up. A good overview on TCP/IP can also be found in RFC 1180, "A TCP/IP Tutorial." Remember, although the term *TCP/IP* technically refers to two specific protocols used in the TCP/IP protocol stack, it is commonly used as it is here to refer also to the entire protocol stack.

The TCP/IP stack consists of five layers, rather than the seven layers in the ISO/OSI model. The session and presentation layers in the ISO/OSI model are subsumed in the application layer in the TCP/IP stack design. This means that application-level protocols must also perform the functions of the session and presentation layers. The network layer in the ISO/OSI model is called the internet layer in the TCP/IP stack, and the data link layer in the ISO/OSI model is called the network interface layer in TCP/IP.

In our discussion of TCP/IP, we use the TCP/IP layer names, not the ISO/OSI layer names. Occasionally, we need to refer to layers in other stack architectures; for this we use the ISO/OSI names because the TCP/IP names don't apply to other network architectures.

The physical layer has the same job here as it does in the ISO/OSI model: to transmit data. It is implemented with transmission mediums and hardware. For transmission, wires, cables, and even radio waves are used; hardware includes items such as UARTs and Ethernet cards.

The network interface layer is similar to its ISO/OSI counterpart, the data link layer, in its responsibilities and how it works. The difference is that error detection is not always implemented in the network interface layer; for example, SLIP does not include error checking. The network interface layer manipulates the hardware so that the device driver can send and receive data frames. Typical protocols implemented in the TCP/IP network interface layer are PPP and SLIP for serial interfaces, and Ethernet for LANs. For networks using the Ethernet network technology, the Address Resolution Protocol (ARP) and Reverse Address Resolution Protocol (RARP), which translate between Internet addresses and hardware Ethernet addresses, are also implemented in the network interface layer.

The internet layer (the network layer in the ISO/OSI model) is responsible for encapsulating data in packets and controlling data flow. As before, a packet contains a header with all the addressing information needed to deliver the packet from a source host to a destination host. As the packet travels along a network, its header is examined at each node by the internet layer, which chooses a route and sends the packet on to the next node. Unlike the ISO/OSI model, a packet at this layer in TCP/IP is called a *datagram* or, more specifically, an *IP datagram.*

IP (Internet Protocol) is the protocol implemented at the internet layer to transmit datagrams (hence, the term *IP datagram*). IP is a connectionless, packet-switching protocol. As mentioned, with a connectionless protocol, no conversation or virtual connection exists between source and destination hosts. The receiving host doesn't know to expect data, and the sending host doesn't know whether the packet ever reaches its final destination.

We described certain aspects of packet-switching, but here's a complete explanation. Packet-switching is a method of delivering data by breaking a data unit into multiple units (packets) that are small enough to be transmitted between a source host and a destination host. The packets are then routed individually, traveling to their destination separately and arriving at different times and possibly out of sequence. The header information in each packet lets the internet layer on the receiving host reassemble the data in the correct order.

Unlike the network layer in the ISO/OSI model, however, the internet layer is responsible for ensuring that each IP datagram it sends to the network interface layer will fit inside a data frame. Most network interface layer protocols have a maximum frame size. If an IP datagram exceeds the maximum frame size of the network interface layer, IP breaks the datagram into fragments that will fit in a data frame, and sends the fragments to the network interface layer. The IP fragments are switched in the same way as non-fragmented packets. At the destination host, the internet layer reassembles all the fragments before presenting the original packet to the transport layer.

Although IP is an unreliable protocol in that it does not guarantee delivery of IP datagrams, it does have a provision for returning error messages when datagrams are discarded. The Internet Control Message Protocol (ICMP) is part of the internet layer, and sends error messages if a datagram is discarded due to age (the packet has been in transmission too long without reaching its destination), size (the packet exceeds the maximum frame size and is flagged not to be fragmented), misrouting (the packet was delivered to the wrong host), and so on. Because ICMP relies on IP for delivery of its error message, the error messages themselves are not guaranteed to arrive. Although error messages are not required or guaranteed to be delivered, however, ICMP does help with early detection of and recovery from errors without adding the overhead that would be required to make IP a reliable protocol.

The Internet Group Message Protocol (IGMP) is another protocol implemented in the internet layer. IGMP is used to implement multicasting; that is, sending data from a single source host to multiple destination hosts.

The transport layer in the TCP/IP protocol stack is responsible for implementing two-way and one-way connections, and directing data to the correct application program. Two protocols are implemented at this layer: Transmission Control Protocol (TCP) and User Datagram Protocol (UDP). TCP is a connection-oriented protocol that offers a reliable byte-stream data delivery service. TCP allows the transport layer to both set up a virtual connection with another host and tear it down when finished. Application programs pass in a stream of data to TCP. On the source host, TCP takes care of breaking up the data into TCP segments for transmission; on the destination host, TCP reassembles the TCP segments into the original byte stream. TCP also guarantees delivery of all data, unless the connection is broken.

UDP, by contrast, is a simple connectionless datagram delivery service. Unlike TCP, it doesn't take responsibility for breaking large data units into smaller ones for transmission or for delivery of data. Before the application layer passes data to the transport layer, it must break data into chunks that fit the maximum size of a UDP datagram. Each time a UDP datagram is sent, a destination host must be specified because a connection is not maintained. UDP datagram delivery is not guaranteed; datagrams may arrive late (out of order) or not arrive at all. It is the responsibility of the application using UDP to verify the delivery of data.

Besides implementing connection-oriented and connectionless services, the transport layer also handles directing data to the correct application program by implementing communications ports. A *port* is an integer that identifies a communications end point, or application program, on a network host. A complete network address includes both an IP address (which identifies a host or a specific computer on the network) and a port (which identifies an application on that host). You see an example of this when you examine the code for the Finger server project later in this chapter.

The application layer in TCP/IP is responsible for all the functions performed by the session, presentation and application layers in the ISO/OSI model, and is implemented in an application program. The protocols used at the application layer vary according to the needs of the application. For example, SMTP is an application-level protocol used by email applications over the Internet. Application layer implementations use the API provided by the TCP/IP protocol stack to establish connections and send and receive messages using one of the two transport protocols, UDP or TCP. Application protocols that use UDP are responsible for

Messages, Segments, Datagrams, Frames, and Packets

Recall that the ISO/OSI networking model defined the terms *message, packet,* and *data frame.* Let's look at the terminology used in the TCP/IP protocol stack. Figure 15-2 shows how these terms are used to describe data at each layer of a TCP/IP stack.

An *application message* is the data stream generated by the application layer. Application messages are of arbitrary length. The TCP transport layer protocol takes an application message and formats it as one or more *TCP segments,* each of which contains a TCP header and some of the application data. A TCP segment is also sometimes called a *transport message* because TCP is a connection-oriented protocol. TCP ensures that each TCP segment satisfies the maximum data size for the network interface layer on the local host, but fragmentation of large TCP segments may still occur as the segment is routed through intermediate hosts to its final destination.

The UDP transport layer protocol accepts chunks of data from an application and formats each chunk into a single *UDP datagram* containing a UDP header and the application data. The application is responsible for splitting its data into chunks that satisfy the maximum data size imposed by the network interface layer.

At the internet layer, IP accepts TCP segments and UDP datagrams and encapsulates them in *IP datagrams,* each of which contains an IP header and the TCP segment or UDP datagram.

At the network interface layer, IP datagrams are encapsulated in *data frames,* or simply *frames,* the format of which depends on the network interface protocol. For example, Ethernet frames contain an Ethernet header, followed by the IP datagram, followed by an Ethernet trailer.

But we've described TCP/IP as a packet-switched network architecture. Where do the packets come in? Well, *packet* is a generic term for a self-contained unit of data. UDP datagrams, IP datagrams, and data frames all satisfy that definition. Packet is most often used in TCP/IP literature as a synonym for an IP datagram. But you'll sometimes see it used to refer to a UDP datagram or an Ethernet frame, as well.

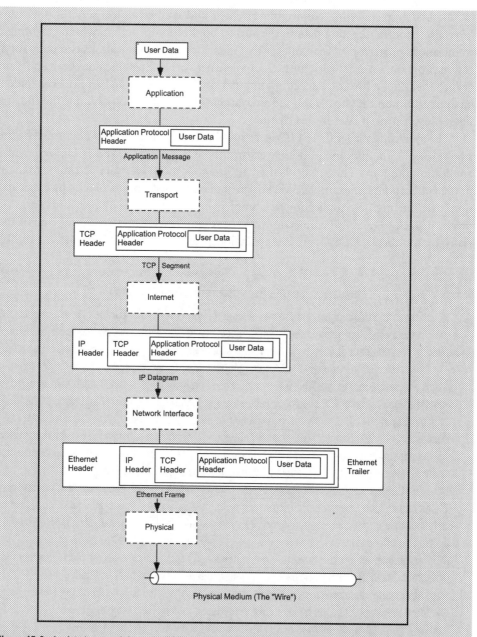

Figure 15-2: As data is passed down the TCP/IP stack, each layer encapsulates the data passed to it by the layer above, adding a header (and sometimes a trailer) that contains information needed by the layer to perform its function. This diagram shows an application using TCP as the transport protocol, running on a host connected to an Ethernet network. An application message, or byte stream, may be divided into multiple TCP segments. Each TCP segment may be fragmented into two or more IP datagrams. The solid lines show actual data flow, down the stack, and across the physical transmission medium.

breaking data into messages, reassembling the data in the correct sequence, and implementing reliability. Application protocols that use TCP can rely on TCP to implement those functions.

Table 15-1 summarizes this overview of the TCP/IP stack.

Table 15-1: The TCP/IP Stack

Layer	Function	Protocols
Application	Application dependent	HTTP, FTP, SMTP, POP3, TELNET, DNS, FINGER, BOOTP, DHCP
Transport	Convert byte streams into TCP segments or UDP datagrams, identify communications end points on hosts, set up and maintain connections	TCP, UDP
Internet	Route, deliver, and fragment IP datagrams	IP, ICMP, IGMP
Network interface	Implement data link protocols and device drivers for hardware	PPP, SLIP, Ethernet, ARP, RARP
Physical	Transport bits, using analog signaling over wire, fiber optics, radio-waves, and so on	Serial line, Ethernet wire

NETWORK INTERFACE LAYER

The network interface layer is implemented in device drivers that encapsulate IP datagrams from the internet layer in data frames and send and receive the frames over the physical network medium. If the destination host is not located on the local network to which the device driver interfaces, the internet layer identifies a gateway host on the local network. The network interface layer sends the frame to the gateway host, which is responsible for forwarding the IP datagram within the frame to the destination host or to another gateway located closer to the destination.

The network interface layer encapsulates the IP datagram with a frame suitable for the physical link used. The frame header typically contains, among other information, a destination address for the local network and a frame type to differentiate between frames that convey control information and frames that transport data. Network interface layer protocols are not necessarily specific to the TCP/IP protocol stack. For instance, PPP and Ethernet are also used as link layer protocols with other network architectures such as Novell IPX/SPX and AppleTalk. These protocols include a header field identifying the internet layer protocol (or network layer protocol, to use the ISO name for the layer) being used. All link layer protocols except SLIP include some type of checksum in the frame for error detection and (possibly) correction.

When the physical layer receives a data frame, it reads it into memory for processing by the network interface layer. The network interface layer checks the frame for errors, strips out the network interface protocol information, and passes the IP datagram up to the internet layer. If the receiving host has more than one network stack installed, the physical layer checks the frame header to see which network layer protocol the packet is addressed to, and then passes the packet to the appropriate network stack.

Let's take a closer look at three popular protocols used at the network interface layer: the SLIP and PPP serial link protocols and the Ethernet LAN protocol.

Serial Link Protocols

Serial link protocols are used on point-to-point networks, or networks that have only two nodes. A serial line that connects two computers is an example of a point-to-point network. Serial link protocols are usually stream oriented; that is, they transfer byte streams without any consideration for data structure boundaries. Serial protocols usually also include some kind of error detection, because point-to-point links are typically used for long-haul networks such as WANs.

Most serial links are slow, ranging from 14.4 to 33.6 Kbaud using a modem, to perhaps 115.2 Kbaud over a direct serial link between hosts. A WAN connection that's using special synchronous serial interfaces, however, can reach speeds from 56 Kbaud to 1.535 Mbps or even 45 Mbps for high-speed backbone connections.

Both SLIP and PPP are used to carry IP datagrams over slow or high-speed serial connections and over short or long-haul point-to-point networks.

SLIP

The Serial Line Internet Protocol (SLIP) is a nonstandard protocol. RFC 1055, which describes SLIP, is identified as a draft and has never been approved as a standard. Although it has never been an official standard, it is popular.

SLIP is simple. It transmits an IP datagram over a serial line as a frame, by marking the end of the frame with a frame delimiter byte, 0xC0. On the receiving end, whenever this frame delimiter byte is detected, the receiver declares that all the data received before this is an IP datagram and sends it up to the internet layer.

So how does the receiver distinguish the frame delimiter byte from a data byte with the same value? SLIP uses an escape character, 0xDB, to signal the beginning of an escape sequence. The second byte in the sequence is 0xDC if the original data byte was 0xC0 (the frame delimiter character), or 0xDD if the original data byte was 0xDB (the escape character). For example, if an original packet contained the following byte sequence:

```
23 5D … C0 34 6A … 75 DB FE 00 04
```

the SLIP frame would contain this:

```
23 5D … DB DC 34 6A … 75 DB DD FE 00 04 C0
```

SLIP does not use checksums. Instead, it relies on the checksum mechanism of the higher-level transport protocols, TCP and UDP. The TCP/IP specification makes checksums in UDP optional, however, which presents us with a problem. If UDP packets without checksums traverse a SLIP link, garbled data might not be detected. So you should not use UDP over a SLIP connection unless you know that your program will always be using a TCP/IP stack that implements checksums for UDP.

When using slow-speed serial lines, such as those used with dialup modems, the overhead required to send TCP/UDP and IP protocol headers can be a deterrent, especially if the payload data is small. Consider that sending a single character, such as a keystroke, may have an overhead of 40 bytes or more. At 40 bytes, the header consumes 40 times as much bandwidth as the data itself. It takes approximately 120 milliseconds to transmit 40 bytes at 33.6 Kbaud (40*10/33600), or a round-trip time of 240 milliseconds to echo the character, which to a user seems sluggish.

Compressed SLIP, or CSLIP, was developed to address this. CSLIP makes sending small messages more efficient by compressing protocol headers. CSLIP, defined by RFC 1144, compresses TCP and IP headers only for TCP segments. UDP datagram headers are not compressed with CSLIP.

CSLIP header compression works as follows. The CSLIP driver caches a copy of the most recent TCP and IP packet headers sent and received. Whenever the driver transmits a packet, it constructs a compressed header that contains only the fields that have changed since the previously transmitted header. Similarly, when a compressed header is received, the driver can construct an uncompressed header using the data from the previously received packet in the cache and the new fields in the compressed header. Typically, not much changes in the TCP and IP headers from one packet to another, and the compressed packet header can be as short as 3 to 5 bytes, which is a significant saving over the 40-byte-plus header of an uncompressed packet. Remember, though, that the data in the packet and the headers of UDP packets are not compressed in this scheme.

PPP

PPP was developed to address the limitations of SLIP. PPP is defined by RFC 1661, "The Point-to-Point Protocol"; RFC 1332, "The PPP Internet Control Protocol (IPCP)"; and ISO International Standard 3309, "Data Communications — High-Level Data Link Control Procedures — Frame Structure." Besides offering multiple protocol support (that is, the capability to transport and deliver data for two or more different network stacks) and 16-bit CRC frame checksums, the PPP specification offers a link management and connection negotiation protocol.

A PPP frame starts with the 0x7E frame delimiter and is followed by the bytes 0xFF and 0x03. The 0xFF byte is an address byte that signals all stations — anyone who listens — to process this frame. The address byte can be used to address specific nodes in a multidrop link, but this feature is not used in TCP/IP-based networks. After the 2-byte header is a 16-bit protocol field that is used to multiplex protocols over the link, followed by up to 1500 bytes of data. The data is followed by a 16-bit CRC; another 0x7E frame delimiter byte terminates the packet. Here's the structure of a PPP frame:

```
7E FF 03 [proto:2] [data:0-1500] [crc:2] 7E
```

The `proto` field contains a protocol identifier that the PPP driver uses for local delivery to the correct protocol in the correct network stack. PPP protocol identifiers used with TCP/IP include the following:

Protocol Identifier	Description
0x0021	IP
0xC021	LCP (Link Control Protocol)
0xC023	PAP (Password Authentication Protocol)
0xC223	CHAP (Challenge Authentication Protocol)
0x8021	IPCP (Internet Protocol Control Protocol)

Frames identified as IP datagrams are delivered to the internet layer. LCP, PAP, CHAP, and IPCP frames are addressed to protocols implemented in the network interface layer and are processed directly by the PPP driver.

PPP also has a flexible escape character mechanism. The escape character is 0x7D, and it causes the inversion of the sixth bit in the byte following the escape character. Whenever the frame delimiter byte or the escape character occur within a PPP frame, they are escaped as we described for SLIP. In addition to these bytes, any character can be escaped to make it possible to use PPP over serial links that are not capable of passing all 256 bytes values. Additional characters that need to be escaped are negotiated at connection time. Usually, ASCII control characters (0x00 to 0x1F) are escaped over PPP links. This provision protects against the possibility of a modem or serial communications driver misinterpreting an ASCII control character. The escape sequences are

Escape sequence	Character
7D 5D	7E
7D 5E	7D
7D 20-3F	00-1F

The link control protocol (LCP) is part of the PPP standard. This protocol is used to establish, configure, and test a serial link. It is responsible for negotiating which characters are included in the escape sequence, as well as what other protocols the link carries. LCP can be used also to negotiate other options, such as encapsulation formats and the periodic sending of test packets to monitor the quality of the connection.

PPP also includes a family of Network Control Protocols. Each NCP is used to negotiate options for one of the various protocols that operate at the network layer. The control protocol used with IP is Internet Protocol Control Protocol (IPCP). IPCP is used to negotiate IP address configuration and IP header compression.

PPP uses IPCP to negotiate the use of IP header compression when the link is established. As long as both hosts support header compression, it is automatically used. This is different than CSLIP/SLIP, in which a user must manually configure each host to specify whether header compression is used. The IP header compression algorithm is the same as that used for CSLIP and is specified in RFC 1144. One common use of PPP is to access a network over a telephone line. Telephone lines are publicly accessible, so the network must validate, or authenticate, a user's logon information before permitting the user to access the network. Two authentication protocols are currently in use: password authentication protocol (PAP) and challenge authentication protocol (CHAP).

PAP is a plain text authentication method. This means that a user's logon and password are sent unencrypted to a host for validation. This is a simple but somewhat insecure method, because someone monitoring the connection could pick the logon and password off the wire on the way to the authenticator. To provide better security for passwords, CHAP (specified in RFC 1994) uses a more sophisticated method of authentication. The server (authenticator) sends the client a plain text, randomly generated challenge. The client uses its password as an encryption key (called the "secret key" in the CHAP specification) to encrypt the challenge with an agreed-upon encryption algorithm, which it then sends as a response to the server. The server verifies the response, and if correct, grants the client access.

One obvious question you might ask yourself at this point is, how hard is it to reverse the encryption algorithm and derive at the secret key (the password). After all, the plain text, randomly generated challenge and the encrypted response are both known.

The default encryption algorithm used in most CHAP implementations is MD5, which is specified in RFC 1321. MD5 is a one-way hashing algorithm that computes a 128-bit number from input it's given, using an intentionally lengthy and computation-intensive algorithm. Since the algorithm is one-way, the key can only be discovered by attempting different keys and applying the algorithm until the encrypted result matches. Because of the large number of possible keys and the computation requirements of the algorithm, this would take an impossibly long time in practical terms. In addition, there are many possible keys that will generate the same encrypted response to a given challenge, further complicating the task of finding the correct key.

PPP versus SLIP

Use PPP rather than SLIP when you have a choice. Although PPP has slightly more protocol overhead than SLIP, PPP also provides automatic configuration and error detection capabilities. If you have to use SLIP, try to ensure that all your applications use TCP as the transport protocol. TCP provides a more reliable connection because UDP does not require the use of checksums.

Ethernet

Local area network (LAN) interfaces differ from point-to-point interfaces in that they have more than two hosts on the same link. This means a frame sent on or to a LAN can be sent to one of several hosts.

A host computer connects to a LAN using a piece of hardware called a network adapter (often also called a network interface card, or NIC). A network adapter is typically more complex and expensive than serial interface hardware, but a LAN typically offers much higher communication rates than serial links. Common LAN transmission rates used are 10, 16, 62.5, and 100 Mbps, but this bandwidth has to be shared among all hosts on a LAN.

Ethernet is the most common LAN interface used for TCP/IP. On an Ethernet network, all nodes are connected by a single wire, usually a coaxial or twisted-pair cable. The network interface layer encapsulates the data in an Ethernet frame. Before sending the frame, the Ethernet card transmits a preamble, which gives the receiver time to synchronize its decoder to the bit stream. The Ethernet frame, shown in Figure 15-3, consists of a 6-byte destination address, a 6-byte source address, a 16-bit packet type field, the data itself, and a 16-bit CRC frame checksum. Each 6-byte Ethernet address is unique and is normally burned into ROM on the Ethernet card by the card's manufacturer. In other words, although network administrators assign IP addresses to network hosts, they don't choose or assign Ethernet addresses. A broadcast frame uses a destination address of all 1s (0xFFFFFFFFFFFF) and is directed to all hosts on the LAN.

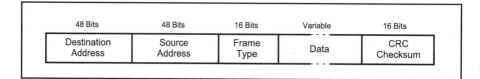

Figure 15-3: The network interface layer is responsible for including this Ethernet header in an Ethernet frame.

A receiver continually monitors the Ethernet frames on the wire. When the receiver sees a frame with a destination that matches its hardware address or a broadcast frame, it reads the frame into a memory buffer for processing by the Ethernet driver (the network interface layer). The CRC is checked before storing the frame in memory; if any errors are detected, the frame is discarded.

The Ethernet driver removes the frame header, checks the packet type, and dispatches it to the appropriate network layer protocol. In our case, the packet type would be an IP datagram, which gets passed to the internet layer of the TCP/IP stack.

Because the network interface layer, or Ethernet driver, was built to communicate to Ethernet hardware addresses, and the internet layer communicates to IP network addresses, a mechanism must translate from one to the other. This mechanism is called the Address Resolution Protocol (ARP), and it is implemented in the network interface layer. Although ARP was developed specifically for TCP/IP, other network layer protocols with similar address translation needs can use ARP as well.

The Ethernet driver maintains a cache of mappings from IP addresses to Ethernet addresses. When an IP datagram is passed in for transmission, the Ethernet driver checks the cache to find the destination host's hardware address. If the address is in the cache, the driver addresses the frame and sends it. If the address isn't in the cache, the Ethernet driver broadcasts an ARP request packet on the LAN, and after receiving a reply with the destination host's address, completes the frame and transmits it.

The ARP request packet contains several fields, which identify the protocol address type (in our case, IP), the IP address, and the hardware address. For the ARP request packet, the hardware field is left empty. The Ethernet driver for each node on the LAN receives the ARP request packet and checks to see whether its IP address matches the requested IP address. The node that finds a match fills in the hardware address field and sends the ARP packet back to the node that requested the mapping.

A mechanism is needed for sharing the wire, or the media, when multiple nodes want to transmit frames at the same time. Ethernet regulates bus traffic using the Carrier Sense Multiple Access with Collision Detect (CSMA/CD) technology. When CSMA/CD is used, each node is responsible for monitoring the communications line. When the node determines that the line is not busy, it starts its transmission. If another node begins a transmission on this line at the same time and a collision results, both nodes cease sending data. To avoid another collision, each node waits a different amount of time before trying to transmit again.

The time to wait is calculated using an exponential delay algorithm. With each successive collision, the backup time increases exponentially. To prevent each host from backing off exactly the same amount of time, a pseudo random number is used to vary the wait period. The random number generator is normally initialized with a seed derived from the hardware address, which is unique.

Eventually, each station involved in the collision will get a turn at sending its packet. When the Ethernet is saturated, however, hosts may occasionally reach a send retry count and discard the packet because of multiple successive collisions. As mentioned previously, packet loss is not a big issue in TCP/IP because upper-level protocols will notice the data loss and resend the packet. A high rate of packet loss on an Ethernet, however, usually indicates that the network is saturated and action needs to be taken to reduce traffic over the segment.

Now that you know how to get IP datagrams on and off a network link, turn your attention to the internet layer.

INTERNET LAYER

The internet layer (sometimes called the IP layer) has primary responsibility for organizing data into packets called IP datagrams and for delivering these packets to the destination host. IP is an unreliable protocol, which you might recall means it does not guarantee delivery of packets. If a packet is lost, an error may or may not be generated; if an error is generated, it may or may not be delivered. It is the responsibility of higher-level protocols to ensure that no data is lost. When you get to the transport layer, you'll see that TCP guarantees data delivery, but the UDP transport protocol does not. Applications that use UDP must either take responsibility for ensuring data delivery in the application protocol or accept the possibility of occasional packet loss. (Packet loss may be acceptable, for example, when sending video or audio data over the Internet.)

To examine the internet layer, we look first at how internet addresses, or IP addresses, are defined and managed. Next, we look at the header for an IP datagram and describe the use of each field in the header. Then we examine how IP manages traffic and routes packets to their destination. We complete our discussion of IP with an overview of fragmentation and the Internet Control Message Protocol (ICMP).

IP Addresses

Because IP is a packet-switched protocol, one of the responsibilities of the internet layer is to switch, or route, IP datagrams based on their internet, or IP, address. The IP address used by the internet layer is a 32-bit number. It is normally shown in *dotted quad* format, in which each of the 4 bytes is expressed as a decimal number, separated by periods. For example, the address 198.162.1.1 is the dotted quad representation of the 32-bit IP address `0xC6A20101`. Each internet node, or host, has a unique address in this address space. The header of each IP datagram contains (among other information) the IP addresses of the source and destination hosts.

IPv6

It's estimated that the current IP address space, which uses 32-bit IP addresses, will be exhausted in the next 5 to 20 years, depending on who's doing the estimating. In 1994, a new standard that uses 128-bit addresses was recommended in RFC 1752, "The Recommendation for the IP Next Generation Protocol." This proposal was approved as an IETF Proposed Standard in 1995. The proposal is referred to as IPv6 (for version 6); the current standard is occasionally referred to as IPv4 (version 4).

IPv6 was designed as an enhancement to IPv4 and is interoperable with IPv4. IPv6 is incrementally deployable, so that individual networks and routers can be converted to IPv6 as needed, in no required order. The standard includes proposals for changes to the IP, ICMP, and DNS (Domain Name System) protocols and proposals for additions to the sockets API used for TCP/IP programming under UNIX. Version 2 (released in January 1996) of the WinSock API used for programming TCP/IP under Windows contains support for IPv6. Because IPv6 is not yet widely deployed, this chapter covers the currently predominant TCP/IP implementation, IPv4.

An IP address has an inherent structure and is split into a network number and a host number. The number of bits used for each part of the address varies depending on the class of the network. Five classes of networks, A through E, are available.

Addresses for Class A networks begin with a 0 in the high-order bit, and have an 8-bit network number and a 24-bit host number. Addresses for Class B networks begin with a 10 in the two high-order bits, and have a 16-bit network number and a 16-bit host number. Addresses for Class C networks begin with a 110 in the three high-order bits, and have a 24-bit network number and an 8-bit host number. Addresses for Class D networks begin with 1110 in the four high-order bits, and are used for multicasting, not for network or host addresses. Addresses for Class E networks begin with 11110 in the five high-order bits, and are reserved for future use. For all classes, a network number or a host number that consists of all 1s is used as a broadcast address; a network or host number of all 0s is normally interpreted as "this" host or "this" network. This design gives us the following range of network and host numbers:

Class	Network Numbers	Host Numbers
Class A	1 – 127	0.0.1 – 255.255.254
Class B	128.0 – 191.255	0.1 – 255.254
Class C	192.0.0 – 223.255.255	1 – 254

With this scheme, the internet layer can quickly separate an IP address into network and host numbers by simply looking at the first 5 bits of the first byte in the IP address.

Network addresses are assigned by Internet Network Information Center (InterNIC). Within a network, the network administrator is responsible for assigning host numbers. A network administrator also has the ability to locally divide the host numbers for a network address into two or more physically distinct subnets. From the outside, a subdivided network is seen as a single Internet network, and all traffic to that network is directed to a single gateway. The physical separation into subnets is visible only locally and is implemented using gateways to connect the subnets.

IP Test Addresses

To run the Network-Aware UPS program in Chapter 14, you had to set up a serial PPP network consisting of an embedded target computer and a Windows computer. How did we select IP addresses for that network? Most likely, your Windows host is already connected to a LAN, such as an Ethernet network. Your network administrator could have given you an unused IP address for the embedded target. But that wouldn't work; the TCP/IP stack would recognize the network number of that IP address as belonging to the LAN and would try to communicate over the Ethernet interface rather than the serial interface. The serial network has to have its own network address, making your Windows machine a multihomed host (see the next sidebar, "Multihoming") with connections to two networks, the Ethernet LAN and the serial network.

Now, your LAN is probably already connected to the Internet through a gateway to an Internet service provider (ISP). When the Windows TCP/IP stack sees packets addressed to a host not on the LAN (the embedded target), the stack directs them to the gateway, which routes them over the Internet based on the network number of the IP address. But we don't want packets intended for our Network-Aware UPS project wandering around the Internet!

InterNIC considered the problem of people setting up temporary test networks and reserved a range of IP addresses in each class of network addresses specifically for testing. These test addresses will never be assigned to real networks on the Internet. If we select one of these test IP addresses for our little serial network, we can safely configure our Windows machine (as described in Appendix C) to route packets addressed to that network over the serial link. If you'd selected an arbitrary IP address instead, your Windows machine would no longer correctly route packets to that arbitrary network on the Internet. And, as a result, you'd no longer be able to converse with hosts on that network — a network that, in accordance with Murphy's Law, would probably include the host referenced by the results of your next Yahoo! search!

Class A addresses reserved for testing are 10.0.0.0 to 10.255.255.255. Class B testing addresses are 172.16.0.0 to 172.31.255.255. Class C testing addresses are 192.168.0.0 to 192.168.255.255. For the Network-Aware UPS project, we selected the Class C test network address 192.168.1, and assigned host numbers of 1 to the Windows machine and 2 to the embedded target.

If you've ever had to configure the network connection on a computer, you've probably had to enter a subnet mask. A *subnet mask* is used by the internet layer on a host to determine which IP addresses are on a local subnet and which IP addresses need to be sent to a gateway to be routed to another subnet. A subnet mask is assigned by the network administrator, depending on how the IP addresses are split and which subnet the gateway is on. A Class C network that is not divided into subnets has a subnet mask of 255.255.255.0. If, for example, this network was divided into two subnets with the 3 high-order bits reserved for host addresses on one subnet and the 5 low-order bits used for the other subnet, the subnet masks would be 255.255.255.31 and 255.255.255.224, respectively.

Multihoming

You might think an IP address is associated with a network host. Thinking that won't get you into trouble most of the time, but an IP address is actually associated with a network interface, not a network host. This distinction is important because one computer can potentially have two, three, or even more network interfaces. A computer may interface to a LAN, a WAN, and a serial connection. A computer with more than one network interface is called a multihomed host. A *multihomed host* has more than one IP address, and has one IP address for each network interface.

Because a multihomed host has an IP address for each network interface, it has the capability to route packets between the networks to which it is connected. For example, if a multihomed host is connected to networks A and B, and a host on network A sends the multihomed host a packet addressed to a host on network B, the network layer on the multihomed host automatically routes the packet to the destination host.

Just because a multihomed host can route packets, however, doesn't necessarily mean it should function as a router. Commercially available routers are specially designed to route packets quickly and support additional routing protocols for conversations between routers to aid in choosing efficient routes. You may use a multihomed host to route packets in low to moderate traffic, but if a lot of traffic exists between the networks, use a dedicated router instead.

The IP Header

The header of an IP datagram includes the information shown in Figure 15-4. Unless IP options (described next), which are used only to debug and test network stacks, are present, the IP header is always 20 bytes in size.

The first 4 bits in the header, the Version field, contain the IP version number. Current systems predominantly implement IPv4, or version 4 of the Internet Protocol. The next 4 bits, the Header Length field, contain the header length, in 32-bit double words. This field normally contains 5 because the IP header without the options field is 20 bytes long.

The next 8 bits contain the Type of Service (TOS) field. This field contains a 3-bit precedence value specifying the importance of the packet. The field also contains flags to tell routers to minimize delay, maximize throughput, maximize reliability, and minimize cost.

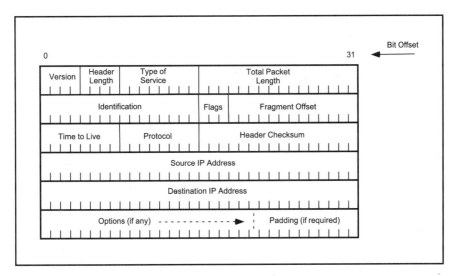

Figure 15-4: The internet layer packages data it receives from the transport layer in a datagram with this IP header. The IP header is always a multiple of 32 bits, so if the variable-length (and rarely present) Options field is not a multiple of 32 bits, the header is padded to a 32-bit multiple.

Today, most TCP/IP implementations simply ignore the TOS field. As the Internet becomes more commercialized and traffic increases, however, this field may become important for regulating the flow of traffic.

The Total Packet Length field is a 16-bit word value and specifies the length of the entire IP datagram, including the header, in bytes. This implies that the theoretical maximum packet size is 65,535 bytes. The maximum transmission unit (MTU) of the underlying network technology, however, is usually much smaller. For example, the Ethernet MTU is 1500 bytes.

The Identification field is a unique 16-bit number generated by the host that originated the IP datagram. If the datagram is later fragmented into two or more packets, each fragment will contain the same identification number. IP uses this field as part of the fragment reassembly process, as you will see in the upcoming "Fragmentation" section.

The Flags and Fragment Offset fields are used to implement fragmentation of datagrams also; these fields are described in the "Fragmentation" section.

The Time to Live (TTL) field contains a value used to prevent a packet from being forwarded forever around the Internet due to some kind of error. This value is decremented by 1 each time the packet is forwarded and is decremented also by the number of seconds (if any) the packet is held before it is forwarded. If the TTL value reaches 0 before the IP datagram is delivered to its destination, the IP datagram is discarded, and an error message is sent to the sending host using ICMP. Most TCP/IP implementations initialize TTL to 30.

The Protocol field identifies the protocol layer to which the data in the IP datagram is to be delivered. The transport layer protocols are assigned a Protocol field value of 6 for TCP packets and 17 for UDP packets. Internet layer protocols are assigned a value of 1 for ICMP packets and 2 for IGMP packets.

The 16-bit Header Checksum contains the 1s complement of the sum of the 16-bit words in the IP header (not the IP datagram). The checksum is generated using a value of 0 for the Header Checksum field. The checksum is verified by every host along the route that the packet takes to its final destination. If a checksum error is detected, the packet is discarded. No error message is generated when a packet is thrown away due to a checksum error.

The Source and Destination IP Address fields contain exactly what their names imply: the IP address of the original sending host and IP address of the destination host, respectively.

The IP Options field is used for testing and debugging networks. This field is always padded to a multiple of 32 bits, so the entire IP header will always be a multiple of 32 bits. Normally, this field is not present in an IP datagram.

Routing and Packet Delivery

At this point, you might be wondering how the internet layer knows how to switch, or route, an IP datagram based on its IP address. Suppose we have a host on an Ethernet network that has a Class C address of 192.168.3.1. The host thus has a host number of 1 and a network number of 192.168.3. Assume that this host is looking at an IP datagram with a destination IP address of 192.168.3.1. Because this destination address matches the host's IP address, the internet layer strips the IP header from the packet and delivers the packet to the protocol specified in the IP header.

Now assume that the host is examining another IP datagram with a destination address of 192.168.3.4. Clearly, this datagram is not for this host, so it has to be routed somewhere. The internet layer looks at the network number of the address, determines that it matches the network number of the Ethernet network it is attached to, and passes the datagram to the network interface layer. The network interface driver determines the Ethernet hardware address for a host with the IP address of 192.168.3.4 by looking into the ARP cache and possibly sending out an ARP request packet to ask for the address.

Now you know how to send an IP datagram to another host on the same network. But how do you send an IP datagram between hosts that are not attached to the same network? For example, how would you send an IP datagram with an IP address of 192.129.43.123 from a host with an IP address of 192.168.3.1?

To aid the internet layer in its routing decisions, most implementations maintain a *routing table*. The internet layer references the routing table to determine which network interface and gateway host to use to route a packet. A routing table for our example might look like this:

Destination	Gateway	Flags	Network Interface
192.168.3.0	192.168.3.1	E	eth0
0.0.0.0	192.168.3.254	EG	eth0

When the internet layer on the host extracts the network number from the IP address of the datagram and finds that the destination address does not match the host's IP address, it consults the routing table. The internet layer searches the routing table from most specific match to least specific, trying to find a matching network number. As you can see, one doesn't exist for 192.129.43.123, and the internet layer defaults to using 0.0.0.0. When used to match networks, the entry 0.0.0.0 means "match any." The flags associated with it, EG, indicate that the packets must be sent over an Ethernet network to a gateway host rather than delivered directly. The network interface is identified as eth0, the attached Ethernet network, and the gateway host is 192.168.3.254. The internet layer has found a way to transmit a datagram with an IP address of 192.129.43.123. After the datagram reaches the gateway, it is the gateway's responsibility to send the datagram on its next hop toward its final destination.

This is a simple example of a typical host that is connected to one LAN and depends on a gateway to deliver packets elsewhere. Let's consider a more complex situation, a sample configuration for a gateway host, or router.

The topology for this example network is shown in Figure 15-5. The gateway is connected to three Ethernet LANs through the interface cards eth0, eth1, and eth2. The gateway also has a PPP connection, ppp0, to an Internet service provider (ISP), which provides access to the Internet.

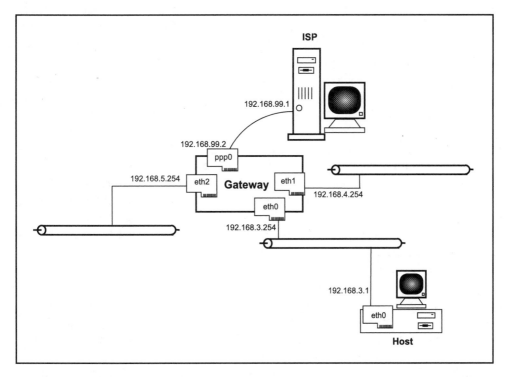

Figure 15-5: This gateway host has connections to three Ethernet LANs and a PPP connection to an Internet service provider. The gateway routes packets between the three LANs and routes Internet traffic to and from the LANs over the PPP connection to the ISP.

The gateway directly routes packets between hosts connected to any one of the three LANs: eth0 with an IP address of 192.168.3.254; eth1 with an IP address of 192.168.4.254; and eth2 with an address of 192.168.5.254. Any traffic directed to other IP addresses is forwarded over the PPP link to the ISP, which routes it over the Internet. Let's take a look at the routing table for this sample gateway host:

Destination	Gateway	Flags	Network Interface
192.168.3.0	192.168.3.254	E	eth0
192.168.4.0	192.168.4.254	E	eth1
192.168.5.0	192.168.5.254	E	eth2
192.168.99.1	192.168.99.2	P	ppp0
0.0.0.0	192.168.99.1	PG ·	ppp0

Packets addressed to hosts on any one of the three LANs can be routed directly, using the network interface to the appropriate LAN. Similarly, any traffic addressed to the host 192.168.99.1 (the ISP) can be routed directly, using the PPP network interface (the P flag on this entry indicates a point-to-point route). Finally, traffic to any other host must be forwarded to the gateway 192.168.99.1 (the ISP) for delivery to its destination. The PG flags on this entry indicate a gateway host connected over a point-to-point route.

When the datagram has been delivered to its destination host, the internet layer on that host verifies the checksum in the IP header, reassembles datagram fragments into the original packet, if necessary, and delivers the packet to the protocol identified in the IP header.

Fragmentation

In addition to routing, the internet layer needs to be able to adapt itself to the requirements of a particular network interface layer. Every network interface protocol has a limit on the maximum frame size it can transmit; for example, the maximum Ethernet frame is 1500 bytes. This limit is called the *maximum transmission unit* (MTU). After the internet layer has determined which network interface to use to transmit the datagram, it may need to fragment the original datagram into two or more smaller datagrams to satisfy the MTU of the network interface layer.

To fragment an IP datagram, the internet layer simply splits the data into several chunks and replicates the IP header in each of the smaller packets. The Flags and Fragment Offset fields in each fragment are then set so that the destination host can reassemble the fragments. Each fragment is then sent independently to the destination host. Any gateway along the way can fragment packets further.

The Flags field consists of 3 bits, two of which are currently used. The first bit in the field is the do not fragment bit, which prevents a packet from being fragmented. This flag is primarily used in network testing, not in network applications. If a packet too large for the MTU is encountered and the do not fragment bit is set, the packet is simply discarded. The second bit in the Flags field is the fragment bit, which identifies a datagram as a fragment. The last bit in the field is the more fragments flag, which is set for every fragment except the last fragment of a packet. The Fragment Offset field identifies the starting offset in the original packet of this fragment. This field is 13 bits wide, which would seem to present a problem because the maximum size of an IP packet is 65,535 bytes. To accommodate this maximum size, packets are always split into fragments that are a multiple of 8 bytes. The Fragment Offset field is multiplied by 8 to obtain the byte offset into the packet.

It is the destination host's responsibility to reassemble the packets. The gateways between the source and destination host simply pass on the IP datagrams without regard to their content. This means some fragments could arrive out of order and others may be missing, especially if they have traveled over different network links to get to the destination. When the destination host receives an IP packet marked as a fragment and with an identification number that is not the same as any packets already being reassembled, it initiates the reassembly process for that packet and starts a reassembly timer. If the timer expires before the last fragment of that packet is received, the partial packet is discarded.

Internet Control Message Protocol

The internet layer uses the Internet Control Message Protocol (ICMP), defined in RFC 792, to report packet delivery errors to the sending host and to send control and information messages to other hosts. Although no standardized application APIs exist for interfacing with the ICMP layer, most TCP/IP implementations include one or more APIs that allow applications to send and receive ICMP datagrams. The application usually has the responsibility to construct (when sending) or interpret (when receiving) the entire ICMP datagram, including the IP header. Most applications that use ICMP are tools for analyzing and debugging network problems, such as the ping program and the traceroute utility. The ping program measures round-trip packet times and checks whether a remote host is alive. The traceroute utility identifies all the hosts a packet is routed through on its way to its final destination.

Two types of ICMP messages are defined: error messages and query messages. Error messages are generated by the internet layer when packet delivery problems are detected. Error messages are always sent to the source host of the packet and include the IP header of the packet that caused the error and the first 8 bytes of data from the packet. ICMP error messages are generated for timeout, destination unreachable, and routing errors. The source host may or may not do anything in response to the error message; the protocol does not require any action.

Query messages report network information or analyze or debug internetworks. For example, the ping program sends an ICMP echo request query to a remote host, which returns an echo reply query message. Similarly, the traceroute program sends an ICMP echo request query with a low TTL (Time to Live) value in the IP header. When the packet times out and is discarded, the router that discards the packet generates an ICMP time exceeded error message. This allows the traceroute program to identify the router that is the first hop along the route to the final destination. The traceroute program then increments TTL and sends the query again to identify the next hop on the route. This process is repeated until the final destination is reached. Other query messages include router solicitation and advertisement messages, which dynamically configure routing tables as routers come online, and address mask request and reply messages, used by hosts on a LAN to obtain the subnet mask for their network segment.

TRANSPORT LAYER

The transport layer sits between the application program and the internet layer. Primarily, the transport layer implements the API that the application layer uses to communicate over the network. In the TCP/IP protocol stack, the transport layer is also responsible for implementing connection-oriented (stream) and connectionless (datagram) services. Finally, the transport layer is responsible for providing communications end points, which allow multiple applications on the same host to communicate simultaneously.

The API used by the application to program the transport layer can vary, depending on the TCP/IP stack implementation. However, the two most popular APIs are Berkeley sockets, named after the UNIX networking API developed at the University of California at Berkeley, and the WinSock API, the Windows TCP/IP programming interface, which is based on Berkeley sockets. You look at the WinSock API when you get to the sample project later in the chapter.

The TCP/IP transport layer provides two protocols. The Transmission Control Protocol, TCP, is a reliable, byte-stream, connection-oriented protocol. The User Datagram Protocol (UDP) is a connectionless, unreliable, datagram delivery service. Application layer protocols work with either TCP or UDP, but not both. For example, the File Transfer Protocol (FTP) runs over TCP, and the Network File Service (NFS) protocol runs on UDP. If you are designing your own application-level protocol, you can choose which transport protocol to use. Most applications use TCP because it's connection-oriented and reliability characteristics make it easier to program. If you use UDP, you have to either implement reliability in the application or design your protocol so it can accept occasional data loss.

Ports and Sockets

Multiple applications can communicate on the same host simultaneously because the transport layer ensures that all data is delivered to the correct application. The transport layer accomplishes this by implementing the concept of a port. A *port* identifies an end point and, in this case, a particular application. Whenever an application program establishes a connection using TCP or sends a datagram using UDP, TCP or UDP assigns the program a unique port number. The combination of a port number and an IP address is called a *socket*. A socket uniquely identifies a specific application on a specific Internet host.

Let's look at a typical scenario. An application that provides a service, called a *server,* waits for an application that uses its service, called a *client,* to initiate a connection and request data (or whatever service is provided). To connect to the server, the client must know the IP address of the host the server is on and the TCP or UDP port number on which the server listens for connections. The server, therefore, normally listens on a *well-known* port number, in other words, a port number that the Internet community has agreed on. For example, HTTP uses port 80, FTP uses port 21, and SMTP uses port 25. Well known Internet port numbers are in the range 0–1023 and can be found in RFC 1700, "Assigned Numbers." The client needs a port number for its end of the connection as well. But because the client port number does not need to be known in advance, the client normally lets the transport layer protocol assign an arbitrary port number for the client connection. So for the connection between the web browser and web server in our UPS project in this chapter, the HTTP server on the embedded target listens on port 80, and the web browser on the Windows machine uses an arbitrary port number — let's suppose it is 3846. The sockets for the connection would then look like this:

Socket	Description
198.162.1.2:80	IP number and port of web server
198.162.1.1:3846	IP number and port of web browser

But what if two clients on host A want to connect simultaneously with a server on host B? Or for that matter, what if one client wants to make two separate connections with the server on host B? Both connections can use the same server port, because each TCP connection (and UDP datagram) is identified by using the server *and* the client socket address. On the server side, the connections have identical socket addresses. On the client side, however, each connection has a different, arbitrarily assigned port number. So the socket addresses for each connection on the client side will be different, which serves to distinguish between the data streams for the two connections.

TCP

As mentioned, TCP implements the connection-oriented transport protocol in the TCP/IP protocol suite. It allows applications on one host to open a connection-oriented communications channel with applications on other hosts. To the application, this communications channel acts as a reliable byte-stream delivery service.

Let's look at some of the components of TCP, such as how sequence numbers and checksums are used to make the connection reliable. TCP also implements a sliding window protocol, which makes it more efficient and increases data throughput over long-distance connections. Finally, we look at how TCP connections are established and examine the fields in the TCP segment header.

Sequence Numbers and Acknowledgments

To provide a stream-oriented channel, TCP has to break the stream into segments, which are passed to the internet layer for IP to process and send on. Each segment is packaged with a TCP header at the beginning of the segment, followed by application data. On the receiving end, TCP turns the segments back into a byte stream that is presented to the application.

To implement a reliable connection, TCP uses sequence numbers to identify each TCP segment. Because a TCP connection is full duplex (data flows simultaneously in both directions), two sequence numbers must be maintained, one for each direction. When the connection is established, each side of the connection generates the initial sequence number for the data it will be sending. Thereafter, the sequence numbers go up by the number of application data bytes sent. For example, suppose host A selects 1200 as the initial sequence number for the data it will be sending over a connection to host B. The first segment host A sends has a sequence number of 1201. If the length of the application data in the first segment is 450 bytes, the sequence number for the second segment sent is 1651. In other words, if you subtract the initial sequence number (which is arbitrary), the sequence number for a TCP segment identifies the byte number in the data stream for the first data byte in that TCP segment.

When the receiver acknowledges data sent to it, it acknowledges the highest sequence number received instead of sending a separate acknowledgment for each sequence number sent. The sender starts a timer when it sends each TCP segment. If the timer expires before the sender receives an acknowledgment, it retransmits the segment.

Using acknowledgments and sequence numbers assures us that the data is transmitted reliably, but it would be inefficient if the sender had to wait for an acknowledgment every time it transmitted a packet of data. The designers realized this as well and implemented a sliding window technique to improve data throughput. The *sliding window* algorithm allows TCP to keep sending data until the data stream is a specific number of bytes, the window size, ahead of the acknowledgments. Typical windows sizes encountered on the Internet are 4K, 8K, and 16K. The benefit is that TCP doesn't have to stop and wait for an acknowledgment before sending another segment. The reason the window size isn't larger is because you don't want to get *too* far ahead of the acknowledgments; otherwise, a timer might expire on a segment way back in the data stream, and TCP would have to resend not only that segment but all segments following it in the data stream. The sliding window algorithm essentially allows the transmitter to send data blindly until it has exhausted the data to be transmitted or the window is full. Under ideal conditions, the receiver acknowledges data fast enough so that the sender stops only when it runs out of data to transmit, never having filled the window. TCP will also dynamically adjust the window size during the life of a connection, depending on traffic conditions. When network traffic is light, the size of the sliding window is expanded to improve throughput. When traffic congestion is high, the window size is reduced to minimize the likelihood of having to resend large amounts of data.

Although acknowledgments can be sent in separate packets, containing no application data, they are usually piggybacked on a segment containing application data, to improve efficiency. Sometimes, especially during retransmission timeouts, it is necessary to send only the acknowledgment to the host on the other end of the connection, if no data is waiting to be sent.

Initiating and Closing a TCP Connection
The goal when establishing a TCP connection is to synchronize the sequence numbers between the two sides. This is accomplished with a three-way handshake, shown in Figure 15-6. The host initiating the connection sends a packet with the SYN (synchronize) flag set. This indicates that the sequence number in this packet is the starting sequence number. The receiver responds by replying with a packet containing several pieces of information. First, it acknowledges receipt of the sender's packet by setting the ACK (acknowledgment) flag. It identifies the packet being acknowledged by setting the acknowledgment number to the sender's beginning sequence number incremented by 1. Finally, it sets the SYN flag indicating that this acknowledgment packet also contains a valid starting sequence number for the receiving side. The sender then acknowledges the receiver's sequence number by sending a packet with the ACK flag set and an acknowledgment number set to the receiver's initial sequence number incremented by 1. After both sides have synchronized their sequence numbers, they are ready to transfer data.

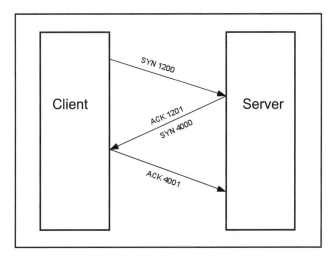

Figure 15-6: To initiate a TCP connection, the hosts must synchronize their sequence numbers. This is done with a three-way handshake between the two hosts.

A connection can be stopped in two ways. The usual way is by using the FIN (finish) flag. Either side of the connection may initiate the close by sending a segment with the FIN flag set. The FIN flag means "I'm not going to send you anymore data, but I'll continue to accept data from you until you send me a FIN flag." The other side responds by acknowledging the FIN packet and sending a FIN of its own. After both sides have sent FINs and received acknowledgments, the TCP connection is terminated.

A more drastic way to shut down a TCP connection is to send a RST (reset) flag. This aborts the connection and releases all resources immediately. A sender can use the RST flag to terminate a connection if it doesn't receive a valid handshake, or either host can use the flag if it must shut down in a hurry. A host may use this method also to kill stale TCP sessions, after a reboot, for example.

The TCP Header

A TCP segment consists of a TCP header followed by application data, if any data is present. The format of the TCP header is shown in Figure 15-7.

The Source and Destination Port fields contain numbers that identify the sending and receiving applications, respectively. The combination of a port number and an IP address is a *socket*. A virtual connection between two applications is uniquely identified by a pair of sockets, one identifying the source and one identifying the destination.

The Sequence Number field identifies the first data byte in the segment by its relative offset from the start of the data stream. The Acknowledgment Number field identifies the sequence number of the next byte of data the sending host expects to receive from the other end of the connection. For example, if the last segment received has a sequence number of 1001 and 320 bytes of data, the sending host expects the acknowledgment number in the next segment to be 1321. The designers of TCP decided to always piggyback both the acknowl-

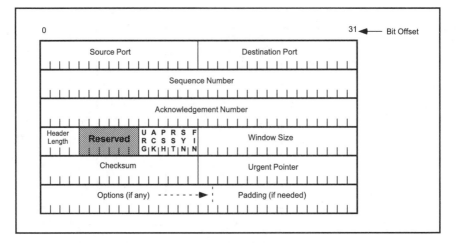

Figure: 15-7: The transport layer constructs TCP segments that include this header and then passes the segments down to the internet layer.

edgment number and the sequence number. Although this may increase overhead, it makes it much easier to decode the packet. Also, by including this information, each packet conveys the state of the connection, which makes the protocol more robust.

The Header Length field is a 4-bit number that specifies the length of the TCP header in 32-bit double words. The TCP header length is normally 5 double words, or 20 bytes.

The Flags field in the TCP header contains six 1-bit flags, of which we have already described the SYN, ACK, FIN, and RST flags. The URG (urgent) flag is set when a value is in the Urgent Pointer field. The PSH (push) flag tells the receiving TCP module to immediately send the segment's data to the destination application, overriding any buffering strategy in effect. The PSH flag is typically used by interactive applications such as Telnet to avoid any delays in users seeing echoed characters, for example.

The Window Size field identifies the size of the sender's sliding window, in bytes. The receiving TCP module uses this information to avoid sending too much data at once and overwhelming the buffering capability of the other end of the connection.

The Checksum field contains an important end-to-end checksum. Remember that IP allows large packets to be split into smaller packets for transmission across the network interface. The IP checksum for each packet handles only the individual IP fragment's IP header, not the data. The transport layer is responsible for verifying that the TCP packet is valid after it has been reassembled. The end-to-end checksum catches data corruption by faulty hardware.

When the URG flag is set, the Urgent Pointer field points to urgent data, sometimes also called *out-of-band data,* in the TCP segment. Urgent data must be processed by the receiving host before any other data. This pointer was originally assigned one meaning (a pointer to the byte following the last byte of urgent data), and was changed in a later RFC to mean a pointer to the last byte of urgent data. Unfortunately, some TCP/IP stacks (notably, implementations derived from the original public domain Berkeley code) use the old interpretation. In addition, no method is available to identify the start of the urgent data. All this makes the use of urgent data in an application problematical.

Finally, the Options field is not normally present in a TCP header. Its presence or absence can be inferred from the header length. If any options are present, the header is padded to a multiple of 32 bits.

UDP

The UDP transport protocol is an unreliable, connectionless protocol, which makes no guarantees. It is simply a wrapper that allows applications to send datagrams to a specific port on a specific host. The application is responsible for breaking the data stream up into datagrams small enough to satisfy the stack requirements for maximum packet size. The application must deal with any lost, duplicated, or out-of-sequence UDP datagrams. Why is this useful?

Sometimes applications do not want the overhead of starting up a connection using TCP and then tearing it down. This can be the case when transaction-based applications have only small amounts of data to send and the time to initialize and tear down a TCP connection is too long. Remember that to start a TCP session, you must send at least three packets, and each must wait for a round-trip delay. With UDP, the application can just send and forget.

Also, with UDP, it is possible to broadcast packets to multiple hosts, something that is not possible with TCP. Broadcasting is sometimes more efficient than setting up and maintaining multiple TCP sessions and replicating the same data.

UDP simply adds a UDP header to the application's data, as shown in Figure 15-8.

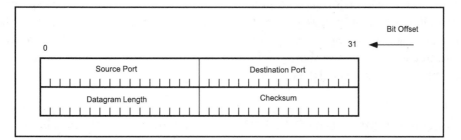

Figure 15-8: A UDP datagram consists of a UDP header followed by data. The UDP header is much simpler than the TCP header because UDP is an unreliable connectionless protocol.

Like the TCP header, the UDP header has Source Port and Destination Port fields so that a UDP packet's source and destination application can be uniquely identified on a particular host. It also contains a Datagram Length field, the value of which is the length of the datagram including the UDP header, and a Checksum field. As in the TCP packet, the checksum implements an end-to-end checksum. Unlike the TCP checksum, the UDP checksum is optional. Although most TCP/IP stacks implement checksums for UDP datagrams, some do not. Therefore, if you are writing an application that uses UDP, you should not depend on data integrity.

APPLICATION LAYER

The application layer is implemented as one or more application programs. Application-layer protocols are the rules applications use when communicating with each other. Most application-level protocols assume the client/server model. Servers listen for requests from clients to perform work or retrieve data. Clients either initiate a TCP connection and then conduct a conversation with the server, following the rules of the protocol, or send a UDP datagram and then wait for a response. Almost all common application-layer protocols use plain ASCII-encoded command strings and responses. This makes it easy to debug; you simply print the strings. It also means there is no need to pack and unpack data in network byte order, as there is for binary data.

We briefly describe several popular application-layer protocols next.

Telnet

Telnet, specified in RFC 854, is a simple protocol for establishing virtual terminal sessions to hosts on the Internet. A client simply opens a TCP connection to a host server. All the data received by the client is displayed on the user's terminal, and any data typed on the user's keyboard is sent to the server. The telnet server, running on a host that can support remote logons, waits for connections on TCP port 23. After a connection is established, the server starts up a logon session on that host. UNIX is a common operating system that allows remote terminal logons through telnet.

In addition to remote logons, a telnet client is useful for debugging servers for other protocols that use TCP as their transport protocol. If a protocol uses commands or requests and generates responses in ASCII, we can use telnet to connect to the server and emulate what a client would do, simply by typing protocol commands at the keyboard. In Chapter 16, "Connecting to the Web," we show you how to use a telnet client to connect to the HTTP server in the Network-Aware UPS project.

Finger

The Finger protocol, described in RFC 1288, is another fairly simple protocol. Finger servers typically run on multiuser operating systems, such as UNIX. A Finger client opens a connection to a Finger server on port 79. If a client sends an empty line, consisting of only a CR-LF sequence, the server simply responds with a listing of all users currently logged on the system and then disconnects. To find out information about one particular user, a Finger client sends the logon name of the user followed by CR LF.

The format of the output from a Finger server is free format. You see how to use Finger in an embedded application later, by examining a Finger server that runs under ETS Kernel.

FTP

RFC 959 specifies the File Transfer Protocol (FTP), which is used, as the name implies, to transfer files across the Internet. FTP stems from the early days of the ARPANET (the government-funded networking project that eventually became the Internet) because the capability to exchange data and files was one of the primary goals of building a wide area network to connect university and government networks. The FTP server listens for client connections on TCP port 21.

Let's look at a few of the commands and responses in FTP. Keep in mind that these are the commands the FTP client sends to the server, not the commands that you, a user, type at a command prompt presented by an FTP client program.

After the connection between the client and server has been established, the client needs to authenticate itself by using the USER and PASS commands. Both commands take arguments, which are plaintext username and password arguments. FTP servers that permit anonymous logons, which allow anyone to connect, use the special ftp or anonymous username and a password that should be your email address. For example:

```
USER anonymous
PASS cyliax@ezcomm.com
```

The initial connection, called the *control connection,* is used to send commands and replies. When a server receives a command, it immediately sends a primary reply indicating the initial success or failure of the command. Some commands require one or more secondary replies, which may, for example, report on the progress or completion of a file transfer. Most commands that transfer data, such as GET and PUT, use a second TCP connection for the data transfer. An FTP server initiates a data connection after receiving a command requesting a data transfer. By default, a data connection is made between port 20 on a server and a port used for the control connection on a client. A client may change the ports used for a data connection by issuing the PORT command, which takes as an argument an IP address (of either the server or the client) and a port number. After the data transfer is complete, a server closes the data connection; that is, a data connection is temporary and is maintained for only the duration of a single data transfer.

Some common data transfer commands are DIR to get a list of all files in a directory, GET to copy a file from a server to a client, and PUT to copy a file from a client to a server. By default, files are transferred in the ASCII character set, with lines terminated by a CR-LF pair. A server and client are responsible for translating between this standardized form and their own internal character set and line terminators. Text files may also be transferred in the EBCDIC character set for efficiency when both hosts use EBCDIC locally. Binary files are transferred in a format called image data type, which treats the data as a bit stream and involves no data translation.

When a client is finished using an FTP server, it sends a QUIT command, which causes the server to close the control connection.

HTTP

Hypertext Transfer Protocol (HTTP) is used to transfer web pages. Web pages can contain quite a rich variety of content, because HTTP provides for a content type specifier that identifies the type of data contained on a page. In addition to standard HTML, web pages can include pictures, Java applets, and audio and video clips, to mention just a few content types. Because the type is identified, a web browser retrieving a page knows how to process the data on the page. HTTP is specified in RFC 1945, and Internet Media Types (content type specifiers) are registered with the IANA (Internet Assigned Numbers Authority) in accordance with RFC 1590.

In a sense, HTTP is like FTP, except instead of dealing with only two file types (binary and text), HTTP can handle multiple types of files and documents. Also, HTTP transfers all its data in-band; that is, it uses the same TCP session to transfer data that it uses for the control channel. FTP, on the other hand, uses separate connections for the command, or control, channel, and the data.

HTTP servers listen to port 80 for TCP connections from clients and then process commands. Some of the commands used are GET, which allows a client to retrieve a document, and POST and PUT, which send data to an HTTP server. Normally, HTTP requires that a server disconnect after each request. This requirement can be very inefficient, however, and the current protocol version allows clients to specify that they would like the connection to persist to process multiple commands.

We describe HTTP and HTTP servers in more detail in Chapter 16, "Connecting to the Web."

SMTP

Simple Mail Transfer Protocol (SMTP) is specified in RFC 821 and is used only to transfer email between hosts. The destination host needs to figure out how to dispose of the received message by either saving it to a user's mail spool file or perhaps sending it to another email host. Like FTP, SMTP is one of the original Internet protocols.

As with other servers, an SMTP server listens for connections on a TCP port (port 25). After a connection is detected, it allows a client to execute commands necessary to send a message. As in an FTP connection, the conversation consists of a series of commands sent by a client and replies sent by an SMTP server. Unlike in an FTP connection, only a single connection is used; the text of the email message is sent over the same connection as the commands.

Let's look at a sample SMTP session to see how an email message is sent. After the connection is accepted by the server, the server sends some status messages:

```
220-serv1.ezcomm.com Sendmail 8.6.12/8.6.12 ready
at Mon, 24 Nov 1997 02:20:43 -0500
220 ESMTP spoken here
```

The client usually identifies itself first using the HELO command. We'll use the prefix ">>> " to identify commands sent by the client.

```
>>> HELO hugo.ezcomm.com
```

The server then acknowledges the client and tells it what features have been enabled:

```
250-serv1.ezcomm.com Hello emma.ezcomm.com
[129.79.238.52], pleased to meet you
    250-EXPN
    250-SIZE
    250 HELP
```

The client then begins the process of sending a message by identifying the message envelope, or the sender and recipient:

```
>>> MAIL From:<cyliax@hugo.ezcomm.com> SIZE=60
250 <cyliax@hugo.ezcomm.com>... Sender ok
>>> RCPT To:<cyliax@ezcomm.com>
250 <cyliax@ezcomm.com>... Recipient ok
```

After the envelope is specified, the client sends the DATA command to request permission to transmit the body of the message:

```
>>> DATA
354 Enter mail, end with "." on a line by itself
>>> this is a test message... -ingo
>>> .
250 CAA07907 Message accepted for delivery
```

That completes the process of sending an email message. The client can now either send another message by introducing a new envelope with the MAIL and RCPT commands or terminate the session with the QUIT command:

```
>>> QUIT
221 serv1.ezcomm.com closing connection
```

The server then disposes of the message(s) in an appropriate matter.

DNS

The Domain Name System (DNS) is used on the Internet to resolve (look up) domain and host names and IP addresses. Several RFCs deal with DNS, but RFC 1035 is the primary specification, describing the details of the domain name system and the protocol used to communicate with DNS servers.

DNS uses a hierarchical naming scheme for computers connected to the Internet. The names are structured like a broad, shallow tree. Below the root node of the tree are the main domains used for grouping organizations on the Internet. You're probably familiar with most of these primary domains; they include com, for commercial businesses; edu, for universities and other educational organizations; gov, for U.S. government organizations; and so on. Below the primary domains, you have one or more levels of subdomains, though in practice it's uncommon to have more than two levels of subdomains. The leaves of the tree are individual host computer names. For example, the name ftp.pharlap.com identifies a computer named ftp (probably an FTP server, from its name) in the subdomain pharlap of the domain com. A special primary domain named arpa is used for reverse name lookup, that is, the process of turning an IP address into a computer and domain name. Below arpa is a tree of network addresses.

DNS is implemented as a distributed database. No one computer on the Internet contains the entire database of host names for the Internet. Maintaining such a huge database would be an impossibility. Instead, the Internet Network Information Center (InterNIC) manages the primary domain names. InterNIC delegates responsibility for assigning names within specific *zones*, or portions of the DNS tree, to particular organizations. These organizations can, in turn, further subdivide the zone and delegate responsibility, until the zones get small enough that one person can manage the responsibility for name assignments within the zone. For example, to resolve the name `ftp.pharlap.com`, a DNS client might first query one of several root DNS servers to find the server that manages the domain `com`. It would then query the `com` name server to find the name server for `pharlap.com`. The name server for `pharlap.com`, which lives on the Class C network maintained at the offices of Phar Lap Software, would be able to resolve the name `ftp` and return the IP address of `ftp.pharlap.com`.

Although a client can iteratively contact several DNS servers in succession, as we just suggested, in practice most clients ask their primary name server to recursively resolve the name or contact other name servers on behalf of the client and return the IP address to the client. For example, if you're running a web browser on the computer named `mymachine.pharlap.com`, and you type `http://www.microsoft.com` in the URL field of the browser, the TCP/IP stack on your machine asks the DNS server on the Phar Lap network to look up `www.microsoft.com`. The local DNS server might have that name in its cache, if someone else (or you) looked it up recently. If not, the local DNS server carries on a succession of conversations with other DNS servers on the Internet, and then finally returns either an error or the resolved IP address to the web browser on `mymachine.pharlap.com`.

DNS can use either UDP or TCP as the transport protocol; DNS servers listen for clients on both UDP port 53 and TCP port 53.

A DNS client is typically implemented transparently in the API used by applications to communicate with the TCP and UDP transport protocols and to perform other network activities. For example, in the Berkeley sockets and WinSock APIs for TCP/IP, the `gethostbyname()` and `gethostbyaddress()` routines use the DNS protocol to request name or IP address lookups, respectively, from the local DNS server.

NETWORK PROGRAMMING FOR ETS KERNEL

ETS Kernel includes a full-featured TCP/IP stack for writing networking applications. The Network-Aware UPS we introduced in Chapter 14, "A Network-Aware UPS," uses the TCP/IP stack and the MicroWeb Server component of ETS Kernel to embed a web server in the UPS application.

In this section, we examine a sample networking application to get an idea of what's involved in adding networking capabilities to an embedded application. We use a Finger server application as an example. (The networking code in the Network-Aware UPS is in the HTTP server component of the MicroWeb Server, and we look at that code in Chapter 16, "Connecting to the Web.")

The Finger protocol is used to retrieve information about a network host. If you specify only the host computer name, the Finger client retrieves a list of all users currently logged on to the host. If you also enter a user name, Finger reports information on that user.

We chose to implement the Finger protocol in our sample because it's a fairly simple program that still illustrates all the network calls needed to implement a server application. Like the Network-Aware UPS project, the connection to our Finger server is over a serial PPP link from a Windows host machine. In case you don't have a Finger client program on your Windows host, we include a Win32 Finger client program with ToolSuite Lite.

The networking API in ETS Kernel is WinSock API, the same API used to write networking applications for Windows. Let's start with a brief summary of how to use WinSock.

WINSOCK API

Over the years, the socket API, which was developed for UNIX by researchers at the University of California at Berkeley, has been popular for TCP/IP-based application. The Berkeley socket interface has been ported to several operating systems. Windows programs use an API called Windows Sockets, or WinSock, to program TCP/IP stacks. The WinSock 1 implementation, which implements the Windows Socket version 1.1 specification, is based on the socket interface in the 4.3 release of the Berkeley Software Distribution (4.3BSD). Having a socket interface under Windows made it easy to port TCP/IP-based applications to Windows, because most applications were originally written to work with the Berkeley socket interface.

A *socket* is a software abstraction used to identify a network connection. A socket contains information about the transport protocol used, the local and remote IP addresses of the two hosts involved in the conversation, and the local and remote transport protocol port numbers. Sockets that use TCP as the transport protocol are called *stream sockets*. Sockets that use UDP are called *datagram sockets.*

Programs can designate sockets as either blocking or nonblocking. For blocking sockets, the APIs wait for network activity (such as making a TCP connection, sending or receiving data, or performing a DNS name lookup) to complete before they return to the calling application. For nonblocking sockets, the APIs return immediately, and it is up to the application to check later to see whether the network operation is complete.

Because BSD uses a preemptive multitasking environment, blocking sockets are a useful paradigm; you simply create a separate thread to perform network activity, and while that thread is blocked waiting for a network operation to complete, the rest of the program can be doing useful work. The blocking sockets paradigm posed a problem, however, for 16-bit Windows, which is a non-preemptive multitasking system. Therefore, WinSock 1 added a number of additional APIs, all prefixed by WSAAsync, to the Berkeley socket APIs. The WSAAsync* APIs are designed to work well with the event-driven, non-preemptive program model of 16-bit Windows.

The Berkeley socket APIs are well-suited for writing network applications for the preemptive multitasking environment offered by Win32 operating systems such as Windows 95, 98, and NT, and ETS Kernel. Because they're suitable, and also because ETS Kernel does not provide the event-driven programming model used for Windows GUI programs, ETS Kernel provides the Berkeley subset of the WinSock 1 API. The APIs are summarized in Table 15-2, grouped by functional category.

Table 15-2: The WinSock APIs

Initializing WinSock

`WSACleanup()`	Called when your application has completed its use of WinSock
`WSAStartup()`	Initializes the WinSock interface

Creating and Closing Sockets

`bind()`	Associates an IP address and port number with a socket
`closesocket()`	Closes the socket connection, if any, and frees the socket handle
`shutdown()`	Stops the transfer of data in one or both directions; this call can be used to ensure that all data transfer is complete before closing the socket
`socket()`	Creates a socket and returns a socket handle

Making TCP Connections

`accept()`	Used by a server to accept a connection request made by a client program
`connect()`	Used by a client to request a connection with a remote host
`listen()`	Used by a server to establish a queue for incoming connection requests on the socket

Sending Data with TCP

`recv()`	Receives stream data over an established connection
`send()`	Sends stream data over an established connection

Sending Data with UDP

`recvfrom()`	Receives a single datagram from any host
`sendto()`	Sends a single datagram to a specific host

Getting or Setting Socket Information

`getpeername()`	Returns the address of the remote host for a connected socket
`getsockname()`	Returns the local address for the socket
`getsockopt()`	Returns the value of a specific socket option
`ioctlsocket()`	Sets the blocking mode of a socket, and obtains information about data available to be read or out-of-band data
`select()`	Polls a socket to determine whether read data is available or whether data can be sent; the call can return immediately, or a timeout value can be specified
`setsockopt()`	Sets the value of a specific socket option

Getting Database Information

`gethostbyaddr()`	Performs a DNS query to obtain information about the specified host IP address
`gethostbyname()`	Performs a DNS query to obtain information about the specified host name or alias
`gethostname()`	Returns the name of the local host
`getprotobyname()`	Looks up information about a protocol name in a local table or disk file
`getprotobynumber()`	Looks up information about a protocol number in a local table or disk file
`getservbyname()`	Looks up information about a service name in a local table or disk file
`getservbyport()`	Looks up information about a service port number in a local table or disk file

(continues)

Table 15-2: The WinSock APIs (*continued*)

Converting the Byte Order	
htonl()	Converts a 32-bit number from host byte order to network byte order
htons()	Converts a 16-bit number from host byte order to network byte order
ntohl()	Converts a 32-bit number from network byte order to host byte order
ntohs()	Converts a 16-bit number from network byte order to host byte order

Manipulating IP Addresses	
inet_addr()	Converts an ASCII dotted decimal IP address to a 4-byte binary IP address in network byte order
inet_ntoa()	Converts a 4-byte binary IP address in network byte order to an ASCII dotted decimal string

Getting and Setting Errors	
WSAGetLastError()	Returns the error value for the last WinSock API called
WSASetLastError()	Sets the error value to be returned by WSAGetLastError()

BUILDING THE FINGER SERVER PROJECT

The Finger server project is located in \TSLITE\PROJECTS\FINGER\FINGSERV. The Finger client project, which is built to run under Windows rather than ETS Kernel, is in \TSLITE\PROJECTS\FINGER\FINGER. Prebuilt executable files, FINGSERV.EXE and FINGER.EXE, respectively, are provided if you want to skip the build step.

To build the Finger server executable from Visual C++ Developer Studio, open the workspace file (FINGSERV.DSW) and click Build|Rebuild All. To build the Finger client executable, open the FINGER.DSW workspace file and click Build|Rebuild All. Chapter 3, "Software Installation and Setup," contains complete details on building the projects.

RUNNING THE FINGER SERVER PROJECT

The Finger project uses the same configuration (cable connections, IP addresses, and so on) that you used to run the Network-Aware UPS program in Chapter 14. If you've already run the Network-Aware UPS, you're ready to go. If not, refer back to Chapter 14 to set up the configuration correctly.

To download and run the Finger server from Developer Studio, open the FINGSERV.DSW workspace and select Build|Execute fingserv.exe. Or, if you prefer, from a DOS prompt set the current directory to \TSLITE\PROJECTS\FINGER\FINGSERV and type the following:

```
runemb release\fingserv
```

After FINGSERV.EXE has been downloaded to the target system, double-click the UPS Connection icon you created in your Dial-Up Networking window, and click the Connect button to initiate the connection with the Finger server on the target system. This process is described in more detail in Chapter 14.

You're now ready to run a Finger client program to get information from the Finger server on the embedded target. Use your favorite Finger client program, or run the Finger client included with ToolSuite Lite. To run the included program, from a DOS prompt on your Windows host type the following commands:

```
cd \tslite\projects\finger\finger\release
finger @192.168.1.2
```

The Finger client connects to the Finger server and prints the response sent by the server, which should look similar to the following:

```
Finger 192.168.1.2:

RUNMODE: WaitHost
CPU: i486
COPROCESSOR: Present
EMULATOR: Not present
RAM: 639 KB, at 0x0,
     15232 KB at 0x100000
MONOCHROME: Not present
VGA: I/O port at 0x3D4,
     0x4000 bytes of screen memory at 0xB8000
FILESYSTEM: Not present
```

Because ETS Kernel is not a multiuser system, our Finger server returns information about the system hardware configuration, rather than returning a list of users currently logged on. To obtain information about a specific hardware item, simply specify its name. For example, if we enter

```
finger vga@192.168.1.2
```

our Finger server returns

```
Finger vga@192.168.1.2:

VGA: I/O port at 0x3D4,
     0x4000 bytes of screen memory at 0xB8000
```

As a comparison, here's the output from a different Finger server running on a typical UNIX host. In response to the command

```
[cyliax@hugo]$ finger @localhost
```

the Finger server returns information about the users who are logged on (note that to generate this sample output, the same user logged on the UNIX system six times):

```
[localhost]
Login     Name            Tty       Idle    Login Time      Office
cyliax    Ingo Cyliax     1         3d      Nov 21 00:19
cyliax    Ingo Cyliax     *p0       4:17    Nov 21 00:19
cyliax    Ingo Cyliax     *p1       1d      Nov 21 00:20
cyliax    Ingo Cyliax     p2                Nov 21 00:27
cyliax    Ingo Cyliax     p3        1:22    Nov 21 00:56
cyliax    Ingo Cyliax     p4                Nov 22 19:25
```

Fingering a specific user of the system (who is not necessarily logged on at the moment) with the `finger lisa@localhost` command returns information about that user:

```
[localhost]
Login: lisa                        Name: Lisa Huffman-Cyliax
Directory: /home/lisa              Shell: /bin/csh
Last login Wed Nov 19 10:29 (EDT) on ttyp3 from localhost
Mail forwarded to lisa@ezcomm.com
No mail.
No Plan.
```

THE FINGER SERVER CODE

Let's look at the source code for the Finger server, which is a typical example of how a server application that uses TCP is constructed. Perusal of the Finger client code is left to you; it's a simple and well-commented program. Although the Finger client is built to run under Windows, the same code could run under ETS Kernel, because both Windows and ETS Kernel provide the WinSock API for network programming.

The Finger server is a multithreaded program. The main thread of execution provides a simple user interface on the target system. The user interface prints Finger queries as they come in, and allows the user to display a summary of all queries received by typing p, or to exit the Finger server program by typing q. The keyboard thread processes keyboard input, and the Finger server thread handles network I/O. We limit the discussion to the networking code in the program.

The Finger server thread is contained in the `FingerThread()` function. This function spends most of its time asleep, listening for client connections on TCP port 79, the Finger well-known (agreed-upon) port. When a Finger client initiates a connection, `FingerThread()` calls `ServiceFingerQuery()` to process the query and send a response.

Setting up a Socket

Let's look first at the code for `FingerThread()` in Listing 15-1. `FingerThread()` establishes a passive TCP connection on which it waits for a client to connect.

Listing 15-1: The FingerThread() function

```
//
// create a TCP socket, put it in non-blocking mode, bind it to the
// finger port, and set up to listen for incoming connections
//
    hListenSock = socket(AF_INET, SOCK_STREAM, IPPROTO_TCP);
    if (hListenSock == INVALID_SOCKET)
    {
        printf("Can't create socket\n");
        goto Err;
    }
    fPolling = 1;
```

```
if (ioctlsocket(hListenSock, FIONBIO, &fPolling) == SOCKET_ERROR)
{
    printf("Can't put socket in non-blocking mode\n");
    goto Err;
}
pServEnt = getservbyname("finger", "tcp");
if (pServEnt == NULL)
{
    LocalPort = htons(IPPORT_FINGER);
    printf("Error %d getting finger port\n", WSAGetLastError());
    printf("Using well-known port %d\n", ntohs(LocalPort));
}
else
    LocalPort = pServEnt->s_port;
LocalAddr.sin_family = AF_INET;
LocalAddr.sin_port = LocalPort;
LocalAddr.sin_addr.s_addr = htonl(INADDR_ANY);
if (bind(hListenSock, (PSOCKADDR) &LocalAddr, sizeof(LocalAddr))
                == SOCKET_ERROR)
{
    printf("Error %d binding to finger port\n",
           WSAGetLastError());
    goto Err;
}
if (listen(hListenSock, SOMAXCONN) == SOCKET_ERROR)
{
    printf("Error %d listening on finger port\n",
           WSAGetLastError());
    goto Err;
}
```

The server uses the socket (AF_INET, SOCK_STREAM, IPPROTO_TCP) call to create a socket and obtain a handle to it. The arguments tell the TCP/IP stack what kind of socket we would like to set up. The first argument specifies the Internet address family (which is always specified for TCP/IP programming; the WinSock API is designed to support other protocol stacks, as well). The second argument specifies that we want a stream socket, that is, a connection-oriented socket that provides a byte-stream delivery service. The last argument selects TCP as the transport layer protocol.

By default, all sockets are created as blocking sockets. We want to use nonblocking sockets for the Finger server for two reasons. First, we want to be able to receive a signal from the main thread when the user types q to exit the program, so that we can close the socket and exit the thread cleanly. If we block indefinitely waiting for the next Finger query, we won't be able to respond in a timely manner to the exit signal. Second, we want to be able to implement timeouts when conversing with the Finger client program, so that if something unexpected happens (for example, the connection of a client that doesn't correctly implement the requirements of the protocol), we won't block forever waiting for the client program to do something. The following call changes the mode of hListenSock from blocking to nonblocking:

```
fPolling = 1;
if (ioctlsocket(hListenSock, FIONBIO, &fPolling) == SOCKET_ERROR)
```

The `ioctlsocket()` function is used to get and set socket options. The `FIONBIO` command sets the blocking mode for the socket; by setting the `fPolling` flag to 1, we select non-blocking mode.

Next, we need to associate the appropriate local IP address and TCP port number with the socket we've just created. With the `getservbyname()` call, we find the well-known port number for the Finger service. We use the `bind()` call to assign the port number and IP address to our socket. The `bind()` call uses a data structure called the `socket_addr` to specify the port and IP address. The Socket API uses this structure as a general-purpose object to store the IP address and the port of a connection. It has three members: the address family (`sin_family`), which has to match that of the socket; the IP address (`sin_addr`); and the port (`sin_port`). We leave the address field of the structure to `INADDR_ANY`, which is shorthand for "Use the host's IP address."

Finally, we put `hListenSock` into a passive listening mode by calling `listen()`. When the socket is in listening mode, TCP acknowledges incoming connection requests for that port and puts them in a queue. Requests are removed from the queue when the application calls `accept()`, as you see in a moment. In addition to the socket handle, the `listen()` function takes a parameter specifying the maximum number of connections that will be kept in the queue. After the queue is filled, any additional connection requests will be refused. If the queue size is set too high, buffer resources are unnecessarily consumed by the stack. `SOMAXCONN` is a WinSock constant that specifies a reasonable maximum queue size of 5 connections.

Waiting for a Connection

After `FingerThread()` has finished initializing the socket to listen for incoming connections from Finger clients, it enters the infinite loop in Listing 15-2, servicing queries from clients and checking for the exit signal from the main thread.

Listing 15-2: FingerThread()'s while() loop

```
//
// Just sit in a loop servicing finger queries, until the main
// thread signals us to terminate.  Because the socket is in
// non-blocking mode we can just poll for remote connections
// inside the loop.
//
   while (TRUE)
   {
//
// Poll for a connection from a remote finger client.  If there
// is one, service the query.
//
      RemoteLen = sizeof(RemoteAddr);
      hConnectSock = accept(hListenSock, (PSOCKADDR)&RemoteAddr,
                     &RemoteLen);
```

```
        if (hConnectSock != INVALID_SOCKET)
            ServiceFingerQuery(hConnectSock, &RemoteAddr);
        else
        {
            ErrVal = WSAGetLastError();
            if (ErrVal != WSAEWOULDBLOCK)
            {
                printf("Error %d accepting connection\n",
                       ErrVal);
                goto Err;
            }
        }

//
// Check if the main thread told us to terminate
//
        if (WaitForSingleObject(hTerminateEvent, 0) == WAIT_OBJECT_0)
            break;

//
// Release the rest of our time slice to avoid chewing up CPU
// cycles continuously polling the socket.
//
        Sleep(10);
    }
```

The accept() function removes the oldest pending connection from the front of the queue and returns a new socket handle, hConnectSock, specifying the connection. The new socket contains the IP address and TCP port number of the Finger client program on the remote host, in addition to the local information we've already placed in hListenSock. The accept() call creates a new socket rather than modifying hListenSock, so the original socket remains available for new incoming connections. hConnectSock is created with the same properties assigned to hListenSock, so it's also a nonblocking socket. If no connections are pending, accept() sets the error to WSAEWOULDBLOCK and returns INVALID_SOCKET for the socket handle.

Each time through the loop, after calling accept() and either processing the new connection by calling ServiceFingerQuery() or noticing that no connections are pending, FingerThread() calls WaitForSingleObject() to check whether the main thread has signaled hTerminateEvent. If the terminate event is signaled, the code breaks out of the loop, closes hListenSock, and exits the thread. Otherwise, it calls sleep(10) to release the rest of its time slice before looping back up to call accept() again. This minimizes the CPU overhead consumed by FingerThread() while waiting for connections from Finger clients.

Servicing the Query

To service a query, Finger calls the ServiceFingerQuery() routine in Listing 15-3. The first part of the routine reads the client's query into a buffer on the stack.

Listing 15-3: The ServiceFingerQuery() routine

```
//
// Read chars into buffer until (1) we get terminating <LF> or <CRLF> or
// (2) we timeout.  Replace the terminating <CRLF> with end-of-string.
//
    memcpy(&RawQuery.FingerAddr, pAddr, sizeof(*pAddr));
    time(&RawQuery.FingerTime);
    fBufOverflow = FALSE;
    for (pBuf = Buf; TRUE; )
    {
        // Read as much data as we can
        nRecv = recv(hSock, pBuf, sizeof(Buf) - (pBuf-Buf), 0);
        if (nRecv == SOCKET_ERROR)
        {
            ErrVal = WSAGetLastError();
            if (ErrVal == WSAEWOULDBLOCK)
                nRecv = 0;
            else
            {
                printf("Error %d receiving finger query\n", ErrVal);
                goto Done;
            }
        }
        else if (nRecv == 0)
        {
            // server is supposed to close the connection!
            printf("Finger client closed connection\n");
            goto Done;
        }
        pBuf += nRecv;

        // Check if it's end of query (<LF> or <CRLF>).
        if (pBuf > Buf && *(pBuf-1) == '\n')
        {
            if (pBuf - Buf >= 2 && *(pBuf-2) == '\r')
                *(pBuf - 2) = 0;
            else
                *(pBuf - 1) = 0;
            break;
        }

        // Check for buffer overflow.  If so just flag it and
        // continue reading the query, saving the last byte in case
        // it's the first byte of a terminating <CRLF> pair.
        if (pBuf - Buf >= sizeof(Buf))
        {
            fBufOverflow = TRUE;
            Buf[0] = Buf[sizeof(Buf) - 1];
            pBuf = &Buf[1];
        }
```

```
         // Check for timeout before complete query received
         time(&CurTime);
         if (CurTime - RawQuery.FingerTime > FINGER_TIMEOUT)
         {
             printf("Timed out waiting for finger query\n");
             goto Done;
         }
    }
```

In spite of the length of this loop, it basically just calls recv() repeatedly, reading received characters into the buffer, until it sees the LF or CR-LF combination, which the Finger protocol specifies as the termination of the client's query. The rest of the code checks for errors, such as the client closing the connection before the entire query is sent, the query overflowing the receive buffer, or the connection exceeding our timeout value of five seconds before the entire query is received.

The recv() function

```
nRecv = recv(hSock, pBuf, sizeof(Buf) - (pBuf-Buf), 0);
```

is an interesting call. For byte-stream (TCP) connections, recv() returns as much data as is available and will fit in the buffer. Because we're using a nonblocking socket, recv() always returns immediately, without waiting for a specific number of bytes to arrive, which is why we call it in a loop. Recv() returns the number of bytes read, or 0 if the connection is closed by the remote host, or SOCKET_ERROR if an error occurred.

After the complete query is received, we break out of the loop and process the query to construct a response string in a buffer. The code is shown in Listing 15-4.

Listing 15-4: Building a query response

```
//
// Construct the appropriate response string to the query.
// We refuse to support @hostname forms of finger queries.
//
    if (fBufOverflow)
    {
        strcpy(Buf, "Query overflowed server's buffer\n");
    }
    else
    {
        // Consume /W, if any
        pBuf = Buf;
        fVerbose = FALSE;
        if (*pBuf == '/' && *(pBuf+1) == 'W')
        {
            fVerbose = TRUE;
            pBuf += 2;
            while (*pBuf == ' ')
                ++ pBuf;
        }
```

```
    // construct reply
    if (strchr(pBuf, '@') != NULL)
        // we don't support @hostname
        strcpy(Buf, "Finger forwarding service denied\n");
    else if (*pBuf == 0)
    {
        // no username — all config info requested
        Buf[0] = 0;
        for (pConfig = pConfigList; pConfig != NULL;
                pConfig = pConfig->pNext)
        {
            sprintf(Buf2, "%s: %s\n", pConfig->pName,
                    pConfig->pInfo);
            if (strlen(Buf) + strlen(Buf2) >= sizeof(Buf))
                // this one won't fit in buffer
                continue;
            strcat(Buf, Buf2);
        }
    }
    else
    {
        // info on specific configuration entry requested
        for (pConfig = pConfigList; pConfig != NULL;
                pConfig = pConfig->pNext)
            if (_stricmp(pBuf, pConfig->pName) == 0)
                break;
        if (pConfig == NULL)
        {
            memmove(Buf, pBuf, strlen(pBuf) + 1);
            strcat(Buf, ": no configuration entry\n");
        }
        else
            sprintf(Buf, "%s: %s\n", pConfig->pName,
                    pConfig->pInfo);
    }

}
```

This code first handles a few provisions in the Finger protocol. The /W flag at the beginning of the query requests a verbose response. A Finger server can also be requested to forward the query to a second host, using the @hostname syntax at the start of the query. Our Finger server refuses to provide this optional service. After these options are consumed, the rest of the query is either null, which means the server should return information on all logged-on users (or in our implementation, all hardware configuration information), or contains the name of a specific user (or hardware component, in our case) that the server should return information on.

After building the response in a buffer, the next step, shown in Listing 15-5, is to send the response to the Finger client.

Listing 15-5: The Send() routine

```
//
// Send the response string to the finger client.  Because
// this is a non-blocking socket, we may have to call send()
// multiple times to transmit all the data.  We use select()
// to wait until more data can be accepted, to avoid calling
// send() repeatedly and consuming CPU cycles.
//
    FD_ZERO(&SendSet);
    FD_SET(hSock, &SendSet);
    for (pBuf = Buf; *pBuf != 0; )
    {
        nSend = send(hSock, pBuf, strlen(pBuf), 0);
        if (nSend == SOCKET_ERROR)
        {
            ErrVal = WSAGetLastError();
            if (ErrVal == WSAEWOULDBLOCK)
                nSend = 0;
            else
            {
                printf("Error %d sending finger response\n", ErrVal);
                goto Done;
            }
        }
        pBuf += nSend;
        if (*pBuf != 0)
            select(0, NULL, &SendSet, NULL, NULL);
    }
```

This code just calls `send()` in a loop until all the data has been sent to the Finger client. `Send()` returns the number of bytes sent (or, more accurately, consumed by the TCP/IP stack; some or all data may actually be buffered locally for a short time before going out over the network). If an error occurs, send() returns SOCKET_ERROR. We ignore the WSAEWOULDBLOCK error; because we're using a nonblocking socket, we expect `send()` to return immediately even if it can't consume any data at the moment. Each time through the loop, we call `select()` to wait until the next time the socket is ready to accept data to be sent. This avoids needlessly consuming CPU cycles calling `send()` repeatedly when the socket's data buffers are already full. The `select()` function is passed three separate lists of sockets to check for readability, writeability, and errors. We're interested in only writing a socket, so we pass NULL for the other two lists. The final NULL argument is a pointer to an optional timeout period; because we don't specify a timeout, `select()` blocks indefinitely until the socket is writeable.

Closing the Connection

After sending all the response data, we close the connection to the client. When we call `closesocket()`, TCP uses the FIN handshake to indicate to the other side that we have no more data to send and want to close the connection. The client side, after noticing that the server has closed the connection, also issues a `closesocket()` and thus completes the FIN handshake, after which the TCP session goes away and the socket resources are reclaimed by the system.

```
//
// Close the connection and exit
//
Done:
    closesocket(hSock);
    return;
```

Although this example is simple, it demonstrates the essentials of the server part of an Internet application.

SUMMARY

We've taken you on a whirlwind tour of networking. We started out by explaining some fundamental concepts such as the ISO/OSI model, a layered network architecture that is the standard for exchanging data on a network. Most network technologies implement either the ISO/OSI architecture or an architecture whose layers map to the ISO/OSI layers.

Next, we discussed some considerations to keep in mind when choosing a protocol stack and network technology to make an embedded system network-aware. Although your choice of a protocol stack will be primarily determined by what network (or networks) you want your system to work with, a likely choice is TCP/IP, because it's the most widely used network architecture worldwide due to the popularity of the Internet. For this reason, we chose to examine the TCP/IP stack layers and protocols.

Finally, we gave an example of what's involved in adding networking to an embedded system using Fingserv, a server program that implements the Finger protocol. The Finger protocol uses the client/server communications model to retrieve information about a network host.

In the next chapter, we discuss HTTP, the application-level protocol used for implementing the web, and HTML, the markup language used by the majority of documents transmitted over the web. We also look at the MicroWeb Server components of ETS Kernel that we used to embed a web server in the UPS application, and look at the code in the Network-Aware UPS that generates the HTML for the UPS web pages.

16

Connecting to the Web

The World Wide Web (or simply, the *web*) was invented in 1990 by Tim Berners-Lee, a computer scientist at CERN, the European Laboratory for Particle Physics (http://www.cern.ch). It was intended as a tool for sharing information in the high-energy physics community, but its more general utility as a widely distributed database for all kinds of information was quickly recognized and its use spread rapidly throughout the Internet community.

The basic idea of the web is to combine computer networking and hypertext media to create a powerful, easy-to-use global information system. *Hypertext* is text that contains links to further information; with computer networks, those links can access information anywhere in the world. Berners-Lee and his coworkers created the first web server and web browser. They defined the Hypertext Transfer Protocol (HTTP) as the protocol used by web browsers and servers to request and transmit resources, or web pages. They defined the Uniform Resource Locator (URL) concept, which combines the name of the Internet node, the name of a single resource, and the name of the protocol used to retrieve the resource into a single unique name. And they defined a document structure called Hypertext Markup Language (HTML), based on the existing Standard Generalized Markup Language (SGML). HTML documents on the web are uniquely identified by a URL and contain hypertext links coded as URLs to other resources on the web. The specifications for HTTP, HTML, and other web standards are maintained by the World Wide Web Consortium (W3C); you can download the latest version of all specifications from http://www.w3.org.

HTTP is an application-level protocol that encodes the conversation between web browsers and web servers. HTTP provides a stateless connection between a client and a server. In practice, this means an HTTP client sends a message to an HTTP server requesting a resource. At some later time, the server asynchronously responds to the request, either by forwarding the resource the client requested or by sending a reply saying that it is unable or unwilling to do so. Initially rudimentary, HTTP has evolved into a feature-rich protocol that is flexible, extensible, and backward-compatible with earlier versions of the protocol.

Note that unlike a conversation using a point-to-point network protocol, an HTTP conversation has no continuously maintained connection between the client and server. After the client issues its request and the server responds, the connection is terminated. Although the client may — and frequently does — go on to request other resources from the same server, each request is a discrete connection. The stateless nature of HTTP is of great benefit to HTTP servers in embedded systems because it dramatically reduces the overhead required to conduct a conversation over a network.

HTML is the lingua franca of the web: All web browsers understand it, and it therefore serves as the basis of a universal GUI for embedded systems applications. The key innovation in HTML is the *hyperlink*, which facilitates the navigation of separate but related documents, without respect to the location of the documents. More precisely, HTML creates links between *resources*. In most cases, resources are documents or some form of text, but a key point for developers of embedded systems is that resources may also represent items such as devices and sensors. Another powerful advantage of HTML is that it enables form-based interactive documents, which makes web content responsive to manipulation by end users. Using HTML forms, users can enter data, access databases, and control devices. Developers benefit from HTML's simple, standardized, programming language.

Because of the huge popularity of the web — after email, a web browser is the most common Internet application — it's desirable to design your embedded systems to connect to the web using the HTTP and HTML standards. Then anyone with a standard web browser can communicate with your system. In this chapter, we describe how HTTP and HTML work and how to use them effectively in an embedded system. We also examine the source code in the Network-Aware UPS that generates the HTML web pages for the UPS system and the source code of the HTTP server component of the ETS Kernel MicroWeb Server.

HTTP IN EMBEDDED APPLICATIONS

What can you do with HTTP in embedded systems? Most importantly, HTTP provides a simple, standard way to transfer files in both directions. You can download files and programs to your embedded applications and also upload data from your embedded system. In either direction, these files can contain any kind of data. HTTP doesn't care about the file's contents, but as you will see later, you can use a message header to easily identify the contents. You can also increase the advantages of the integrated networking support included in most real-time operating systems. Adding HTTP server functionality to network-aware embedded systems makes them instantly accessible to the millions of desktop and notebook systems that integrate web browser software.

A strength of HTTP is that the elements of the protocol itself are plain ASCII text. HTTP conversations may be directly observed without passing through an interpreter or special hardware. The textual nature of HTTP is valuable to developers of embedded systems because it simplifies the debugging process for devices deployed across network topologies. Although HTTP itself is text based, we alluded to the fact that it imposes no inherent limits on the types of data that may be exchanged between an HTTP client and an HTTP server. In the applications you examine in this chapter, we use HTTP to arbitrate the transfer of HTML documents that include nontextual content. Using the same techniques, you can transmit HTML documents that include a variety of data formats, such as binaries, animation, still images, and audio files.

The capability to format and transfer HTML documents from an embedded web server confers a great advantage on many embedded applications. Often, embedded devices lack support for keyboard input and video display output. Providing an easy-to-use, convenient, and powerful user interface to an embedded device is a challenging task. Web browsers and standard HTML form-based interfaces solve these problems for developers of embedded systems, enabling them to concentrate on application-specific functionality and feature sets. This design strategy was demonstrated in Chapter 14, where we used HTML and a web browser running on a Windows-based desktop system to implement the user interface for the Network-Aware UPS.

Coke Machines on the Web

Dozens of soda machines are connected to the Internet (enter `+coke+machine` in the Yahoo! search engine to find them). One of the earliest was the Coke machine in the computer science department of Carnegie-Mellon University.

This Coke machine was located in a central location, some distance from the offices used by many of the staff and students. You might take a five-minute walk to get a Coke, only to find that the machine was empty or that your Coke was warm because that column in the machine had just been refilled. Some enterprising students set out to remedy this problem in 1982.

They wired the Coke machine to detect each light that lit when a column ran out and that flashed for a few seconds each time a Coke was sold. This detection circuit was connected by an RS-232 interface to a computer connected to the CMU network (and from there to the entire Internet). The students wrote software that polled the Coke machine once a second and determined — using the knowledge of how many Cokes fit in a filled column and the data collected about when Cokes were sold and when a column went empty — which columns were empty and which columns had Cokes that had been in the machine the longest and were therefore the coldest. This information was available to anyone on the CMU network (and by extension, anyone on the Internet) through a Finger server (like the project you examined in Chapter 15, "Networking"). To find out whether a trip to the Coke machine would produce a cold Coke, and if so which column to purchase your Coke from, all you had to do was *finger* (run a Finger client) the Coke machine from your office. A descendant of the original CMU Coke machine is still connected at `http://www.cs.cmu.edu/~coke/`.

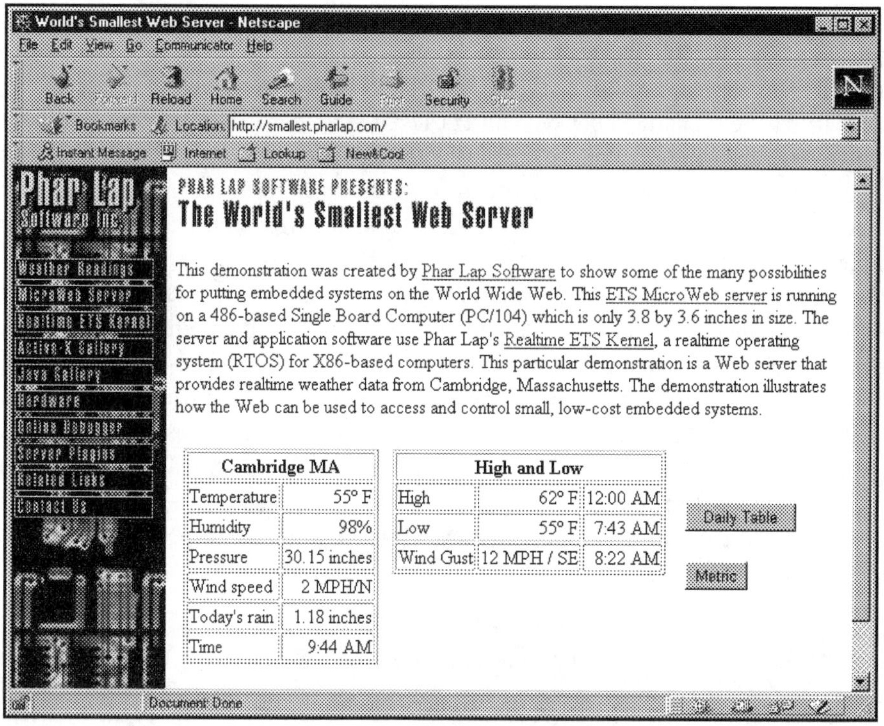

Figure 16-1: Phar Lap's weather station is an example of an embedded system providing up-to-the-second data over the web using HTTP and HTML.

For an example of an embedded system using HTTP, point your web browser to `http://smallest.pharlap.com` to display the web page shown in Figure 16-1. This embedded system, billed as the "world's smallest web server" (it runs on a PC/104 SBC that measures 3.6" x 3.8"), is connected to a Davis Instruments weather station on the roof of Phar Lap's offices in Cambridge, Massachusetts. The system provides real-time weather data to web browsers on demand.

To get an idea of the power of providing data in real time using HTML and HTTP, enter the `http://smallest.pharlap.com/debug/` URL in your web browser to display the page shown in Figure 16-2.

From this online debugger page, you can examine system memory, look at the code running in the system, display the active threads in the system, and more, using a standard web browser running anywhere in the world. Poke around a bit to see how much detail `smallest.pharlap.com` provides, using the same techniques to generate web pages on demand that we show you in the Network-Aware UPS.

Thousands of embedded systems are connected to the Internet. For example, go to the Yahoo! search engine and enter `WebCam` to display hundreds of sites that provide real-time images from systems with cameras connected to the web. You can use a web browser to collect data from your embedded system; download new data or software updates to your embedded

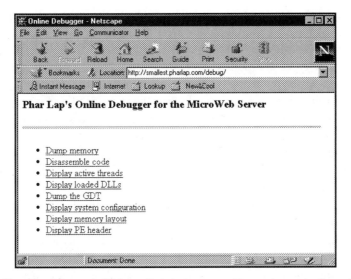

Figure 16-2: The online debugger built into smallest.pharlap.com enables you to examine the system's internals remotely, using a standard web browser.

system; reconfigure your embedded system; debug your embedded system; or do anything else you can think of that utilizes the capability to pass data back and forth over a network.

THE HTTP PROTOCOL

HTTP is an application-level protocol that uses TCP for the transport layer protocol. The most current version of HTTP, 1.1, is described in RFC 2068. Check this document if you want the full details. We use version 1.1 in our explorations and examples, but be aware that support for HTTP 1.1 may not be fully implemented across all platforms. In general, this won't be an insurmountable problem for your applications, because HTTP clients and servers are backward-compatible with earlier protocol versions.

HTTP uses the client/server networking model we covered in Chapter 15, "Networking." The HTTP server waits for connections on a well-known TCP port, port 80. HTTP clients initiate connections on port 80, and after the connection is established, send a request for a specific resource. The web server sends a response that indicates an error condition, or indicates success and includes the requested resource; then the web server closes the connection. HTTP resources are most often HTML documents but can be almost any type of data — pictures in various formats, audio data, binary executables, zip files, and so on.

WEB BROWSERS

A browser takes its name from the fact that it enables the user to navigate (browse) web content using hypertext links in HTML documents. Besides navigating using links, the browser also formats and displays HTML-encoded web pages retrieved from HTTP servers. Typical browsers can render and display HTML documents and GIF images directly, but may also require the services of external agents on the browser's host system to handle novel resource content. In particular, audio and video resources are usually played by an external application. Most browsers accept plug-in components that extend their functionality and allow them to handle new types of resource content. Because a web browser must be capable of understanding and displaying many types of content, it is a large, complex program.

The browser initiates resource retrieval when the user specifies a resource to fetch. The Uniform Resource Locator (URL) is the web name for a particular resource. Users can specify a URL by clicking a hyperlink or by typing a URL. The browser parses the URL and extracts the protocol (most often HTTP), the hostname (the server on which the resource resides), and the Universal Resource Identifier, or URI (the path and name of the desired resource on the specified server).

The browser then initiates a connection with the server for the specified protocol on the specified network host. Web browsers typically support several protocols in addition to HTTP (for example, FTP and SMTP), but we restrict our discussion to HTTP. An HTTP server listens for connections on TCP port 80, so the browser initiates a connection to that port. After the connection is established, the browser sends a request message that includes headers optionally identifying the user and listing accepted resource types. The server sends a response message that consists of a status line followed by one or more header fields and the requested resource.

When the browser receives this response, it first reads and decodes the status line to make sure the server could process the request properly. The status code consists of three decimal digits; any code in the range 2xx signifies success. On finding a successful status code, the browser reads and parses the header section up to a terminating blank line and extracts the resource type, the type of encoding, and the length. If the browser can handle the resource type and the encoding, it reads and appropriately processes the resource. If the resource type is suitable for screen display (for example, an HTML document and a GIF image), the browser renders and displays it. Finally, the resource is cached locally so that if the user browses back to the same page later, the browser has the option of loading it from the cache rather than over the network if the content hasn't changed. (The browser determines whether the content is unchanged with an HTTP request for only the header fields for the resource; one of the header fields gives the last change date for the resource content.)

HTML documents may embed images, called *inline graphics*. These are displayed along with the text in the HTML document but are downloaded asynchronously over separate HTTP connections, because they can add considerably to download times for an HTML page. After all document content has been retrieved, rendered, and displayed, the browser is ready to process the next user-requested link. Downloading a complex document is an iterative process and can require many HTTP transactions between the browser and server.

Web Servers

A web server is a much simpler program than a web browser. The server opens a passive TCP connection on the well-known HTTP port, port 80, and stands by waiting to accept connections. After accepting a connection, the server reads and parses the request line. If the action requested by the browser is not implemented or the URI is unavailable, the server returns an error status and closes the connection. Otherwise, the server proceeds by opening the resource indicated by the URI, which may be a resource in a disk file or a resource constructed in memory by a program or a subroutine. Before sending the data, the server builds an appropriate header section for the resource and sends it followed by a blank line. Finally, it sends the resource data and closes the connection. Web servers also implement HTTP features such as authentication and uploading files from clients.

URLs and URIs

Uniform Resource Locators (URLs) are used to locate resources on the Internet. The basic format of a URL is

```
protocol://hostname[:port]/pathname
```

The *protocol* field specifies the application-layer protocol to be used to access the resource. Following is a short list of common protocols:

http	HTTP protocol
ftp	FTP protocol
mailto	SMTP mail protocol
telnet	Telnet protocol

Following the protocol field, the *hostname* field specifies the name or IP address of the host computer that houses the requested resource. The *port* field is optional, and specifies the TCP port on which to request a connection with the host. If the port is not specified, the well-known port for the specified protocol is used.

Following the hostname field, the *pathname* field identifies a resource on the host. This subfield of the URL is known as the Universal Resource Identifier (URI). For example, the URL `http://smallest.pharlap.com/dir1/dir2/index.htm` means that we want to use the HTTP protocol to make a connection to `smallest.pharlap.com` on port 80 (the well-known port for HTTP). The resource we are interested in is located with the pathname `/dir1/dir2/index.htm`.

The HTTP protocol concerns itself only with the URI part of the URL. The remaining portion of the URL identifies the destination of the message and the protocol used to convey it. HTTP is one of several protocols you can specify in a URL.

HTTP Messages

HTTP messages are either requests sent from a client to a server or responses sent from a server to a client. The format of a message is

```
start-line
message-headers
CR LF
message-body
```

A request has three components: the start-line, the message-headers, and the message-body. The start-line is required; the message-headers and the message-body are optional.

The *start-line* is either a request-line, for requests sent from client to server, or a status-line, for responses sent from server to client. We cover these in the sections that follow on requests and responses.

The *message-headers* are zero or more lines of text, each containing one message-header terminated by CR LF (a carriage return character, 0x0D, and a linefeed character, 0x0A). The message-headers section is terminated by a blank line, containing only CR LF. Message headers are divided into four categories: *general-headers*, which are used in both requests and responses; *request-headers*, used only in requests; *response-headers*, used only in responses; and *entity-headers*, which are used in both requests and responses, and which define information about the entity, or resource, included in the message-body. The format of a message-header is:

```
field-name: field-value
```

Although you may send message-headers in any order, the recommended practice is to send general-headers first, followed by either request-headers or response-headers and ending with entity-headers. The HTTP 1.1 field-names for the general-header category are:

```
Cache-Control
Connection
Date
Pragma
Transfer-Encoding
Upgrade
Via
```

The HTTP 1.1 field-names for the entity-header category are:

```
Allow
Content-Base
Content-Encoding
Content-Language
Content-Length
Content-Location
Content-MD5
Content-Range
Content-Type
Etag
Expires
Last-Modified
```

The *message-body,* if present, contains the resource. The unencoded resource is called the *entity-body.* The message-body contains the unencoded entity-body or the entity-body encoded as indicated by the `Transfer-Encoding` header field.

The length of the message-body is specified either by a `Transfer-Encoding` header field or a `Content-Length` header field. If neither header field is present, the length is indicated by the server closing the connection for a response message. A request message must include a header field indicating the length of the message-body; closing the connection is not an option for the client because that would make it impossible for the server to send a response.

Request Messages

After the HTTP server accepts the client's connection, the client sends an HTTP request to the server. The format of an HTTP request message is

```
request-line
message-headers
CR LF
message-body
```

The request-line is required; the message-headers and the message-body are optional (except as noted later for simple requests conforming to the HTTP 0.9 specification). If the request does not include headers or a body, the request-line must be followed by a blank line containing only CR LF to terminate the request.

The *request-line* is a single line of text that has three fields and is terminated with CR LF.

```
method request-URI HTTP-version
```

The *method* indicates the action to be performed on the resource identified by the *request-URI*. Following is a list of methods that the client can use and the HTTP version in which they were introduced:

Method	Version
GET	0.9
HEAD	1.0
POST	1.0
PUT	1.1
DELETE	1.1
TRACE	1.1
OPTIONS	1.1

Only the POST and PUT methods can include a message-body.

The GET method causes the server to send the client the resource specified by the URI.

The HEAD method is similar to GET, but the server sends only the header section of the response, omitting the entity-body or the resource itself. This is useful if the client wants to know whether the resource has changed since the last time it was retrieved or the type or encoding of the resource without trying to retrieve the resource.

Whereas the GET and HEAD methods deal with retrieving resources from the server, the POST and PUT methods allow the client to send data to the server. Clients use PUT to send a resource to the server so that it can be stored there. The request headers and entity-body describe and contain the resource to be sent, respectively. The server-side implementation of the PUT method is application-dependent. If the server has a file system, it can simply store the PUT resource at the specified URI. In an embedded system, this method could be used to apply software updates to the system.

The POST method is also used to send data to the server but is designed to submit records to a database engine rather than to save resources as files. The POST method is typically used when you fill out an HTML form. For example, when using a web-based online ordering system, you enter information in the fields and click the Submit button in the form. The web browser sends an HTTP request to the server using the POST method, with the form data included as the entity-body in the request. The server receives the POST, processes the field data, and performs whatever database update function is implemented for that web page. You see an example of HTML forms when you examine the code in the Network-Aware UPS later in this chapter.

The DELETE method deletes files on the HTTP server's host computer and is mostly used by web authoring and maintenance tools. Both PUT and DELETE have the potential to be destructive, and many Internet service providers choose to disable these methods on their servers.

The TRACE method requests that the server reflect the message back to the client, with the request-line replaced with a status-line of 200 OK or an error status if appropriate. This method is used by clients for testing connections, in particular to test the effect of any message forwarding or caching by proxy servers in the request chain.

The OPTIONS method requests information about the communications options available for the requested URI. The response sent by the server includes message-headers containing information about the resource, specifically information related to transmission of the resource, but does not include a message-body.

The second field in the request-line, *request-URI*, identifies a resource on the server. In many server implementations, the URI identifies a file in the server's file system space. Note, however, that URIs are purely symbolic identifiers that merely specify a resource, not necessarily a file. The server can construct the resource dynamically when it receives the request; that's what the code in the Network-Aware UPS does. The server could also use URIs to identify specific physical devices, such as an indicator light. For example, you could implement one URI named /light/on and another named /light/off. If you send this request:

```
GET /light/on
```

the server implementation interprets the symbolic URI, turns the light on, and perhaps sends a response message to the client confirming that the light has been turned on. Similarly, the request message:

```
GET /light/off
```

could turn the light off again.

This clever but simple technique is a key tool for developers of embedded systems. You can use simple textual HTTP directives to implement control functions in embedded devices that do not have file storage for resources. The symbolic URIs are mapped to actions, devices, and monitoring tasks.

The third field in the request line is *HTTP-version*. It is of the form HTTP/version.revision and identifies the protocol version assumed by the message format. Omitting the HTTP-version field in the request line indicates that you are using HTTP version 0.9 or older, and that you want to use the simple request and response format specified for version 0.9. A simple request is a request that contains only a request-line and can specify only the GET method. The simple request has no message-header or message-body section. A response to a simple request is just a message-body, with no start-line or message-headers.

If the server does not implement the version of the protocol specified in the request line, it may respond with an error message indicating that it does not support the requested version or that it is simply confused. The client then tries successively older versions of the protocol, until it discovers one that the server implements. All servers understand version 0.9, so it is the lowest common denominator, and virtually all servers understand version 1.0.

The message-headers follow the request-line in an HTTP request message. The *message-headers* in a request can include any field-names from the general-header, request-header, and entity-header categories. The HTTP 1.1 field-names for the request-header category are:

```
Accept
Accept-Charset
Accept-Encoding
Accept-Language
Authorization
From
Host
If-Modified-Since
If-Match
If-None-Match
If-Range
If-Unmodified-Since
Max-Forwards
Proxy-Authorization
Range
Referer
User-Agent
```

Finally, the *message-body* (the last section of the HTTP request message), if present, contains data to be sent to the server. This data might be form-oriented information sent along with the POST method, or it may be the content of a resource to be stored using the PUT method.

Response Messages

The format of the response message sent by the server to the client is

```
status-line
message-headers
CR LF
message-body
```

The status-line is required; the message-headers and the message-body are optional. Unlike a request, however, a response almost always includes message-headers and a message-body. Most error responses sent by a server include a message-body that contains HTML-formatted text explaining the error. A few errors do not include a message-body; see the HTTP specification for details.

The server uses the *status-line* to inform the client of the disposition of the request. The status-line has three fields and is terminated by a CR LF:

```
HTTP-version status-code reason-phrase
```

The *HTTP-version* field indicates the HTTP version the server is using for the response. This field has the same format as the HTTP-version field in the request line and may be used to negotiate the highest version of the HTTP protocol common to both the client and the server.

The *status-code* field consists of a three-digit code that the server uses to indicate the status of the request. Many application-layer protocols such as SMTP and FTP use these three-digit status codes. The first digit of the code indicates the severity of the status or error; the second and third digits encode a specific error. In practice, the first digit in the code is the most important. Status code groups specified for HTTP 1.1 are

- 1*xx*: **Informational.** The request was received and the process is continuing.

- 2*xx*: **Success.** The response fulfills the client's request.

- 3*xx*: **Redirection.** The request can't be satisfied because the resource has moved or must be accessed in some other way. Further action is required by the client.

- 4*xx*: **Client error.** The request is incorrectly formatted or cannot be fulfilled because the client is not permitted access to the resource.

- 5*xx*: **Server error.** The request appears to be valid, but the server cannot fulfill the request because of an internal error or lack of a necessary feature.

Codes 4*xx* and 5*xx* indicate that an error has occurred. A client error means that the server did not understand the client's request message. The request was probably illegally formatted. A server error could mean that a resource is not available, or that the server is out of memory or can't perform the request for some other reason. The last field in the status line, *reason-phrase*, is a textual string representing the status code. The string is used for information only and provides a human-readable format for the error code. Table 16-1 shows the complete list of status codes specified for HTTP 1.1.

Table 16-1: Status Codes and Recommended Reason-Phrases

Status Code	Reason-Phrase
100	Continue
101	Switching Protocols
200	OK
201	Created
202	Accepted
203	Non-Authoritative Information
204	No Content

continues

Table 16-1: Status Codes and Recommended Reason-Phrases (*continued*)

Status Code	Reason-Phrase
205	Reset Content
206	Partial Content
300	Multiple Choices
301	Moved Permanently
302	Moved Temporarily
303	See Other
304	Not Modified
305	Use Proxy
400	Bad Request
401	Unauthorized
402	Payment Required
403	Forbidden
404	Not Found
405	Method Not Allowed
406	Not Acceptable
407	Proxy Authentication Required
408	Request Time-out
409	Conflict
410	Gone
411	Length Required
412	Precondition Failed
413	Request Entity Too Large
414	Request-URI Too Large
415	Unsupported Media Type
500	Internal Server Error
501	Not Implemented
502	Bad Gateway
503	Service Unavailable
504	Gateway Time-out
505	HTTP Version Not Supported

The *message-headers* in a response can include any field-names from the general-header, response-header, and entity-header categories. The HTTP 1.1 field-names for the response-header category are:

```
Age
Location
Proxy-Authenticate
Public
```

```
Retry-After
Server
Vary
Warning
WWW-Authenticate
```

The *message-body* sent following the message-headers contains either the requested resource or an HTML-formatted message giving more detail about the status-code.

Message Headers

The creators of HTTP intentionally built upon protocols and practices in widespread use at the time. In particular, the headers are based on the Multipurpose Internet Mail Extensions (MIME) headers (specified in RFC 1521) used for email messages. Headers act like variables: They associate a symbolic field-name with a field-value. Now let's examine a few of the more commonly used HTTP headers in a bit more detail.

The HTTP RFC commonly refers to header field-names simply as headers; for example, "the `Content-Type` header" as opposed to "the header containing the `Content-Type` field name." Since this usage is more readable, we follow the same convention here.

The `Content-Type` header specifies the media type contained in the requested resource. The header has the following format:

```
Content-Type: media_type [;options]
```

where *media_type* describes the encoding of the resource in the message section. Media types may be any of the Internet Media Types registered with the Internet Assigned Numbers Authority (IANA), as specified in RFC 2048. Some common media types are

`text/plain`	Simple text document
`text/html`	HTML document
`text/postscript`	PostScript document
`image/gif`	GIF encoded image
`image/tiff`	TIFF encoded image
`application/zip`	ZIP archive

The `Content-Length` header specifies the length of the resource, in bytes:

```
Content-Length: digits
```

The `Date` header specifies the time and date when a message was created. The `Date` header information must be in one of the following formats:

```
Date:   day-of-week, day month year hh:mm:ss GMT
Date:   day-of-week, day-month-year hh:mm:ss GMT
Date:   day-of-week month day hh:mm:ss year
```

The `Server` header identifies the server software that generated the response. The basic format of the `Server` header is

```
Server: server-information
```

The *server-information* field normally contains a product name followed by a colon and a version number. Clients can use this information to exploit features or implement workarounds for problems found in a specific implementation of the server software.

The User-Agent header identifies the client software to the server:

```
User-Agent: client-information
```

In addition to anticipating protocol implementation problems by the client, the server can use this information for statistics.

The From header identifies the email address of the user of the client program:

```
From: email-address-of-user
```

The user's email address is usually logged in the servers access log file and can be used for statistics. It should not be used for authentication because most client implementations enable the user to configure this information. The server may also use this information to communicate with the user by email. For example, a server might notify the user if resources retrieved in the past have changed. Less altruistically, some marketing organizations use this information to build mailing lists for sending Internet junk mail, or spam.

To send implementation-specific directives, you use the Pragma header:

```
Pragma: directive
```

This header is used to extend the functionality of the HTTP protocol without adding extra headers to the protocol definition. Sometimes these extensions are added for testing and evaluation. The Pragma header is also an excellent way to add application-specific functionality to HTTP. If a client or server implementation does not understand the directive in the Pragma header, it will ignore the directive and not consider it a syntax or protocol error. The pragma directives specified in HTTP 1.1 include the following:

```
No-cache
Hold-connection
```

The Last-Modified header gives the data and time a resource was last modified:

```
Last-Modified: date
```

Clients and proxy servers can use this information to decide whether cached versions of the resource are still up-to-date.

The If-Modified-Since header is sent with the client request to instruct the server not to include the content of the resource in the response unless the content is newer than the specified date:

```
If-Modified-Since: date
```

In addition to the headers covered here, several others are specified by the HTTP RFC; we listed their field-names previously. If you want more information, check the HTTP RFC to find out what each of the headers do and mean.

Using Telnet to Debug HTTP

Telnet is an Internet application that acts like a virtual terminal. You give it a host name and a TCP port number, and it opens a TCP connection. Any commands you type are sent to the server on the other host, and any responses sent by the server are printed on your display. Telnet can understand standard terminal escape sequences, such as the widely used DEC VT100 terminal commands. Telnet client programs are provided for most operating systems; for example, they are included as standard applications with all Windows and UNIX operating systems.

Telnet is primarily intended for interactive connections to Internet hosts. For example, it is frequently used for remote logon to a character-based command shell, such as one of the UNIX shells. Because HTTP, like most application-level protocols in TCP/IP, is an ASCII-only protocol, however, you can easily use a telnet client to debug an HTTP server. You connect to the HTTP server on TCP port 80 with telnet and then type the request message; telnet prints the response message on your display. For example, we'll use telnet to connect to the Internet host `smallest.pharlap.com`, and display the HTML for the top-level web page. In other words, instead of typing `http://smallest.pharlap.com/` in a browser, we'll use telnet to connect to port 80 on host `smallest.pharlap.com`:

```
[cyliax@hugo]$ telnet smallest.pharlap.com 80
Telnet responds with:Trying 192.233.86.137...
Connected to smallest.pharlap.com.
Escape character is '^]'.
```

Then we'll use the GET method to retrieve the / URI (the top level web page on the server). Essentially, you'll emulate what an HTTP client does during an HTTP session:

```
GET /

<HTML>
<HEAD>
<TITLE>World's Smallest Web Server</TITLE>
</HEAD>
<FRAMESET COLS="140,*" BORDER=0>
<FRAME SRC="nav.htm" MARGINWIDTH=0 NORESIZE>
<FRAME SRC="weather/current.htm" NAME="mane">
<!-- Get it?  Horsey's have manes!  -->
</FRAMESET>
<NOFRAMES>
<TABLE><TR VALIGN=top>
<TD>
<!--#include file="nav.htm"-->
</TD><TD>
<!--#include file="weather.htm"-->
</TD></TR></TABLE>
</NOFRAMES>
</HTML>
Connection closed by foreign host.
```

You used the simple HTTP 0.9 form of the request. Because you didn't enter an HTTP version number on the request line, the server returned the resource (the HTML document) with no status line or headers. Notice that you have to enter a blank line after the GET command to terminate the request before the server sends its response.

Now let's look at a full request and response. We connect to the same port and host and receive the same response:

```
[cyliax@hugo]$ telnet smallest.pharlap.com 80
Trying 192.233.86.137...
Connected to smallest.pharlap.com.
Escape character is '^]'.
```

This time, you use the GET method to stipulate that you are an HTTP 1.1 client on the request line. As a result, you get back a status line and several header lines in the response, before the message body, which contains the HTML page.

```
GET / http/1.1

HTTP/1.0 200 OK
Date: Fri, 15 May 1998 14:43:01 GMT
MIME-Version: 1.0
Server: MicroWeb/1.0
Content-Type: text/html
Content-Length: 414
Last-Modified: Wed, 11 Jun 1997 21:09:10 GMT

<HTML>
<HEAD>
<TITLE>World's Smallest Web Server</TITLE>
</HEAD>
<FRAMESET COLS="140,*" BORDER=0>
<FRAME SRC="nav.htm" MARGINWIDTH=0 NORESIZE>
<FRAME SRC="weather/current.htm" NAME="mane">
<!- Get it?  Horsey's have manes!  -->
</FRAMESET>
<NOFRAMES>
<TABLE><TR VALIGN=top>
<TD>
<!-#include file="nav.htm"-->
</TD><TD>
<!-#include file="weather.htm"-->
</TD></TR></TABLE>
</NOFRAMES>
</HTML>
Connection closed by foreign host.
```

Using telnet to look at and debug protocols is an effective tool because you can observe the protocol conversation. You may want to experiment with variations of this technique. For example, use telnet to connect to an Internet mail server. The well-known port for this service is port 25. See whether you can send an email message to yourself, using the SMTP protocol, which is covered in Chapter 15, "Networking."

PERSISTENT CONNECTIONS

Before HTTP 1.1, a separate TCP connection was required for each client request. Because web pages often contain several embedded links to inline images and other associated data, a client often has to make multiple requests of the same server to completely display a single web page. In these circumstances, the overhead of opening and closing each TCP connection becomes significant.

HTTP 1.1 introduced persistent connections. If both the client and server implement HTTP 1.1 or later, the connection is persistent by default. The server does not automatically close the TCP connection after replying to a single request. Rather, the connection stays open until either the client or the server signals a close using the `Connection` header. This permits the client to send multiple requests and then initiate the closing of the connection. In addition, the client is permitted to *pipeline* requests — send multiple requests without waiting for a response — to achieve better throughput. The server is required to respond to pipelined requests in the order received.

Although connections are expected to persist with HTTP 1.1, the specification explicitly notes that both client and server must be prepared to gracefully handle an unsignaled close of the connection.

CACHING

Caching of resources generally occurs at the client and greatly improves performance. For example, in resources that use inline graphics for icons, remembering which icons you have fetched and storing them in memory or on the disk (if you have one) is highly advantageous. Caching speeds up resource loading at the client by reusing the relatively static data stored locally. This technique is so popular that most web browsers store everything they retrieve in a disk cache, which is typically several megabytes in size.

A proxy server can also help at an organization level. A *proxy server* is an HTTP server that relays client HTTP requests. Sometimes proxy servers are used to facilitate HTTP communications in which individual workstations don't have direct Internet access, such as workstations protected by firewalls. In other network topology schemes, the gateway between the intranet and Internet may forbid routing of application-layer protocols between networks. In these cases, the HTTP server on the platform that stands between a workstation and an Internet connection can be configured to act as a proxy server. In this role, the proxy server accepts connections from HTTP clients on an internal network and then itself acts as an HTTP client to retrieve resources from external HTTP servers.

A proxy server can be configured also to cache resources that internal clients have requested on a disk drive. In this case, the proxy server is called a *caching proxy server*. Commercial HTTP servers such as Netscape's Enterprise Server provide these features. By caching resources on a caching proxy server, you can dramatically speed up access to frequently requested resources because LAN-based internal networks are usually an order of magnitude faster (10 Mbps Ethernet versus an Internet connection that might be anything from a 14.4 Kbps modem up to a 1.4 Mbps cable modem connection).

To avoid returning stale (out-of-date) data from a cache, clients and proxy servers normally use the HEAD method to obtain the Last-Modified-Date header for the resource to decide whether the cache resource is up-to-date. If the cached copy of the resource is stale, the client or proxy server uses the GET method to obtain a new copy of the resource.

SECURE HTTP

You can enhance security in HTTP in three ways. You can restrict which clients can connect to your HTTP server (based on their IP addresses), you can use passwords to protect resources on a server, and you can encrypt the data in the HTTP session. All three methods can be used separately or in combination.

The first technique, restricting access to your HTTP server based on the client's identity, is the easiest to implement. The server examines the IP address of the client. If the address is in the list of acceptable Internet addresses, the server allows the client to make requests. Otherwise, the server simply closes the TCP session.

To implement password access to protected resources, HTTP provides a method that can be used to authenticate the client for access to resources on the server. The server tells the client that authentication is required to access a resource by returning the status code 401 or 407 and a WWW-Authenticate header in the response message. The WWW-Authenticate header has the basic format of

```
WWW-Authenticate: type realm="realm_name"
```

The *type* field specifies the authentication method the server wants to use. The *realm* identifies the group of resources on the server that are protected with this particular authentication method. The client uses the Authorization header in the request message to send a *cookie* containing a password or other authentication information to the server. The basic format is as follows:

```
Authorization: type cookie
```

Using the Basic authentication method, the client sends the user's logon and password for the particular realm the client wants to access. The logon and password are encoded using base64 encoding. This authentication method is not very secure because an attacker can find out the cookie for a realm and use it to gain access.

A stronger authentication method, called the Digest method, is described in RFC 2068. Unlike the Basic method, the Digest method does not send the logon and password in clear text as the cookie. For more details on this method, refer to RFC 2069, which describes the various encryption algorithms and the mechanisms used.

The last technique for making HTTP more secure is to encrypt all the traffic between the client and the server. This technique uses the Secure Sockets Layer (SSL) mechanism to establish a session key, and then encrypts all traffic over a TCP connection in both directions. The application-layer protocol, in this case HTTP, is not aware that encryption is taking place.

The details of how SSL establishes the session are complex, and we don't discuss them here. Commercial HTTP applications that use SSL also use the RSA encryption algorithm, which requires a license to implement. Commercial HTTP servers that use SSL can be obtained from Netscape and Microsoft. For more information on SSL and how it is used with HTTP, check out `http://home.netscape.com/newsref/std/SSL.html`.

HTML IN EMBEDDED APPLICATIONS

Since its inception, HTML has been continuously revised and expanded. As of this writing, the World Wide Web Consortium's (W3C) most recent, officially released version of HTML is 3.2. Currently, both Microsoft and Netscape are developing and testing features that extend the HTML 3.2 standard. Many of these features are included in HTML 4.0, released as a draft in 1996 by the W3C. HTML 4.0 will probably accrete several additional features before it is approved as a standard. If you want to learn about the content of HTML 4.0 and its features, download the most recent HTML 4.0 draft from W3C's web site, `http://www.w3c.org/`.

So what does HTML have to do with embedded systems programming, you might ask. Here's the answer: HTML is a universal formatting language that implements interactive network-based applications, making it a natural choice for quickly, easily, and reliably equipping embedded systems with form-driven device interfaces. We show you how to do exactly this, and explain why you should want to do so.

Using HTML in an embedded systems interface design has two benefits: cost savings and universal access. Both benefits accrue because developers using HTML can rely on off-the-shelf web browsers to view and interact with embedded devices. Not only does this relieve designers of embedded systems of the responsibility of providing the interface code, it makes embedded devices accessible from virtually anywhere. With web browsers bundled in every major desktop operating system (Windows, Mac OS, and UNIX all provide integrated browsers), an embedded GUI enjoys consistent appearance and behavior across a variety of browser hosts. In this sense, HTML is the basis of a universal GUI for embedded systems.

Contrast this to the time and effort required to build a proprietary GUI application for each of the various desktops that must communicate with an embedded system, and the economic benefits are sharply focused. The greatest advantage of HTML is that all user-interface management is delegated to the browser. By adding HTML support to your embedded applications, you can omit expensive display interface and user I/O hardware from an embedded system, and instead make the user interface available by remote access from any web browser.

We won't try to teach you HTML here; many excellent books have been written on that subject. One that we found useful is *HTML: The Definitive Guide*, by Chuck Musciano and Bill Kennedy (O'Reilly & Associates, Inc., 1997).

DYNAMIC HTML

Web pages don't have to be static data, stored in files on disk. In embedded systems, web pages usually shouldn't be static data. The value in using the HTTP and HTML standards to connect your embedded system to the web lies in making your web pages reflect the current state of the system and in enabling you to interact directly with the system in real time. To do that, you must construct your web pages dynamically, at the time the request is received from the client system. That way, the client always sees the most recent data about the system.

Common Gateway Interface (CGI) is a standard method for building web pages on-the-fly (as they are requested) and is widely used in multiprocessing operating systems such as UNIX. Using CGI, a web server constructs a page dynamically by spawning a separate process when a particular page is requested. The process is responsible for reading any parameters passed along with the URI, constructing the web page, and passing the web page back to the server to return to the client. The CGI process that builds the web page can be anything from a C program to a Perl script or a shell script.

In embedded systems, which frequently are multithreaded but not multiprocess, spawning a separate process to handle a request for a web page doesn't always make sense. Instead, commercial web servers for embedded systems frequently have proprietary hooks that allow the application to get control when a web page is requested and construct the data for the web page dynamically. In ETS Kernel, the HTTP server invokes an application-provided callback when a web page is requested; the application can read the resource from disk, construct it in memory, or do anything else that makes sense to build the page. In addition, the HTML-On-The-Fly library routines included in the ETS Kernel MicroWeb Server simplifies the task of dynamically building HTML to present data about your embedded system. You see how this works in detail when you examine the code in the Network-Aware UPS later in the chapter.

ETS KERNEL HTTP SERVER

The Network-Aware UPS project uses the HTTP server and the HTML-On-The-Fly components of the MicroWeb Server included with ETS Kernel. In this section, you look at the source code for the HTTP server. The full version of ToolSuite includes source code for all components of the MicroWeb Server, but ToolSuite Lite includes the HTTP server only in binary form (in the HTTPSERV.LIB file), so the source code you look at here isn't on the CD-ROM.

The interface to the HTTP server is defined in the HTTPSERV.H header file. The application calls two APIs in the HTTP server: StartWebServer() and StopWebServer(). StartWebServer() initializes the WinSock programming interface to the TCP/IP stack, initializes the HTTP server, and spawns a server thread that starts listening on port 80 (the well-known HTTP port) for client connections. StopWebServer() shuts down the HTTP server, releases all resources allocated to the server, and calls the WSACleanup() WinSock function.

The application must provide several callback functions for use by the HTTP server. These functions are called when client connections or errors occur. Because the HTTP server creates a separate thread to handle each client connection, these functions execute in the context of a thread created by the HTTP server. Most of these functions must be reentrant, because multiple client connections, handled by multiple threads, can occur simultaneously. The callback functions are

```
void __cdecl GetURI(REQ_INPUTS *pInp, REQ_OUTPUTS *pOutp)
void __cdecl PostURI(REQ_INPUTS *pInp, REQ_OUTPUTS *pOutp)
void __cdecl LogRequest(REQUEST_RECORD *pReq)
void __cdecl WebServerError(BOOL fFatal, char *pErrMsg)
```

The GetURI() callback is invoked when a GET or a HEAD method is received from a client. This callback function is responsible for loading the resource in a memory buffer, setting variables that allow the HTTP server to construct standard headers for the response message, and specifying any additional headers that need to be included in the response. In the full version of ToolSuite, sample programs load resources from disk and construct resources dynamically in memory. In the Network-Aware UPS, we always construct resources in memory; we never load them from disk. PostURI() is called when a POST method is received from a client. This function handles the data included with the request message, and then, like the GetURI() function, constructs the response resource and headers. Because the HTTP server implements HTTP 1.0, there is no provision to handle the PUT, DELETE, TRACE, and OPTIONS methods.

The REQ_INPUTS structure in Listing 16-1 is in the HTTPSERV.H header file and contains complete information about the request message received from the client.

Listing 16-1: The REQ_INPUTS structure

```
//
// Input parameters to GetURI() and PostURI().
// All members are optional except pURI and pPath.
//
typedef struct {
    char    *pURI;            // original URI in the request
    char    *pPath;           // DOS-compatible file path (the URI up to
                              // any ';' or '?' character, with escapes
                              // replaced and '/' changed  to '\')
    char    *pParams;         // start of params or NULL if none
                              // (anything past an initial ';' and up
                              // to any '?', with escapes replaced)
    char    *pQuery;          // the query or NULL if none (anything
                              // past the '?' character in the URI,
                              // with escapes replaced)
    char    *pFrom;           // text from "From:" header or NULL
// all fields below this are used only by POST method (PostURI())
    int     ContentLength;    // length of Entity-Body (could be 0)
    char    *pEntityBody;     // Entity-Body or NULL if
                              // ContentLength == 0
    char    *pContentType;    // text from "Content-Type:" or NULL
    char    *pContentEncoding; // text from "Content-Encoding:" or NULL
    IN_ADDR LocalIpAddr;      // local IP address for this connection
// except the following which is used only by GetURI()
    BOOL    fHeadMethod;      // T ==> HEAD request.  The GetURI() routine
                              // only needs to fill in the  information
                              // about the entity (particularly length and
                              // last modified time), but can leave
                              // pEntityBody set to NULL.  Reading in the
                              // entity body is allowed, and the HTTP
                              // server will correctly free it if present.
} REQ_INPUTS;
```

The `REQ_OUTPUTS` structure in Listing 16-2 must be filled in by the callback to give the HTTP server the information it needs to construct the response message to send to the client.

Listing 16-2: The REQ_OUTPUTS structure

```
//
// Output parameters from GetURI() and PostURI()
// If the URI is successfully read:
//    All members are optional except LastModTime and ContentLength. If
//    ContentLength is nonzero, pEntityBody should be non-NULL. If
//    StatusCode isn't set, standard "200 OK" status is sent to client.
// If an error occurs:
//    All members are optional except StatusCode. For most errors,
//    the HTTP spec recommends also sending a short HTML entity-body
//    describing the error (check the HTTP spec for details). If a
//    non-NULL entity-body is returned for an error, set the
//    LastModTime to the current time.
//
typedef struct {
    time_t LastModTime;         // the last modified time for the
                                // content, or the current time() if
                                // unknown, in time_t format (seconds
                                // since 00:00:00 GMT 1-Jan 1970)
    int     ContentLength;      // length of Entity-Body (could be 0)
    char    *pEntityBody;       // ptr to Entity-Body, NULL if
                                // ContentLength==0. The memory should
                                // be malloc()'d, and it is the caller's
                                // responsibility to free() it
    time_t Expires;             // "Expires:" date, in time_t format, or 0
    char    ContentType[64];    // "Content-Type:" text or empty str
    char    ContentEncoding[64]; // "Content-Encoding:" text or empty string
    char    StatusCode[64];     // Status Code string to send or
                                // empty string to send default
                                // "200 OK". If error, this MUST be
                                // set to an appropriate string.
    char    HeaderFields[256];  // extra header fields, each terminated
                                // by \r\n (e.g. "Pragma: no-cache\r\n")
} REQ_OUTPUTS;
```

After the client connection is terminated, `LogRequest()` is called to let the application log requests to a database or perform any other tracking desired for HTTP connections. Entry to this function is serialized by placing it in a critical section in the HTTP server; this can be performed without affecting service to clients because `LogRequest()` is called after the client connection is closed. Since `LogRequest()` is called by one thread at a time, it doesn't need to be reentrant.

`WebServerError()` is called to notify the application when an error is detected in the HTTP server. Most errors are due to improperly terminated connections or another client error that requires no action. If an internal error occurs in the HTTP server and recovery is not possible, the server shuts itself down (stops listening for connections) before calling `WebServerError()` and sets the `fFatal` flag to indicate the occurrence of a fatal error.

The main loop of the HTTP server is in `HttpThread()`, a thread that initializes a TCP socket for port 80 and listens for connections. The code to initialize the socket is almost identical to the code you saw for the Finger server in Chapter 15, "Networking," so we don't reproduce it here. Let's look at the loop that waits to receive client connections in Listing 16-3.

Listing 16-3: Polling for HTTP connections

```
//
// Just sit in a loop servicing HTTP queries, until the main thread
// signals us to terminate.  Because the socket is in non-blocking
// mode we can just poll for remote connections inside the loop.
//
   while (TRUE)
   {

// Check if the main thread told us to terminate
      if (WaitForSingleObject(hTerminateEvent, 0) == WAIT_OBJECT_0)
         break;

//
// Poll for a connection from a remote HTTP client.  If there is one,
// create a thread to service the request.  We create a thread for
// each request to improve response times and minimize the chance we
// would overflow the pending connection queue in the stack and have
// connection requests refused.
//
      RemoteLen = sizeof(RemoteAddr);
      hSock = accept(hListenSock, (PSOCKADDR)&RemoteAddr,&RemoteLen);
      if (hSock == INVALID_SOCKET)
      {
         ErrVal = WSAGetLastError();
         if (ErrVal != WSAEWOULDBLOCK)
            SendError(FALSE, NULL, "Error %d accept()ing "
                      "connection", ErrVal);
         // Relinquish time slice to any other runnable threads, so we
         // don't hog the CPU just checking for connections.  Sleep(0)
         // doesn't allow lower priority threads to run.
         Sleep(10);
         continue;
      }
      else
      {
         pConnect = malloc(sizeof(HTTP_CONNECT));
         if (pConnect == NULL)
         {
            SendError(FALSE, &RemoteAddr, "Can't malloc() "
               "memory for thread connect struct");
            closesocket(hSock);
            continue;
         }
```

```
    pConnect->hSock = hSock;
    memcpy(&pConnect->RemoteAddr, &RemoteAddr, sizeof(RemoteAddr));
    pConnect->pBuf = pConnect->Buf;
    time(&pConnect->CliRequestTime);
    if (!StartThread((void(*)(void *))ServiceRequestThread,
                     pConnect))
    {
        SendError(FALSE, &RemoteAddr, "Unable to "
            "create thread to service connection");
        closesocket(hSock);
        free(pConnect);
        continue;
    }
  }
}
```

Each time through the loop, we call `WaitForSingleObject()` to check whether an event object used to notify the thread of server shutdown has been signaled. We then call the WinSock `accept()` function to check for a pending client connection. If no connection is pending, we call `Sleep()` to release the rest of the time slice to any other threads waiting to run, and then continue with another loop iteration. If a connection is pending, we call `StartThread()` to create a new thread to service the request, passing it `ServiceRequestThread()` as the initial thread function and a pointer to an `HTTP_CONNECT` structure containing the socket handle for the connection, the address of the client, and the time at which the connection was established. `StartThread()` performs a small amount of bookkeeping and calls `beginthread()` to create the thread. Having created the thread, we continue at the top of the loop.

Spawning threads is a common way to implement transaction-based servers, especially HTTP servers. Using separate threads to handle connections and transactions improves performance and simplifies coding. To handle simultaneous clients, a single-threaded server would have to multiplex several sockets: one for each open connection plus one for the listening port.

`ServiceRequestThread()` starts by setting a thread debug name that includes the client's IP address, to simplify the task of identifying threads from the debugger. (If you use your web browser to look at `http://smallest.pharlap.com/debug/` and click "Display active threads," you'll see any active HTTP connection threads, in addition to the other threads in the system. At a minimum, an HTTP connection thread will be handling your request for the active threads page; the IP address will be either the IP address of your machine or the IP address of a proxy server — probably your ISP — making the request on your behalf.) `ServiceRequestThread()` then initializes the contents of the `REQ_INPUTS` and `REQ_OUTPUTS` structures, which it will pass to the appropriate callback for the request method.

Next, `ServiceRequestThread()` reads the request-line (the first line of the request message) and parses it to obtain the URI, the requested method, and the HTTP version the client supports:

```
//
// Read the first request line and parse it.  We support these methods:
//    GET - retrieve data from URI
//    HEAD - get info about URI
//    POST - accept subordinate of URI
//
    pLine1 = ReadRequestLine(pConnect, &ReqOutp, &fSendResponse);
    if (pLine1 == NULL)
    {
        if (fSendResponse)
            goto RESPOND;
        goto DONE;
    }
    if (strncmp(pLine1->pLineText, "GET ", 4) == 0)
    {
        Method = METHOD_GET;
        pURI = pLine1->pLineText + 4;
    }
    else if (strncmp(pLine1->pLineText, "HEAD ", 5) == 0)
    {
        Method = METHOD_HEAD;
        ReqInp.fHeadMethod = TRUE;
        pURI = pLine1->pLineText + 5;
    }
    else if (strncmp(pLine1->pLineText, "POST ", 5) == 0)
    {
        Method = METHOD_POST;
        pURI = pLine1->pLineText + 5;
    }
    else
    {
        strcpy(ReqOutp.StatusCode, pStat501);
        HtmlErrorPage(&ReqOutp, "Unrecognized method: %s",
                    pLine1->pLineText);
        goto RESPOND;
    }
    pHttpVer = strstr(pLine1->pLineText, "HTTP/");
    if (pHttpVer != NULL)
        fHttp10 = *(pHttpVer + 5) > '0';
```

The ReadRequestLine() function calls recv() in a loop, and buffers receive data in a buffer allocated in the HTTP_CONNECT structure. Its logic is similar to the read function you saw in the Finger server in Chapter 15, so we won't examine it here. If the requested method is not one of the HTTP 1.0 methods (GET, HEAD, and POST), we call HtmlErrorPage() to send a response with an error status (501 Not Implemented) and an HTML-formatted page identifying the unrecognized method. Otherwise, we set a flag (initialized to FALSE at the top of the function) indicating whether the client supports HTTP version 1.0 or later.

Next, if the client supports HTTP 1.0 or later, we enter a loop reading header lines and processing the headers used by the server, until we read the end of the message-headers section. This is mostly string manipulation code, so we won't reproduce it here. The headers in the request message used by the HTTP server are `If-Modified-Since`, `Content-Encoding`, `Content-Type`, `Content-Length`, and `From`. Any other headers are ignored.

After reading any headers in the message, if the request is a `POST` method and the `Content-Length` header specified a length greater than zero, we read the `POST` data (the entity-body):

```
//
// If POST method, read the entity-body, if any, sent by the client
//
    if (Method == METHOD_POST && ReqInp.ContentLength > 0)
    {
        if ((ReqInp.pEntityBody = malloc(ReqInp.ContentLength))==NULL)
        {
            SendError(FALSE, &pConnect->RemoteAddr, "Can't malloc "
                "memory for POSTed entity-body");
            strcpy(ReqOutp.StatusCode, pStat500);
            HtmlErrorPage(&ReqOutp, "Server error, unable to "
                    "allocate memory");
            goto RESPOND;
        }
        if (!ReadEntity(pConnect, &ReqInp, &ReqOutp, &fSendResponse))
        {
            if (fSendResponse)
                goto RESPOND;
            goto DONE;
        }
    }
```

The `ReadEntity()` function simply calls `recv()` in a loop to read the entity-body portion of the request message. If an error occurs, `ReadEntity()` sets the `fSendResponse` flag to indicate whether it has constructed an error response in the `ReqOutp` structure or whether the connection should be closed without sending a response.

We've now finished reading and parsing the request message. The next step is to parse the URI and then call the appropriate callback for the method as shown in Listing 16-4.

Listing 16-4: The ParseURI() function

```
//
// Parse the URI into its pieces and process the method. Note we do NOT
// serialize calls to PostURI() and GetURI() (in the interests of server
// responsiveness), so they must be written to be reentrant.
//
    if (!ParseURI(pConnect, pURI, &ReqInp, &ReqOutp))
        goto RESPOND;
    AddrSize = sizeof(LocalAddr);
    if (getsockname(pConnect->hSock, (LPSOCKADDR) &LocalAddr,
                    &AddrSize) == SOCKET_ERROR)
        ReqInp.LocalIpAddr.s_addr = htonl(INADDR_NONE);
    else
        ReqInp.LocalIpAddr = LocalAddr.sin_addr;
```

```
    if (Method != METHOD_POST)
        GetURI(&ReqInp, &ReqOutp);
    else
    {
        // Find out what type of POST we are dealing with.
        if ( ReqInp.pContentType &&
             strnicmp(ReqInp.pContentType, FORM_URL_ENCODED,
                      strlen(FORM_URL_ENCODED)) == 0 )

            // Rebuild pInp to hold a standard POST.
            RetVal = GetURLEncodedPostInfo(&ReqInp) ;

        else if ( ReqInp.pContentType &&
                  strnicmp(ReqInp.pContentType, MULTIPART_FORM_DATA,
                           strlen(MULTIPART_FORM_DATA)) == 0 )

            // Rebuild pInp to hold a multipart POST.
            RetVal = GetMultiPartPostInfo(&ReqInp) ;

        else
        {
            // It is possible for a POST to have no content-type.
            // If this is the case, we will not process it.  We will
            // let the application parse the fields of ReqInp.
        }

        // If there was a problem handling the POST, we should call
        // SendError() to let the application know there was a  problem.
        // We should also build an HTML page describing the error.
        if ( RetVal != FORM_NO_ERR )
        {
            HandlePostError(RetVal, &pConnect->RemoteAddr, &ReqInp,
                            &ReqOutp) ;
            goto RESPOND ;
        }

        PostURI(&ReqInp, &ReqOutp);
    }
```

The ParseURI() function initializes the pURI, pPath, pParams, and pQuery members of the REQ_INPUTS structure. The pURI member points to a buffer containing the original URI, as it was received in the request message. A URI is composed of a required path component, followed by an optional semicolon (;) and a parameters component, followed by an optional question mark (?) and a query component. These components are stored in buffers pointed to by pPath, pParams, and pQuery, respectively. In addition, any escaped characters in the original URI are converted back to the original characters in the component buffers, and the path component has backslash (\) substituted for forward slash (/) characters, to make pPath easy to use as input to DOS-compatible file system APIs.

The appropriate method handler function is then called: GetURI() for the GET or HEAD method or PostURI() for the POST method. For the POST method, we first do any processing required on encoded or multipart content to provide the PostURI() function with an unencoded, complete entity-body.

When the callback function returns, we're ready to send a response to the client, using the contents of the REQ_OUTPUTS structure. First, as shown in Listing 16-5, we check to make sure the structure contains complete information and to not return the entity-body in the response if it's not needed.

Listing 16-5: Preparing the response message

```
//
// Method was processed successfully.  Now decide whether we
// actually include the entity-body (if any) in our response, based
// on conditions which vary for each method.
//
    if (ReqOutp.LastModTime > time(NULL))
        // future times for current content are not permitted.
        time(&ReqOutp.LastModTime);
    if (ReqOutp.StatusCode[0] == EOS)
        strcpy(ReqOutp.StatusCode, pStat200);
    switch(Method)
    {
    case METHOD_HEAD:
        // Send all the info about the entity, but not the entity-body
        if (ReqOutp.pEntityBody != NULL)
        {
            free(ReqOutp.pEntityBody);
            ReqOutp.pEntityBody = NULL;
        }
        break;
    case METHOD_GET:
        // Don't send the entity-body, or any info about it, if
        // the last-modified date is earlier than the if-modified-since
        // date (which is set to 0 if none) AND the length, if
        // specified (0 if unspecified), is unchanged.
        if (ReqOutp.LastModTime <= ModSinceTime &&
                ReqOutp.pEntityBody != NULL &&
                (ModSinceLen == 0 ||
                ModSinceLen == ReqOutp.ContentLength))
        {
            free(ReqOutp.pEntityBody);
            ReqOutp.pEntityBody = NULL;
            ReqOutp.ContentLength = 0;
            ReqOutp.ContentType[0] = EOS;
            ReqOutp.ContentEncoding[0] = EOS;
            strcpy(ReqOutp.StatusCode, pStat304);
        }
        break;
```

```
case METHOD_POST:
    // although POST is mostly used to send data to the server,
    // it may also return an entity-body (preferably of type
    // "text/html") describing how to access a resource that
    // has been created as a result of the POST.  If there
    // is such an entity-body, we always send it.
    break;
}
```

We don't return an entity-body in the response if the request was a HEAD method or if it was a GET method with an If-Modified-Since header and the resource date is older than the date specified in the header.

Next, if the client supports HTTP 1.0 or later, we send a status line and the message-headers section. We won't reproduce the code here; it's a relatively straightforward series of calls to a SendResponse() function that, in turn, calls the WinSock send() API to send data to the client. The message headers the server will send, if appropriate, are Date, MIME-Version, Server, Content-Type, Content-Encoding, Content-Length, Last-Modified, Expires, and any additional headers specified by the application code in the method callback.

Finally, we send the entity-body portion of the response message, close the connection with the client, and call the LogRequest() callback in the application program:

```
//
// Send the entity body (if any).
//
    if (ReqOutp.pEntityBody != NULL)
    {
        if (!SendResponse(pConnect, ReqOutp.pEntityBody,
                        ReqOutp.ContentLength))
            goto DONE;
    }
    fSentResponse = TRUE;

DONE:

// Close the connection
    closesocket(pConnect->hSock);

//
// Log the request if it was successfully received and replied to.
// We serialize calls to this function to make the application
// easier to write, since now that the response has been sent it
// won't impact performance to wait here.
//
    if (fSentResponse)
    {
        EnterCriticalSection(&csLog);
        SendRequestLog(pConnect, pLine1, ReqOutp.StatusCode);
        LeaveCriticalSection(&csLog);
    }
```

Notice that we enter a critical section to call `SendRequestLog()`, which constructs a `REQUEST_RECORD` structure and calls `LogRequest()`. We have finished servicing the request and closed the connection with the client, so the thread has nothing else to do before exiting; therefore, blocking here will not affect responsiveness. Entering a critical section allows the `LogRequest()` function to be non-reentrant.

When `LogRequest()` returns, we free any allocated memory blocks and exit from the thread. This code is straightforward, so we don't reproduce it here.

HTML-ON-THE-FLY IN THE NETWORK-AWARE UPS

The code to construct web pages in the Network-Aware UPS is located in the `WEBMEM.C` file. This file includes the callbacks used by the HTTP server, in particular `GetURI()`. The code that builds the web pages in memory uses the ETS Kernel HTML-On-The-Fly library to help construct the HTML tags

As you probably know, an HTML document is comprised of HTML tags enclosed in angle brackets (<>) and text to be displayed by the web browser. Although some tags (such as <P>, the new paragraph tag) stand alone, most tags operate on a range of text enclosed in start and end tags, where the end tag is the same as the start tag but with a leading forward slash. For example, the contents of a complete HTML document are delimited by the <HTML> and </HTML> tags.

The interface to the HTML-On-The-Fly library is defined in three header files: `HTML.H`, `HTMLFORM.H`, and `HTMLPAGE.H`. The `HTML.H` file contains defines for various tags and options, which are used as inputs to the HTML generation routines, and prototypes for the APIs that generate properly formatted HTML tags; these function names all begin with `html_`. The `HTMLFORM.H` file contains defines and API prototypes for generating HTML forms; the form functions all begin with `form_`. The `HTMLPAGE.H` file contains defines and prototypes for APIs that build and manage HTML pages, or documents; these function names begin with `hpg_`.

Let's start by examining the `GetURI()` function that the HTTP server calls when a GET or POST method is received:

```
void __cdecl GetURI(REQ_INPUTS *pInp, REQ_OUTPUTS *pOutp)
{
    PAGE_ENT *pPageEnt;

// Initialize the output structure members to default values
    hpg_SetDefOutput(pInp, pOutp);

//
// Look up the URI in our page table structures to see if we can
// generate the HTML page.
//
    pPageEnt = hpg_PtableLoc(TopPageTable, pInp, pOutp);
    if (pPageEnt == NULL)
        return;
```

```
//
// Call the function to generate the HTML page. We have to enter a
// critical section to do this, because the HTML-on-the-fly library is
// not reentrant and this function may be reentered by different threads.
//
    EnterCriticalSection(&csHtml);
    ((HTML_FUNCP) pPageEnt->ptr) (pInp, pOutp);
    LeaveCriticalSection(&csHtml);

    return;
}
```

GetURI() first calls hpg_SetDefaultOutput() to initialize the contents of the REQ_OUTPUTS structure to a null entity-body, a Content-Type of text/html, and a Last-Modified-Time of the current time. GetURI() then calls hpg_PtableLoc() to look up the requested URI in the page directory structures that start with the root page directory, TopPageTable:

```
PAGE_ENT TopPageTable[] =
{
"", (void *)TopPage,              NULL,
"ups.htm", (void *)UpsInterface,  "UPS Interface",
"about.htm", (void *)AboutUps,    "About this UPS system",
"onepixel.gif", (void*)onepixel,  NULL,
NULL
};
```

The PAGE_ENT structure is defined in the HTMLPAGE.H file. Each structure contains the name of the resource, followed by a pointer to the function that generates the resource, followed by a string used for the hyperlink to the page (or NULL if no link is desired), as you'll see in a moment. If the resource is a directory that can contain other resources, it's identified by a trailing forward slash (/) in the resource name, and the pointer is a pointer to another array of PAGE_ENT structures. This supports arbitrary levels of directories in a resource name; we don't use this feature in the Network-Aware UPS.

In the TopPageTable array, we have four resources, corresponding to the /, /ups.htm, /about.htm, and /onepixel.gif URIs. The first three resources are HTML documents that make up the user interface to the UPS system. The onepixel.gif resource is referenced by the ups.htm web page; it isn't intended to be viewed as a standalone web page.

The hpg_PtableLoc() function returns a pointer to the PAGE_ENT structure for the requested URI. GetURI() just calls the function referenced in the PAGE_ENT structure to generate the resource in a memory buffer. Because the HTML-On-The-Fly library is not reentrant, we enter a critical section to call the page generation function. The page generation function stores its results in the REQ_OUTPUTS structure; when the function returns, GetURI() returns to the HTTP server, which sends the response message to the client.

The top-level page (the page referenced by the / URI) is generated by the TopPage() function:

```
//
// Generates the HTML for the top level page.  The top level
// page just has some text describing the UPS system, and
// links to other pages defined by the TopPageTable structure.
//
BOOL __cdecl TopPage(REQ_INPUTS *pInp, REQ_OUTPUTS *pOutp)
{
    if (!hpg_DirectoryPage(pInp, pOutp, TopPageTable,
        "UPS Project 3",
        "This system simulates a UPS which reports status "
        "and accepts simulated inputs through an HTML page. "
        "Embedding a web server into the system allows "
        "any web browser to act as a user interface to the "
        "UPS.\n"))
        return FALSE;
    return hpg_DonePage(pOutp);
}
```

The `TopPage()` function calls `hpg_DirectoryPage()`, which generates the HTML document shown next. The call to `hpg_DonePage()` closes the document by adding the `</BODY>` and `</HTML>` end tags, and completes the contents of the REQ_OUTPUTS structure.

```
<HTML><HEAD><TITLE>UPS Project 3</TITLE>
This system simulates a UPS which reports status and accepts
simulated inputs through an HTML page. Embedding a web server
into the system allows any web browser to act as a user interface
to the UPS.
</HEAD>
<BODY>
<HR>
<UL>
<LI><A HREF="ups.htm">UPS Interface</A>
<LI><A HREF="about.htm">About this UPS system</A>
</UL>
</BODY></HTML>
```

The document title and text were passed as arguments to `hpg_DirectoryPage()`. The list of hyperlinks to other pages in the directory is generated from the data in the `TopPageTable` array, which was also passed to `hgp_DirectoryPage()`.

The `AboutUps()` function generates a simple page containing a text message describing the UPS system:

```
//
// Function that generates the "About UPS" web page.  This
// is a very simple page with just text in it.
//
BOOL __cdecl AboutUps(REQ_INPUTS *pInp, REQ_OUTPUTS *pOutp)
{
```

```
//
// Open an empty HTML document first
//
    if (!hpg_CreatePage(pOutp))
        return FALSE;

//
// Build the HTML document
//
    html_brtext(HTML_TITLE, "UPS Project 3");
    html_text("\n");
    html_endtag(HTML_HEAD "\n");
    html_tag(HTML_BODY "\n");
    html_text("This UPS project reports the UPS status and "
              "allows remote users to simulate inputs via a "
              "web interface.  It uses the ETS MicroWeb "
              "Server to provide HTML pages to any standard "
              "web browser.");

//
// Return the completed HTML document
//
    return hpg_DonePage(pOutp);
}
```

The call to `hpg_CreatePage()` initializes the HTML-On-The-Fy library and creates the <HTML> and <HEAD> tags that start the document. The `html_brtext()` call creates text bracketed by start and end tags, in this case <TITLE> and </TITLE>. The `html_endtag()` call creates the end tag for the document head. (The new lines inserted in the document are for readability when viewing the document source, as you will in a moment.) Next, we call `html_tag()` to create the <BODY> tag that starts the main body of the document, and then call `html_text()` to write the text we want to display. The call to `hpg_DonePage()` closes the document by adding the </BODY> and </HTML> end tags, and completes the REQ_OUTPUTS structure. The generated HTML is shown next:

```
<HTML><HEAD><TITLE>UPS Project 3</TITLE>
</HEAD>
<BODY>
This UPS project reports the UPS status and allows remote users
to simulate inputs via a web interface.  It uses the ETS MicroWeb
Server to provide HTML pages to any standard web browser.
</BODY></HTML>
```

The most complex page generated by the UPS system is the user-interface page, shown in Figure 16-3, which enables the user to simulate inputs and view the status of the UPS.

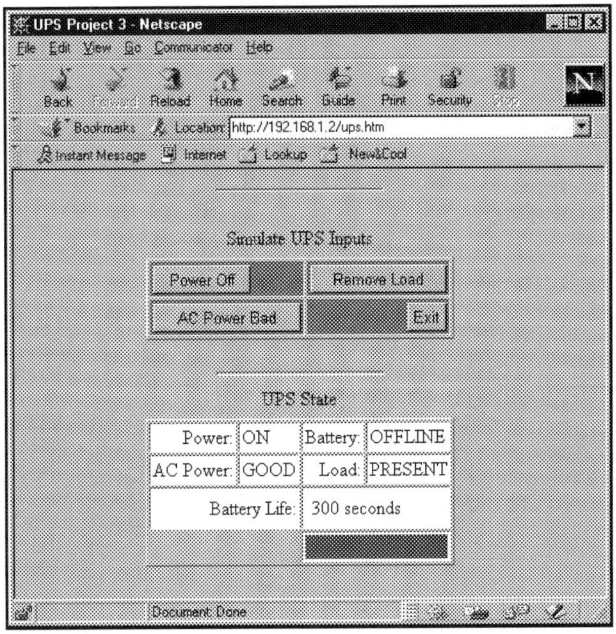

Figure 16-3: The UPS user-interface page.

This page is generated by the `UpsInterface()` function. Look first at the HTML generated by this function, so you can refer to it as you go through the code:

```
<HTML><HEAD><TITLE>UPS Project 3</TITLE></HEAD>
<BODY bgcolor=silver text=black>
<CENTER>

<HR width="30%">
<FORM METHOD="GET" ACTION="ups.htm">
 <TABLE BORDER=1 CELLPADDING=2 HSPACE=2 VSPACE=4 bgcolor=olive>
  <CAPTION>Simulate UPS Inputs</CAPTION>
  <TR ALIGN=left>
   <TD><INPUT TYPE="submit" NAME="button" VALUE="Power On"></TD>
   <TD ALIGN=right><INPUT TYPE="submit" NAME="button"
                   VALUE="Add Load"></TD>
  </TR>
  <TR ALIGN=left>
   <TD><INPUT TYPE="submit" NAME="button" VALUE="AC Power Bad"></TD>
   <TD ALIGN=right><INPUT TYPE="submit" NAME="button" VALUE="Exit"></TD>
  </TR>
 </TABLE>
</FORM>
```

```html
<HR width="30%">
<TABLE BORDER=1 CELLPADDING=2 HSPACE=2 VSPACE=4 bgcolor=white>
 <CAPTION>UPS State</CAPTION>
 <TR ALIGN=right>
  <TD>Power:</TD>
  <TD ALIGN=left>OFF</TD>
  <TD>Battery:</TD>
  <TD ALIGN=left>OFFLINE</TD>
 </TR>
 <TR ALIGN=right>
  <TD>AC Power:</TD>
  <TD ALIGN=left>GOOD</TD>
  <TD>Load:</TD>
  <TD ALIGN=left>ABSENT</TD>
 </TR>
 <TR ALIGN=right>
  <TD COLSPAN=2>Battery Life:</TD>
  <TD COLSPAN=2 ALIGN=left>
   <TABLE>
    <TR>
     <TD>300 seconds</TD>
    </TR>
   </TABLE>
  </TD>
 </TR>
 <TR ALIGN=left>
  <TD COLSPAN=2></TD>
  <TD COLSPAN=2><img src="onepixel.gif" width="100%" height=20></TD>
 </TR>
</TABLE>

</CENTER>
</BODY></HTML>
```

UpsInterface() first calls hpg_CreatePage() to initialize the HTML-On-The-Fly library and start the document with the <HTML> and <HEAD> tags. Because we initialize the HTML document immediately, if any errors occur we can generate an error message in the HTML document and return an error status (along with the document explaining the error) in the response message. With the document initialized, UpsInterface() next parses the query portion of the URI to determine which button (if any) on the web page was clicked.

```c
//
// Determine the appropriate command to the event subsystem, based
// on which form button was pressed.  If no button was pressed,
// just send the STATUS command.
//
   Event.Event = EVENT_STATUS;
   if (pInp->pQuery != NULL && *pInp->pQuery != 0)
   {
```

```
    // decode parameter list to get form button
    if (form_decode(FormFields, &Event, pInp->pQuery, ErrMsg))
    {
        html_text("Error parsing query string: %s\n", ErrMsg);
        goto DONE_NO_REFRESH;
    }
}
```

This code selects the appropriate simulated event to send to the event subsystem, according to which button the user clicked. If no query string is in the URI, no button was clicked, so we send EVENT_STATUS, which doesn't simulate any UPS events but requests the event subsystem to send back the UPS state.

If there is a query string, it's passed to the form_decode() function along with a pointer to a UPS_EVENT structure and the following FormFields array of FIELD_LIST structures (defined in HTMLFORM.H):

```
FIELD_LIST FormFields[] =
{
"button=Power On", (char *)EVENT_POWER,
                    offsetof(UPS_EVENT, Event),
"button=Power Off", (char *)EVENT_POWER,
                    offsetof(UPS_EVENT, Event),
"button=Add Load", (char *)EVENT_LOAD,
                    offsetof(UPS_EVENT, Event),
"button=Remove Load", (char *)EVENT_LOAD,
                    offsetof(UPS_EVENT, Event),
"button=AC Power Good", (char *)EVENT_AC,
                    offsetof(UPS_EVENT, Event),
"button=AC Power Bad", (char *)EVENT_AC,
                    offsetof(UPS_EVENT, Event),
"button=Exit", (char *)EVENT_EXIT,
                    offsetof(UPS_EVENT, Event),
NULL
};
```

Each structure in the array contains a string that appears in the query if the corresponding form button is clicked, a simulated event to send to the event subsystem, and the offset of the Event member in the UPS_EVENT structure. The form_decode() function uses this table to determine which simulated event to store in the UPS_EVENT structure passed to the function.

With the Event UPS_EVENT structure (both the structure variable and one of the structure members are named Event) filled in, the next task is to send the simulated event to the event subsystem for processing, and wait for the event subsystem to return the UPS state, which we need to generate the web page. We examined this code in Chapter 14, "A Network-Aware UPS," so we won't reproduce it here. Basically, we call MsgWrite() to add the simulated event to the message queue that the event subsystem uses as input. Then we read the UPS state information from the status pipe that the event subsystem writes to after simulating the input. If the UPS state information is not sent within a timeout period of one second, we send an error page as the response message to the client.

After we've received the latest UPS state information from the event subsystem, we're ready to construct the HTML for the user-interface page. First, we create the document title, end the document head, and start the document body, just as we did in the AboutUps() function. The only difference is that we use html_tagwopt() to add some color options to the BODY tag. Then we create a CENTER tag to center the contents of the web page in the browser window; we output the end tag for CENTER at the end of the document.

```
//
// now build the page.
//
    html_brtext(HTML_TITLE, "UPS Project 3");
    html_endtag(HTML_HEAD "\n");
    html_tagwopt(HTML_BODY "\n",
                 " bgcolor=%s", "silver",
                 " text=%s", "black",
                 NULL);
    html_tag(HTML_CENTER "\n");
```

Next, we create the simulated inputs section of the web page:

```
//
// buttons;  put them in a table to format them
//
    html_tagwopt("\n" HTML_HORZRULE "\n", " width=\"30%s\"", "%", NULL);
    html_tagwopt(HTML_FORM "\n",
                 OPT_METHOD, "GET",
                 OPT_ACTION, "ups.htm",
                 NULL);
    html_tagwopt(" " HTML_TABLE "\n",
                 OPT_BORDER, 1,
                 OPT_CELLPADDING, 2,
                 OPT_HSPACE, 2,
                 OPT_VSPACE, 4,
                 " bgcolor=%s", "olive",
                 NULL);
    html_text("  ");
    html_brtext(HTML_CAPTION, "Simulate UPS Inputs");
    html_text("\n");

    html_tagwopt("  " HTML_ROW "\n", OPT_ALIGN, "left", NULL);
    html_tag("    " HTML_CELL);
    form_named_button("button", Status.State & STATE_POWER_ON ?
                      "Power Off" : "Power On");
    html_endtag(HTML_CELL "\n");
    html_tagwopt("    " HTML_CELL, OPT_ALIGN, "right", NULL);
    form_named_button("button", Status.State & STATE_LOAD_PRESENT ?
                      "Remove Load" : "Add Load");
    html_endtag(HTML_CELL "\n");
    html_text("  ");
    html_endtag(HTML_ROW "\n");
```

```
html_tagwopt("  " HTML_ROW "\n", OPT_ALIGN, "left", NULL);
html_tag("   " HTML_CELL);
form_named_button("button", Status.State & STATE_AC_BAD ?
                  "AC Power Good" : "AC Power Bad");
html_endtag(HTML_CELL "\n");
html_tagwopt("    " HTML_CELL, OPT_ALIGN, "right", NULL);
form_named_button("button", "Exit");
html_endtag(HTML_CELL "\n");
html_text("  ");
html_endtag(HTML_ROW "\n");

html_text(" ");
html_endtag(HTML_TABLE "\n");
html_endtag(HTML_FORM "\n");
```

We start by creating an HR (horizontal rule) tag to set off this area of the page. Then we open an HTML form. We need to create a form because input buttons can exist only within forms. The form options specify the method (GET) used to send form data and the URI (ups.htm) to request. Next, we start an HTML table; the table enables us to nicely format the button display in a two-by-two grid. The options for the TABLE tag specify the spacing around rows and columns, the background color, and the border width. We use a table caption to create a title (Simulate UPS Inputs) for this section of the document. As we output the tags, we add new lines and leading spaces to make the HTML more readable when you view the document source.

Next, we create the two rows of the table, each with two cells. Within each table cell, we call form_named_button() to create the INPUT tag that (along with its options) specifies the button and its label. When the button is clicked, the browser appends button=label as a query to the URI, allowing the web server to determine which button was clicked, as you saw previously. Then we output the end tags for the table and the form.

Next, we create the document section that displays the current UPS state information:

```
//
// Put the UPS state in a table
//
    html_tagwopt("\n" HTML_HORZRULE "\n", " width=\"30%s\"", "%", NULL);
    html_tagwopt(HTML_TABLE "\n",
                 OPT_BORDER, 1,
                 OPT_CELLPADDING, 2,
                 OPT_HSPACE, 2,
                 OPT_VSPACE, 4,
                 " bgcolor=%s","white",
                 NULL);
    html_text(" ");
    html_brtext(HTML_CAPTION, "UPS State");
    html_text("\n");

    html_tagwopt(" " HTML_ROW "\n", OPT_ALIGN, "right", NULL);
    html_text("  ");
    html_brtext(HTML_CELL, "Power:");
    html_text("\n");
```

```
html_tagwopt("  " HTML_CELL, OPT_ALIGN, "left", NULL);
html_text(Status.State & STATE_POWER_ON ? "ON" : "OFF");
html_endtag(HTML_CELL "\n");
html_text("  ");
html_brtext(HTML_CELL, "Battery:");
html_text("\n");
html_tagwopt("  " HTML_CELL, OPT_ALIGN, "left", NULL);
html_text(Status.State & STATE_BATT_ON ? "ONLINE" : "OFFLINE");
html_endtag(HTML_CELL "\n");
html_text("  ");
html_endtag(HTML_ROW "\n");

html_tagwopt(" " HTML_ROW "\n", OPT_ALIGN, "right", NULL);
html_text("  ");
html_brtext(HTML_CELL, "AC Power:");
html_text("\n");
html_tagwopt("  " HTML_CELL, OPT_ALIGN, "left", NULL);
html_text(Status.State & STATE_AC_BAD ? "BAD" : "GOOD");
html_endtag(HTML_CELL "\n");
html_text("  ");
html_brtext(HTML_CELL, "Load:");
html_text("\n");
html_tagwopt("  " HTML_CELL, OPT_ALIGN, "left", NULL);
html_text(Status.State & STATE_LOAD_PRESENT ? "PRESENT" : "ABSENT");
html_endtag(HTML_CELL "\n");
html_text("  ");
html_endtag(HTML_ROW "\n");

html_tagwopt(" " HTML_ROW "\n", OPT_ALIGN, "right", NULL);
html_tagwopt("  " HTML_CELL, OPT_COLSPAN, 2, NULL);
html_text("Battery Life:");
html_endtag(HTML_CELL "\n");
html_tagwopt("  " HTML_CELL "\n",
             OPT_COLSPAN, 2,
             OPT_ALIGN, "left",
             NULL);
// we need this hack of putting a table on the row
// above the thermometer bar for battery life, to
// make the thermometer bar display correctly in Netscape.
if (Status.msBatteryLife > Status.msMaxLife)
    Status.msBatteryLife = Status.msMaxLife;
html_tag("    " HTML_TABLE "\n");
html_tag("     " HTML_ROW "\n");
html_tag("      " HTML_CELL);
html_text("%d seconds", Status.msBatteryLife/1000);
html_endtag(HTML_CELL "\n");
html_text("     ");
html_endtag(HTML_ROW "\n");
html_text("    ");
html_endtag(HTML_TABLE "\n");
```

```
html_text("   ");
html_endtag(HTML_CELL "\n");
html_text(" ");
html_endtag(HTML_ROW "\n");

html_tagwopt("  " HTML_ROW "\n",
             OPT_ALIGN, "left",
             NULL);
html_tagwopt("   " HTML_CELL, OPT_COLSPAN, 2, NULL);
html_endtag(HTML_CELL "\n");
html_tagwopt("   " HTML_CELL, OPT_COLSPAN, 2, NULL);
// Note this thermometer bar has only been tested with
// Netscape 4.0 and Explorer 4.0, and may not display
// correctly with other browsers.
Percent = Status.msBatteryLife*100/Status.msMaxLife;
if (Percent == 0)
    Percent = 1;  // Netscape can't cope with 0% image width
html_rawtext("<img src=\"onepixel.gif\" width=\"");
html_text("%d", Percent);
html_rawtext("%\" height=20>");
html_endtag(HTML_CELL "\n");
html_text(" ");
html_endtag(HTML_ROW "\n");
html_endtag(HTML_TABLE "\n");
```

Again, we use a horizontal rule to set off this section of the document. We create a table to hold the state information and a table caption as a title for the section. The code to create the table rows and cells is self-explanatory, until we get to the battery life section of the table. HTML cells have an option that enables you to specify that the cell spans multiple columns; we use this to obtain the larger area needed to display the battery life. But the text showing the battery life in seconds, which is a single cell (spanning two columns) of the outer table, is placed inside an inner table. This apparently needless code is a workaround for a bug in the Netscape 4.0 browser; without the inner table, the bar graph for battery life in the next row of the table won't display correctly.

The last row of the table contains two double-width cells; the first one is empty, and the second contains the battery life bar graph. The bar graph is generated with an IMG (image) tag that references the onepixel.gif resource, a GIF file containing a single red pixel. The width and height options to IMG enable you to specify the area that the image will fill; the browser either clips or (as in this case) replicates the image to fill the specified area. We specify the height as a number of pixels and the width as a percentage of the cell width, depending on how much battery life remains.

When the browser sees the IMG tag, it sends a second request message to the server in the UPS to get the onepixel.gif resource. This resource is just a GIF file. Because the UPS system doesn't have a disk drive, however, we can't load a resource from disk. Instead, because onepixel.gif is a small file (just 800 bytes), we use some linker switches to link it into the data segment for the UPS executable. The linker also creates global symbols identifying the start and end locations of the file in memory. The onepixel() function that generates the onepixel.gif resource uses these symbols to copy the resource from the data segment to the memory buffer allocated for the resource. This doesn't have anything to do with HTML, so we won't show you the linker switches and the code for onepixel() here. In Chapter 17, "Java," we use the same trick for resources that are Java class files; in that chapter, we give you a complete description of how the linker switches and the code that returns the onepixel.gif resource works.

Finally, if there's an error message (there isn't an error in Figure 16-3 and in the HTML reproduced previously), we generate a third section of the document, with a table containing a single cell with the error message in it:

```
if (Status.ErrLen > 0)
{
    html_tag("\n" HTML_PARA "\n");
    html_tagwopt(HTML_HORZRULE "\n", " width=\"30%s\"", "%", NULL);
    html_tagwopt(HTML_TABLE "\n",
                OPT_BORDER, 1,
                OPT_CELLPADDING, 2,
                OPT_HSPACE, 2,
                OPT_VSPACE, 4,
                " width=\"80%s\"", "%",
                " bgcolor=%s","white",
                NULL);
    html_brtext(HTML_CAPTION, "UPS Error");
    html_text("\n");

    html_tagwopt(" " HTML_ROW "\n", OPT_ALIGN, "left", NULL);
    html_text("   ");
    html_brtext(HTML_CELL, ErrMsg);
    html_text("\n ");
    html_endtag(HTML_ROW "\n");
    html_endtag(HTML_TABLE "\n");
}

html_text("\n");
html_endtag(HTML_CENTER "\n");
```

That's the end of the document, so we output the end tag for the CENTER tag.

Before returning the HTML document to GetURI(), we add some header fields to be sent with the response message:

```
//
// Don't let this page be cached by the web browser, because its look
// changes depending on UPS state.  Also, have the web browser
// automatically reload the page every 5 seconds so UPS state gets
// automatically tracked.
//
    strcpy(pOutp->HeaderFields, "pragma: no-cache\r\n");
```

```
    strcat(pOutp->HeaderFields,
            "Expires: Thu, 01 Jan 1970 12:00:00 GMT\r\n");
    pHostEnt = gethostbyaddr((char *)&pInp->LocalIpAddr,
                              sizeof(pInp->LocalIpAddr), PF_INET);
    if (pHostEnt != NULL)
        pHostName = pHostEnt->h_name;
    else
        pHostName = inet_ntoa(pInp->LocalIpAddr);
    if (pHostName != NULL)
    {
        strcat(pOutp->HeaderFields, "Refresh: 5; URL=http://");
        strcat(pOutp->HeaderFields, pHostName);
        strcat(pOutp->HeaderFields, "/ups.htm\r\n");
    }


    return hpg_DonePage(pOutp);
```

This adds the following headers to the HTTP response message sent to the browser:

```
Refresh: 5; URL=http//192.68.1.2/ups.htm
Pragma: no-cache
Expires: Thu, 01 Jan 1970 12:00:00 GMT
```

The `Refresh` header tells the browser to request a new copy of the web page every five seconds. This allows the displayed page to automatically track the UPS state, showing the battery discharging or recharging. The `Pragma: no-cache` header instructs the browser and any proxy servers to always request the page from the UPS system rather than cache the page locally. This ensures that the user doesn't see out-of-data UPS state information. Because not all browsers recognize the `no-cache` pragma, we add the `Expires` header with the oldest date supported by HTTP; the combination of these two headers disables caching with the Netscape Navigator and Microsoft Internet Explorer browsers, and should work with other browsers.

SUMMARY

In this chapter, we introduced HTTP, the protocol used to transfer web documents. We showed how you can use HTTP as a general multimedia document transfer protocol and explored the advantages of using HTTP in embedded systems applications. We also described the advantages of generating HTML documents to provide a user interface to an embedded system. Because web browsers are found anywhere computers are connected to the Internet, using HTML permits you to leverage existing standards to provide a user interface without having to write GUI software, either on your embedded system or on another platform with connectivity to your embedded system.

The Network-Aware UPS uses the HTTP server and the HTML-On-The-Fly library included with ETS Kernel to provide a user interface to the UPS system. Using any standard web browser, you can view the current status of the UPS and simulate inputs to the UPS.

In Chapter 17, we expand our discussion of web standards by looking at the Java programming language and environment and by adding a Java applet to the UPS system.

17

Java

An emerging standard in embedded systems development is the Java programming language. Java is the brainchild of Sun Microsystems, which for years has embraced networking as the optimal computing paradigm, having as its mantra, "the network is the computer." Java is the programming language that supports Sun's vision of network computing.

Originally, though, Java was intended to control consumer electronic devices such as cell phones and pagers. These are classic embedded systems, and the designers of Java intended to build a simple, object-oriented, network-savvy, interpreted, robust, secure, architecture-neutral, portable, high-performance, multithreaded, dynamic language. To make Java attractive to programmers, Sun incorporated a syntax and structure similar to that of C. Despite Sun's intentions, though, Java simply didn't prove suitable for small, electronic devices, largely because it was big and slow. The processing power and amount of memory needed to use Java applications in such devices was too costly.

Arguably, the most important of Sun's goals when designing Java were platform independence and built-in networking. A program that can run unmodified on several diverse hardware and software platforms is ideal for a networked environment, in which users want to be able to download and run applications on any machine in the office. And a language with built-in, standardized networking support on any platform is a boon to developers who want to build distributed programs that communicate over the network and take advantage of the resources available on the network.

Fortuitously, when Java was in the final stages of development, interest in the newly commercialized Internet was reaching a fever pitch. Sun used this opportunity to tout Java as a language designed for the Internet, and they succeeded in making the two inseparable in many minds. By the time Java was released in the spring of 1996, expectations were high because the industry largely saw Java as the tool that would take the Internet to the next level of functionality.

Although Java never became as ubiquitous on the Web as initially expected, Java and its cousin JavaScript, a Java-like language created by Netscape for writing scripts in web pages, are common fixtures on most commercial Web sites today.

So why should embedded developers be interested in Java? One reason is an increasing market demand to adapt embedded devices for communication over the Internet. To meet this requirement, it makes sense to consider the language many developers are using to build Internet applications. Another reason is that as the prices for memory chips and 32-bit processors decline, the sizable overhead that initially made Java too costly for use in embedded systems is no longer the problem it once was. With the cost penalties for using Java diminishing, its many advantages make it worth considering as an embedded platform.

To introduce you to Java, this chapter describes the Java language and platform model, how it uses computer resources, and its advantages and limitations. We also provide an example of the use of a Java applet for monitoring the UPS project developed in previous chapters. We don't attempt to teach you Java programming, but many worthy books are available on this topic. One good introductory book is *Java in a Nutshell,* as well as its companion volume, *Java Examples in a Nutshell,* both by David Flanagan (O'Reilly & Associates, 1997).

A LANGUAGE AND A PLATFORM

Java is unique in that it is a programming language that uses its own virtual machine, the Java Virtual Machine, or JVM, as its software platform. Java is a programming language in the same sense that C and BASIC, for example, are languages: It consists of a coherent set of high-level instructions that can be executed by a computer. Unlike other languages, however, Java isn't compiled to machine code that runs on a specific operating system and processor. Rather, it's compiled to bytecodes that the JVM interprets.

The Java language was designed from the ground up as an object-oriented language with a simple, yet powerful, syntax. Its simplicity makes it easy to learn and makes programs easier to maintain; it's significantly easier to learn Java than to learn C++, for example. With the exception of the primitive numeric, character, and Boolean data types, everything else in Java, including strings and arrays, are objects. Java has no global data; all data is contained within an object or as a local variable in a method (a function member of a class). In keeping with the design goals of robustness and security, Java is also a strongly typed language, which permits extensive compile-time checking for type mismatch problems. Java has built-in statements for synchronizing program threads and for handling and throwing (generating) exceptions.

The JVM is a layer of software that runs on top of a host operating system and provides a single, consistent API to Java programs. The JVM loads the compiled bytecode files (called *class files*), dynamically loading and linking additional class files as necessary. The program executes entirely within the environment provided by the JVM, obtaining all of its services from the JVM. The Java API that the program uses to obtain services is defined by Sun and consists of a set of classes, organized in groups called *packages.*

The Java 1.0 API was defined by Sun's Java Development Kit (JDK) 1.0, which was released in January 1996. The current version is JDK 1.1, released in February 1997; JDK 1.2 was in beta as this book was being finalized, in the fall of 1998. The Java 1.1 API consists of 23 packages, including packages for graphics (java.awt), networking (java.net), remote method invocation (java.rmi), input and output (java.io), security (java.security), and core·language classes (java.lang), which include fundamental capabilities such as string manipulation, thread control, and exception processing.

Ideally, you write your Java program, compile it to bytecodes, and debug and test it in your favorite JVM. After your program is working, it should run in any JVM that conforms to Sun's definition for the Java API, regardless of the underlying hardware and operating system platform. If you write a program to the Java 1.0 API, it should run in any JVM 1.0 or later environment; if you write to Java 1.1, it should run under any JVM 1.1 or later environment.

The real world, however, always has complications. You can compile a Java program in more than one way , and you can choose more than one kind of Java environment. In this section, we summarize the available compiler and environment options.

PLATFORM ALTERNATIVES

In the less than two years since Sun released JDK 1.0, a number of options for executing Java programs in an embedded product have surfaced.

Java Virtual Machines

The most straightforward approach is to run Java programs the way Sun originally intended, on a Java Virtual Machine. To achieve this goal, you have two options. The easiest solution is to use a RTOS that already includes a JVM for running Java programs. If this is not possible, you can license the JVM from Sun and port it to the RTOS of your choice.

Porting the JVM yourself, however, creates two difficulties. First, Sun charges a six-figure licensing fee for the JVM, so licensing is not a viable option unless you're building either a very high-volume product or a product with an extremely high price tag. Second, porting the JVM to a new environment requires months of work. Although Sun designed the JVM with porting in mind, it's a large and complex piece of code (the JVM plus the class libraries for the Java API are several megabytes). And it's not feasible to carve it up into smaller chunks to simplify porting and reduce memory requirements. Sun wants all Java platforms to be full implementations so that they can achieve their goal of "write once, run everywhere." The JVM was not designed to be split; in any case, if you've selected Java for your product, you probably want to take advantage of the full-featured JVM environment.

The host operating system to which you are porting the JVM must provide at least simple context-switching support, a memory allocator, a file system, graphics support for the Abstract Window Toolkit, and standard network protocols. When porting the JVM to your real-time operating system, you must do the following:

- Map the Abstract Window Toolkit (AWT) to the graphics support in the host system

- Map the networking classes to the native networking code on the system

- Map the file-related I/O classes to the host file system
- Port the platform-dependent part of the Java Virtual Machine to the host operating system calls for memory allocation and thread management

In addition, your embedded system must be full-featured enough to work with the JVM paradigm. To run Java programs, the JVM must be able to load them. Unlike a traditional embedded system, you don't just burn the application and OS into ROM. A JVM wants to load class files (bytecode files) either from a file system or over a network. Your embedded Java system will need either a network connection or a file storage device such as a hard disk or a flash disk.

PersonalJava and EmbeddedJava

Sun recognizes that the memory and other resources required to support a full JVM implementation significantly limit the number of embedded systems for which Java can be considered. With the goal of increasing the use of Java in embedded systems, Sun has defined two subsets of the Java API: the PersonalJava API, and the EmbeddedJava API. JavaSoft, the Sun Microsystems division charged with developing and promoting Java, defined two embedded subsets in an attempt to better serve both the higher-end and lower-end embedded markets; the uses JavaSoft recommends for PersonalJava and EmbeddedJava, however, overlap considerably, so it's not always clear which is the appropriate choice for a particular embedded system.

The PersonalJava API is designed for building networked applications that users download from a network or the Internet and run on home, office, and mobile consumer devices such as handheld computers, set-top boxes, game consoles, mobile handheld devices, and smart telephones. PersonalJava devices will usually have sophisticated graphical user interfaces.

The EmbeddedJava API is an interface designed for embedded devices with either no display or a simple alphanumeric display, such as mobile telephones, pagers, process control devices, instrumentation, office peripherals, network routers, and network switches. EmbeddedJava is optimized for building applications with small memory footprints that run on real-time operating systems. Unlike PersonalJava, EmbeddedJava is scaleable; that is, developers can leave out components of the JVM that the application doesn't require. Systems that implement a subset of EmbeddedJava, however, can't necessarily run Java applets that were designed to run in the full EmbeddedJava or PersonalJava environment.

The draft of the PersonalJava API was released for public review in June 1997. It was finalized and officially published in early October 1997. The draft of the EmbeddedJava API was released for public review in early 1998, and the final version was published in mid-1998.

In general, both the PersonalJava API and the EmbeddedJava API are designed to provide only features required by an embedded device. Both APIs are a subset of the Java API that was released in the JDK 1.1, supplemented by a small number of new APIs designed to meet the needs of networked embedded applications. Java APIs introduced after JDK 1.1 will not automatically become a part of either PersonalJava or EmbeddedJava. Applications written to the EmbeddedJava API can run also under PersonalJava and Java, and applications written to the PersonalJava API can run also under Java.

As is the Java API and the JVM, both the PersonalJava API and the EmbeddedJava API are designed to be ported to multiple RTOSs, and several RTOS vendors such as Wind River, ISI, and Microtec have announced support for PersonalJava and EmbeddedJava. For RAM-based systems, Sun envisions developers building PersonalJava and EmbeddedJava applications exactly like they build Java applications and running interpreted bytecodes on the target system. For ROM-based systems, Sun has a tool (JavaCodeCompact) that converts Java bytecodes to C source code. You then compile the C source code, and link it with other C code used in your application, the Java Virtual Machine, and the RTOS to produce the final ROM image. This model provides good performance because you run machine code rather than interpreted bytecodes.

Sun has not introduced any new debugging solutions with the PersonalJava and EmbeddedJava APIs. Instead, they expect developers to debug their applications on the desktop. If it's necessary to debug on the target system, you'll probably have to embed debug code to print or log to a file information about the progress of the program.

Despite having ambitious and worthwhile goals, PersonalJava and EmbeddedJava are very new, not fully developed, and not well understood by the community of embedded systems developers. They offer the potential to use Java in interesting ways in embedded devices, but it's too soon to say just what effect they'll have on embedded software development.

JavaOS

A third software platform alternative is to license JavaOS from Sun and port it to the processor of your choice. JavaOS is an operating system based on the Java language and built by Sun's JavaSoft division. JavaOS for SPARC, x86, and StrongARM are available for licensing directly from Sun Microsystems. JavaOS 1.0 was announced in March 1997.

Sun's objective in building JavaOS was to reduce the overhead Java programs required by removing the requirement for a host operating system underneath the JVM. The idea is to reduce memory requirements by removing a software layer, which also makes the system run faster because fewer layers of translation exist. (Presumably, an unstated goal was to provide Sun with an entree to the real-time operating system business.) According to JavaSoft, a complete JavaOS system is designed to run on a hardware platform with a minimum of 4MB of either ROM or disk storage and 4MB of RAM.

JavaOS has a layered architecture; according to JavaSoft, each layer can be updated independently. The bottom two layers, which are platform-specific and compiled into machine code, are the microkernel and the Java Virtual Machine. The platform-independent portion of JavaOS is written in Java, and consists of four layers: the graphics system, the windowing system, the device drivers and device driver interface, and the network classes.

It's interesting that JavaSoft chose to write device drivers in Java. To support operations not possible from within Java, they created two support classes written in C, which are available to device drivers but not to application code. The Memory class enables drivers to access and modify specific bytes and words of storage. The Interrupt class handles interrupt dispatching.

To port the JavaOS to your hardware platform, you'll need to bring up the microkernel and the JVM using traditional embedded techniques. In theory, the rest of the layers should work without modification. You also have to make the graphics and network device drivers work; that task may be straightforward or require a significant amount of work, depending on whether or not you use hardware directly supported by Sun.

Java One Processors

In addition to being a software platform, Java is also a hardware platform. Sun Microelectronics, the semiconductor division of Sun, has developed a set of processors optimized to run Java programs. Sun refers to its chip architecture as Java One.

The Java One architecture is implemented using picoJava, a microprocessor core that is used across all Java chips. Processors based on picoJava natively execute Java bytecode, and Sun claims they can also execute legacy C/C++ code as efficiently as comparable RISC architectures. The picoJava core can be licensed from Sun by other microprocessor manufacturers. In addition, Sun sells its own CPU based on the picoJava core, the microJava 701 microprocessor.

Because picoJava-based microprocessors are designed as general-purpose microprocessors in addition to being, as Sun phrases it, Java-centric, they can run the operating system of your choice. You can use them with JavaOS or with any RTOS with support for a JVM. But whatever your choice of OS, your Java programs will run faster on a Java chip than on another chip with a JVM, because the bytecode interpreter portion of the JVM won't be needed — instead, Java bytecodes will execute as native instructions on the processor.

The microJava 701 processor was announced in October 1997, with chip availability targeted for the second half of 1998. It's too early to tell whether this innovative architecture will win industry acceptance.

JavaBeans

The JavaBeans API is a component framework defined by Sun for creating reusable, modular software components that can be plugged together to create a custom application. It's not a model widely used in embedded systems development, so we describe it only briefly.

In one sense, JavaBeans competes with other component frameworks such as ActiveX from Microsoft and CORBA (Common Object Request Broker Architecture) from an industry consortium; Sun designed it to also interoperate with other frameworks. So, for example, a Java bean can be placed in an ActiveX wrapper and manipulated by a Windows program just like an ActiveX component.

To develop a Java bean, you write a Java program that conforms to basic rules defined by Sun, and you use the JavaBeans API to create an interface that allows your bean to plug into any conforming *beanbox* (Sun's term for its sample program that can manipulate beans).

JavaScript

JavaScript, while sharing a name and a certain appearance with Java, is actually unrelated, except in name. JavaScript was developed by Netscape Communications, and its name was originally LiveScript. (Netscape has a compiled, server-side version of LiveScript called LiveWire.) Java and JavaScript look similar at a superficial level, and a partnership with Sun produced the JavaScript name.

JavaScript is a platform-independent, event-driven interpreted programming language. Because it's interpreted, and because of its simplicity compared to Java, JavaScript is used primarily as a scripting language for web programming. In particular, it's useful for adding interactivity to the World Wide Web because scripts can be embedded into HTML files simply by using the appropriate HTML tag.

JavaScript is much simpler and smaller than Java and cannot be used to create applets or standalone programs. It uses an object-like syntax, with object and attribute references similar to what might be found in Java. It typically runs on web browsers, but can also be used on web servers. JavaScript is useful for writing code that interacts with HTML elements on web pages; Java applets are useful for creating independent windows with their own graphics within a web page.

Client-side JavaScript deals mostly with objects typically found on a web page, such as forms, text boxes, and buttons. LiveWire (server-side JavaScript) facilitates the handling of requests from clients and supports connectivity to web databases. In other words, it's possible to use LiveWire for programming in place of using a scripting language such as Perl and the Common Gateway Interface, or CGI.

It's important to understand that a Java-enabled web browser is not automatically enabled for JavaScript, and vice versa. The two languages require separate interpreters, licensed from Sun (for Java) and Netscape (for JavaScript). Future browsers, however, will likely incorporate both.

COMPILER ALTERNATIVES

You have three alternatives for compiling Java code for the available software and hardware platforms: bytecode, Just-in-Time, and native code compilers. In this section, we look at the advantages and limitations of each.

Bytecode Compilers

Most Java programs are compiled to bytecode and executed on a JVM. Figure 17-1 depicts how this works. The Java source code is compiled by a Java bytecode compiler. The resulting program runs on top of a JVM. If the program is an applet embedded in an HTML page, the JVM is integrated into a web browser. If the program is a standalone application, the JVM runs on top of the host operating system. The JVM then interprets the bytecodes to execute the program.

Although better than interpreted source code, the performance of interpreted bytecode still lags significantly behind code that is fully compiled to binary instructions. The fastest you can probably expect an interpreted Java program to run is five to ten times slower than a compiled C program. For this reason, many programmers don't consider it worthwhile to learn an interpreted language. However, while this may have been true in an era of slow 8- and 16-bit processors, it may not necessarily continue to be true. Fast 32-bit chips are often an affordable and suitable way to overcome performance problems, and designers are continually working to improve the efficiency of the interpreter. You may find that the time-to-market

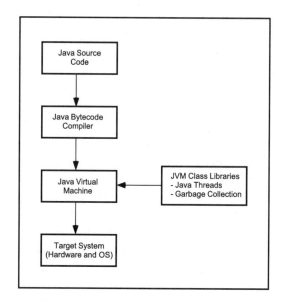

Figure 17-1: Interpreted Java solutions provide the write-once, run-anywhere facilities associated with Java on desktop systems.

advantage offered by the built-in functionality of the JVM outweighs the extra cost of using a faster processor to accommodate the overhead of interpreted code.

Just-in-Time Compilers

Sun realized that for many applications, the performance penalty of interpreted Java would be too great to overlook. In fact, if this was the only way of executing Java programs, the language might have been viewed as interesting but ultimately impractical. The roadblock Sun faced in improving performance was portability. Conventional wisdom said that it was impossible to have the performance associated with compilation and the platform independence associated with interpreted Java. Sun's solution was just-in-time, or JIT, compilers, a concept introduced in the 1960s that has been used for interpreted languages such as Lisp and Smalltalk. A JIT compiler offered the best of both worlds. Let's see how this works.

A Java program is first compiled using a bytecode compiler. This produces a platform-independent program. Next, you put the program on a target machine not with a JVM but rather with a machine-specific JIT compiler. When the program is executed, instead of the JVM interpreting the bytecode, the JIT compiler translates the bytecode into machine code on-the-fly.

As you might anticipate, a performance hit occurs the first time an application executes. After the program is compiled, however, it can execute as quickly as a compiled application. Some JIT compiler vendors, such as Microsoft, claim to attain C-like performance on Java code processed through its JIT after the initial compilation process. This improved performance comes at a price, though. A typical JIT compiler requires a half to 1MB of disk space on the target. For a desktop computer with a gigabyte or more of disk space, this extra software doesn't pose a problem. For an embedded device with little or no mass storage, this may not be a possible solution. You could avoid the disk space requirement by putting the JIT compiler into ROM. This approach makes the device somewhat more expensive because you have to purchase additional ROM and a JIT compiler license, but it's a way to boost performance without consuming disk space.

Java JIT compilers have been written for the leading general-purpose microprocessor architectures, such as Intel and SPARC. Most programming languages other than Java don't use a JIT compiler because speed, not platform independence, is the only consideration. As interest in Java for embedded purposes increases, JIT compilers will almost certainly be developed for other families of microprocessors.

Native Java Compilers

If a program will be embedded into one type of device, platform independence may not be necessary, and a native Java compiler may be your best bet. Sun has tried mightily to resist native compilation, recognizing that it negates platform independence, but it is giving in to the inevitable in embedded systems. Native compilers are available for Intel and Motorola processors, primarily from the GNU community, and more are coming from other compiler vendors. Because of the speed and memory size advantages, native compilation is likely to become popular for some classes of embedded systems. In addition, using native compilation makes it possible to mix Java with code written in other languages, as shown in Figure 17-2.

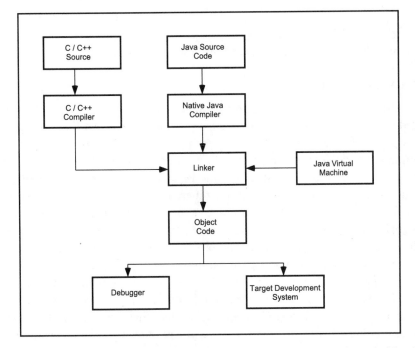

Figure 17-2: Native compilers provide significant application performance benefits over interpreted Java Virtual Machine solutions. In addition, compiling Java to object format enables solid multilanguage support.

ADVANTAGES FOR EMBEDDED DEVELOPMENT

The Java language had the advantage of being designed by a small and focused team that understood and embraced the vision of networked computing. Although initial implementations of the language had some flaws, many of which have since been addressed, there were few technical compromises in the vision. The result is a language uniquely designed for devices whose primary purpose is to communicate with one another.

A number of technical advantages might lead developers of embedded systems to choose Java. These advantages (several of which apply to building programs in general, not just to embedded development) follow:

- Processor independence
- Object-oriented programming
- Security and secure operations
- Memory management
- Garbage collection
- Networking
- Dynamic configuration
- Exception handling
- Threading
- Graphics

In the sections that follow, we explore each of these advantages.

PROCESSOR INDEPENDENCE

The first advantage of Java, processor independence, might seem to have little relevance in embedded systems. Traditionally, an embedded program is designed for and runs on a specific microprocessor, and portability in C-based applications can be assured for the most part by recompiling or cross-compiling programs for other platforms.

But Sun sees the world differently. In its model, an application may be stored on one system, yet downloaded and run on an entirely different one; devices may download pieces of programs from different locations to run on one processor; or different processors may run a single application, passing data between each other across the network. Using Java, an embedded system can be a general-purpose communications device, capable of downloading and running programs that let it do specific things.

This is a new model for embedded systems, but one toward which some developers are migrating. For example, vendors of TV set-top boxes have announced plans to incorporate JVMs so users can receive, through Java applets, content that supports the TV show they are watching as they are watching it. For example, if you're watching a football game, supporting content might be the player statistics; if you're watching a movie, supporting content might be background information on the actors. JVMs are also being incorporated into cellular telephones so users can receive stock quotes, game scores, and other timely information.

After we accept that this is an appropriate design and implementation model for some embedded devices, other advantages become apparent. One is that you have more flexibility in choosing your development platform. You do not need to develop on the same platform as the target platform or worry about cross-compiling, because Java bytecode runs on any operating system for which a JVM exists. A second advantage is that virtually all testing and debugging can occur independently of the target device. Some data inputs and hardware interaction, however, will require testing on the target (or a very good simulation). And because individual JVMs sometimes have compatibility problems, you should test a program on all platforms for which it is intended. Generally, though, you don't need sophisticated and expensive host-target development environments, with logic probes, ICEs, and other debugging tools.

OBJECT-ORIENTED PROGRAMMING

Object-oriented design and programming have come into mainstream use in the 1990s. An *object* is the encapsulation of code and data into a structure that supports encapsulation, inheritance, and polymorphism. In practice, these features mean that a programmer can work with instructions at a high level of abstraction and assume that the object can execute the instructions at a low level. An object can seamlessly model real-life objects. A hardware switch, for example, can be implemented in software using a switch object, which contains all the data and code needed to control and operate the switch.

Java is a pure object-oriented language. All code and data is part of a class, with no provision for global variables or code to exist independently of a class. An object is an instance of a class, and objects are manipulated by calling the methods, or functions, that are part of the class. An object's methods operate on the object's data. Java classes are organized in a hierarchy, with a subclass capable of inheriting behavior from its superclass and extending the superclass to add functionality specific to the subclass. The object model lets you define data structures corresponding to real-life objects, making the translation between what a program has to do and how it is implemented largely transparent, as described previously.

Java's class hierarchy has 6 major classes (23 classes in all) called *packages*. To make use of any objects in any packages, you simply include that package in your declarations. You also have full inheritance in the class hierarchy. Any object instantiated from deep in the hierarchy has access to all the methods defined higher up in the hierarchy.

The advantages of object-oriented design and programming are speed of development and code maintainability. Much object-oriented development can be done by reusing and modifying code from the existing class libraries, rather than creating new structures. This speeds development. The best testimony to this may be that the developers of Sun's Java Workshop, a Java IDE written entirely in Java, were able to build a full-featured graphical IDE in a few months. An object-oriented approach also encourages a natural structure to the program, making it highly readable and easy to modify and enhance.

Security and Secure Operations

Thanks to the JVM, a Java application is isolated from contact with any aspect of the operating system or hardware, so little chance exists of a computer virus or other surreptitious code gaining control of the device. The virtual machine is a layer of protection between the host device and software that may be of unknown quality and reliability.

In addition, the Java designers removed the concept of pointer variables from the language. Java programs cannot access arbitrary memory locations; they can only read or write objects created by the Java memory management system. With the strong typing enforced by the Java compiler, it's theoretically impossible to access memory outside the memory regions allocated to the program. This restriction makes it extremely difficult to write malicious programs.

Granted, this protection is not complete; researchers have found holes in the Java security model, some of which Sun has addressed. It is possible for talented but unscrupulous programmers to write programs that intentionally but indirectly modify the contents of memory or acquire passwords or other information from a host computer. However, the JVM does afford a level of protection that may not be possible with code running directly on the hardware.

Even tighter restrictions are imposed on Java applets, which are designed to be downloaded from the Internet and therefore are considered to be untrusted code, unless the applet includes the digital signature of a host you've designated as trusted. A JVM runs untrusted code such as applets in an area of memory it calls a *sandbox*. It allocates each applet resources and privileges, and restricts it to those allocations. In addition to these restrictions, the sandbox model imposes the following limitations:

- Reading from and writing to the file system on the local computer is not permitted.

- Networking operations are restricted. The untrusted code is not permitted to create a network connection to any computer except the one from which it was downloaded. It also cannot listen for or accept connections on any port number less than 1024 (which is the port number space reserved for well-known ports used for standard Internet protocols).

- Spawning new processes or dynamically loading native code libraries (as opposed to Java classes) is not permitted.

- Accessing or creating threads outside the thread group in which the untrusted code is running is not permitted.

Memory Management

Memory management is a far simpler concept in Java than in other languages because Java doesn't use pointers. All memory is dynamically allocated as an object is instantiated. As we noted previously, access to individual memory addresses was viewed by Java's designers as a potential security risk and, as a result, is not permitted. Add to this the fact that Sun's networking model assumes you may not know the target processor, and referencing individual memory addresses becomes unnecessary. Eliminating pointers results in not only increased security but also simpler programming and fewer bugs.

To understand how Java allocates memory, consider a comparison to the C language. In C, data can be accessed by value or by reference. In practice, virtually everything that's not a primitive data type is accessed by reference, using pointers, for the sake of flexibility and control. Consequently, the difference between value and reference becomes very clear, especially because you have to use a different notation (* and &) to access data by reference. To use the two different access methods, you have to clearly understand what they are and why you should use one or the other.

In Java, storing by value and reference is seamless, especially because the notation is the same. The only thing that differentiates access by value, and access by reference is the data type itself — all primitive data types are always accessed by value, and all objects, including strings, arrays, and file streams, are always accessed by reference. Variables declared as a primitive data type contain the value of the variable. Variables declared as an object contain a reference to the object (that is, the address of the object), not the object itself. Merely declaring an object variable does not allocate memory for the object; you have to use the new keyword to allocate memory and create the object.

The primary difference between the two approaches is that it's not possible to do pointer arithmetic or other operations on Java memory addresses, as you would with C. Addresses for objects in Java are relative (or virtual) addresses arbitrarily assigned in the virtual machine, so there is no reason why you might want the pointer address.

GARBAGE COLLECTION

Garbage collection is the automated process of searching through memory for unreferenced memory and reclaiming it for the free memory list. The JVM uses garbage collection to return memory to the system when it's no longer in use.

When a Java program declares and instantiates an object or an array, it simply makes a request of the JVM, which accesses the underlying system memory (usually, but not always, through the host operating system) and allocates the memory. Java's garbage collection system typically works by searching through memory for objects and then checking their reference lists. It counts how many variables in a program are currently referencing each object. When the reference count for a particular object is zero, it knows that the object is no longer in use and its memory can be reclaimed. As a result, you don't have to manually deallocate memory as you do in C, where it is a necessary, time-consuming, and error-prone detail. Java handles the process automatically and accurately, removing a common source of errors in C/C++ programs.

NETWORKING

Because embedded systems are often networked today, using a language with built-in networking support saves a great deal of time and effort in implementing networking protocols and communications routines. In the case of Java, networking classes include TCP/IP stream and datagram routines for using TCP and UDP, methods for HTTP and URL services, and code for error checking and recovery features.

Although networking is possible from other languages, such as C, those languages require special add-on packages, DLLs, or other library modules that must be provided by the operating system or by third-party vendors. Special add-ons often require knowledge of the operating system or third-party tools, unlike Java's standardized, built-in, networking support.

Java includes networking packages out of necessity. Because the designers couldn't make any assumptions about the networking facilities available on an underlying operating system, they had to include integrated networking class libraries to ensure that Java programs would work on all platforms.

Dynamic Configuration

Dynamic configuration is the customizing or reconfiguring of a system at start-up. Systems that have to load special hardware configurations, network parameters, or utilities at boot time to support specific uses often use dynamic configuration.

Java supports dynamic configuration with dynamic binding. When you compile to byte-code the individual class files that make up a program, none of the references between your class files, or to classes in JVM packages such as graphics, networking, and core language support, are resolved. When the JVM loads your program, it dynamically loads and binds (that is, links) all classes referenced by your program. Hence, all you have to do to change a system's configuration is update the corresponding class file. The next time the system boots, the JVM automatically binds the new file to your program and the new configuration is executed.

Exception Handling

Unlike in many desktop operating systems and applications, in an embedded system it is often unacceptable to reboot. We expect to be able to make a telephone call or watch TV, for example, without technical interruptions. This means that virtually all embedded programs have to be robust enough to intercept errors and prevent them from crashing the program or, worse yet, the entire device.

Program errors and bugs occur for a number of reasons. Relatively few are due to inherent logic errors. Instead, most programs crash because of unexpected inputs or because the program can't call upon system resources needed to complete a specific operation.

You have to anticipate problems like these and be able to trap them so they don't cause greater problems. You can trap and handle errors in virtually any programming language, but having facilities for doing so built in, as they are in Java, helps enormously. This is particularly the case in Java because it's a language designed for data communications, which tends to produce a large number of errors because of the uncertain inputs inherent in communications.

In Java, errors are signaled by throwing (generating) an exception. Using a language statement (with the keywords `try`, `catch`, and `finally`) designed for exception handling, programs can arrange to group their error-handling code in a few centralized locations. The `try` block of the statement is the normal flow of program execution. When an exception occurs in the `try` block (including nested levels of subroutines), control is passed to the `catch` block of code. The `finally` block of code is always executed, regardless of whether or not an exception occurs. Unhandled exceptions propagate up the call stack to the JVM and terminate the program. No more will you have to arrange to manually return error conditions up through several layers of function calls. Instead, when an error occurs, the code detecting the error simply throws an exception. This greatly simplifies error-handling code in applications, resulting in better error handling and more robust code.

THREADING

Most operating systems offer the capability for a single process to generate and manage multiple threads that perform different program activities independently of one another. Few programming languages provide direct support for managing threads, however; it typically requires direct operating system calls. Java, on the other hand, provides facilities for spawning, managing, and synchronizing threads directly in the language. As with other Java features, this was a necessity because the designers couldn't be certain that the underlying operating system would support multithreading.

Developers are using threads in more and more programs as a way to meet requirements that a program accomplish different, often unrelated tasks. Because Java has built-in language support for threads, creating multithreaded programs is easier and more natural with Java than it is with other languages.

GRAPHICS

The JVM includes an extensive graphics and windowing support package called the Abstract Windowing Toolkit (AWT). Using AWT, you can quickly and easily create sophisticated, powerful graphical user interfaces in your programs. For embedded systems that need an elaborate user interface, this can offer a huge savings in development time that translates into much quicker time to market.

LIMITATIONS OF JAVA

In computing, as in life, there is no such thing as a free lunch, and Java doesn't violate that axiom. Every advantage in Java comes with a corresponding cost. Following are some of its primary disadvantages and limitations:

- Performance
- Garbage collection overhead
- JVM overhead
- Hardware access
- Language immaturity

We discuss these disadvantages and limitations next.

PERFORMANCE

As we noted previously, you can expect interpreted Java bytecode to run five to ten times slower than the equivalent program written in C or C++. For some embedded systems, that performance hit isn't a problem because the system isn't CPU-bound. More often than not, however, slower execution speeds translate into unacceptable response times. Several possible solutions are available to mitigate the speed problem:

- **Use a faster, more powerful processor to get the system response time back into the acceptable range.** This solution will raise your per-system cost.

- **Use a native Java compiler (if one is available for your processor) to get better performance.** By doing this, you give up the platform-independent advantages of Java, but most embedded systems run on only one platform anyway.

- **Incorporate a JIT (just-in-time) compiler in your system, so that Java classes get compiled as they are loaded.** This solution may increase system costs if you have to add extra memory to the system to accommodate the JIT compiler. Also, if pieces of your system are loaded incrementally as needed, you must carefully control when program loading can happen, so that the pause that occurs when a class is compiled on loading doesn't affect system response times.

GARBAGE COLLECTION OVERHEAD

We noted that the automatic memory allocation and garbage collection feature in Java is a boon because it removes a common source of program bugs and simplifies the programmer's job. The problem with garbage collection from the perspective of a real-time system, however, is that it *is* automatic: You have limited control over when garbage collection is performed.

When the garbage collector runs, it freezes processing by the rest of the system. That's because it has to move objects around in memory, and it has to update all program variables that reference (point to) those objects before the program can run again. Depending on the amount of memory and the speed of the processor, garbage collection can freeze processing for as much as tenths of a second. Clearly, this is unacceptable for hard real-time systems, and problematic at best even for soft real-time systems.

Garbage collection can be initiated in three ways. First, the JVM has a background garbage collection thread. This thread tends to start garbage collection if it sees that the system is idle. A background garbage collection can be preempted if an event occurs to wake up another thread, but the garbage collector is not preempted instantly; it has to update all references to objects that have already been moved before it can let another thread run.

Second, if the JVM does not find enough memory to satisfy a memory allocation request, it initiates a non-preemptive garbage collection. The rest of the system is disabled until the garbage collection operation completes.

Finally, an application can request a garbage collection by calling the `system.gc()` method. So if you know the system isn't going to be performing any time-critical tasks for a while, you can initiate a garbage collection in the hope of avoiding one later at a more critical time.

At first glance, this intractable problem would seem to rule out the use of Java in hard real-time systems. That's not entirely true, as you'll see in a moment. But because garbage collection is more easily incorporated in soft real-time systems, let's look first at workarounds that can mitigate the effect of garbage collection in soft real-time systems. (You might also want to use some of these techniques in a hard real-time system, but none of them are sufficient by themselves to guarantee hard real-time response times.)

- Try to design your program so that it allocates all its objects up front, rather than continuously creating and destroying objects. Then the heap will remain in a quiescent state after initialization, and garbage collection won't consume any time.

- Call `system.gc()` whenever you know the system won't be doing any time-critical operations for half a second or so. This will help you avoid automatic garbage collection occurring at an inopportune time.

- Add extra memory to your system, so the heap always has lots of free memory. This will help keep the heap from getting fragmented, so that garbage collection will execute faster. It will also help avoid the non-preemptive garbage collection that occurs when a memory allocation request can't be satisfied.

- Some JVMs implement an incremental garbage collection algorithm that doesn't attempt to compact the entire heap each time garbage collection is performed. This tends to decrease the time spent for each garbage collection, although the frequency of garbage collection operations tends to increase. An incremental algorithm helps to reduce average system response times, although the worst case remains the same, because it's always possible that a full garbage collection will be required to satisfy a memory allocation request.

- If you use a faster processor, the execution time required for performing garbage collection decreases.

Now let's consider how we could handle garbage collection in the context of a hard real-time system. We have only two alternatives to suggest here. As you'll see, both solutions obviate the platform-independent characteristic of Java programs; your hard real-time Java application isn't going to run in any environment but your own.

- Imagine a JVM that gives the application more control over garbage collection. For example, for a real-time system, it's preferable for the memory allocator to throw an exception rather than initiate a non-preemptive garbage collection. The application can catch and deal with an out-of-memory exception, but it can't do anything about missed deadlines due to garbage collection. Similarly, providing an interface to the garbage collector that synchronizes automatic garbage collections with the requirements of the rest of the system helps avoid the system freezing unexpectedly. And using an incremental algorithm that can be quickly preempted if necessary is a requirement for hard real-time. We're aware of only one JVM that claims to provide real-time garbage collection: PERC (Portable Executive for Reliable Control), from

NewMonics. PERC is not a modification of Sun's JVM. It was written from the ground up to provide real-time support. We haven't used this JVM, but you should consider it if you want to use Java in a hard real-time system.

- Another alternative is a mixed Java and C/C++ system. All time-critical code is put in C/C++ threads, and less critical operations such as user interface and networking are put in Java threads. By making the C/C++ threads a higher priority than Java threads, you can ensure real-time system response. One company promoting this strategy is Negev Software Industries (NSI) of Dimona, Israel. NSI's JVM is called Java Software Coprocessor (JSCP), and the entire JVM runs on a single thread of the underlying RTOS. The JVM, rather than the RTOS, provides the threading support for the Java code. The RTOS provides the threading support for the C/C++ code that implements the real-time part of the system. You can license JSCP and port it to run on the RTOS of your choice.

Garbage collection poses one of the more difficult problems with using Java in embedded systems. Perhaps as Java becomes more popular in the embedded world, Java vendors will begin to provide JVMs that better satisfy the requirements of a hard real-time system.

JVM OVERHEAD

We've talked about a number of built-in features of a JVM, such as graphics and networking, that help you get Java programs to market quicker. The flip side of all those features is the memory overhead of a JVM. Because a JVM comes in one monolithic chunk (you must have a complete implementation to achieve the portability goal of using Java), the JVM memory footprint can't be reduced. Existing JVMs have a minimum memory footprint of 2MB and up.

Presumably, your Java program is using some of the features that are consuming memory. And because there's so much in the JVM, individual Java applications tend to be small, which can be a big advantage if you're building a system that dynamically downloads and runs multiple applications over a network. But the fact remains that Java does not have the configurability and scalability that has traditionally been the hallmark of embedded operating systems.

HARDWARE ACCESS

Java's method of achieving portability and security means that it lacks the capability to interface directly with hardware. The Java Virtual Machine is just that, a virtual machine — a software abstraction of the hardware that only makes it appear that the connection is a direct one. The virtual machine controls the interface with the actual hardware, and you are forced by definition to deal with the virtual machine.

But this isn't an insurmountable limitation. Much as C programs often use in-line assembly to get around a performance bottleneck, so, too, can Java programs use C to gain direct access to the hardware.

Getting Java and C to work together can be accomplished in a couple of ways. First, you can use native methods, which are written in C/C++ (or another language), but when called are loaded into the same memory space and run in the same context as the JVM. Because they are compiled to machine code, native methods run faster and can access hardware directly. The second option is native processes, which are standalone programs that run independently of the JVM, in their own memory space. Native processes and Java code communicate with each other through sockets, like the sockets used for communication endpoints in networking. After you select a mixed language approach, though, the platform independence and possibly security features offered by Java are out the window.

The Java processors, described previously in this chapter, can be considered hardware implementations of the interpreter component of the software JVM. Java programs can run directly on these processors and manipulate the hardware (note, however, that Sun had to add a few special-purpose instructions to the language to work with these processors directly).

LANGUAGE IMMATURITY

Java was released in May 1996, and beta versions were available a few months before. The first major revision, the Java Development Kit (JDK) 1.1, came out a year later. By the standards of programming languages, Java is still young and immature. Virtually all languages intended for general use have required several years to achieve a level of maturity needed to reliably write production applications.

If Java hadn't been developed by a small team, certain errors and omissions may have been discovered and addressed. And after Java was fielded, it was immediately put to many more uses than were originally envisioned. All of this means that initial implementations of Java, while remarkably robust and useful, fell short in several areas. These areas included security, size, and performance.

In continuing its development, Sun has a three-phase strategy for promoting Java as a universal language and computing platform. The first phase is the use of Java for programs that duplicate existing business or enterprise functions, such as email, calendars, and word processors. For these applications, Java will compete with traditional programming languages and traditional ways of developing applications.

The second phase is to offer Java to corporations as a way to build custom applications for internal use. IS departments often build custom applications using a language that must be compiled and, therefore, platform-specific. This, in turn, results in porting, compiling, and maintaining separate copies of the program for each platform. By using Java, IS departments would have to write and maintain only a single copy of each program.

The last phase, which is also still in the process of getting off the ground, is to define Java APIs and language features for use in traditional embedded devices, such as cellular telephones, set-top boxes, and printers.

So embedded uses of Java are last on Sun's priority list. Sun is continuing to develop the language for these uses, but this development takes a back seat to desktop and enterprise uses. Given Sun's priorities, it will likely be some time before all the embedded concerns are addressed. Until that time, programmers of embedded systems will have to make use of workarounds, compromises, and third-party solutions.

Programming tools for Java development are also still evolving. Compilers and development tools are available from several sources, such as Symantec, Microsoft, and Sun. And Sun is no longer your only choice for JVMs and JITs; several other vendors provide competitive offerings. Companies have been slower to develop testing and debugging tools. Rudimentary products are on the market from debugging vendors Parasoft and NuMega Technologies. Parasoft's jtest automatically generates test cases for testing Java modules, and NuMega's JCheck provides visibility of program behavior in the JVM. Neither addresses more than a small part of the debugging process, and both are intended for desktop development, although they can be used for more of the embedded development process.

We still have no cross-debugging solutions of the sort traditionally used by developers of embedded systems to bring up programs on the target hardware. Because you'll probably have to write the hardware-specific parts of your application in C/C++ anyway, your best bet is to debug that code with a C/C++ cross-debugger, and debug the Java code on your target system by popping up dialog boxes, keeping a log file, or other similar techniques.

THE JAVA-ENABLED UPS

To demonstrate the use of a Java applet on a web page, we took the Network-Aware UPS project from Chapter 14 and replaced the HTML in the user interface page with a Java applet. You can build compelling user interfaces easily in Java because of the powerful graphics support built into the JVM in the web browser. In the Java-Enabled UPS, we simply replicated the user interface from the Network-Aware UPS, but the buttons, tables, and bar graph look different because they're drawn by the Java graphics package rather than the web browser's HTML engine. In addition, because of the built-in networking support in Java, it's easy for an applet to dynamically update the page display by retrieving new data from the web server. We use this capability to refresh the web page every 2 seconds, tracking any changes in UPS state.

BUILDING THE JAVA-ENABLED UPS PROJECT

The Java-Enabled UPS is located in \TSLITE\PROJECTS\UPS4. A prebuilt executable, UPS4.EXE, is provided if you want to skip the build step. To build the executable, first use your favorite Java compiler to compile the Ups4.java file. For example, with Symantec Visual Café for Java, type the following from a DOS command prompt:

```
sj Ups4.java
```

After you've compiled the Java applet to produce the Ups4.class and BarGraph.class class files (we also provide prebuilt copies of these files in case you don't have a Java compiler), use Visual C++ Developer Studio to open the UPS4.DSW workspace file, and then click Build|Rebuild All. Chapter 3, "Software Installation and Setup," contains complete details on building the projects.

RUNNING THE JAVA-ENABLED UPS PROJECT

Before downloading and running UPS4.EXE, you must correctly connect the target system to the host computer, and you must configure Windows for the networking connection. This setup procedure is identical to that required for the Network-Aware UPS; refer back to Chapter 14 for detailed instructions.

After you have everything correctly configured, download and execute the Java-Enabled UPS by selecting Build|Execute ups4.exe from Developer Studio. Alternatively, from a DOS command prompt, set the current directory to \TSLITE\PROJECTS\UPS4 and type the following:

```
runemb release\ups4
```

After UPS4.EXE has been downloaded to the target system, double-click the UPS Connection icon in your Dial-Up Networking window and connect to the embedded UPS system, as described in Chapter 14.

After the connection is established between the Windows host and the UPS system, start a web browser that supports Java 1.1 to display web pages from the Java-Enabled UPS. Although Sun released JDK 1.1 in February 1997, not all web browsers support it — and those that do may offer only incomplete support. If your browser is not Java 1.1-compatible, you'll probably get an error message to the effect that the applet calls an unsupported method. These types of problems should be expected when using new technology. We tested with Netscape Navigator and Microsoft Internet Explorer.

If you use Netscape Navigator, you must have version 4.04 with the JDK 1.1 patch or the JDK 1.1 release of 4.05 or later. One version 4.05 release (with no distinguishing characteristics that we could find) does not support JDK 1.1. If you have that version, the applet will not load because of unimplemented methods; get a newer version from Netscape's web site.

If you use Microsoft Internet Explorer, you must have version 4.01 with service pack SP1 or later. Internet Explorer 4.0, which is JDK 1.1-compatible, takes upwards of 5 seconds to make a TCP connection with the URL.openStream() method, which is used by the applet in the Java-Enabled UPS. Because the applet attempts to retrieve the UPS status from the UPS system every 2 seconds, the applet won't work with Internet Explorer 4.0.

From your Java 1.1-compatible browser, type http://192.168.1.2/ as the destination URL in the Address, Location, or URL box. This retrieves the home page from the UPS system (the test IP addresses used are explained in detail in Chapter 14). Click the UPS Interface link to display the UPS interface page with the Java applet, which is shown in Figure 17-3. The first time you load the UPS interface page, a delay occurs while the browser initializes the JVM and loads the JVM packages (class libraries) referenced by the UPS Java applet.

As with the Network-Aware UPS, add a load, turn on the power to the load, and simulate an AC power failure to start the battery discharging. The Java applet updates the display every two seconds, enabling you to see the battery discharging, as shown in Figure 17-4.

Feel free to experiment with simulating various inputs to the UPS system. If you let the battery discharge completely and then attempt to add a load, the UPS system generates an error message and the applet displays a UPS error message in a third area, below the UPS state display.

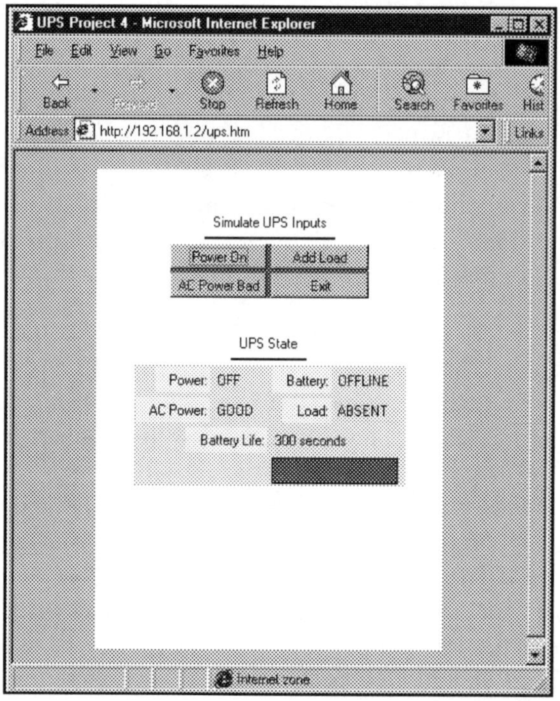

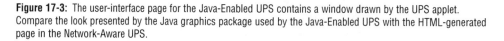

Figure 17-3: The user-interface page for the Java-Enabled UPS contains a window drawn by the UPS applet. Compare the look presented by the Java graphics package used by the Java-Enabled UPS with the HTML-generated page in the Network-Aware UPS.

When you have finished exercising the UPS system, click the Exit button to terminate the application. As shown in Figure 17-5, the Java-Enabled UPS uses the error-reporting mechanism to report termination.

When the UPS system closes the network connection and terminates, the Windows Dial-Up Networking program displays a window titled Reestablish Connection, which tells you that the connection was terminated and asks whether you want to reconnect. Click Cancel to terminate the Dial-Up Networking connection on the host side.

A QUICK TOUR OF THE SOURCE

To create the Java-Enabled UPS from the Network-Aware UPS, we modified some of the code in WEBMEM.C and added the Java applet source file Ups4.java. Recall from Chapter 16, "Connecting to the Web," that the UpsInterface() function in WEBMEM.C generated the UPS interface page. The function still does, but it's a much simpler page now, as you can see by selecting View|Source from Internet Explorer (or View|Document Source from Netscape), as shown in Figure 17-6. All the page does now is use the APPLET tag, which defines a window size and instructs the browser to load the Ups4.class Java applet and give it that window for its user interface.

The ups.htm web page is generated by the UpsInterface() function in Listing 17-1.

Listing 17-1: The UpsInterface() function

```
//
// In this version, the "UPS Interface" page just loads a Java
// applet which provides the actual interface.
//
BOOL __cdecl UpsInterface(REQ_INPUTS *pInp, REQ_OUTPUTS *pOutp)
{
    if (!hpg_CreatePage(pOutp))
        return FALSE;
    html_brtext(HTML_TITLE, "UPS Project 4");
    html_endtag(HTML_HEAD "\n");
    html_tagwopt(HTML_BODY "\n", " bgcolor=%s", "silver",
                " text=%s", "black", NULL);
    html_tag(HTML_CENTER "\n");
    html_rawtext("\n<APPLET code=\"Ups4.class\" width=300 height=400\n"
                "           alt=\"The Ups4.class applet can't run in this"
                " web browser\">\n Java is not enabled in your web"
                " browser!\n</APPLET>\n");

    html_text("\n");
    html_endtag(HTML_CENTER "\n");
    return hpg_DonePage(pOutp);
}
```

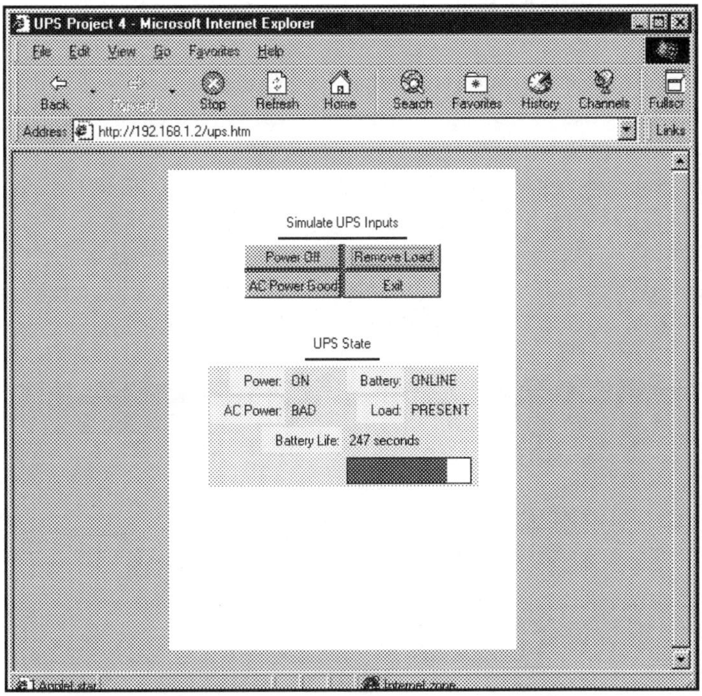

Figure 17-4: As the battery discharges, the Java applet requests new UPS state information from the UPS system every 2 seconds and updates the display accordingly.

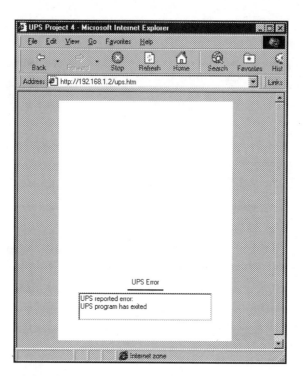

Figure 17-5: When you instruct the Java-Enabled UPS simulation to exit, the exit status is reported in the error box.

The HTML-on-the-fly library functions we saw in Chapter 16 are used to create most of the tags on the page. The `html_rawtext()` function is used to create the APPLET tag, which has a more complex syntax than the other tags.

When the web browser processes the APPLET tag, it requests the web page containing the `Ups4.class` Java class file from the web server on the network host with IP address `192.168.1.2`. (After loading `Ups4.class`, it also requests the `BarGraph.class` class file, which is referenced by `Ups4.class`.) Although the UPS system could store these class files in a file system on disk, we don't want to add a disk drive to the UPS (which otherwise has no

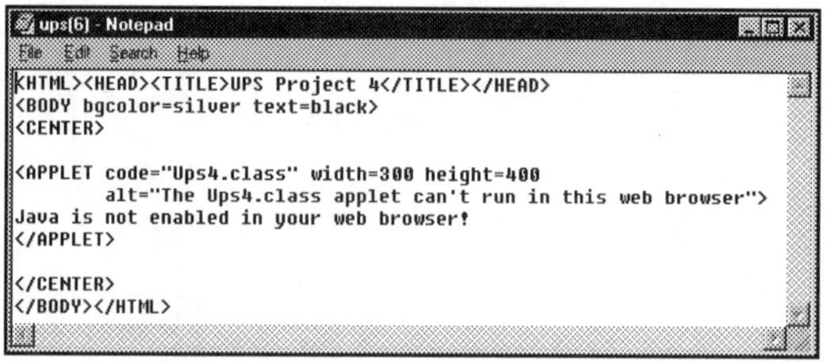

```
HTML><HEAD><TITLE>UPS Project 4</TITLE></HEAD>
<BODY bgcolor=silver text=black>
<CENTER>

<APPLET code="Ups4.class" width=300 height=400
        alt="The Ups4.class applet can't run in this web browser">
Java is not enabled in your web browser!
</APPLET>

</CENTER>
</BODY></HTML>
```

Figure 17-6: In the Java-Enabled UPS, the ups.htm web page generated by the UpsInterface() function contains an APPLET tag instructing the web browser to load and run the Ups4.class Java applet.

need for file storage) for only these two files! Instead, we chose to store images of Ups4.class and BarGraph.class in memory, embedded in the data for the UPS4.EXE program. When the browser requests the web pages containing the class files from the web server in the UPS, the web server retrieves them from memory rather than loading them from the disk.

The class files are embedded in the program's data with the help of a linker switch. As you might recall from Chapter 3, when the Developer Studio project was created, Embedded StudioExpress automatically created a link file. The bottom of that link file has room for additional linker commands. Let's look at the linker switches we added to UPS4.LNK:

```
! Add any additional linker commands here.
-lib utilsmt
-segment UPS4_CLASS class=RDATA ro file=Ups4.class
-segment BARGRAPH_CLASS class=RDATA ro file=BarGraph.class
```

The first switch just links in the multithreaded version of the UTILS library, which contains the speaker utility routine we use to beep the speaker when the UPS battery is discharging. Following that are two -SEGMENT switches that store the two Java class files in the data for UPS4.EXE. Each -SEGMENT switch creates a new segment with the specified name; the FILE= argument to the switch tells the linker to store the named file in the segment. The CLASS= argument has nothing to do with Java classes; it specifies the class of the segment, and the linker uses this information for ordering segments in memory. The RDATA class is one of the data segment classes in ETS Kernel applications. The RO argument is a segment attribute, specifying that the segment is read-only.

But how does the web server find these files in memory when a web browser requests them? The linker creates global symbols, accessible by code, that define the start and end of each segment in memory. The Ups4Class() function, which returns the web page for Ups4.class, uses these symbols.

```
//
// function that returns in-memory file Ups4.class
//
#define SEG_BEGIN(sname) _p_SEG_##sname##_BEGIN
#define SEG_END(sname) _p_SEG_##sname##_END

BOOL __cdecl Ups4Class(REQ_INPUTS *pInp, REQ_OUTPUTS *pOutp)
{
    extern char SEG_BEGIN(UPS4_CLASS), SEG_END(UPS4_CLASS);
    int len;
    len = &SEG_END(UPS4_CLASS) - &SEG_BEGIN(UPS4_CLASS) + 1;
    if ((pOutp->pEntityBody = malloc(len)) == NULL)
    {
        hpg_ErrorPage(pOutp, pErr500, "Server error: out of memory");
        return FALSE;
    }
    memcpy(pOutp->pEntityBody, &SEG_BEGIN(UPS4_CLASS), len);
    pOutp->ContentLength = len;
    strcpy(pOutp->ContentType, "application/java-applet");
    return TRUE;
}
```

The symbols are the segment name, prefixed with _p_SEG, and postfixed with _BEGIN or _END, as appropriate. Taking the address of the symbol names with the C & operator gives the addresses of the first and last bytes in the segment. Ups4Class() allocates a memory buffer, copies the file image to the allocated buffer, and returns the buffer address, buffer length, and a web page content type of application/java-applet to the web server. The server then transmits the web page over the network to the web browser.

After loading the Java applet, the JVM in the web browser invokes the Ups4.init() applet method. The source code for both the Ups4 and BarGraph classes are in the Ups4.java file (when this file is compiled, the compiler produces both class files). The class definition for Ups4 follows.

```
public class Ups4 extends Applet implements Runnable
{
private Panel InputHdr;
private Panel Inputs;
private Button PowerButton;
private Button LoadButton;
private Button ACPowerButton;
private Button ExitButton;
private Panel StateHdr;
private Panel State;
private Label PowerValue;
private Label BatteryValue;
private Label ACPowerValue;
private Label LoadValue;
private Label BattLifeValue;
private BarGraph BattBarGraph;
private Panel ErrorHdr;
private TextArea Error;
private Thread StateThread = null;
```

As required for an applet, Ups4 is an extension, or subclass, of the Applet class, which is in the java.applet package included with the JVM. (The full name of the Applet class is java.applet.Applet; we can use the shorter name because we use an import java.applet.* statement at the top of the file.) The implements Runnable clause means the Ups4 class implements the java.lang.Runnable interface. The Runnable interface defines the run() method required for use with the Thread class. Because Ups4 is multithreaded, it needs a run() method.

At the top of the class definition, we've placed all the fields of the class, most of which are used to construct the user interface. The exception is StateThread, the thread we create to update the UPS state every 2 seconds. All the fields are declared private, which means they can be accessed by only the methods of the Ups4 class.

The user interface is constructed using the Java GUI building blocks called *components*, each of which is a subclass of java.awt.Component.*. The components are added to *containers*, which are used to arrange, or lay out, the components. Because a container is also a component, containers can be placed within containers. In Ups4, we use Panel containers for each of the primary areas on the applet window, and place `Button`, `Label`, and `TextArea` components within the `Panel` containers. The applet is itself a container, so all the `Panel` containers are laid out within the applet window. Figure 17-7 shows the container and component hierarchy created by the `Ups4` applet. The user interface we're building is shown in Figure 17-3.

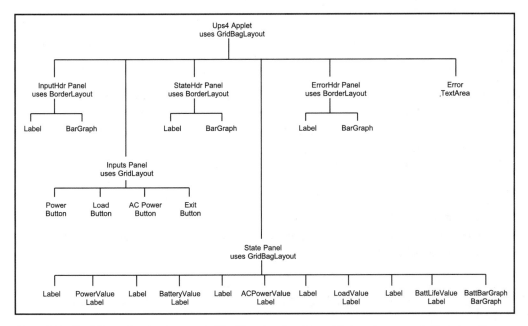

Figure 17-7: The GUI user interface is created with a hierarchy of container objects and component objects from the java.awt package. The leaves of the tree are the components, which contain the text or graphics data to display. The diagram shows the layout manager used by each container object to position components on the display.

The entry point for all Java applets is the `init()` method in Listing 17-2. The `init()` method for `Ups4` creates the user interface and the thread that updates UPS state information every two seconds.

Listing 17-2: The init() method

```
public void init()
{
    Label tempLab;
    Dimension tempDim;
    Color hdrBackColor = new Color(240, 240, 240);
    Color inputBackColor = new Color(250, 0, 0);
    Color stateBackColor = new Color(220, 220, 220);
    Color stateLabelColor = new Color(250, 250, 150);
    Color stateValueColor = stateBackColor;

// Make the background for the entire applet white
    this.setBackground(Color.white);
```

```
// Initialize the constraints for the applet layout.
   this.setLayout(new GridBagLayout());
   GridBagConstraints cUps4 = new GridBagConstraints();
   cUps4.fill = GridBagConstraints.NONE;
   cUps4.gridwidth = 1; cUps4.gridheight = 1;
   cUps4.anchor = GridBagConstraints.CENTER;
```

Init() first sets the background color for the applet window to white. Then it sets the layout manager for the Ups4 applet to GridBagLayout. The GridBagLayout layout manager allows fairly flexible control over components with variable-sized cells. We'll use this layout manager to position all the panels we create.

We then create cUps4, a GridBagConstraints object we'll use to instruct the layout manager how to position each panel. We'll fine-tune the constraints for each panel, but we initialize the object here with our basic set of constraints: the fill field is set to none because we don't resize any of the panels. The gridwidth and gridheight fields select the number of columns and rows of the grid pattern used to display each panel; we'll put each panel in a single cell of the grid. The anchor field is used to control the component position when the display area is larger than the component. We want all our panels centered within their grid cells.

The first panel in the applet is the InputHdr panel, which contains a Label component for the header text for the simulated input buttons and a BarGraph component used to draw an underscore to set off the text.

```
//
// The InputHdr panel contains the header text for the input buttons,
// plus an underline which we just draw with a very thin bar graph.
//
   cUps4.gridx = 0; cUps4.gridy = 0;
   cUps4.insets = new Insets(2,2,2,2);
   InputHdr = new Panel();
   InputHdr.setBackground(hdrBackColor);
   InputHdr.setLayout(new BorderLayout(0, 2));
   this.add(InputHdr, cUps4);
   tempLab = new Label("Simulate UPS Inputs", Label.CENTER);
   InputHdr.add(tempLab, "Center");
   tempDim = tempLab.getPreferredSize();
   InputHdr.add(new BarGraph(tempDim.width, 1), "South");
```

We set the cUps4 constraints object to position the InputHdr panel in row 0, column 0 of the grid, with 2 pixels of padding space (the insets field) next to each edge of the panel. We then create the InputHdr panel, set its background color and layout manager, and call the add() method to set the layout constraints for the panel.

We use the BorderLayout layout manager to position components within the InputHdr panel. This layout manager can place components against the four edges of the container and in the center of the container. We place the Label component in the center of the InputHdr panel and the BarGraph component on the bottom (South) edge of the panel.

The Label component contains a single line of text. Unlike all the other components and containers we use, the BarGraph component is not part of the java.awt package; we created it to display the battery life bar graph. We use it here to draw a rule 1 pixel in height and the width of the Label component.

The Inputs panel, which contains the four Button components used to simulate UPS inputs, is the next panel in the applet.

```
//
// The Inputs panel contains the four buttons used to simulate UPS inputs.
//
    cUps4.gridx = 0; cUps4.gridy = 1;
    cUps4.insets = new Insets(2,2,25,2);
    Inputs = new Panel();
    Inputs.setBackground(inputBackColor);
    Inputs.setLayout(new GridLayout(2, 2, 4, 3));
    this.add(Inputs, cUps4);
    PowerButton = new Button("Power Xxx");
    PowerButton.setForeground(Color.black);
    PowerButton.setBackground(Color.lightGray);
    Inputs.add(PowerButton);
```

The Inputs panel is placed in row 1, column 0 of the applet's grid; in other words, in the cell below the InputHdr panel. The top, left, and right padding for the panel is 2 pixels, but we put 25 pixels of padding below the panel. (Notice that we create a new Insets object here, losing the reference to the previous Insets object we created when setting constraints for the InputHdr panel. In a C++ program, this would result in a memory leak; in Java, the garbage collector will take care of reclaiming the memory used by the previous Insets object.)

We use the GridLayout layout manager to position components within the Inputs panel. GridLayout arranges components in an evenly-spaced grid with specific dimensions, as opposed to the sort of free-form grid used by GridBagLayout. This is ideal for our buttons, which we want to be of uniform size. We specify a 2 x 2 grid, with 4 pixels of space between columns and 3 pixels between rows.

We then add four Button objects to the Inputs panel; we've reproduced the code for only the Power On/Off button here. Because we're not going to allow dynamic resizing of components (to keep the code simple), we initialize the text for the button to the maximum size we'll need. That way, when the layout managers for the panels and the applet figure out how big to make each component, we'll have enough space reserved for the maximum size button label.

Next is the StateHdr panel, for the header text of the UPS state table; the panel contains a Label component and a BarGraph component to draw a rule, just like the InputHdr panel. Then we create the State panel, which contains the Label and BarGraph components used to display the state of the UPS system.

```
//
// The State panel is a table containing all the UPS state information.
//
    cUps4.gridx = 0; cUps4.gridy = 3;
    cUps4.insets = new Insets(2,2,25,2);
    State = new Panel();
    State.setBackground(stateBackColor);
```

```
State.setLayout(new GridBagLayout());
this.add(State, cUps4);
GridBagConstraints cState = new GridBagConstraints();
cState.fill = GridBagConstraints.NONE;
cState.insets = new Insets(2,2,2,2);
cState.gridwidth = 1; cState.gridheight = 1;

// Power
tempLab = new Label("Power:", Label.RIGHT);
tempLab.setBackground(stateLabelColor);
cState.gridx = 0; cState.gridy = 0;
cState.anchor = GridBagConstraints.EAST;
State.add(tempLab, cState);
PowerValue = new Label("XXX", Label.LEFT);
PowerValue.setBackground(stateValueColor);
cState.gridx = 1; cState.gridy = 0;
cState.anchor = GridBagConstraints.WEST;
State.add(PowerValue, cState);
```

The State panel is placed in row 3, column 0 of the applet's grid, in the cell below the StateHdr panel. We set the StateHdr panel, like the Inputs panel, so that the top, left, and right padding is 2 pixels, with 25 pixels of padding below the panel.

The State panel needs the flexibility offered by the GridBagLayout layout manager. We initialize cState, the GridBagConstraints object used for setting layout constraints on components within the State panel, to not support dynamic resizing of components, to put 2-pixel spacing around each edge of the component, and to position each component in a single cell of the grid.

The state of the UPS power to the load is displayed using two Label components. We position the "Power:" text right-justified within the label display area and position the PowerValue component's text (which will be either "ON" or "OFF") left-justified within the label display area. In addition, we use the State panel layout constraints to right-justify (EAST) and left-justify (WEST) the labels themselves within their respective grid cells. The labels are placed in columns 0 and 1 of row 0.

We skip the code that displays the battery, AC power, and load state. The last item in the UPS state is the battery life.

```
// Battery Life
tempLab = new Label("Battery Life:", Label.RIGHT);
tempLab.setBackground(stateLabelColor);
cState.gridx = 0; cState.gridy = 2;
cState.gridwidth = 2;
cState.anchor = GridBagConstraints.EAST;
State.add(tempLab, cState);
BattLifeValue = new Label("nnnnn seconds", Label.LEFT);
BattLifeValue.setBackground(stateValueColor);
cState.gridx = 2; cState.gridy = 2;
cState.anchor = GridBagConstraints.WEST;
State.add(BattLifeValue, cState);
```

```
// bar graph for Battery Life
tempDim = BattLifeValue.getPreferredSize();
BattBarGraph = new BarGraph(tempDim.width + 20, tempDim.height);
BattBarGraph.setBackground(Color.white);
cState.gridx = 2; cState.gridy = 3;
cState.gridwidth = 2;
cState.anchor = GridBagConstraints.WEST;
State.add(BattBarGraph, cState);
```

The text for the two labels used to display battery life is longer than the other UPS state components, so we set the `gridwidth` field in `cState` to 2 to allow the labels to use two cell widths in the grid. As before, both the text and the label components are right- and left-justified.

The battery life bar graph is positioned in columns 2 and 3 on row 3 of the grid. We want to make the bar graph as wide as possible without throwing off the look of the entire state table display. The cell grids have no fixed size; the layout manager makes the grid just large enough to accommodate the size of all the components in the grid. So we obtain the width of the `BattLifeValue` component, which occupies the two cells immediately above the bar graph, and increase that width by 20 pixels, a value determined by trial and error to get the table display to look good. We give the bar graph the same height as the label components to obtain a balanced look.

At the bottom of the applet window, we place the `Panel` container for the error message header and the `TextArea` component for the actual text of the error message. These components are hidden unless an error message must be displayed, which is why they don't appear in Figure 17-3. The error message components are used also to display a message when the UPS system exits; refer to Figure 17-5 to see them used for that purpose.

The code to set up the `ErrorHdr` panel is just like the code we saw for the `InputHdr` panel. The error message text is displayed in a `TextArea` component.

```
// The Error text area
    cUps4.gridx = 0; cUps4.gridy = 5;
    cUps4.insets = new Insets(2,2,2,2);
    Error = new TextArea("", 2, 35, TextArea.SCROLLBARS_BOTH);
    Error.setBackground(Color.white);
    this.add(Error, cUps4);
```

A `TextArea` component can display arbitrary-length strings. We give the component 2 rows and 35 columns of display area, and request both horizontal and vertical scrollbars, if necessary, to allow the user to see the entire text of long messages.

With the display components all created and laid out, the next step is to query the UPS system to obtain the state of the UPS and correctly initialize the contents of all the display components.

```
//
// Now request UPS state information
// to initialize the display contents
// correctly.  Make sure the error
// text area and header are initially
```

```
// visible; they must be visible the
// first time the display is painted
// or we can't make them visible later.
//
    GetUpsState(null);
    ErrorHdr.setVisible(true);
    Error.setVisible(true);
```

The GetUpsState() method, which we'll see in a moment, communicates over the network to the UPS system to obtain the UPS state and modifies the contents of the display components accordingly. GetUpsState() sets the error message components to invisible if there's no error message (which is usually the case). When the init() method terminates, all components that we want to be able to make visible later must be displayed, so we force the error message components to be visible.

The last task the init() method performs is creating a thread to query the UPS system and update the display every 2 seconds.

```
//
// Create a thread to automatically query the UPS target for state
// information and update the display every 2 seconds.  This thread is
// terminated by the main thread when an error occurrs on the UPS system
// or the UPS system exits.
//
    StateThread = new Thread(this);
    StateThread.start();
```

Using the this keyword creates a new thread of execution in the Ups4 Applet object. We call the start() method to begin thread execution. A thread always begins by calling the run() method for the object.

```
//
// The run method for the thread.  Just sits in a loop getting UPS state
// every 2 seconds and updating the display.
//
public void run()
{
    while (true)
    {
        try { Thread.sleep(2000); }
        catch (InterruptedException e) {}
        GetUpsState(null);
    }
}
```

This thread couldn't be much simpler. It just sits in an infinite loop, sleeping for 2 seconds each time through the loop and then calling GetUpsState() to query the UPS system for state information and to update the applet display. The Thread.sleep() method can throw an InterruptedException, so we have to arrange to catch it or the compiler will flag an error. We don't need to do anything if an exception is thrown, however; we just continue our normal processing.

Now let's see what happens when a button is pressed.

```
//
// Handle button presses.  Just send the command corresponding to the
// button to the UPS and process the returned UPS state.
//
public boolean action(Event event, Object arg)
{
    if (event.target == PowerButton)
        return GetUpsState(PowerButton);
    else if (event.target == ACPowerButton)
        return GetUpsState(ACPowerButton);
    else if (event.target == LoadButton)
        return GetUpsState(LoadButton);
    else if (event.target == ExitButton)
        return GetUpsState(ExitButton);
    else
        return false;
}
```

You handle events in Java by overriding the appropriate method of the Component class; for button presses, you override the action() method. The action() method returns true if it handles the event or false if not, in which case the event is passed to the container of the component to see whether that container wants to process it.

We handle the four button presses by calling GetUpsState() to send a command to the UPS system and update the UPS state display after the command is processed. If any event other than one of the four button presses is passed, we return false.

Now let's look at the GetUpsState() method. GetUpsState() communicates with the UPS system using the built-in networking support in the JVM. Because we already have a web server on the UPS, we elected to send commands and get back UPS state information using the HTTP protocol. We send commands using the HTML forms paradigm, by appending ?button=value to the URL. The web page containing the state information (javaups.htm) is just plaintext with comma-separated fields. The page has no HTML tags because it's not intended for display by a web browser.

This is a quick, easy solution that works well. The only downside with using HTTP is that it doesn't maintain a connection; each time we want to get state information, we have to open a new connection, get the web page, and close the connection. This unnecessary connection setup and shutdown makes the program slower. As an exercise, you could make the program faster if you defined a private protocol that kept a connection open and allowed you to send commands and get the status at any time. This would be easy to do on the Java side, using the powerful networking support in the java.net package. You'd open the connection in the init() method and close it in the destroy() method, and then just send commands and get the UPS status whenever you needed to. On the UPS target side, start with the Finger server code introduced in Chapter 15, "Networking," and modify it to use a specific port number you select for your protocol. Keep the connection open until the client (the applet) closes it.

Then define a simple ASCII protocol that allows you to send commands from the client and send the UPS status from the server.

Let's look at the basic flow of control in `GetUpsState()` in Listing 17-3, with the networking code stripped out.

Listing 17-3: The GetUpsState() method

```java
public synchronized boolean GetUpsState(Button b)
{
    InputStream in = null;
    String UpsState = "";
    String ServerError = "UPS reported error:\n";
    String FormatError = "Bad format in state string returned by UPS:\n";

    try
    {
        // Clear any old errors in the error text area.
        Error.setText("");

... networking and display update code removed ...

    catch (Exception e)
    {
        if (e.getMessage().equals(""))
            Error.appendText("Unknown exception in GetUpsState().\n");
        else
            Error.appendText(e.getMessage() + "\n");
    }

//
// Close network connection and update visibility of error
// message text area no matter what happens
//
    finally
    {
        if (in != null)
        {
            try { in.close(); }
            catch (Exception e) {}
        }
        ErrorHdr.setVisible(!Error.getText().equals(""));
        Error.setVisible(!Error.getText().equals(""));
    }

    return true;
}
```

Notice that GetUpsState() is declared as a synchronized method. Only one thread at a time can be executing in a synchronized method; any other threads that attempt to call the method will block until the first thread exits the method. Because we don't want two threads attempting to communicate with the UPS system simultaneously, we declare GetUpsState() synchronized.

The networking code is enclosed in a try block, so we can catch any exceptions that are thrown. Because the Exception class is the base class for all Java exceptions, this catch() statement catches any exception that is thrown. If the exception has a message, we display it in the Error component of the display; otherwise, we display a message stating that we received an unknown exception. Notice that we append text to the Error component, rather than replacing existing text. We clear the text in the Error component at the top of the try block; if we've already written a message to it before the exception was thrown, we want to be able to see the original error message in addition to the error message about the exception.

In the finally block, which executes whether or not an exception is thrown, we close the network connection if one was established. Then we make the ErrorHdr and Error components visible or hidden depending on whether text is present in the Error component.

Now let's look at Listing 17-4 and the networking code in GetUpsState().

Listing 17-4: Making an HTTP request in GetUpsState()

```
String command = "";
if (b != null)
{
    // Netscape implementation of URL class doesn't substitute
    // %20 for spaces, so we have to do it by hand.
    command = "?button=";
    int idx, idxSpace;
    for (idx = 0, idxSpace = 0; idxSpace >= 0; idx = idxSpace + 1)
    {
        idxSpace = b.getLabel().indexOf(" ", idx);
        if (idxSpace < 0)
            command += b.getLabel().substring(idx);
        else
        {
            command += b.getLabel().substring(idx, idxSpace);
            command += "%20";
        }
    }
}
URL StateUrl = new URL(getCodeBase().getProtocol(),
                    getCodeBase().getHost(),
                    "/javaups.htm" + command);
in = StateUrl.openStream();
byte[] buffer = new byte[4096];
int bytes_read;
```

```
while ((bytes_read = in.read(buffer)) != -1)
{
    UpsState += new String(buffer, 0, bytes_read);
}
```

The first thing we do is construct the URL, which will look like this:

```
http://192.168.1.2/javaups.htm[?Button=name]
```

where the `?Button=name` portion is optional and present only if the user pressed a button in the applet window. The JVM networking code supplies the protocol (HTTP) and the host name for the connection from which the Java applet was loaded. We append `javaups.htm`, the name of the web page on the UPS system used to interface with the Java applet, and the button name. The only complexity is that the button name can contain spaces (for example, "Power On"). The HTTP protocol specifies that spaces should be encoded as `%20` in the URI (the portion of the URL, following the host name, that is passed to the web server). The JVM networking code should handle that substitution, but the JVM in Netscape Navigator doesn't replace the spaces, so we have to do it ourselves.

After the URL has been constructed, making the HTTP connection and reading the web page is trivial — the JVM does all the work. We call the `URL.openStream()` method to open the HTTP connection and create an input stream, and then just call the `InputStream.read()` method in a loop, appending data to the `UpsState` string, until `read()` returns -1, indicating that the connection has been closed.

The UPS state information returned by the UPS system is encoded as ASCII comma-delimited text. We can see the contents of the web page (`javaups.htm`) that the Java applet requests by displaying it in the web browser, as shown in Figure 17-8.

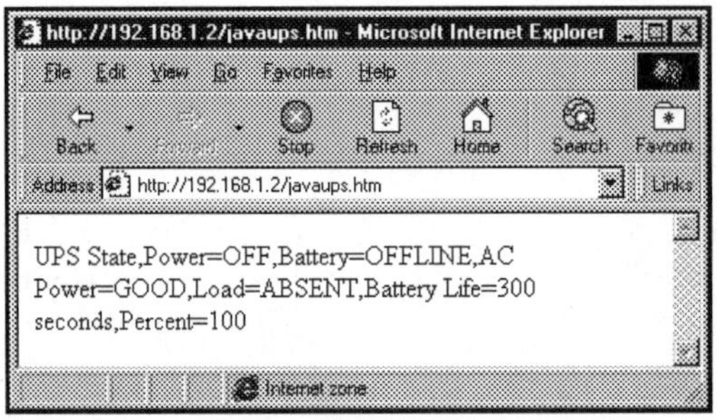

Figure 17-8: Type the name of the javaups.htm web page directly into the browser Address, URL, or Location box to view the ASCII text that the Java applet has to parse. The UPS state is encoded as a sequence of comma-delimited fields. The state information starts with the string "UPS State,"; the applet considers any other string an error.

Now let's take a look at the UPS function that generates the `javaups.htm` web page: `JavaUpsInterface()` in the WEBMEM.C file. Listing 17-5 shows the code that handles the processing of the URI.

Listing 17-5: The JavaUpsInterface() function

```
//
// Determine the appropriate command to the event subsystem, based
// on which form button was pressed.  If no button was pressed,
// just send the STATUS command.
//
    Event.Event = EVENT_STATUS;
    if (pInp->pQuery != NULL && *pInp->pQuery != 0)
    {
        // decode parameter list to get form button
        if (form_decode(FormFields, &Event, pInp->pQuery, ErrMsg))
        {
            sprintf(Output, "Error parsing query string: %s\n", ErrMsg);
            goto DONE;
        }
    }

//
// Send the command to the event subsystem, and wait for the
// response.  If we time out on the communication, we just
// return an error message for our HTML page.
//
    StartTime = GetTickCount();
    while (TRUE)
    {
        if (MsgWrite(hEventQueue, &Event, FALSE) == 1)
            break;
        Sleep(10);
        if (GetTickCount() - StartTime > EVENT_TIMEOUT)
        {
            strcpy(Output, "Server error: timeout sending to "
                    "event thread");
            goto DONE;
        }
    }
    if (Event.Event == EVENT_EXIT)
    {
        strcpy(Output, "UPS program has exited");
        goto DONE;
    }
    ElapsedTime = GetTickCount() - StartTime;
    if (ElapsedTime > EVENT_TIMEOUT ||
        WaitForSingleObject(hStatusPipeRead,
                    EVENT_TIMEOUT - ElapsedTime) != WAIT_OBJECT_0)
    {
        strcpy(Output, "Server error: timeout receiving from "
                    "event thread");
        goto DONE;
    }
```

```
if (!ReadFile(hStatusPipeRead, &Status, sizeof(Status), &Len,
          NULL) || Len != sizeof(Status))
{
    strcpy(Output, "Server error: read error receiving from "
            "event thread");
    goto DONE;
}
if (Status.ErrLen > 0)
{
    ElapsedTime = GetTickCount() - StartTime;
    if (ElapsedTime > EVENT_TIMEOUT ||
        WaitForSingleObject(hStatusPipeRead,
              EVENT_TIMEOUT - ElapsedTime) != WAIT_OBJECT_0)
    {
        strcpy(Output, "Server error: timeout receiving from "
                "event thread\n");
        goto DONE;
    }
    if (!ReadFile(hStatusPipeRead, ErrMsg, Status.ErrLen, &Len,
              NULL) || Len != Status.ErrLen)
    {
        strcpy(Output, "Server error: read error receiving from "
                "event thread\n");
        goto DONE;
    }
}
```

Notice that this code is essentially identical to the code in Chapter 16, "Connecting to the Web," for the `UpsInterface()` function of the Network-Aware UPS. The only difference is that the Network-Aware UPS returns errors as HTML, but the Java-Enabled UPS returns only an ASCII error message. We call `form_decode()` to parse the `?Button=name` query in the URI, call `MsgWrite()` to write a simulated event to the message queue, and call `ReadFile()` to read the UPS status from the status pipe.

Having read the `UPS_STATUS` structure sent by the event subsystem, we turn that into the ASCII string we saw in Figure 17-8 and return it as the contents of the web page as shown in Listing 17-6.

Listing 17-6: The UPS state string

```
//
// Construct the UPS state string to send to the Java applet.
//
    strcpy(Output, "UPS State,Power=");
    strcat(Output, Status.State & STATE_POWER_ON ? "ON" : "OFF");
    strcat(Output, ",Battery=");
    strcat(Output, Status.State & STATE_BATT_ON ? "ONLINE" : "OFFLINE");
    strcat(Output, ",AC Power=");
    strcat(Output, Status.State & STATE_AC_BAD ? "BAD" : "GOOD");
    strcat(Output, ",Load=");
```

```
    strcat(Output, Status.State & STATE_LOAD_PRESENT ? "PRESENT" :
                                                       "ABSENT");
    if (Status.msBatteryLife > Status.msMaxLife)
        Status.msBatteryLife = Status.msMaxLife;
    sprintf(&Output[strlen(Output)], ",Battery Life=%d seconds,"
            "Percent=%d", Status.msBatteryLife/1000,
        Status.msBatteryLife*100/Status.msMaxLife);
    if (Status.ErrLen > 0)
    {
        strcat(Output, ",Error=");
        strcat(Output, ErrMsg);
    }

DONE:
//
// Set the contents of the web page in the output struct
//
    if (Output[0] == 0)
        return FALSE;
    pOutp->pEntityBody = malloc(sizeof(Output) + 1);
    if (pOutp->pEntityBody == NULL)
        return FALSE;
    strcpy(pOutp->pEntityBody, Output);
    pOutp->ContentLength = strlen(pOutp->pEntityBody);
```

This is only a series of string concatenations; we don't need HTML tags because this page isn't intended for viewing by a browser. Having constructed the string, we call `malloc()` to allocate a buffer for the string, as required by the interface to the web server, and return the string to the web server for transmission to the applet.

Now let's look at Listing 17-7 to see how the `GetUpsState()` method in the Java applet processes the first few fields of this information.

Listing 17-7: GetUpsState() processes the state string

```
//
// Process the UPS state string.  If we don't get the expected "UPS
// State," at the beginning of the string, just display the text in the
// Error text area and hide all the other containers.  Stop the
// the thread that periodically updates UPS state.
//
    int idxVal,idxComma;
    if (!UpsState.startsWith("UPS State,"))
    {
        InputHdr.setVisible(false);
        Inputs.setVisible(false);
        StateHdr.setVisible(false);
        State.setVisible(false);
        StateThread.stop();
        throw new Exception(ServerError + UpsState);
    }
```

```
        idxComma = UpsState.indexOf(",");
        if (idxComma < 0)
            throw new Exception(FormatError + UpsState);

        // process Power=ON|OFF, substring
        if (!UpsState.startsWith("Power=", ++idxComma))
            throw new Exception(FormatError + UpsState);
        idxVal = UpsState.indexOf("=", idxComma);
        if (idxVal < 0)
            throw new Exception(FormatError + UpsState);
        ++ idxVal;
        idxComma = UpsState.indexOf(",", idxVal);
        if (idxComma < 0)
            throw new Exception(FormatError + UpsState);
        PowerValue.setText(UpsState.substring(idxVal, idxComma));
PowerButton.setLabel(UpsState.regionMatches(idxVal,"ON",0,2)
                            ? "Power Off" : "Power On");
```

If we don't see "UPS State," at the beginning of the string, we assume that the UPS system has returned an error message instead of the UPS state information. In that case, we copy the error message to the `Error` component and hide the `InputHdr`, `Inputs`, `StateHdr`, and `State` containers because we no longer have valid UPS state information.

Assuming that the string looks as we expect, we start parsing the string to extract the information. For the power state, we use the value (`ON` or `OFF`) to update the `PowerValue` text in the state table, and update the `PowerButton` button label in the simulated inputs table in the display. Throughout the parsing process, we throw exceptions if a formatting error is encountered in the state string.

Skipping the display update for the battery, AC power, and load states, let's look at the code to handle the battery life bar graph.

```
// process Percent=nnn[,] substring
if (!UpsState.startsWith("Percent=", ++idxComma))
    throw new Exception(FormatError + UpsState);
idxVal = UpsState.indexOf("=", idxComma);
if (idxVal < 0)
    throw new Exception(FormatError + UpsState);
++ idxVal;
idxComma = UpsState.indexOf(",", idxVal);
if (idxComma < 0)
    BattBarGraph.setPercent(Integer.valueOf(
            UpsState.substring(idxVal)).intValue());
else
    BattBarGraph.setPercent(Integer.valueOf(
            UpsState.substring(idxVal, idxComma)).intValue());
```

Having extracted the percentage of remaining battery life from the state string, we convert the percentage to an integer and call the `setPercent()` member of the `BarGraph` class to update the bar graph display.

That's how easy it is to write networking code in Java. Almost all the work in GetUpsState() involved parsing strings. Even the string manipulation code was simpler than equivalent C code, thanks to the powerful string manipulation capabilities built into Java.

Notice that no code in GetUpsState() explicitly repaints the applet window. Instead, each component automatically requests a repaint whenever its contents change. To see how this works, let's examine the implementation of the BarGraph component in Listing 17-8, found at the end of the Ups4.java file.

Listing 17-8: The BarGraph component

```
//
// This class displays a bar graph
//
class BarGraph extends Component
{
private int width,height;
private int percent;
private Dimension preferredSize;
private Color backgroundColor;
private Color foregroundColor;
private Color outlineColor;

// Construct the object
public BarGraph(int width, int height)
{
    this.width = width;
    this.height = height;
    backgroundColor = Color.lightGray;
    foregroundColor = Color.red;
    outlineColor = Color.black;
    percent = 100;
    preferredSize = new Dimension(width + 1, height + 1);
}

public Dimension getPreferredSize()
{
    return preferredSize;
}

public Dimension getMinimumSize()
{
    return getPreferredSize();
}

public void setForeground(Color c)
{
    foregroundColor = c;
    super.setForeground(c);
}
```

```
public void setBackground(Color c)
{
    backgroundColor = c;
    super.setBackground(c);
}

public void setPercent(int percent)
{
    if (percent < 0)
        this.percent = 0;
    else if (percent > 100)
        this.percent = 100;
    else
        this.percent = percent;
    repaint();
}

// Display the object
public void paint(Graphics g)
{
    int x = width * percent / 100;

    g.setColor(foregroundColor);
    g.fillRect(0, 0, x, height);
    g.setColor(backgroundColor);
    g.fillRect(x, 0, width - x, height);
    g.setColor(outlineColor);
    g.drawRect(0, 0, width, height);
}
```

The BarGraph class is derived from the Component class, as are all components. The class constructor requires a width and a height, in pixels, for the bar graph; it simply initializes the class fields with the bar graph dimensions and colors, and sets the bar to 100 percent.

After implementing some methods, required for all components, to return the component dimensions and set the foreground and background colors, we encounter setPercent(), the method that the Ups4 class calls to change the bar length in the graph. The setPercent() method updates the percent field of the class, and then calls the repaint() method to request a repaint of the component as soon as possible.

When the JVM is ready to refresh the display, it calls the paint() method to allow the component to update the display. The paint() method is passed a Graphics object, which contains information about the placement of the component and methods to draw graphics primitives. We use the fillRect() and drawRect() methods to draw the bar graph. Notice that the starting coordinates of the rectangle are relative to the location of the BarGraph component.

SUMMARY

Java is generating a lot of interest in the world of high-end embedded system development, especially for devices that provide data communications features. Most real-time OS vendors are offering some version of the JVM for use on their platforms, and many are implementing the PersonalJava and EmbeddedJava APIs.

Java is not only a programming language but also a platform. It provides a complete environment within which Java programs execute. Because the Java platform is feature-rich, well-defined, and has been ported to run on top of many different operating systems, Java programs are platform independent.

As you've seen, platform independence hasn't been achieved for embedded systems. Embedded devices tend to have requirements, such as direct access to hardware, that can't be satisfied by the Java platform. After you add some C or assembly code into the application, it's no longer device independent.

Java has a number of other benefits, however, that make compelling arguments for its use in embedded systems. Its feature-rich environment, particularly in the area of network programming and graphical user interfaces, means certain classes of applications can be developed and brought to market much more quickly with Java than with traditional embedded languages such as C and C++. For many products, the advantages of faster time to market outweigh Java's disadvantages of greater memory overhead and slower execution speed.

Possibly the two biggest problems with using Java in an embedded device are the affect of garbage collection on real-time response and the lack of debugging tools for bringing up Java programs on the target hardware. By separating your application into a Java piece and a C/C++ piece, you can go a long way toward solving both of these problems. If you create all the real-time code and all the hardware-manipulation code in C/C++, you can debug the hardware-specific code with your C++ debugger, and the real-time code won't be affected by Java's garbage collector. If you then code the user interface and the network communications in Java, you leverage the built-in support in Java to develop your application faster and can debug the device-independent Java code on a desktop machine.

Java offers a number of different alternatives for designing, building, and executing programs. As in any design effort, however, weighing project considerations such as time to market, cost, existing skills, advantages, and tradeoffs is important. No one approach is ideal. And although the market for Internet and web devices is unknown, understanding the advantages and limitations of Java and how to leverage them in embedded software design may be one of your most important activities of the next few years.

18

Floating-Point Programming

Ordinarily, a CPU works with numbers that mathematicians call *integers* — any positive or negative whole number, including zero. The world, however, is full of fractional quantities. Weights, temperatures, speeds, luminosities, and all the other millions of dimensions that anyone might measure are rarely nice round, whole numbers. For fractional values, a CPU uses floating-point numbers.

Floating point is used also for very large numbers. Integers have a much smaller dynamic range than floating-point numbers. For example, a 32-bit integer can represent numbers in the range -2^{31} to $2^{31} - 1$ (approximately -2.15×10^9 to 2.15×10^9). In comparison, a 32-bit floating-point variable using the IEEE Standard 754 data format can represent numbers in the approximate range 1.18×10^{-38} to 3.4×10^{38}. In addition, 64-bit integers can be used only with difficulty in C on a 32-bit machine, however, 64-bit floating-point variables, which can represent numbers in the range 2.23×10^{-308} to 1.7×10^{308}, are supported by all C compilers.

Note: Because integers are stored in two's complement format, the range of negative and positive numbers differs, so when listing the range of an integer data format, you show the entire range from negative to positive. IEEE 754 floating-point numbers use a separate sign bit, so the range of positive and negative numbers is identical. When listing the range of a floating-point data format, you express it in terms of smallest and largest magnitude. This allows you to see the smallest fraction (closest to zero) that can be represented by the data format.

We begin this chapter with a review of floating-point numbers and floating-point notation: what they are and how they work. We provide guidelines to help you determine whether your embedded system needs floating-point support. Then we discuss floating-point hardware and software, and the advantages of using each. Finally, we present a program that demonstrates the performance difference between floating-point hardware and floating-point software.

SCIENTIFIC NOTATION TERMINOLOGY

Floating-point numbers are represented in scientific notation. Let's quickly review the terminology you learned in school. An example should bring it all back to you. 32325 in scientific notation is

```
3.2325 × 10⁴
```

The number 3.2325 is called the *mantissa* (or the *significand*), and 4 (the power to which 10 is raised) is called the *exponent* (or the *characteristic*).

Computers, like people, use scientific notation to represent floating-point numbers. Computers, however, work in a binary (base 2) number system, not the base 10 system used here. For example, the number 1100101 in scientific notation is

```
1.100101 × 2⁶
```

Well, we cheated a little to make this example clearer. A binary number wouldn't have the 2 or the 6. The scientific notation for 1100101 *really* is this:

```
1.100101 × 10¹¹⁰
```

That may look a little weird. But if you glance back to the first example of scientific notation we gave, you'll see that the *structure* is identical. The example has a mantissa, an exponent, and even a radix point. A *radix point* separates the integer and fractional parts of the number. In base 10, a radix point is known as a decimal point; in base 2, it's called a binary point.

Numbers to the left of the radix point are multiplied by the base to the power n, where n is 0 for the number next to the radix point, 1 for the next number, and so on. For the fractional part of the number, n is -1 for the number just to the right of the radix point, -2 for the next number, and so on. So, you can express 2324.13 as

```
2 × 10³ + 3 × 10² + 2 × 10¹ + 4 × 10⁰ + 1 × 10⁻¹ + 3 × 10⁻²
```

where, if you recall, $10^0 = 1$. In fact, any number raised to the 0 power is 1.

This same pattern applies to writing a binary number in floating-point notation. For example, 10110.101 is equal to

```
1 × 2⁴ + 0 × 2³ + 1 × 2² + 1 × 2¹ + 0 × 2⁰ + 1 × 2⁻¹ + 0 × 2⁻² + 1 × 2⁻³
```

Finally, a number in scientific notation is said to be *normalized* if one nonzero digit is to the left of the radix point. For example, the normalized form of the binary number 10110.101 is 1.0110101×2^4.

FLOATING-POINT SUPPORT ON EMBEDDED SYSTEMS

The nature of an application dictates whether you'll need floating-point support for your embedded application. Many embedded systems require only integer mathematics; adding floating-point support would be overkill. For example, the POS system in Chapter 5 needed to perform arithmetic calculations on product prices. Rather than using floating-point arithmetic and representing prices as a whole-number dollar part and a fractional cents part, we chose to represent prices as integer cents. We wrote the arithmetic calculations in the code carefully to detect integer overflow and correctly round fractional cent values, and we wrote the display code to manually insert the radix point. By adding this small amount of extra logic to the code, we were able to avoid the need for floating-point support in the system.

Some embedded systems, however, must deal with real-world information that is not easily represented by integers. If you need to perform very precise calculations (that is, maintain a large number of significant digits), process data that includes nonintegral values, or manipulate data with a very wide range of values that can't all be represented in 32-bit or 64-bit integers, you must use floating point. For example, you need floating-point capabilities to build systems such as the following:

- Signal processing equipment frequently uses filtering, transform, or spectral analysis algorithms that require real numbers (that is, numbers that have both an integer and a fractional part).

- Robotics and computer numerical control (CNC) applications need precision for positioning accuracy and trigonometric functions for axis positioning.

- Navigation equipment uses trigonometric functions for calculating position.

- Data acquisition equipment often needs to scale, reduce, or compress large amounts of data as it is collected, using numerical algorithms that require floating point.

- Systems with complex graphic displays use floating-point algorithms for operations such as rotation, scaling, and interpolation.

FLOATING-POINT DATA FORMATS

We base our discussion of floating-point numbers on the IEEE 754 standard, which is by far the most widely accepted standard for floating-point data formats and operations. (IEEE 854, a more generalized standard based on IEEE 754, uses the same data formats.) We are not aware of any floating-point hardware and software vendors that do not support IEEE 754.

A floating-point number consists of three fields:

- **A sign field.** The value of this single-bit field indicates the sign of the mantissa. A 1 in this field indicates a negative mantissa; a 0 indicates a positive mantissa.

- **An exponent field.** This field holds the binary exponent.
- **A mantissa field.** This field holds the binary mantissa.

The size of the sign field is always 1 bit. The size of the exponent and mantissa fields depends on the floating-point data type and is what differentiates one floating-point data type from another.

IEEE 754 specifies three floating-point data types:

- **Single precision.** The format for this data type occupies 32 bits and provides 7 decimal digits of precision. (That is, only the 7 most significant digits of the base 10 representation of the number are accurate.) The C data type `float` uses this format.

- **Double precision.** The format for this data type occupies 64 bits and provides 15 to 16 decimal digits of precision. The C data type `double` uses this format.

- **Extended precision.** The format for this data type occupies 80 bits and provides 15 to 16 decimal digits of precision. No C data type corresponds to the extended-precision floating-point data type. Floating-point processors typically promote all numbers to extended precision for intermediate calculations to minimize any loss of precision during the calculation.

Table 18-1 summarizes the different floating-point number formats, showing how many bits are used to store the exponent and the mantissa, as well as the approximate range of equivalent decimal numbers.

Table 18-1: Floating-Point Data Types

Format	Exponent Bits	Mantissa Bits	Range
Single	8	23	1.18×10^{-38} to 3.40×10^{38}
Double	11	52	2.23×10^{-308} to 1.79×10^{308}
Extended	15	64	3.37×10^{-4932} to 1.18×10^{4932}

You may have wondered why the sign field is associated with the mantissa. What about the sign of the exponent? Can't a floating-point number have a negative exponent? Where's the sign for the exponent? The answer is that it's in the exponent.

EXPONENT FORMAT

The exponent for floating-point numbers is stored in *biased*, or *excess*, format. This means the value of the exponent is added to a bias — a uniform deviation from a particular point of reference — and then stored in the exponent field.

For example, suppose you have a number that you want to store in single-precision floating-point format; the number has an exponent of 32. Single-precision floating-point numbers use a bias of +127. The value of the exponent when stored will be

```
127 + 32 = 159 = 10011111₂
```

Now suppose we have a number whose exponent's value is −32. In this case, the value of the exponent when stored will be

```
127 + (-32) = 95 = 1011111₂
```

which should answer the question posed earlier regarding the whereabouts of the exponent's sign. Using bias format, the sign of the exponent is implicitly stored in the value of the exponent itself. A value of 127 or greater (in decimal) indicates a positive exponent; a value of 126 or less indicates a negative exponent.

Why use a bias number format for the exponent? It turns out that this notation simplifies the comparison of exponents. The bias (127 for single precision, 1023 for double precision, 16383 for extended precision) is chosen to force the biased exponent to be a positive value. When comparing two floating-point numbers, an FPU (floating-point unit, also known as a floating-point coprocessor) can simply perform an unsigned comparison of the two exponents to determine which has the larger magnitude. We discuss FPUs in the section "Floating-Point Hardware and Software."

MANTISSA FORMAT

Floating-point numbers are always processed and stored in normalized form by an FPU. That is, the mantissa always assumes the format

```
1.ff...f
```

where the leading bit (the integer bit) is always 1, followed by n fractional bits, where the value of n depends on the data format.

Always keeping numbers in normalized form offers two advantages: It maximizes the number of significant bits stored, and it makes comparisons between two numbers easier. Normalization maximizes precision for three reasons. First, the position of the binary point is always known; it follows the first bit in the mantissa. Therefore, you do not need to use space to store the position of the binary point, which means more bits are available to store the mantissa. Second, because the leading bit is always 1, it's not necessary to store it, which adds one extra bit of precision. IEEE Standard 754 specifies eliminating the leading 1 bit for single- and double-precision data formats and including the leading 1 bit in the extended-precision data format. Finally, normalizing small values (whose magnitude is less than 1) eliminates leading zeros, which maximizes the number of significant bits stored in the mantissa.

Normalization makes comparisons simple (and therefore fast) because the FPU can first compare the exponents (which, as you saw earlier, is a simple unsigned comparison). If the exponents are not equal, the number with the larger exponent has the larger magnitude because the mantissas in a normalized binary floating-point number are always between 1 and 2. If the exponents are equal, the FPU performs an unsigned comparison of the two mantissas; again, the number with the larger magnitude has the larger mantissa.

NUMBER HOLES

It's easy to forget the fact that an FPU, no matter how precise, can never be infinitely precise. Some numbers can be precisely represented in floating-point format, but an infinite number of real numbers are out there. (In fact, an infinite number of them are between 1 and 2.) Even the extended real format can represent only a finite number of numbers.

Look at it this way. Suppose you're using double-precision format in all your calculations. That means you have about 16 decimal digits of accuracy. For example, the decimal number 0.11111111111111111 is stored in double-precision format as 0x3FBC71C71C71C71C. The number 0.11111111111111112 is stored as 0x3FBC71C71C71C71D — 1 bit bigger. Pretty accurate, but notice that this means all the numbers between 0.11111111111111111 and 0.11111111111111112 cannot be represented, and there are an infinite number of such numbers.

As it turns out, the size of *holes* (the distance between numbers that can be represented exactly) is nonuniform. That is, bigger holes exist between some numbers than others. In fact, as you move along the number line to numbers with larger and larger magnitudes, the holes get bigger and bigger. (This is easy to see when you consider the fact that, as the exponent gets bigger and bigger, the value of the least significant bit in the mantissa gets bigger and bigger also. For example, the double-precision format is unable to tell the difference between 0.22222222222222221 and 0.22222222222222222; both are stored as 0x3FCC71C71C71C71C.)

This discussion of precision and number holes leads us into the topic of error control — an area of deep interest for anyone doing serious work in mathematics on a computer. Given that a computer's representation of a floating-point number is finite, it follows that when the result of an operation is a number that cannot be represented exactly, a small amount of error is introduced. And when a particular algorithm consists of lots and lots of floating-point calculations, those tiny errors can accumulate to a significant error. With the application of error-control techniques, inaccuracies in calculations can be kept to a minimum. This topic is too complex to address here; for further reading, you might find the following books useful:

- *Computer Methods for Science and Engineering*, by Robert LaFara (Hayden Books, 1973).
- *Numerical Recipes in C: The Art of Scientific Computing*, by William Press, B. Flannery, S. Tukolsky, and W. Vetterling (Cambridge University Press, 1989). Note: Versions of Numerical Recipes are available for other languages, and all books in this family are highly recommended.
- *The Art of Computer Programming. Volume 2: Seminumerical Algorithms, Third Edition*, by Donald Knuth. (Addison-Wesley Publishing Co., 1997). This is the quintessential work on computer mathematics.

SPECIAL NUMBERS

Floating-point hardware and software that is compliant with IEEE Standard 754 provide several types of special numbers that can help you deal with some peculiarities of programming with floating-point numbers. Members of this class of special numbers are recognized by their unique encodings. The types of special numbers are the following:

- Positive and negative zero
- Positive and negative infinity
- Denormals
- NaN (Not-a-Number)

Zero and Infinity

Because floating-point data formats include a separate sign bit, zero can have either a positive or a negative sign. For computation, the value of zero always behaves identically, regardless of sign, so you can ignore the signed property of zero. For different computations that produce a zero, IEEE Standard 754 has a table that shows whether the result is positive or negative zero.

IEEE-compliant FPUs and emulation libraries have a representation for both positive and negative infinity. Any floating-point number whose exponent field is all ones and whose mantissa field is all zeros is interpreted as an infinity. The sign of the infinity is the sign of the mantissa. The result of a computational overflow or a divide-by-zero operation is infinity.

IEEE-compliant floating-point systems let you perform mathematics with infinity. You can compare infinities; you can add infinities (but only if they have the same sign), you can take the arctangent of infinity to receive the result of $\pi/2$, and so on. IEEE Standard 754 includes a table showing mathematical operations that can be performed on infinity and the results.

Denormals

As you saw previously, an FPU is required (by IEEE Standard 754) to store and manipulate numbers in normalized form. Sometimes, however, an FPU can't normalize a number for storage in the format used by a particular data type.

Why? The reason is that the number is outside the range of representable numbers for that data type. Recall that the format for each floating-point data type allocates a fixed number of bits for the exponent field. Couple that with the fact that the normalization process shifts the mantissa and changes the value of the exponent to keep the overall value of the number unchanged. (If you shift the mantissa left, you must decrease the exponent; if you shift the mantissa right, you must increase the exponent.) Sometimes, a number gets so small that trying to shift the mantissa left will cause the exponent to become less than the lowest value it can represent. The number cannot be normalized.

Numbers in a specific range (depending on the data type) can be represented in the data format, just not in normalized form. The exponent is set to the smallest possible value for the data format (the biased exponent is zero), and the integer bit of the mantissa is zero. As the values get smaller, more and more of the most significant fractional bits are also zero. Such numbers are called *denormals,* or *denormalized numbers.* Some FPUs can work with denormals, which can be advantageous if the application deals with extremely small (close to zero) numbers. In effect, the range of representable numbers for the data type is extended at the low (small) end of the range. Calculations can continue to take place if a particular algorithm has generated a denormal. Note that a denormal loses precision (as compared to a normalized number) because the most significant nonzero bit is not shifted to the binary point; it is some distance to the right of the binary point (which cause one or more bits of precision to "fall off the end" on the right.)

It's not possible to extend the range at the high end. If a number is too large to be represented in normalized form, you'd need more than one bit in the integer part of the number, the part to the left of the binary point. Because the data formats specified by IEEE Standard 754 assume a binary point to the right of the most significant bit and have no space to store the explicit position of a binary point, you can't represent numbers with more than one bit to the left of the binary point.

Not-a-Number (NaN)

NaN is used to indicate an exceptional condition and is recognized by an exponent of all ones and a nonzero mantissa. (A zero mantissa field indicates an infinity.) There are two kinds of NaNs: signaling NaNs and quiet NaNs.

A *signaling NaN* is never generated by an FPU or a floating-point library. It's used by software to inform the FPU or library that something's wrong. When the FPU or library sees a signaling NaN as a factor in a floating-point operation, an exception is thrown. Following is an example of how you can use a signaling NaN.

Suppose you've written a program in C that uses floating-point numbers. Inadvertently, you write a routine that uses one of the floating-point variables before that variable has been initialized. Fortunately, the compiler has been smart enough to preload all variables with the value for a signaling NaN. Consequently, when the program attempts to do anything with the variable — such as add it and another variable or subtract it — the FPU signals an exception and you catch the bug more quickly. If the variable hadn't been preloaded with a NaN, it might have been filled with random bits that looked like a valid floating-point number — and the program would appear to be working correctly.

A *quiet NaN*, in contrast, is created by the FPU as the result of an invalid operation for which exceptions are masked. Quiet NaNs are propagated also through subsequent arithmetic operations. Consequently, software can determine that a particular operation was invalid if the result is a quiet NaN. For example, division by zero might produce a quiet NaN, depending on how the FPU is programmed.

> **Note:** As you'll see, producing a quiet NaN isn't the only way an FPU can notify software that an invalid operation has occurred. Most FPUs can be programmed to generate a floating-point exception (which triggers an interrupt) whenever software attempts an invalid operation.

FLOATING-POINT HARDWARE AND SOFTWARE

Now that you know how to use floating-point capability in an embedded application, it's time to see how you get that capability in your application.

Developers of desktop systems assume that floating-point capability is just *there*. They don't have to ask for it specifically. The CPUs of modern desktop systems include an on-chip

FPU, and desktop compilers (aware of the FPU's presence) emit the proper code to use the floating-point hardware.

Some embedded processors have on-chip floating-point units as well, so the developer of an embedded system can, if need be, choose hardware that gives the same ease of use that a desktop developer enjoys. Embedded processors that do not have integrated FPUs are less expensive and therefore offer a low-cost alternative CPU for applications that don't need floating point.

Some applications need floating point, but not to the extent that floating-point hardware is necessary. For this situation, you can opt to include a floating-point emulation library, which performs all the floating-point mathematics that would otherwise be performed by an FPU.

The developer of embedded systems, therefore, can choose between floating-point support or not. And for systems that require floating point, the developer can choose between floating point performed in hardware or in software. Let's look at these two alternatives.

HARDWARE

Years ago, floating-point hardware in a system was a separate processing unit. For example, early IBM PCs included an empty socket, into which you plugged what was called the *floating-point coprocessor*. It was called a coprocessor because it worked alongside the CPU. Another name for the floating-point coprocessor was *floating-point unit*, or FPU. We use floating-point coprocessor and FPU synonymously.

An FPU is a processing unit in its own right. You program an FPU just like you program a CPU. The FPU fetches instructions and data, parses and executes the instructions, and thereby performs floating-point operations on the data.

Inside an FPU are registers that hold the data being operated on, flags registers that record the results of comparisons, and status and control registers that allow software to query and modify the internal state of the FPU.

The instructions in the repertoire of most FPUs can be divided into six categories:

- **Data transfer operations** move data into and out of the FPU (they are the coprocessor's load and store operations). Most instructions in this category transfer data between the coprocessor's internal registers and the system's memory. Some FPUs have instructions that can transfer data directly between the FPU's registers and the CPU's registers.

- **Nontranscendental operations** include addition, subtraction, multiplication, and division. Some other mathematical functions in this category are square root, absolute value, and rounding a floating-point number to an integer.

- **Comparison operations** are self-explanatory. Comparison instructions allow a program to compare two numbers, and (usually with the help of additional instructions in the Control operations category) pass the result to the CPU's flags. Consequently, a program can compare numbers and execute a conditional branch instruction based on the outcome of the comparison.

- **Transcendental operations** provide the fundamental trigonometric functions — sine, cosine, and tangent — as well as the inverse trigonometric functions — arcsine, arccosine, and arctangent. Also in this group are the exponentiation (raising a number to a power) and logarithm functions.

  > **Note:** Some FPUs include only a subset of all the transcendental functions. In most cases, the instructions provided are sufficient so that — with a little additional programming — an intrepid programmer can derive the missing functions from those provided. For example, the 80387 and earlier coprocessors from Intel include the arctangent as the sole inverse trigonometric function. But, using well-known identity relationships, you can derive arcsine and arccosine from the arctangent function. Luckily, if you do all your work in a high-level language (such as C or C++), you don't have to worry about any of this because the compiler takes care of it for you.

- **Constants** are a source of often-used mathematical constants. These constants range from the mundane 0.0 and 1.0, to the more esoteric π and e. For example, the 80x87 instruction FLDPI loads one of the FPU's registers with the constant π. (Every FPU we've encountered provides such constants at the highest precision that the FPU can support. In other words, FLDPI won't load 3.14159; rather, it will load something like 3.14159265358979323846 or better.)

- **Control operations** perform no mathematical functions. Rather, they let the programmer control the way that the floating-point hardware operates. For example, on the Intel 80x87 FPUs, instructions in this category allow the programmer to select which rounding algorithm the FPU will use to round (or truncate) the results of mathematical operations. In addition, the 80x87's FSTSW instruction (also in this group) will transfer the FPU's status register either to a memory location or the CPU's AX register. The FPU's status register carries the results of comparison instructions. Using FSTSW, a program can use the results of a comparison operation to control a conditional branch instruction executing in the CPU.

Floating-Point Exceptions

Just as an errant program may attempt an invalid operation on a CPU, so too it may attempt an invalid calculation on an FPU. When an FPU determines that an invalid calculation was requested, it either generates an exception to allow a software ISR to handle the situation, or it produces a result (such as infinity or NaN) that denotes an error condition and sets flags in a status register that software can read to determine more about what caused the error. Which action is taken by the FPU depends on whether or not software has programmed the FPU to mask the exception.

The invalid operations that can cause an FPU error are in two categories: stack operations and arithmetic operations. Invalid stack operations occur only on an FPU, such as the Intel 80x87, that organizes its internal floating-point registers as a stack. On the 80x87, one register — labeled ST(0) — is the top of the stack. Store a value in ST(0), and the contents of the other registers are pushed down. Read a value from ST(0), and the contents of the other registers are popped up. Software produces an invalid operation called a *stack overflow* if it attempts to push more numbers onto the stack than it can hold. (The stack has eight registers. Pushing nine numbers onto the stack creates an invalid operation.) Similarly, software creates an invalid operation called a *stack underflow* if it attempts to pop a number off an empty stack. If stack overflow and underflow conditions are masked, the destination register contents are set to NaN.

When software attempts an operation that is either mathematically impossible or has a result that can't be represented by the FPU, it's an invalid arithmetic operation. IEEE Standard 854 defines a number of invalid arithmetic operations that should be handled by an FPU. These include the following:

- **Divide by zero.** This operation either triggers a divide-by-zero exception or results in a value of infinity or negative infinity if the exception is masked.

- **Numeric overflow and underflow.** An overflow occurs when the magnitude of the result exceeds the largest magnitude that can be represented in the selected data format. Overflow either generates an overflow exception or results in a value of infinity or negative infinity if the exception is masked. An underflow occurs when the magnitude of the result is below the smallest magnitude that can be represented in the selected data format. Underflow either generates an underflow exception or results in a denormal value or a value of zero if the exception is masked.

- **Inexact result.** When the result of an arithmetic operation cannot be exactly represented in the data format, a precision (inexact result) condition results. This condition is quite common; an infinite amount of numbers cannot be precisely represented, and a finite number can be precisely represented. Therefore, most applications mask this exception, in which case the FPU rounds the result to the nearest representable value.

- **Miscellaneous arithmetic operations.** These include taking the square root of a negative number, dividing infinity by infinity, and multiplying infinity by zero, depending on the FPU you're using. These operations either generate an exception or result in a NaN value if the exception is masked.

If an unmasked invalid operation occurs, the FPU generates an exception. The floating-point exception ISR can examine the registers of the FPU and determine what caused the exception. The ISR might even be able to correct the problem — replacing what would have been an erroneous result with a useable approximation. If the problem can't be corrected, the program is typically terminated with an error or reset and restarted from a known safe point.

Connecting an FPU to a CPU

As mentioned, the floating-point coprocessor began life as a separate processing unit. Most systems with FPU support had an FPU socket somewhere on the motherboard. You could plug in an FPU chip if you needed floating-point support, or leave it empty if floating-point hardware wasn't required.

On such systems, the CPU and FPU were closely coupled. They shared the same data, address, and control buses. In addition, the CPU and FPU received the same clock signals, as well as signals indicating a system reset. Consequently, the two were synchronized with one another. Other directly connected lines between the CPU and FPU carried the signals that allowed the two processors to manage arbitration of the address and data buses. (In other words, the FPU could take over the address and data buses as needed.) Finally, the interrupt out line of the FPU was tied into the interrupt system of the CPU so that a floating-point exception would generate a CPU interrupt.

Because the CPU and FPU shared the same data and address buses, both processors saw the same instruction stream. FPU instructions began with an identifying byte. When the CPU fetched a floating-point instruction, the CPU would recognize it as such and ignore it, but the FPU would begin processing it.

Today, integration has pushed the FPU onto the same chip as the CPU in most systems (desktop as well as embedded). Nevertheless, the functionality has remained the same from the programmer's perspective. In fact, chip designers have striven to maintain backward compatibility, so that the new integrated CPU/FPU works just like its ancestors...only faster.

SOFTWARE

For applications that need floating-point support but not an FPU, you can use *floating-point emulation software.* This software is typically provided in the form of a library linked in to the final application. A programmer writes the same floating-point code regardless of whether the software or the FPU will be performing all the floating-point mathematics.

A floating-point emulation library can provide floating-point capabilities in two ways. One way is to simply link in a collection of floating-point routines that perform all fundamental floating-point operations (nontranscendental, transcendental, and so on), and then generate function calls into the library for every floating-point operation in the application.

The developer simply sets a switch in the compiler at compile time, and the compiler compiles the high-level language's floating-point operations into the floating-point library's function calls. When the final executable is created, the linker links in the needed routines from the library.

For example, suppose you had a section of C code that looked like this:

```
float a,b,c;
a=22.0f; b=7.0f;
c=a/b;    /* Approx. Pi */
```

When this section of code was compiled, the emitted assembly code might look like this:

```
MOV   EAX,OFFSET C   ; Address of result
MOV   EBX,OFFSET A   ; Address of numerator
MOV   ECX,OFFSET B   ; Address of denominator
JSR   FltDivide      ; Call floating-divide
```

The addresses of the two operands and the result are placed in CPU registers (the OFFSET operator returns the address of a symbol). Then the FltDivide routine in the floating-point library is called.

The other way a floating-point emulation library provides floating-point capabilities is to emulate the behavior of an FPU, which requires a little assistance from the CPU. Many CPUs generate a no-coprocessor exception if the program attempts to execute a floating-point instruction and an FPU is not present. If this exception is available, the compiler can simply translate the floating-point operations into FPU instructions. Here's how it works: When the code runs, anytime a floating-point instruction is executed, the exception handler is triggered. The library has an area of memory set aside that simulates the FPU's register stack. It even has internal representations of the status and control words, the registers that software programs use to control the operation of the FPU. The handler (by examining the stack) can determine what instruction caused the exception, and emulate the action of that instruction. The application software is never aware that an FPU doesn't exist, because everything that happens in response to the execution of an FPU instruction is precisely what would happen if an FPU were present.

Look back at the C source code we showed for a simple division operation. If that code were compiled in a system that used a floating-point emulator, the output of the compiler would look something like this (we're presuming the presence of an 80x87-style processor):

```
FLD    A  ; Push numerator
FLD    B  ; Push denominator
FDIVP     ; Divide and pop
FSTP   C  ; Store and pop
```

As each instruction is executed, an exception is generated, and the exception handler calls the emulator library to handle each specific instruction. The first instruction causes the emulator to push the floating-point value in A onto the emulator's simulation of the 80x87's register stack. The second instruction does the same with the value in B. Next, the divide instruction performs the division and pops the stack so that only the quotient remains in the top register. Finally, the FSTP instruction stores the register and pops the last value off the stack.

Both schemes described have advantages and disadvantages. Compiling floating-point operations into floating-point library calls is slightly faster than the second scheme because no run-time translation occurs. Remember, in the second scheme, the emulator must first determine which instruction is being executed and then do the floating-point work. Also, the emulator must not only perform the floating-point code, but also emulate the internal behavior of a floating-point coprocessor; that emulation consumes processing time.

On the other hand, the emulation scheme provides a nice combination of flexibility and portability. You can run an application using an emulator on a system without an FPU. Or you can run the same application (without recompiling) on a system with an FPU, in which case the application runs much faster.

Inside the 80387

The Intel 80387 was the floating-point coprocessor for Intel's 32-bit 80386. The integrated FPU of all Intel 32-bit 80x86 processors (including the Pentium) are derivatives of the 80387. (The 80387 is descended from the 80287, which in turn is descended from the 8087. Each is an improvement — adding instructions and increasing processing power — over its preceding model.)

Inside the 80387 are 8 data registers, each 80 bits long and capable of holding a variety of numeric data types, ranging from simple signed integers to an extended floating-point value. Floating-point instructions can address each register independently or treat the entire set as a stack. For example, the following assembly language code is a simple routine for multiplying two numbers:

```
FLD   val1      ;Load (push) first value onto stack
FLD   val2      ;Load (push) second value
FMUL  ST(1),ST  ;Multiply and pop
```

The floating-point number `val1` is pushed onto the top of the stack by the first instruction. The second instruction pushes `val2` on top of the stack. At this point, the top two items on the stack are `val2` and `val1` (`val2` is the topmost). The final instruction performs two actions. First, it multiplies the second register on the stack (identified by `ST(1)`) by the topmost register (`ST`), and places the result in `ST(1)`. Then it pops the stack. What had been on the top (`val2`) is discarded. The registers' contents are shifted up — what had been in `ST(1)` is now loaded into `ST`.

Three other registers in the 80387 are of interest to programmers:

- **The control register.** Software can modify the contents of this register and thereby control how the FPU performs rounding, control the FPU's internal precision, and enable or disable certain floating-point exceptions.

- **The status register.** This is the FPU's counterpart to the CPU's flags register. Various fields in this register are updated by the FPU to reflect the outcome of floating-point operations.

- **The tags register.** This register is divided into 8 fields of 2 bits each. Each field's value indicates the contents of one of the data registers — whether the data register is empty, holds a valid number, holds zero, or holds a special value (such as a denormal or infinity). Exception-handling software can read this register and ascertain what's in each of the data registers, without having to read those registers individually and decode their contents.

Fortunately, you won't have to worry about the internal details of the FPU when you write programs that use floating point — the compiler takes care of those details for you. We didn't force you to write assembly language to program the PC hardware; we won't force you to write assembly language when you build programs that use floating point.

WHY USE FLOATING-POINT EMULATION SOFTWARE?

The reason for using floating-point emulation software rather than an FPU is economics. A separate FPU takes up board space; a CPU with integrated FPU is more expensive than one without.

Price is always an issue in embedded systems design. If a chip suits your application and doesn't have an integrated FPU, you save a few cents per unit and save significantly overall in large-volume applications. On the other hand, emulation software runs much more slowly than FPU hardware; we compare the two when we run the programming project for this chapter. If your application needs to perform floating-point calculations only occasionally, using emulation software to reduce system cost makes sense. In floating-point-intensive applications, however, the performance penalty for using emulation is likely to be so prohibitive that you have to use FPU hardware instead.

A BITMAP FILTER

As an example of floating-point operations in action, and as a way to demonstrate the performance differences between using an FPU and a floating-point emulator library, we created a bitmap filter program. FILTER performs a simple, image-processing function: It reads a bitmap file, passes the image through a low-pass spatial filter, and writes the result out as another bitmap file. The low-pass filter removes high-frequency image information created by sharp lines or distinct differences between adjacent pixels and has a smoothing or blurring effect on the image.

> **Note:** This filter algorithm is a member of a larger class of operations called convolutions. A more complete description of the spatial filter algorithm — as well as other image processing algorithms — is in *Practical Image Processing in C,* by Craig A. Lindley (John Wiley & Sons, 1991).

HOW THE BITMAP FILTER PROJECT WORKS

The bitmap filter application is exceedingly simple — so simple that there's no user interaction. The program, FILTER.EXE, reads a file named INPUT.BMP, processes it, writes a resulting file named OUTPUT.BMP, and displays the time taken to perform the processing. The filter program uses the host file I/O feature of ETS Kernel to read and write files in the current directory on the host computer, so you don't have to bother copying files to and from the boot floppy disk in the target computer. We supplied an INPUT.BMP file in the project directory.

Before we step you through the application, you should be aware of a few limitations. First, the application can read *only* 24-bit bitmap files. The program simply rejects any other bitmap format — and any other graphics file format. Second, although the application processes any 24-bit bitmap file, be aware that such files can be large. Because the application must keep a source and destination bitmap image in memory during processing, you might ask the application to process a bitmap image that the target computer does not have the memory to handle. If this happens, the application reports a memory allocation failure.

To work as described, FILTER uses a pair of memory buffers. The source buffer holds the original image — that is, the picture to be modified; the destination buffer holds the resulting image after applying the low-pass filter. To explain how FILTER works, presume for the moment that the images are in grayscale and each byte in memory represents a single pixel in the image. (For an RGB image, the same algorithm is applied separately to the red, green, and blue components of each pixel in the image.)

The spatial filter algorithm works by moving through the image, processing a pixel at a time, and writing it to the destination buffer. The destination pixel's value is the weighted sum of the corresponding source pixel *and* the source pixel's *neighborhood*, which is a pixel's eight immediately adjacent pixels. Each 3 × 3 matrix (a pixel and its neighborhood) is multiplied by a 3 × 3 convolution kernel, and the result is written to the destination pixel. This process is illustrated in Figure 18-1.

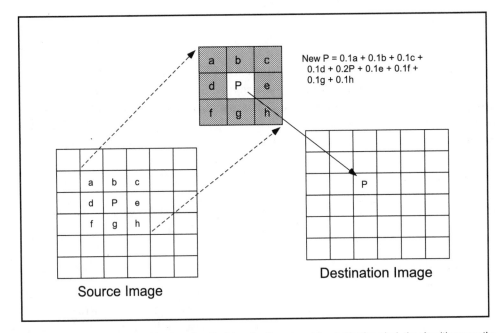

Figure 18-1: The spatial filter algorithm in action. To determine the value of the destination pixel, the algorithm uses the weighting formula shown at the top of the figure.

We selected this algorithm because it involves repeated floating-point multiplications, plus conversions between integer and floating-point values. We added timing routines to the code to calculate the time it takes to process an image.

We run the program first using the hardware FPU and then using the ETS Kernel floating-point emulator. Because the ETS Kernel floating-point emulator works by disassembling FPU instructions (as is required for any Win32-compatible OS), we can use the same executable to run with both floating-point hardware and floating-point software emulation.

BUILDING THE BITMAP FILTER PROJECT

The filter project is in TSLITE\PROJECTS\FILTER. A prebuilt executable, FILTER.EXE, is provided if you want to skip the build step. To build the executable from Visual C++ Developer

Studio, open the workspace file (`FILTER.DSW`) and click Build|Rebuild All. Chapter 3, "Software Installation and Setup," contains complete details on building the projects.

RUNNING THE BITMAP FILTER PROJECT

Before you run the application, make certain the current directory is `\TSLITE\PROJECTS\FILTER`. This is the location of the `INPUT.BMP` file, which is used as input to `FILTER.EXE`. If you run the project from Developer Studio by selecting Build|Execute filter.exe, the current directory is always the project directory. If you run the program from a DOS box, set the current directory to the project directory and run FILTER by typing:

```
runemb release\filter
```

The `FILTER.EXE` program is built with the ETS Kernel floating-point emulator linked in. If a hardware FPU is present on the target system, ETS Kernel turns off emulation and the floating-point instructions in the program are executed by the FPU. If the target has no FPU, the emulator automatically emulates all floating-point instructions.

To see the difference that a floating-point coprocessor can make, run the application twice — once using the FPU and once using the emulator. Your target system must have a coprocessor. If it doesn't, you'll only be able to run with the emulator. (This happens automatically; you don't have to do anything.) If you're not sure whether your target has a floating-point coprocessor, you can find out by running the Finger Server project, which responds to a Finger query with information about the hardware in the target system, as discussed in Chapter 15, "Networking." Or you can boot MS-DOS on the target system and run Microsoft's `MSD.EXE` system diagnostic utility. Or you can just run the FILTER program and see whether it runs in a few seconds (in which case, your system has a coprocessor) or a few minutes.

Assuming that your target system has a coprocessor, just run FILTER normally to execute using the hardware FPU:

```
runemb release\filter
```

The application is transferred to the target system and immediately begins running, processing the `INPUT.BMP` file that is in the same directory and shown in Figure 18-2.

As far as user feedback goes, `FILTER.EXE` is exceedingly boring. It doesn't appear to do anything while it's processing the image through the spatial filter. When the processing is complete, the program displays an execution time on the host system. For example:

```
Milliseconds = 10130
```

The application then writes the `OUTPUT.BMP` file to the current directory on the host computer. The filtered image is shown in Figure 18-3.

You can see the effect of the smoothed image also by launching the Windows Paint application, loading `INPUT.BMP` and then loading `OUTPUT.BMP`. The image in the output file is slightly blurred, with much less contrast than the picture in the input file.

Write down the number of milliseconds the program reports. This is the time it took to execute the smoothing algorithm using the target system's floating-point coprocessor.

Figure 18-2: INPUT.BMP, the original bitmap image.

Now force the application to use the floating-point emulator. Remove the ETS Monitor boot disk from your target machine and put it in the floppy drive on your host machine. From an MS-DOS command prompt on the host machine, type the following:

```
cfigkern -emu always a:\diskkern.bin
```

This command configures ETS Monitor on the boot floppy so that applications use the floating-point emulator — even if an FPU is present.

Now return the boot floppy to the target's drive, reboot the machine, and run the FILTER.EXE program again. Record the reported time, which will be the time it takes the program to execute the smoothing algorithm using floating-point emulation software. Compare this result to the previous result.

Figure 18-3: The image after it has been passed through the spatial filter. Notice that it is not as sharp as Figure 18-2.

We ran `FILTER.EXE` on a 25-MHz 386SX machine with a 387SX coprocessor. Using the coprocessor, the application took 10130 milliseconds — a little over 10 seconds. Using the floating-point emulation software, however, the application took 424967 milliseconds, or about 7 minutes!

Now, admittedly, we timed a portion of an application that was intensely floating-point dependent. Most applications use a mixture of floating-point and integer processing, and consequently the presence of an FPU won't have as much effect as it does here. Still, you should always assess how much floating-point processing your application will be doing, and determine how much of an effect it will have on overall application performance. That assessment will help you decide whether you need a hardware FPU on your target system or whether you can use a software emulator to reduce the system cost.

Finally, you should reconfigure ETS Monitor on your boot disk to put it back the way it was. Place the boot disk in your host system's floppy drive and enter the following command:

```
cfigkern -emu auto a:\diskkern.bin
```

This returns ETS Monitor to its default setting for the floating-point emulator. Specifically, the `auto` mode means that applications will use a floating-point coprocessor if one is present on the target machine and will use the floating-point emulator if one isn't.

A Quick Tour of the Source

When you run FILTER, it does the following:

1. Reads in the source bitmap file.

2. Processes the source bitmap and records the results into the destination bitmap. (All processing at this stage occurs in memory.)

3. Writes the destination bitmap file.

Our interest lies in the second step. To explain steps one and three, we would have to describe the internals of 24-bit BMP files and the routines used to read and write them, which is tangential to our focus. If you're interested, however, check out the source code, which is provided in the `\TSLITE\PROJECTS\FILTER` directory. You're welcome to extract whatever routines you want for your own applications. (The file that contains the source code for reading and writing 24-bit BMP files is `BMPPACK.C`.)

The source code for the image-processing portion of the application is in `BMPFILT.C`. The `dofilter()` routine, in Listing 18-1, performs the smoothing operation.

Listing 18-1: The dofilter() routine

```
/*
** FILTER
*/
int dofilter(BitmapHeader *srcbitmapheader,
             BitmapHeader *destbitmapheader)
```

```
{
    ULONG imagesize;          /* Size of data area */
    ULONG linelength;         /* Length of a scanline in bytes */
    ULONG tlinelength;        /* True line length */
    ULONG height;             /* Image height local */
    ULONG width;              /* Image width local */
    ULONG i;                  /* Loop index */
    unsigned j,k;             /* More loop indexes */
    float fpsum;              /* Convolution value for each pixel */
    DWORD millis;             /* Milliseconds */

/*
** In operations involving pointers, we use the following
** locals to save on structure member access.
*/
    BYTE *srcptr;             /* Source pointer */
    BYTE *destptr;            /* Destination pointer */

/* Allocate space for the destination bitmap's data. Then clear it. */
    imagesize=srcbitmapheader->biSizeImage;
    destbitmapheader->biDataPtr=(BYTE *)malloc(imagesize);
    if(destbitmapheader->biDataPtr==(BYTE *)NULL)
    {
        printf("**Error allocating memory\n");
        return(FALSE);
    }
    memset((void *)destbitmapheader->biDataPtr,0,imagesize);

/*
** Copy the source header's data (less the pointer) into the
** destination's header data
*/
    memmove((void *)destbitmapheader, (void *)srcbitmapheader,
            BITMAP_HEADER_ON_DISK);

/*
** Set up for processing....copy the edges of the image from source to
** destination. First copy the top and bottom lines.
*/
    height=srcbitmapheader->biHeight;    /* Set up locals */
    width=srcbitmapheader->biWidth;
    linelength=width*3;                      /* 3 bytes per pixel */
/*
** The following bit of trickery is necessary because
** 24-bit bitmap files are stored in such a way that
** each scanline begins on a 4-byte boundary. So, the
** *true* linelength is sometimes a little bit larger
** than the linelength.
*/
```

```
   tlinelength=linelength;
   while((tlinelength % 4)!=0)
       ++tlinelength;
/* Begin copy */
   srcptr=srcbitmapheader->biDataPtr;
   destptr=destbitmapheader->biDataPtr;
   memmove((void *)destptr, (void *)srcptr,    /* Bottom */
           tlinelength);
   srcptr+=tlinelength*(height-1);
   destptr+=tlinelength*(height-1);
   memmove((void *)destptr, (void *)srcptr,    /* Top */
           tlinelength);

/*
** Now copy the left and right edges from source to destination.
*/
   srcptr=srcbitmapheader->biDataPtr+tlinelength;
   destptr=destbitmapheader->biDataPtr+tlinelength;
   for(i=0;i<(height-1);i++)
   {
       /* Move "left" column */
       destptr[0]=srcptr[0];
       destptr[1]=srcptr[1];
       destptr[2]=srcptr[2];
       /* Move "right" column */
       destptr[linelength-3]=srcptr[linelength-3];
       destptr[linelength-2]=srcptr[linelength-2];
       destptr[linelength-1]=srcptr[linelength-1];
       destptr+=tlinelength;
       srcptr+=tlinelength;
   }

/*
** Start timing
*/
   millis=GetTickCount();

/*
** Filtering begins here. We process for each "plane" in the
** image (red, green, and blue). For each pixel, we perform
** a digital laplacian convolution. Each pixel's value is
** altered based on the weighted sum of its value plus the
** values of its neighbors. The weights are chosen so as
** to smooth or blur the final image.
*/
   for(j=0;j<3;j++)    /* For each plane */
   {
       srcptr=srcbitmapheader->biDataPtr+tlinelength+3+j;
       destptr=destbitmapheader->biDataPtr+tlinelength+3+j;
```

```
    for(k=1;k<height-1;k++)    /* For each scanline */
    {
        i=0;
        /*
        ** Following while loop hits each pixel.
        ** Note that we stop at linelength-6. We
        ** stop an extra 3 short because the
        ** srcptr and destptr have been "shifted
        ** left" 1 pixel (3 bytes) to account for
        ** the unprocessed left column.
        */
        while(i<linelength-6)
        {
            fpsum=0.1f*srcptr[i-tlinelength-3] +
                  0.1f*srcptr[i-tlinelength] +
                  0.1f*srcptr[i-tlinelength+3] +
                  0.1f*srcptr[i-3] +
                  0.20f*srcptr[i] +
                  0.1f*srcptr[i+3] +
                  0.1f*srcptr[i+tlinelength+3] +
                  0.1f*srcptr[i+tlinelength] +
                  0.1f*srcptr[i+tlinelength-3];
            /*
            ** If the new value is whiter than white, make
            ** it white.
            */
            if(fpsum>255)
                fpsum=255;

            /* Store the new pixel */
            destptr[i]=(BYTE)fpsum;

            /* Advance to next pixel. */
            i+=3;
        }
        /*
        ** Advance to next line
        */
        srcptr+=tlinelength;
        destptr+=tlinelength;
    }
}
/* Finish timing. Report results */
    millis=GetTickCount()-millis;
    printf("Milliseconds = %d\n",millis);

/* All done. Go home */
    return(TRUE);
}
```

The `dofilter()` routine accepts two arguments: `srcbitmapheader` and `destbitmapheader`. Both are pointers to data structures (of type `BitmapHeader`) that hold an internal representation of a bitmap file. The `dofilter()` routine processes the contents of `srcbitmapheader`, writing the results to `destbitmapheader`. (The contents of `destbitmapheader` ultimately become the processed `.BMP` file.)

The `BitmapHeader` structure consists of two parts. One carries information about the bitmap file's attributes — width, height, bits per pixel, and so on. The other part carries the bitmap image itself. The memory for this second portion must be allocated for the destination bitmap, which is the first thing that `dofilter()` does.

Next, `dofilter()` copies the bitmap's attributes from source to destination. This information can be copied unchanged because the destination bitmap's attributes will be the same as the source bitmap's attributes. The two bitmaps will not differ in dimensions or pixel depth — only certain pixel values will be modified.

Because the filtering algorithm requires a neighborhood of the source pixel to produce a destination pixel, pixels around the edge of the picture pose a problem. Such pixels — because they are on the edge — don't have a full neighborhood. The `dofilter()` routine takes the easy way out, and simply copies edge pixels from source to destination unchanged. First, the routine uses `memmove()` to copy the top and bottom edges. Because the pixels in the image are stored by row rather than by column, the left and right edges are copied a pixel at a time.

At this point, `dofilter()` is about to enter the filtering algorithm. Consequently, the routine calls `GetTickCount()` and stores the value in the `millis` variable. `GetTickCount()` returns the number of milliseconds since the system was booted. As you'll see, `dofilter()` calls the routine again when the processing is finished, and subtracts the earlier time (in `millis`) from the later time to determine the total execution time. You can run the application with and without the math coprocessor enabled and see the time difference.

The smoothing algorithm consists of two nested `for()` loops. Within the innermost `for()` loop is a `while` loop. The outer `for()` loop processes each color plane; an RGB image has three planes: red, green, and blue. (In other words, the code within the outer `for()` loop is executed once for all the red pixels, once for all the green pixels, and once for all the blue pixels.)

The next `for()` loop processes each scan line. Within that `for()` loop is the `while()` loop that processes each pixel. One expression does most of the work in the algorithm — the multiterm, weighted summation that yields the value `fpsum` (which ultimately becomes the value of the destination pixel). This summation includes nine floating-point multiplications and eight floating-point additions. The routine performs a sanity check, making sure that the result in `fpsum` is not greater than 255 — the maximum in a given color plane for any pixel. If so, the routine substitutes 255 and then stores the value in the destination pixel. (Note the conversion from floating-point to `BYTE` data type. `BYTE` is a `typedef` for `unsigned char`.)

At the end of the routine, `dofilter()` calls `GetTickCount()`, subtracts the value from the earlier call to `GetTickCount()`, and reports the difference as the elapsed time.

SUMMARY

In this chapter, we introduced floating-point numbers, and took you on an abbreviated tour of the mathematics behind them. Although many embedded applications require only integer math support, some demand floating-point capabilities, and still others appear to require floating-point support when integer support is sufficient. As always, to control costs and keep your projects on schedule, it's important to take the time to review the project's requirements, analyze your options, and make the right decision.

If you decide that your embedded application needs floating-point support, your next step is to determine how that support is provided: through an FPU (hardware) or floating-point emulation (software). You saw that an FPU has the advantage of speed, but using emulation reduces per-system cost and has the advantage of flexibility and portability.

To illustrate the performance difference between an application running on an FPU and an application using a floating-point emulator, we created a small image-processing program that made heavy use of some basic floating-point operations. ToolSuite Lite enabled us to run the application first using hardware floating-point support, and then using software support. Then, with the help of the timer built into the PC hardware, we measured the difference. When deciding whether you need an FPU or software emulation in your system, you can benchmark a simple simulation of the floating-point algorithms in your application in this fashion to obtain performance statistics.

19

Dynamic Link Libraries

Many operating systems, such as UNIX, Microsoft Windows, and OS/2, implement dynamic libraries. Microsoft Windows and OS/2, however, refer to them as *dynamic link libraries,* or DLLs. Programs can link dynamically to a DLL when they are executed or while they are running. In contrast, programs can link to an object library only during compilation or linkage — before you create the executable. This style of linking is called *static linking,* and object libraries are often referred to as *static libraries.*

Dynamic link libraries and static libraries are similar in that both are a set of executable routines containing code and data. Programs that use static libraries resolve external references at link time and, therefore, contain everything they need to run. Programs that rely on dynamic link libraries, however, resolve external references every time they run. Intuitively, it may seem that a self-contained program executable is best for an embedded system. DLLs, however, have several advantages that make them worthy of consideration for use in embedded systems. In this chapter, we discuss the advantages, explain how to use DLLs in your applications, and demonstrate implementing DLLs in an example program.

WHAT IS A DLL?

A DLL is an executable file but not a stand-alone executable; it can't be run by itself. It contains a collection of functions that other programs can use. These functions are exported from the DLL; that is, the DLL contains an *export table* listing the routines that a program can call. A program can load and use a DLL in two ways: implicitly or explicitly.

Implicit DLL loading occurs when the program calls the functions by name, like a normal function call. When the program is built, it is linked not with a static library but with an import library that identifies the DLL name and its functions. The linker builds an *import table* in the program executable identifying the DLL, the called functions, and where they are referenced in the program. When the system loads the program, it sees the import table, automatically finds and loads the referenced DLL, and then resolves (or links) the references to the functions in the DLL. Because the linking is performed at load time rather than program build time, it is called *dynamic linking.*

DLLs can have import tables, too. A DLL's import table can reference functions in other DLLs and in the main executable. For the latter, the main program must then have an export table; otherwise, the DLL wouldn't be able to import functions from the main program. When a program is loaded, all implicitly referenced DLLs (DLLs referenced in the program's import table), are automatically loaded. The system loads also any DLLs implicitly referenced by the DLLs that were just loaded. This process continues until all the import tables in all the executables (both the main program and all DLLs) have been processed.

Explicit DLL loading occurs when code (in a program or a DLL) makes a system call to explicitly load a specific DLL. But how does the program then call functions in the DLL? If the program called them by name, the functions would be in the import table and the DLL would have been implicitly loaded. Instead, the program makes another system call to obtain a pointer to a function in the DLL. Using the function pointer, the program can call the function indirectly. By making another system call, you can unload explicitly loaded DLLs to free up the memory they occupy.

Implicitly loaded DLLs are widely used on desktop systems such as Windows and UNIX. One reason for their popularity is that different modules (different DLLs) can be updated independently. This is particularly useful when different companies provide different modules, such as third-party libraries of functions, a C run-time library from a compiler vendor, and APIs provided by the operating system. In fact, all Win32 APIs are referenced as DLLs by Windows programs. When a new version of the operating system is released, existing programs continue to work unchanged. A second reason for using DLLs on desktop systems is code sharing. If more than one process uses the same DLL, the code in that DLL can be shared; you don't have to load the DLL twice, which results in a memory usage savings.

Independent module releases and code sharing, however, are of limited benefit in embedded systems. It's more common to simply replace entire embedded systems with new hardware and software than it is to upgrade individual software modules in the field. Similarly, few embedded systems use multiprocessing, so code sharing between processes is unnecessary.

Nevertheless, using DLLs in embedded systems has some benefits, as you see in the following section. You also see that explicitly loaded DLLs are more common than implicitly loaded DLLs because the former can be loaded and unloaded when needed, to make memory available for other purposes.

ADVANTAGES OF USING DLLS

The modular characteristic of DLLs results in several benefits when you use DLLs in embedded systems. The benefits are in the following areas:

- **Memory requirements.** Using DLLs, you can load and unload portions of your program as needed. You can use this capability to reduce the system's overall memory requirements, as long as all the code in the system never needs to be available simultaneously.

- **System upgrades.** You can upgrade individual DLL modules independently from the rest of the system.

- **System configuration and customization.** You can easily configure different versions of your system with different hardware configurations, connection requirements, and so on by using a DLL to hold all the customization and configuration information.

MEMORY REQUIREMENTS

Memory is a precious resource in an embedded system. You can make judicious use of this resource by storing infrequently used code in a DLL on disk and loading it only when needed. This can be an attractive option, particularly if the disk is a device that can be accessed quickly, such as an SSD. For example, suppose your system must dial out to a central office once a week to download new data. You could put in a DLL the code that conducts the conversation with the central office and updates the local database. Then you load the DLL once a week, when you perform the update; the rest of the time, the code isn't loaded, freeing memory for other uses.

SYSTEM UPGRADES

Upgrading an embedded application — no matter how major or minor the changes — usually entails updating the application code, testing and debugging the software, recompiling and re-linking the software and libraries, and finally burning and replacing ROMs.

Compare that to upgrading an application using a DLL. For a third-party DLL, whether it adds features or corrects a bug, you simply copy or download a new version of the DLL to the system's storage device and reboot the system. When the application runs, it loads the new DLL and all the changes take effect.

To upgrade an application using a DLL you wrote, you have to update the code and recompile it as you would any program. But updating a DLL is less work than updating an application. A DLL is usually much smaller than a full-fledged program, and updating and recompiling a small, isolated module is easier and faster than working on the larger program. Also, after you've recompiled a DLL, you simply copy or download it to the system's storage device, reboot the system, and the new functionality takes effect. You don't burn ROMs and make an on-site visit to replace them.

One of the most common reasons to upgrade a system is to update or install new device drivers. Operating systems have to work with an array of hardware, such as printers, keyboards and keypads, monitors, and communication devices, from a variety of vendors. Supporting all possible peripherals would make the footprint of an operating system unnecessarily large because the embedded system it ran on would use only a fraction of its capabilities. Normally, you include only the device drivers needed for the hardware configuration.

If each device driver is built as a separate DLL, rather than statically linked to the operating system, you simplify the process of upgrading or adding new hardware devices. Rather than rebuilding the complete operating system and application, you simply replace the old driver DLL with the new driver. When the system reboots, it automatically uses the new driver, without the need for additional system changes.

SYSTEM CONFIGURATION AND CUSTOMIZATION

Some embedded systems are marketed in a variety of configurations, allowing the customer to select the features they need. When you give customers this flexibility, however, your manufacturing department must be able to easily customize and then manufacture the system.

Using DLLs can simplify the manufacturing of multiple system configurations. First, you design your software so that each optional component is in a separate DLL. Then to configure the system software, you store on the system disk only the DLLs corresponding to selected features rather than re-linking and installing a custom software version for each system. When the main portion of the application runs, it locates and loads only the DLLs needed for the particular configuration.

You can use various methods in the main application to decide which DLLs should be loaded. You can simply look for all DLLs the system supports and load only those present on the disk. Or you can use an ASCII initialization file, similar to the .INI files in Windows 3.1, to configure the system. The application would read the .INI file, interpret each line of the file, and load only the DLLs referenced by commands in the .INI file. Because the initialization file is in ASCII, configuring a system requires only that you edit the initialization file to select features.

DISADVANTAGES OF USING DLLS

We can think of three disadvantages to using DLLs. First, building an application as a main executable and several DLLs is more complex than linking a single, monolithic .EXE file because you have to design the interfaces, set up the build to create multiple files, and define all the imports and exports for the .EXE and each DLL. After you have the interfaces and build framework in place, however, developing and maintaining an application with DLLs is no more difficult than without DLLs. Second, if a DLL contains a large library of functions but your application needs only a few functions, using a DLL wastes memory. That's because the entire DLL is always loaded, regardless of how much or how little of it is used. With statically linked libraries, only functions that are used are linked into the final executable file. Third, loading a DLL takes time. If your application loads and unloads DLLs explicitly at run-time, you must be careful when performing the load operation to avoid affecting the system response times.

If you need a modular and flexible system, whether for configurability, field upgrade potential, or dynamic loading of code to support rarely needed functionality, consider using DLLs. Otherwise, there's no reason to add to system complexity by using DLLs.

USING DLLS WITH ETS KERNEL

Under ETS Kernel, you enable support for DLLs by linking the DLL loader into your application (using the `@ldr.emb` linker command file). Because the DLL loader is inside the application, implicit loading of DLLs referenced by the main `.EXE` is not supported; that is, you can't have an import table in your executable. Instead, DLLs are explicitly managed, using the `LoadLibrary()`, `FreeLibrary()`, and `GetProcAddress()` Win32 APIs.

Although implicit loading is not supported for the main executable, it is supported for DLLs. That is, if you explicitly load DLL A with a `LoadLibrary(a.dll)` call, and DLL A imports functions from DLL B, which in turn imports functions from DLL C, both `B.DLL` and `C.DLL` are automatically loaded as well.

Although the executable can't have an import table, it can have an export table. This is desirable when DLLs need to call functions in the main program. For example, all Win32, Kernel, and C library APIs are linked into the main executable. For a DLL to call these functions, they must be exported from the `.EXE` file and imported by the DLL. We show you how this works when we get to the sample project later in the chapter.

To load a DLL explicitly, you use the `LoadLibrary()` call. The syntax is

```
DllHandle = LoadLibrary(DllName);
```

`LoadLibrary()` takes a single argument, a pointer to a DLL name string. It returns a DLL handle if the DLL is successfully loaded or NULL if the load call fails. If the call fails, you can call `GetLastError()` for additional error information.

The DLL name string can be a complete path or the DLL file name. If just the DLL file name is given, ETS Kernel searches for the DLL in several locations, in the following order:

- First, if the program was downloaded from a host system, ETS Kernel searches the host system directory from which the program was loaded.

- Second, ETS Kernel searches the current directory of the program.

- Third, ETS Kernel searches the directories specified in the PATH environment variable (if the PATH variable exists).

After the DLL has been successfully loaded and initialized, you must determine the address of the functions you want to call. You do this by calling the `GetProcAddress()` function. Its syntax is

```
FunctionPointer = GetProcAddress(DllHandle, FunctionName);
```

`GetProcAddress()` takes two parameters: the DLL handle returned by the `LoadLibrary()` call, and a pointer to a function name string. `GetProcAddress()` returns a pointer to the function or NULL if the function is not exported by the DLL. If the call fails, you can call `GetLastError()` for additional error information.

Finally, when the application no longer needs the DLL, we request that the DLL be unloaded by calling `FreeLibrary()`, which takes the handle to the DLL as an argument:

```
FreeLibrary(DllHandle);
```

`FreeLibrary()` frees all memory allocated to the DLL and to any DLLs implicitly loaded by the DLL.

Because a DLL is a collection of functions with no `main()` routine, normally the first code to execute in a DLL is whichever one of its exported functions the application calls first. However, DLLs can include an initialization routine, called an attach function, that is automatically called when the DLL is loaded into memory.

The attach function has the following syntax, as defined by Win32:

```
BOOL __stdcall DllEntryPoint(HANDLE hDll, DWORD Reason, void *Reserved)
```

The name of the function is arbitrary (though `DllEntryPoint` is customary), but the calling convention (`__stdcall`) and parameter syntax are required. The first parameter is a handle for the DLL. The `Reason` parameter identifies the reason the attach routine is being called and is one of four values: `DLL_PROCESS_ATTACH`, `DLL_PROCESS_DETACH`, `DLL_THREAD_ATTACH`, and `DLL_THREAD_DETACH`. The third parameter is unused.

The four values for `Reason` correspond to the four times a DLL attach routine can be called. `DLL_PROCESS_ATTACH` means the DLL has just been loaded by `LoadLibrary()`; the attach routine in the DLL is called before the `LoadLibrary()` call returns to the main program. This call allows the DLL to perform any one-time initialization required when it is loaded. `DLL_PROCESS_DETACH` means the DLL is being unloaded by a `FreeLibrary()` call; this enables the DLL to perform any cleanup required before it is removed from memory. `DLL_THREAD_ATTACH` means the application has just created a new thread; this enables the DLL to perform any required per-thread initialization. Finally, `DLL_THREAD_DETACH` means an application thread is about to terminate; the DLL can then perform any per-thread cleanup.

The return value from `DllEntryPoint()` is used only when `Reason` is `DLL_PROCESS_ATTACH` (the DLL is being loaded by a `LoadLibrary()` call). If the attach routine returns TRUE, the DLL load succeeds. If the attach routine returns FALSE, the DLL is unloaded from memory and `LoadLibrary()` returns an error to the application.

The presence or absence of a DLL attach routine is indicated by whether or not the DLL file has an entry point. If the DLL has an entry point, it has an attach routine. If the DLL has no entry point, it doesn't have an attach routine.

We don't use DLL attach routines in the programming project in this chapter. Following, however, is a sample DLL attach routine:

```
BOOL __stdcall DllEntryPoint(HANDLE hDll, DWORD Reason, void *Reserved)
{
    switch(Reason)
    {
    case DLL_PROCESS_ATTACH:
        printf("DLL just got loaded\n");
        if (!DllInit())
            return FALSE;
        break;
```

```
            case DLL_PROCESS_DETACH:
                printf("DLL is being unloaded\n");
                DllCleanup();
                break;
            case DLL_THREAD_ATTACH:
                printf("Thread just got created\n");
                NewThreadInit();
                break;
            case DLL_THREAD_DETACH:
                printf("Thread about to be terminated\n");
                ThreadCleanup();
                break;
        }
        return TRUE;
    }
```

We show you how to build DLLs and how to specify exports and imports in both the main executable and in DLLs when we describe the programming project later in this chapter.

THE ENCDEC PROJECT

In the ENCDEC project, we demonstrate how you can dynamically load and unload DLLs as needed to implement functionality that is required only occasionally. ENCDEC simulates an application that occasionally needs to send and receive email messages. When email messages include binary files as attachments, the attachment is encoded in an ASCII representation, using one of two encoding algorithms. The most popular of these algorithms is base64 encoding. An older encoding used primarily on UNIX systems is uuencode. The ENCDEC program is capable of encoding binary files using the base64 or uuencode algorithms, and decoding uuencode or base64-encoded files back to their original binary form.

Because we're simply demonstrating how to use DLLs, ENCDEC doesn't actually send or receive email. ENCDEC is a command-line driven program; you give it input and output file names, specify an encoding algorithm, and specify whether you want the input file encoded or decoded. Each of the four possible file translations — base64 encoding, base64 decoding, uuencode encoding, and uuencode decoding — is implemented in a separate DLL. ENCDEC loads the appropriate DLL to handle the specified file translation.

By keeping the code to process email messages in one or more DLLs, you can avoid consuming memory for code that rarely runs. When email processing is required, you load the appropriate code, do the work, and then unload the code again to free up memory.

BUILDING THE **ENCDEC** PROJECT

The project is located in \TSLITE\PROJECTS\ENCDEC. As usual, we've included prebuilt executable and DLL files in the RELEASE subdirectory, so you can skip the build step if you want.

The workspace for this project is more complicated than the workspaces for the other projects in this book because it builds an .EXE file and four .DLL files. From Developer Studio, open the ENCDEC.DSW workspace file. As shown in Figure 19-1, the workspace contains five

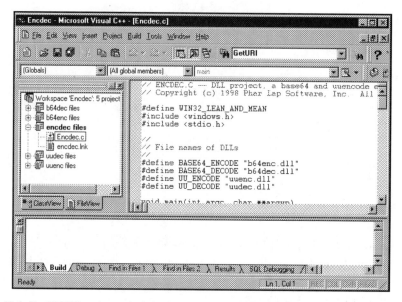

Figure 19-1: The ENCDEC workspace includes four projects, one that builds the .EXE file and one to build each .DLL file.

separate projects. The encdec project builds the main executable program, ENCDEC.EXE. The b64dec, b64enc, uudec, and uuenc projects build the four .DLL files.

In a workspace with multiple projects, you can build only the active project. The active project is identified in bold in the FileView and ClassView windows of Developer Studio; in Figure 19-1, encdec is the active project. To select a new active project, click Project|Set Active Project.

To build the files for this project, first click Project|Set Active Project to make encdec the active project. Next, click Build|Rebuild All to build the ENCDEC.EXE file. Then for each DLL project in turn, make it active and click Build|Rebuild All to build a DLL file.

Because this workspace is organized differently than the workspaces used by the other projects in the book, let's examine the differences. We created the ENCDEC.DSW workspace by creating a new ETS project normally, as described in Chapter 3. Then, from within the workspace, we created four new projects of type "Win32 Dynamic-Link Library" to hold each DLL project file. The directory structure is organized such that each DLL project is a subdirectory in the ENCDEC project directory; for example, the B64DEC project files are in the \TSLITE\PROJECTS\ENCDEC\B64DEC directory.

The encdec project must be built before the DLL projects because, when using DLLs, you must specify the imports and exports in the .EXE and .DLL files. ENCDEC.EXE doesn't import any functions from the DLLs; as noted previously, that's not permitted with ETS Kernel. Instead, as you see when we examine the source code, ENCDEC.EXE calls GetProcAddress() to get the addresses of functions exported from the DLLs. ENCDEC.EXE, however, has to export from the executable the C run-time library functions needed by the DLLs. You can't link a separate copy of the C run-time library into each DLL. Doing so would waste memory, and separate run-time libraries would each attempt to maintain a separate heap, data structures for open files, and so on, leading to all sorts of problems.

So, we need to export a handful of C run-time library functions from ENCDEC.EXE and import them into each .DLL file. If we explicitly specified the function names in each project, we'd have to update five projects each time we wanted to add or remove a function name. Instead, we specify the function names once, in the encdec project. When we build ENCDEC.EXE, we also build an import library, ENCDEC.LIB, which is an input file to build each DLL. An import library contains function names and identifies the executable or DLL from which they are exported; the linker uses that information to build an import table in the DLL. That's why we have to build the encdec project first.

The function names exported by ENCDEC.EXE are identified at the end of the ENCDEC.LNK file generated by ETS Project Wizard when we created the project. We edited the file to add the following linker commands:

```
! Add any additional linker commands here.
-export _fclose=fclose
-export _feof=feof
-export _ferror=ferror
-export _fgets=fgets
-export _fopen=fopen
-export _fprintf=fprintf
-export _fread=fread
-export _fwrite=fwrite
-export _printf=printf
-export _strncmp=strncmp
-makedeffile encdec.def
```

Each -EXPORT switch adds a function to the export table for ENCDEC.EXE. In accordance with Microsoft convention, we export the functions by their unmangled names, without the underscore added by the compiler. (Although C mangled names have only an underscore added and are thus easy to read, C++ mangled names are almost impossible to read; hence we use the convention that functions are exported by their unmangled name.) The name to the left of the equal sign is the mangled name, the name the linker has in the program's symbol table. The name to the right of the equal sign is the unmangled name, the name the linker will place in the export table.

The last switch, -MAKEDEFFILE, creates a .DEF file in a format readable by Microsoft's LIB utility. The LIB program reads the .DEF file and processes it to produce an import library, ENCDEC.LIB. This is accomplished by adding a post-build step to the encdec project, as shown in Figure 19-2. Click Project|Settings, select the encdec project, and click the Post-build step tab to see the LIB command line.

Each DLL is linked with the Microsoft linker rather than the ToolSuite LinkLoc linker. Because DLLs are loaded dynamically into RAM at run-time and are relocated according to the load address, the embedded features of LinkLoc for locating and ROMing programs aren't needed. Also, configuring DLL projects to use the LinkLoc linker is awkward, so we use the Microsoft linker. To see the settings used to build B64DEC.DLL, click Project|Settings and select

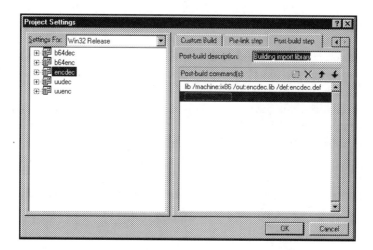

Figure 19-2: The post-build step for the ENCDEC project runs LIB to read the ENCDEC.DEF file produced by the linker and create an ENCDEC.LIB import library file.

the b64dec project. Then click the C/C++ tab and select the Code Generation category to display the information shown in Figure 19-3. We configured the DLL projects to use the multithreaded DLL C run-time library, so they won't link in the static C run-time library. We won't use the multithreaded DLL run-time library either, but selecting the DLL library rather than the static library avoids linking in the latter. We'll actually get the C run-time library functions we need by importing them from ENCDEC.EXE.

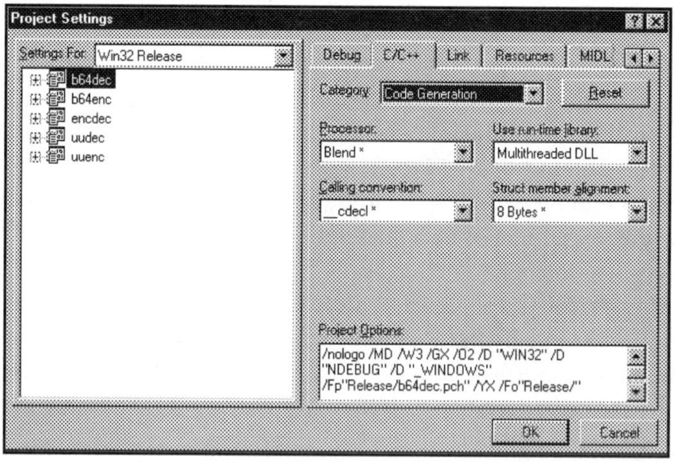

Figure 19-3: The DLLs are compiled to use the multithreaded DLL run-time library rather than the static run-time library.

Now click the Link tab and select the General category, as shown in Figure 19-4. We checked the Ignore all default libraries box because we don't want to link in any static libraries. In the Object/library modules text box, we deleted all libraries except `kernel32.lib`, the import library for Win32 functions; including this allows you to import Win32 functions from the main executable (though we don't use this capability in this project). Then we added `..\encdec.lib` to the list. This is the import library created when we built `ENCDEC.EXE`, and it contains the references to the C run-time library functions used by the DLLs. Finally, because `B64DEC.DLL` doesn't have a DLL attach routine, we added the `/noentry` switch to the Project Options text box. (If your DLL had an attach function, you would select the Output category and enter the name of the attach function in the Entry-point symbol text box.)

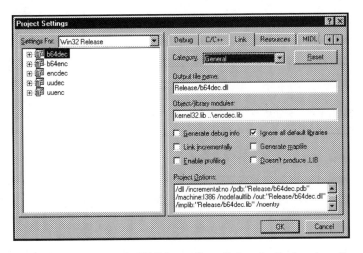

Figure 19-4: The DLL projects link the ENCDEC.LIB import library file from the directory above (the project directory for ENCDEC), ignore all default libraries, and specify the /noentry switch because they don't have a DLL attach routine.

Finally, as shown in Figure 19-5, we also added a post-build step to the `b64dec` project. Click the Post-build step tab to display this information. After the DLL is built, we copy the `B64DEC.DLL` file to the `Release` subdirectory for the `encdec` project, the directory where the `ENCDEC.EXE` file is located. By placing the DLL in the same directory as the `.EXE` file, we don't have to give a file path when calling `LoadLibrary()` to load the DLL; the system automatically looks in the directory from which `ENCDEC.EXE` was loaded. We also specified a similar post-build command for the Win32 Debug settings for each project, to copy the DLL to the `Debug` subdirectory.

We took care of the imports (C run-time library functions) needed by `B64DEC.DLL` by including `ENCDEC.LIB` in the link. But what about functions that `B64DEC.DLL` exports? If we look at the `B64DEC.C` source file, we see that the exported function, `TranslateFile()`, is defined with the `__declspec(dllexport)` attribute:

```
BOOL __declspec(dllexport) TranslateFile(char *pInName, char *pOutName)
```

The compiler passes that attribute information along to the linker, which in turn uses it to automatically add the unmangled name for the `TranslateFile()` function to the export table.

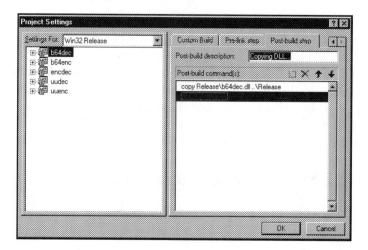

Figure 19-5: The post-build step for the b64dec project copies the DLL file to the Release subdirectory for the encdec project. When the executable runs, the DLL loader looks in the directory from which the ENCDEC.EXE file is loaded to find the DLL files.

Microsoft Visual C++ includes the DUMPBIN.EXE command-line tool for examining the contents of executable files (both .EXE files and .DLL files). If you run DUMPBIN with no arguments, it prints a list of switches to enable viewing different sections of the executable file. We use the following DOS command line to display the import and export tables for B64DEC.DLL:

```
dumpbin /imports /exports b64dec.dll
```

This command prints the following information in the DOS box:

```
Microsoft (R) COFF Binary File Dumper Version 6.00.8168
Copyright (C) Microsoft Corp 1992-1998. All rights reserved.


Dump of file b64dec.dll

File Type: DLL

  Section contains the following exports for b64dec.dll

          0 characteristics
   3623CA95 time date stamp Tue Oct 13 17:48:05 1998
       0.00 version
          1 ordinal base
          1 number of functions
          1 number of names

    ordinal hint RVA        name

          1     0 00001000 TranslateFile
```

```
Section contains the following imports:

  encdec.exe
                  10002000 Import Address Table
                  10002040 Import Name Table
                         0 time date stamp
                         0 Index of first forwarder reference

                         6    fread
                         0    fclose
                         8    printf
                         4    fopen
                         7    fwrite

  Summary

                  1000 .data
                  1000 .rdata
                  1000 .reloc
                  1000 .text
```

As expected, one function, `TranslateFile()`, is exported from B64DEC.DLL, and several C run-time library functions are imported from the ENCDEC.EXE file.

RUNNING THE **ENCDEC** PROJECT

ENCDEC reads and writes files on the host system, using the ETS Kernel host file system support. To run ENCDEC, you specify four required parameters on the command line:

```
runemb encdec infile outfile enc|dec b64|uu
```

The *infile* and *outfile* arguments specify the input and output files, respectively. The third argument is the operation to be performed on the input file: `enc` specifies that the file should be encoded, and `dec` specifies that the file should be decoded. Finally, the fourth argument specifies which algorithm to use: `uu` for the uuencode algorithm or `base64` for the base64 algorithm.

Based on the selected encoding algorithm and whether to encode or decode, ENCDEC loads the appropriate DLL and translates *infile* to *outfile*. In this project, for convenience, we use the remote file system feature rather than the target's local file system. In a fully functional embedded system, we would load the DLLs from a local hard disk drive or SSD.

Let's run the program. Because this program uses command-line parameters, we demonstrate running it from a DOS prompt. (You can specify command-line parameters when running the program from Developer Studio. To run from Developer Studio, click Project|Settings, click the Debug tab, and enter the command-line arguments in the Program arguments text box. Because using command-line parameters from Developer Studio is tedious, we run the program from DOS.) First, set the current directory to \TSLITE\PROJECTS\DLL. Then enter the following command to encode the ENCDEC.OBJ binary file using base64 encoding:

```
runemb release\encdec release\encdec.obj encdec.b64 enc b64
```

After the program is downloaded and starts running, it prints the following:

```
Loading DLL: b64enc.dll
Encoding release\encdec.obj ==> encdec.b64 ... Done
```

This command instructs ENCDEC to read the ENCDEC.OBJ file from the RELEASE subdirectory, encode it using the base64 algorithm, and write the output to the ENCDEC.B64 file in the current directory. The resulting file contains a sequence of 72-character encoded lines; the first two lines of the file are shown next. You may get some differences in the first line of the file because of a time stamp in bytes 4 – 7 of the object file or because of compiler differences if you compiled the object file with a version of Visual C++ other than 6.0.

```
TAEbAAUFKjZzCgAAXAAAAAAAAAuZHJlY3R2ZQAAAAAAAAAJgAAAEwEAAAAAAAAAAAAAAA
AAAAChAALnRleHQAAAAAAAAAAAAAFACAAByBAAAwgYAAAAAAAzAAAAIBBQYC5kYXRhAAAA
```

Now let's decode it again. Type the following command:

```
runemb release\encdec encdec.b64 encdec.obj dec b64
```

This command decodes our ENCDEC.B64 file to create the ENCDEC.OBJ file in the current directory. The newly created object file should be identical to the object file we started with in the RELEASE subdirectory.

Feel free to play with ENCDEC, encoding and decoding files with both the base64 and uuencode algorithms. If you want to test ENCDEC working with other programs, send yourself some email with a binary file attached. Edit the resulting email source to clip out the base64-encoded portion and write it to a separate file. Then use ENCDEC to decode it and obtain the original binary file you emailed to yourself. Similarly, if you have access to a UNIX system, use the uuencode program to encode a binary file with the uuencode program. Then run ENCDEC to decode it, and compare the result with the original binary file.

A QUICK TOUR OF THE SOURCE

To begin our examination of the source code to ENCDEC, look at Listing 19-1. This shows the start of the main() routine in the ENCDEC.C file that's used to build ENCDEC.EXE.

Listing 19-1: The main() routine

```
//
// File names of DLLs
//
#define BASE64_ENCODE "b64enc.dll"
#define BASE64_DECODE "b64dec.dll"
#define UU_ENCODE "uuenc.dll"
#define UU_DECODE "uudec.dll"

void main(int argc, char **argvp)
{
    BOOL    fEncode;        // T ==> encoding, F ==> decoding
    BOOL    fBase64;        // T ==> base64 format, F ==> uuencode format
    FILE    *hInfile;       // input file handle
```

```
    FILE    *hOutfile;        // output file handle
    char    YesNo;            // answer to question
    char    DllName[64];      // name of DLL to load
    HANDLE  hDll;             // handle of loaded DLL
    BOOL (*pTranslate)(char *pInName, char *pOutName);

//
// Extract command line arguments, open the input file and
// create the output file.
//
    if (argc < 5)
    {
USAGE:
        printf("Usage: encdec infile outfile enc|dec b64|uu\n");
        return;
    }
    if (stricmp(argvp[3], "enc") == 0)
        fEncode = TRUE;
    else if (stricmp(argvp[3], "dec") == 0)
        fEncode = FALSE;
    else
    {
        printf("Invalid encode/decode argument\n");
        goto USAGE;
    }
    if (stricmp(argvp[4], "b64") == 0)
        fBase64 = TRUE;
    else if (stricmp(argvp[4], "uu") == 0)
        fBase64 = FALSE;
    else
    {
        printf("Invalid format argument\n");
        goto USAGE;
    }
    hInfile = fopen(argvp[1], "rb");
    if (hInfile == NULL)
    {
        printf("Can't open input file: %s\n", argvp[1]);
        goto USAGE;
    }
    fclose(hInfile);
    hOutfile = fopen(argvp[2], "rb");
    if (hOutfile != NULL)
    {
        fclose(hOutfile);
        printf("Output file %s exists; overwrite it (y|n)? ",
                argvp[2]);
        scanf("%1s", &YesNo);
        if (YesNo != 'y')
            return;
    }
```

This straightforward code parses the command-line arguments. If the command-line syntax is correct, the code opens the input file to verify that it exists. If the file doesn't exist, an error is flagged. The code then attempts to open the output file, and if it exists, asks the user whether it's okay to overwrite the existing output file. Then any opened files are closed. As you see shortly, different DLLs use different conventions to open files, so we let the DLLs open the files to perform the I/O.

Because ENCDEC.EXE is not linked with the local file system, all file I/O is automatically redirected to the host file system. Both the input file and the output file are opened on the host system.

Now look at the rest of the ENCDEC.C source code, which is shown in Listing 19-2.

Listing 19-2: ENCDEC.C

```
//
// Load the DLL
//
    if (fBase64)
        strcpy(DllName, fEncode ? BASE64_ENCODE : BASE64_DECODE);
    else
        strcpy(DllName, fEncode ? UU_ENCODE : UU_DECODE);
    printf("Loading DLL: %s\n", DllName);
    hDll = LoadLibrary(DllName);
    if (hDll == NULL)
    {
        printf("Error %d loading DLL\n", GetLastError());
        return;
    }
    pTranslate = (BOOL (*)(char *, char *)) GetProcAddress(hDll,
                "TranslateFile");
    if (pTranslate == NULL)
    {
        printf("Error %d getting address of procedure TranslateFile\n",
            GetLastError());
        goto EXIT;
    }

//
// Do the encode/decode
//
    printf("%s %s ==> %s ... ", fEncode ? "Encoding" : "Decoding",
        argvp[1], argvp[2]);
    if (!(*pTranslate)(argvp[1], argvp[2]))
    {
        printf("Error translating file\n");
        goto EXIT;
    }
    printf("Done\n");
```

```
//
// Unload DLL and exit
//
EXIT:
    FreeLibrary(hDll);
    return;
}
```

Based on the command-line arguments, the code selects the name of the DLL and calls LoadLibrary() to load it. As with the input and output files, the DLL files are loaded from the host file system because we didn't link the local file system into ENCDEC.EXE. Recall that in the build step, we copied the DLL files to the same directory as the ENCDEC.EXE file, so we don't have to specify a path; they will be found by the standard search algorithm for locating DLL files.

After the DLL is loaded, we call GetProcAddress() to get a pointer to the TranslateFile() function in the DLL. We use the same function name in all the DLLs to simplify the logic in ENCDEC.C. After obtaining the function pointer, we call the translate function, passing it pointers to the input and output file names. The translate function returns TRUE for success or FALSE if an error occurs.

Finally, we call FreeLibrary() to unload the DLL, and then exit the program. Because ENCDEC terminates after the file translation is performed, it isn't necessary to unload the DLL. But in a real system, it would be important to unload the DLL after processing was complete to free memory for other uses.

Because all the DLLs are similar in function, you look at only one in detail. The B64ENC.DLL file is built from the B64ENC\B64ENC.C file, and encodes the input file using the base64 algorithm.

Base64 encoding works by translating groups of 3 binary characters (24 bits) into 4 ASCII characters. Each ASCII character therefore represents 6 bits of the original data, and the binary values 0 – 63 are mapped to 64 characters in the ASCII character set: the letters $A - Z$ and $a - z$, the numbers 0 – 9, and the two symbols + and /. The specification for base64 encoding is located in RFC 2045, part one of the MIME (Multipurpose Internet Mail Extensions) request for comments.

The B64ENC.C file contains just one function, TranslateFile(), shown in Listing 19-3. It reads the input file, encodes it, and writes the results to the output file.

Listing 19-3: The TranslateFile() function

```
//
// The ASCII encodings of the binary values 0 - 63
//
char B64Encode[64] = {
'A','B','C','D','E','F','G','H','I','J','K','L','M','N','O','P',
'Q','R','S','T','U','V','W','X','Y','Z',
'a','b','c','d','e','f','g','h','i','j','k','l','m','n','o','p',
'q','r','s','t','u','v','w','x','y','z',
'0','1','2','3','4','5','6','7','8','9',
'+','/'};
```

```
//
// Encodes an input file using base64, writing the results
// to the output file.
//
// Base64 encoding is specified in RFC2045, part one of the
// Multipurpose Internet Mail Extensions (MIME).
//
// Returns TRUE if success, FALSE if error
//
BOOL __declspec(dllexport) TranslateFile(char *pInName, char *pOutName)
{
    FILE    *hInfile, *hOutfile;
    char    Buf[18*3];          // buffers input characters
    char    *pBuf, *pEndBuf;    // ptrs within Buf
    size_t  nRead;              // number of chars read into Buf
    char    Encoded[4];         // output (encoded) chars
    int     nch;                // number of output chars
    int     i;

//
// Open the input file and create the output file. Base64
// always uses <CR><LF> to terminate lines, regardless
// of what the local OS conventions for text are, so it's
// easiest to manipulate the files in binary mode.
//
    hInfile = fopen(pInName, "rb");
    if (hInfile == NULL)
    {
        printf("Can't open input file: %s\n", pInName);
        return FALSE;
    }
    hOutfile = fopen(pOutName, "wb");
    if (hOutfile == NULL)
    {
        fclose(hInfile);
        printf("Can't create output file: %s\n", pOutName);
        return FALSE;
    }

//
// Loop, reading data from the input file and encoding it,
// until we hit end of file.
//
    while (TRUE)
    {
//
// Read the next 18*3 (or less, if end-of-file) input chars,
// which we will use to create the next line of the output
// file, consisting of 18*4 (or less) ASCII chars terminated
```

```
// by <CR><LF>.   (The base64 spec limits output lines to no
// more than 76 chars;   we write 18*4 or 72 chars/line.)
//
// When we hit end-of-file, we're done.
//
        nRead = fread(Buf, 1, sizeof(Buf), hInfile);
        if (nRead <= 0)
        {
            if (feof(hInfile) != 0)
                break;
            printf("Error %d reading input file\n", ferror(hInfile));
            goto FAILURE;
        }
        pBuf = Buf;
        pEndBuf = pBuf + nRead;

//
// Loop, converting 3 input chars at a time into 4 output chars,
// and writing them to the output file, until the buffer is empty.
//
        while (pBuf < pEndBuf)
        {
//
// Split the next 3 input bytes (or 1 or 2, if end-of-file)
// into 4 bytes with binary values 0-63.
//
            Encoded[0] = ((BYTE)*pBuf) >> 2;
            Encoded[1] = (*pBuf++ & 0x3) << 4;
            if (pBuf >= pEndBuf)
            {
                Encoded[2] = Encoded[3] = '=';
                nch = 2;
            }
            else
            {
                Encoded[1] |= ((BYTE)*pBuf) >> 4;
                Encoded[2] = (*pBuf++ & 0xF) << 2;
                if (pBuf >= pEndBuf)
                {
                    Encoded[3] = '=';
                    nch = 3;
                }
                else
                {
                    Encoded[2] |= ((BYTE)*pBuf) >> 6;
                    Encoded[3] = *pBuf++ & 0x3F;
                    nch = 4;
                }
            }
```

```
        //
        // Convert the binary values 0-63 to ASCII.
        //
                for (i = 0; i < nch; ++ i)
                    Encoded[i] = B64Encode[Encoded[i]];


        //
        // Write the 4 encoded bytes to the output file.
        //
                if (fwrite(Encoded, 1, 4, hOutfile) != 4)
                {
                    printf("Error %d writing to output file\n",
                        ferror(hOutfile));
                    goto FAILURE;
                }
            }


        //
        // Write a <CR><LF> to the output file to terminate the line.
        //
            Encoded[0] = '\r';
            Encoded[1] = '\n';
            if (fwrite(Encoded, 1, 2, hOutfile) != 2)
            {
                printf("Error %d writing to output file\n",
                    ferror(hOutfile));
                goto FAILURE;
            }
        }


    //
    // return success
    //
        fclose(hInfile);
        fclose(hOutfile);
        return TRUE;

    FAILURE:
        fclose(hInfile);
        fclose(hOutfile);
        return FALSE;
    }
```

TranslateFile() opens both the input file and the output file in binary mode. Because base64 encoding specifies that the lines in the encoded ASCII file should be terminated by CR LF, it's best to handle line termination explicitly in the code, rather than using text file I/O mode and depending on the default ASCII file line termination used by your operating system. That way, if your code is ported to an operating system that doesn't use CR LF for line termination (such as UNIX), it will continue to work.

Next, we enter a loop, reading bytes from the input file and converting them to lines of text in the output file. Each time through the loop, we read 54 bytes from the input file, which is converted to 72 ASCII characters, or one line, in the output file. The base64 specification limits the encoded line length to no more than 76 characters; we chose 72 characters to be conservative.

At the end of the input file, if we have only 1 input byte to encode, we have 2 unused output bytes to set; if we have only 2 input bytes, we have 1 unused output byte. The unused output bytes at the end of a base64-encode file are set to the ASCII = character.

Finally, we close the input and output files and return.

SUMMARY

In this chapter, you've seen that you can use dynamic link libraries (DLLs) to make your application software modular and flexible. In embedded systems, these features make DLLs attractive for dynamic loading and unloading of infrequently needed code, for easily upgrading software on deployed systems, and for simplifying the configuring and customizing of systems.

20

C++ Exceptions and Structured Exceptions

odern compilers have built-in support for handling errors and unexpected events. In this chapter, we look at two such mechanisms: C++ exception handling and structured exception handling. C++ exception handling is part of the ANSI standard for C++ and provides C++ programs with a way for low-level code to communicate unexpected events directly to high-level code. Structured exception handling is an error-reporting mechanism implemented in Win32 operating systems and can be used by both C and C++ programs. Structured exceptions provide a simple means for applications to handle CPU exceptions; structured exception handling is also the foundation on which Win32 compilers implement C++ exceptions.

C++ exceptions are a software error-reporting mechanism. When an error occurs, software can throw an exception, which can be any C++ object or data type. The system scans back up the call stack, looking for the first function that has arranged to catch that particular exception object. If the outermost function is reached without encountering a catch handler for the thrown object, the runtime library function terminate(), which terminates the application, is called. C++ exceptions provide an attractive alternative to passing error codes back up through many layers of function calls or storing error codes in global variables that are supposed to be examined by higher-level code.

Structured exceptions are used to report CPU exceptions. As you saw in Chapter 9, "Interrupts," CPU exceptions are a kind of interrupt signaled by the CPU when software attempts to perform an invalid operation, such as dividing by zero, executing an illegal opcode, or accessing memory outside the memory region allocated to the program. When a CPU exception occurs, the Win32 structured exception processing code scans up the call stack looking for a function that has arranged, using the __except keyword, to handle that particular exception. If the outermost function is reached without finding a handler for the exception, the C run-time library prints an error message and terminates the program. Adding structured exception handling to your embedded system helps make it robust; you can arrange to catch exceptions caused by programming errors and either shut down the system gracefully or restart the system. You can handle processor exceptions also by writing an ISR, as described in Chapter 9, but structured exception handling is easier to implement. In addition, structured exception handling enables you to provide localized protection to specific blocks of code and handle the same exception in different ways in different parts of your program.

In this chapter, we show you how to use C++ exception handling and structured exception handling in your own programs. We also enhance the Network-Aware UPS project from Chapter 14 to create a Restartable UPS project that implements both C++ and structured exception handling. You use these powerful mechanisms to easily build a system that can catch abnormal events and restart itself, important capabilities in a system that must be fail-safe.

BENEFITS OF EXCEPTION HANDLING

Exception handling provides a method to handle errors and CPU exceptions in a clean way. Let's consider software error control first.

The traditional error-reporting technique involves returning error codes from functions. That method works well if the caller of the function wants to process the error condition immediately. Frequently, however, programs are deeply nested in many layers of function calls when an error occurs. For appropriate error handling to occur, the error code must be propagated up to one of the outer functions. Many intervening functions may also be able to generate errors, which complicates matters. The programmer has to come up with a complicated, and therefore mistake-prone, error-reporting technique that can combine potential error conditions from many different sources. This approach is so tedious that it's often tempting for the programmer to simply ignore error returns from functions, assuming they will always succeed. You've probably encountered the classic null pointer reference that results from using the return value from a malloc() call without checking for a NULL error value first.

Another technique commonly used by general-purpose libraries of functions is returning only a success or failure condition from each function and reporting more detailed error codes in a global variable. For example, several functions in the ANSI C run-time library report errors in the errno global variable. Similarly, the Win32 APIs just return a success or failure condition, and applications obtain an error code by calling the GetLastError() function. Although this approach helps alleviate the problem of combining error codes from several sources as you propagate errors up through nested function calls, it requires a bit of extra code wherever you need to properly handle an error — the code to retrieve the error code. Again, it's tempting when writing code that has to check for errors after every function call to take shortcuts and not bother retrieving the error code. As a result, even if the error is detected and reported, the error message reports only that a particular function returned an error, not what the error code is. This makes it much more difficult to diagnose a problem without running it under a debugger, which is often impossible to do in the field.

The designers of C++ incorporated a software exception mechanism into the language to simplify error control. (Most object-oriented languages have a similar mechanism; we used Java exceptions in the Java applet we wrote in Chapter 17.) The basic idea is that a block of code can be *guarded* with a language statement. Each guarded block of code is associated with one or more exception handlers. If an exception is *thrown* by code within the guarded block or by any functions called by the guarded block of code, the appropriate exception handler *catches* the exception and continues processing in the context of the high-level function. You can see the advantage. You can be down any arbitrary number of nested function calls, and software can simply throw an exception to transfer control directly to an exception handler in an upper-level function. There's no need to propagate error return codes back up through all those nested function calls.

CPU exceptions are also difficult to handle by traditional methods. Because a CPU exception is an interrupt, you have to write an ISR to get control when the interrupt occurs. If your application doesn't handle the exception, an operating system ISR terminates your program with an error message.

The problem with writing ISRs to handle CPU exceptions is that you get control directly from the code that caused the exception. If the exception is in low-level code (which is usually the case), determining the best course of action is difficult. As with software errors, CPU exceptions are most easily handled by high-level code. But with CPU exceptions, you don't even have the option of passing the exception up through nested function calls to the top layer; the code that caused the exception can't continue to execute unless you first correct the cause of the exception. Therefore, application handling of exceptions is usually limited to attempting to save data and then restarting the program or terminating cleanly. Performing this process reliably is difficult, however, because it's hard to know what code is safe to execute after a CPU exception, which is indicative of a program error or corrupted data.

Win32 structured exception handling addresses this problem with a control mechanism similar to C++ software exceptions. Using special language statements (different statements from those used for C++ exceptions), programs can mark a guarded block of code with an associated CPU exception handler. When a CPU exception occurs in the guarded block of code or in any function called by the guarded code, control is passed directly to the exception handler in the context of the high-level function. The application program does not need to include an ISR. The high-level code, which can best decide how to recover from an exception, gets control directly; this allows the same exception to be handled differently by different parts of the program. For example, a low-level string copy function in a library can be used by both a database subsystem and a user-interface display subsystem. Each of those subsystems can have separate guarded blocks of code at a high level; if an exception occurs in the string copy function, control is passed to whichever subsystem is up the nested call stack. The database and user-interface subsystems can choose to handle the exception in different ways.

EXCEPTION HANDLING IN EMBEDDED SYSTEMS

By using C++ exceptions and structured exceptions, you can write cleaner code and make your embedded applications more robust. Cleaner code is possible because error-handling code can be concentrated in a few central locations rather than sprinkled throughout the application. Systems can be made more robust by passing errors directly to upper-level code where better choices can be made about how to recover from the error.

ROBUST CODE

Catching errors at a high level permits you to decide at the application level how to handle error conditions. Some errors may not need handling, while others may require only that the particular function be retried because a transient error caused the condition. For example, if a mathematics exception occurs, you may be able to ignore the error in some instances and try a different algorithm requiring less precision in other instances.

Still other errors might warrant restarting a system. Using exception handling, however, it's possible to shutdown and restart a system in response to an error without discontinuing service to a user. The capability to easily pass errors to the top-level code in a system lets you perform an orderly system reset, shutting down each subsystem in turn to allow data to be saved and possibly preserving the current subsystem state so that it can pick up where it left off when the system restarts. After each subsystem is cleanly terminated, you can restart the system and continue to provide uninterrupted service to the user.

CLEAN CODE

Using exceptions makes code cleaner because it allows you to use a more structured method of layering error recovery. Most software projects are divided into modules. With exception handling, you can specify a default error mechanism with each module. If the default error mechanism is not applicable, the module can easily pass the error to higher-level code for processing.

Without this structured method of error control, you have to sprinkle error code throughout your application. You also have to remember to check global error variables after making a call that can cause an error, or you have to combine possible error values from different functions and propagate the error upward, with the result that you need error-handling code after virtually every function call.

C++ EXCEPTION HANDLING

C++ exception handling is implemented with the `try`, `throw`, and `catch` language statements. A guarded block of code is marked with the `try` statement. Following the `try` statement, you may have one or more `catch` statements (exception handlers) that catch different exception types, where an exception type may be any valid data type, including a C++ class. If an ellipsis (...) is entered for the exception type, the `catch` statement handles any type of exception; this syntax may be used only in the last `catch` handler for the `try` block. If no exceptions are thrown during execution of the guarded section of code, no `catch` statements are executed, and execution continues at the program statement following the last `catch` statement for that `try` block.

When software detects an error condition, it signals an exception with a `throw` statement. The `throw` has the same syntax as a normal function return; its operand is an expression that evaluates to a specific data type and value. Unlike function returns, a single function can have multiple `throw` statements with expressions that can evaluate to different data types.

When an exception is thrown, the `throw` operand creates an exception object (if the object is a C++ class, the constructor function runs). The run-time library then starts unwinding the call stack, examining each `try` block it encounters to see whether a `catch` statement can handle the thrown object. If no appropriate handler is found, the unwinding continues until the outermost `try` block is found. The run-time library `terminate()` function is then called; it, in turn, calls `abort()` to kill the program. You can install a custom termination function by calling `set_terminate()`.

When a matching `catch` statement is found, program execution is resumed with the first program statement in the `catch` statement. A thrown exception is the only way to enter a `catch` statement; you can't jump into a `catch` statement with a `goto` statement, for example. When the code in the `catch` statement has run, execution continues with the statement following the last `catch` statement in the `try` block. The code in the `catch` statement can re-throw the exception to be handled by higher-level code, using a `throw` statement with no operand.

While the C++ exception-handling code is unwinding the call stack after a thrown exception, it automatically calls the destructor functions for all local objects constructed before the exception was thrown. This important feature ensures that objects are correctly deleted, no memory leaks occur, and so on.

Let's look at a simple program that uses C++ exception handling:

```
#include <iostream.h>
void GenerateException(int ExcepNum);

void main(void)
{
    cout << "Entering first try block\n";
    try
    {
        GenerateException(0);
        cout << "First try block completed\n";
    }
    catch (char *pStr)
    {
        cout << "Exception: " << pStr << "\n";
    }
    catch (int ErrorCode)
    {
        cout << "Exception: " << ErrorCode << "\n";
    }
    cout << "Entering second try block\n";
```

```
    try
    {
        GenerateException(1);
        cout << "Second try block completed\n";
    }
    catch (char *pStr)
    {
        cout << "Exception: " << pStr << "\n";
    }
    catch (int ErrorCode)
    {
        cout << "Exception: " << ErrorCode << "\n";
    }
    cout << "Exiting program\n";
}

void GenerateException(int ExcepNum)
{
    if (ExcepNum == 0)
        throw "A string exception";
    else
        throw 100;
}
```

Running this program produces the following output:

```
Entering first try block
Exception: A string exception
Entering second try block
Exception: 100
Exiting program
```

As you can see, we didn't get to the last statement of guarded code in either `try` block. Instead, the exception thrown by `GenerateException()` caused control to be passed directly to the appropriate exception handler in the `try` block (depending on the data type of the thrown object). After the exception handler ran, control continued with the next statement following the end of the `try` block.

Note: This program is so trivial that we didn't bother to create a Developer Studio project for it. If you want to run it, type the source code in an editor, calling the file FOO.CPP. You can create a Developer Studio project, but it's simpler to build and run the program under ToolSuite Lite by typing the following:

```
cl /GX /c foo.cpp
linkloc @vc.emb @strucexc.emb foo
runemb foo
```

The same program can run native under Windows. To build FOO.EXE as a Windows console application, type `cl /GX foo.cpp`. The /GX compiler switch enables C++ exception handling.

STRUCTURED EXCEPTION HANDLING

Structured exceptions are a Win32 mechanism for handling CPU exceptions in C and C++. By implementing a method for dealing with processor exceptions in C and C++, we don't have to write interrupt service routines to handle these exceptions.

STRUCTURED EXCEPTIONS IN C

Win32 structured exceptions are implemented in C using the __try and __except reserved keywords. The syntax is similar to the C++ exceptions syntax, but with two important differences. The syntax for a C structured exception __try block is

```
__try
{
    guarded-statement-block
}
__except (exception-filter)
{
    handler-statement-block
}
```

The differences are in the __except statement in the __try block. First, only one __except statement can be in a C __try block, unlike C++ exceptions, which allow multiple catch statements in a try block. Second, data types are not used to control whether an __except handler executes, as they are in the C++ catch statement. Instead, the __except statement includes an expression used as a filter; the result of evaluating the filter expression determines whether the exception handler runs.

As with C++ exceptions, the guarded block of code executes to completion unless a CPU exception occurs. If an exception occurs, the Win32 structured exception-handling code unwinds the call stack, looking for a __try block. When it finds one, it evaluates the exception filter expression, which must resolve to one of three values (defined in the Visual C++ EXCPT.H header file):

- **EXCEPTION_CONTINUE_SEARCH.** This value instructs the Win32 exception-handling code to continue unwinding the stack, looking for outer-level __try blocks.

- **EXCEPTION_CONTINUE_EXECUTION.** This value instructs the exception-handling code to ignore the exception and continue execution with the code that caused the exception. (Presumably, the exception filter expression has either determined that the exception is innocuous or taken some action to remove the source of the exception.)

- **EXCEPTION_EXECUTE_HANDLER.** The exception handler statement block is executed. Control then continues with the first program statement following the __try block.

If all exception filters evaluate to EXCEPTION_CONTINUE_SEARCH, when the exception-handling code reaches the outermost __try block, it invokes the default system exception handler, which prints an error message and terminates the program.

Let's look first at a simple example to see how structured exception handling works:

```
#define WIN32_LEAN_AND_MEAN
#include <windows.h>
#include <stdio.h>

void main(void)
{
    printf("Entering __try block\n");
    __try
    {
        int i,j=0;
        i = 1/j;
        printf("__try block completed\n");
    }
    __except((GetExceptionCode() == EXCEPTION_INT_DIVIDE_BY_ZERO) ?
            EXCEPTION_EXECUTE_HANDLER : EXCEPTION_CONTINUE_SEARCH)
    {
        printf("A divide by zero exception occurred\n");
    }
    printf("Exiting program\n");
}
```

This program produces the following output:

```
Entering __try block
A divide by zero exception occurred
Exiting program
```

The guarded block of code performs an integer divide-by-zero. Notice that the last statement (the `printf()`) in the guarded block does not execute; instead, control passes to the `__except` statement. The `GetExceptionCode()` function, which may be called only within an exception filter, returns a value identifying the exception that occurred (possible values are defined in the Visual C++ WINBASE.H header file). In this case, the exception is the one we are looking for, so we return EXCEPTION_EXECUTE_HANDLER and the handler runs and prints its error message. Execution then resumes with the statement following the `__try` block (the `printf()` that says the program is exiting).

Note: This trivial program is not included on the CD-ROM. If you want to run it, type the source code in an editor, calling the file FOO.C. You can create a Developer Studio project, but it's simpler to build and run the program under ToolSuite Lite by typing the following:

```
cl /c foo.c
linkloc @vc.emb @strucexc.emb foo
runemb foo
```

The same program can run native under Windows. To build FOO.EXE as a Windows console application, type `cl foo.c`.

Now let's look at a more elaborate example. This structured exception project is in \TSLITE\PROJECTS\STRUCEXC. To build the program from Developer Studio, open the work-space file (STRUCEXC.DSW) and click Build|Rebuild All. A prebuilt executable, STRUCEXC.EXE, is provided if you want to skip the build step. To run the program, click Build|Execute strucexc.exe from Developer Studio. Or from a DOS command prompt, set the current directory to \TSLITE\PROJECTS\STRUCEXC and type runemb release\strucexc.

The source code for the project, in the STRUCEXC.C file, is reproduced in Listing 20-1.

Listing 20-1: STRUCEXC.C

```
int main()
{
    int    Result;

    if (!IntDivide(10, 2, &Result))
        printf("Result of 10/2 is divide-by-zero exception!\n");
    else
        printf("Result of 10/2 is %d\n", Result);

    if (!IntDivide(10, 0, &Result))
        printf("Result of 10/0 is divide-by-zero exception!\n");
    else
        printf("Result of 10/0 is %d\n", Result);

    if (CauseGPFault())
        printf("CauseGPFault succeeded!\n");
    else
        printf("CauseGPFault failed!\n");

    printf("Exiting from main\n");
    return 0;
}

// Returns TRUE if success, FALSE if divide-by-zero exception occurs
BOOL IntDivide(int Dividend, int Divisor, int *Result)
{
    __try
    {
        *Result = DoDivide(Dividend, Divisor);
        return TRUE;
    }
    __except (ExceptionFilter(GetExceptionCode(),
            GetExceptionInformation()))
    {
        return FALSE;
    }
}

int DoDivide(int Dividend, int Divisor)
{
    return Dividend/Divisor;
}
//
// This routine intentionally causes a GP fault. Because it uses
```

```
// the same exception filter as IntDivide, it never returns — the
// filter lets the OS handler that kills the program run.
//
BOOL CauseGPFault()
{
    __try
    {
        char *p = NULL;
        *p = 0;
        return TRUE;
    }
    __except (ExceptionFilter(GetExceptionCode(), GetExceptionInformation()))
    {
        return FALSE;
    }
}


//
// This function analyzes the reason for an exception and returns one of
// the following values:
//    EXCEPTION_EXECUTE_HANDLER — run body of except() handler
//    EXCEPTION_CONTINUE_SEARCH — continue down chain of handlers to find
//            one that can handle it (the system handler at the end of
//            the chain kills the program)
//    EXCEPTION_CONTINUE_EXECUTION — let original code that caused the
//            exception continue to execute (because the filter fixed the
//            cause of the exception or the exception can be ignored)
//
int ExceptionFilter(ULONG ExcepCode, EXCEPTION_POINTERS *pExcepInfo)
{
    EXCEPTION_RECORD *pExcepRecord;
    CONTEXT          *pContext;

    pExcepRecord = pExcepInfo->ExceptionRecord;
    pContext = pExcepInfo->ContextRecord;

// If it's a divide by zero, let the body of the except() handler run.
    if (ExcepCode == EXCEPTION_INT_DIVIDE_BY_ZERO)
        return EXCEPTION_EXECUTE_HANDLER;

//
// For any other exception, just print out some information about
// the exception and then let the OS kill the program.
//
    printf("Got exception 0x%08X, Flags = 0x%08X, "
            "CS:EIP = %0X:%08X\n", ExcepCode,
            pExcepRecord->ExceptionFlags,
            pContext->SegCs, pContext->Eip);
    return EXCEPTION_CONTINUE_SEARCH;
}
```

Running the program produces the following output in the DOS box on the host computer:

```
Result of 10/2 is 5
Result of 10/0 is divide-by-zero exception!
Got exception 0xC0000005, Flags = 0x00000000, CS:EIP = 18:000108D6

Abnormal program termination at Mon Sep 28 17:39:29 1998
Warning RUNEMB.342220: target halted on exception 13: General protection
fault

Target state at the time of exception:
EAX=00000000   EBX=00000000   ECX=0001E8D4   EDX=00000000
ESI=00000000   EDI=00000000   EBP=00023094   ESP=00023068
DS=0020  SS=0020  ES=0020  FS=0028  GS=0020
CS:EIP=0018:000108D6   EFLAGS=00000246   Mode=Protected
GDT Base=00001C04   GDT Limit=018F   IDT Addr=00001D94   IDT Limit=07FF
Event Code=000D   Event Value=00010000

Stack Frame Dump:

Level 0: 000108D6
Level 1: 000107DA
```

The first thing this program does is call IntDivide() twice, once with good input and once with bad input (a zero divisor). The IntDivide() function calls DoDivide() from a guarded block of code to perform the division. If DoDivide() returns normally, IntDivide() returns TRUE to indicate that the division was successfully performed. If the exception handler runs, IntDivide() returns FALSE to indicate a divide-by-zero exception occurred. As expected, the output indicates that the first division succeeded and the second caused the divide-by-zero exception.

In this program, the exception filter is a call to the ExceptionFilter() function. We pass ExceptionFilter() the exception code and also a pointer to an EXCEPTION_POINTERS structure obtained by calling GetExceptionInformation(). The EXCEPTION_POINTERS structure, defined in the Visual C++ WINNT.H header file, contains pointers to an exception record and a CPU context record:

```
typedef struct _EXCEPTION_POINTERS {
    PEXCEPTION_RECORD ExceptionRecord;
    PCONTEXT ContextRecord;
} EXCEPTION_POINTERS, *PEXCEPTION_POINTERS;
```

Both the CONTEXT structure and the EXCEPTION_RECORD structure are also defined in WINNT.H. The more interesting of these two structures is the CONTEXT structure, which contains the application context at the time the exception occurred. We reproduce the CONTEXT structure next, with the lengthy comments stripped:

```
typedef struct _CONTEXT {

    DWORD ContextFlags;

    DWORD    Dr0;
    DWORD    Dr1;
    DWORD    Dr2;
    DWORD    Dr3;
    DWORD    Dr6;
    DWORD    Dr7;

    FLOATING_SAVE_AREA FloatSave;

    DWORD    SegGs;
    DWORD    SegFs;
    DWORD    SegEs;
    DWORD    SegDs;

    DWORD    Edi;
    DWORD    Esi;
    DWORD    Ebx;
    DWORD    Edx;
    DWORD    Ecx;
    DWORD    Eax;

    DWORD    Ebp;
    DWORD    Eip;
    DWORD    SegCs;
    DWORD    Eflags;
    DWORD    Esp;
    DWORD    SegSs;

} CONTEXT;
```

This structure contains the values of the CPU registers (except the system registers, which are not used by application programs) at the time the exception occurred. You can use this structure to obtain information about the program that caused the exception. (When you debug a program, the Developer Studio debugger uses this structure to display the current program location, register contents, and so on.) But you can do more than examine information from this structure: You can also change it! Based on the exception, the exception filter can change the contents of registers and then return EXCEPTION_CONTINUE_EXECUTION. The operating system structured exception code will transfer control back to the application, using the new register values. You can even change the instruction pointer and stack pointer.

ExceptionFilter() returns one of the three allowed values for an exception filter. In this case, because we are writing a filter explicitly for a divide-by-zero exception, we return EXCEPTION_EXECUTE_HANDLER if a divide-by-zero exception occurs. If any other exception occurs, we print the CS:EIP (the instruction pointer) of the instruction that caused the exception, and return EXCEPTION_CONTINUE_SEARCH to let the run-time library exception handler run (which terminates the program).

When the two calls to IntDivide() have completed, the program calls CauseGPFault(). This function causes a general protection exception by dereferencing a null pointer. The code that causes the exception is inside a guarded block of code; again, we use the ExceptionFilter() function as the exception filter expression. This time, because ExceptionFilter() is coded to recognize only a divide-by-zero exception, the filter routine prints the exception code, the exception flags, and the CS:EIP location of the instruction that caused the exception. It returns EXCEPTION_CONTINUE_SEARCH, which results in the run-time library exception handler getting control (because no outer __try blocks in the program can handle a general protection exception). The run-time library prints the register dump and stack frame dump shown in the program output, and terminates the program. Notice that CauseGPFault() never regains control and never returns, so the rest of the code in main() (which called CauseGPFault()) never executes.

STRUCTURED EXCEPTIONS IN C++

You can't mix the use of the __try and __except C structured exception keywords with the try, catch, and throw C++ exception keywords. Therefore, how can C++ programs handle CPU exceptions? Two techniques are supported under Visual C++. First, recall that the catch syntax uses an ellipsis (...) as the operand to catch any C++ exception. An ellipsis catch handler also catches structured exceptions. With this method, however, no information is provided about the type or nature of the exception.

A more useful method for catching structured exceptions in C++ programs is installing an exception translation function. To specify a translation function, you call _set_se_translator() with the name of the translation function as the argument. The translation function is invoked when a structured exception occurs and is passed an exception code and a pointer to an EXCEPTION_POINTERS structure (the same two arguments we passed to the ExceptionFilter() function in the STRUCEXC project described previously). The translation function can package whatever information is required into an application-defined object, and throw the object as a C++ exception. Because the translation function runs in the context of the function that caused the exception, the C++ exception-handling code unwinds the stack until it finds a catch handler that can accept the structured exception object. The catch handler can then process the structured exception appropriately, using the information packaged by the translation function. We use this technique in the Restartable UPS project described next.

A RESTARTABLE UPS

To demonstrate the use of C++ exceptions and structured exceptions, we took the Network-Aware UPS project from Chapter 14, recoded parts of it in C++, and added some exception-handling code. The resulting program catches all C++ exceptions and structured exceptions, prints an appropriate error message, performs an orderly shutdown of the UPS system, and then restarts the system to provide uninterrupted service to the user.

BUILDING THE RESTARTABLE UPS PROJECT

The Restartable UPS code is located in \TSLITE\PROJECTS\UPS5. To build the Restartable UPS project, open the UPS4.DSW workspace file in Microsoft Developer Studio and select Build|Rebuild All. Chapter 3, "Software Installation and Setup," contains complete details on building the project. Or if you want to skip the build step, use the prebuilt executable, UPS4.EXE, which is installed in the RELEASE subdirectory.

RUNNING THE RESTARTABLE UPS PROJECT

Before downloading and running UPS5.EXE, you must connect the target system to the host computer and configure Windows for the networking connection. The setup procedure is identical to that required for the Network-Aware UPS; refer to Chapter 14 for detailed instructions.

After you have everything correctly configured, download and execute the Restartable UPS by selecting Build|Execute ups5.exe from Developer Studio. Alternatively, from a DOS command prompt, set the current directory to \TSLITE\PROJECTS\UPS5 and type the following:

```
runemb release\ups5
```

After UPS5.EXE has been downloaded to the target system, double-click the UPS Connection icon in your Dial-Up Networking window and connect to the embedded UPS system, as described in Chapter 14.

After the connection has been established between the Windows host and the UPS system, start your favorite web browser to display the web pages from the Restartable UPS. Type http://192.168.1.2/ in the Address, Location, or URL web browser window to display the UPS home page. Click UPS Interface to display the interface page shown in Figure 20-1.

To demonstrate the capabilities introduced in this version of the UPS project, we added two buttons to the user interface. The Reset UPS button causes the UPS software to throw a C++ exception. The Cause GP Fault button instructs the UPS to dereference a null pointer, which causes a general protection exception because of the null pointer protection feature in ETS Kernel. The UPS software catches both C++ exceptions and structured exceptions, performs an orderly shutdown of the system, and then restarts the system.

Test the program and throw a C++ exception by clicking the Reset UPS button. The UPS system returns the web page in Figure 20-2 (which contains instructions on how to reconnect after the system reset) and then performs the system shutdown and restart.

The Restartable UPS project includes some diagnostic printf() statements to let you see what's happening. These messages are displayed in the DOS box on the host system as shown in Figure 20-3, using the host console I/O support in ETS Kernel.

The catch handler for C++ exceptions prints a message identifying the C++ exception that occurred; in this case, the exception was generated as a result of clicking the Reset UPS button. The system then tells you when it begins the shutdown process, when it begins the restart process, and when the restart is complete and it is ready to accept a new dial-up networking connection from the host.

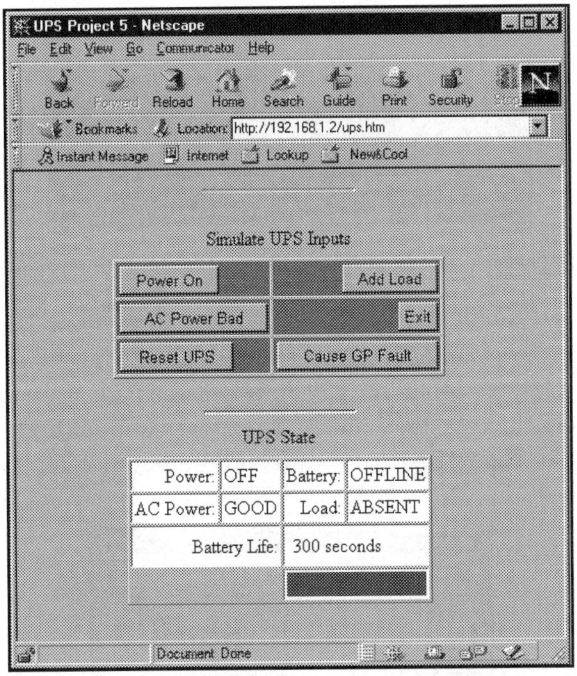

Figure 20-1: The user interface to the Restartable UPS includes two new buttons: Reset UPS and Cause GP Fault.

When the UPS system has successfully restarted, click the Reconnect button in the Reestablish Connection window shown in Figure 20-4. The Dial-Up Networking software automatically pops up this window when the UPS system shuts down and terminates the PPP connection to the host.

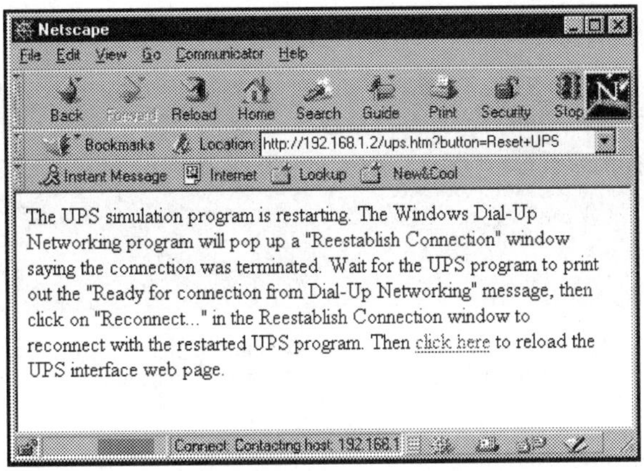

Figure 20-2: When you click the Reset UPS button, the UPS system returns a web page containing reconnect instructions.

Figure 20-3: Messages printed in the host system's DOS box let you track the restarting process in the Restartable UPS.

After the connection is reestablished, click the hyperlink (the "click here" text) on the web page shown in Figure 20-2 to display the UPS interface web page again. Now click the Cause GP Fault button to test the code that catches structured exceptions. The UPS system again returns the web page in Figure 20-2 with instructions on how to reconnect after the reset.

Figure 20-4: After the UPS restart is complete, click the Reconnect button to establish a new connection to the UPS system.

The reconnect procedure is the same as it was after a C++ exception; the cause of the reset is different, not the reset itself. The messages printed in the host DOS box, shown in Figure 20-5, identify the cause of the reset.

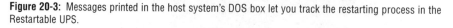

Figure 20-5: When the UPS system catches a structured exception, it prints an error message identifying the type of the exception and the address of the instruction causing the exception before it restarts the system.

A QUICK TOUR OF THE SOURCE

The UPS.C module from previous UPS projects is replaced with a C++ module, UPS.CPP, to support the C++ exception-handling mechanism. The InitializeUps() function has changed slightly; because the event subsystem is now implemented as a class, we have to create the event subsystem object during initialization:

```
//
// Create the event object and initialize the event subsystem.
//
    pUpsEvent = new CUpsEvent();
    if (pUpsEvent == 0)
    {
        printf("Error creating event object\n");
        goto CLOSE_PIPE;
    }
    if (!pUpsEvent->InitEventsys())
    {
        printf("Error initializing event subsystem\n");
        goto DELETE_EVENT;
    }
```

After creating the object, we call the InitEventsys() function to initialize the event subsystem.

The main() function, shown in Listing 20-2, is where you find the code to handle C++ exceptions and structured exceptions.

Listing 20-2: The main() function in UPS.CPP

```
void main(int argc, char **argvp)
{
//
// Initialize the system
//
INIT:
    if (!InitializeUps(argc, argvp))
        return;

//
// Process events until the user tells us to exit, or a C++ exception or
// a structured exception occurs.  For exceptions, we print an error
// message and then restart the program; a UPS should never die!
//
    _set_se_translator(SeTranslate);
    try
    {
        pUpsEvent->EventLoop();
    }
    catch(char *pMsg)
    {
        // a C++ exception the EventLoop threw
        printf("C++ exception: %s\n", pMsg);
        goto RESTART;
    }
```

```
        catch(SE_EXCEPTION se)
        {
            // a C structured exception occurred
            if (PrintException(se))
                goto RESTART;
            else
                throw;
        }
        catch(...)
        {
            printf("An unexpected C++ exception occurred.\n");
            goto RESTART;
        }

//
// User pressed Exit button.  Cleanup and exit.
//
        CleanupUps();
        return;

RESTART:
        printf("Shutting down UPS.\n");
        CleanupUps();
        printf("Restarting UPS.\n");
        goto INIT;
    }
```

After initializing the system, we call _set_se_translator() to install the SeTranslate() function to translate structured exceptions to C++ exceptions. We then enter a guarded block of code to call the event loop, the main flow of control in the program. This will allow us to catch all exceptions thrown in the main thread of the UPS program by the event loop or the functions it calls. Because this is the only try block in the program, we won't be able to catch any exceptions thrown in any of the other program threads. To catch exceptions in other threads, we'd need to add try blocks in the top-level function for each of the other threads.

Three catch handlers are in this try block. The first handler catches C++ exceptions thrown as type char *; in this relatively simple program, we just throw all C++ exceptions as error message strings. We print the string in the host DOS box, identifying it as a C++ exception, and jump down to restart the program.

The second catch handler catches exceptions of type SE_EXCEPTION, a structure defined at the top of the UPS.CPP file.

```
    //
    // Structure used to throw a C structured exception to a
    // C++ exception handler.
    //
    typedef struct {
      unsigned int ExcepCode;      // structured exception that occurred
      DWORD Eip;                   // EIP at the time of the exception
    } SE_EXCEPTION;
```

This structure is thrown by the SeTranslate() function you'll see in a moment, and it contains the exception code for the structured exception and the address of the assembly language instruction that caused the exception. The handler calls PrintException() to print an error message identifying the structured exception. If PrintException() returns TRUE, we restart the system, just as we did in the C++ exception handler. If PrintException() returns FALSE, we re-throw the structured exception to let the C run-time library handle it. The PrintException() function returns FALSE if a debug exception occurs, because debug exceptions are used only for debugging and aren't indicative of a bug in the application.

The third handler is an ellipsis catch handler, which catches any other type of exception. We don't expect any other types of exceptions because we don't throw any other types in this program. In a system like a UPS that can't be allowed to crash, however, it's best to make sure you can catch any type of exception, in case a software library you're using throws an exception you don't expect. This handler just prints a message that an unknown C++ exception occurred and then restarts the program.

To restart the UPS, we simply call CleanupUps() to shut down all subsystems cleanly, and then jump back to the start of main() to call InitializeUps() again to bring the system back up.

Let's take a look at the SeTranslate() function that translates structured exceptions to C++ exceptions:

```
//
// Translate function called by C run-time library when a
// structured exception occurs.  We re-throw the exception as
// a C++ exception.
//
void SeTranslate(unsigned int Excep, _EXCEPTION_POINTERS *pExcepInfo)
{
    SE_EXCEPTION se;

    //
    // Just pass the exception code and the EIP at the time of the
    // exception to our C++ exception handler.  Our C++ handler doesn't
    // need any of the rest of the exception context.
    //
    se.ExcepCode = Excep;
    se.Eip = pExcepInfo->ContextRecord->Eip;
    throw se;
}
```

Recall that this function runs in the context of the code that caused the structured exception. All we have to do is package the information we need for our error printout (the exception type and the instruction pointer) in an SE_EXCEPTION structure, and then throw the SE_EXCEPTION structure as a C++ exception.

Now let's look at the CleanupUps() function in UPS.CPP. This function looks similar to its predecessor in the Network-Aware UPS, but it has two important differences:

```
//
// Clean up for program exit
//
void CleanupUps(void)
{
//
// Close down subsystems.
//
    CleanupTimersys();
    CleanupWebsys();
    delete pUpsEvent;

//
// Close pipe handles and delete event queue.
//
    CloseHandle(hStatusPipeRead);
    CloseHandle(hStatusPipeWrite);
    MsgQueueDelete(hEventQueue);
    return;
}
```

Because the event subsystem is a C++ object, we shut it down by deleting the object; the class destructor takes care of any necessary cleanup.

The Restartable UPS differs from the Network-Aware UPS also in that we delete the message queue. In the Network-Aware UPS, we didn't bother to terminate the timer thread when exiting and, as a result, we couldn't delete the message queue, which was used by the timer thread. But now that we're supporting system shutdown and restart, it's no longer acceptable to be lazy about deleting objects. If we used the old code, each time the UPS was restarted we'd be leaving an orphaned timer thread and message queue behind, unnecessarily consuming system resources. So in the Restartable UPS, we exit the timer thread and delete the message queue. We won't reproduce the code that terminates the timer thread; it's in the TIMER.C file and is similar to the code used to terminate the beep thread, which we discussed in Chapter 12, "Multitasking."

Before leaving the code in UPS.CPP, note that the FatalErr() function from the Network-Aware UPS is gone. When fatal errors occur, the system throws a C++ exception rather than calling the FatalErr() function, which could only shut down the system, not restart it.

Now let's move on to the event subsystem, which is in the EVENT.CPP file. The C++ class constructor and destructor are new for the Restartable UPS:

```
//
// Constructor just sets the subsystem initialized flag to FALSE.
//
CUpsEvent::CUpsEvent(void)
{
    m_fInitialized = FALSE;
}
```

```
//
// Destructor cleans up if the initialize routine was called.
//
CUpsEvent::~CUpsEvent(void)
{
    if (m_fInitialized)
        CleanupEventsys();
}
```

The class constructor just sets a member variable to indicate that the subsystem is not yet initialized. We don't perform the subsystem initialization inside the constructor because the initialization code can report errors; a constructor can't pass any information back to the code creating the object. That's why the UpsInitialize() function calls the InitEventsys() function explicitly after creating the event subsystem object.

The class destructor does clean up the event subsystem as long as the subsystem has been initialized. We won't bother to look at the InitEventsys() and CleanupEventsys() code; it's substantially similar to the code in the Network-Aware UPS, except that the global variables have become member variables in the event subsystem class.

The event loop in Listing 20-3 is similar to the code we've seen previously, but the loop has two new events that correspond to the two new buttons on the user interface.

Listing 20-3: The EventLoop()

```
//
// Main event loop.  Just loops, waiting for events (either commands
// from the remote web browser, or timer events  generated by the timer
// subsystem) to occur and processing them. Exits when an EXIT command
// is received.
//
void CUpsEvent::EventLoop(void)
{
    UPS_EVENT NextEvent;     // next event to process
    char    ErrMsg[256];     // error message (if any)

//
// Loop, getting events and updating the system state accordingly,
// until we get an exit event.
//
    while (TRUE)
    {
//
// Read the next event from the event queue.  This call blocks until
// there is an event to read.
//
        if (MsgRead(hEventQueue, &NextEvent, TRUE) != 1)
            throw "Unexpected error while reading event queue";
```

```
        //
        // Process the event.
        //
                ErrMsg[0] = 0;
                if (NextEvent.Event >= 0 && NextEvent.Event < NEVENTS)
                    // event that can cause state change occurred
                    GetNextState(NextEvent.Event, ErrMsg);
                else
                {
                    switch(NextEvent.Event)
                    {
        case EVENT_TIMER:
                        // update globals for time passing
                        ProcessTimers(NextEvent.u.Msecs);
                        break;
        case EVENT_STATUS:
                        // nothing to do but send response
                        break;
        case EVENT_EXIT:
                        // exit program
                        return;
        case EVENT_RESET:
                        // throw the reset to the C++ exception handler
                        throw NextEvent.u.pMsg;
        case EVENT_GPFAULT:
                        // cause a GP fault, which will cause a C structured
                        // exception, which will get re-thrown by our translate
                        // function as a C++ exception.
                        {
                            char *p = NULL;
                            *p = 0;
                        }
        default:
                        printf("Invalid event code: %d\n", NextEvent.Event);
                        throw "Event subsystem got an invalid event code";
                    }
                }


        //
        // Any event except a timer event was from a command sent
        // by the web server subsystem.  Send status back to the
        // web server thread so it can create a new web page to send
        // back to the remote browser.
        //
                if (NextEvent.Event != EVENT_TIMER)
                    SendStatus(ErrMsg);
            }
        }
```

The EVENT_RESET event, generated by the web server subsystem when the Reset UPS button is clicked, causes the event loop to throw a C++ exception with an error message string as an operand. The code to process EVENT_GPFAULT dereferences a null pointer to cause a general protection exception. As you saw previously, the structured exception this generates will be translated into a C++ exception that UPS.CPP can handle. Notice that in the event loop and elsewhere in the event subsystem, fatal errors are now handled by throwing a C++ exception, rather than by calling the FatalErr() function.

You may be wondering why the web server subsystem sends these two new events to the event subsystem, instead of throwing an exception itself. The reason is that the web server subsystem executes in the context of a different thread. Although we could arrange to catch exceptions in other threads as well, interthread communication is simplified if we only throw and catch exceptions in the main thread.

Finally, the web server subsystem in WEBMEM.C has some straightforward changes to the UpsInterface() function to add the two new buttons to the user interface page, generate the text for the restart web page, and pass the two new events for the event subsystem in response to those buttons being clicked. The new code is easy to understand, so we won't reproduce it here.

SUMMARY

Judicious use of C++ exceptions in your embedded system can greatly simplify error reporting and make your code more robust and easier to maintain. Similarly, using the Win32 structured exception support to catch CPU exceptions caused by your application enables you to perform an orderly shutdown without losing data and optionally restart the system, rather than letting the system crash in response to a program bug.

We enhanced the UPS project in this chapter to catch both C++ and structured exceptions. This allowed us to automatically restart the system when a fatal error condition or a program bug occurred, instead of shutting down the system and losing power to any loads connected to the UPS. Using these techniques in your own embedded systems will substantially increase their reliability.

21

ROMing an Application

N
ow that you know how to design, develop, and debug an embedded application, it's time for the final step: putting your program into ROM. We start with a few notes about how ROM is used in embedded systems. Then, because the term *ROM* describes many different devices, we review the most common types of ROM, how they're programmed, and how they're used in typical systems. We also describe the debugging process for a program in ROM and how typical PC embedded systems start a program in ROM. Then we briefly examine the facilities in the full version of TNT Embedded ToolSuite that help you create an application that runs in ROM.

USING ROM IN EMBEDDED SYSTEMS

Although it's perfectly normal to download an application program into target system memory during development and debugging, shipping your workstation and program loader along with the target system probably isn't a good idea. Almost by definition, an embedded system is self-contained and begins running when you turn on the power.

The typical way to achieve automatic start-up is to store all system software in nonvolatile memory, such as ROM, and then automatically run that software when, or very soon after, the system power goes on. Unlike a desktop system, an embedded system doesn't require any user input to select or start the main program.

The most straightforward way to use ROM is to put the application's code in it and run the program directly from ROM. Constant data values, such as lookup tables, calibration curves, messages, and bitmaps, can also benefit from ROM storage. On a larger scale, ROM-based file systems can give rapid access to read-only programs and data through the familiar file I/O functions used to access read/write file systems.

Storing a program in ROM has two benefits. First, the system can start more quickly; because the program is already in ROM, ready to execute, you don't need to wait while the program is loaded from disk into RAM. Second, a cost savings is associated with using ROM. Memory chips are much cheaper than disk drives or other forms of nonvolatile storage (presuming you need megabytes, rather than gigabytes, of storage). Your system will cost less, consume less power, and have a smaller footprint if you don't include a disk drive. Assuming your system doesn't need a disk drive for other reasons, it makes sense to place your operating system and application in ROM so you can dispense with a disk.

ROM storage also has several limitations, the most obvious of which is that you cannot use self-modifying code. ROM devices typically have much slower access times than DRAM, a disadvantage only partially offset by instruction prefetching and caching. And ROM devices typically have only byte-wide access, versus 32-bit wide access to DRAM. Although Intel x86 processors (among others) can fetch multibyte values from a byte-wide ROM, using this convenient feature incurs a 2:1 (on systems with 16-bit buses) or 4:1 (on systems with 32-bit buses) performance slowdown when fetching multibyte values from memory. In systems where one or more of these limitations causes problems, programs are often stored in ROM and then loaded from ROM to RAM at start-up. Although this approach incurs additional cost (for RAM chips) over a system that executes directly from ROM, it retains a cost and start-up time advantage over systems that boot from disk.

Even programs that run from ROM need to use RAM as well. The program data, the stack, and the heap must be in RAM because they must be written as well as read. This need to use both ROM and RAM places additional requirements on your compiler, linker, and other development tools. First, final program addresses must be assigned at build time because the code is stored in read-only memory, where no relocation is possible. Contrast this with tools for building desktop applications, which typically have no facility for specifying program addresses because the programs are relocated at load time based on where in memory the operating system loads them. Second, the tools must be capable of separately locating code and data rather than storing them contiguously as is usual on desktop systems because the code runs from ROM and the data is stored in RAM. Third, initialized data needs to be copied from ROM to RAM at start-up time; good development tools can do this for you automatically and ideally can store the initialized data in compressed form in ROM to save space. Finally, not all data needs to go in RAM. Any read-only data, such as bitmaps, read-only tables, and read-only file systems, can be stored in ROM. Large amounts of read-only data should definitely be stored in ROM to save on costly RAM. To accomplish this, the development tools must differentiate between read-only data and variable data and allow you to locate them independently.

TYPES OF ROM

Several types of ROM are available: mask-programmed ROMs, fusible-link ROMs, EPROMs, EEPROMs, and flash memory. A key difference between the different types of ROM is how you program them; that is, how you store programs and data in read-only memory. At one extreme are mask-programmed ROMs, which receive their bit patterns during the manufacturing process. At the other end of the spectrum is flash memory, which can be programmed while the embedded system is running.

In this section, you look at each type in more detail.

MASK-PROGRAMMED AND FUSIBLE-LINK ROMS

Mask-programmed ROMs are essentially custom chips built around your program and data. The chip foundry generates a custom mask layer that creates storage circuits holding the specified bits. These ROMs are very dense because each memory cell is wired to a 1 or a 0. Mask-programmed ROMs have the same cost model as standard ICs: a large one-time cost and delay before the first chip comes off the manufacturing line, followed by a vast quantity of very inexpensive copies.

Laser-trimmed ROMs are a variation of mask-programmed ROMs but with a standard mask layer. To store bits, a laser cuts portions of the top layer of metallization. Because the laser trimming is performed on a chip with a standard mask, the one-time cost and delay for each unique part number is much less. The per-chip cost, however, is higher, because the laser trimming step is performed in the manufacturing process. The laser trimming operations occur just before the chip is packaged and bonded to the external pins.

Fusible-link ROMs move the chip production process into your office. Each bit position has an exposed part of the top-layer metallization, called a *fuse,* that can be opened by applying a specified programming current. Some variations have antifuses that close when a specified programming voltage is applied. In either case, a fusible-link ROM is usually referred to as a PROM (programmable ROM) because the bit patterns are loaded after manufacturing is complete.

> **Note:** The common phrases *burning a PROM* or *blowing a PROM* started in the early days when programming fusible-link PROMs involved at least a little bit of heat, if not fire and smoke.

It's worth noting that fusible-link ROMs have been largely supplanted by OTP (one time programmable) EPROMs, which are available at higher densities and lower costs. Current fusible-link PROMs are specialized for very high speed and rather low density, limiting them to specialized applications.

In short, mask-programmed ROMs are appropriate for thoroughly debugged programs that will be used in huge volumes. Laser-trimmed ROMs and fusible-link ROMs are appropriate for lower volume applications because it takes longer to program them and the per-chip cost is higher. All three types of ROM can be used in high-reliability applications, because high-energy radiation cannot change the stored bit patterns.

EPROMS

Ultraviolet-erasable PROMs, or EPROMs (and rarely, UVEPROMs) store each data bit as a collection of electrons on the insulated gate of a CMOS field-effect transistor (FET). EPROMs are programmed similar to fusible-link PROMs: a high programming voltage stores each bit by temporarily breaking down the insulation layer and injecting a charge into the gate. Unlike fusible-link PROMs, though, EPROMs are programmed through a quartz window in the chip package. When you see a chip with a window, it's an EPROM!

Erasing an EPROM requires 5 to 30 minutes, depending on both the device circuitry and the UV flux intensity. The UV wavelengths that supply enough energy to dissipate the stored charges are precisely the wavelengths that can severely damage eyes and skin, so you must remove the device from its socket and put it in an EPROM eraser with a light shield to protect bystanders. After erasure, all bits are a logic 1.

Because EPROMs can be erased by exposure to ultraviolet radiation, the window must be covered by an opaque label during normal operation to prevent light from disturbing the chip's circuitry. Ordinary fluorescent lights emit enough UV radiation to slowly erase the bits, and high-intensity desk lights can inject a charge into other parts of the circuitry.

Typically, the chips are removed from the circuit for both erasure and programming, but they can be programmed in circuit if the system hardware provides the requisite programming voltages and circuitry. You can erase and reprogram EPROMs several thousand times, with the upper limit set by chip design, total UV exposure, and programming technique. Data storage is typically assured for ten years, although many manufacturers grant this assurance only if you use approved device programmers (machines that store programs and data in read-only memory) and no other.

The term OTP EPROMs, mentioned previously, is an oxymoron because they are not erasable. OTP EPROMs are UV-erasable EPROMS but in an opaque package. Lacking a quartz window, you cannot erase these parts! The main motivation for using an OTP EPROM is that they cost less. OTP EPROMs use plastic packaging similar to that used for conventional chips, rather than specialized plastic or ceramic packages with quartz windows. Therefore, you can use the same chip technology in a final system as in the prototypes, which can be critical for high-reliability systems that must use only approved parts.

EPROMs are currently the most common type of PROM, although flash memory is gaining fast.

EEPROMs

The EEPROM (electrically erasable PROM) takes EPROM technology one step further by erasing and writing to the storage cells with an electric field rather than UV radiation. Current chips include on-chip voltage generators to erase and write to the cells. They also implement a programming algorithm in hardware to handle all internal details and present a status bit that indicates when the programming cycle is complete. As a result of all the steps implemented in hardware, EEPROM chips are similar to static RAM chips, except they have agonizingly slow write times of about 10 ms (that's milliseconds, not micro- or nanoseconds).

An EEPROM's data retention is typically ten years and, because the programming hardware is on-chip, you need not worry about using an approved programmer. EEPROMs can be reprogrammed tens of thousands of times versus thousands of times for EPROMs.

EEPROMs allow in-circuit erasing and programming at the byte level and, therefore, are the most flexible type of ROM and the most expensive. The length of time it takes to program EEPROMs makes them best suited for applications that store small amounts of data during a protracted interval. The ease with which EEPROMs can be erased makes them ill-suited for applications that must maintain critical data. A program crash that writes random patterns throughout the CPU's memory address space can instantly destroy months of painstaking and irreplaceable data collection. We'll discuss the hazards of in-circuit programmability later; for now, be careful!

FLASH MEMORY

Flash memory is a compromise between EPROM and EEPROM. Like an EEPROM, flash memory is erased electrically but in large blocks rather than byte by byte. Some devices allow you to erase their entire contents; others permit erasing independent blocks of 512 bytes or more.

Flash write times are faster than EEPROM write times because a whole block of data can be programmed in the time it takes to program a single byte in an EEPROM. Flash chips include a buffer that stores an entire data block and hardware that transfers it to nonvolatile storage cells. You must write an entire block, however, before storing data in another block: Flash memory is not well suited for random write-addressing patterns.

Because flash memory does not require a quartz window and need not be removed from the circuit board for programming or erasure, it uses ordinary plastic packages and comes in a variety of sizes ranging from standard DIPs to surface mount packages.

Flash memories allow typically 10,000 to 100,000 erase and programming cycles, with some devices specified for 1,000,000 cycles. Data retention is usually more than ten years but is also affected by the number of programming cycles.

As we noted in Chapter 7, "File Systems," many chip manufacturers are devoting extensive development efforts to their flash memory lines, resulting in high (and increasing) data density, improved cost effectiveness, and greater flexibility. For example, Intel's flash memory chips store 64Mbits using their StrataFlash technology, which doubles storage densities. For many embedded applications, flash memory is hard to beat.

PROGRAMMING PROMS

Mask-programmed and laser-trimmed ROMs arrive with your program and data already in place. All other types of PROMs begin life with all their bits erased, so you must program, or burn, your bits into them using a programmer. A *programmer,* or *device programmer,* is a machine that stores, or programs, bits into a nominally read-only memory chip, not a person who creates the bit patterns in the first place. To somewhat reduce the confusion, we will use the word software, rather than program, when referring to an application. This is an area where operator overloading has gone mad!

DEVICE PROGRAMMERS

Device programmers are available in two types: PROM programmers and Universal programmers. Both are used to burn software into PROMs, EPROMs, and flash memories, but Universal programmers can burn software also into programmable logic devices (PLDs) such as programmable logic arrays (PALs) and field-programmable gate arrays (FPGAs). PROM programmers are generally less expensive than Universal programmers but obviously not as flexible. Prices range from a few hundred dollars for the former to many thousands of dollars for the latter; you may find that you start with an inexpensive PROM programmer and later add a fancy Universal programmer to your collection.

Although most device programmers download their data from a PC or similar host system to a target PROM, some have a standalone mode. Standalone programmers are handy in the field because they can read, verify, edit, and reprogram memory devices without host system support. You operate standalone programmers using a small front panel display. Many standalone programmers store data in nonvolatile memory, which is particularly useful when you want to create several PROMs holding the same data.

Device programmer vendors are constantly playing catch-up with chip manufacturers. Although new PROMs have different capacities, come in different packages, and require different programming algorithms, they are useless without a device programmer to fill them with bits. However, usually only a few certified device programmers are capable of handling a new type of PROM when it is introduced. Worse, PROM manufacturers do not guarantee the reliability of their devices if they are burned in a nonapproved programmer.

Two useful metrics you can use to evaluate a device programmer are whether the vendor supports new devices quickly and how much it costs to get the programmer updated to the latest capabilities. Device programmer vendors typically publish a list of devices they can program, and many make algorithm updates available on their Web sites, ready to download into their programmers.

INPUT FILES FOR DEVICE PROGRAMMERS

The first requirement for burning a PROM is that the device programmer must be able to handle the file format produced by the linker or locator software. The most common file formats for PROM devices are Motorola HEX and Intel HEX; PLDs tend to use JEDEC format. These human-readable files contain location information and data, along with checksums and other error-detection mechanisms. If all else fails, most device programmers can also read binary image files, the raw binary bits that will fill the PROM.

The second requirement for burning a PROM is a method for mapping the file produced by the linker or locator to the physical memory device. The software producing the data files writes a logical image without concern for whether it fits into one or more PROM devices. How the data files map to the physical devices depends on the embedded system's hardware design. Most device programmers know how to deal with several standard layouts, and it behooves you to take one of those approaches in your system.

For simple microcontroller systems with a 1-byte data bus, a small program, and a single PROM, the device programmer simply burns each byte of the file into the corresponding byte of the PROM.

Slightly more ambitious microcontroller systems may have a program that requires two or more PROMs. The usual hardware addressing arrangement in this case locates the second PROM just after the first one. Knowing that, the device programmer reads the file and, if it requires more than one PROM, distributes the data accordingly. For example, if the file requires two PROMs, the device programmer stores the data in the lower addresses in the first PROM and the data in the higher addresses in the second PROM. Because the device programmer can detect that more than one PROM is required for the data, and distribute the data across multiple PROMs, including more than one PROM in a system is easy. This capability also means that if you're burning chips for many systems, you may find it faster and easier to program all chips in the first set and then all in the second set, rather than program the first chip of each set, then the next chip in each set, and so on.

More complex embedded systems with separate CPUs use a different hardware mapping design called *byte interleaving,* or *splitting,* that maps a 16- or 32-bit data bus onto 8-bit PROMs. In effect, each PROM supplies one bus byte: a 16-bit system has two PROMs and a 32-bit system has four. The device programmer reads the data file provided and splits the data for the separate PROMs. You can also combine 16-bit and 32-bit mappings in a split system with multiple sets.

When handling programmed memory devices, you must carefully keep track of which PROM goes in which socket. For example, a 32-bit system with two sets of single-byte PROMs requires eight PROMs. For a functional system, you must insert the chips in only 1 of 8! (8 factorial = 40,320) possible ways.

Most device programmers can compute a checksum for each PROM based on the data it contains, and some can automatically insert that checksum at a specified address in the device. It's a good idea to write the checksum on the PROM's label. This provides both a good check that you've performed the job and aids in identifying PROMs in the field.

In-Circuit Programmers

Before, burning ROMs using a device programmer was the only way to do the job, but no longer. You can now burn certain ROMs such as flash and EEPROM using an in-circuit programmer. Furthermore, non-socketed flash and EEPROM chips must use in-circuit programming because they are not removable.

Two types of in-circuit programmers are available. The simplest is an adapter that connects the target system's PROMs to a device programmer that loads the data from a PC or similar host system; the target system's CPU remains inert during the entire process. A more complex variation allows the target CPU to control the device programmer and the burning-in of data received from a host system.

The latter approach has a chicken-and-egg paradox: Where does the target CPU find the program that tells it how to burn a program into its memory? The usual solution is a small boot PROM that contains just enough code to load and burn the final application. When the boot PROM itself needs to be reprogrammed, it can be either removed from a socket and programmed in a programmer, or programmed through an adapter. Some larger flash memory devices include an independently programmed boot block that serves the same purpose as a separate boot PROM, without requiring another memory chip or device on the board.

If a system can program its own PROMs, it can also accidentally erase or overwrite those PROMs. Many EEPROMs and flash memory devices use locking mechanisms to help prevent such accidents. When the device is locked, writing to the device has no effect — unless the CPU unlocks the device by writing a particular sequence of data to certain memory addresses. When the CPU unlocks the memory device, it may be erased or programmed. The chip documentation describes the procedure and usually includes sample code to help you get started.

After the memory is unlocked, programming is generally a matter of writing the new data block to the appropriate memory locations and instructing the device (by issuing a block programming instruction or whatever the device requires) to program the data. Because flash and EEPROM programming takes such a long time compared to reading, the programming software must poll the memory to determine when the programming is complete. Unfortunately, each PROM manufacturer uses proprietary protocols to indicate the beginning and end of programming mode, so you must consult the documentation again.

When device programming is complete, be sure to disable programming mode. This is generally accomplished by writing yet another sequence of data to certain memory addresses.

In-the-Field Software Updates

Before flash memory and EEPROMs, updating software in the field usually meant sending to the customer's site a field engineer, who opened the box and installed new PROMs. Some customers could install the PROMs themselves or even burn and install new PROMs from data files sent by mail. Lacking those choices, the only alternative was returning the unit for the update.

Using in-circuit programmable memory devices, it is now possible to update software in ROM without opening the box, either at the end of the production line or at the customer's site. Some issues with this approach, however, bear closer examination.

First, is in-circuit programmability a benefit? You know it's convenient. New PROM data can arrive on a floppy disk or through a parallel port, a serial port, or network connection. If the network connects to the Internet, authorized persons can update the program from a remote location. Still, in-circuit programmability is not without its challenges. A system that can update its own PROMs can also scribble random bits into the PROMs due to a software bug or a hardware glitch. (However, accidental overwrites can be avoided by selecting PROMs with memory-locking devices, and being careful to ensure that software sets the lock after each programming operation.) It is also harder to keep track of which software version is in control of the system — the EPROM chips no longer have labels.

Remember, too, that flash memory and EEPROM devices can't be read while they're being programmed, which means the CPU cannot execute the code to program a PROM from one section of a PROM while programming another section of a PROM. The code to program a PROM must run from RAM or a separate PROM device. This can pose a challenge in small systems without much RAM. It's not as likely to be an issue in larger embedded systems with separate boot PROMs or CPUs that can hold the key part of the device programming routine in RAM or a code cache, respectively, while the flash memory or EEPROM is unavailable. (Intel has recently introduced flash devices that allow reading during programming, but the majority of available devices do not support this.)

In addition, you must provide a recovery routine to handle any programming failures that may occur and leave the system with invalid or partial data in a PROM. Checksums or CRC values provide a way to detect data errors; a few device programmers can write such values into specified addresses of each memory device. If the embedded system has sufficient storage to hold the previous version of the application while programming the PROMs with a new version, the recovery routine can resume operation with the old code: an older version of the system is preferable to a boat anchor.

DEBUGGING PROGRAMS IN ROM

Although your program should be completely debugged before you commit it to ROM, you may find one last error after you screw the lid down on what you think is the final version. In other words, you'll probably have to do some debugging of the program running from ROM. In this section, we describe some common options for debugging programs in ROM.

First, you can't simply insert a breakpoint instruction to halt execution and regain control of the program at a specific point. Some processors, notably the Intel x86 CPUs (from the 386 onward), include debugging hardware that compares the current instruction address to the contents of a register; when the CPU attempts to fetch an instruction from that address, the hardware invokes a software debugger. The x86 hardware can also invoke a debugger on data reads from and writes to specific addresses, and (for Pentium and higher processors) on I/O accesses to specific ports. Make sure your debugging solution is capable of using hardware support for debugging in ROM.

If you are accustomed to debugging with the full source code displayed and display-by-name access to each variable, remember that the system's ROMs contain none of that information. You must store the symbol table for a particular set of ROMs on a separate system and use a debugger that can access that information while debugging the program in ROM. Worse, if your application (or its start-up routine) copies data from ROM to RAM, the debugger must be capable of using the actual addresses at the time of execution.

An in-circuit emulator may be the most effective way to debug a program in ROM because it replaces the CPU with a probe that gives you complete access to and control of the entire system. As we described in Chapter 4, "Debugging," using an ICE, you can set breakpoints at any memory or I/O address, trace real-time execution through a routine, and examine all variables and ports. Unfortunately, ICE hardware is expensive, generally limited to a single CPU family, and tends to lag behind leading-edge CPU capabilities.

If all else fails, you can use the traditional crash-and-burn technique: after a crash, you insert a few debug statements into the failing program, burn a new set of PROMs, and try again. Getting status information from the system may be difficult, but even a few spare I/O pins or an LED can work wonders when you don't have (or can't use) a display. Replacing the PROMs with either a ROM emulator or nonvolatile RAM greatly reduces the lengthy erase-and-burn part of the cycle. A ROM emulator is a small hardware gadget containing a block of RAM that you plug into the target's ROM socket. The emulator makes the RAM appear as ROM on the target system, but a host system can easily download new versions of the program over a serial or parallel cable. Nonvolatile RAM is essentially a battery-powered RAM package that you can carry from one system to another; it resembles an EPROM in footprint, an EEPROM in convenience, and a RAM in writing speed. We've debugged many ROMed systems in the field with no other support available.

A debugger running on the host can write programs and data into the ROM emulator or nonvolatile RAM, set breakpoints, and (for most ROM emulators) reset and restart the target system through the cable connecting the host to the ROM emulator. The target system can't change the contents of what it sees as ROM, so the program and debugging kernel are protected from inadvertent damage. Some ROM emulators allow the target to communicate with the host by accessing specific memory addresses.

After you have used crash-and-burn debugging, you will begin to appreciate the virtues of higher-powered technology. Being able to use the simplest techniques, however, gives you a considerable edge when that ICE isn't available!

PC BOOT METHODS

Now that you have seen how to get a program into ROM and get it working, you can examine the mechanisms that start the program when you turn the system on or after a system reset. Because it's not feasible to describe all the embedded processors and platforms on the market, we use the PC architecture as an illustration of the boot techniques you'll find on other systems.

The processor begins execution at a fixed location in memory after a power-up or reset; the address depends on the CPU. Code in ROM at that location performs fundamental hardware initializations (for example, enabling the system's RAM) before invoking a higher-level routine to set up the rest of the system. In a standard PC-compatible system, this code is the BIOS (basic input/output system). It has some well-defined hooks that can invoke external programs to perform additional setup at various points of the process. When the BIOS completes its hardware initialization, it attempts to load a boot program first from the floppy disk and then from the hard disk; the boot program then loads the operating system into RAM.

When you build an embedded PC, you have three choices for initializing the hardware and software in your system: a boot jump ROM, a BIOS extension boot, and a ROM-based file system boot. In addition to these options, you could build a dedicated desktop system that uses a standard PC operating system such as MS-DOS or Windows and write your application as a DOS or Windows program. This last method is the easiest and quickest to implement but can't provide real-time capabilities and also results in the most costly system to manufacture because you must purchase a DOS or Windows license and your system must include enough hardware for the needs of the operating system. Therefore, let's look at the first three choices.

BOOT JUMP ROM

A boot jump ROM is ROM mapped to the starting instruction address for the CPU. It contains the first software to execute, so it must initialize the system from the ground up. Intel x86 CPUs begin execution at an address 16 bytes below the top of the memory address space.

Because PC-compatible systems locate the BIOS ROM just below 1MB in the memory address space, for backward compatibility with the original IBM PC, standard PC system boards map hardware addresses such that a single 64K ROM responds to addresses in the 64K regions just below 1MB and just below the top of memory.

Typically, the boot jump ROM initialization begins by putting the CPU in an acceptable state: setting up the memory management unit, mapping RAM and ROM addresses, and defining hardware protection levels. The routine next identifies and initializes the system board's support chipset, which may include PCI bus setup, and then probes for peripherals on the system board. Those peripherals include video display interfaces, the keyboard and mouse interfaces, sound boards, SCSI controllers, and any other hardware that will be used by the system. After the system hardware is initialized, the boot code either loads the operating system and application code into RAM from a nonvolatile storage device, or jumps to the entry point in ROM for the operating system and application code.

Writing your own boot jump code minimizes your system costs because you don't have to license start-up software. But it can be extremely difficult code to write and debug. It's difficult to write because PC motherboard chipsets have no standardized interface, and new versions with different interfaces are released every few months. This means finding and adapting existing code is difficult; you usually have to write the boot jump code from scratch — which is why few companies specialize in writing BIOSs for PCs. Boot jump code is difficult to debug because it's the first code to run and you have no debug software available on the target system. You either have to use an ICE or the crash-and-burn technique we described previously.

For the x86 embedded processors, such as the Intel 386EX and the National NS486, the peripherals and chipset logic are included in the main CPU. This makes writing initialization code easier because the interface is standardized and reasonably well documented. In addition, most real-time operating systems, such as ETS Kernel, include working initialization code for those processors, so you can start with that and adapt it to suit your needs.

BIOS EXTENSION BOOT

If you're building a standard PC-compatible motherboard or purchasing off-the-shelf boards such as PC/104 boards, you'll most likely opt to use a standard PC BIOS. After the PC BIOS initializes most of the system's hardware, it scans the PC's memory address space for BIOS extensions. If you define part of your program as a BIOS extension, it can take control during this scan, perform whatever setup your code requires, and then return control to complete the rest of the standard BIOS initialization.

Code implementing a PC BIOS extension begins at any 2K address boundary between 0xC0000 and 0xDF800, inclusive, or at address 0xE0000. The first 2 bytes of an extension are 0x55 and 0xAA, and the third byte indicates the number of 512-byte blocks the BIOS extension software occupies. All bytes in the extension, starting with the fourth byte, must add up to 0x00, so you must compute and include a checksum byte somewhere in your code and data.

When the BIOS finds a valid extension, it executes a far CALL to the fourth byte of the extension; the first instruction of your code must be the next byte after the extension's length byte. When your routine is finished, it returns control to the BIOS through a far RET instruction.

After the BIOS completes the system initialization, it executes an INT 19h (in real mode) to boot from drive C: or A:. Your BIOS extension can capture the INT 19h vector, regain control of a functional system, and decide whether to allow a normal disk boot. Your code can run a program from ROM, boot from a network, or do whatever needs doing.

In particular, you can require a user password to boot from an external disk. This provides a straightforward way to prevent casual booting from random floppies while allowing system PROM updates using standard hardware.

Booting from a BIOS extension requires a BIOS license for each system, which adds to the cost of the system. The BIOS software is tailored to a specific board, however, and initializes all the hardware found on this board and used in a standard PC. This can be vitally important if your system includes a PCI bus: The BIOS handles the probing of all PCI bus resources, reads the Plug-and-Play configuration data, and configures the system in a well-tested, standard way. This alone may justify paying the BIOS licensing fee.

ROM-based File System Boot

From the programmer's perspective, booting from a read-only file system in ROM is the simplest way to boot a standard PC. A solid-state disk (SSD) driver, typically installed as a BIOS extension, simulates a PC-DOS file system in a block of ROM. When the BIOS executes INT 19h, the SSD driver loads the operating system directly from ROM. In other words, this is a specific instance of a BIOS extension boot, but you have even less code to write because the board vendor provides the SSD driver.

Because the SSD gets control as part of the normal BIOS boot sequence, all of the usual initializations are complete and no special handling is required. The SSD driver is a standard software component — sometimes delivered on an ISA or a PC/104 board with all the ROM it uses — and plugs directly into a standard system.

An SSD is typically implemented with flash memory and sometimes includes write protection to prevent inadvertent damage to the boot program areas. The simplest method of initializing the SSD ROM is to boot from a floppy and copy the files using the DOS COPY command, although you can use many other ROM programming methods described previously.

After you set up a system, you can duplicate it by pulling the memory chips (if the flash memory is removable), reading their contents in a device programmer, burning copies directly into blank chips, and putting the copies in new systems. This eliminates the gymnastics of booting and copying files on each target system.

One disadvantage of booting from an SSD is that it requires at least slightly more flash memory for a given program size than direct booting because the DOS file system uses FAT and directory entries in addition to your program and data. Booting from an SSD is also marginally slower because the BIOS must scan for and initialize all system hardware before booting. And, of course, you must buy and install the SSD hardware and drivers.

However, using an SSD enables you to concentrate on the unique part of your system and leave the details to the drivers. This may improve your time to market enough to justify the additional expenses.

TOOLSUITE SUPPORT FOR ROM

The ToolSuite Lite edition on the CD-ROM accompanying this book can't place applications in ROM. The full TNT Embedded ToolSuite product, however, includes extensive ROM support for many of the variations discussed in this chapter.

The ToolSuite linker can separate the various segments of an application program, place them at specific ROM and RAM addresses, and create ROM images for systems using multiple ROMs. All popular PROM programmer file formats are supported. The linker can create a compressed copy of initialized data in ROM, and a supplied start-up routine automatically uncompresses and copies the initialized data from ROM to RAM at system start-up. When creating ROM output files, the linker can also create separate symbol files for use by debuggers when debugging the application in ROM.

All the PC boot methods described previously are supported in ToolSuite. The product includes initialization code for the Intel 386EX and National NS486 embedded processors. Also included is built-in support for several boards based on those processors, including the Forth-Systeme Modul 386EX, the Intel/Radisys 386EX Explorer Board, and the National Semiconductor NS486SXF Evaluation Board. ToolSuite includes support for several popular PC/104 system boards with special features, such as solid-state disks or special download capabilities.

The Microsoft and Inprise (formerly Borland) debuggers supported by ToolSuite can be used normally to debug applications in ROM; breakpoints and watchpoints are set automatically using the hardware debug registers on the x86 chips. ToolSuite has integrated source-level debugging support for the software debuggers used with three popular ICEs: the Applied Microsystems CodeTAP-386EX, the Microtek PowerPack 386EX Emulator, and the Microtek PowerPack NS486 Emulator. ToolSuite also works with ROM emulators and includes built-in support for the virtual serial port feature in the Grammar Engine PromICE ROM emulator, which enables you to download and debug applications, without the need for a parallel or a serial debug port on the target system.

SUMMARY

The majority of embedded systems place at least part of their software in ROM in the final system. This chapter showed you the uses for ROM in embedded systems, outlined the types of ROM available, and described how to go about the process of burning your software into ROM. We also described debugging techniques to use with applications in ROM. Finally, we cited different options available to boot, or start up, a system from ROM, using the PC platform as a specific illustration.

A Hardware Resource Guide

Many companies sell SBCs, in-circuit emulators, and ROM emulators compatible with 32-bit PC architecture. We list here some that we're familiar with and some that we discovered while researching this book. You can find additional companies that sell hardware and software products for embedded development on the following web sites: Real-time Gazette Online at `http://www.realtime-magazine.com`, EG3 at `http://www.eg3.com`, and Tech On-line at `http://www.techonline.com`.

SINGLE-BOARD COMPUTERS

AAEON Electronics, Inc.

x86-based SBCs
3 Crown Plaza
Hazlet, NJ 07730
732-203-9300
http://www.aaeon.com

Adaptive Systems, Inc.

Business-card-size, modular embedded computers for handheld x86 products
6315 Monarch Park Place, Suite B
Longmont, CO 80503
303-247-2327
http://www.adaptivesystems.com

Adastra Systems Corporation

SBCs using 486 and Pentium processors
3988 Trust Way
Hayward, CA 94545
510-732-6900
http://www.adastra.com

Advantech Co., Ltd

SBCs with processors ranging from 386 to Pentium
1260 Memorex Drive
Santa Clara, CA 95050
408-982-1715
http://www.advantech.com/epc

Ampro Computers, Inc.

PC-compatible SBCs and expansion modules
4757 Hellyer Avenue
San Jose, CA 95138
408-360-0200
http://www.ampro.com

Analog & Digital Peripherals, Inc.

All-on-One embedded PC
P.O. Box 499
Troy, OH 45373
937-339-2241
http://www.adpi.com

Arcom Control Systems

SBCs
13510 South Oak Street
Kansas City, MO 64145
816-941-7025
http://www.arcomcontrols.com

Arise Industrial Computer, Inc.

SBCs and expansion peripherals
453 Ravendale, Drive, #F
Mountain View, CA 94043
650-428-0868
http://www.arisecomputer.com

Axiom Technology, Inc.

SBCs, various Intel processors and peripherals
16801 E. Gale Avenue, Unit D
City of Industry, CA 91745
626-934-1199
http://www.axiomtek.com

Cell Computing, Inc.

Small form factor embedded computing solutions
2099 Gateway Place, Suite 750
San Jose, CA 95110-1017
408-967-8800
http://www.cellcomputing.com

Densitron International PLC

Industrial SBCs
10430-2 Pioneer Boulevard
Santa Fe Springs, CA 90670
562-941-5000
http://www.densitron.com

EMAC, Inc.

SBCs; PC-104 systems; 386, 486 and Pentium processors
11 Emac Way
Carbondale, IL 62901
618-529-4525
http://www.emacinc.com

Embedtec Corporation

Embedded PCs and SBCs supporting a wide variety of bus architectures
20045 Stevens Creek Boulevard
Cupertino, CA 95014
408-253-0250
http://www.embedtec.com

Forth-Systeme GmbH

2.1" x 3.2" small-sized CPU module with up to 4MB SRAM
P.O. Box 1103
D-79200 Breisach, Germany
+ 49 (0) 7667-908-0

General Micro Systems, Inc.

Embedded computers using a variety of processors
P.O. Box 3689
8358 Maple Place
Rancho Cucamonga, CA 91730
909-980-4863
http://www.gms4vme.com

Industrial CPU Systems, Inc.

Industrial SBCs
111-D W. Dyer Road
Santa Ana, CA 92707
714-957-2815
http://www.icpu.com

INSIDE Technology USA, Inc.

PC-compatible SBCs for embedded control and industrial applications
8 Prestige Circle, Suite 116
Allen, TX 75002
972-390-8593
http://www.inside-usa.com

JK Microsystems, Inc.

Single-board PCs for embedded DOS applications
1902 East 8th Street
Davis, CA 95616
510-236-1151
http://www.jkmicro.com

Megatel Computer Corporation

Embedded PCs
125 Wendall Avenue
Weston, Ontario
M9N 3K9 Canada
416-245-2953
http://www.megatel.ca

Micro Industries Corporation

16- and 32-bit PC-compatible embedded computers
8399 Green Meadows Drive North
Westerville, OH 43081-9486
740-548-7878
http://www.microindustries.com

Microbus, Inc.

x86 SBCs
10849 Kinghurst, Suite 105
Houston, TX 77099
281-568-4744
http://www.microbus.com

Micro/sys

Embedded PCs
3447 Ocean View Boulevard
Glendale, CA 91208
818-244-4600
http://www.embeddedsys.com

New Micros, Inc.

Embedded SBCs for a variety of processors
1601 Chalk Hill Road
Dallas, TX 75212
214-339-2204
http://www.newmicros.com

Octagon Systems Corporation

Industrial embedded PCs
6510 West 91st Avenue
Westminster, CO 80030-2915
303-430-1500
http://www.octa.com

or Industrial Computers, Inc.

SBCs and industrial computer solutions
11150 Main Street, Suite 100
Fairfax, VA 22030
800-361-0441
http://www.or-computers.com

RadiSys Corporation

Embedded PCs
5445 NE Dawson Creek Drive
Hillsboro, OR 97124
503-615-1100
http://www.radisys.com

Real Time Devices, Inc.

*Compact solutions for data acquisition
and embedded control*
200 Innovation Boulevard
P.O. Box 906
State College, PA 16804
814-234-8087
http://www.rtdusa.com

R.L.C. Enterprises, Inc.

*386EX single-board computers with a
variety of on-board peripherals*
5425 El Camino Real
Atascadero, CA 93422
805-466-9717
http://www.RLC.com

S-MOS Systems

*CARDIO credit-card-sized embeddable
x86 computers*
150 River Oaks Parkway
San Jose, CA 95134
408-922-0200
http://www.smos.com

Teknor Industrial Computers, Inc.

*High-end Compact PCI, PICMG,
PCI/ISA, and PC/104 computers*
7900 Glade Road, Suite 100
Boca Raton, FL 33434
561-883-6191
http://www.teknor.com

Texas Micro, Inc.

SBCs using 486 and Pentium II processors
5959 Corporate Drive
Houston, TX 77036
713-541-8200
http://www.texasmicro.com

VersaLogic Corporation

*Industrial computers for embedded and
industrial control applications*
3888 Stewart Road
Eugene, OR 97402
800-824-3163
http://www.versalogic.com

Vesta Technology, Inc.

*SBC engines with a variety of on-board
peripherals*
11465 I-70 Frontage Road North
Wheat Ridge, CO 80033
303-422-8088
http://www.sbc2000.com

WinSystems, Inc.

*Embedded PCs for use in industrial
applications*
715 Stadium Drive
Arlington, TX 76011
817-274-7553
http://www.winsystems.com

ZF MicroSystems, Inc.

IBM-compatible SBC for embedded control
1052 Elwell Court
Palo Alto, CA 94303
650-965-3800
http://www.zfmicro.com

Ziatech Corporation

CompactPCI and STD-32 industrial computers
1050 Southwood Drive
San Luis Obispo, CA 93401
805-541-0488
http://www.ziatech.com

HARDWARE DEBUGGING TOOLS

American Arium

In-circuit emulators for Pentium processors
14281 Chambers Road
Tustin, CA 92780
714-731-1661
http://www.arium.com

EmuTec, Inc.

In-circuit emulators
Everett Mutual Tower, Suite 901
P.O. Box 3035
Everett, WA 98203
425-267-9604
http://www.emutec.com

Grammar Engine, Inc.

ROM emulators
921 Eastwind Drive, Suite 122
Westerville OH 43801
614-899-7878
http://www.gei.com

Microtek International

In-circuit emulators for many Intel processors (and others)
3305 NW Aloclek Drive
Hillsboro, OR 97124
503-645-7333
http://www.microtekintl.com

Nohau Corporation

In-circuit emulators for a variety of processors
51 East Campbell Avenue
Campbell, CA 95008-2053
408-866-1820
http://www.nohau.com

Softaid

In-circuit emulators for 80186, 386EX, 8088, and others
8310 Guilford Road
Columbia, MD 21046
410-290-7760
http://www.softaid.com

Tech Tools

ROM, EPROM, and flash emulators
P.O. Box 462101
Garland, TX 75046-2101
972-272-9392
http://www.tech-tools.com

B

APIs

ETS Kernel APIs are comprised of three categories of APIs: Win32, WinSock, and kernel APIs. In particular, ETS Kernel includes support for a subset of the Win32 console APIs defined by Microsoft Windows; support for the Berkeley subset of the WinSock 1.1. API; and support for kernel APIs that provide access to kernel functionality not available through the Win32 API. (You can think of the kernel APIs as extensions to the Win32 API that provide additional real-time capabilities and low-level access to hardware and the operating system.) In addition, because the C run-time library in Microsoft Visual C++ is implemented on top of the Win32 API, virtually all the routines in the library are supported. In this appendix, we list the supported functions in each category, starting with those in the C run-time library.

Due to space limitations, we don't provide complete documentation on the APIs in this appendix. The \TSLITE\DOCS\APIS.DOC file included on the CD-ROM has complete documentation on the kernel and WinSock APIs. The online help files included with Microsoft Visual C++ have complete documentation on the C run-time library routines and the Win32 APIs.

C RUN-TIME LIBRARY ROUTINES

Table B-1 lists the C run-time library routines supported for the Microsoft Visual C++ compiler. The commercial version of TNT Embedded ToolSuite supports a similar list of routines for the Inprise (formerly Borland) C++ compiler.

Table B-1: Supported C Run-Time Library Routines

abort	_cprintf	fopen
abs	_cputs	_fpclass
_access	_creat	_fpieee_flt
acos	_cscanf	_fpreset
_alloca	ctime	fprintf
asctime	difftime	fputc
asin	_disable	_fputchar
assert	div	fputs
atan	_dup	fread
atan2	_dup2	free
atexit	_ecvt	freopen
atof	_enable	frexp
atoi	_endthread	fscanf
atol	_endthreadex	fseek
_beginthread	_eof	fsetpos
_beginthreadex	_exit	_fsopen
bsearch	exp	_fstat
_cabs	_expand	ftell
calloc	fabs	_ftime
ceil	fclose	_fullpath
_cexit	_fcloseall	_futime
_c_exit	_fcvt	fwrite
_cgets	_fdopen	_gcvt
_chdir	feof	getc
_chdrive	ferror	_getch
_chgsign	fflush	getchar
_chmod	fgetc	_getche
_chsize	_fgetchar	_getcwd
_clear87	fgetpos	_getdcwd
clearerr	fgets	_getdrive
_clearfp	_filelength	_getdrives
clock	_fileno	getenv
_close	_findclose	_get_osfhandle
_commit	_findfirst	_getpid
_control87	_findnext	gets
_controlfp	_finite	_getw
_copysign	floor	gmtime
cos	_flushall	_heapchk
cosh	fmod	_heapwalk

continues

Table B-1: Supported C Run-Time Library Routines (*continued*)

_hypot	_ltoa	remove
_inp	_makepath	rename
_inpd	malloc	rewind
_inpw	_matherr	_rmdir
isalnum	__max	_rmtmp
isalpha	_memccpy	_rotl
__isascii	memchr	_rotr
_isatty	memcmp	_scalb
iscntrl	memcpy	scanf
__iscsym	_memicmp	_searchenv
__iscsymf	memmove	setbuf
isdigit	memset	_setjmp
isgraph	__min	_setmode
islower	_mkdir	setvbuf
_isnan	_mktemp	sin
isprint	mktime	sinh
ispunct	modf	_snprintf
isspace	_msize	_sopen
isupper	_nextafter	_splitpath
isxdigit	_onexit	sprintf
_itoa	_open	sqrt
_j0	_open_osfhandle	srand
_j1	_outp	sscanf
_jn	_outpd	_stat
_kbhit	_outpw	_status87
labs	perror	_statusfp
ldexp	_pipe	strcat
ldiv	pow	strchr
_lfind	printf	strcmp
localeconv	putc	_strcmpi
localtime	_putch	strcpy
log	putchar	strcspn
log10	_putenv	_strdate
_logb	puts	_strdup
longjmp	_putw	_strerror
_lrotl	qsort	strerror
_lrotr	rand	strftime
_lsearch	_read	_stricmp
_lseek	realloc	strlen

continues

Table B-1: Supported C Run-Time Library Routines (*continued*)

_strlwr	strxfrm	_unlink
strncat	_swab	_utime
strncmp	tan	va_arg
strncpy	tanh	va_end
_strnicmp	_tell	va_start
_strnset	_tempnam	vfprintf
strpbrk	time	vfwprintf
strrchr	tmpfile	vprintf
_strrev	tmpnam	_vsnprintf
_strset	__toascii	_vsnwprintf
strspn	_tolower	vsprintf
strstr	_toupper	vswprintf
_strtime	_tzset	vwprintf
strtod	_ultoa	_write
strtok	_umask	_y0
strtol	ungetc	_y1
strtoul	_ungetch	_yn
_strupr		

WIN32 APIS

The C constants, data structures, and function prototypes for the Win32 APIs are defined in the WINDOWS.H file included with Visual C++. Any source file that calls a Win32 function must include WINDOWS.H. You must define the symbol WIN32 (or WIN32_LEAN_AND_MEAN) before including WINDOWS.H.

Table B-2 lists the Win32 APIs supported by ETS Kernel. The functionality of each API matches the functionality documented by Microsoft, with any differences noted in footnotes. APIs not listed in this table are not supported, though they may have a stub (do-nothing) implementation to resolve references by the compiler run-time libraries. Only ANSI strings are supported in ETS Kernel. The Win32 APIs have no Unicode implementation.

Table B-2: Supported Win32 APIs

CancelWaitableTimer	CreateEvent
CloseHandle	CreateFile
CompareFileTime	CreateMutex
CompareString	CreatePipe
CreateDirectory	CreateSemaphore

continues

Table B-2: Supported WIN32 APIs (*continued*)

CreateThread	GetLargestConsoleWindowSize
CreateWaitableTimer	GetLastError
DebugBreak	GetLocalTime*
DeleteCriticalSection	GetLogicalDrives
DeleteFile	GetLogicalDriveStrings
DosDateTimeToFileTime	GetModuleFileName
DuplicateHandle	GetModuleHandle
EnterCriticalSection	GetNumberOfConsoleInputEvents
ExitProcess	GetProcAddress
ExitThread	GetProcessHeap
FatalAppExit	GetShortPathName
FileTimeToDosDateTime	GetStdHandle
FileTimeToLocalFileTime*	GetSystemTime*
FileTimeToSystemTime	GetSystemTimeAsFileTime*
FindClose	GetThreadContext
FindFirstFile	GetThreadPriority
FindNextFile	GetThreadTimes
FlushFileBuffers	GetTickCount
FreeLibrary	GetVersion
GetCommandLine	GetVersionEx
GetConsoleMode	GlobalAlloc
GetConsoleScreenBufferInfo	GlobalFree
GetCurrentDirectory	GlobalSize
GetCurrentProcess	HeapValidate
GetCurrentProcessId	HeapWalk
GetCurrentThread	InitializeCriticalSection
GetCurrentThreadId	InterlockedCompareExchange
GetDiskFreeSpace	InterlockedDecrement
GetDriveType	InterlockedExchange
GetEnvironmentStrings	InterlockedExchangeAdd
GetEnvironmentVariable	InterlockedIncrement
GetExitCodeThread	LeaveCriticalSection
GetFileAttributes	LoadLibrary
GetFileInformationByHandle	LocalAlloc
GetFileSize	LocalFileTimeToFileTime*
GetFileTime	LocalFree
GetFileType	LocalReAlloc
GetFullPathName	LocalSize

continues

* System Time and Local Time are the same under ETS Kernel.

Table B-2: Supported WIN32 APIs (*continued*)

MoveFile	SetFileAttributes
OpenEvent	SetFilePointer
OpenMutex	SetFileTime
OpenSemaphore	SetLastError
OpenWaitableTimer	SetLocalTime*
OutputDebugString	SetStdHandle
PeekConsoleInput	SetSystemTime*
PeekNamedPipe	SetThreadContext
PulseEvent	SetThreadPriority
QueryPerformanceCounter	SetUnhandledExceptionFilter
QueryPerformanceFrequency	SetWaitableTimer
RaiseException	Sleep
ReadConsole	SuspendThread
ReadConsoleInput	SystemTimeToFileTime*
ReadFile	TerminateThread
ReadProcessMemory	TlsAlloc
ReleaseMutex	TlsFree
ReleaseSemaphore	TlsGetValue
RemoveDirectory	TlsSetValue
ResetEvent	TryEnterCriticalSection
ResumeThread	UnhandledExceptionFilter
RtlUnwind	VirtualAlloc
RtlZeroMemory	VirtualFree
ScrollConsoleScreenBuffer	VirtualQuery
SetConsoleCursorPosition	VkKeyScan
SetConsoleMode	WaitForMultipleObjects
SetCurrentDirectory	WaitForSingleObject
SetEndOfFile	WriteConsole
SetEnvironmentVariable	WriteConsoleOutput
SetEvent	WriteFile

* System Time and Local Time are the same under ETS Kernel.

WINSOCK APIS

The WinSock (Windows Sockets) 1.1 APIs supported by ETS Kernel are listed in Table B-3. Complete documentation on these APIs is in the `\TSLITE\DOCS\APIS.DOC` file.

Table B-3: Supported WinSock APIs

C Routine	Description
accept()	Accept a connection on a socket
bind()	Associate a local address with a socket
closesocket()	Close a socket
connect()	Establish a connection to a peer
gethostbyaddr()	Get host information corresponding to an IP address
gethostbyname()	Get host information corresponding to a hostname
gethostname()	Return the standard host name for the local machine
getpeername()	Get the IP address of the peer to which a socket is connected
getprotobyname()	Get protocol information corresponding to a protocol name
getprotobynumber()	Get protocol information corresponding to a protocol number
getservbyname()	Get service information corresponding to a service name and protocol
getservbyport()	Get service information corresponding to a port and protocol
getsockname()	Get the local IP address for a socket
getsockopt()	Retrieve a socket option
htonl()	Convert a u_long from host to network byte order
htons()	Convert a u_short from host to network byte order
inet_addr()	Convert a string containing a dotted address into an in_addr
inet_ntoa()	Convert a network address into a string in dotted format
ioctlsocket()	Control the mode of a socket
listen()	Establish a socket to listen for incoming connection
ntohl()	Convert a u_long from network to host byte order
ntohs()	Convert a u_short from network to host byte order
recv()	Receive data from a socket
recvfrom()	Receive a datagram and store the source address
select()	Determine the status of one or more sockets, waiting if necessary
send()	Send data on a connected socket
sendto()	Send a datagram to a specific destination
setsockopt()	Set a socket option
shutdown()	Disable sends and/or receives on a socket
socket()	Create a socket
WSACleanup()	Terminate use of Windows Sockets
WSAGetLastError()	Get the error status for the last operation that failed
WSASetLastError()	Set the error code which can be retrieved by WSAGetLastError()
WSAStartup()	Initialize Windows Sockets, using highest compatible version

KERNEL APIS

Kernel APIs defined for only ETS Kernel (that is, not for part of a larger standard) are listed below. The shaded APIs are supported only in the commercial version of TNT Embedded ToolSuite, not in the ToolSuite Lite version on the CD-ROM. Complete documentation on these APIs is in the \TSLITE\DOCS\APIS.DOC file.

EtsAddSubsysData

Add Record of Internal Data for Remote Debugging

```
void EtsAddSubsysData(SUBSYS_DATA *p);
```

EtsAtoi

Convert ASCII to Integer

```
int EtsAtoi(const char *str);
```

EtsBsearch

Binary Search of Sorted Array

```
void * EtsBsearch(const void *key, const void *base, unsigned int num,
                unsigned int width,
          int (__cdecl *compare)(const void *elem1, const void *elem2));
```

EtsCallExitHandlers

Call Registered Exit Functions

```
void EtsCallExitHandlers(ETS_EXIT_EVENT_RECORD *pRec);
```

EtsCheckISRPriority

Compare Current Thread Priority to ISR Priority

```
int EtsCheckISRPriority(void);
```

EtsClearISRPriority

Unlock the ETS Scheduler

```
void EtsClearISRPriority();
```

EtsClearLogEnd

Enable Overwriting Existing Entries in Event Log

```
void EtsClearLogEnd();
```

EtsCSAccessConfigurationRegister

Read or Write a PC Card Configuration Register

```
int EtsCSAccessConfigurationRegister(size_t size, conf_reg_t *reg)
```

EtsCSAdjustResourceInfo

Identify Resources to the ETS PC Card Support Package

```
int EtsCSAdjustResourceInfo(size_t size, adjust_t *adj);
```

EtsCSGetCardServicesInfo

Return Information About the ETS PC Card Support Package

```
int EtsCSGetCardServicesInfo(size_t size, servinfo_t *info)
```

EtsCSGetConfigurationInfo

Get Description of PC Card Socket and Configuration

```
EtsCSGetConfigurationInfo(client_handle_t *handle, size_t size,
                config_info_t *config);
```

EtsCSGetFirstClient

Get Handle of Registered Client

```
EtsCSGetFirstClient(client_handle_t *handle, size_t size,
                client_req_t *req);
```

EtsCSGetFirstConfigurationInfo

Get Description of PC Card Socket and Configuration

```
EtsCSGetFirstConfigurationInfo(client_handle_t *handle,
                char *zClientName, size_t size,
                config_info_t *config);
```

EtsCSGetFirstTuple

Get First Tuple from CIS

```
int EtsCSGetFirstTuple(size_t size, tuple_t *tuple)
```

EtsCSGetNextClient

Get Handle of Registered Client

```
EtsCSGetNextClient(client_handle_t *handle, size_t size,
                client_req_t *req);
```

EtsCSGetNextConfigurationInfo

Get Description of PC Card Socket and Configuration

```
EtsCSGetNextConfigurationInfo(client_handle_t *handle,
                char *zClientName, size_t size,
                config_info_t *config);
```

EtsCSGetNextTuple

Get Next Tuple from CIS

```
int EtsCSGetNextTuple(size_t size, tuple_t *tuple)
```

EtsCSGetStatus

Get Current Status of PC Card and Socket

```
EtsCSGetStatus(size_t size, status_t *status);
```

EtsCSGetTupleData

Get Data Associated with Returned Tuple

```
EtsCSGetTupleData(size_t size, tuple_t *tuple)
```

EtsCSIsACard

Query Card Information Structure on PC Card

```
int EtsCSIsACard(isa_db_t *db, unsigned int size, isa_req_t *req);
```

EtsCSMapMemPage

Map Memory Area of PC Card into Window

```
EtsCSMapMemPage(window_handle_t win, size_t size, memreq_t *req);
```

EtsCSModifyConfiguration

Modify Configuration of a PC Card and Socket

```
EtsCSModifyConfiguration(size_t size, modconf_t *mod);
```

EtsCSModifyWindow

Change Attributes or Access Speed of a Window

```
EtsCSModifyWindow(window_handle_t win, size_t size, modwin_t *req);
```

EtsCSParseTuple

Interpret Tuple Data

```
int EtsCSParseTuple(union cisparse_t *parse, unsigned int size,
            struct tuple_t *tuple);
```

EtsCSRegisterClient

Register Client with Client Services

```
EtsCSRegisterClient(client_handle_t *handle,
            event_handler_t event_handler,
            size_t req_size, client_reg_t *req);
```

EtsCSReleaseConfiguration

Remove Configuration Information for Card

```
EtsCSReleaseConfiguration(client_handle_t handle, size_t size,
                          relconf_t *req);
```

EtsCSReleaseIO

Release I/O Addresses

```
EtsCSReleaseIO(client_handle_t handle, size_t size, io_req_t *req);
```

EtsCSReleaseIRQ

Release Interrupt Request Line

```
EtsCSReleaseIRQ(client_handle_t handle, size_t size, irq_req_t *req);
```

EtsCSReleaseWindow

Release Block of System Address Space

```
EtsCSReleaseWindow(window_handle_t win);
```

EtsCSReportError

Interpret Tuple Data

```
int EtsCSReportError(size_t size, errrep_t *req);
```

EtsCSRequestConfiguration

Configure PC Card and Socket

```
EtsCSRequestConfiguration(client_handle_t handle, size_t size,
                          config_req_t *req);
```

EtsCSRequestIO

Allocate I/O Addresses

```
EtsCSRequestIO(client_handle_t handle, size_t size, io_req_t *req);
```

EtsCSRequestIRQ

Reserve Interrupt Request Line

```
EtsCSRequestIRQ(client_handle_t handle, void *pointer, size_t size,
                irq_req_t *req);
```

EtsCSRequestWindow

Assign Window to PC Card and Socket

```
EtsCSRequestWindow(client_handle_t *phandle, size_t size,
                   win_req_t *req);
```

EtsCSValidateCIS

Validate Card Information Structure (CIS)

```
EtsCSValidateCIS(size_t size, cisinfo_t *info);
```

EtsDisableThreadStackOvfCheck

Disable Thread Stack Overflow Checking

```
DWORD EtsDisableThreadStackOvfCheck(void);
```

EtsDisableThreadTimeCounting

Stop Per-Thread CPU Utilization Counting

```
DWORD EtsDisableThreadTimeCounting(void);
```

EtsDisplayError

Display Error Message on Host and Target Consoles

```
void EtsDisplayError(BYTE *pErrMsg);
```

EtsDumpThreads

Display Information about Active Threads

```
void EtsDumpThreads(void (__cdecl *pUserPrintfFunc) (char *, ...));
```

EtsEnableLog

Enable or Disable Event Logging

```
BOOL EtsEnableLog(BOOL fEnableLogging);
```

EtsEnableThreadStackOvfCheck

Enable Thread Stack Overflow Checking

```
DWORD EtsEnableThreadStackOvfCheck(void);
```

EtsEnableThreadTimeCounting

Start Per-Thread CPU Utilization Counting

```
DWORD EtsEnableThreadTimeCounting(void);
```

EtsEnumerateThreads

Call Specified Function for Each Active Thread

```
DWORD EtsEnumerateThreads(THREADENUMFUNCP pIterFunc);
```

EtsEnumerateThreadTimeCounts

Call Specified Function with Thread ID and Time Count

```
DWORD EtsEnumerateThreadTimeCounts(THREADTIMEFUNCP pIterFunc);
```

EtsEnumLogEntries

Return Pointer to Next Logged Event

```
EVENT_LOG_ENTRY *EtsEnumLogEntries(EVENT_LOG_ENTRY *Event);
```

EtsExitProcess

Terminate Program

```
void EtsExitProcess(UINT uExitCode);
```

EtsForceThreadFuncCall

Force Function Call When Thread is Scheduled

```
int EtsForceThreadFuncCall(HANDLE hThread, FORCEFUNCPTR pFunc,
                           DWORD Arg);
```

EtsFormatLogEvent

Convert Binary Event Log Record to ASCII

```
int EtsFormatLogEvent(EVENT_LOG_ENTRY *Event, LPSTR Buffer, int BuffSize);
```

EtsFreeUnusedThreadBlocks

Give Free Thread Block List Back to Memory Allocator

```
void EtsFreeUnusedThreadBlocks(void);
```

EtsGetCritSecDebugName

Get ASCII Name of Critical Section for Debugging

```
DWORD EtsGetCritSecDebugName(void *pCritSec, char *pNameBuf,
                             int lenNameBuf);
```

EtsGetDebugName

Get ASCII Debug Description of the Specified Win32 IPC Object

```
EtsGetDebugName(HANDLE hObject, char *pNameBuf, int lenNameBuf);
```

EtsGetKernelRunMode

Get Run Mode Configured into Kernel

```
DWORD EtsGetKernelRunMode(void);
```

EtsGetMemoryStats

Get Target Memory Usage Statistics

```
void EtsGetMemoryStats(PETSMEMORYSTATS lpms);
```

EtsGetRealtimeEventLogMask

Return Mask for Realtime Event Log

```
DWORD EtsGetRealtimeEventLogMask(void);
```

EtsGetRTCTime

Get the Current Time From External Real-time Clock

```
BOOL EtsGetRTCTime(SYSTEMTIME *pTime);
```

EtsGetSubsysLogFlags

Return Events Being Logged

```
DWORD EtsGetSubsysLogFlags(void);
```

EtsGetSystemInfo

Get Configuration Information

```
void EtsGetSystemInfo(EK_KERNELINFO *pKernelInfo,
                      EK_SYSTEMINFO *pSystemInfo);
```

EtsGetThreadDebugName

Get ASCII Name of Thread

```
DWORD EtsGetThreadDebugName(HANDLE hThread, char *pNameBuf,
                           int lenNameBuf);
```

EtsGetTimerPeriod

Get Frequency of Time-of-Day Clock

```
unsigned long EtsGetTimerPeriod(void);
```

EtsGetTimeSlice

Get Length of Multitasking Time Slice

```
DWORD EtsGetTimeSlice(void);
```

EtsGetVsbVarsPointer

Get Pointer to Kernel VSB_VARS Structure

```
VSB_VARS *EtsGetVsbVarsPointer(void);
```

EtsHostGetCommandLine

Get Passed-in Command Line from Host

```
DWORD EtsHostGetCommandLine(PSTR pBuffer, DWORD NumBytes,
                            DWORD *pBytesRead);
```

EtsHostGetCommandLineLen

Return Length of Passed-in Command Line from Host

```
DWORD EtsHostGetCommandLineLen(void);
```

EtsHostGetEnvSize

Return Size of Environment from Host

```
DWORD EtsHostGetEnvSize(void);
```

EtsHostGetEnvStrings

Return Environment from Host

```
DWORD EtsHostGetEnvStrings(PSTR pBuffer, DWORD NumBytes,
                           DWORD *pBytesRead);
```

EtsInitializeLogBuffer

Initialize Event Logging

```
BOOL EtsInitializeLogBuffer(DWORD BuffSize);
```

EtsInp

Read Byte from Specified Input Port

```
int EtsInp(unsigned port);
```

EtsInpw

Read Word from Specified Input Port

```
int EtsInpw(unsigned port);
```

EtsLogEvent

Write Event to Log

```
BOOL EtsLogEvent(DWORD EventId, DWORD argc, ...);
```

EtsLogEventFromBuff

Write Event from Buffer to Log

```
BOOL EtsLogEventFromBuff(DWORD EventId, DWORD Size, LPVOID Buffer);
```

EtsLtoa

Convert Long to ASCII

```
unsigned char * EtsLtoa(unsigned long value, unsigned char *bp,
                        int radix);
```

EtsMailBody

Specify Content of Mail Message Body

```
int EtsMailBody(HANDLE h, char *body);
```

EtsMailClose

Terminate the Mail Connection

```
int EtsMailClose(HANDLE h);
```

EtsMailFrom

Specify Originator of Mail Message

```
int EtsMailFrom(HANDLE h, char *pFrom);
```

EtsMailHeader

Specify One Field of a Mail Header

```
int EtsMailHeader(HANDLE h, char *fieldname, char *fieldbody);
```

EtsMailOpen

Initiate a Mail Connection to Remote Host

```
HANDLE EtsMailOpen(char *pHostName, char *pName );
```

EtsMailSendMessage

Send a Mail Message

```
int EtsMailSendMessage(char *server, char *me, char *from , char *to,
                       char *subject, char *body);
```

EtsMailTo

Specify Recipient of Mail Message

```
int EtsMailTo(HANDLE h, char *pTo);
```

EtsMarkTimeSlice

Note Timer Tick in Multitasking Environment

```
void EtsMarkTimeSlice(DWORD msElapsed);
```

EtsMemcpy

Copy Bytes to Memory

```
void * EtsMemcpy(void *s1, const void *s2, unsigned int n);
```

EtsMemmove

Copy Bytes to Memory

```
void * EtsMemmove(void *s1, const void *s2, unsigned int n);
```

EtsMemset

Fill Memory Locations

```
void * EtsMemset(void *s, int c, unsigned int n);
```

EtsMoveThreadToFront

Move a Thread in Front of Same-Priority Peers

```
DWORD EtsMoveThreadToFront(HANDLE hThread);
```

EtsOutp

Write Byte to Specified Output Port

```
int EtsOutp(unsigned port, int databyte);
```

EtsOutpw

Write Word to Specified Output Port

```
int EtsOutpw(unsigned port, unsigned dataword);
```

EtsPcCardGetATA

Get Configuration of PC Card ATA Disk

```
int EtsPcCardGetATA(int portnum, int *pIO, int *pCTL, int *pIRQ);
```

EtsPcCardGetATACount

Return Number of PC Card ATA Disks in System

```
int EtsPcCardGetATACount(void);
```

EtsPcCardGetSerialPort

Get Configuration of Serial Port PC Card

```
int EtsPcCardGetSerialPort(int portnum, int *pIO, int *pIRQ);
```

EtsPcCardGetSerialPortCount

Return Number of Serial Port PC Cards in System

```
int EtsPcCardGetSerialPOrtCount(void);
```

EtsPCICall

Directly Access the PCI BIOS

```
int EtsPCICall(EK_PCIREGS *pRegs);
```

EtsPCIFindDevice

Query PCI BIOS About a Specific Device

```
int EtsPCIFindDevice(unsigned short deviceID, unsigned short vendorID,
              unsigned short index, EK_PCIDEVICE *pDev);
```

EtsPCIFindDeviceByClass

Query PCI BIOS about Presence of a Specific Device Type

```
int EtsPCIFindDeviceByClass(unsigned long pciClass, unsigned short index,
              EK_PCIDEVICE *pDev);
```

EtsPCIInit

Check for Presence of PCI BIOS and 32-bit Entry Point

```
int EtsPCIInit(EK_PCIBIOSINFO *pInfo);
```

EtsPCIReadCfgByte

Read Byte from PCI Configuration Register

```
int EtsPCIReadCfgByte(unsigned regIndex, EK_PCIDEVICE *pDev);
```

EtsPCIReadCfgDWord

Read Double Word from PCI Configuration Register

```
int EtsPCIReadCfgDWord(unsigned regIndex, EK_PCIDEVICE *pDev);
```

EtsPCIReadCfgWord

Read Word from PCI Configuration Register

```
int EtsPCIReadCfgWord(unsigned regIndex, EK_PCIDEVICE *pDev);
```

EtsPCIReadConfig

Read from PCI Configuration Register

```
int EtsPCIReadConfig(int type, unsigned regIndex, EK_PCIDEVICE *pDev);
```

EtsPCIWriteCfgByte

Write Byte to PCI Configuration Register

```
int EtsPCIWriteCfgByte(unsigned regIndex, unsigned valueToWrite,
                EK_PCIDEVICE *pDev);
```

EtsPCIWriteCfgDWord

Write Double Word to PCI Configuration Register

```
int EtsPCIWriteCfgDWord(unsigned regIndex, unsigned valueToWrite,
                EK_PCIDEVICE *pDev);
```

EtsPCIWriteCfgWord

Write Word to PCI Configuration Register

```
int EtsPCIWriteCfgWord(unsigned regIndex, unsigned valueToWrite,
                EK_PCIDEVICE *pDev);
```

EtsPCIWriteConfig

Write to PCI Configuration Register

```
int EtsPCIWriteConfig(int type, unsigned regIndex,
                unsigned valueToWrite, EK_PCIDEVICE *pDev);
```

EtsPicEnable

Enable or Disable an IRQ on the 8259 PIC

```
int EtsPicEnable(int hardwareIRQNum, int newState);
```

EtsPicEOI

Issue an EOI for the Specified Hardware IRQ

```
void EtsPicEOI(int hardwareIRQNum);
```

EtsPicGetIRQIntNumber

Get Interrupt Vector Corresponding to Hardware IRQ

```
int EtsPicGetIRQIntNumber(int hardwareIRQNum);
```

EtsQueryFileHandle

Query File Handle

```
int EtsQueryFileHandle(HANDLE FileHandle);
```

EtsReadThreadInternalInfo

Get Internal Information About a Thread Specified by Handle

```
DWORD EtsReadThreadInternalInfo(HANDLE hThread,
                ETSTHREADINFO *pInfoBlock);
```

EtsReadThreadInternalInfoId

Get Internal Information About a Thread Specified by ID

```
DWORD EtsReadThreadInternalInfoId(DWORD id, ETSTHREADINFO *pInfoBlock);
```

EtsReadThreadTimeCount

Get Time Count for Thread Specified by Handle

```
DWORD EtsReadThreadTimeCount(HANDLE hThread, union _LARGE_INTEGER
                             *pCountVar);
```

EtsReadThreadTimeCountId

Get Time Count for Thread Specified by Thread ID

```
DWORD EtsReadThreadTimeCountId(DWORD id union _LARGE_INTEGER *pCountVar);
```

EtsRegisterCallback

Register Device Driver Callback

```
BOOL EtsRegisterCallback(WORD Type, ETS_CALLBACK pCallback,
                         DWORD ulOpaque, BOOL bAdd);
```

EtsResetSystemTimeFromRTC

Resynchronize In-Memory Time

```
BOOL EtsResetSystemTimeFromRTC(void);
```

EtsResetThreadTimeCounts

Set Time Count for All Threads to Zero

```
DWORD EtsResetThreadTimeCounts(void);
```

EtsRestoreExceptionHandler

Restore Specified Exception Vector

```
BOOL EtsRestoreExceptionHandler(unsigned IntNumber,
                                PETSHANDLERINFO pSaveArea);
```

EtsRestoreIDTHandler

Restore Contents of IDT Entry

```
BOOL EtsRestoreIDTHandler(unsigned IntNumber, BYTE *pSaveArea);
```

EtsRestoreInterruptHandler

Restore Specified Interrupt Vector

```
BOOL EtsRestoreInterruptHandler(unsigned IntNumber,
                                PETSHANDLERINFO pSaveArea);
```

EtsSaveExceptionHandler

Save Specified Exception Vector

```
BOOL EtsSaveExceptionHandler(unsigned IntNumber,
                             PETSHANDLERINFO pSaveArea);
```

EtsSaveIDTHandler

Save Contents of IDT Entry

```
BOOL EtsSaveIDTHandler(unsigned IntNumber, BYTE *pSaveArea);
```

EtsSaveInterruptHandler

Save Specified Interrupt Vector

```
BOOL EtsSaveInterruptHandler(unsigned IntNumber,
                             PETSHANDLERINFO pSaveArea);
```

EtsSelectConsole

Select Host or Target Console

```
int EtsSelectConsole(int Type);
```

EtsSelectFileSystem

Select Host or Target File System

```
int EtsSelectFileSystem(int Type);
```

EtsSetCritSecDebugName

Set ASCII Name of Critical Section for Debugging

```
DWORD EtsSetCritSecDebugName(void *pCritSec, char *pName);
```

EtsSetDebugName

Assign an ASCII Debug Description to the Specified Win32 IPC Object

```
DWORD EtsSetDebugName(HANDLE hObject, char *pName);
```

EtsSetExceptionHandler

Install C Function as Exception Handler

```
BOOL EtsSetExceptionHandler(unsigned IntNumber, PETSINTHANDLER pHandler);
```

EtsSetIDTHandler

Install Function as IDT Interrupt Handler

```
BOOL EtsSetIDTHandler(unsigned IntNumber, PVOID pHandler);
```

EtsSetInterruptFlag

Enable or Disable All Hardware Interrupts

```
int EtsSetInterruptFlag(int newIntFlagState);
```

EtsSetInterruptHandler

Install C Function as Interrupt Handler

```
BOOL EtsSetInterruptHandler(unsigned IntNumber, PETSINTHANDLER pHandler);
```

EtsSetISRPriority

Lock the ETS Scheduler

```
void EtsSetISRPriority();
```

EtsSetLogEnd

Disable Overwriting Existing Entries in Event Log

```
void EtsSetLogEnd();
```

EtsSetLogOutput

Specify Console Output of Event Log

```
WORD EtsSetLogOutput(WORD wOutput);
```

EtsSetRealtimeEventLogMask

Specify Mask for Realtime Event Log

```
DWORD EtsSetRealtimeEventLogMask(DWORD NewMask);
```

EtsSetSubsysLogFlags

Specify Events Being Logged

```
DWORD EtsSetSubsysLogFlags(DWORD Flags);
```

EtsSetThreadDebugName

Set ASCII Name of Thread

```
DWORD EtsSetThreadDebugName(HANDLE hThread, char *pName);
```

EtsSetTimerPeriod

Specify Frequency of Time-of-Day Clock

```
void EtsSetTimerPeriod(unsigned long Period);
```

EtsSetTimeSlice

Specify Length of Multitasking Time Slice

```
DWORD EtsSetTimeSlice(DWORD msSliceLen);
```

EtsStrcat

Concatenate Strings

```
char * EtsStrcat(char *s1, const char *s2);
```

EtsStrchr

Find Character in String

```
char * EtsStrchr(const char *s1, int c);
```

EtsStrcmp

Compare Strings

```
int EtsStrcmp(const char *s1, const char *s2);
```

EtsStrcpy

Copy String

```
char * EtsStrcpy(char *s1, const char *s2);
```

EtsStricmp

Compare Strings

```
int EtsStricmp(const char *s1, const char *s2);
```

EtsStrlen

Determine Length of String

```
unsigned int EtsStrlen(const char *s1);
```

EtsStrncmp

Compare Partial Strings

```
int EtsStrncmp(const char *s1, const char *s2, unsigned int n);
```

EtsStrncpy

Copy Partial String

```
char * EtsStrncpy(char *s1, const char *s2, unsigned int n);
```

EtsTCPBringDeviceDown

Bring Down Device Driver

```
int EtsTCPBringDeviceDown(DEVHANDLE hDevice)
```

EtsTCPBringDeviceUp

Initialize Device Driver

```
int EtsTCPBringDeviceUp(DEVHANDLE hDevice)
```

EtsTCPConfigureDevice

Set New Configuration for Device Driver

```
int EtsTCPConfigureDevice(DEVHANDLE hDevice, EK_TCPIPCFG *pTCPCfg,
                          void *pExtendedInfo);
```

EtsTCPGetDeviceCfg

Get Base Configuration Info for Device Driver

```
EK_TCPIPCFG *EtsTCPGetDeviceCfg(DEVHANDLE hDevice)
```

EtsTCPGetDeviceExtendedInfo

Get Extended Configuration Info for Device Driver

```
void *EtsTCPGetDeviceExtendedInfo(DEVHANDLE hDevice)
```

EtsTCPGetDeviceHandle

Get Handle for Installed Device Driver

```
DEVHANDLE EtsTCPGetDeviceHandle(char *pDeviceName)
```

EtsTCPGetDeviceInstanceInfo

Get Device Ethernet Info

```
void *EtsTCPGetDeviceInstanceInfo(DEVHANDLE hDevice);
```

EtsTCPGetDeviceStatus

Get Status of Network Device

```
int cdecl EtsTCPGetDeviceStatus(DEVHANDLE hDevice, void *pDeviceStatus);
```

EtsTCPGetStackCfg

Get Stack Configuration Info

```
void cdecl EtsTCPGetStackCfg(EK_TCPSTACKCFG *stkCfg,
                             EK_TCPDNSCFG *dnsCfg,
                             EK_TCPGATEWAYCFG *gwCfg);
```

EtsTCPRegisterDevice

Register Device

```
DEVHANDLE EtsTCPRegisterDevice(int type, int ID, ...)
```

EtsTCPSetDefaultGateway

Set Default Gateway for PPP/CSLIP Connection

```
void EtsTCPSetDefaultGateway(DEVHANDLE hDevice)
```

EtsTCPSetDeviceEthernetInfo

Set Device Ethernet Info

```
int EtsTCPSetDeviceEthernetInfo(DEVHANDLE hDevice, char *EnetAddr);
```

EtsTCPSetDeviceInstanceInfo

Set Device Instance Info

```
int EtsTCPSetDeviceInstanceInfo(DEVHANDLE hDevice, int Instance,
                     void *hInstance);
```

EtsTCPSetStackCfg

Set Stack Configuration Info

```
void cdecl EtsTCPSetStackCfg(EK_TCPSTACKCFG *stkCfg,
                     EK_TCPDNSCFG *dnsCfg,
                     EK_TCPGATEWAYCFG *gwCfg);
```

EtsTestCritSecOwner

Does Current Thread Own Specified Critical Section?

```
DWORD EtsTestCritSecOwner(void *pCrit);
```

EtsToupper

Convert Character to Uppercase

```
int EtsToupper(int c);
```

form_button

Put an Unnamed Submit Button on an HTML Form

```
void form_button(char *descp);
```

form_decode

Decode Data from a Form

```
int form_decode(FIELD_LIST *ftp, void *structp, char *stringp,
            char *emsgp);
```

form_hidden

Put a Hidden Field on an HTML Form

```
void form_hidden(char *namep, char *valuep);
```

form_input_box

Put a Text Input Box on an HTML Form

```
void form_input_box(char *namep, int width, char *defaultp,
            char *labelp);
```

form_named_button

Put a Named Submit Button on an HTML Form

```
void form_named_button(char *namep, char *descp);
```

form_radio_button

Put a Radio Button on an HTML Form

```
void form_radio_button(char *namep, char *labelp, char *descp,
                       int checkedf);
```

FtpAuthenticate

Authenticate an FTP Client

```
int FtpAuthenticate (char *pUserName, char *pPassword);
```

FtpLogSession

Record Each FTP Session

```
void FtpLogSession(USER_RECORD *pReq);
```

FtpServerError

Report FTP Server Errors

```
void FtpServerError(BOOL fFatal, char *pErrMsg);
```

FtpStartServer

Initialize FTP Server

```
BOOL FtpStartServer(FTP_CONFIG *pFtpCfg);
```

FtpStopServer

Shutdown FTP Server

```
void FtpStopServer(void);
```

GetURI

Process an HTTP GET or HEAD Request

```
void GetURI(REQ_INPUTS *pInp, REQ_OUTPUTS *pOutp);
```

hpg_CreatePage

Create Empty HTML Page

```
BOOL hpg_CreatePage(REQ_OUTPUTS *pOutp);
```

hpg_DirectoryPage

Build HTML Page for a Directory

```
BOOL hpg_DirectoryPage(REQ_INPUTS *pInp, REQ_OUTPUTS *pOutp,
                       PAGE_ENT *pPageTable, char *pHeaderText,
                       char *pPageText, ...);
```

hpg_DirNeedsSlash

Build HTML Error Page and Status Code for Directory Missing '/'

```
BOOL hpg_DirNeedsSlash(REQ_INPUTS *pInp, REQ_OUTPUTS *pOutp);
```

hpg_DonePage

Complete an HTML Page

```
BOOL hpg_DonePage(REQ_OUTPUTS *pOutp);
```

hpg_ErrorPage

Build an HTML Error Page

```
void hpg_ErrorPage(REQ_OUTPUTS *pOutp, const char *pStatusCode,
                   const char *pFormat, ...);
```

hpg_LoadDlls

Load and Initialize DLL Plug-Ins

```
PAGE_ENT * hpg_LoadDlls(char *pTableDll, char *pLoadPath);
```

hpg_MemGifFile

Process In-Memory GIF File

```
BOOL hpg_MemGifFile(REQ_OUTPUTS *pOutp, char *startp, char *endp);
```

hpg_MemHtmlFile

Process In-Memory HTML File

```
BOOL hpg_MemHtmlFile(REQ_OUTPUTS *pOutp, char *startp, char *endp);
```

hpg_PtableLoc

Locate URI in Page Tables

```
PAGE_ENT * hpg_PtableLoc(PAGE_ENT *pStartTable, REQ_INPUTS *pInp,
                         REQ_OUTPUTS *pOutp);
```

hpg_SetDefOutput

Set Output Page Structure to Default Values

```
void hpg_SetDefOutput(REQ_INPUTS *pInp, REQ_OUTPUTS *pOutp);
```

html_brtext

Put Bracketed Text into an HTML Document

```
void html_brtext(char *tagp, char *fmtp, ...);
```

html_endtag

Put an End Tag into an HTML Document

```
void html_endtag(char *tagp, ...);
```

html_fclose

Close an HTML File

```
int html_fclose(void);
```

html_fopen

Open an HTML File

```
HTML_HANDLE html_fopen(char *fnamep);
```

html_incfile

Include Text File in an HTML Document

```
int html_incfile(char *fnamep);
```

html_sethtmlpage

Specify Current HTML Page

```
HTML_HANDLE html_sethtmlpage(HTML_HANDLE hNewPage);
```

html_strclose

Close an In-Memory HTML String

```
char * html_strclose(void);
```

html_stropen

Open an In-Memory HTML String

```
HTML_HANDLE html_stropen(int isize, int gsize);
```

html_tag

Put a Tag into an HTML Document

```
void html_tag(char *tagp, ...);
```

html_tagtext

Put a Tag Followed by Text into an HTML Document

```
void html_tagtext(char *tagp, char *fmtp, ...);
```

html_tagwopt

Put a Tag with Options into an HTML Document

```
void html_tagwopt(char *tagp, ...);
```

html_text

Put Formatted Text into an HTML Document

```
void html_text(char *fmtp, ...);
```

html_textn

Put Text into an HTML Document

```
void html_textn(char *textp, int n);
```

LogRequest

Record Each Processed HTTP Request

```
void LogRequest(REQUEST_RECORD *pREQ);
```

PostURI

Process an HTTP POST Request

```
void PostURI(REQ_INPUTS *pInp, REQ_OUTPUTS *pOutp);
```

StartWebServer

Initialize the HTTP Server

```
BOOL StartWebServer(short Port);
```

StopWebServer

Shutdown the HTTP Server

```
void StopWebServer(void);
```

WebServerError

Handle MicroWeb Server Errors

```
void WebServerError(BOOL fFatal, char *pErrMsg);
```

WebServerInfo

Handle MicroWeb Server Messages

```
void WebServerInfo(char *pErrMsg);
```

WebServerWarning

Handle MicroWeb Server Warnings

```
void WebServerWarning(char *pErrMsg);
```

C

Configuring Serial Networking Connections for Windows

This appendix documents the steps necessary to set up a serial networking connection using a direct cable connection (no phone lines or modems) between a Windows 95, 98, or NT 4.0 machine and an embedded target running ETS Kernel. You need to do this to run the projects described in Chapter 14, "A Network-Aware UPS," Chapter 15, "Networking," Chapter 17, "Java," and Chapter 20, "C++ Exceptions and Structured Exceptions."

You configure the connection to use TCP/IP over PPP. The connection is initiated by the Windows computer; that is, you run the embedded target first, and it listens for incoming PPP connections. Then, you use the Windows Dial-Up Networking utility to initiate the PPP connection with the embedded target. Finally, you run the Windows program (usually a web browser) that communicates with the embedded target.

You use 192.168.1.1 as the IP address for the Windows machine, and 192.168.1.2 as the IP address for the embedded target. These IP addresses were selected because they're reserved for testing, as we described in Chapter 15. For all the screen shots and instructions, we assume that you use the COM1 serial port on the Windows computer for the network cable connection. If you use a different serial port, adjust the instructions accordingly.

We show you the wiring connections required to use a null modem cable for a network connection. Then we document the three steps needed to set up a Windows dial-up networking connection. First, you install a serial driver that can run over a direct cable connection. Second, you install the Windows Dial-Up Networking software component. Finally, you create and configure a Dial-Up Networking connection entry.

NULL MODEM CABLE SPECIFICATIONS

To make a direct connection between the two computers, you need a null modem cable. You can purchase a LapLink-compatible null modem cable at any computer store. If you want to make your own cable or check a cable you've purchased to make sure it has all the required connections, refer to Table C-1 for the required wiring. Most PCs have 9-pin serial connectors, but in case you have an older computer with a 25-pin connector, we show the pinouts for both kinds of connectors.

Table C-1: Required Connections in a Null Modem Cable

Signal	9-Pin	25-Pin		25-Pin	9-Pin	Signal
GND	5	7	⟷	7	5	GND
TX	3	2	⟷	3	2	RX
RX	2	3	⟷	2	3	TX
RTS	7	4	⟷	5	8	CTS
CTS	8	5	⟷	4	7	RTS
DSR	6	6	⟷	20	4	DTR
DTR	4	20	⟷	6	6	DSR

INSTALLING A SERIAL DRIVER FOR A DIRECT CONNECTION

To install a new serial driver, double-click the Modems icon in the Control Panel to display the Install New Modem dialog box. Under Windows 98, the first dialog box asks whether you want to run the Hardware Installation Wizard. Check the "Don't run the Hardware Installation Wizard" box, and then click Next. Under all three versions of Windows, you now see an Install New Modem dialog box that asks whether you want Windows to try to detect your modem. Check the "Don't detect my modem; I will select it from a list" box, and then click Next.

The dialog box shown in Figure C-1 is displayed next. Notice that when "Standard Modem Types" is selected in the Manufacturers area, a driver named "Dial-Up Networking Serial Cable between 2 PCs" is available.

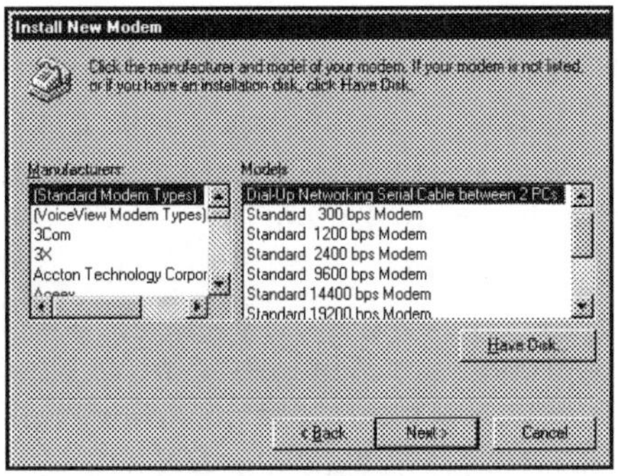

Figure C-1: For Windows NT 4.0, select the dial-up networking driver and then click Next. For Windows 95 and 98, click the Have Disk button to install the driver from the CD-ROM.

For Windows NT 4.0, select the "Dial-Up Networking Serial Cable between 2 PCs" driver and then click Next.

For Windows 95 and 98, the "Dial-Up Networking Serial Cable between 2 PCs" driver won't work for a PPP networking connection. Instead, you have to install a serial driver included on the CD-ROM. This driver was compiled by Kevin L. Wells. Other versions of this driver are available on Kevin's web site, `http://www.vt.edu:10021/K/kewells/net/index.html`. Please note that Kevin cannot provide support for the driver; all support for the software in this book is provided through the `http://www.pharlap.com/book/` web site.

The driver is a Windows device information file (INF) named `W95DIRCT.INF` and is located in the `\TSLITE\BIN` directory. Click the Have Disk button shown in Figure C-1 to display the Install From Disk dialog box. Type `C:\TSLITE\BIN` in the text box. Because `W95DIRCT.INF` is the only INF file in that directory, the install program automatically opens it and displays the dialog box shown in Figure C-2. Select the Direct Connection driver, and then click the Next button.

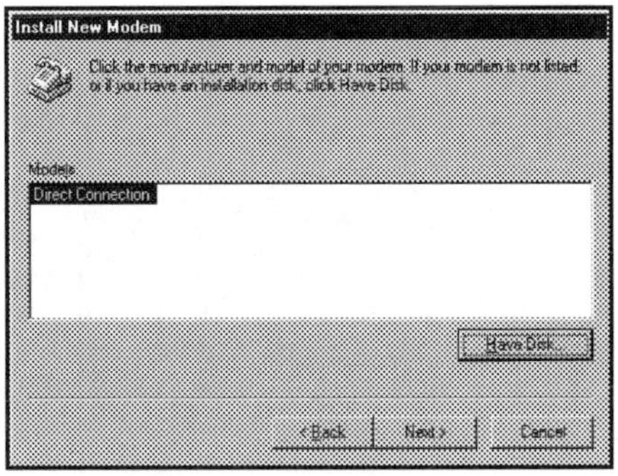

Figure C-2: For Windows 95 and 98, the Direct Connection driver from the W95DIRCT.INF file is the one we want. Click the Next button.

Under all three versions of Windows, you now see another Install New Modem dialog box, which asks you to "Select the port to use with this modem." Choose the serial port on the Windows machine to which the null modem cable will be connected, and then click Next. Windows installs the driver. When the final Install New Modem dialog box appears, click the Finish button to complete the driver installation.

After installation is complete, a Modems Properties dialog box should appear. If it does not, double-click the Modems icon in the Control Panel to display it. Select the driver you just installed (either "Direct Connection" for Windows 95 or 98 or "Dial-Up Networking Serial Cable between 2 PCs" for Windows NT 4.0), and then click Properties to configure the driver. On the General tab of the dialog box shown in Figure C-3, verify that the correct serial port is selected, and then select 57600 baud as the maximum communications speed.

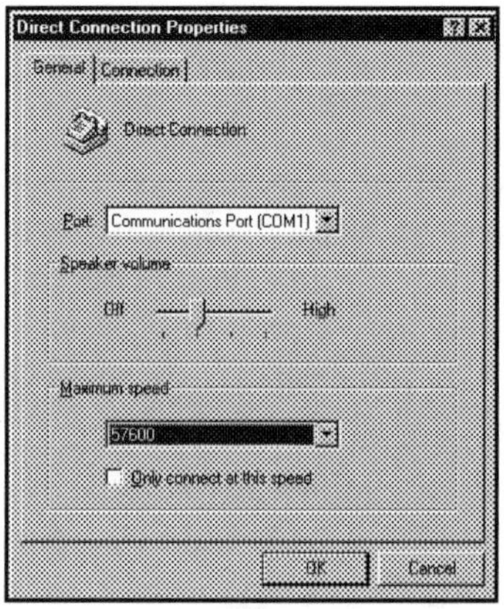

Figure C-3: Select 57600 as the maximum communications speed.

On the Connection tab shown in Figure C-4, select 8 data bits, no parity, and one stop bit, and remove all check marks from the check boxes in the Call preferences area.

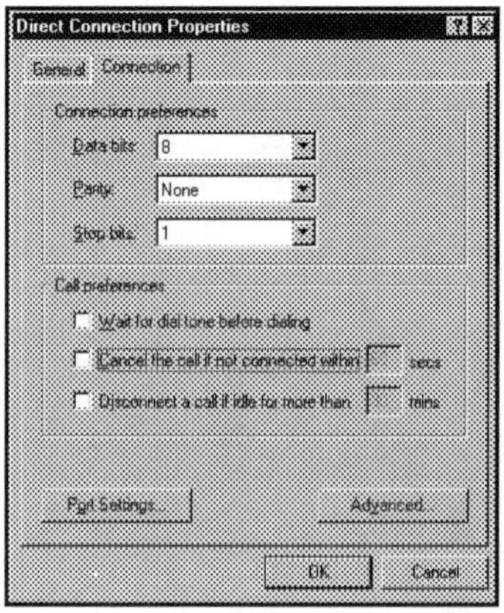

Figure C-4: Select 8 data bits, no parity, 1 stop bit.

Click the Advanced button to display the dialog box shown in Figure C-5. Select RTS/CTS hardware flow control, and make sure the "Use error control" box does not contain a check mark.

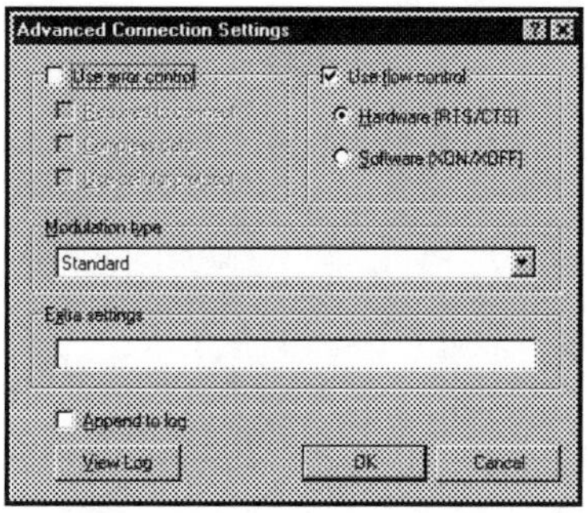

Figure C-5: Select RTS/CTS flow control and no error control.

Click OK twice to return to the Modems Properties dialog box. Click the Close button to exit the Modems setup program.

INSTALLING DIAL-UP NETWORKING

The steps required to install Dial-Up Networking differ in Windows NT 4.0 and Windows 95 and 98, so we describe them in separate sections.

DIAL-UP NETWORKING IN WINDOWS 95 AND 98

In Windows 95 and 98, you now need to make sure Dial-Up Networking is installed. Double-click Add/Remove Programs in the Control Panel to display the dialog box shown in Figure C-6. Select the Windows Setup tab.

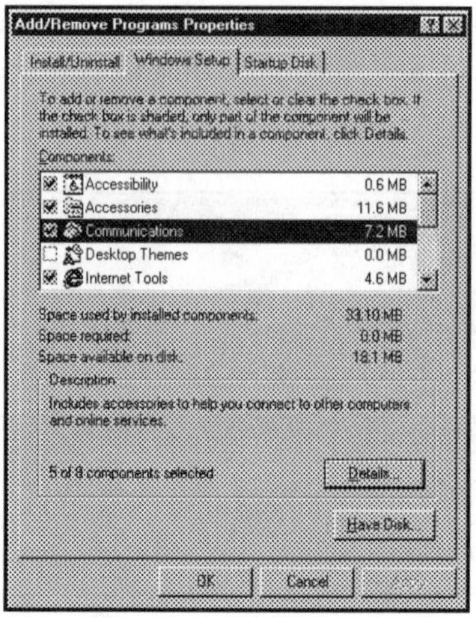

Figure C-6: The Dial-Up Networking utility is part of the Communications component.

Highlight the Communications component, and then click Details to display the dialog box shown in Figure C-7.

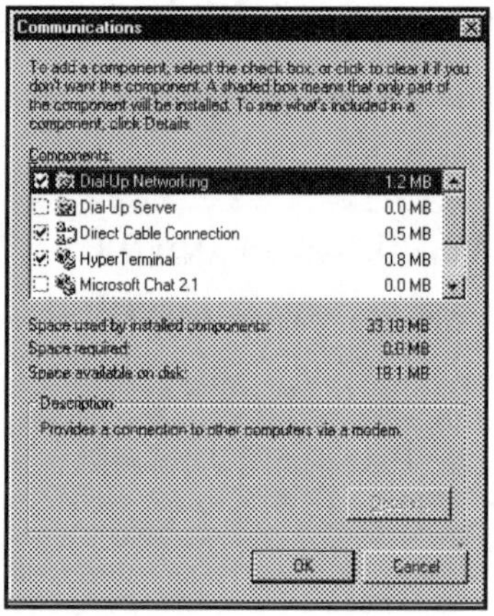

Figure C-7: Install Dial-Up Networking if necessary.

Make sure that Dial-Up Networking has a check mark. If it does, click the Cancel button. If Dial-Up Networking does not have a check mark, click it to add one, and then click the OK button; when you return to the Add/Remove Programs Properties dialog box, click the Apply button to install Dial-Up Networking, and follow the instructions.

DIAL-UP NETWORKING IN WINDOWS NT 4.0

Under Windows 4.0, select Start|Programs|Accessories|Dial-Up Networking. If the Dial-Up Networking software is not installed, Windows asks whether you want to install it. Click the

Install button and follow the instructions. Next, you must install the Remote Access Services (RAS) component of Dial-Up Networking — if it's not already installed — and then configure it. Double-click the Network icon in the Control Panel, and then click the Services tab.

If RAS was already installed, select Remote Access Service and then click the Properties button to display the Remote Access Setup dialog box in Figure C-8. If RAS is not in the list of installed services, click the Add button to install the Remote Access Service. The Add RAS Device dialog box appears. Select the "Dial-Up Networking Serial Cable between 2 PCs" driver, and then click OK to advance to the Remote Access Setup dialog box shown in Figure C-8.

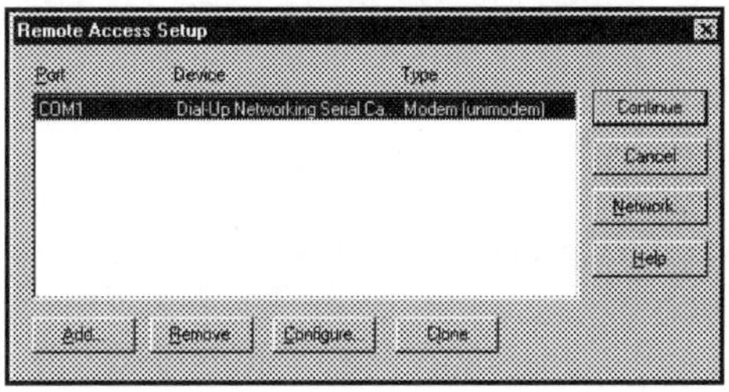

Figure C-8: Select the "Dial-Up Networking Serial Cable between 2 PCs" driver. Click Configure and then Network to complete the Remote Access Service setup.

Click the Configure button to display the Configure Port Usage dialog box. Click to select the "Dial out only" radio button in the Port Usage area of the dialog box, and then click OK.

Next, click the Network button to display the Network Configuration dialog box. Check the "TCP/IP box", and uncheck the "NetBEUI" and "IPX" boxes. Then click OK.

Now click the Continue button to finish the setup and return to the Network dialog box. Click the Close button. Windows asks you to reboot; close any open windows and click OK to restart your system.

CREATING A DIAL-UP NETWORKING CONNECTION

The steps required to create a new Dial-Up Networking connection entry differ in Windows NT 4.0 and Windows 95 and 98, so we describe them in separate sections.

A NEW CONNECTION IN WINDOWS 95 AND 98

For Windows 98 users, select Start|Programs|Accessories|Communications|Dial-Up Networking (for Windows 95, select Start|Programs|Accessories|Dial-Up Networking) to display the Dial-Up Networking window. Double-click the Make New Connection icon to display the dialog box shown in Figure C-9.

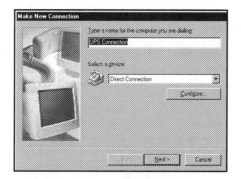

Figure C-9: Select the Direct Connection serial driver, and name your connection UPS Connection.

Type a name for the connection, and make sure "Direct Connection" is selected as the device. Click the Next button to display another Make New Connection dialog box that asks you to enter a telephone number. You must enter 5557777 as the phone number because it's used as part of the PPP connection setup conversation and the projects are configured to expect 5557777. Click Next to get to the dialog box that says you have completed setting up the connection, and then click Finish to return to the Dial-Up Networking window.

Next, right-click the UPS Connection icon you just created and select Properties to display the dialog box shown in Figure C-10.

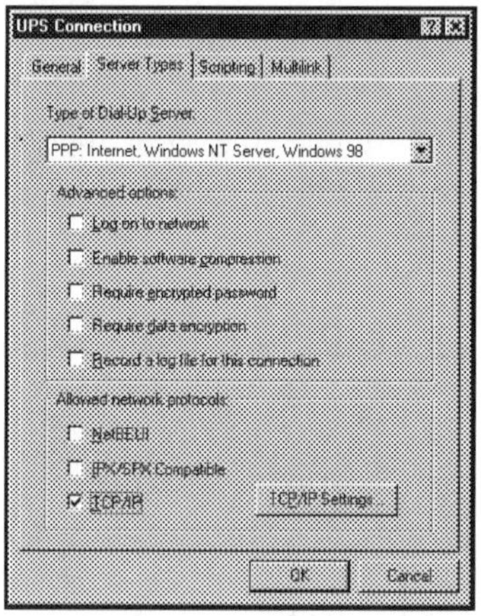

Figure C-10: Select the PPP dial-up server, check the TCP/IP box, and make sure no options in the Advanced area have check marks.

Click the Server Types tab. Under Type of Dial-Up Server, select "PPP: Internet, Windows NT Server, Windows 98." Make sure no boxes in the Advanced options area have check marks. In the Allowed network protocols area, make sure only the TCP/IP box has a check mark. Then click TCP/IP Settings to display the dialog box shown in Figure C-11.

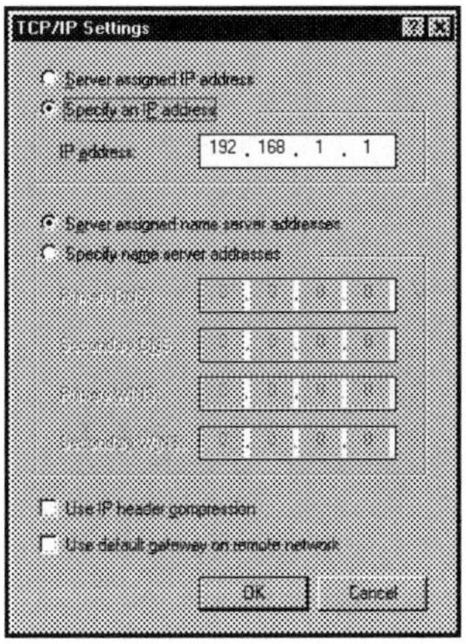

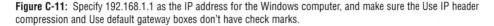

Figure C-11: Specify 192.168.1.1 as the IP address for the Windows computer, and make sure the Use IP header compression and Use default gateway boxes don't have check marks.

Click to select the "Specify an IP address" radio button, and then type 192.168.1.1 for the IP address. Click to select the "Server assigned name server addresses" radio button. Make sure the "Use IP header compression" and "Use default gateway on remote network" boxes do not have a check mark. Click OK to return to the previous dialog box, and click OK again to complete the connection configuration.

You've created a UPS Connection connection entry in the Dial-Up Networking phone book. You can use this connection icon to make PPP connections to the embedded target machine, as described in Chapter 14.

A New Connection in Windows NT 4.0

For Windows NT 4.0 users, select Start|Programs|Accessories|Dial-Up Networking to display the Dial-Up Networking dialog box. Then click the New button to display the dialog box shown in Figure C-12. (If you don't have any entries in your Dial-Up Networking phone book, you'll get a New Phonebook Entry Wizard dialog box that wants to guide you through creating a connection. Check the "I know all about phonebook entries" check box, and then click Finish to display the dialog box in Figure C-12.)

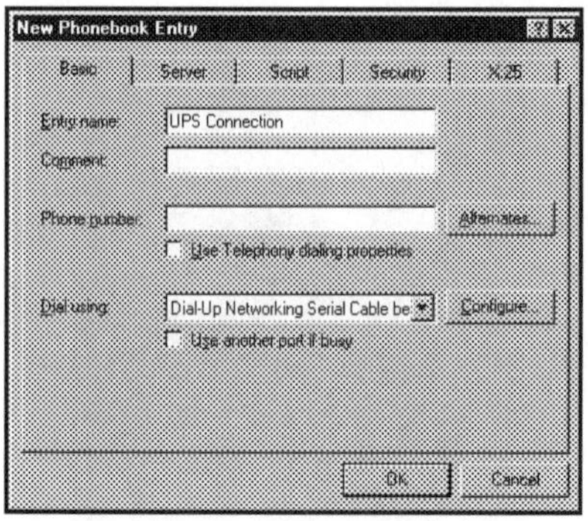

Figure C-12: On the Basic tab, name the entry UPS Connection.

Type UPS Connection as the name of the phonebook entry, make sure "Dial-Up Networking Serial Cable between 2 PCs" is selected as the driver, and make sure the "Use another port if busy" box doesn't have a check mark. Then click the Server tab, which is shown in Figure C-13.

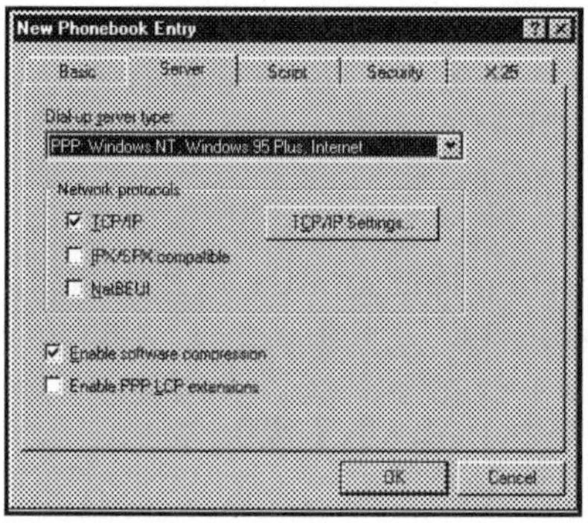

Figure C-13: On the Server tab, select PPP and TCP/IP. Make sure the "Enable PPP LCP extensions" box doesn't have a check mark.

For the Dial-up server type, select "PPP: Windows NT, Windows 95 Plus, Internet." Make sure the "Enable PPP LCP extensions" box doesn't have a check mark. Select the TCP/IP network protocol, and click the TCP/IP Settings button to display the dialog box shown in Figure C-14.

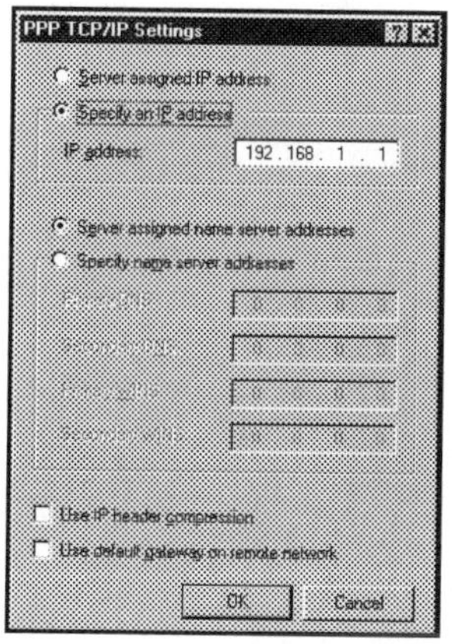

Figure C-14: Specify 192.168.1.1 as the IP address, and make sure the two check boxes don't have check marks.

Click to select the "Specify an IP address" radio button, and type 192.168.1.1 as the IP address. Click to select the "Server assigned name server addresses" radio button. Make sure the "Use IP header compression" and "Use default gateway on remote network" boxes don't have check marks. Then click OK to return to the New Phonebook Entry dialog box.

Now click the Script tab. In the After dialing (login) area, choose "None." Then click the Security tab. In the Authentication and encryption policy area, choose "Accept any authentication including clear text."

Finally, click OK to return to the Dial-Up Connection dialog box. From here, you can select the UPS Connection entry you just created and click the Dial button to connect to one of the networking projects, as described in Chapter 14. Remember that the networking executables shipped on the CD-ROM are built to work with Windows 95 and 98. For Windows NT, you must edit the SetupSerialConnection() function to change the line

```
SEArray[0].Expect = "5557777\x0D";
```

to read

```
SEArray[0].Expect = "CLIENT";
```

and then rebuild the program. We describe this in more detail in Chapter 14.

Development Methodologies
for Real-Time and
Embedded Systems

In Chapter 2, "Designing and Developing Your Real-Time System," we presented practical methods for developing embedded systems. For those who prefer to use a formal methodology, this appendix provides six methodologies for designing real-time embedded systems. We encourage you to investigate these methodologies and have provided references to sources of detailed information.

Most of the methodologies presented here follow the basic theme of analysis, design, and implementation, and then augment those phases with their own steps. Some methodologies add steps that specifically address the integration of hardware and software. Other methodologies provide explicit testing phases. Most importantly in regards to real-time systems, some methodologies include steps that involve analyzing a system's timing requirements as an aid in properly implementing processes (or threads) in the final software.

Perhaps you'll find that one of the methodologies presented here suits your particular work style.

OCTOPUS

The Octopus methodology is intended for real-time and embedded systems. Described in detail in *Object-Oriented Technology for Real-Time Systems: A Practical*

Approach Using OMT and Fusion, by Maher Awad, Juha Kuusela, and Jergen Ziegler (Prentice Hall, 1996), Octopus is based on concepts from the earlier object-oriented design methodologies of OMT (object modeling technique) and Fusion. OMT was developed by a group led by James Rumbaugh at General Electric's Research and Development Center. The primary reference is *Object-Oriented Modeling and Design,* by James Rumbaugh, Michael Blaha, William Premerlani, Frederick Eddy, and Bill Lorensen (Prentice Hall, 1991). The Fusion methodology is described in *Object-Oriented Development: The Fusion Method,* by Derek Coleman, Stephanie Bodoff, and Patrick Arnold (Prentice Hall, 1994).

Real-time embedded system development with Octopus includes these five phases:

- **System requirements:** Define the overall goals of the system.

- **System architecture:** Divide the system into manageable subsystems.

- **Subsystem analysis:** Analyze each subsystem to determine the task (or tasks) it performs. Construct an overall structure of the subsystem.

- **Subsystem design:** Define the precise internals of each subsystem.

- **Subsystem implementation:** Code the subsystem models defined in the subsystem design phase.

Octopus also defines a *hardware wrapper,* which is software that serves as an interface between higher-level software and the hardware. The wrapper has two benefits. First, it enables you to proceed with development of subsystems before the final hardware is in place. You can define interfaces to the hardware wrapper rather than interfaces to the hardware. Second, it improves the portability of the overall system. Because the wrapper insulates the rest of the system from the hardware, a change in the hardware requires only a change in the wrapper. The wrapper itself is treated as another subsystem, so that the analysis, design, and implementation of the wrapper proceeds as with any other subsystem in the overall application. (Octopus encourages construction of the wrapper to proceed in parallel with other subsystems, so that it becomes available as early in the project lifecycle as possible.)

We know of no software toolsets on the market that automate the Octopus methodology. Nokia, Inc., however, maintains a web site (`http://www.nrc.nokia.com/octopus/tutorial/`) that includes an online Octopus tutorial.

ELLISON

In her book *Developing Real-Time Embedded Software in a Market-Driven Company* (John Wiley and Sons, 1994), Dr. Karen Ellison takes the reader through an example project, and in so doing introduces a development process that is a thoughtful combination of elements from other methodologies. Dr. Ellison's approach is less formal and more practical than other methodologies and is geared toward real-time embedded projects.

Development using Dr. Ellison's methodology proceeds through the following phases:

- **Requirements analysis phase:** Determine what the final system is supposed to accomplish. This phase is similar in scope to the initial phase of the Octopus method.

- **Design phase:** Flesh out the top-level architecture of the project. The components (or, if you will, subsystems) are determined, without regard to internal details or whether a particular component accomplishes its function in hardware or software.

- **Performance analysis:** Ascertain whether the design (at this point) will meet performance requirements. The developer "walks through" modeled system activities, estimating execution times for steps within each activity. A high degree of accuracy is not encouraged at this step (that is taken care of later, in the task planning phase). Rather, the idea is to verify that the design's performance is in the ballpark. Dr. Ellison adds this phase (missing in many methodologies), which is particularly useful in the design of embedded systems for which the software's execution must meet performance specifications.

- **Component specification:** Flesh out the internal details of the components determined in the design phase. Partition components into manageable chunks.

- **Task planning:** Determine the individual processes and threads (tasks), and apply mathematical formulae to determine a suitable scheduling algorithm to meet performance requirements. This step specifically addresses multitasking real-time systems.

- **Development testing:** Perform unit testing, in which individual software components are tested as independent units, and integration testing, in which software components are tested in combination with one another.

Note that Dr. Ellison does not address the coding phase. Dr. Ellison's contention is that the coding should be straightforward if the previous steps are followed.

As with the Octopus methodology, no CASE tools implement Dr. Ellison's methodology. The book, however, is a wealth of useful information and should be on the shelf of every engineer of embedded and real-time systems.

OBJECTGEODE

ObjectGeode is both a methodology and a CASE toolset developed by Verilog, Inc. The steps in the ObjectGeode development process include:

- **Requirements analysis:** Examine the system from the perspective of system users and begin to explore the internal components (referred to as *actors*) within the system to determine the flow of information among the components.

- **Design:** Define the overall architecture of the system and provide detailed descriptions of individual software objects within the system.

- **Test design:** Perform unit and integration testing. This step takes place as part of the design phase.

- **Targeting:** Define the connections between the software and the hardware.

- **Testing:** Execute the finished product to seek out bugs. The testing (that is, the data sent to the system, the sequence in which the data is presented, and so on) is guided by the information derived in the test design phase.

ObjectGeode specifies an iterative development process. The results of the testing phase are used to determine whether the system performs as specified (in which case the system is validated and can be shipped) or whether significant errors have been detected. In the latter case, the developer would return to one of the earlier phases (perhaps as far back as the analysis phase).

ObjectGeode has used notation based on the OMT methodology, but is (at the time of this writing) making the transition to the unified modeling language (UML). UML is the synthesis of object-oriented notations from several popular object-oriented methodologies. It is catching on as the de facto standard object-oriented modeling language. Elements have been added to UML to make it suitable for real-time development and the details of this can be found at Rational Software's web site: `http://www.rational.com`. The ObjectGeode toolset has the capability to generate C or C++ code directly from the models developed in the analysis and design phases. Currently, the toolset supports such real-time operating systems as Chorus, pSOS, VRTX, VxWorks, Win32, and several UNIX variants. You'll find more information at Verilog's web site: `http://www.verilogusa.com`.

ROOM

ROOM, which stands for Real-time Object-Oriented Modeling, is a methodology designed from the ground up to support the development of real-time systems. ROOM is described in great detail in the book *Real-Time Object-Oriented Modeling,* by Brian Selic, Garth Gullekson, Paul Ward, and Jim McGee (John Wiley and Sons, 1994). ROOM focuses primarily on the design and implementation phases. (The ROOM book provides little explanation for the analysis phase, which it refers to as "model development heuristics.")

ROOM defines a combination textual and graphical language for describing the structure and behavior of the objects, or actors, that make up the system being designed. The textual language is similar to C++ in structure and provides information that could not easily be captured in graphical notation (such as data types). The graphical language is a combination state chart, which defines the behavior of a particular actor, and object-interaction diagram, which describes how objects are connected to one another.

ObjecTime, Inc., whose founders developed ROOM, sell software tools that enable developers to create ROOM-based models. The true power of the system lies in the fact that ROOM models are executable. Consequently, a developer can craft a system using the ROOM tools, and execute that model without writing a line of low-level code.

The ObjecTime tools create C or C++ source code from ROOM models. ObjecTime has integrated its tools with several popular real- time operating systems, including Lynx, pSOS, VRTX, and VxWorks. For more information, see ObjecTime's web site at `http://www.objectime.com`.

SHLAER-MELLOR

The Shlaer-Mellor OOA/OOD (object-oriented analysis/object-oriented design) methodology is named after its creators — Sally Shlaer and Stephen Mellor. The foundational books for the Shlaer-Mellor method are *Object-Oriented Analysis: Modeling the World in Data* and

Object Lifecycles: Modeling the World in States, both by Sally Shlaer and Stephen Mellor (Yourdon Press, 1989 and 1992, respectively). A good introduction to the Shlaer-Mellor method (with a focus on its application to embedded systems) is in the April 1996 issue of *Embedded Systems Programming* magazine. The article is "Migration from Structured to OO Methodologies," by Sally Shlaer and Steve Mellor.

The Shlaer-Mellor methodology was designed to provide an easy transition from structured development techniques to object-oriented development techniques. Progress through the methodology takes the developer through analysis, design, and implementation. The Shlaer-Mellor methodology is complex and uses a variety of interrelated graphical diagrams for capturing various aspects of the system under development.

The methodology's authors have founded Project Technology, a company that markets software tools for automating development using the Shlaer-Mellor method. BridgePoint, the flagship tool, enables developers to build, verify, and execute models used in the Shlaer-Mellor methodology. More recently, the company released ProjectStart Model Libraries, which are blueprints for building Shlaer-Mellor models for real-time systems. The ProjectStart models act as generic starting points that developers can use for system design.

You'll find more information at ProjectTechnology's web site at http://www.projtech.com.

K-FLOW AND GOO

Barry Kauler, on staff at the University of Western Australia, is the author of a novel object-oriented modeling system called K-Flow, which he has expanded into the GOO (graphical object-oriented) methodology. The original definition of K-Flow appeared in *Object-Oriented Flow Design for Embedded Systems,* by Barry Kauler (Karda Prints, 1996). GOO is described in *Flow Design for Embedded Systems: A Radical New Unified Object-Oriented Methodology,* by Barry Kauler (R&D Books, 1997).

What makes Professor Kauler's K-Flow methodology unique is that he designed it for building small embedded systems. The author's first book included the software framework necessary to implement applications developed using K-Flow running on 8051 8-bit microcontrollers.

The GOO methodology is much less formal than other methodologies and is best described as a work in progress. Still, the author has greatly enhanced the graphical notation used in the methodology and has even created a Windows-based diagramming tool that can generate C code directly from diagrams. More information is available at http://www.goofee.com.

Index

Real-Time Programming Online

Visit http://www.pharlap.com/book for...

• Real-time embedded programming news • ToolSuite Lite updates and errata • Hardware partners list • The Embedded WebFarm

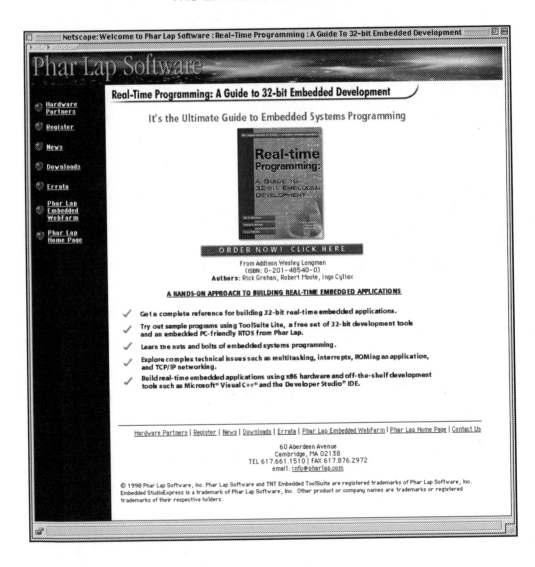

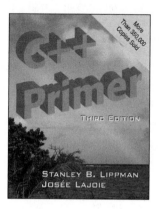

PHAR LAP SOFTWARE, INC. BINARY LICENSE AGREEMENT

By purchasing the book Real-Time Programming: A Guide to 32-bit Embedded Development (the "Book") you have selected "ToolSuite Lite™", a limited function version of the product "TNT Embedded ToolSuite®", contained on the CD-ROM included therewith. BY OPENING THE CD-ROM PACKAGE YOU, AS LICENSEE, ACCEPT AND ARE BOUND BY THIS AGREEMENT; IF YOU DO NOT ACCEPT THIS AGREEMENT, RETURN THE BOOK AND CD-ROM (UNOPENED) TO THE DEALER FOR A FULL REFUND.

LICENSE

Effective on your acceptance of this Agreement, under this License you may:

- Use ToolSuite Lite™ on a single machine and copy it for backup or support of that use.

- Link the library and object files contained in its \LIB directory (the "Library Files") and incorporate the example code and programs contained in the \EXAMPLES directory (the "Projects") with any program(s) you develop. The Library Files, when linked with your program, are the "ETS™ Kernel"; your program, when linked with the ETS™ Kernel, is an "Embedded Application". You may not link or include any of the library and object files contained in its \MONITOR directory with or in your programs or any Embedded Application.

- Develop any number of Embedded Applications, all for your internal use on a single target computer system. You may not distribute or sublicense any Embedded Applications.

- Transfer all copies of ToolSuite Lite™ and the License to a third party, if you also transfer your copy of the Book to that party and that party accepts this Agreement.

The License self-terminates on any use or transfer of ToolSuite Lite™ or any copy thereof in violation of or other than as expressly permitted by this License. On its termination, you must destroy and cease all use of ToolSuite Lite™ and all copies thereof.

LIMITED WARRANTY AND LIMITATION OF REMEDIES

TOOLSUITE LITE™ IS PROVIDED "AS IS" AND WITHOUT WARRANTY, EXPRESSED OR IMPLIED, INCLUDING BUT NOT LIMITED TO THE IMPLIED WARRANTIES OF MERCHANTABILITY AND FITNESS FOR A PARTICULAR PURPOSE AND WARRANTIES OF PERFORMANCE OR OPERATION. IN NO EVENT WILL PHAR LAP OR ITS PUBLISHERS, AUTHORS, LICENSORS OR DEALERS BE LIABLE FOR ANY DAMAGES, INCLUDING INCIDENTAL OR CONSEQUENTIAL DAMAGES, EVEN IF ADVISED OF THEIR POSSIBILITY, OR FOR ANY CLAIM BY ANY PARTY.

GENERAL TERMS

This Agreement is the entire agreement between you and Phar Lap, superseding all prior communications, oral or written. Only a written agreement signed by you and Phar Lap can modify it. The provisions of this Agreement are severable. This Agreement is governed by the laws of The Commonwealth of Massachusetts, excluding all conflict of laws provisions. You and Phar Lap hereby disclaim the provisions of the U.N. Convention for the International Sale of Goods. You shall not permit export of ToolSuite Lite™ or any direct products thereof to any country to which export is then controlled by the U.S. Bureau of Export Administration without that agency's prior written approval. Under Title 48 of the Code of Federal Regulations, U.S. Government offices, branches, and agencies shall use ToolSuite Lite™ only as a "commercial item" and with only those rights granted hereunder.